PENGUIN CLASSICS

# THE WAR WITH HANNIBAL

ADVISORY EDITOR: BETTY RADICE

TITUS LIVIUS was born in 59 BC at Patavium (Padua) but later moved to Rome. He lived in an eventful age but little is known about his life, which seems to have been occupied exlusively in literary work. When he was aged about thirty he began to write his *History of Rome*, consisting of 142 books of which thirty-five survive. He continued working on it for over forty years until his death in AD 17.

AUBREY DE SÉLINCOURT, scholar and translator, translated Livy's *The Early History of Rome* (Books I–V) and *The War With Hannibal* (Books XXI–XXX), *The Histories* of Herodotus and *The Campaigns of Alexander* by Arrian, all for the Penguin Classics. He was born in 1896 and educated at Rugby, and University College, Oxford. A schoolmaster of genius for twenty-six years, he retired in 1947 to the Isle of Wight where he lived until his death in 1962.

BETTY RADICE read classics at Oxford, then married and, in the intervals of bringing up a family, tutored in classics, philosophy and English. She became joint editor of the Penguin Classics in 1964. She translated Pliny's *Letters*, Livy's *Rome and Italy*, the Latin comedies of Terence, *the Letters of Abelard and Heloise* and Erasmus's *Praise of Folly*, and also wrote the Introductions to Horace's *The Complete Odes and Epodes* and *The Poems* of Propertius, all for Penguin Classics. She also edited and introduced Edward Gibbon's *Memoirs of My Life* for the Penguin English Library. She edited and annotated her translation of the younger Pliny's works for the Loeb Library of Classics, and translated from Italian, Renaissance Latin and Greek for the Officina Bodoni of Verona. She collaborated as a translator in the Collected Works of Erasmus and was the author of the Penguin Reference book *Who's Who in the Ancient World*. Betty Radice was an honorary fellow of St Hilda's College, Oxford, and a vice-president of the Classical Association. She died in 1985.

# LIVY

# THE WAR WITH HANNIBAL

Books XXI–XXX of
*The History of Rome from its Foundation*

*

*Translated by*
AUBREY DE SÉLINCOURT

*Edited with an Introduction by*
BETTY RADICE

PENGUIN BOOKS

PENGUIN BOOKS

Published by the Penguin Group
Penguin Books Ltd, 80 Strand, London WC2R 0RL, England
Penguin Putnam Inc., 375 Hudson Street, New York, New York 10014, USA
Penguin Books Australia Ltd, 250 Camberwell Road, Camberwell, Victoria 3124, Australia
Penguin Books Canada Ltd, 10 Alcorn Avenue, Toronto, Ontario, Canada M4V 3B2
Penguin Books India (P) Ltd, 11 Community Centre, Panchsheel Park, New Delhi – 110 017, India
Penguin Books (NZ) Ltd, Cnr Rosedale and Airborne Roads, Albany, Auckland, New Zealand
Penguin Books (South Africa) (Pty) Ltd, 24 Sturdee Avenue, Rosebank 2196, South Africa

Penguin Books Ltd, Registered Offices: 80 Strand, London WC2R 0RL, England

www.penguin.com

This translation first published 1965
Reprinted with an Index 1972

055



Printed and bound in Great Britain by Clays Ltd, Elcograf S.p.A.

Set in Monotype Bembo



ISBN-13: 978–0–14–044145–1

www.greenpenguin.co.uk

MIX
Paper | Supporting responsible forestry
FSC www.fsc.org FSC® C018072

Penguin Books is committed to a sustainable future for our business, our readers and our planet. This book is made from Forest Stewardship Council™ certified paper.

# TABLE OF CONTENTS

| | |
|---|---|
| Introduction | 7 |
| Book xxi | 23 |
| Book xxii | 93 |
| Book xxiii | 167 |
| Book xxiv | 231 |
| Book xxv | 293 |
| Book xxvi | 355 |
| Book xxvii | 425 |
| Book xxviii | 497 |
| Book xxix | 565 |
| Book xxx | 619 |
| Maps | 677 |
| Chronological Index | 685 |
| Index | 689 |

# MAPS


| | |
|---|---|
| Spain during the war with Hannibal | 677 |
| Hannibal's Crossing of the Alps | 678 |
| North Italy | 679 |
| Central Italy | 680 |
| South Italy and Sicily | 681 |
| Central Greece | 682 |
| Africa and Numidia | 683 |
| Plan of Syracuse | 684 |

# INTRODUCTION

*Put Hannibal in the scales: how many pounds will that peerless*
*General mark up today? This is the man for whom Africa*
*Was too small a continent, though it stretched from the surf-beaten*
*Ocean shores of Morocco east to the steamy Nile,*
*To tribal Ethiopia, and new elephants' habitats.*
*Now Spain swells his empire, now he surmounts*
*The Pyrenees. Nature sets in his path*
*High Alpine passes, blizzards of snow: but he splits*
*The very rocks asunder, moves mountains with vinegar.*
*Now Italy is his, yet still he forces on:*
*'We have accomplished nothing,' he cries, 'till we have stormed*
*The gates of Rome, till our Carthaginian standard*
*Is set in the City's heart.' A fine sight it must have been,*
*Fit subject for caricature – the one-eyed commander*
*Perched on his monstrous beast! Alas, alas for glory,*
*What an end was here: the defeat, the ignominious*
*Headlong flight into exile, everyone gawping at*
*The once-mighty Hannibal turned humble hanger-on,*
*Sitting outside the door of a petty Eastern despot*
*Till His Majesty deign to wake. No sword, no spear,*
*No battle-flung stone was to snuff the fiery spirit*
*That once had wrecked a world: those crushing defeats,*
*Those rivers of spilt blood were all wiped out by a*
*Ring, a poisoned ring. On, on, you madman, drive*
*Over your savage Alps, to thrill young schoolboys*
*And supply a theme for speech-day recitations!*

Juvenal, *Satire X*, lines 147–67.

(TRANSLATED BY PETER GREEN)

All military commanders who have been masters of strategy and great leaders of men have left their legends to inspire or to intimidate later generations, and something unforgettable about Hannibal could fire the imagination of the Romans whenever they thought of their historic past. Even Juvenal, an embittered satirist writing on the vanity of human wishes, cannot stifle a grudging admiration for the enemy at the gates of Rome three centuries before his own day.

*Hannibal ad portas* became part of the tradition as a nursery threat or a rallying-cry, much as Boney's name was used in nineteenth-century homes and survives in sea-shanties. For a comparable episode in English history which retains its power to stir public sentiment, we must go back to the defeat of the Spanish Armada, though those of us who remember the years 1939–45 can surely recognize the moment when a Hannibal stood at our gates and there seemed nothing to hold him but the obstinacy of the people's refusal to accept defeat.

Ten books out of Livy's *History of Rome* were devoted to the seventeen years of the second war between Rome and Carthage, and these ten have come down to us practically intact among the thirty-five survivors of the original 142. Livy's plan for the whole grouped the books in fives,[1] and we are fortunate in having these two groups which form a single unit. The first five (Books XXI–XXV) cover the rising tide of Carthaginian successes, and the Roman disasters of the Ticinus, Trebia, Lake Trasimene, and Cannae, culminating in a crippling defeat for the Roman armies in Spain. Then the tide turns, Rome takes the initiative, and Book XXX ends with the victory over Hannibal at Zama.

Livy was born at Patavium (Padua) in 59 B.C., moved to Rome and started on his history about the age of thirty, and continued to work on it for over forty years until his death in A.D. 17. Little is known of his life; like Virgil and Horace he was inspired by deep patriotic feeling and gratitude to Augustus for the security he enjoyed after the civil wars. Tacitus (*Annals* IV: 34) says he was friendly with Augustus, who appreciated his objectivity as well as his eloquence, and Suetonius (*Claudius* 41) mentions how he encouraged the Emperor Claudius in his own attempts to write a History of Rome. Quintilian more than once quotes the gibe of Livy's contemporary, the critic Asinius Pollio, about his *patavinitas*, his provincialism (*Instit.*

1. The first five were translated by Aubrey de Sélincourt for the Penguin Classics under the title *The Early History of Rome*.

*Orat.* I: 5, 56; VIII I, 3). This refers probably to the north-Italian accent and idiom which offended the Roman purist, though it may also indicate a certain lack of sophistication and a simplicity of judgement. But Pliny's story of the Spaniard who came to Rome only to have one look at Livy (*Letters* II: 3) suggests that he was well known in the capital as a literary figure. His position as a writer was soon firmly established; by Martial's day the History existed in 'potted' as well as in its complete form (*Epigrams* XIV: 190), and Livy was the main source used by Silius Italicus for his mammoth epic on the second Punic war. A book of Livy kept Pliny reading at Misenum instead of going to see the eruption of Vesuvius – a fact which has provoked incredulous comment in classrooms ever since.

It was presumably from the use of Livy in the schools that the teachers of rhetoric quoted by Juvenal chose Hannibal as a stock subject for debate: the pupil must discuss 'whether Hannibal should make straight for the City from the field of Cannae or play safe after the rain and thunder and lead around his cohorts, all dripping after the storm' (Juvenal *Sat.* VII: 161). Elsewhere Juvenal compares the pampered ladies of his times with the women whose hands were hardened with spinning wool when 'Hannibal was near the City and their husbands stood to arms at the Colline Gate' (*Sat.* VI: 290); and his famous denunciation of military ambition quoted above is his answer to Livy's emotional patriotism.

Along with Plutarch (who was himself indebted to Livy), Seneca, and Cicero, Livy was an inspiration to the European scholars who welcomed the humanism of the classical world. The dramatic episode of the gold rings taken from the dead after Cannae was something Dante remembered from '*Livio .. che non erra*' (quoted on p. 180). The names of Livy's heroes, including that of Hannibal himself, appear among the classical references in Petrarch's *Sonnets* (see especially 103, 104, and 186), and Petrarch always hoped to discover some of the lost books of Livy; one of his Latin letters to the illustrious dead is addressed to Livy to tell him so. Less happily, he wrote a Latin epic (*Africa*) on Scipio Africanus. By the middle of the sixteenth century Livy was translated into French, Italian,

Spanish, and German; Philemon Holland's celebrated English version appeared in 1600. Montaigne, as one would expect, found a wealth of material in Roman history to illustrate his arguments, and though he says more than once that his favourite authors are Plutarch and Seneca, he quotes Livy on the Punic wars as well as on the early legends of Rome. The complex characters of both Scipio and Hannibal interest him, and on the latter he quotes Livy with Petrarch and Silius Italicus. Livy's imaginative descriptions of certain episodes in the war are reproduced almost as Livy wrote them: the bitterly cold weather at the time of the battle of the Trebia, and Hannibal's measures to lessen its effects on his men, and the grim scene of the dead at Cannae who had buried their heads in the earth to end their sufferings. (pp. 81 and 151).[1]

The romantic episode of Sophonisba's marriage and death (Book XXX) provided a subject for one of the earliest Italian renaissance tragedies (Trissino's *Sofonisba*, 1515) and later for several playwrights during the seventeenth and eighteenth centuries, among them Corneille, Nathaniel Lee, and James Thomson.[2] Political writers as far removed in time and thought as Machiavelli and Montesquieu have found illustrations for their arguments in *The History of Rome*. *Discorsi sopra la prima deca di Tito Livio* was published in 1513 as a preliminary to *The Prince*; while Montesquieu wrote against the tyranny of princes, and Livy's early books were the basis of *Considérations sur les causes de la grandeur des Romains et de leur décadence* which he wrote in 1734. Later on Rousseau made his own translation of speeches selected from Livy, and these were used, with Cicero and Plutarch, as models by the idealist speakers in the French Revolution, who found inspiration in the history of the republics of Greece and Rome.

In this country Livy has always been read in the schools and still is, though his difficulties of style have not always endeared him to the young. For the nineteenth-century reformists he

1. See Montaigne's *Essays*, translated by J. M. Cohen (Penguin Classics). Reference to Scipio is made on pp. 337, 382, and 398; Hannibal: 121 and 123; the Trebia: p. 122; Cannae: p. 326.

2. One line at least of his play survives: 'Oh! Sophonisba! Sophonisba! Oh!' (*The Oxford Dictionary of Quotations*).

and his heroes must have embodied all the virtues of their public school ideal – patriotism, public spirit, dignity, and self-control. These are not amongst the more popular virtues today, but Livy remains a great writer whose themes can still appeal; if proof is needed it lies in the success of an excellent popular book on Hannibal,[1] published in 1960 and inspired by a re-reading of Dr Arnold of Rugby's *The Second Punic War*.

As a historian Livy has never ranked high since Niebuhr drew the distinction between first- and second-hand information; it has long been accepted that a historian writing long after the events he describes cannot be taken at his face value, but every effort must be made to penetrate through his statements to his sources. For Livy's early history this is practically impossible. It is scarcely credible now that Macaulay's *Lays of Ancient Rome* were intended to be read as a reconstruction of the ballad-sources which Macaulay believed the 'man of fine imagination' drew upon,[2] though the *Lays* themselves remain a supreme example of a fine imagination at work and can never lose their appeal for anyone who enjoys a stirring poem. But for his account of the war with Hannibal, Livy could have used good first-hand sources. There were the records of senatorial decrees, kept in the Treasury, and the *annales maximi*, the annual records of state elections, ceremonies, festivals, portents, visits of ambassadors, and the like, gathered into eighty books by Publius Mucius Scaevola in 115 B.C. from the lists put up each year by the *pontifex maximus*. There is, however, no evidence that Livy ever consulted them. He preferred to follow the later annalists such as Claudius Quadrigarius and Valerius Antias, cited eight times in Books XXV–XXX; Coelius Antipater, author of a monograph on the Second War; Quintus Fabius Pictor, senator and historian who took an active part in the war himself (see pp. 101 and 157) and wrote a history of Rome in Greek; and above all, the Greek historian Polybius, whose *Universal History* in forty books starts with the war with Hannibal. Polybius was born about 203 B.C. and died in 120, and he must have spoken to people who took part in the war. He had had political and military experience in Greece and

1. Leonard Cottrell, *Enemy of Rome*, Evans Brothers, 1960.
2. See Macaulay's Preface to the *Lays of Ancient Rome*.

moved in the cultured circle surrounding the Scipios in Rome. He was widely travelled and observant, and luckily for us, that part of his history which Livy follows closely for the second half of the war has survived in great part for comparison.

Livy is only following the general practice of ancient historians when he does not cite his authorities except where they conflict. But he can reasonably be charged with an unscientific approach to them and a sad lack of ability to judge their relative merits. On p. 62 he quotes varying estimates of the size of Hannibal's army, including that of Polybius who had actually seen the figures on the temple of Juno near Croton, but Livy does not refer to this nor imply that Polybius's total is most likely to be reliable.[1] He also has an irritating trick of following one source almost to the end of an episode and then casting doubt on it by mentioning alternative possibilities; the scientific approach would be to evaluate the sources first. This makes for great confusion in the chronology of the campaigns in Spain: for example, in his account of the siege of Saguntum Livy apparently follows Coelius Antipater and only afterwards (p. 38) states that there is a conflicting version of the date – in fact that of Polybius, though he is not named. Again, on p. 465 Livy says that Coelius alone has three different accounts of the death of Marcellus: but Livy himself does not feel he might try to choose between them. And it is tantalizing to be told that the words of a poem by Livius Andronicus 'were no doubt good enough for those rude and uncultivated days, but were I to quote them now they would sound unpleasing and graceless.' (p. 479.)

The annalistic method of approach determines the structure of Livy's history; every year has its elections, prodigies observed, disposal of the armed forces, and the events in each sphere – Italy, Spain, Greece, and North Africa. This is not always the clearest way of setting out a logical sequence of events; the reader sometimes feels as though he were reading a serial novel by Dickens, where several groups of characters

1. 'I found near Lacinium the bronze tablet on which Hannibal had drawn up this list during the time when he was in this region of Italy, and judging it to be an entirely reliable authority, decided to follow it.' *Polybius* III: 33: 18.

all have to have their quota in each new instalment, and he must keep turning back to remind himself how things stood. Sometimes we cannot see the wood for the trees, and wonder if Livy himself grasped clearly that the endless marchings to and fro in central Italy after Cannae were part of a deliberate policy of Hannibal's to wear down the Romans by detaching the Italian cities, instead of risking a naval defeat by having troops sent over from Carthage: meanwhile the home government was to pursue the war actively in Spain, Sardinia, Sicily, and the Illyrian coast through the alliance with Philip V of Macedon. (In this Hannibal miscalculated the temper of the Italian cities – some were won over, but most saw little advantage in exchanging allegiance to Rome, however unwilling, for submission to a semitic intruder. But it took many years of Fabian tactics followed by Scipionic strategy for this policy to be defeated.)

Again, in his annual records of elections Livy never says explicitly that the appointment of a dictator with military authority and of a master of Horse lapsed after Cannae, as a direct result of the impossible situation before the battle when Minucius Rufus, as master of Horse, claimed equal powers with the dictator. Henceforth a dictator was appointed only for special work as censor to hold elections, and the office was abolished in 200. A historian with a firmer grasp of historical trends would also have pointed out the effects of the war on constitutional practice; since the popular assemblies were too clumsy and infrequent for urgent decisions, the power of the tribune became less effective and the Senate ruled as a supreme war council – an oligarchy based on its prestige, then at its highest. As the statutory five praetors and two consuls were not enough for all the necessary commands, the constitutional interval between offices was dropped and commands could also be retained by a proconsul or propraetor. So Fabius Maximus was consul in 215, 214, and 209, and Marcellus commanded continuously in Sicily from 214 to 211. Scipio went out to Spain in 210 as a *privatus cum imperio*, and retained his command until 201. Nowhere does Livy say there was anything extraordinary in these deviations from the normal.

Nor is Livy a military historian; the tactics described in his battle scenes are rarely clear, and obviously not intended for a specialist reader. On p. 641 Mago is defeated somewhere 'in Insubrian Gaul' in a battle which suspiciously resembles an engagement in Spain described on pp. 498 ff. The site is never made clear; what interests Livy is the parley between the Roman leaders on the eve of battle and the dramatic entry of Mago's elephants. His confused topography is notorious. On p. 569 Hippo Regius is cited in error for Hippo Diarrhytus, and on p. 514 a battle in Spain takes place between forces said earlier to be stationed more than a hundred miles apart. The route followed by Hannibal in his crossing of the Alps is still as fruitful a topic of debate as it was in Juvenal's day.[1] Here, however, I think we must be careful not to criticize Livy unfairly as an 'armchair historian'. Polybius claims to have crossed the Alps by Hannibal's route, but his description is no clearer than Livy's: and he has less justification.[2] Polybius of course travelled widely, first on state and military missions, and then under the patronage of Scipio Aemilianus. Livy on the other hand is the only Roman historian who never held any office of state which would take him abroad or enable him to move freely inside Italy. He knows Rome, and the river Po near his native Padua (p. 73) but the Romans did not travel for the mere pleasure of sightseeing, and Livy's youth was spent in an Italy torn by civil war. Trevelyan's dictum that the historian needs better boots rather than better books would have been incomprehensible to him.

Livy's aim in writing his history is clearly stated in his preface to the first book. He wishes to make a worthy contri-

1. See pp. 54 ff. and map p. 678. The best discussions of all the available evidence is in Gavin de Beer's *Alps and Elephants* (Nelson, 1955), reprinted in a French edition, *Route Annibal* (éditions Nelson, 1962). He argues convincingly for a route crossing the Aygues (Livy's Arar) and passing via the Drône – Col de Grimone – upper Durance – Col de la Traversette to Turin. Leonard Cottrell (op. cit.) takes the same view. Both books have excellent photographs. For a different view see P. G. Walsh, *Livy: His Historical Aims and Methods* (C.U.P.); F. W. Walbank, J.R.S.46, (1956), pp. 37 ff.

2. 'On these matters I can speak with confidence; I have inquired about the circumstances from eye-witnesses and personally inspected the country, and actually crossed the Alps to learn and see for myself.' *Polybius* III: 48: 12.

bution to the task of 'putting on record the story of the greatest nation in the world'. Later on he emphasizes his moral purpose. 'The study of history is the best medicine for a sick mind; for in history you have a record of the infinite variety of human experience plainly set out for all to see: and in that record you can find for yourself and your country both examples and warnings: fine things to take as models, base things, rotten through and through, to avoid. I hope my passion for Rome's past has not impaired my judgement; for I do honestly believe that no country has ever been greater and purer than ours or richer in good citizens and noble deeds; none has been free for so many generations from the vices of avarice and luxury; nowhere have thrift and plain living been for so long held in such esteem. Indeed, poverty with us went hand in hand with contentment. Of late years wealth has made us greedy, and self-indulgence has brought us, through every form of sensual excess, to be, if I may so put it, in love with death both individual and collective.'[1]

Like Horace and Virgil he looks to the past for the moral standards which he found lacking in Augustan Rome; 'I shall find antiquity a rewarding study, if only because, while I am absorbed in it, I shall be able to turn my eyes from the troubles which for so long have tormented the modern world . . .' This is his escape from the sophistication of the capital which Ovid and Propertius knew and loved; and in his country's triumph over Carthage he must have seen her finest hour. The defeat at Cannae left Rome 'without a force in the field, without a commander, without a single soldier, Apulia and Samnium in Hannibal's hands, and now nearly the whole of Italy overrun. No other nation in the world could have suffered so tremendous a series of disasters, and not been overwhelmed' (p. 154). This is written from the heart with a right and proper pride. It was not so much superior generalship which won the war as the stubborn determination of Romans and loyal allied Italians, fighting together with confidence in their constitution and hopes for the future.

Paradoxically, Livy's sense of the dramatic leads him sometimes to talk loosely of 'all the Italians' going over to Hannibal.

1. *The Early History of Rome*, p. 18.

In fact, only the Bruttians were Hannibal's allies from the start, in hope of plundering the Greek cities in their midst; but Rhegium was always loyal to Rome, and Petelia was only brought over after an eleven-month siege (p. 204). Hannibal had been disappointed in the Cisalpine Gauls, and Mago had only lukewarm Gallic support in 205 (p. 572). And against the list of defections after Cannae must be set the fact that Hannibal failed to win over the Latins; Latin prisoners were liberated without ransom after Hannibal's victory at Lake Trasimene (p. 101) and he tried in vain to induce the citizens of Nuceria to join his army (p. 184). Yet after nine years' fighting only twelve of the thirty Latin colonies refused further help to Rome, and their punishment was simply to be ignored. 'They were punished by silence – a silence which was felt to be most in accord with the dignity of Rome' (p. 440). Five years later their position was brought up again in the Senate and the towns duly taxed to make up their arrears in money and men. By contrast, seven towns in Etruria voluntarily contributed equipment for Scipio's expedition to Sicily and Africa in 205 (p. 562).

The next century was to see Italian hopes belied, the decay of the small Italian farmer and the drift to the towns, the emergence of a Roman plutocracy, and the growing dissatisfaction of the Italians with their burdens of taxation and military service. Livy himself was only one generation removed from the cruel war in which Italian 'allies' fought to gain full political equality with Roman citizens, and his romantic patriotism, coupled with his political conservatism, naturally led to nostalgia for a time when Romans and Italians were truly united in a common cause.

Impartiality is rare in a historian of strong feeling, and Livy's admiration for his ideal Roman–Italian type has led one critic at least to declare roundly that 'his main fault is a too uncritical patriotism.'[1] He is not particularly interested in racial types – he has neither Herodotus's lively curiosity for human vagaries nor Tacitus's ability to investigate a primitive people. The Celtic temperament of the Gauls for him is always unreliable and deficient in stamina, the Carthaginians are treacherous, the Numidians amorous and the Campanians proud and sybaritic.

1. P. G. Walsh, op. cit., p. 36.

Nor can he see, as Thucydides and Sallust did, that war in itself corrupts, that reprisals follow atrocities, and that ultimately neither combatant can be free from guilt. He is unwilling to censure any Roman leader, even for brutality like that of Marcellus in Sicily; he concludes a harrowing description of the appalling massacre at Henna with what reads like a conscious parrying of criticism: 'Thus Henna was held – by a criminal act or a necessary one, call it what you will' (p. 279). Pleminius may be condemned for the Roman atrocities at Locri (p. 588), but Scipio is exonerated from blame although he leaves Pleminius in command (p. 596). Masinissa is another of Livy's heroes, all that a noble ally should be: Livy treats him tenderly over the affair with Sophonisba, and produces a remarkable argument in justification of his desertion from Carthage in 207: 'The reason for his sudden change of sides was not, at the time, entirely clear; but that he had acted, even then, on reasonable grounds, was proved later by his unswerving loyalty to Rome down to his extreme old age' (p. 519).

Livy is in fact a romantic historian. He sees the war with Carthage largely as a conflict of personalities – on the one side his Roman heroes, on the other Hannibal. It could even be argued that Hannibal is the true romantic hero. Certainly he dominates the stage from first to last, and no one on the Carthaginian side approaches him in stature; we watch him pitting his resources against one Roman commander after another, Sempronius at the Trebia, Flaminius at Lake Trasimene, Paullus at Cannae, Marcellus at Nola – until the young Scipio is ready to meet him in the field at Zama. At one point (p. 512) Livy pays high tribute to his personal magnetism, and one cannot help feeling that he was fascinated by the personality of this alien, un-Roman figure, his country's arch enemy who was possessed of qualities which the sober historian is impelled to admire. So perhaps may Virgil in the later books of the Aeneid have found himself making Turnus a more compelling romantic personality than his true hero Aeneas.

But Livy's highest conscious admiration is for Scipio – like Aeneas, the *fatalis dux*, the man destined to command from the moment of his passionate outburst among the survivors of

Cannae (p. 153). Five years later he offered himself for the command in Spain after the disaster in which both his father and his uncle had been killed. He was then twenty-four, and from then on the issue of the war and the fate of Hannibal were in his hands. As we follow his fortunes in Spain, Sicily, and Africa, we are held by the spell of his personal charm, which could captivate 'not only the barbaric Syphax . . . but even his bitterest enemy Hasdrubal' (p. 521), make the volatile Numidian Masinissa his devoted follower, quell mutinous troops, and compel a reluctant Senate of older men to let him carry out his bold strategy of taking the war out of Italy.

Livy certainly disapproves of Scipio's practice of working on credulous minds by representing himself as divinely inspired (p. 379), and he may have thought the long hair and unconventional dress of his hero another unnecessary affectation, but he is convinced of Scipio's powers, his energy and resourcefulness, his imagination and ability to learn from his opponent, qualities which Livy takes pains to display in the speeches he gives Scipio at dramatic moments in the war. The most telling of these are Scipio's reply to the personal attack on him in the Senate by the old Fabius Maximus (p. 556), and the words spoken at his meeting with Hannibal before the battle of Zama (p. 657). Here Livy succeeds in making his readers feel that the real conflict lies in this last fatal interview; the victory after the battle, the peace terms, and Scipio's triumph are historical events which round off the action, but this exchange is the true climax of the drama of the war.

Livy's faults as a scientific historian do not detract from his greatness as a writer, but they prompt the question whether he should have been writing history at all. His gifts are positive and original; but would they have had better scope if he had written at a time when the historical novel was a popular accepted form?

Like a novelist he subordinated historical precision to the demands of character and plot. He indulged freely in invention and imagination in order to present a living picture. He would have disclaimed the title of a 'historian' in the modern sense. He had no wish to spend long years burrowing for irrefutable but trivial facts and to secure himself against criticism by burying them again in unreadable monographs. Like Scott, he wanted to be read, and he wanted the public to enjoy reading him. His success was immediate and universal; he became a classic.[1]

As R. M. Ogilvie points out, the heyday of the historical novel is to be found in periods when there is 'a widespread interest in the past, unaccompanied by widespread or specialized learning'. Today popular interest has shifted to imaginative historical biography, or to psychological novels where historical characters and their motives are subjected to detailed analysis. In these fields one thinks of Rex Warner on Caesar, Robert Graves on Claudius, *Memoirs of Hadrian*, and *The Sword of Pleasure*. There are excellent novels of action written for young people; but no one writes today as Scott and Livy did, with the conviction that there are lessons to be learned from history and that the rise or downfall of their characters provides practical examples for the conduct of our daily lives. Perhaps Kipling was the last person to do so when, out of his love of Sussex, he created *Puck of Pook's Hill* to teach the continuity of history. It may be that a touch of *patavinitas* is essential for writing of this kind.

If we compare *The War with Hannibal* with the old serious-minded historical novels, such as *Romola*, *The Cloister and the Hearth*, and *Salammbo*, it is clear that Livy's power to relive the past is remarkable. He never falls into the error of trying to create atmosphere by lifting pages from Baedeker – George Eliot and Lord Lytton earnestly did their best with Florence and Pompeii, but the dead stones never speak. Instead, he keeps description to a minimum and recreates the spirit of Rome by entering into the feelings of the people of the time, so that his readers can share the panic as Hannibal approaches Rome, the wild rejoicing after the victory of the Metaurus, and even the overheard comments of the bystanders at the triumph of Livius and Nero (p. 508). He can make us feel what it is like to suffer a long siege, to lie on a battlefield wounded and dying, to be trapped in a panic-stricken crowd, and to face action cold and wet and hungry. All his great battle-accounts are memorable for some individual reaction or mass emotion. So it is

1. From 'Sir Walter Scott and Livy', a Third Programme talk by R. M. Ogilvie; printed in *Listener*, 3 November 1960.

impossible to think of Cannae without seeing the consul Paullus, sitting on a stone, bleeding from his wounds and refusing the offer of a horse; and at Lake Trasimene there is the horror of fighting in the fog with mud and water underfoot until 'at last the heat of the sun dispersed the mist, and in the clear morning light hills and plain revealed to their eyes the terrible truth that the Roman army was almost totally destroyed' (p. 100). We can forgive Livy his inaccuracies over the crossing of the Alps when we remember the scenes he has described – the elephants crossing the river, the stumbling horses, the terrible descent over the newly-fallen snow, and Hannibal's unremitting efforts to hearten his exhausted men. This is imaginative writing of the highest order, and there is not a book amongst the ten without scenes of similar power placed with masterly skill at strategic points in the narrative.

Individual episodes too are selected for a purpose; the survivors of Cannae are compelled to break away by the sheer personality of a junior officer, Publius Sempronius Tuditanus, and when they reach safety in Canusium they are provided with food and clothing and money by a wealthy Apulian woman, Busa, whom the Senate afterwards honoured. In 212, 'with all Spain apparently lost and both armies wiped out, one man restored the shattered fortunes of Rome' – Lucius Septimius, who took over the command of the remnant. These are names Livy wishes to be remembered and admired.

Finally, no one can fail to be impressed by the solid achievement of a constitutional government; whatever the stresses of war, annual elections and the periodic census are held, levies for the army organized, and claims for exemption given a fair hearing. Taxes are collected in due order and only one case of profiteering is reported and prosecuted (p. 296). At the outbreak of the war in 218 Rome had six legions; the following year there were eleven, and in 211, despite the estimated loss of 50,000 Romans and allies at Cannae, there were twenty-three legions serving. The financial strain was immense, but the country's credit was maintained. In 215 private companies undertook to supply the army in Spain for deferred payment, and even before the end of the war, one third of the money borrowed from individual citizens six years previously was repaid (pp. 402 and

586). In this record of courage and constancy Livy saw the continuity which he could not express clearly in his year-by-year report of the war's detailed progress, and this is what gives *The War with Hannibal* a true dramatic unity. The theme was there for Livy, in the records of his predecessors, but what he made of it was his own.

When Aubrey de Sélincourt died he had almost finished translating *The War with Hannibal*. Some of it was in typescript, some in manuscript; the last twelve chapters were not translated, and none of the work was revised. I have completed the translation, added footnotes to the few he left, and supplied maps and a chronological index. In revising the translation to make it conform with the Oxford Text of Walters and Conway I have done no more than remove the ambiguities and inconsistencies he would have removed himself had he lived, so that this translation can be read essentially as he left it, in the freely-moving, eloquent prose he wrote with wonderful ease. The manuscripts he left in his clear handwriting were almost entirely free from after-thoughts and corrections; he could read a half-page of Livy, carry it in his head and put the translation down on paper in its finished form. This suggests to me a real affinity with his subject; neither de Sélincourt nor Livy would suffer the forward surge of the narrative to be held up by details like the exact spelling of a disputed Spanish place-name. Both were masters of prose style, both were humanists and scholars, and this translation should do something to restore Livy's reputation as the 'man of fine imagination' who was an inspiration to European learning in the past. Perhaps Aubrey de Sélincourt would also have wished it to help the teacher to 'remember the purpose of his duties, and impress upon his pupil the qualities of Hannibal and Scipio rather than the date of the fall of Carthage, and not so much where Marcellus died as why it was inconsistent with his duty that he should die there. Let him be taught not so much the facts of history as how to judge them.'[1]

I should like to thank Mrs de Sélincourt for her confidence in my ability to edit her husband's work, Dr E. V. Rieu for his

1. Montaigne, *Essays*, p. 62.

constant encouragement, Sir Gavin de Beer and Mr R. M. Ogilvie for permission to quote their views, Dr Peter Green for a quotation from his forthcoming translation of Juvenal's *Satires*, my husband and Thomas Radice for advice, and Mr E. F. Watling for invaluable help with proofs.

B.R.

*Highgate, 1963*

The reprint of 1972 includes a comprehensive index prepared by Jean Maund. Her task was not easy, as Aubrey de Sélincourt often reduced three Roman names to one, to keep the narrative moving; these are all now indexed in full under the names used in the translation. I should like to extend my thanks to Mrs Maund for her contribution. It is her speed and accuracy, plus her determination not to be defeated by the multiplicity of Hannos, Hasdrubals and Magos in the Carthaginian forces, that have made this index useful and informative for students of Livy.

B.R.

*1972*

# BOOK XXI

1. Most historians have prefaced their work by stressing the importance of the period they propose to deal with; and I may well, at this point, follow their example and declare that I am now about to tell the story of the most memorable war in history: that, namely, which was fought by Carthage under the leadership of Hannibal against Rome.

A number of things contributed to give this war its unique character: in the first place, it was fought between peoples unrivalled throughout previous history in material resources, and themselves at the peak of their prosperity and power; secondly, it was a struggle between old antagonists, each of whom had learned, in the first Punic War, to appreciate the military capabilities of the other; thirdly, the final issue hung so much in doubt that the eventual victors came nearer to destruction than their adversaries. Moreover, high passions were at work throughout, and mutual hatred was hardly less sharp a weapon than the sword; on the Roman side there was rage at the unprovoked attack by a previously beaten enemy; on the Carthaginian, bitter resentment at what was felt to be the grasping and tyrannical attitude of their conquerors. The intensity of the feeling is illustrated by an anecdote of Hannibal's boyhood: his father Hamilcar, after the campaign in Africa, was about to carry his troops over into Spain, when Hannibal, then about nine years old, begged, with all the childish arts he could muster, to be allowed to accompany him; whereupon Hamilcar, who was preparing to offer sacrifice for a successful outcome, led the boy to the altar and made him solemnly swear, with his hand upon the sacred victim, that as soon as he was old enough he would be the enemy of the Roman people. Hamilcar was a proud man and the loss of Sicily and Sardinia was a cruel blow to his pride; he remembered, moreover, that Sicily had been surrendered too soon, before the situation had become really desperate, and that Rome, taking advantage of internal troubles in Africa, had tricked Carthage into the loss of Sardinia, and then had added insult to injury by the imposition of a tribute. 2. All this rankled in his mind, and his conduct of affairs during the five years of the war in Africa, following hard upon the signature of peace with Rome, and subsequently during the nine years he spent in extending Carthaginian influence in Spain, made it clear enough that his ultimate object was an enterprise of far greater moment, and that if he had lived the invasion of Italy would have taken place under Hamilcar's leadership, instead of, as actually happened, under Hannibal's. That the war was postponed was due to Hamilcar's timely death and the fact that Hannibal was still too young to assume command.

The interval between father and son was filled by Hasdrubal, who commanded the Carthaginian armies for some eight years. Gossip had it that as a very young man he had won the personal favour and affection of Hamilcar, who in course of time and in recognition of his other qualities had married him to his daughter; and that he obtained command of the army on the strength of the relationship thus established, against the wishes of the leading men in Carthage, but strongly supported by the Barca[1] faction whose influence both with the army and the common people was very great. His policy aimed at peaceful expansion rather than conquest; avoiding the direct use of force he preferred to extend Carthaginian power by establishing friendly relations with local princes and thus winning the support of the various peoples under their control. A pacific policy, however, did not save him from a violent end, for he was murdered by a native in revenge for his master whom Hasdrubal had killed. The murderer was seized by the bystanders but showed no sign either of fear or remorse; even under torture the expression on his face never changed, and one might have imagined that triumph had so far subdued his pain that he was actually smiling.

It was with Hasdrubal, because of his extraordinary flair for exercising influence upon the Spanish peoples and thus bringing them under Carthaginian sway, that the Romans had renewed the treaty of peace, fixing the river Ebro as the boundary

1. i.e. the supporters of Hamilcar, surnamed Barca, 'the Thunderer'. (A. de S.)

between their respective spheres and establishing the neutrality of Saguntum as a sort of buffer state.

3. The question of Hasdrubal's successor was quickly decided. The military vote was in favour of the young Hannibal, who was at once escorted to headquarters, where he was unanimously and enthusiastically acclaimed, and there is little doubt that the army's choice was supported by the mass of the people in Carthage. Years before, when Hannibal was little more than a boy, Hasdrubal had written home to request his presence with the troops, and the propriety of the request had been debated in the Carthaginian Senate. The Barca party was in favour of granting it, urging the wisdom of accustoming the young man to active service, with a view to his ultimate succession to his father's position, but the opposite view was taken by their opponents. 'I think,' said Hanno, the leader of the anti-Barca faction, 'that Hasdrubal's request is a fair one – but, at the same time, that it ought not to be granted.' Such ambiguity made everyone stare, so Hanno went on to explain himself. 'Hasdrubal,' he said, 'sees in the matter nothing but the due payment of a debt: he himself surrendered the flower of his youth for the delectation of Hannibal's father; now he asks a similar favour from the son. What could be more just? But heaven forbid that under the veil of a military training we should subject our young men to the lusts of our generals. Moreover, we are surely not afraid of a little delay in allowing Hamilcar's son to see with his own eyes the excessive power his father wielded – a power not unlike that of a reigning monarch – or of being too slow to pay homage to the son of a king whose son-in-law was made heir to the command of our armies. No: my proposal is that this young fellow be kept at home, and be taught, in proper subjection to the law and its officers, to live on equal terms with his peers. Otherwise we may well find that this small spark may one day kindle a great fire.' 4. Most of the nobility supported Hanno; but they were few and, as usually happens, wisdom was forced to yield to numbers. Hannibal was sent to Spain, where the troops received him with unanimous enthusiasm, the old soldiers feeling that in the person of this young man Hamilcar himself was restored to them. In the features and expression of the son's face

they saw the father once again, the same vigour in his look, the same fire in his eyes. Very soon he no longer needed to rely upon his father's memory to make himself beloved and obeyed: his own qualities were sufficient. Power to command and readiness to obey are rare associates; but in Hannibal they were perfectly united, and their union made him as much valued by his commander as by his men. Hasdrubal preferred him to all other officers in any action which called for vigour and courage, and under his leadership the men invariably showed to the best advantage both dash and confidence. Reckless in courting danger, he showed superb tactical ability once it was upon him. Indefatigable both physically and mentally, he could endure with equal ease excessive heat or excessive cold; he ate and drank not to flatter his appetites but only so much as would sustain his bodily strength. His time for waking, like his time for sleeping, was never determined by daylight or darkness: when his work was done, then, and then only, he rested, without need, moreover, of silence or a soft bed to woo sleep to his eyes. Often he was seen lying in his cloak on the bare ground amongst the common soldiers on sentry or picket duty. His accoutrement, like the horses he rode, was always conspicuous, but not his clothes, which were like those of any other officer of his rank and standing. Mounted or unmounted he was unequalled as a fighting man, always the first to attack, the last to leave the field. So much for his virtues – and they were great; but no less great were his faults: inhuman cruelty, a more than Punic perfidy, a total disregard of truth, honour, and religion, of the sanctity of an oath and of all that other men hold sacred. Such was the complex character of the man who for three years served under Hasdrubal's command, doing and seeing everything which could help to equip him as a great military leader.

5. From the very first day of his command Hannibal acted as if he had definite instructions to take Italy as his sphere of operations and to make war on Rome. Speed was of the essence of his plan. The premature deaths of Hamilcar and Hasdrubal reminded him that he was not himself immune from accident if he delayed. So without hesitation he determined to attack Saguntum. As an attack upon this town was certain to rouse

Rome to action, he first invaded the territory of the Olcades, a tribe lying south of the Ebro, within the Carthaginian sphere of influence though not actually under Carthaginian control; by this move he hoped to distract attention from his real purpose and to give the impression that by the conquest of neighbouring tribes he had been led on, in an inevitable chain of events, to war with Saguntum. Carteia, the wealthy capital of the Olcades, was stormed and sacked: the lesser neighbouring settlements were scared into submission and forced to pay tribute, and the victorious army retired with its plunder to winter in New Carthage, where by a generous distribution of the captured material and prompt settlement of arrears of pay Hannibal further strengthened the bond between himself and his troops, both native and foreign.

At the beginning of the following spring operations were pushed forward against the Vaccaei, and their towns of Hermandica and Arbocala taken by assault, the latter after a protracted defence by the large and determined population. Fugitives from Hermandica joined forces with those of the Olcades who after the defeat of the previous summer had lost their homes, and together they stirred the Carpetani to action. Hannibal had returned from his expedition against the Vaccaei and was near the Tagus, when they set upon his column, encumbered as it was with loot, and threw it into confusion. Avoiding direct retaliation, Hannibal took up a position on the river bank and waited for dark; then, when all movement had ceased and there was no sound from the enemy's camp, he forded the river and took up a new position, constructing his defences in such a way as to leave the enemy an opportunity to follow him over. His intention was to attack them as they were crossing, and with this in view he instructed his mounted troops to set upon them as soon as they saw them in the water. His infantry and elephants (forty in number) he posted on the bank. The enemy force, raised as it was by the addition of the fugitives to 100,000 men, would have been invincible in a straight fight on open ground; they were a proud and warlike people, so, relying upon their superiority in numbers and convinced not only that Hannibal's withdrawal was due to fear of defeat but also that nothing but the river barrier lay between themselves and victory, they raised their war-cry and, without waiting for orders, plunged helter-skelter into the water. A strong contingent of Carthaginian cavalry promptly dashed in to meet them, and battle was joined in midstream. It was an unequal struggle, for the unmounted Spaniards, unable to get a firm foothold in the treacherous shallows, would have been an easy prey to the confident assault of a mounted trooper, even had he been unarmed, while the cavalrymen, for their part, with full command over their movements and their weapons, sitting firm on their mounts even where the stream ran strongest, set effectually to work with both javelins and swords. Many of the enemy were drowned; some, swept downstream by the powerful current, were trampled to death by the elephants, while the remainder tried to save themselves by returning to their own bank of the river; but while they were still at sixes and sevens and doing what they could to collect their scattered units, Hannibal led his men in mass formation into the river, crossed, and before they could recover their breath drove them in disorder from the bank. He ravaged the countryside, and a few days later the Carpetani surrendered and were added to the list of conquered peoples. The whole of Spain south of the Ebro, with the exception of Saguntum, was now in Carthaginian hands.

6. Hannibal was not yet actually at war with Saguntum, but as a preliminary to it he was already beginning to sow seeds of discontent amongst the neighbouring tribes, notably the Turdetani. He soon presented himself to them as their supporter in the quarrel he had himself organized, and when it became obvious to the Saguntines that Hannibal intended not to negotiate but to resort to force, they sent representatives to Rome to ask for assistance in the war which was now clearly inevitable. The consuls of that year,[1] Publius Cornelius Scipio and Tiberius Sempronius Longus, brought the Saguntine envoys before the Senate and opened the debate; the decision was taken to send envoys to Spain with instructions to look into the situation of their allies, and, if circumstances seemed to warrant it, to make a formal demand to Hannibal to keep his

1. i.e. 218 B.C. The siege of Saguntum must have started in 219. See p. 38 where Livy tries to solve the difficulty.

hands off Saguntum; they were then to cross to Africa and lay before the government in Carthage the first complaints of Rome's allies in Spain. But before the Roman envoys had had time even to start on their mission, news came that operations against Saguntum had begun. No one had expected this decisive move so soon.

The Senate met to reconsider the situation. Opinions were divided. Some proposed that Spain and Africa should be allotted to the consuls as their respective spheres of operation and that total war, by sea and land, should be undertaken; others preferred to concentrate wholly against Hannibal in Spain; others, again, expressed the view that it would be wiser to await the return of the envoys from Spain, as so serious a step as war with Carthage ought not to be taken without full deliberation. It was this last, and most cautious, proposal which was adopted, and hastened the despatch of Publius Valerius Flaccus and Quintus Baebius Tamphilus to Saguntum with instructions to approach Hannibal and then, if he refused to stop his operations against the town, to proceed to Carthage and demand the surrender of the Carthaginian commander on the charge of a breach of the treaty between the two powers.

7. Meanwhile, during these discussions and preparations in Rome, the assault upon Saguntum was proceeding with all the means at Hannibal's command. The town, situated about a mile from the sea, was by far the most prosperous settlement south of the Ebro. The inhabitants are said to have come originally from the island of Zacynthus, with a certain admixture of Rutulians from Ardea; but in any case the place had rapidly risen to its present importance by the qualities of its people, building their prosperity partly upon the produce of the sea and of the soil, partly upon the increase of their numbers, partly, again, upon the reverence for principle which was the essence of their training, and which led them to remain loyal to an ally even if such loyalty should involve their own destruction.

Hannibal, having invaded Saguntine territory and done wholesale damage to growing crops, launched a triple assault on the town. In one section of the defences there was a slope down into a comparatively broad and level stretch of ground, and it was here that Hannibal determined to bring up his 'mantlets' under the protection of which the battering-rams might be brought into action against the walls. The ground at some little distance from the walls was, indeed, level enough to enable the mantlets to be moved into position; nevertheless the manoeuvre was by no means successful when it came to the point of action. There were several reasons for its failure: first, the menace in that sector of a fortified tower of great height and strength; secondly, the fact that the wall itself had been raised to a greater height than elsewhere to protect a spot otherwise susceptible of attack, and, lastly, the more vigorous resistance of the picked troops which had been detailed to undertake the most difficult and dangerous tasks in the defence. For a time they kept the attackers at bay by missile weapons, and left no place safe for their pioneers, but soon, no longer content only with the flash of spears in defence of the tower and walls, they were moved to make a series of sorties against the enemy posts and assault works. In the skirmishes which ensued the losses on each side were about equal, but the situation quickly changed when Hannibal, rashly riding up to within range of the wall, was severely wounded in the thigh by a javelin. At this all the troops in his vicinity wavered and broke and the various assault-machines came near to being abandoned altogether. 8. For the following few days operations quietened down into something resembling a siege, to give Hannibal's wound time to heal; the hand-to-hand encounters stopped, though there was no slackening on either side in the preparation of means for assault or defence. Thus the struggle soon began afresh with greater vigour than before; and in a number of sectors, often at spots where the ground did not admit the construction of siege-works, battering-rams were moved up under the protection of mantlets. Numerically the Carthaginians were at a great advantage, the evidence suggesting that the army amounted to 150,000 men; the town's defenders, on the contrary, found themselves stretched beyond reasonable limits by the multifarious calls upon their energies, and were hardly sufficient for their tasks. Already the rams were in action and doing serious damage in many sectors; one section of the wall had been so far breached by continuous falls of masonry that a way had been opened into the town. Soon afterwards three towers together with the stretch of wall between them had crashed to the ground. For a moment the Carthaginians had thought that the town was theirs, and troops of both sides dashed forward through the breach, as if the now vanished wall had screened not the defenders only, but the attackers too. The fight which ensued bore no resemblance to the sort of tip-and-run affairs which in the course of protracted siege-operations one side or the other often seeks a chance of bringing on: it was a pitched battle, a major engagement such as might have been fought in the open field, though in fact the combatants were pinned between the fallen masonry of the wall and the near-by buildings of the town. Hope on the one side, the courage of despair on the other, were raised to the highest pitch, Hannibal's men confident that one final push would deliver the town into their hands, the Saguntines stoutly resisting the threat to their now defenceless home, while not a man of them would give an inch of ground lest an enemy soldier should press forward into the place where he had stood. Casualties increased as the fighting grew hotter; so closely were the men on either side pressed together that no missile could miss its mark. The Saguntines included in their armoury a sort of javelin called a *falarica*: it had a rounded shaft of fir and an iron head. Just below the head the shaft was square, as in the Roman *pilum*. Round this portion of the shaft they bound tow smeared with pitch. The iron head of this weapon, being three feet long, was capable of going through a man's body, armour and all; but the most alarming thing about it was, that even when it stuck in a man's shield without penetrating his flesh, the blazing tow and pitch, lighted before it was hurled, and fanned by its motion through the air to a fiercer flame, compelled the victim to drop his weapons and so left him exposed and defenceless against its successors.

9. For a long time the struggle was indecisive. The Saguntines drew courage from the fact that the defence of the town had been more successful than they had dared to hope, while their adversaries, robbed of the expected victory, felt themselves beaten. In these circumstances the defenders suddenly raised a cheer and thrust the invader back amongst the ruins of the wall; here the Carthaginian force found itself in difficulties,

lost its cohesion, and was finally flung out, completely overpowered, and compelled to seek the protection of its own camp.

Meanwhile news came that the envoys from Rome had arrived, and they were met on the coast by a party sent by Hannibal to warn them of the danger of proceeding any farther inland: for the numerous tribes were both highly incensed and up in arms, and Hannibal, moreover, had no time in his present difficult circumstances to give audience to a delegation. When it became clear that the envoys, refused a hearing at Saguntum, were determined to go on to Carthage, Hannibal forestalled them by writing to the leaders of his party there and urging them to prepare the minds of his supporters and prevent them from allowing the opposing faction to make any conciliatory gesture towards Rome.

10. As a result of this, though the delegation was at least granted an audience, it proved as fruitless and ineffectual as the previous one. In the Carthaginian senate the only man to speak for the existing treaty was Hanno: the other members were solidly against him, and he was listened to in dead silence – not indeed the silence of assent, but the silence due to his personal position and importance. In the name of the gods who protect the sanctity of treaties he begged them not to provoke a Roman as well as a Saguntine war. He had solemnly warned them not to allow a son of Hamilcar to go out to the Carthaginian armies. Had he not said that the very ghost of that man, let alone his son, was incapable of living in peace, and that never, so long as a single heir of the name and blood of the Barcas survived, could the treaty with Rome be safe from peril? 'Yet you,' he continued, 'sent to join our troops this dangerous and ambitious man, hot with the desire for power and seeing but one way to its acquisition – a life in arms amongst the soldiery, spent in provoking an endless succession of wars. The fire was there, and you fed it; yes, you piled fuel on the flames which are burning you now. By the terms of our treaty with Rome, Saguntum is a neutral town, and your armies are besieging it; soon Roman legions will be besieging Carthage, led by those same gods who in the former war blessed their revenge for the rupture of the terms of peace. Are you

so ignorant of Rome - and of Carthage - of the portion fate has decreed for them and for ourselves? Envoys who came from one allied people, and on behalf of another, your truly admirable Commander-in-Chief, in defiance of international law, refused to admit to his presence. Denied the reception which the representatives even of an enemy can expect to be granted, they have come here to you, asking for satisfaction according to the treaty between our two nations. They demand the surrender of the man responsible for a criminal act. Their demands are mild, their first steps slow and cautious; but for that very reason I fear that once they set their hands to work, their resentment against us will be the more bitter and prolonged. Remember Hamilcar's defeat off the Aegates islands and afterwards at Eryx, and the miseries you suffered through twenty-four years of warfare by land and sea. Then it was not this boy who commanded our armies, but his father Hamilcar – that second Mars, as his friends like to think him. None the less, though the terms of the treaty excluded us from Italy, we did not keep our hands off Tarentum, just as now history is repeating itself at Saguntum. Because of that act the gods themselves shared in the victory, and the technical question of who it was that broke the treaty was decided by the result of the war, which, like a just judge, gave victory to those who had right on their side. It is against Carthage that Hannibal is now moving his engines of war; it is our own walls he is battering with his rams. The ruins of Saguntum – would I were a false prophet! – will fall upon our own heads, and the war we started with Saguntum will have to be fought against Rome.

'Shall we then surrender Hannibal? My opinion, I know, will carry little weight, because his father and I were always bitterly opposed. I was glad when Hamilcar died – and why? because if he lived, war with Rome was inevitable; and this son of his, with the devil in his heart and the torch in his hand to kindle its flames, I hate and abhor. I do indeed demand his surrender, to atone for the treaty he broke; nay more, if there were no question of giving him up, I should demand his removal to the remotest corner of the world, his banishment to some spot from which no word of him – not even the sound of

1. In 241, at the end of the First War.

his name – could ever reach us, nor he himself ever again disturb our peace.

'This, then, is my proposal: that representatives be sent immediately to Rome with instructions to satisfy the Senate's demands; that a second delegation should approach Hannibal with our orders to withdraw from Saguntum, and then deliver his person to the Romans in accordance with the treaty; and, finally, that a third delegation should be entrusted with reparations to the people of Saguntum.'

11. When Hanno had ended, there was no need for anyone to refute his arguments, as the senate was almost unanimously on Hannibal's side; indeed the feeling was that he had spoken like an enemy of his country even more than the Roman envoy, Valerius Flaccus. The reply to the Roman delegation, therefore, was to fix the blame for hostilities not upon Hannibal but on the Saguntines, and to add that Rome would be acting improperly if she let her concern for Saguntum take precedence over her long-standing treaty of friendship with Carthage.

In all this diplomatic activity the Romans were letting time slip by. Hannibal, however, was by no means altogether idle. His men were exhausted by their recent fighting and engineering labours in the field, so he allowed them a few days' rest, having posted parties to guard the various operational devices. But all the time he was working on their morale, fanning in them the flames of wrath against the enemy, or rousing their greed with the hope of rich rewards; to this he put the finishing touch in an address, in which he announced his intention of turning over to the troops everything of value they could find when the town should be taken. The effect of the announcement was electric: if at that moment the signal for assault had been given, nothing could have stood against them. The Saguntines, meanwhile, were using the pause in the fighting to the best possible effect: during the several days which passed without a move by either side, they worked day and night to rebuild the section of wall, the destruction of which had laid the town open to the enemy.

But the lull was soon over, and the next assault was a more violent one. This time, the din of battle seemed to be everywhere at once, so that the defenders hardly knew where first, or best, to concentrate their defence. Hannibal in person was urging his men to fresh efforts at a point where they were bringing into action a mobile tower higher than any section of the fortifications of the town. This machine was dragged up; by means of the catapults and stone-throwers with which each storey was equipped, the walls were cleared of defenders and Hannibal seized the opportunity of sending a party of some 500 African troops armed with picks to undermine the wall. It was not a difficult task, as the wall was of old-fashioned construction, the stones not being cemented but set in clay, and for this reason portions of it fell for some distance on both sides of the actual point of impact, so that columns of men were enabled to enter the town over the fallen rubble. They occupied an elevated point within the walls, and brought their artillery into position; then they built defences round the point they had seized, thus giving themselves a sort of fort, or stronghold, in the heart of the town from which to threaten the inhabitants. The Saguntines replied by constructing a fresh wall farther in, to protect the as yet uncaptured portion of the town. On both sides operations both offensive and defensive were carried on with the greatest vigour, but the difficulties of the Saguntines were growing: their efforts to save the central portions of the town from the enemy's advance gradually diminished what of it they could still control; at the same time supplies were running low, and hope of succour from outside, with the Romans, on whom alone they could rely, still far away and all the neighbouring country in enemy hands, was day by day growing less.

Their gloomy forebodings were temporarily relieved by the sudden departure of Hannibal on an expedition against the Oretani and Carpetani. These two peoples, in surprise and anger at the severity of Hannibal's demand for troops, had seized and retained the officers in charge of recruitment, thus giving reason to fear that they might be contemplating rebellion. But Hannibal was too quick for them, and, taken by surprise, they abandoned all thought of resistance.

12. Actually, however, there was no relaxation of the pressure on the town, for Maharbal, son of Himilco, whom Hannibal had left in command, carried on offensive operations with such

vigour that Hannibal's absence was hardly noticed by anyone – friend or foe. This officer fought a number of successful actions, destroyed a further stretch of wall by employing three rams, and was able to show Hannibal on his return widespread devastation and much newly tumbled masonry amongst the town's defences. Without further delay Hannibal pressed forward right up to the central stronghold; there was a savage struggle with heavy losses on both sides, and a portion of the stronghold fell into his hands.

At this juncture two men, Alco of Saguntum and a Spaniard named Alorcus, attempted to end hostilities, though the hope was a slender one. The former, thinking that an appeal for mercy might have some effect, without the knowledge of his compatriots, slipped out of the town under cover of darkness and presented himself before Hannibal. But his tears were of no avail, so when he found the victorious general obdurate and the terms of surrender cruelly harsh, he changed his tactics, and, without further pleading, remained with the Carthaginians as a deserter, declaring that it would be death to treat for peace upon such conditions. The terms were, that the Saguntines should make full reparation to the Turdetani, deliver to Hannibal all the gold and silver in their possession, leave the town only with what they wore on their backs, and make a home for themselves in such place as Hannibal chose to indicate. Alco having denied that the Saguntines would accept these terms, the Spaniard Alorcus who at that time was serving in Hannibal's army, though he held a semi-official position as 'friend and guest' of the Saguntines, undertook to negotiate in the belief that where all else is lost the will to resist is inevitably lost too. Having openly handed over his arms to the enemy guards, he passed through the fortifications of the town and by his own request was taken to the officer in command. A motley crowd immediately gathered, but they were cleared out of the way and Alorcus was given a hearing. 13. 'If,' he began, 'your fellow-citizen Alco, having gone to Hannibal to try to obtain terms of peace, had returned to you with the terms which were offered, this visit of mine would not have been necessary: I should not have come to you either as a deserter, or to speak on Hannibal's behalf. But Alco has deserted you: the fault may be his, or it may be yours – his, if he only pretended to be afraid; yours, if there is real danger in this town for messengers who bring back the truth. For this reason, I have presumed upon the old ties of guest-friendship between us to come here and try to persuade you that it is, indeed, peace of a sort which is offered you. At least you are offered your lives. That I am saying what I say for nobody's benefit but your own, is sufficiently proved by the fact that I made no mention to you of peace either while your own resources were still adequate to maintain resistance, or while you continued to hope for assistance from Rome. That time is now gone by: you can no longer hope for succour; your own arms and your own walls can no longer defend you. I bring you, therefore, an offer of peace – not, indeed, a fair one, but the best obtainable. Nor need you wholly despair, if only you will listen to what it is in the proper spirit, as coming from the victor to the vanquished – if, that is, all you possess now being Hannibal's property, you are prepared not to consider as a loss what is taken from you, but rather to consider what is left you as pure gain. Your town, largely in ruins, is almost wholly in Hannibal's hands. This you must surrender to him; but he leaves you your land, and will indicate a site where you may build a new town. Your gold and silver, both national and private property, must all be surrendered. Your own lives and persons, those of your wives and children, will be spared, if you leave the town with not more than two suits of clothes apiece, and unarmed.

'Such are the demands of your victorious enemy; and, however harsh they may be, you are not in a position to refuse them. Personally, I have some hope that, once he finds all opposition removed, he may make some concessions; none the less I put it to you that it is better to face their full severity than to let your wives and children be dragged away to slavery before your eyes (as the custom of war allows) and then to have your throats cut.'

14. Crowds had been gradually gathering, and the Saguntine senate had become not unlike a general assembly of the populace. Suddenly, however, the leaders of the senate, before an answer could be given, left their places, collected all the precious metal from public buildings and private houses they could

find, and flung it into a fire hastily kindled for the purpose in the Forum, and themselves leapt after it into the flames. Throughout the town there was consternation, only to be increased by a sudden and dreadful sound from the direction of the citadel: the tower, long battered by the rams, had fallen, and over its ruins a company of Carthaginian troops was pressing forward. When they signalled that the way was clear and that there was no further opposition from the regular guard-posts and pickets, Hannibal knew that his moment had come: launching a full-scale assault he overwhelmed the town, having issued orders that no man of military age should be spared. It was a barbarous order, though hardly avoidable, as the event proved; for how was it possible to show mercy to men who in desperation either fought to the death or set fire to their own houses and burned themselves alive together with their wives and children?

15. The plunder taken from the captured town was very great. Much of value had been deliberately destroyed by its owners, and in the general butchery the fury of combat had made little distinction of age; all prisoners, moreover, became the property of the soldiers who took them; but in spite of this authorities agree that a considerable sum was realized by the sale of valuables and that a large quantity of costly furniture and rich materials was sent to Carthage.

Some writers[1] have stated that Saguntum fell in the eighth month after the beginning of hostilities, and that Hannibal then withdrew to New Carthage for the winter, and finally reached Italy five months after leaving that place. If this is so, then Publius Cornelius and Tiberius Sempronius could not have been the consuls to whom the Saguntine envoys were sent at the beginning of hostilities; for they both fought against Hannibal during their year of office, one on the river Ticinus, the other a little later on the Trebia. The dates do not fit, and we must either conclude that the events concerned were compressed into a shorter space of time than these writers suppose, or that Saguntum was not first attacked, but actually taken, at the beginning of the year in which Cornelius and Sempronius entered upon office. The battle of the Trebia cannot be put as late as

1. Notably Polybius.

the consulships of Gnaeus Servilius and Gaius Flaminius, because Flaminius entered office at Ariminum and was elected under the auspices of Sempronius who had gone to Rome to hold the elections after the battle of the Trebia, and had then rejoined his troops in their winter quarters.

16. The return to Rome of the delegation to Carthage with a report that the Carthaginian government refused to negotiate coincided almost exactly with the news of the fall of Saguntum. The effect on the Senate was shattering: grief, and pity for the dreadful and undeserved fate of a friendly people, shame at the failure to send them succour, anger against Carthage, the fear which seemed to suggest that the enemy was already at the gates of Rome and threatening to destroy her, all combined in a conflict of emotions which made calm deliberation impossible. They knew they had never had to face a fiercer or more warlike foe – and that, too, at a time when Rome herself was least prepared for a great military effort. Their recent campaigns against Sardinia, for instance, or Corsica, or Istria, or Illyria had been only minor affairs, mere pin-pricks, and no real test of Roman arms, while their engagements with the Gauls had been more in the nature of casual skirmishing than of regular war. Carthage was a very different matter. She had long been an enemy to Rome, and her troops, trained in twenty-three years of hard and consistently successful warfare in Spain, and accustomed to obey a commander of supreme enterprise and skill, were now crossing the Ebro fresh from the destruction of a powerful and wealthy town; they were bringing with them innumerable Spaniards already battle-hungry, and would soon be raising the Gauls, with their insatiable appetite for blood. War was coming, and it would have to be fought in Italy, in defence of the walls of Rome, and against the world in arms.

17. The regions in which the two consuls were respectively to operate had already been fixed as Spain, on the one hand, and Africa and Sicily on the other. Lots were drawn, and the former fell to Cornelius, the latter to Sempronius. A decree was passed to raise six legions for the current year, with as many allied troops as each consul thought fit, and to mobilize as strong a fleet as possible. 24,000 Roman infantry were enrolled and 1,800 cavalry; allied troops consisted of 40,000 infantry

and 4,400 cavalry. The strength of the fleet was 220 quinquiremes and twenty light craft.

The question of a declaration of war was then put to the assembled people of Rome. The vote was in favour, whereupon business was suspended throughout the city for a period of public prayer, and the gods were petitioned for a happy and successful outcome of the war.

The forces were divided between the two consuls as follows: two legions, each consisting of 4,000 infantry and 300 cavalry, were assigned to Sempronius, together with 16,000 allied foot, 1,800 horse, 160 warships, and twelve light vessels. In command of these contingents he was sent to Sicily with instructions to cross into Africa if his colleague Cornelius proved strong enough to prevent Hannibal from entering Italy. To Cornelius fewer troops were assigned, because the praetor Lucius Manlius was also being sent to Gaul with a not inconsiderable force; his naval strength was cut most severely, because it was not expected that a sea-borne invasion would be attempted or that Hannibal was contemplating naval warfare. The number of his ships was accordingly reduced to 60 quinquiremes. His other forces consisted of two Roman legions with their regular cavalry attached, 14,000 allied foot, and 1,600 horse. In Cisalpine Gaul were stationed two Roman legions, 10,000 allied infantry 1,000 allied cavalry, and 600 Roman cavalry, all intended for the war with Carthage.

18. These preparations made and all being in order for the outbreak of hostilities, the Senate sent another delegation to Carthage. Its members were all oldish men – Quintus Fabius, Marcus Livius, Lucius Aemilius, Gaius Licinius, and Quintus Baebius – and their instructions were to ask the Carthaginian senate whether Hannibal's attack on Saguntum had been in accordance with government policy. If the Carthaginians admitted the apparent direction of their actions and defended them as the result of official policy, then the Roman delegation was to declare war.

The envoys duly arrived. They were given audience in the senate, and Fabius without further words put the single question they had been instructed to ask. One of the Carthaginian senators thereupon said: 'Your previous embassy, gentlemen, when you demanded the person of Hannibal for attacking Saguntum, as you supposed, on his own initiative, was a somewhat ill-considered one; the object of your present embassy, though expressed for the moment in milder terms, is in fact a more serious matter. On the former occasion Hannibal was accused and the surrender of his person demanded; now you are trying to extort from us a confession of guilt, and at the same time seeking immediate reparation as if we had already confessed. Now in my view the proper question is not whether Saguntum was attacked as a matter of state policy or on the whim of a single individual, but whether that attack was, in the circumstances, legal or illegal. The inquiry into whether one of our own citizens acted arbitrarily or not – and perhaps his subsequent punishment – is a matter for ourselves alone; with you we have only a single point in dispute, namely the legality of the act under the terms of the treaty between us. Very well, then: since it is your pleasure to discriminate between what army-commanders do by government orders and what they do on their own initiative, consider the following facts. Your consul Gaius Lutatius signed with us a treaty by the terms of which neither side was to interfere with the allies of the other – but no mention in this connexion was made of Saguntum, which was not, at that time, in alliance with Rome. You will say, perhaps, that the treaty entered into with Hasdrubal debarred us from attacking Saguntum – to which my only reply will be words you have yourselves put into my mouth. For did you not deny that you were bound by a treaty which was entered into without either the sanction of the Senate or the approbation of the people? And did you not in consequence negotiate a fresh one which had the national authority behind it? If, then, you do not consider your treaties are binding unless they are signed with the full authority of the State, we, for our part, shall refuse to recognize the treaty negotiated by Hasdrubal without our knowledge or consent. I would ask you, therefore, to say no more about Saguntum or the river Ebro; let your minds, rather, now at last deliver themselves of the real thought they have long been big with.'

Fabius, in answer, laid his hand on the fold of his toga, where he had gathered it at the breast, and, 'Here,' he said, 'we bring you peace and war. Take which you will.' Scarcely had he spoken, when the answer no less proudly rang out: 'Whichever you please – we do not care.' Fabius let the gathered folds fall, and cried: 'We give you war.' The Carthaginian senators replied, as one man: 'We accept it; and in the same spirit we will fight it to the end.'

19. This direct challenge followed by the declaration of war seemed more in keeping with the dignity of Rome than an argument upon points of law, particularly at the present juncture, when Saguntum had just been destroyed. As to the actual rights and wrongs of the matter, there was no comparison between Hasdrubal's treaty and the earlier one concluded by Lutatius, which was altered; for in the latter an additional clause was included to the effect that it should hold good only if it obtained popular assent, whereas in Hasdrubal's treaty there was no such proviso: for years during Hasdrubal's lifetime it was tacitly accepted and was not altered even after his death. Even if the terms of the former treaty continued to be observed, there was sufficient protection for Saguntum in the clause 'excepting the allies of both parties'; this had not been qualified by any such phrase as 'present allies', or 'possible future ones', but since there was nothing to prevent the acquisition of new allies, it was clearly unjust to suppose either that no state should be taken into the Roman alliance for services rendered, or that, having been so taken, it should not be defended against aggression. The only stipulation was that no state allied to Carthage should be excited to revolt, or received into the Roman alliance if it rebelled of its own accord.

According to the instructions given them in Rome, the Roman delegation then proceeded to Spain with the object of persuading the various Spanish communities to accept the friendship of Rome, or at least of detaching them from the Carthaginian interest. The Bargusii, to whom they first applied, had already had enough of Carthaginian control, and gave them, in consequence, a favourable reception; and this success enabled them to excite a desire for change in a number of the tribes south of the Ebro. The Volciani, however, to whom they next applied, administered a severe check to the success of the embassy, and by an answer which soon became famous throughout the country turned the other communities from all thoughts of alliance with Rome. When their council had met to hear the delegates, the eldest member said: 'Men of Rome, it seems hardly decent to ask us to prefer your friendship to that of Carthage, considering the precedent of those who have been rash enough to do so. Was not your betrayal of your friends in Saguntum even more brutal than their destruction by their enemies the Carthaginians? I suggest you look for allies in some spot where what happened to Saguntum has never been heard of. The fall of that town will be a signal and melancholy warning to the peoples of Spain never to count upon Roman friendship nor to trust Rome's word.' The delegation was then told to quit the neighbourhood forthwith and it never subsequently met with any more favourable reception by the council of any of the Spanish towns. After a fruitless tour of the country it crossed into Gaul.

20. In Gaul, the envoys were faced with the strange and alarming spectacle of the natives attending the council (such was their custom) in full armour. The spokesman for Rome began by extolling the glories and virtues of his country and the extent of its dominion, and went on to ask his hearers not to allow the Carthaginian army, if it attempted to invade Italy, to pass through their territory. The request is said to have been met with such a roar of anger and such shouts of laughter from the young warriors present, that the magistrates and older men had difficulty in restoring order. In their view it was both impudent and ridiculous to suppose that the Gallic people, to save Italy from war, would be willing to draw it upon themselves and to offer their own cornlands, instead of somebody else's, to be trampled and ravaged by hostile armies. But quiet was at last restored, and the request was answered by the statement that, as Rome had never helped Gaul nor Carthage ever injured her, there was no good reason for the Gauls to fight either on one side or the other. They added, moreover, that they had heard that men of their nation were being expelled from territories on the Italian frontier and forced by Rome to pay tribute, amongst other indignities. The result of attempted negotiations in other Gallic communities was much

the same, and the Roman delegates heard no really friendly or pacific word until they reached Massilia,[1] where, as the result of their allies' loyal and diligent inquiries, they learned that Hannibal had already successfully worked upon the Gallic tribes and determined their attitude. It was added, however, that not even to Hannibal would the Gallic peoples, with their warlike and independent spirit, prove very tractable friends unless he mollified their chiefs from time to time with presents of gold – which all Gauls coveted.

Their tour of Spain and Gaul completed, the envoys returned to Rome. The consuls, not long before, had left for their respective provinces, and the Roman world was tense with excitement. War was coming, and rumour had it that the Carthaginians had already crossed the Ebro.

21. After the capture of Saguntum Hannibal had retired to winter quarters in New Carthage. News was brought him of the various activities in Rome and Carthage and of the decisions which had been made, so when he learned that he was himself the cause of the coming war as well as the commander-in-chief of the Carthaginian armies, he determined to act swiftly. As soon as he had completed the division and sale of the remainder of the captured material, he summoned a meeting of his Spanish troops, and addressed them as follows: 'My friends, no doubt you see as well as I do that, with all the Spanish peoples subject to our influence, one of two courses is open to us: either we must stop fighting and disband our armies, or pursue our conquests elsewhere. By doing the latter, and by seeking plunder and renown from the conquest of other countries, the Spanish peoples will reap the harvest not only of peace but of victory. Since, therefore, we are soon to fight a campaign in distant parts and nobody knows when you may see your homes and loved ones again, I have decided to grant leave of absence to any man who wishes to visit his family. Your orders are to return to duty at the beginning of spring, in order that, with God's help, we may begin a war which will fill your pockets with gold and carry your fame to the world's end.'

Most of the men were already feeling the separation from

1. Marseilles.

their families and looking forward sadly to a longer separation to come; so the unexpected offer of leave was very welcome. The whole winter was a time of inactivity between two periods of hard service, one completed, the other still to be faced, and the respite gave the troops fresh strength, both physical and moral, to endure again all that might be required of them. At the beginning of spring they reassembled according to orders.

After reviewing his auxiliary troops Hannibal went to Gades[1] to pay his vows to the Tyrian Hercules in the temple there, and swore to express further obligations to that god, should his affairs prosper. His next concern was the twofold task of perfecting his offensive and defensive measures. To obviate the danger of a Roman invasion of Africa by way of Sicily while he was marching for Italy through Spain and the Gallic provinces, he took the precaution of stationing a powerful force in the island. As this necessitated reinforcements, he asked for a fresh contingent of African troops, mostly light-armed spearmen, intending to employ African troops in Spain and Spanish troops in Africa in the belief that service by each in a foreign country would provide a sort of mutual guarantee of good behaviour. He sent 13,850 targeteers to Africa together with 870 slingers from the Balearic Islands and 1,200 cavalrymen of various nationality, some to serve in different parts of Africa, some to garrison Carthage; at the same time he dispatched officers to raise troops from the states dependent upon him, with orders that 4,000 picked men should be moved to Carthage to strengthen the garrison there and also to act as hostages. 22. Spain moreover was not to be neglected, especially in view of the recent Roman attempt to seduce the leading men of the various Spanish peoples from their allegiance, and the defence of the country was put into the capable hands of his brother Hasdrubal. The troops under his command were mainly African: 11,850 African foot, 300 Ligurians, and 500 from the Balearics. To these were added 450 Libyphoenician horse – men of mixed blood, half Punic half African – about 1,800 Numidians and Moors from the Atlantic coast, and a small force of 200 horse from the Ilergetes in Spain. Finally, there were twenty-one elephants, to make the land-forces

1. Cadiz.

complete. Furthermore, as it seemed likely that the Romans might attempt to repeat their former successes by sea, Hasdrubal was given for coastal defence a fleet of fifty quinquiremes, two quadriremes, and five triremes, though of these only thirty-two quinquiremes and five triremes were actually fitted out and manned.

From Gades Hannibal returned to the army's quarters in New Carthage, and then proceeded by way of Etovissa to the river Ebro and the coast. Here, the story goes, he had a dream: a young man of godlike aspect told him he had been sent by God to guide him to Italy, and bade him follow, and in all places keep his eyes fixed upon him. Conquering his fear, he followed the divine guide, looking neither to right nor left, nor behind, until overcome by a natural human curiosity and eager to know what it was he had been forbidden to see behind him, he was unable to control his eyes any longer. He looked round, and saw a monstrous snake, gliding; and in its path trees and bushes were tumbling in dreadful ruin, while a storm-cloud loomed up behind with the crash of thunder. He asked in his dream what that fearful commotion might be and what was the meaning of the sign, and a voice said in answer that it signified the laying waste of Italy, and that he must go forward without further questioning and allow what needs must be to remain in darkness.

23. Encouraged by his dream he proceeded to cross the Ebro, dividing his forces into three detachments. A party had already been sent ahead to Gaul with instructions to reconnoitre the Alpine passes and to endeavour to obtain by bribes the favour of the Gallic chieftains whose territories lay along the route the army would probably follow. The force with which he crossed the river amounted to 90,000 foot and 12,000 horse. The next objectives were the Ilergetes, Bargusii, Ausetani, and the district of Lacetania on the foothills of the Pyrenees; this whole coastal area Hannibal put in charge of Hanno, to keep control of the passes between the provinces of Spain and Gaul, assigning him a force of 10,000 infantry for the purpose. The march through the passes of the Pyrenees then began.

By this time Hannibal's foreign troops had become fairly sure of his ultimate objective – the invasion of Italy; and as a result the contingent from the Carpetani, 3,000 strong, refused to proceed, in alarm, supposedly, less at the actual prospect of the fighting than of the length of the march and the well-nigh impossible passage of the Alps. To recall the deserters or to detain them by force might have adversely affected the morale of his other foreign troops, wild and undisciplined as they were, so Hannibal dismissed over 7,000 of his men whom he knew to be resentful at the prospect of the campaign ahead of them, and pretended that the deserters had also been dismissed for the same reason. 24. Then, to prevent the undermining of discipline by idleness and delay, he proceeded forthwith to cross the Pyrenees with the rest of his troops and encamped near the town of Iliberis.

The Gauls were aware that Italy was Hannibal's objective; nevertheless the news of the subjection of the Spanish peoples beyond the Pyrenees and the occupation of their country by a powerful force so alarmed them that, in fear of being themselves reduced to slavery, a number of their tribes flew to arms and concentrated at the town of Ruscino. Hannibal, to whom the only danger in this situation seemed to be a possible delay, sent a delegation to the Gallic chieftains with instructions to tell them that he desired a conference, for which purpose either he would advance to Ruscino, or they, if they preferred, could approach Iliberis, to facilitate a meeting. He would be glad to receive them in his own camp, or – alternatively – was equally willing to come to them without hesitation, as he had entered Gaul not as an enemy but as a friend and had no intention, unless they compelled him, of drawing the sword before he was in Italy. The message was duly delivered; the Gallic chieftains promptly moved with their men to Iliberis and were easily persuaded to meet Hannibal, whereupon the presents they received soon induced them to let the Carthaginian army move on past Ruscino and through their territory without molestation.

25. Meanwhile, before any news had reached Rome subsequent to the report of the envoys from Massilia that Hannibal had crossed the Ebro, the Boii incited their neighbours the Insubrian Gauls to join them in revolt – almost as if Hannibal were already over the Alps. The reason for their defection was

not so much their long-standing hostility to Rome as resentment at the recent planting on Gallic soil of the two settlements of Placentia and Cremona, near the river Po. Hurriedly mobilizing their forces they invaded that district and caused so much alarm and confusion that not only the rural population but even the three Roman officials who were superintending the assignment of land in the new settlement fled to Mutina, lest the walls of Placentia should prove an insufficient protection. The three officials were probably Gaius Lutatius, Gaius Servilius, and Titus Annius, though some annals have Quintus Acilius and Gaius Herennius in place of the two last, and others Publius Cornelius Asina and Gaius Papirius Maso. About Lutatius there is no discrepancy in the records. There is also some doubt about whether the envoys sent to demand reparations from the Boii were subjected to violence, or whether it was the three officials engaged upon the partition of agricultural land who were assaulted.

The Gauls were no great hands at military tactics and without any experience in siege warfare; against those shut up in Mutina they did nothing and no attempt was made to storm the defences. In these circumstances negotiations for a truce were opened – or so it was pretended. The Roman envoys, invited by the Gallic chiefs to a conference, were seized – an action which violated not only the accepted conventions of international procedure but also the specific guarantees given on the occasion – and the Gauls refused to release them unless their hostages were restored.

At the news of the envoys' plight and of the danger to Mutina and its garrison, the praetor Lucius Manlius started for the town with a relief-party. Indignation prevented proper precautions being taken. Most of the neighbourhood was uncultivated, and his road lay through woods. He had no scouts out, and the result was that he fell into a trap and suffered severe losses before he managed to struggle clear into open country. There he halted, and properly fortified his position; and his men, in spite of their losses – probably some 500 killed – recovered their morale when they found that the enemy seemed to have no heart for a concerted attack. They proceeded on their way, and so long as their route led through open country, there was no further sign of the enemy; once again, however, the moment they got into woodland, the rear of the column was attacked. Discipline went to pieces, and panic spread; six standards were lost and 700 men killed. It was not till the force emerged from the trackless and difficult wooded country that the Gauls stopped their alarming tactics and the Roman column could breathe freely. Thereafter, marching through open country, they had no difficulty in protecting themselves, and proceeded to Tannetum, a village near the Po, where they temporarily fortified a position. This, together with such provisions as could be brought down the river and the assistance of the Brixian Gauls, kept them in comparative safety against the daily increasing numbers of the enemy.

26. In Rome the report of this unexpected trouble, and the knowledge that the Roman government now had a war with Gaul as well as with Carthage on its hands, called for prompt action. The Senate ordered fresh troops to be raised, and instructed the praetor Gaius Atilius to march to Manlius's relief with one Roman legion and 5,000 allied troops. The enemy having dispersed in alarm, the force reached Tannetum unmolested.

At the same time Cornelius Scipio, having raised a fresh legion in place of the one which had been ordered out with the praetor, sailed from Rome with sixty warships. Coasting Etruria and Liguria, he went on past the mountains of the Salyes until he reached Massilia, where he established himself on the easternmost of the several mouths of the Rhône. He was not yet by any means sure that Hannibal had crossed the Pyrenees, though he was soon to learn that he was already preparing to cross the Rhône. As he did not know where he was likely to make contact with him, and his men had not yet recovered from the effects of their rough voyage, he took the precaution of sending out a reconnoitring party of 300 mounted troops, with local guides and supported by a Gallic contingent, to find out all they could and to watch the enemy's movements without risking an encounter. Hannibal had by now reached the territory of the Volcae, having either scared or bribed the other tribes into submission. The Volcae were a powerful people with settlements on both banks of the Rhône, but as they distrusted their ability to keep the Carthaginians from reaching the river they had decided to make use of it as a barrier to their further advance. With this in view nearly all of them had crossed over and were now holding the farther, or eastern, bank. The other tribes in the neighbourhood of the river, and even such men of the Volcae who had not abandoned their homes, Hannibal induced by the offer of presents to construct boats and rafts and to collect others from wherever they could find them. The natives themselves were only too eager to see Hannibal safely across and to have their own territory relieved as quickly as possible from the burden of his numerous army; so it was not long before an immense number of craft was assembled, big and small – the latter roughly-built boats for local use, while at the same time the Gauls set about constructing canoes hollowed from a single tree-trunk. The Carthaginian soldiers soon followed suit. The work was easy and timber abundant, and, as the only requirement was something that would float and carry a load, the result was the rapid construction of a number of rough and more or less shapeless hulls, which would at least take them and their gear across the river.

27. As soon as preparations were complete, they were deterred from proceeding by an assembly in force of the enemy, both horse and foot, who were thronging the farther bank of the river. To circumvent this menace, Hannibal sent Hanno, the son of Bomilcar, with a party of men, mostly Spanish, a day's journey up the river; his instructions were to start soon after dark and, on the first opportunity, to cross over, attracting as little attention as possible, and then, by an outflanking movement, to attack the enemy in the rear when occasion offered. Information was given by the Gallic guides that some twenty-five miles upstream there was a convenient place for crossing, where the river was broader and shallower as it was split into two channels by a small island. Timber was quickly cut and rafts constructed to carry the men over, together with their horses and gear, the Spanish troops making no bones about swimming across with their shields beneath them and their clothes stowed in leather bags. The rest of the force crossed on the rafts, lashed together to form a bridge. Camp was then

pitched near the river bank, and the men were given a day's rest to recover from their night march and subsequent labours, their commanding officer being anxious to avoid any sort of miscarriage in the operation. Next day they got on the move again, and raised a smoke signal to indicate that they were across the river and not far away. Hannibal saw the signal, and gave immediate orders for his own men to begin their passage of the river. For the infantrymen the boats were already prepared; most of the cavalry was got across with the men swimming by the side of their horses, a line of larger craft being stationed just above them to break the force of the current, and to make easier going for the rafts and boats farther downstream. Many of the horses were attached by lines to boats' sterns, while the rest were ferried across ready saddled and bridled, for instant use by their riders on the farther side.

28. The Gallic warriors came surging to the river bank, howling and singing as their custom was, shaking their shields above their heads and brandishing their spears, in spite of the menace which confronted them of those innumerable hostile craft, rendered yet more alarming by the roar of the stream and the cries of the soldiers and sailors struggling to overcome the fierce current and the shouts of encouragement from their comrades awaiting their turn to cross. All this was bad enough; but suddenly, from behind, a more terrible sound assailed their ears – the triumphant shout of Hanno's men. Their camp had been captured, and a moment later Hanno himself was upon them: they were caught between two deadly menaces, the thousands of armed men landing on the river bank and a second army unexpectedly pressing upon their rear. After one fruitless attempt at active resistance they forced a way out of the trap as best they could and dispersed in confusion to their villages. Hannibal, now convinced that there was more smoke than fire in Gallic resistance, completed at leisure the passage of the river, and pitched camp.

Various methods were, I believe, employed to get the elephants across; at any rate there are differing accounts of how it was done. According to one account, the beasts were herded close to the bank, and a notably ferocious one was then goaded by his driver, who promptly plunged into the water; the furious animal pursued him as he swam for his life and so drew the rest of the herd after him. Despite their terror at finding themselves in deep water, they were all carried to the farther bank by the sheer force of the current. It is more generally thought that they were ferried across on rafts – surely a safer method, and also, to judge by the result, a more likely one. The method was to prepare a big float, 200 feet long and 50 feet wide, which was held in position against the current by a number of strong cables led to the bank upstream; it was then covered with soil like a bridge, to induce the elephants to walk on to it without fear, as if they were still on land. To this float a second raft, of the same width but only half the length, and suitable for towing across the river, was attached. The elephants, the females leading, were driven on to the float – supposing it to be a solid road – and then passed on to the raft, when the ropes which lightly attached it to the float were immediately cast off, and it was towed over to the farther bank by rowing-boats. When the first batch had been landed, others were fetched and brought over. None of the animals showed any alarm so long as they were on what seemed the solid bridge: panic began only when the raft was cast off and they found themselves being carried into deep water; it was then that they showed fright, those nearest the edge backing away from the water and causing much jostling and confusion amongst their companions, until their very terror, at the sight of water all around them, seemed to freeze them into stillness. A few completely lost their heads and fell into the water; their riders were flung off, but the beasts themselves, stabilized by their weight, struggled on bit by bit till they found shallow water, and so got ashore.

29. While this operation was in progress, Hannibal had sent a party of 500 Numidian horsemen to try to find out the location, strength, and intentions of the Roman force. The Numidians were met by the party of 300 Roman cavalrymen, who had been sent, as I have already mentioned, from the mouth of the Rhône to reconnoitre. The fight which followed was, in spite of the small numbers engaged, a surprisingly savage one; many were wounded and the losses in killed were about equal on both sides. It was only when the Romans had already had nearly enough that the Numidians broke and fled,

and so gave them the victory. Roman losses, including the Gallic auxiliaries, amounted to 160; those of the Numidians to over 200. This preliminary skirmish might be taken as an omen of what was to come – portending final victory for Rome, but at the same time a victory far from bloodless and won only after a struggle of which the issue was to be long in doubt.

When the troops returned after this engagement to their respective commanders, Scipio could be sure of only one thing, namely that he must adjust his own movements to the actions and strategy of the enemy. Hannibal, for his part, was still hesitating between continuing his march straight into Italy, and offering battle to the first Roman force that chanced to lie in his way; he was, however, dissuaded from an immediate trial of strength with Scipio by the arrival of a delegation from the Boii with their chieftain Magalus, who promised to serve him as guides and to share his dangers, at the same time expressing the opinion that the invasion of Italy should be his sole objective, to be undertaken without any frittering away of his strength.

The rank and file of the Carthaginian army had a wholesome respect for Roman arms, as the former war was not yet forgotten; but they were much more alarmed by the prospect of the long march and, especially, of the passage of the Alps – about which stories were told dreadful enough to frighten anyone, particularly the inexperienced. 30. In view of this, Hannibal, once he had made his decision to go ahead and to make straight for Italy, paraded his troops and delivered an address calculated to work upon their feelings by a judicious mixture of reproof and encouragement. 'What sudden panic is this,' he said, 'which has entered those breasts where fear has never been? Year after year you have fought with me, and won; and you never left Spain until all the lands and peoples between the two seas were subject to our power. When the Roman people demanded the surrender of the "criminal" – whoever it might have been – who laid siege to Saguntum, you were justly angry and crossed the Ebro bent upon obliterating the very name of Rome and setting the world free. Then, at least, none of you thought of the journey long, though it stretched from the setting to the rising sun; but now, when you can see that much the greater part of the distance is already behind you – when you have made your way through the wild tribes and over the passes of the Pyrenees, when you have tamed the violence of the mighty Rhône and crossed it in face of those countless Gallic warriors who would fain have stopped you; when, finally, you have the Alps in sight, and know that the other side of them is Italian soil: now, I repeat, at the very gateway of the enemy's country, you come to a halt – exhausted! What do you think the Alps *are*? Are they anything worse than high mountains? Say, if you will, that they are higher than the Pyrenees, but what of it? No part of earth reaches the sky; no height is insuperable to men. Moreover, the Alps are not desert: men live there, they till the ground; there are animals there, living creatures. If a small party can cross them, surely armies can? The envoys you see with us did not, in order to get over, soar into the air on wings. Moreover, their own forebears were immigrants – they were countryfolk from Italy, who often crossed these same mountains safely enough – hordes of them, with their women and children, whole peoples on the move. Surely, then, for an army of soldiers, with nothing to carry but their military gear, no waste should be too wild to cross, no hills too high to climb. Remember Saguntum, and those eight long months of toil and peril endured to the end. It is not Saguntum now, but Rome, the mightiest city of the world,[1] you aim to conquer: how can you feel that anything, however hard, however dangerous, can make you hesitate? Why, even the Gauls once captured Rome – and you despair of being able even to get near it. Either confess, then, that you have less spirit and courage than a people you have again and again defeated during these latter days, or steel your hearts to march forward, to halt only on Mars' Field between the Tiber and the walls of Rome.'

31. Hannibal's words were not without effect. When he had ended, he gave the order for his men to rest and prepare themselves for the march.

The army moved on the following day. The route Hannibal chose was along the Rhône valley towards central Gaul.[2] This

1. True perhaps for Livy's day, but certainly not for Hannibal's.
2. See map p. 678.

was not the more direct route to the Alps, but Hannibal preferred it as the farther he got from the coast the less likely he was to encounter Roman resistance, and he had no wish for a trial of strength until he reached Italy. Four days later he was at the junction of the Isaras[1] and the Rhône, both of which flow down from the Alps and embrace a stretch of country known as the Island. In this neighbourhood was the territory of the Allobroges, a people even in those days inferior to none in Gaul for power and fame. At the time of Hannibal's arrival the country was split by internal discord, two brothers disputing for the throne; the elder, Brancus, had been king, but an attempt was being made by his younger brother to depose him, with the support of the young nobles and the claim that might, in this case, was right. The two rivals seized the opportunity of Hannibal's presence to refer to him the decision of the quarrel, and he, acting as arbitrator, and supporting the views of the council and the leading men, restored the throne to Brancus. In recognition of this service he was assisted by a gift of provisions and supplies of all sorts, especially of clothing, which it was essential to lay in against the notorious cold of the high Alps.

The business of the Allobroges settled, Hannibal's objective was now the mountains themselves. Still avoiding the most direct route, he turned left to the territory of the Tricastini, proceeding thence past the borders of the Vocontii to the Tricorii and finding nothing to stop him until he reached the river Druentia.[2] This Alpine stream is more awkward to cross than any other river in Gaul; in spite of its volume of water nothing can float on it, because, not being contained by banks, it is split up into a number of constantly changing channels, where the shallows and deep potholes, dangerous to a man on foot, shift from day to day; add the stones and gravel swept down by the rapid current, and it is clear that anyone who enters it will find a foothold by no means firm or safe. On this occasion the stream was swollen by rains, with the result that the crossing was a scene of extraordinary confusion, the rank and file adding to the very real and actual dangers by

1. Probably the present River Aygues, but this is disputed.
2. The present River Drôme.

their own disorderly clamour and desperate haste to get over.

32. The consul Publius Cornelius had reached Hannibal's position on the Rhône three days too late. His troops were in battle order, and his intention was to engage immediately; but all he found was an empty encampment. As it became clear to him that Hannibal had too long a start to be easily overtaken, he rejoined his fleet, thinking that the better and safer course would be to confront Hannibal on his descent of the Alps into northern Italy. At the same time, as he was unwilling to leave his own province of Spain without a Roman force to protect it, he sent the greater part of his army there under the command of his brother Gnaeus Scipio, with instructions not only to support against Hasdrubal the Spanish peoples who were already friendly to Rome and to win others to her alliance, but also, if he could, to drive Hasdrubal from Spain altogether. He himself meanwhile returned with quite a small force to Genoa intending to defend Italy with the troops already stationed in the vicinity of the Po.

From the Druentia Hannibal advanced towards the Alps mainly through open country, and reached the foothills without encountering any opposition from the local tribes. The nature of the mountains was not, of course, unknown to his men by rumour and report – and rumour commonly exaggerates the truth; yet in this case all tales were eclipsed by the reality. The dreadful vision was now before their eyes: the towering peaks, the snow-clad pinnacles soaring to the sky, the rude huts clinging to the rocks, beasts and cattle shrivelled and parched with cold, the people with their wild and ragged hair, all nature, animate and inanimate, stiff with frost: all this, and other sights the horror of which words cannot express, gave a fresh edge to their apprehension. As the column moved forward up the first slopes, there appeared, right above their heads, ensconced upon their eminences, the local tribesmen, wild men of the mountains, who, if they had chosen to lurk in clefts of the hills, might well have sprung out from ambush upon the marching column and inflicted untold losses and disaster.

Hannibal soon ordered a halt and sent his Gallic guides forward to reconnoitre. Informed that he could not get through there, he encamped in the best stretch of fairly level ground he could find, hemmed in though it was by savagely broken rocks and precipitous cliffs. Later he learned from the same guides, whose way of life and language were much like those of the local tribesmen, and who had been able, in consequence, to listen to their deliberations, that the pass was held only in the daytime, and that at nightfall the natives dispersed to their homes. In view of this information, at dawn next morning he approached the eminences where the tribesmen were on watch as if with the intention of openly trying to force a passage through the defile during the hours of daylight. During the rest of the day he concealed his actual purpose; his men fortified the position where they had originally halted, and it was not till he was sure that the tribesmen had abandoned the heights and gone off guard that his real intention became evident. Leaving the baggage in camp with all the cavalry and most of the infantry, and kindling, for a blind, more fires than the numbers actually left in camp would justify, he assembled a force of light-armed infantrymen, all men picked for their courage and determination, swiftly cleared the defile, and established himself on the heights which the tribesmen had been holding. 33. At dawn next morning camp was broken up and the rest of the army moved forward.

The tribesmen were beginning to muster at their usual look-out station on the heights when, to their astonishment, they saw the Carthaginian assault-troops right above their heads and already in possession of it, while another army of them was passing through along the track. The two things together were such a shock to them that for the moment they were frozen into immobility; soon, however, the sight of the enemy's own difficulties restored their confidence. In the narrow pass the marching column was rapidly losing cohesion; there was great confusion and excitement amongst the men, and still more amongst the terrified horses, so the tribesmen, in the hope that any hostile action by themselves would be enough to complete their discomfiture, came swarming down the rocky and precipitous slopes, sure-footed as they were from long familiarity with their wild and trackless terrain. The Carthaginians thus found themselves facing two enemies – the hostile tribesmen and the terrible difficulty of their position in the narrow defile. It was a case of every man for himself, and in their struggles to get clear of danger they were fighting with each other rather than with the enemy. It was the horses, more than anything else, which created havoc in the column: terrified by the din, echoing and re-echoing from the hollow cliffs and woods, they were soon out of control, while those which were struck or wounded lashed out in an agony of fear, causing serious losses both of men and gear of all descriptions. In the confusion many non-combatants, and not a few soldiers, were flung over the sheer cliffs which bounded each side of the pass, and fell to their deaths thousands of feet below; but it was worst for the pack-animals – loads and all, they went tumbling over the edge almost like falling masonry.

All this was a shocking spectacle; nevertheless Hannibal, watching from above, stayed for the moment where he was and kept his assault-troops in check, lest their joining the column should only add to the confusion. But when he saw the column break up, and realized that even to get the men through safely would not help him much if all their gear were lost, he knew it was time to act. Hurrying down from his position on the heights, he scattered the hostile tribesmen with a single charge. His arrival did, indeed, increase the confusion amongst his own men, but only for a moment; for once the enemy had fled and the track was clear, order was restored, and it was not long before the whole army, unmolested and almost in silence, was brought safely through. The chief fortified village of the district, together with the neighbouring hamlets, was then captured, and the cattle and grain taken from these places proved sufficient to feed the army for three days. As the tribesmen had learnt their lesson, and the going was now comparatively easy, the army during these three days made considerable progress.

34. Coming to the territory of another mountain tribe, a numerous one for this sort of country, Hannibal encountered no open resistance, but fell into a cunningly laid trap. In fact he nearly succumbed to the very tactics in which he himself excelled. The elders of the fortified villages presented themselves in the guise of envoys, and declared that the wholesome

example of others' suffering had taught them to prefer the friendship of the Carthaginians to the risk of learning at first hand of their military might. They were willing, in consequence, to submit to Hannibal's orders, to supply him with guides and provisions, and to offer hostages as a guarantee of their good faith. Hannibal was too cautious to take what they said at its face value, but was unwilling to reject the offer out of hand, lest a refusal should drive them into open hostility; accordingly he replied in friendly terms, accepted the hostages, and made use of the supplies the natives had offered; he then followed their guides – but with proper precautions, and by no means proceeding in loose order, as he might have done in friendly territory.

At the head of the column were the cavalry and elephants; Hannibal himself, with the pick of the infantry, brought up the rear, keeping his eyes open and alert for every contingency. Before long the column found itself on a narrowing track, one side of which was overhung by a precipitous wall of rock, and it was suddenly attacked. The natives, springing from their places of concealment, fiercely assaulted front and rear, leaping into the fray, hurling missiles, rolling down rocks from the heights above. The worst pressure was on Hannibal's rear; to meet it, his infantry faced-about – and it was clear enough that, had not the rear of the column been adequately protected, the Carthaginian losses would have been appalling. Even as it was the moment was critical, and disaster only just averted; for Hannibal hesitated to send his own division into the pass – to do so would have deprived the infantry of such support as he was himself providing for the cavalry – and his hesitation enabled the tribesmen to deliver a flank attack, cut the whole column in two, and establish themselves on the track. As a result, Hannibal, for one night, found himself cut off from his cavalry and baggage-train. 35. Next day, however, as enemy activity weakened, a junction was effected between the two halves of the column and the defile was successfully passed, though not without losses, especially amongst the pack-animals.

Thenceforward there was no concerted opposition, the natives confining themselves to mere raids, in small parties, on front or rear, as the nature of the ground dictated, or as groups of stragglers, left behind or pressing on ahead of the column as the case might be, offered a tempting prey. The elephants proved both a blessing and a curse: for though getting them along the narrow and precipitous tracks caused serious delay, they were none the less a protection to the troops, as the natives, never having seen such creatures before, were afraid to come near them.

On the ninth day the army reached the summit.[1] Most of the climb had been over trackless mountain-sides; frequently a wrong route was taken – sometimes through the deliberate deception of the guides, or, again, when some likely-looking valley would be entered by guess-work, without knowledge of whither it led. There was a two days' halt on the summit, to rest the men after the exhausting climb and the fighting. Some of the pack-animals which had fallen amongst the rocks managed, by following the army's tracks, to find their way into camp. The troops had indeed endured hardships enough; but there was worse to come. It was the season of the setting of the Pleiades:[2] winter was near – and it began to snow. Getting on the move at dawn, the army struggled slowly forward over snow-covered ground, the hopelessness of utter exhaustion in every face. Seeing their despair, Hannibal rode ahead and at a point of vantage which afforded a prospect of a vast extent of country, he gave the order to halt, pointing to Italy far below, and the Po Valley beyond the foothills of the Alps. 'My men,' he said, 'you are at this moment passing the protective barrier of Italy – nay more, you are walking over the very walls of Rome. Henceforward all will be easy going – no more hills to climb. After a fight or two you will have the capital of Italy, the citadel of Rome, in the hollow of your hands.'

The march continued, more or less without molestation from the natives, who confined themselves to petty raids when they saw a chance of stealing something. Unfortunately, however, as in most parts of the Alps the descent on the Italian side, being shorter, is correspondingly steeper, the going was much more difficult than it had been during the ascent. The

1. Probably the Col de la Traversette (9,680 feet).
2. Late October.

track was almost everywhere precipitous, narrow, and slippery; it was impossible for a man to keep his feet; the least stumble meant a fall, and a fall a slide, so that there was indescribable confusion, men and beasts stumbling and slipping on top of each other.

36. Soon they found themselves on the edge of a precipice – a narrow cliff falling away so sheer that even a lightly-armed soldier could hardly have got down it by feeling his way and clinging to such bushes and stumps as presented themselves. It must always have been a most awkward spot, but a recent landslide had converted it on this occasion to a perpendicular drop of nearly a thousand feet. On the brink the cavalry drew rein – their journey seemed to be over. Hannibal, in the rear, did not yet know what had brought the column to a halt; but when the message was passed to him that there was no possibility of proceeding, he went in person to reconnoitre. It was clear to him that a detour would have to be made, however long it might prove to be, over the trackless and untrodden slopes in the vicinity. But even so he was no luckier; progress was impossible, for though there was good foothold in the quite shallow layer of soft fresh snow which had covered the old snow underneath, nevertheless as soon as it had been trampled and dispersed by the feet of all those men and animals, there was left to tread upon only the bare ice and liquid slush of melting snow underneath. The result was a horrible struggle, the ice affording no foothold in any case, and least of all on a steep slope; when a man tried by hands or knees to get on his feet again, even those useless supports slipped from under him and let him down; there were no stumps or roots anywhere to afford a purchase to either foot or hand; in short, there was nothing for it but to roll and slither on the smooth ice and melting snow. Sometimes the mules' weight would drive their hoofs through into the lower layer of old snow; they would fall and, once down, lashing savagely out in their struggles to rise, they would break right through it, so that as often as not they were held as in a vice by a thick layer of hard ice.

37. When it became apparent that both men and beasts were wearing themselves out to no purpose, a space was cleared –

with the greatest labour because of the amount of snow to be dug and carted away – and camp was pitched, high up on the ridge. The next task was to construct some sort of passable track down the precipice, for by no other route could the army proceed. It was necessary to cut through rock, a problem they solved by the ingenious application of heat and moisture; large trees were felled and lopped, and a huge pile of timber erected; this, with the opportune help of a strong wind, was set on fire, and when the rock was sufficiently heated the men's rations of sour wine were flung upon it, to render it friable. They then got to work with picks on the heated rock, and opened a sort of zigzag track, to minimize the steepness of the descent, and were able, in consequence, to get the pack animals, and even the elephants, down it.

Four days were spent in the neighbourhood of this precipice; the animals came near to dying of starvation, for on most of the peaks nothing grows, or, if there is any pasture, the snow covers it. Lower down there are sunny hills and valleys and woods with streams flowing by: country, in fact, more worthy for men to dwell in. There the beasts were put out to pasture, and the troops given three days' rest to recover from the fatigue of their road-building. Thence the descent was continued to the plains – a kindlier region, with kindlier inhabitants.

38. The march to Italy was much as I have described it. The army reached the frontier in the fifth month, as some records have it, after leaving New Carthage. The crossing of the Alps took fifteen days. There is great difference of opinion about the size of Hannibal's army on his arrival in Italy; the highest recorded estimate puts it at 100,000 infantry and 20,000 cavalry; the lowest at 20,000 infantry and 6,000 cavalry.[1] I should myself be most inclined to accept the statement of Lucius Cincius Alimentus (who mentions in his account that he was taken prisoner by Hannibal), if only he did not confuse the issue by the addition of Gallic and Ligurian troops. These included, he puts the total numbers of the army led into Italy

1. So Polybius (III: 33) who says the figures were recorded by Hannibal in an inscription he saw himself at the temple of Lacinian Juno near Croton. See p. 234 and p. 564.

at 80,000 infantry and 10,000 cavalry; but I think it more likely – and some writers support my view – that the Gauls and Ligurians joined voluntarily later. Alimentus further states that he learned from Hannibal himself that, after crossing the Rhône, he lost 36,000 men and an enormous number of horses and pack-animals, having descended into Italy by way of the Ligurian Taurini, on the borders of Gallic territory. As this latter fact is generally accepted, I cannot understand why there should be any doubt about the route he followed over the Alps, or why it is often supposed that he crossed by the Pennine Alps[1] (which got their name by the fact of his crossing) farther north. The historian Coelius Antipater says that he crossed by Mt Cremo;[2] but neither of these routes would have brought him to the Taurini – they would have led through the territory of the hill-dwelling Salassi to the Libuan Gauls. Nor is it likely that those more northern passes into Gaul were then open; the route, especially, which leads to the Pennine Alps would have been blocked by half-German tribes, and there is another thing which anyone inclined to believe in the Pennine route might do well to consider: the fact, namely, that the Veragri, who live thereabouts, know nothing of the derivation of the name 'Pennine' from the circumstance of the 'Punic' crossing. On the contrary, they derive the name from Penninus, the divinity to whom they have consecrated a shrine on the mountain top.

39. Conveniently for the start of Hannibal's operations, war had broken out between the Taurini and the Insubrian Gauls. Hannibal was not, however, in a position to use his troops in armed support of either party, as they were not yet fully recovered from their tribulations – and the early stages of convalescence are often worse than the disease. The men had become as filthy and unkempt as savages, and the sudden change from labour to leisure, from starvation to plenty, from dirt and misery to decent living had affected them in various ways. It was this that offered the consul Cornelius Scipio a chance of coming to grips with them before they were properly fit again, and for that reason, after reaching Pisae,[3] he

1. Perhaps the Great St Bernard.
2. Perhaps the Little St Bernard.
3. On p. 56 Livy says he returned to Genoa.

had hurried northward to the Po, having taken over from Manlius and Atilius a body of inexperienced troops still somewhat bewildered by their recent defeat by the Gauls. However, by the time he reached Placentia Hannibal had moved on, and had already taken by storm the chief town of the Taurini, who had refused to ally themselves with him; he might moreover have secured by intimidation the support – or even the willing support – of the Gauls in the neighbourhood of the Po, had not the consul's appearance surprised them while they were still looking round for the best moment to secede. At the same time Hannibal left the Taurini, thinking that his actual presence would induce the Gauls who had not made up their minds which side to take, to follow him.

The rival armies were now almost within sight of each other. So far neither of the commanders fully knew the quality of his antagonist, yet they confronted each other not without a certain feeling of mutual respect. The name of Hannibal had been a famous one in Rome even before the destruction of Saguntum; and Hannibal for his part could not but believe in the genius of Scipio simply because he, of all men, had been chosen to oppose him. Moreover, the feats recently performed by each increased the other's admiration – Hannibal's daring and successful passage of the Alps, Scipio's masterly speed in meeting his antagonist in Italy, after being left behind in Gaul.

Scipio was the first to cross the Po. He took up a position on the river Ticinus, and, before advancing to battle, addressed his troops in the following hortatory words.

40. 'My men,' he said, 'there would be no call for a speech from me, if I were leading into action the army which I commanded in Gaul. The cavalrymen who so splendidly routed the enemy horse on the Rhône would need no words of exhortation; nor would those legions with whom I pursued Hannibal and wrung from him what was as good as a victory – the admission, namely, that he was running away and refusing battle. But, as things are, that army, levied for Spanish service, is doing its duty, under the command of my deputy, my brother Gnaeus, in the country where the Senate and people of Rome wished it to serve. I, for my part, have freely offered myself for service here, so that you might have a consul to

lead you against Hannibal and the Carthaginians. You and I are as yet unacquainted with each other; so my words must be few.

'My men, let me tell you of the sort of warfare you must expect: it will be against an enemy you defeated in the last war both on land and at sea; an enemy from whom you have exacted tribute for twenty years; an enemy from whom you took Sicily and Sardinia as prizes of war. You, therefore, will enter upon it with the high hearts of victors, they in the despondency of beaten men. Nay more, their readiness to fight at all is due not to courage but necessity – unless you imagine that an enemy who declined combat when his army was still intact, has better hopes of success now that he has lost two thirds of his troops during the passage of the Alps. Perhaps you will answer that though they are few they are nevertheless brave and strong – that they are irresistible fighters. Nonsense! They are the ghosts and shadows of men; already half dead with hunger, cold, dirt, and neglect; all their strength has been crushed and beaten out of them by the Alpine crags. Cold has dried them up, snowstorms have frozen their sinews stiff, their hands and feet are frostbitten, their horses lamed and enfeebled; and they have not a weapon amongst them which is not damaged or broken. What an army! Why, you will not be facing an enemy at all, but only the dregs of what once were men. My chief fear is that we shall have to admit that it was the Alps, not you, who conquered Hannibal. Ah well! perhaps it was right that the gods, without human aid, should have fought the first stages of a war with treaty-breakers like these; we who – after heaven – have suffered from their treachery have the duty only of bringing that war to its conclusion.

41. 'I am not afraid that you will suspect me of concealing my real feelings, and of exaggerating the facts merely to encourage you. I was at liberty, had I wished, to go with my army into Spain, and I had already started thither. In Spain – my own allotted sphere of action – I should have had my brother to advise me and to share my perils; I should have had an easier campaign on my hands, with Hasdrubal instead of Hannibal as my antagonist; nevertheless, as I was sailing along the Gallic coast I had news of Hannibal, and landed; I ordered my cavalry

forward, I moved up to the Rhône. The cavalry was offered a chance of action – I seized it, and won. Hannibal's infantry I could not overtake on land – like an army in flight they were going too fast; so I returned to my fleet and with all possible speed accomplished the long voyage and the long march, to meet him here at the foot of the Alps. Does it look as if, while trying to escape a fight with this terrible foe, I have now encountered him accidentally? Is it not more likely that I have deliberately planted myself in his path, and am challenging him to fight? I want to find out if during these last twenty years the earth has suddenly produced a new race of Carthaginians – or if they are still like those whom you ransomed at Eryx for eighteen denarii a head. I want to know if this man Hannibal can substantiate his claim to be the rival of Hercules[1] – that world-traveller and mighty man of valour – or if he has just been left by his father as a tax-paying underling, or even as a slave, of the Roman people. Were he not haunted by his guilt over Saguntum, he might well reflect upon his conquered country, or at least upon his own father and family – upon the treaties signed by the hand of Hamilcar, who at the bidding of a Roman consul marched his garrison down from their fortress on Mt Eryx, and in grief and rage accepted the harsh conditions – the evacuation of Sicily and the payment of a tribute to Rome – imposed on his vanquished countrymen:

'For these reasons I expect you to fight not only with your usual valour, but with the added force of indignation and anger, as if you saw your own slaves coming suddenly in arms against you. We might, on Eryx, have starved the enemy to death – the most terrible of punishments; we might have sent our victorious fleet to Africa, and in a couple of days blotted Carthage from the map without a blow in return. Instead, we listened to their cries for mercy, and pardoned them. We lifted the blockade, and made peace; and as if that were not enough, we gave them our protection when they were involved in the African war.

'And now, they repay our generosity by following a young commander drunk with ambition, and coming to attack our

1. Hercules was said to have crossed the Alps with the cattle of Geryon.

country. Would that the coming struggle were for your glory only, and not also for your lives! But you must fight not, as once, for the possession of Sicily and Sardinia, but in defence of Italy. There is no other army behind us, to stop Hannibal if we fail; there are no more Alps to give us time to mobilize fresh defences. It is here, my men, that we must make our stand, as if we were fighting before the walls of Rome. I call upon each one of you to remember that he is protecting, not his own body, but the lives of his wife and little children – and then to go beyond his personal cares in the full realization that the eyes of the Senate and people of Rome are upon us now. On our hands and hearts today will depend the future fortune of that great City and of the Roman Empire.'

42. Unlike Scipio, Hannibal thought that deeds would be a better encouragement to his men than words. He formed his troops into a circle, and had some prisoners, whom he had captured in the mountains, brought into the middle of it in chains. Gallic weapons were laid on the ground in front of them, and an interpreter was told to ask if any of them would be willing to fight in single combat if he were released from his chains and offered a horse, together with the weapons, as the prize of victory. Every one of them declared himself eager to fight, and when lots were cast there was not a man but hoped that the luck would come his way. When it did, the lucky one leapt exultantly upon the sword and shield, glorying in the congratulations of his comrades and dancing the wild dances of his people. During the actual combats, the feeling both amongst the prisoners themselves and the Carthaginian spectators was such that the fortune of the victors seemed hardly more worthy of praise than the brave death of the defeated.

43. It proved a stimulating spectacle, and when several pairs had fought the parade was dismissed. Later Hannibal called another meeting of all ranks, and addressed them (we are told) in the following words:

'My soldiers, just now, as you were watching other men's fate, you were not unmoved; only think with similar feelings of what is in store for yourselves, and victory is already in our hands. What you have seen was more than a spectacle for your entertainment: it was a sort of image, or allegory, of your own condition. It may indeed be that fate has laid upon you heavier chains and harsher necessities than upon those prisoners of ours. North and south the sea hems you in; you have not a single ship even to escape in with your lives; facing you is the Po, a greater and more turbulent river than the Rhône. Behind you is the Alpine barrier, which even in the freshness and flower of your strength you almost failed to cross. Here then, where you have first come face to face with the enemy, you must conquer or die. But have courage! Circumstances compel you to fight; but those same circumstances offer you in the event of victory nobler rewards than a man might pray for, even from the immortal gods. The prize would be great enough, were we only to recover by the strength of our hands the islands of Sicily and Sardinia which our fathers lost; but all the heaped wealth of Rome, won in her long career of conquest, will be yours; those rich possessions – yes, and the possessors too. Forward then, and win this splendid prize! and with God's blessing draw your swords! You have chased cattle long enough in the wild mountains of Lusitania and Celtiberia, with nothing to show for the long years of toil and danger; since then you have travelled far, over mountains, across rivers, through peoples in arms, and it is time that you fought a campaign with money in it and all good things, and earned a rich reward for your efforts. Here Fortune has granted you an end to your sweat and tears; and here she will pay you worthily for your long service in the field. You need not imagine that victory will be as hard to win as the fame of our antagonists might suggest. Fortune is fickle: often a despised enemy has fought to the death, and a feather in the scale has brought defeat to famous nations and their kings. Take away the blinding brilliance of the name, and in what can the Romans be compared with you? To say nothing of your twenty years of brave and successful service in the field, you have come to this place from the Pillars of Hercules, from the Atlantic Ocean and the farthest limits of the world, thrusting your victorious way through all the wild and warlike nations of Spain and Gaul; and now you will be facing an army of raw recruits, beaten this very summer to its knees and penned in by the Gauls – an army and a commander still strangers to one another. And what a commander! Am I to compare myself with him – that six months' general who abandoned his own troops – when I, born and bred on active service, in my illustrious father's tent, subdued Spain and Gaul and vanquished not only the wild Alpine tribes but – a much harder task – the Alps themselves? Show Scipio now the soldiers of Rome and of Carthage without their standards, and I would wager he couldn't tell which were his own. Now as for me, my men, there is not one of you who has not with his own eyes seen me strike a blow in battle; I have watched and witnessed your valour in the field, and your acts of courage I know by heart, with every detail of when and where they took place: and this, surely, is not a thing of small importance. I was your pupil before I was your commander; I shall advance into the line with soldiers I have a thousand times praised and rewarded; and the enemy we shall meet are raw troops with a raw general, neither knowing anything of the other.

44. 'Wherever I look, I see high hearts and strong arms: I see my veteran infantry, my cavalry, native and Numidian, all drawn from nations of noble blood; I see my brave and loyal allies; and, lastly, you, my fellow countrymen of Carthage, whom just resentment as well as patriotism has inspired to fight. We are the aggressors, we the invaders of Italy – and for that reason shall fight with a courage and audacity corresponding to our hopes – with the well-known confidence of him who strikes the first blow. Anger, the sense of unmerited injury, will spur you on and give you added fire: remember how they demanded the surrender of my person – of me, your commander – as a criminal, and later of every man amongst you who might have fought at Saguntum. Had you been given up they would certainly have put you to death with the cruellest tortures. The Romans are a proud and merciless people; they claim to make the world their own and subject to their will. They demand the right to dictate to us who our friends should be and who our enemies. They circumscribe our liberties, barring us in behind barriers of rivers or mountains beyond which we may not pass – but they do not themselves observe the limits they have set. "Do not cross the Ebro," they say; "keep your hands off Saguntum." "But is Saguntum on

the Ebro?" you say. "Then don't go anywhere – stay where you are!"

"It is not enough," you say, "that you steal our ancient possessions Sicily and Sardinia. Must you have Spain too? If I abandon Spain, you will cross into Africa." *Will*, indeed! Why, of the two consuls elected this year they have already sent one to Africa, the other to Spain. We have nothing left in the world but what we can win with our swords. Timidity and cowardice are for men who can see safety at their backs – who can retreat without molestation along some easy road and find refuge in the familiar fields of their native land; but they are not for you: you must be brave; for you there is no middle way between victory and death – put all hope of it from you, and either conquer, or, should fortune hesitate to favour you, meet death in battle rather than in flight.

'Think on these things; carry them printed on your minds and hearts. Then – I repeat – success is already yours. God has given to man no sharper spur to victory than contempt of death.'

45. Such were the two orations with which the rival commanders sought to inflame the spirit of their men.

Scipio's first move was to throw a bridge over the Ticinus and to construct a blockhouse to protect it. Hannibal, while the work was in progress, sent a squadron of Numidian cavalry, 500 strong, under Maharbal to devastate the land of the local tribesmen who were friendly to Rome, with special instructions to spare, so far as possible, Gallic property and to urge the Gallic chieftains to turn against their Roman masters. When the bridge was finished the Roman force crossed and took up a position five miles from Victumulae in the territory of the Insubres. Hannibal's army lay close by, and when he saw that a battle was imminent he hurriedly recalled Maharbal's squadron and summoned another meeting of his troops. This time, in the belief that all his previous warnings and exhortations had been insufficient if he was to get the best out of his men, he promised certain specific rewards, in order further to arouse their fighting spirit. One promise was the gift of land either in Italy, Africa, or Spain, according to choice, the land to be free of tax for the recipient and his children; secondly, he was prepared to give an equivalent in money to whoever preferred it; thirdly, members of allied nations who wished to become Carthaginian citizens would be enabled to do so; lastly, if any of them preferred to return home, he promised to do his utmost to secure their position there, so that they should not wish to see the situation of any of their countrymen exchanged for their own. He further offered their liberty to slaves who had accompanied their masters on service, promising the masters two slaves for each one thus lost. To prove the genuineness of these offers, taking a lamb in his left hand and a stone in his right, he prayed to Jupiter and the other gods that, if he broke his word, they would serve him as he was about to serve the lamb – whereupon he crushed the animal's head with the stone. The gesture succeeded: the entire army, convinced that God himself was now the guarantor of their hopes, and feeling that nothing delayed the realization of them except the fact that they were not yet fighting, as one man with one voice demanded instant action.

46. The Romans, for their part, were by no means so eager to engage. For one thing, they had been alarmed recently by certain ominous events: a wolf had got into the camp, mauled those he met, and escaped unhurt; and bees had swarmed on a tree which overhung the commander's tent. Proper steps were taken to avert these omens, and then Scipio moved: advancing with his cavalry and light-armed spearmen to reconnoitre the enemy's position and get what information he could at close range about the nature and strength of their forces, he unexpectedly fell in with Hannibal and his own cavalry who were out on a similar reconnaissance. At first neither force was aware of the other, and for each the first sign of an approaching enemy was the cloud of dust raised by the movement of horses and men over the dry ground. Both columns halted and prepared to engage.

Scipio posted his spearmen and Gallic cavalry in the front line, with the Roman troops and the pick of the allies in support. The native (or 'bridled') cavalry formed the centre of Hannibal's line, with the Numidian horse on the wings. Hardly had the battle-cry been raised, when Scipio's spearmen broke and ran, hoping to save themselves amongst the support-troops in the rear. For a time the respective cavalry formations maintained an equal struggle, until Scipio's squadrons found themselves seriously handicapped by the spearmen – infantry troops – who had got mixed up with them. Many fell from their horses, or dismounted to bring aid to hard-pressed comrades; to a great extent things were assuming the aspect of an infantry battle, when suddenly the Numidian horse, which had formed the enemy wings, executed a circling movement and appeared in the Roman rear. It was a severe blow to the Roman morale, and the situation was made worse by the fact that Scipio was wounded, and saved from death only by the intervention of his young son. This was the boy who was later to win the glory of bringing the war to a successful conclusion, and by his splendid victory over Hannibal and the Carthaginians to earn the title of Africanus.

The rout of the spearmen – the first object of the Numidians' attack – was pretty complete; the cavalry, on the other hand, maintained cohesion, forming a screen round the wounded consul whom they protected with their persons as well as with their swords, and bringing him into camp without any sort of confusion and in perfectly good order. Coelius Antipater gives the honour of saving Scipio's life to a Ligurian slave; I myself prefer to believe that it was his son, basing my belief on the testimony of the greater number of historians, and on popular tradition.

47. This was the first battle of the war, and it showed clearly that in cavalry the Carthaginians had the advantage. From that it followed that open country, like that between the Po and the Alps, was not suitable for effective Roman resistance. Accordingly next night the order was given to pack up as quietly as possible and break camp. All speed was made towards the Po, Scipio's intention being to get his men across on the floating bridge, which had not yet been broken up, without the confusion inevitably caused by enemy pursuit. The army reached Placentia before Hannibal knew it had left the Ticinus; he succeeded, however, in capturing some 600 stragglers who were still on the hither bank of the Po, engaged in breaking up the floating bridge – and taking their time over it. He could not cross by it himself, because the floats at either end had already

been cast off and the whole thing was drifting downstream. Coelius Antipater tells us that Mago[1] with the cavalry and Spanish infantry promptly swam the river, using a line of elephants to check the force of the current, while Hannibal got the rest of his troops across by means of a ford higher up. But anyone who knows the Po[2] will find this account hard to believe: it is unlikely that mounted troops could get the better of the very strong current without losing their horses and gear, even though the Spaniards may all have swum across on bladders. Moreover, to find a ford suitable for the crossing of a heavily laden army would have meant a long trek lasting many days. I prefer to follow the authorities who state that within two days they found, not without difficulty, a place where a bridge of rafts could be constructed, and that the light-armed Spanish cavalry under Mago was sent over it in advance of the main body. Hannibal waited in the neighbourhood of the river while he received delegations from the Gauls, and crossed later with his heavier infantry, Mago, meanwhile, proceeding towards the enemy at Placentia, a day's march from the Po. A few days later Hannibal fortified a position six miles from Placentia, and the day after that deployed his force in sight of the Romans and offered battle.

48. During the following night there was an unpleasant incident in the Roman camp – disturbing rather than actually serious: it was the work of the Gallic auxiliaries, some 2,000 of whom with 200 of their mounted troops killed the sentries on duty at the gates and deserted to Hannibal. Hannibal gave them a friendly reception, raised their hopes of rich rewards, and sent them off to their various communities with instructions to try to turn popular feeling against Rome. Scipio was afraid that the murder of the sentries might prove to be the signal for a universal Gallic revolt, and that the whole people might catch the infection and rush to arms; so in spite of the fact that his wound was still troublesome, late the following night he quietly broke camp and proceeded towards the river Trebia where he took up a fresh position on higher ground in hilly country, less suitable for cavalry to manoeuvre in. This time

1. Hannibal's brother.
2. A rare occasion when Livy shows that he has seen a site himself.

he was less successful in escaping observation; Hannibal sent his Numidians after him, followed by his whole cavalry force, and would certainly have caused havoc in Scipio's rear, had not the Numidians allowed their greed for plunder to divert them into his abandoned camp. There they ransacked everything but found nothing to compensate for the delay. Valuable time had been lost, and the enemy meanwhile had slipped through their fingers. When they saw that the Romans had already crossed the Trebia and were marking out their new camp, they did succeed in killing a few stragglers who had not yet got over the river.

Scipio's wound had been made intolerably painful by the jolting it had received on the march; for this reason, added to his wish to wait for his colleague, who he now knew had been recalled from Sicily, he determined to fortify a permanent defensive position on the safest spot he could find near the river. Hannibal took up his own position close by; he was elated by the success of his cavalry, but at the same time anxious about his supplies: indeed, the problem of supplies was growing every day more acute, as he never had anything prepared in advance and was marching through enemy territory. In these circumstances he sent a demand to the little settlement of Clastidium, where the Romans had amassed a large store of grain. Hannibal was preparing to assault the place, when a good chance appeared of its being betrayed to him – as indeed it was, and for the insignificant sum of 400 gold pieces. The commander of the garrison who accepted this bribe was one Dasius, from Brundisium. Clastidium was Hannibal's granary while his troops remained on the Trebia. Wishing, at the beginning of his campaign, to gain a reputation for clemency, he used no harsh measures against the prisoners who had given themselves up with the garrison.

49. On the Trebia the war by land had come to a temporary halt; but meanwhile both before and after the arrival of the consul Sempronius there had been activity around Sicily and the islands off the Italian coast. Twenty quinquiremes with a thousand fighting troops had been sent from Carthage to raid the coast; nine of them made the Liparae islands, eight Vulcan Islands, while three were swept off their course into the Straits.

They were seen from Messana, and Hiero, King of Syracuse, who was awaiting the Roman consul there, despatched twelve warships against them. The three quinquiremes offered no resistance, and were captured and brought into the harbour at Messana. It was learned from the captured crews that, in addition to the twenty ships of their own fleet, another squadron, of thirty-five quinquiremes, was on its way to Sicily, to raise trouble there amongst the former friends of Carthage. The primary objective of this second fleet was Lilybaeum, and, presumably, it had been wrecked on the Aegates during the same spell of bad weather which had scattered the first fleet. Hiero sent a written report of this information to the praetor Marcus Aemilius, who was in charge of affairs in Sicily, and urged him to hold Lilybaeum with a strong garrison. At the same time military officers were sent to the various neighbouring communities with orders to keep careful watch; above all, Lilybaeum was to be held, and in addition to these preparations a general order was issued to the effect that the naval allies should stock their vessels with ten days' cooked food, and, at the given signal, instantly embark. Further, watch was to be kept from look-outs all along the coast for the approach of the enemy fleet. The Carthaginians intended to reach Lilybaeum just before dawn, and for that reason had deliberately lingered on the way; but since they were approaching under sail and the moon was still up they were spotted some way off-shore, and the signal was immediately given from the look-outs. At the same time there was a call to arms in the town, and the ships were manned. Some of the troops were stationed on the walls and at the gates, some ordered to serve with the fleet. The Carthaginians soon saw that they had lost the advantage of surprise, so until daybreak they lay off the harbour and employed the interval in stowing their sails and preparing their ships for battle. Then, as soon as it was light, they withdrew farther off-shore, to have open water to fight in and to enable the enemy fleet to get out of the harbour without obstruction. The Romans, for their part, were no less eager to engage, as the number and quality of their men gave them as much confidence as the memory of past actions in those same waters. 50. Once they were in the open sea, the object of the Romans was to fight it out at close quarters as soon as might be; but not so their antagonists, who employed elusive tactics, relying on seamanship rather than brute force and preferring to pit ship against ship instead of man against man. For the Carthaginian fleet, though well manned, carried few soldiers, with the result that when one of their vessels was grappled by an enemy, she was at a serious disadvantage in mere fighting strength. Once this became apparent, the disparity in the numbers of the fighting personnel was as great a tonic to the Romans as it was a discouragement to their adversaries. Seven Carthaginian ships were quickly surrounded; the rest made off. 1,700 soldiers and sailors were taken prisoner, amongst them three Carthaginians of noble rank. The Roman fleet suffered no damage, except for one ship which was holed, but managed to get back into harbour.

Before the news of this battle was known in Messana, the consul Sempronius arrived in the town. At the entrance to the straits Hiero met him with a fleet in battle order, went aboard his ship, and congratulated him on his safe arrival with his army and fleet, adding his good wishes for a successful expedition into Sicily. He then gave him a full account of the conditions there and of the Carthaginian designs, and promised the people of Rome assistance as loyal as he had rendered them when he was a young man during the first Punic War. He offered to supply the consul's legionaries and the naval allies with provisions and clothing free of charge, adding that Lilybaeum and the maritime communities were in great danger, and that to some of them a change would be not unwelcome. In view of this Sempronius determined to sail to Lilybaeum without a moment's delay. Hiero and his fleet accompanied him, and on the way thither news was brought them of the battle at Lilybaeum and the defeat and capture of the enemy ships.

51. Arrived at the town, Sempronius dismissed Hiero and the royal fleet, left the praetor to guard the Sicilian coast, and sailed for Malta, which was in Carthaginian hands. Hamilcar, the son of Gisgo, commander of the island's garrison, surrendered with nearly 2,000 men, and the island and town passed into Roman control. A few days later Sempronius returned to

Lilybaeum, where his prisoners of war, together with those taken by the praetor, with the exception of the noblemen amongst them, were sold at public auction.

Enough now seemed to have been done to secure the eastern parts of Sicily, so Sempronius crossed to the Vulcan Islands where a Carthaginian squadron was said to be stationed. No enemy was, however, found there, for the squadron had already sailed for Italy and was, at that moment, threatening the town of Vibo after heavy and destructive raids on its territory. News of these raids was brought to Sempronius on his way back to Sicily, and at the same time he received letters from the Senate reporting Hannibal's descent into Italy and instructing him to proceed at the first possible moment to the assistance of Scipio.

Sempronius now had a good deal on his hands, and had to act promptly. His army he sent by sea to Ariminum on the Adriatic; to his second-in-command Pomponius he assigned twenty-five warships for the defence of Vibo and the Italian coast, and manned a fleet of fifty ships for the praetor Aemilius. Then, having settled affairs in Sicily, he sailed with ten ships along the Italian coast to Ariminum, whence he proceeded with his army and joined Scipio on the Trebia.

52. The whole military strength of Rome, and both consuls, were now facing Hannibal. It was therefore clear that unless that strength proved adequate, there was no hope of saving the Roman dominion. None the less, counsels were divided: one consul influenced, no doubt, by his wound and by his ill success in the cavalry engagement, urged caution and delay; the other, feeling, as he did, fresh and ready for anything, demanded instant action. The Gallic tribes between the Trebia and the Po were, in the present circumstances, sitting on the fence: a struggle being imminent between two mighty nations, they were unwilling to declare their allegiance outright, and looked for the favour of the winning side. The Romans accepted readily enough this attitude, provided no actually hostile move was made, but Hannibal, on the contrary, violently resented it, urging that it was the Gauls themselves who had invited him into Italy to liberate them. His indignation against them, combined with the need to get provisions

for his men, induced him to send out a force of 2,000 infantry and 1,000 cavalry, mostly Numidians with an admixture of Gauls, to raid the whole district as far as the Po. The Gauls, unable to resist, were driven by this act of aggression to make up their minds; accordingly they at once turned their sympathies towards the party they hoped would defend them, sent a delegation to Roman headquarters and begged aid for their unfortunate country which was suffering only for its inhabitants' excessive loyalty to Rome. Scipio, however, found the request untimely, and disliked the matter of it; he had no reason to trust the Gauls, remembering, as he did, their many acts of treachery, in particular, not to mention others which time might have obliterated, the recent perfidy of the Boii. Sempronius, on the other hand, expressed the opinion that to offer assistance to the first who asked for it would prove the strongest possible bond for keeping the Gallic tribes loyal to Rome. Then, while his colleague was still hesitating, he despatched his own cavalry, supported by about a thousand infantry spearmen, with orders to protect Gallic territory on the other side of the Trebia. This force surprised Hannibal's raiders while they were scattered about over the countryside and mostly quite unfit for action as they were loaded with plunder and in no sort of order. They were thrown into complete confusion, many were killed and the remnants driven in flight right up to the outposts of the Carthaginian camp. From the camp the enemy came pouring out in force, and Sempronius's men were compelled to retire, until with the arrival of reinforcements they were able to renew the offensive. After that there was a ding-dong struggle, the Romans now advancing, now giving ground. It ended with the honours more or less even, though report favoured, on the whole, a Roman victory.

53. To Sempronius, however, there was no doubt about the matter at all. He was beside himself with delight. He had won a famous victory – and with his cavalry, the very arm in which Scipio had suffered defeat. He was convinced that the morale of the troops was now fully restored; that there was not a man apart from his colleague who wished to delay a general engagement. As for Scipio, it was his mind that was sick rather than

his body – the mere memory of his wound made him shrink from the thought of blood and battle. But because one man was sick, was that a reason for the rest to behave like dotards? No, no: further procrastination and shilly-shallying were out of the question. Were they waiting for a third consul and yet another army? The enemy camp was on Italian soil – almost within sight of Rome; the enemy objective was not the recovery of Sicily and Sardinia, nor of Spain north of the Ebro – it was the expulsion of the Romans from the land where they had been born and bred. 'Can you not hear,' he cried, 'the groans of our fathers who were wont to fight around the walls of Carthage, at the sight of their sons cowering here, in Italy, behind their defences, though two consuls and two consular armies are in the field? What would those brave men feel at the thought of all the country between the Alps and the Apennines being controlled by Hannibal?'

So Sempronius went on, urging his point of view by the sick-bed of his colleague and passionately haranguing the officers at headquarters as if addressing the troops. An additional reason for his urgency was, no doubt, the approach of the consular elections; for he had no desire that the fighting should be put off until new consuls were in control, and he himself, while his colleague lay sick, should lose the chance of gaining the glory. Scipio continued to protest, but to no purpose; the order was given to prepare for action without delay.

Hannibal was well aware of what the proper Roman strategy ought to have been, and he had hardly dared to hope that the consuls would make any rash or ill-considered move. Now, however, that facts had confirmed the report that one of them was a proud and passionate man, rendered even more so by his recent success against the raiders, he was convinced that luck was with him and that a battle was imminent. He took every possible measure to ensure that he should not lose his chance; now was the moment, while the Roman troops were still raw, and the better of their two commanders was still incapacitated by his wound. The Gauls moreover were still full of fight, and he knew that thousands of them would lose their enthusiasm for his cause in proportion as they were drawn further and further from their homes. For these and similar reasons he both expected that a fight was coming, and was determined, should the Romans hold back, to provoke one; accordingly, when his Gallic spies (it was safer to use Gauls in this capacity, as they were serving in both camps) reported that the Romans were ready for action, he began to look around for a suitable place to set a trap.

54. Between the armies was the stream, running between high banks and edged for some distance by a dense growth of marsh plants, together with the brambles and scrub which usually cover waste ground. Hannibal rode round on his horse minutely examining the terrain, and when he found a place which afforded adequate concealment for cavalry, he summoned his brother Mago. 'This,' he said, 'is the spot you must occupy. Choose a hundred men from the infantry, and a hundred from the cavalry, and bring them to me early tonight. Meanwhile the troops may rest.' The staff meeting was then dismissed, and soon Mago reported with the men he had picked. 'I can see,' said Hannibal, 'that you have brought me some tough fellows; but as you will all need quantity as well as quality, I want each of you to select nine others like yourselves from the cavalry squadrons and infantry companies. Mago will show you where to set your trap. The enemy, you will find, has no eye for this sort of stratagem.'

Mago's thousand horse and thousand foot were in this way sent off, and Hannibal issued orders to the Numidian cavalry to cross the Trebia at dawn, advance to the enemy position, and lure him to engage by an attack with missiles on his guard-posts; then, once the fight was on, they were to give ground gradually and so draw him to cross the river. The orders to the commanders of other units, infantry and cavalry, were to see that all their men had a good meal, after which they were to arm, saddle their horses, and await the signal.

Sempronius was thirsting for action: to meet the Numidians' raid on his guard-posts he at once led out his whole cavalry force – the arm in which he felt the greatest confidence; these were followed first by 6,000 infantry and finally by the entire army, and stationed in the spot previously determined upon.

There, between Alps and Apennines, it was a snowy winter's day, and the cold was increased by the proximity of rivers and marsh; men and horses had left the shelter of camp without a moment's warning – they had eaten nothing, taken no sort of precautions against the cold. There was not a spark of warmth in their bodies; and the nearer they approached the chilling breath of the water, the more bitterly cold it became. But worse was to come, for when in pursuit of the Numidians they actually entered the river – it had rained in the night and the water was up to their breasts – the cold so numbed them that after struggling across they could hardly hold their weapons. In fact, they were exhausted and, as the day wore on, hunger was added to fatigue.

55. Meanwhile Hannibal's troops were warming themselves by great fires in front of their tents. Rations of oil had been distributed for the men to rub themselves with, to keep them supple; they had all breakfasted at leisure; so that when word came that the Romans were across the river, it was a fresh and eager army that ran to its stations in the line.

In the van of his force Hannibal posted the Baliares and the light-armed foot, about 8,000 strong; supporting them were the heavier infantry – the flower of his troops. On the wings were 10,000 mounted troops, with the elephants beyond them – half on the right, half on the left. Sempronius posted his cavalry on the flanks of his infantry – having recalled them for the purpose; for in their disorderly chase after the Numidian raiding-party they had received an unexpected check from a sudden rally of the enemy. The total Roman strength at the beginning of this battle was 18,000 legionaries, 20,000 allied troops of the Latin name, and certain contingents provided by the Cenomani, the only Gallic nation to remain loyal.

The action was opened by Hannibal's Baliares. They were met by the superior weight of the Roman legionaries and quickly withdrawn to the wings, where they greatly increased the pressure on the Roman cavalry, which was already fighting against odds – for they were tired men, while their antagonists were fresh, and more than double their number. Now, however, on top of that, the Baliares almost overwhelmed them with a cloud of javelins. The elephants, too, on the extreme wings caused wide-spread confusion, as the horses were terrified by the sight and smell of these strange beasts they had never seen before. As for the infantry, the Roman foot showed no lack of spirit, but they were physically weak compared with the enemy, who had entered the fight refreshed with food and rest, unlike themselves, half frozen as they were, and faint with hunger. None the less sheer courage might have carried them through if they had had only the Carthaginian infantry to contend with; but as it was, the Baliares, after the repulse of the Roman mounted troops, were attacking them on the flanks with missiles, and the elephants had by now forced a way right into their line. Finally, Mago and his Numidians, once the line had – all unaware – moved forward beyond their place of concealment, appeared suddenly in their rear with almost shattering effect. Yet even in this terrible situation the Roman line for some time held firm – even, what was least of all to be expected, against the elephants. The light-armed foot, specially brought in to deal with them, drove them off with their javelins, followed up, and pierced them again in the soft skin under their tails. 56. Under this treatment the brutes were getting out of hand and looked like turning in panic against their own masters, so Hannibal had them removed from the centre and transferred to the left wing, against the Gallic auxiliaries. The auxiliaries promptly broke and fled, thus adding a fresh cause of alarm for the hard-pressed Romans.

In these circumstances a body of some 10,000 Romans – who were now completely encircled – took the only way of escape they could find and hacked a passage with the edge of the sword right through the African centre, supported, as it was, by its allied Gallic contingents. The river barred the way back to camp, and it was raining so hard that they could not see at what point in the mêlée they could best help their friends, so they took the shortest route to Placentia. Subsequently a number of other groups, at various points, succeeded in breaking out; those who made for the river were either drowned or cut down as they hesitated on the brink; others, scattered in flight over the countryside, made for Placentia on the tracks of the retreating column. A few, emboldened by sheer terror of death by the sword to plunge into the water, got across and reached the camp.

Rain, sleet, and intolerable cold carried off many of the pack-animals and nearly all the elephants. At the river-bank the Carthaginians ceased their pursuit, and on their return to camp the men were so benumbed with cold that they could hardly feel pleasure in their victory. Accordingly the following night they allowed the garrison in Scipio's camp and most of the remaining troops to cross the Trebia on rafts unmolested: either they were unaware of the movement because of the noise of the torrential rain, or else too exhausted for further effort, and suffering from wounds, as many were, they pretended to have noticed nothing. Scipio led his force quietly to Placentia. There was no opposition. From Placentia he crossed the Po and proceeded to Cremona, to spare one town the heavy burden of two armies wintering in it.

57. In Rome the news of this disastrous defeat caused such panic that people fancied that at any moment Hannibal would be at the city gates. There was no hope, it seemed, nothing to help them defend the gates and walls from assault. One consul had been beaten at the Ticinus, the other recalled from Sicily, and now the two together, with the combined force of both consular armies, had been defeated too. What other commanders, what other troops could be summoned to their defence? Such was the state of feeling when Sempronius himself arrived in Rome. His journey had been hazardous in the extreme: raiding parties of the Carthaginian horse were all over the countryside, and he had managed to come through by sheer audacity, without any fixed plan or hope of resisting if he were recognized. Once in Rome, he presided at the consular elections – the one essential thing in the present circumstances still to be done – and returned to Placentia. The new consuls were Gnaeus Servilius and Gaius Flaminius.

Even in their winter quarters the Romans were not unmolested. Numidian raiders were constantly on the warpath, and – in the wilder and rougher regions – Celtiberian and Lusitanian as well. All supply-routes were consequently closed, except for what could be brought by boat up the Po.

Near Placentia there was an important trading-post, well fortified and strongly guarded, which Hannibal planned to surprise. He knew that his best chance of success lay in concealing his design, so with a force of mounted and light-armed troops he approached the place under cover of darkness. But the sentries on guard saw him, and such a din immediately arose from inside the fortress that it could be heard even in Placentia. Just before dawn the consul arrived on the scene with a squadron of horse, in advance of the legionaries who had orders to follow in battle array. Meanwhile the mounted troops of either side engaged each other, and in the course of the skirmish Hannibal was wounded and had to leave the field. This was a severe blow to the enemy morale and contributed, no doubt, to the successful defence of the fortress. After a few days' rest, and before his wound was properly healed, Hannibal proceeded to attack Victumulae, another trading-post which the Romans had fortified during the war with the Gauls. The place had subsequently become populous, all sorts flocking thither from the neighbouring tribes, and at the time we are speaking of the fear of raids had driven almost everyone off the land to the shelter of its walls. On Hannibal's approach this large and mixed population, emboldened by the report of the brave defence of the other trading-post near Placentia, flew to arms and marched out to meet him. Their long straggling line encountered his troops on the road – there was no attempt to form into battle order; they were no better than an undisciplined mob, while their antagonists were trained soldiers under an experienced commander, each enjoying the confidence of the other. They were easily routed – all 35,000 of them – though Hannibal's force was a mere handful.

Next day the fortress surrendered and was taken over by a Carthaginian garrison. All were ordered to lay down their arms, and as soon as the order was obeyed the signal was given to the victors to plunder the place as if it had been a city captured by assault. Of all the horrors which in circumstances of this sort historians like to record, not one was omitted: those unhappy people were the victims of every form of lust, cruelty, and inhuman beastliness. Such, then, were the activities of Hannibal during the winter.

58. While the weather remained intolerably cold, the troops, after this, were allowed to rest; but it was not for long, and at the first, doubtful signs of spring Hannibal set out for Etruria, determined, if he could, by force or persuasion to win the

Etruscans, like the Gauls and Ligurians, to his cause. Crossing the Apennines he encountered weather almost worse than the horrible conditions he had found in the Alps. Heavy rain and a violent wind right in their faces made progress impossible; they could not hold their weapons, and, if they tried to struggle on, the wind spun them round and flung them off their feet. The strength of it made it impossible to breathe, so all they could do was to turn their backs to it, crouching on the ground. Then the sky seemed to burst in a roar of sound, and between the horrific thunderclaps lightning flashed. They were blinded and deafened and benumbed with terror. Then, when the rain at last stopped, it blew harder than ever, and they felt that the one essential thing was to get some sort of shelter erected on the spot. But this was only a fresh beginning of their troubles; for they could not open out the canvas or get anything to stand, or, if they did, it promptly blew away, everything going in shreds down the wind. Soon the moisture whipped off by the wind froze in the icy air above the peaks, and there was so heavy a fall of hail and snow that the men dropped all their gear and flung themselves face downward on the ground, where they lay smothered rather than protected by whatever they could find to cover them. So intense was the cold that followed, that of all that miserable heap of prostrate men and beasts not one, however much he wished, was able for a long time to raise himself from where he lay – scarcely indeed could they bend their joints, both muscles and limbs being frozen stiff. At long last they managed to get some life and movement back into their bodies and revived a little; a few fires were kindled here and there, but even then every man was too weak to assist his comrades. For two days they stayed in that dreadful place, unable to budge. Many men and beasts perished, including seven of the elephants which had survived the battle of the Trebia.

59. Having descended the range, Hannibal moved back towards Placentia, and halted after a march of some ten miles. Next day, with a force of 12,000 foot and 5,000 horse, he offered battle to Sempronius, who had now returned from Rome and was willing once again to try his luck. That day there was no engagement, and the opposing forces remained

some three miles apart; but on the day following the clash came. The fight was a violent one and fought with varying fortune: at the first onset the Romans had so much the better of it that they chased the enemy back to his camp and were soon actually assaulting the camp itself. Hannibal posted a handful of men to defend the rampart and entrances and concentrated the rest of his force in the centre of the fortified area, giving them instructions to look alive and await the signal for a sortie. Things remained like this till about the ninth hour of the day,[1] and then Sempronius, seeing that he had wearied his men to no purpose and that there was little hope of taking the camp, gave the order for withdrawal. Hannibal, the moment he heard the bugle sound and saw the assault slacken and the enemy beginning to withdraw, ordered out his mounted troops on both wings and himself rapidly took the field with the flower of his infantry. The ensuing engagement might have been as bloody and as closely contested as any ever fought, if there had been enough daylight left to allow it to continue; both sides were indeed on fire with passion and fought accordingly, but night put an end to the struggle. The losses, in consequence, were hardly commensurate with the violence of the fighting; and, like the honours, they were about equal on both sides. Neither side lost more than 600 infantrymen, and only half that number of cavalry; but the Romans suffered beyond their actual numerical losses in that some men of the order of knights together with five general officers and three commanders of their allied troops were amongst the dead.[2]

After this battle Hannibal moved into Liguria and Sempronius to Luca. The Ligurians had waylaid and captured two Roman quaestors, Gaius Fulvius and Lucius Lucretius, and also two general officers and five knights, mostly sons of senators: all these they handed over to Hannibal on his arrival, thinking thereby to strengthen the bonds of friendship between themselves and him.

60. While events in Italy were taking this course, Gnaeus Cornelius Scipio had been sent to Spain with combined naval

1. i.e. about 3 p.m.

2. This account must have come from a late source and may be fictitious.

and military forces. Starting from the mouth of the Rhône he sailed westward past the Pyrenees and brought up at Emporiae, where he disembarked his troops and proceeded, partly by renewing former treaties of friendship, partly by negotiating new ones, to extend the Roman influence from the Laeetani right down the coast as far as the Ebro. The reputation for clemency which he gained as a result of this policy was useful to him not only in his dealings with the maritime states but also amongst the less civilized tribes inland and in the mountains; with these tribes he succeeded in concluding an offensive and defensive alliance, and raised a number of strong auxiliary contingents from amongst them. The defence of Spain north of the Ebro was in the hands of Hanno, to whom Hannibal had entrusted it; Hanno accordingly, deciding to move quickly before the entire region could pass under Roman control, took up a position within sight of Scipio and prepared for action. Scipio, for his part, was equally unwilling to postpone a clash, knowing as he did, that he would have both Hanno and Hasdrubal to deal with, and preferring to face them one at a time rather than both together. The fight was by no means a desperate one: 6,000 of Hanno's men were killed and 2,000 taken prisoner, together with the garrison of his camp – which was subsequently stormed, the commander himself and a number of leading men being captured. The neighbouring town of Cissis was also taken, but it was a small place and yielded the captors little of any value – only cheap native household stuff and low-quality slaves. The camp, on the other hand, proved a rich prize for Scipio's men: for nearly all the valuables belonging both to the defeated army and to Hannibal's army serving in Italy had been left behind south of the Pyrenees, to enable the men to travel light.

61. Hasdrubal had crossed the Ebro before he heard the news of his colleague's defeat. His intention was to challenge the Roman army with his force of 8,000 foot and 1,000 horse, immediately it appeared; but when he learned of the disaster at Cissis and the loss of Hanno's camp, he changed his route and proceeded towards the coast. Not far from Tarraco he fell in with large numbers of sailors and of soldiers attached to Scipio's fleet: success usually makes people careless, and all these men

were strolling at their ease about the countryside. They paid for their negligence however, for Hasdrubal, sending his mounted troops in all directions to round them up, drove them with great slaughter, and in even greater confusion, back to their ships. Then, not daring to wait longer in that neighbourhood lest he should be surprised by Scipio, he withdrew to the other side of the Ebro.

Scipio, on the report of a new enemy, lost no time in getting on the move. He punished a few of the ships' captains for neglecting their duty, left a fair-sized garrison at Tarraco, and returned with the fleet to Emporiae. Scarcely had he gone, when Hasdrubal appeared; he persuaded the Ilergetes, a people who had given hostages to Scipio, to revolt, and with the assistance of their fighting men harried the fields and crops of tribes which had remained faithful to Rome. Then, when Scipio moved out from his winter quarters, he withdrew once more south of the Ebro.

Scipio attacked the Ilergetes, now abandoned by the man who had inspired their defection. He forced them to take refuge within the defences of Atanagrum, the capital town of the district, and then laid siege to the place. A few days later they surrendered; whereupon Scipio, having demanded an increased number of hostages and imposed a fine, received them back within the dominion of Rome. He then proceeded against another people allied to Carthage, the Ausetani, near the Ebro; while he was blockading their town, their neighbours, the Laeetani, attempted to come to their aid under cover of darkness, but quite near the town, just as they were hoping to enter, they were surprised and caught. Twelve thousand were killed. The survivors, nearly all without their arms, scattered and fled, and found their way home again. As for the Ausetani blocked up behind their walls, the one thing which saved them was the weather which rendered assault impossible: during the thirty days of the siege the snow seldom lay less than four feet deep, and it so buried the Roman sheds and mantlets that it was often enough by itself a sufficient shield against blazing brands thrown by the defenders. Finally, when their chief, Amusicus, had fled to Hasdrubal, the place was surrendered, upon an agreed payment of twenty talents of silver. Scipio then returned to winter quarters at Tarraco.

62. In the course of that winter many queer things happened in Rome and the country round it – or at least they were said to have happened, and believed, on small evidence, to have happened, as is the way when men's minds are shaken by superstitious fears. A six-months-old baby, of good family, had shouted 'Victory!' in the vegetable market; in the cattle market an ox had walked up three pairs of stairs, and then when the lodgers screamed, was so frightened that he leapt out of the window; shapes like shining ships had appeared in the sky; the Temple of Hope in the vegetable market had been struck by lightning; at Lanuvium a spear had moved of its own accord, and a crow had swooped down on to the shrine of Juno and perched on the Sacred Couch; near Amiternum forms in the likeness of men, dressed in white, had frequently been seen – they approached no one but kept their distance; in Picenum it had rained stones; at Caere the divination tablets had ominously grown smaller, and in Gaul a wolf had pulled a sentry's sword out of its sheath and run off with it.

The Board of Ten was instructed to consult the Sacred Books in view of these prodigies – except in the case of the rain of stones at Picenum. To deal with this latter, a nine-day period of supplication was proclaimed. Almost the entire community was engaged in the business of purification: in the first place the City was ceremonially purged, and sacrificial victims of the greater sort were offered to the gods specified in the Sacred Books. A gift of gold, forty pounds in weight, was carried to the temple of Juno at Lanuvium; a bronze statue was dedicated by the married women to Juno on the Aventine; at Caere, where the divination tablets had shrunk, a 'Strewing of Couches'[1] was ordered, and public prayers to Fortune on Mt Algidus; at Rome, too, another Strewing of Couches was ordered in honour of Youth, and prayers, again, at the shrine of Hercules, first by named individuals, then by the whole people before all the Couches where the gods had been invited to recline. Five victims of the greater sort were sacrificed to Genius, and Gaius Atilius Serranus the praetor was commanded

1. A *lectisternium*, or banquet offered to the gods, at which their images were placed on couches (*pulvinaria*).

to make certain solemn vows to be duly fulfilled if during the next ten years the state should suffer no grievous change. These vows and expiatory rites, authorized by the Sibylline Books, considerably relieved the public mind from its superstitious fears.

63. Flaminius, one of the consuls designate, to whom the lot had assigned the command of the legions wintering at Placentia, wrote to the consul Sempronius instructing him to see that the troops were at Ariminum on the Ides of March. He had formed the plan to enter upon his duties as consul not in Rome but with his troops in the field, and the reason for this breach with custom was the memory of his quarrel with the Senate both during his tenure of office as tribune and again during his previous consulship – the quarrels, that is, about the abrogation of his consulship and then, later, about his right to an official triumph. He had further exasperated the Senate by the introduction of a new measure by the tribune Claudius; this measure, which Flaminius alone of the senatorial party supported, was designed to render illegal the possession by a senator, or the son of a senator, of any sea-going vessel of more than 300 amphoras'[1] capacity, the size which was deemed sufficient for carrying the produce of an estate, any form of trade being considered beneath a senator's dignity. The proposed measure met with violent opposition and made Flaminius, who supported it, highly unpopular with the senatorial party; on the masses, however, the effect was just the opposite, and it procured for Flaminius a second consulship.

In view of all this Flaminius fully expected that the Senate would detain him in Rome, either by falsifying the auspices or by making him wait for the Latin Festival and perform other tiresome duties such as are expected from a consul; so he pretended to have business somewhere in the country and slipped away to his 'province' before his formal investiture. The revelation of what he had done made the Senate, already angry, much angrier: 'Flaminius' – such was the cry – 'is now at war not only with the Senate but with the gods. Once, for the neglect of the due ceremonial at his assumption of office,

1. An amphora, or two-handed wine jar, was a standard liquid measure of about six gallons.

both gods and men had recalled him from the field, and he had disobeyed the call; now his conscience pricks him for that contempt, and he dares not perform his solemn vows on the Capitol. He shrinks from visiting the temple of Jupiter Greatest and Best on his first day of office; from confronting the hostile eyes of the Senate which he abhors, and from asking its advice; from proclaiming the Latin Festival and celebrating on the Alban Mount the annual sacrifice to Latin Jove; from taking the auspices as custom demands and going to the Capitol to offer his prayers and thence proceeding to his duties abroad like a Roman commander in his general's cloak, like a Roman consul attended by his lictors. Instead of this he creeps away unseen, like a camp-boy – no mark of his high office upon him, no lictors in attendance – as if he were a criminal under sentence of exile. Does he fancy it is more consonant with his dignity to enter office at Ariminum instead of in Rome: to assume his official robe in a common inn rather than in the presence of his own household gods?'

The Senate voted unanimously for his recall – that he should be dragged back if necessary and compelled to perform in person all the duties of his office, both human and divine, before setting out again to join his army in the field. Terentius and Antistius were instructed to convey to him the Senate's wishes, but they had no more effect upon him than the letters written him by the Senate in his previous consulship. A few days later he entered upon office, and while he was sacrificing a calf, the animal, after being struck by the knife, escaped from the officials' hands and spattered the bystanders with blood. There was consternation everywhere, especially amongst those present who were too far from the altar to know exactly what had caused the alarm. Most people took the incident as an omen of coming disaster.

After this Flaminius took over two legions from Sempronius the out-going consul, and two others from the praetor Atilius, and the march to Etruria through the passes of the Apennines began.

# BOOK XXII

1. Spring was now at hand when Hannibal moved from his winter quarters. His attempt to cross the Apennines had already once been frustrated by the intolerable weather, and the attitude of the Gauls was making it very dangerous to stay where he was; these people had expected to enrich themselves by plunder, but now, when their hopes of plundering other men's territory were gone and they realized instead that their own lands were to be the scene of operations, with the additional burden of having the armies of both sides quartered there for the winter, they forgot their hatred of Rome and turned all the force of their resentment against Hannibal. Gallic chieftains frequently plotted against his life, but it was their own mutual treachery that saved him; for they would inform against each other as frivolously as they would themselves conspire. None the less Hannibal had had to protect himself by adopting disguises of various sorts, such as changing his clothes or his head-gear.[1] The anxiety this caused him was a further reason for moving earlier than he would otherwise have done.

About this time on the Ides of March, Gnaeus Servilius entered upon his consulship in Rome. When he made his report to the Senate on the state of public affairs, anger against Flaminius flamed up afresh. They had elected – so they put it – two consuls, but had, in effect, only one; for how could Flaminius who had flouted both custom and religion be deemed to have any legal authority at all? Roman officials went abroad only when the guardian deities of their own homes and of the State had sanctioned their authority: only when the Latin Festival had been celebrated; when sacrifice had been offered on the Alban Mount; when their vows had been duly performed on the Capitol. How could a man who had no official position take the auspices? or, having left the City without their sanction, how could he pretend to take them, for the first time, upon foreign soil? All this was a cause of anxiety; and the

1. Polybius says he had several changes of wig.

alarm was increased by reports of unnatural things occurring simultaneously in widely separated localities. In Sicily some soldiers' javelins had burst into flames; the same had happened in Sardinia to a cavalry officer's staff while he was inspecting the guards around the defences of the town; the gleam of fire had been seen at many points on the sea-shore; two shields had sweated blood, some soldiers had been struck by lightning, the sun had appeared to be diminished in size; at Praeneste it had rained red-hot stones and at Arpi shields had been seen in the sky and the sun locked in combat with the moon; two moons rose, in daylight, at Capena, and at Caere the waters had flowed mixed with blood; even Hercules' Spring had flecks of blood in it, and near Antium reapers had seen bloodstained wheat fall into their baskets; at Falerii the sky split and gaped wide, while through the aperture a great light shone; the divination tablets had shrunk, and one of them had turned up bearing the words, *Mars shakes his spear.* About the same time in Rome the statue of Mars on the Appian Way and the images of the wolves had broken into sweat, while at Capua the sky had looked as if it were on fire and the moon seemed to be falling in a shower of rain. Apart from these portents there were certain minor prodigies which were not without effect on people's minds: some goats grew wool; a hen turned into a cock, a cock into a hen. All these phenomena were reported in detail to the Senate, and the witnesses to each brought in, whereupon the consul asked the opinion of the House upon the measures which religion required should be taken. It was decreed that, as an act of purification, sacrifice should be offered both of sucklings and of grown victims, and that three days of public prayer should be held at all shrines; the Board of Ten were to consult the Books, and everything else should be done according to what the Divine Writings revealed as the gods' pleasure. On the advice of the Board it was decided to present to Jupiter a golden thunderbolt weighing fifty pounds, and gifts of silver to Juno and Minerva, and to offer sacrifices of full-grown victims to Queen Juno on the Aventine and to Juno Protectress at Lanuvium; it was further ordained that the married women should collect what money each individually could contribute and offer it to Queen Juno on the Aventine, and that a Strewing of Couches should be held; in addition, that even the freedwomen should organize a collection, according to what each could afford, to pay for an offering to Feronia. This done, the Board of Ten presided over a major sacrifice in the forum at Ardea. Lastly, sacrifice was offered in December at the shrine of Saturn in Rome, a Strewing of Couches was proclaimed, at which senators officiated, and a public banquet held; throughout the city for a day and a night Saturn was honoured by the joyful crying of his name, and the people were ordered to keep that day as a public holiday, then and thereafter.

2. While the consul Servilius was occupied in Rome with these propitiatory ceremonies and with raising troops, Hannibal moved out of his winter camp. He had learned of Flaminius's arrival at Arretium, and though he had been informed of a longer but better route for his march, he decided not to take it; instead, he took the shorter route through country which the Arno had recently flooded to a greater extent than usual. His order of march was to place the Spaniards and Africans, the backbone of his veteran troops, in the van, accompanied by their baggage, to ensure their having what they needed should they be compelled, at any point, to halt; the cavalry brought up the rear, with the Gauls in the middle. Mago and his light Numidian horse were detailed to keep the column together, especially to keep a check on the Gauls in case (living up to the national character) they should become sick of the hardships involved in a long march and be tempted to slip away, or to refuse to proceed. The troops in the van, so long as their guides could keep ahead of them, had a rough time, wading through deep pits and holes filled by swirling eddies from the river, now half drowned in the soft mud, now sinking over head and ears in the water; nevertheless they managed to follow the standards; but the Gauls were quite incapable of keeping their feet or of extricating themselves once the eddies had sucked them in; without spirit to spur them to effort or hope to give them courage, some dragged themselves along in a state of wretched exhaustion, while others simply lay helpless and hopeless and died where they had fallen, amongst the bodies of the drowned or drowning animals. What contributed most of all to the men's exhaustion was the lack of

sleep through four days and three nights. The entire region was flooded, and when not a dry spot could be found on which to rest their weary bodies, they piled their gear in heaps and lay on top of it. All they wanted was something which was not under water, and the heaped corpses of the pack-animals which had fallen and perished all along the route often gave them a bed of sorts for a few minutes' rest. Hannibal himself caught some infection of the eyes, the result of the dangerous alternations of heat and cold in the early spring weather; he rode the one surviving elephant, to keep himself as far above the water as he could, but in the end lack of sleep combined with the marsh climate and its nocturnal damps affected his head, and, as there was neither the place nor the time to seek a cure, he lost the sight of an eye.

3. Many men and many beasts found a miserable death in the swamps, but as soon as the army was through and Hannibal could find a dry spot, he halted and encamped. He had sent scouts in advance of the column, and already knew by their reports that the Roman forces were near Arretium; he proceeded accordingly with the utmost diligence to collect information on every matter which it was vital for him to know – Flaminius's plans and general attitude to the campaign, the lie of the country, the means of access, the possible sources of supply. The region (the Etruscan plains between Faesulae and Arretium) was amongst the most productive in Italy, rich in cattle, grain, and everything else. Flaminius, still remembering his former consulship, was as arrogant as ever, with but scant respect even for the gods, let alone the laws of his country or the majesty of the Senate. His innate recklessness had been further nourished by the successes he had achieved in war and politics, so it was pretty clear that, on the present occasion, he would act with headlong impetuosity and with no thought of restraint by God or man. Hannibal, in order to foster for his own advantage Flaminius's defects of character, prepared to bait him and prick him to action; leaving the Roman camp on his left he made for Faesulae, harrying and devastating Etruscan territory with the intention of forcing upon Flaminius the spectacle of as much damage as fire and sword could produce. Flaminius, for his part, could never have remained inactive

even had the enemy done so, still less now that everything his friends possessed was being ruined or carried off almost before his eyes. It was, he felt, the gravest reflection upon himself that a Carthaginian army should be roaming at large through central Italy, marching without any attempt at resistance to attack the very walls of Rome. At a meeting of his staff all his officers urged a policy of caution; any spectacular move would, they declared, be dangerous; he should wait for the other consul, so that the two of them might join forces and cooperate in the coming campaign – two heads, two hearts being better than one. Meanwhile they suggested that the cavalry and light auxiliaries might be used to check the widespread enemy depredations. Flaminius was furious; he precipitately left the meeting and gave the order to march and to prepare for immediate action. 'So be it!' he exclaimed with bitter irony; 'let us stay here before the walls of Arretium where our country is, and the guardian spirits of our homes! Hannibal is at liberty to escape us and make Italy a desert – let him march to Rome leaving fire and ruin behind him! We have no intention of moving until the Senate summons Flaminius from Arretium as once it summoned Camillus from Veii!'

In the act of giving the order to have the standards lifted, and just as he had sprung into the saddle, his horse stumbled and threw him. All who saw the accident were much alarmed by the bad omen; but there was more to come, for at that moment word was brought that one of the standards, despite every effort of the standard-bearer to pull it out of the ground, refused to budge. Flaminius turned to the man who brought the message and asked him if he also, perchance, had a letter from the Senate in his pocket, forbidding him to engage. 'Be off with you,' he cried; 'tell them to *dig* it out, if they are too weak with fright to pull it up.'

Thereupon the column began to move. The officers, in addition to the fact that they disapproved of Flaminius's policy, were greatly disheartened by the two bad omens; the men, on the contrary, thoroughly appreciated their commander's independence and audacity, buoyed up, as they were, by hope, however baseless.

4. Hannibal, determined to inflame his antagonist and drive

him to avenge the sufferings of his allies, left nothing undone to reduce to a desert the whole stretch of country between Cortona and Lake Trasimene. His army had now reached a place which nature herself had made a trap for the unwary. Between the mountains of Cortona, where they slope down to the lake, and the lake itself there is only a very narrow path, an opening just wide enough to get through – deliberately designed, it would seem, for its sinister purpose. Further on is a somewhat wider area of level ground, and at the eastern end rises the barrier of the mountains. Here, at the eastern exit, Hannibal took up a position, in full view, with his African and Spanish veterans; his light troops, including the Baliares, he concealed amongst the mountains north of the lake, and stationed his cavalry, also hidden by hills, close to the narrow western entrance, so that they could block it the instant the Romans had passed within. Thus, with the lake on one side and the mountains on the other, all egress would be barred.

Flaminius had reached the lake at sunset the previous day. On the day following, in the uncertain light of early dawn, he entered the narrow pass. No sort of reconnaissance had been made. When his column began to open out on reaching the wider area of level ground north of the lake, he was aware only of those enemy units which were in the direct line of his advance; of the units concealed in his rear and in the hills above him he had no inkling whatever. Hannibal had achieved his object: as soon as he had his antagonist penned in by the lake and the mountains and surrounded, front, rear, and flank, by his own men, he gave the order for a simultaneous attack by all units. Down they came from the hills, each man by the nearest way, taking the Romans totally unprepared. The unexpectedness of the attack was, moreover, increased by the morning mist from the lake, lying thicker on the low ground than on the hills; the units on the hills could see each other well enough, and were able, in consequence, the better to coordinate their attack.

By the battle-cry which arose on every side of them the Romans knew they were surrounded before they could see that the trap had closed. Fighting began in front and on their flanks before the column had time to form into line of battle, before even their weapons could be made ready, or swords drawn. 5. In the general shock and confusion Flaminius, so far as such an emergency permitted, kept a cool head, and tried as well as time and place allowed to reduce the chaos in the ranks to some sort of order, as each man swung this way or that to face the shouts of triumph or calls for help that met his ears. Wherever he could make his voice heard, or force a way through the press, he encouraged his men and urged them to stand firm, crying out that no prayers would save them now, but only their own strength and their own valour. They must cut their way through with the sword, and the greater their courage the less would be their peril. But the din of the mêlée was so great that not a word either of exhortation or command could be heard. In the chaos that reigned not a soldier could recognize his own standard or knew his place in the ranks – indeed, they were almost too bemused to get proper control over their swords and shields, while to some their very armour and weapons proved not a defence but a fatal encumbrance. In that enveloping mist ears were a better guide than eyes: it was sounds, not sights, they turned to face – the groans of wounded men, the thud or ring of blows on body or shield, the shout of onslaught, the cry of fear. Some, flying for their lives, found themselves caught in a jam of their own men still standing their ground; others, trying to return to the fight, were forced back again by a crowd of fugitives. In every direction attempts to break out failed. The mountains on one flank, the lake on the other, hemmed them in, while in front of them and behind stood the formations of the enemy. When at last it was clear to all that the one hope of life lay in their own individual swords, the nature of the struggle was transformed: no man now waited for orders or exhortation: each became his own commander, dependent on his own efforts alone. Familiar tactics, the well-known disposition of forces, were flung to the winds; legion, cohort, company no longer had any significance; if formations there were, chance alone made them, to fight in front or rear was a matter for the spirit in each breast to decide. So great was the fury of the struggle, so totally absorbed was every man in its grim immediacy, that no one even noticed the earthquake which ruined large parts of many

Italian towns, altered the course of swift rivers, brought the sea flooding into estuaries and started avalanches in the mountains.

6. For three long and bloody hours the fight continued, and most furiously of all around the person of Flaminius. His best troops kept constantly at his side, and he was always quick to bring support to any point where he saw his men in trouble or likely to be overwhelmed. His dress and equipment made him a conspicuous figure, and the enemy attacks were as determined as the efforts to save him; and so it continued, until a mounted trooper, an Insubrian named Ducarius, recognized his face. Calling to his fellow-tribesmen, 'There is the consul,' he cried, 'who destroyed our legions and laid our town and our fields in ruin! I will offer him as a sacrifice to the ghosts of our people foully slain!' Putting spurs to his horse he galloped through the thickest of the press, cut down the armour-bearer who had tried to check his murderous intent, and drove his lance through Flaminius's body. Only the shields of some veterans of the reserve prevented him from stripping the corpse.

For a large part of the Roman army the consul's death was the beginning of the end. Panic ensued, and neither lake nor mountains could stop the wild rush for safety. Men tried blindly to escape by any possible way, however steep, however narrow; arms were flung away, men fell and others fell on top of them; many, finding nowhere to turn to save their skins, plunged into the edge of the lake till the water was up to their necks, while a few in desperation tried to swim for it – a forlorn hope indeed over that broad lake, and they were either drowned, or, struggling back exhausted into shallow water were butchered wholesale by the mounted troops who rode in to meet them.

Some 6,000 of the leading column succeeded by a vigorous effort in breaking through and got clear of the pass without knowing anything of the situation in their rear; they halted on an eminence, whence they could hear shouts and the clash of arms, but the mist was too thick for them to see the progress of the battle or to know what was happening. All was nearly over when at last the heat of the sun dispersed the mist, and in the clear morning light hills and plain revealed to their eyes the terrible truth that the Roman army was almost totally destroyed. Hurriedly, lest the enemy cavalry should see them and give chase, they plucked the standards from the ground and made off with all the speed they could muster. Next day they surrendered to Maharbal, who with the Carthaginian cavalry had overtaken them before dawn; hunger was by then staring them in the face, and Maharbal had promised to let them go with a garment apiece on condition of giving up their arms. Hannibal, however, with a truly Punic disregard for the sanctity of a promise, put them all into chains.

7. Such was the famous fight at Lake Trasimene, one of the few memorable disasters to Roman arms. The Roman dead amounted to 15,000; 10,000, scattered in flight throughout Etruria, found their way back to Rome by various ways. Of the enemy 2,500 were killed; many on both sides died of wounds. Some writers have estimated the casualties, both our own and the enemy's, at many times the number; I myself, apart from my unwillingness to exaggerate on insufficient evidence, that all too common vice of historians, have based my account on Fabius,[1] a contemporary witness of these events. All prisoners of the Latin name Hannibal liberated without ransom; Roman prisoners he put in chains. He then gave orders that the bodies of his own men should be picked out from the heaps of enemy dead and given burial. He also wished to honour Flaminius with burial, but, though his body was searched for with all diligence, it was never found.

When news of the disaster first arrived in Rome, terror and confusion swept the city. People thronged into the forum, women roamed the streets asking whom they met the meaning of the dreadful tidings which had so suddenly come and what had happened to the army. The crowds swelled to the proportions of a mass meeting, and when they turned to the place of assembly and the Senate-house and began to call for the city magistrates, then, and only then, just before sunset, the praetor Marcus Pomponius gave his answer: 'We have been beaten,' he said, 'in a great battle.' From him, they could get no further or more definite information; but rumour was rife, and by scraps of talk picked up from one another they took home the story that the consul and a great part of the army had been

1. Quintus Fabius Pictor. cf. p. 157.

killed; the few survivors were either at large scattered over Etruria, or prisoners in enemy hands. For every calamity suffered by the beaten army there was a separate fear to torture the minds of all those who had relatives serving under Flaminius, ignorant as they were of the fate of their loved ones. No one knew what to hope for or what to dread.

During the next few days the crowd at the city gates was composed of more women than men, waiting and hoping for the sight of some loved face, or at least for news. They pressed around any chance comer, hungry for tidings, and nothing could tear them away, especially if it was a friend or acquaintance, until they had tried to get every detail from beginning to end. The expression on their faces as they walked away told plainly enough the nature of the news they had received, as did the people who, as they returned home, pressed round them to congratulate or to console. It was the women who were the most affected – either by joy or grief: one woman, we are told, suddenly confronted at her door by a son who had come home alive, died before his eyes; another who had been wrongly informed that her son had been killed, was sitting sadly in her house when the young man suddenly came in; the shock of excessive joy killed her.

The praetors kept the Senate sitting from sunrise to sunset for several days, to debate the question of what leader they could find and what forces they could raise to continue resistance against the victorious enemy.

8. Before their plans were fully matured, news came of a fresh disaster: 4,000 mounted troops under the propraetor Gaius Centennius had been sent by the consul Servilius to the support of his colleague, and the whole force had been cut off by Hannibal in Umbria, where it had gone after hearing the news of Trasimene. The report of this new defeat affected people in various ways: some, having a greater cause for sickness at heart, found it a small thing compared with what had gone before; others could not weigh the gravity of what had happened as an isolated event, but only in the context of circumstances: a sick body is more sensitive to the least pain than a healthy one, and in the same way the seriousness of any reverse for their suffering and afflicted country must, they felt, be

weighed not by its intrinsic magnitude but against their present weakness which could not endure any additional burden. The government accordingly had recourse to the appointment of a dictator, a remedy which for many years had been neither wanted nor applied. There were, however, difficulties: the consul, by whom alone a dictator could be nominated, was not in Rome, and it was not easy to send letters, or a messenger, to him through enemy-occupied country; so, as the people could not themselves elect a dictator, they took the hitherto unprecedented step of appointing Quintus Fabius Maximus as acting-dictator, with Marcus Minucius Rufus as his master of Horse. The two men were entrusted by the Senate with the task of strengthening the defences on the city walls, posting garrisons wherever they should see fit, and destroying the bridges. The defence of Italy had failed – the war henceforward would be at home, to save the City.

9. Hannibal marched straight through Umbria to Spoletium. Having devastated the surrounding country he attempted an assault upon the town, but was repulsed with heavy loss, a reverse which, to judge by the strength of one small settlement he had failed to take, gave him some idea of what the power and resources of Rome herself must be. Accordingly he turned into the territory of Picenum, a very rich agricultural district well stocked, in addition, with potential booty of all kinds, which his rapacious and needy troops eagerly seized. Here he remained in camp for a number of days, till his men had recovered from the fatigue of their winter marches, their troubles in the swamps of the Arno, and a battle which, though its result was satisfactory, had been neither light nor easy.

When his troops had rested long enough – and in any case they preferred raiding and plundering to inactivity and leisure – Hannibal proceeded to harry the territory of Praetutia and Hadria, going on from there to the Marsi, Marrucini, and Peligni, and the district on the Apulian border around Arpi and Luceria. The consul Servilius, after a few skirmishes with the Gauls and the capture of one inconsiderable town, having learned of the defeat of Flaminius and his army, set out for Rome. The walls of the capital were in danger, and he would not be absent at this crisis of its fate.

This was Fabius's second dictatorship. On the day he entered office he called a meeting of the Senate. Beginning with a reference to religious matters, he informed the House that Flaminius's error had sprung not so much from temerity and lack of experience as from neglect of the traditional ceremonies, especially the taking of the auspices; he went on to urge that the gods themselves should be consulted as to the proper form the appeasement of their wrath should take, and obtained a resolution that the Board of Ten should be instructed to consult the Sibylline Books, a rare measure except when unnatural events of the most dreadful kind were brought to the Senate's notice. The Books were duly inspected, and the Board made its report: first, the offering made to Mars, in view of the present war, had been incorrectly performed, and must therefore be performed afresh and on a greater scale; secondly, Great Games should be vowed to Jupiter and a shrine to Venus Erycina and to Mens;[1] thirdly, public prayer should be held, and a Strewing of Couches; and, lastly, a vow should be made to hold a Sacred Spring[2] if the war went well and the country 'remained in the same state' as before hostilities began. As Fabius would be occupied with military affairs, the Senate instructed the praetor Marcus Aemilius to see that these measures were carried out promptly, and according to the directions of the College of Pontiffs.

10. When these decrees had been passed, Lucius Cornelius Lentulus, the *pontifex maximus*, expressed the opinion, which was supported by the College of Praetors, that the necessary first step was to lay the question of vowing a Sacred Spring before the people, as that measure could not be taken without their direct approval. The antique formula in which the question was put went as follows: 'Is it your will and pleasure that this be so done? If the Commonwealth of the Quirites, the people of Rome, shall five years hence have been preserved, as I wish it may, in health and safety from these present wars,

1. Mens ('mind' or 'purpose') together with Piety, Valour, and Good Faith, is mentioned also by Cicero as being a quality 'by which a man can be elevated to godhead', and therefore as an object of worship. (A. de S.)

2. An offering to the gods of the produce of the coming Spring.

namely the war which the Roman people is waging with the people of Carthage, and the wars with the Gauls on this side of the Alps: then the Roman people vows as a gift whatsoever the spring shall have brought it from its herds of swine, its flocks of sheep, of goats, and oxen; and whatsoever shall not be yet dedicated to any god, shall be sacrificed to Jupiter from the day the Senate and people may command. He who shall sacrifice, let him sacrifice when and by what rite he will; in what form he may do it, let it be considered rightly done. If that which ought to be sacrificed should die, let it be exempted from the rites, and let no blame be attached. If any man unknowingly hurt or kill it, let it not be held against him. If any man shall steal it, let no guilt be on the people therefore, nor upon him from whom it was stolen. If unknowingly he sacrifice on a forbidden day, let the offering be held lawful, and if he be slave or free, and if he sacrifice by night or by day, let it be considered lawful. If a sacrifice shall be performed before the Senate and people shall have ordered it, let the people be acquitted and free from blame.'

On the same account Great Games were vowed, at a cost of 333,333⅓ *asses*; three hundred oxen were to be sacrificed to Jupiter, and white oxen and other victims to many other gods. The vows made, a period of public prayer was decreed, in which not only the city folk with their families participated, but also those of the rural population who, having property of their own, were therefore interested in the stability of the country as a whole. A Strewing of Couches was then held, under the supervision of the Board; six couches were exhibited, one for Jupiter and Juno, another for Neptune and Minerva, another for Mars and Venus, another for Apollo and Diana, another for Vulcan and Vesta, and the last for Mercury and Ceres. The final ceremony was the dedication of shrines: the dictator, Quintus Fabius Maximus, dedicated one to Venus Erycina, in accordance with the instructions found in the Sacred Books to the effect that the ceremony should be performed by the highest officer of state. The praetor Otacilius dedicated another shrine to Mens.

11. The completion of these religious duties was at once followed by practical measures, and the dictator opened the

debate in the Senate on the number and nature of the forces required to oppose the victorious enemy. A decree was passed authorizing him, first, to take over the army of the consul Servilius and, secondly, to enrol from citizens and allies as many fresh troops, both horse and foot, as he thought fit. Lastly, he was to take all measures which he believed to be for the national safety. Fabius accordingly declared his intention of adding two fresh legions to Servilius's army; they were raised by the master of Horse and ordered by the dictator to report at Tibur on a given date. Further orders were issued for the inhabitants of unfortified towns to move into places of safety, while everyone whose land was in a part of the country likely to be traversed by Hannibal was to leave it, having first burnt all buildings and destroyed all crops to prevent supplies from falling into enemy hands.

Fabius then set out along the Flaminian Way to meet the consul and his troops, and as soon as he came in sight of the column near Ocriculum on the Tiber, and of the consul riding towards him with his cavalry, he sent an officer to remind him that he must present himself to the dictator without his lictors. The order was obeyed; and, as length of time had almost blotted the meaning of the dictatorship from the memories of citizens and allies alike, this meeting of the two men provided a splendid exhibition of its majesty. Almost immediately afterwards letters arrived from Rome reporting the capture near the harbour of Cosa by a Carthaginian squadron of some merchant vessels carrying supplies from Ostia to the army in Spain. The consul was given orders to go to Ostia at once, to man with fighting troops and allied seamen all ships either there or up the river near Rome, and to use them for the pursuit of the enemy squadron and the defence of the Italian coast. In Rome a large force was enlisted; even freedmen, if they had children and were of military age, had taken the oath. Of this force, raised in the capital, all under thirty-five years of age were sent to serve with the fleet; the remainder were left to guard the city.

12. The dictator, after taking over the consul's army from the second-in-command Fulvius Flaccus, marched through Sabine territory to Tibur, where the recruits had been ordered to

assemble; from there he went on to Praeneste, then took to by-roads, finally coming out on to the Latin Way, and thence proceeding towards the enemy. All roads had been reconnoitred with the utmost thoroughness, and he was determined, short of absolute necessity, to run no risks anywhere. On the day he first encamped within sight of the enemy, not far from Arpi, Hannibal immediately moved out and offered battle, but was disappointed to see no sort of activity or bustle in the Roman camp: all was quiet, so, muttering that the Romans' martial spirit was cowed at last, that they were beaten men who had openly yielded their claim to valour and glory, he returned to camp. However, despite these taunts, a certain anxiety, which he would not have cared to express, began to trouble him: would he not have to deal in future with a commander very different from Sempronius and Flaminius? and had not defeat at last taught the Romans to look for a commander of his own quality? Even at this early stage Fabius's caution aroused his respect; but he had not yet had evidence of his unshakeable perseverance. He began, therefore, with tactics deliberately designed to provoke retaliation – constantly shifting his position, devastating before his opponent's eyes the fields and crops of friendly peoples. Now, in double-quick time, his column would disappear from sight; now, again, a detachment would suddenly take up a concealed position at some bend in the road, on the chance of surprising Fabius should he come down on to the plain.

Fabius himself kept moving on high ground only, never far from the enemy, with the object of maintaining contact but avoiding a clash. So far as circumstances allowed he kept his men within their defences; wood and fodder were never collected by small parties, and always within a restricted area; a small detached force of cavalry and light troops, specially designed to meet sudden emergencies, adequately protected his own men and provided at the same time a weapon of offence against casual enemy raiders. He steadily refused to stake all on a general engagement, but at the same time minor skirmishes, of no great moment, on favourable ground and with a safe refuge within reach, gradually accustomed his men, shaken as they were by their previous defeats, at last to feel fewer doubts about either their fighting spirit or their luck.

All this was sound strategy; nevertheless it could hardly have been opposed more bitterly by Hannibal himself than it was by the master of Horse, who was prevented from hurling the country into ruin only by the fact of his inferior rank: presumptuous and precipitate, unable to bridle his tongue, he began, first privately, then openly, to insult his superior, accusing him of the faults which a jaundiced view might have seen in what were, in fact, his virtues, calling his delaying tactics a shrinking from action and his caution timidity. In short, he tried to exalt himself by denigrating his superior – an iniquitous practice which has become only more common by its frequent success.

13. Hannibal crossed from the territory of the Hirpini into Samnium, devastated the country round Beneventum, and captured Telesia. These and other acts were a deliberate continuation of his policy of provoking Fabius in the hope that anger at all these unmerited sufferings inflicted upon allied peoples might draw him down to a fair trial of strength.

Amongst the great number of Italian prisoners whom Hannibal had set at liberty after the battle of Trasimene were three Campanians of good standing, who had already on many occasions been lured by presents and promises to attempt to win over their people to the Carthaginian cause. These three men now assured Hannibal that if he moved into Campania, he might have a chance of getting possession of Capua. Hannibal hesitated, his feelings alternating between mistrust and confidence; Capua was a great prize, but the men who had given the information were hardly of a sort to inspire full trust. None the less they did induce him to leave Samnium and make for Campania. As for the three men, he warned them to do all they could to support their words with deeds, told them to come back to him with more of their compatriots, including some of the leading citizens, and dismissed them. He then ordered a guide to lead him into the territory of Casinum, as he had been informed by people familiar with the country that the occupation of the pass would cut the route by which the Romans could bring aid to their allies. His pronunciation, however, did not take kindly to Latin names, with the result that the guide thought he said 'Casilinum'; he accordingly went in the wrong direction, coming down by way of Allifae, Calatia, and Cales into the plain of Stella, where seeing on every side a barrier of mountains and rivers, he sent for the guide and asked where on earth he was. The guide answered that he would lodge that day at Casilinum, whereupon Hannibal realized the mistake and knew that Casinum was miles away in a different direction. He had the guide scourged and crucified as an example to others, took up a position which he strongly fortified, and sent a squadron of cavalry under Maharbal to raid Falernian territory. The raid was a destructive one, and caused immense damage to property as far as Sinuessa, and terror and confusion over a still wider area. Nevertheless not even the panic caused by these depredations, not even the flames of war on every side of them, could move Rome's allies from their allegiance. And why? – because they were subject to a just and moderate rule, and were willing to obey their betters. That, surely, is the one true bond of loyalty.

14. Mutiny in the Roman army very nearly broke out again when, with Hannibal encamped on the Volturnus and the smoke of conflagrations rising on every hand from the farms in this loveliest region of all Italy, Fabius still kept his troops moving along the ridges of Mount Massicus. For a few days previously murmurs had been quieted, for the column had been kept going more quickly than usual and the men had supposed that the object of the haste was to save Campania from devastation; but when they reached the farthest limit of the ridge and had the enemy actually in sight burning the houses in Falernian territory and the farms of the settlers around Sinuessa, and there was still no word said of action, Minucius could contain himself no longer. 'Are we here,' he cried, 'merely to enjoy the pleasant spectacle of our friends being butchered and their houses burned? Are we not ashamed, if for none else, at least for these citizens of ours, whom Romans of old sent out as settlers to guard this frontier from Samnite aggression? It is not by their neighbours the Samnites that the flames are kindled now, but by a foreigner from Carthage, whom our own procrastination and inertia have allowed to come here from the ends of the world! Our fathers thought

it an insult to their power that Carthaginian fleets should cruise off their coast – and are we so degenerate as to see unmoved that same coast full of Numidians and Moors, out to destroy us? Once in our indignation at the attack on Saguntum we appealed not to men only but to the gods who guard the sanctity of treaties: now we watch Hannibal scaling the walls of towns in a Roman colony – and do nothing! Smoke from burning farms and smouldering crops drifts into our faces, blinds our eyes; the pitiful cries of our friends ring in our ears – it is we they beg, more often than the gods, to succour them. In answer, our army goes strolling like cattle through summer pastures in the hills and devious paths, lurking in woods, half-hidden in clouds. If Camillus had intended to recover Rome from the Gauls by wandering around the peaks and passes, as this modern Camillus – our grand dictator, sought out to save us in time of peril – is going about his task of recovering Italy from Hannibal, Rome would today be a Gallic town. Many a time have our ancestors saved Rome – but, if we continue these delays, I fear they will have saved it only for the benefit of Hannibal and the Carthaginians. But Camillus, that true Roman, when the news reached him at Veii that by the authority of the Senate and the people's will he had been named dictator – did *he* sit on the Janiculum (it was high enough!) and watch the enemy from his chair? No: he marched down into the plain, and on that very day within the city walls, where the Gallic Tombs[1] now stand, he cut them to pieces, and again near Gabii on the day which followed. And, years later, when we were sent under the yoke by the Samnites at the Caudine Forks,[2] how did Lucius Papirius Cursor set us free and place the yoke, in his turn, on the proud Samnites' necks? By marching this way and that along the ridges of Samnium? No indeed! but by bringing his armed might to bear in the siege of Luceria, and giving the once victorious foe no rest. Again – not long ago – what but speed of action gave victory to Gaius Lutatius? Remember how he surprised and overwhelmed the enemy fleet the day after he saw it – a fleet loaded with supplies and

1. The place where the Gauls were said to have burnt those who died of plague during their siege of Rome in 390 B.C.

2. In 321 B.C.

encumbered with its own gear and all the apparatus of war. To imagine a war can be won by doing nothing whatever but pray, is folly: soldiers must be armed; they must be led into the field of battle; you must meet your enemy man against man. Rome's power grew by action and daring – not by these do-nothing tactics, which the faint-hearted call caution.'

Many officers and cavalrymen of the Roman army crowded round Minucius as he delivered his presumptuous harangue, and the substance of it even came to the ears of the common soldiers. Had the matter been put to a general vote, there is little doubt that the army would have declared a preference to serve under Minucius rather than Fabius.

15. Fabius, for his part, had as keen an eye on his own troops as on the enemy; and his first act was to show that their attitude had not weakened his resolution. He knew perfectly well that his delaying tactics were by now unpopular in Rome as well as in the army; none the less he remained inflexible, continuing the same line of policy throughout the rest of the summer, with the object of forcing Hannibal, robbed of the hope of the battle he so eagerly desired, to look about for somewhere to winter in – the country where he now was, with its fruit-trees, vineyards, and other produce which was agreeable rather than necessary, offering only seasonal, but not permanent, supplies. This information was brought him by his scouts.

Once he was confident that Hannibal would use the same pass as before when he withdrew from Falernian territory, Fabius occupied Mt Callicula and Casilinum with a fairly strong force – Casilinum is on the boundary between Falernum and Campania, and the river Volturnus runs through the town. Leaving the garrison there, he led the rest of his troops back along the same high ground, having sent Lucius Hostilius Mancinus with 400 allied horse to reconnoitre. Mancinus was one of the many young officers who had often listened to Minucius's angry and presumptuous harangues, and they had not been without their influence upon him. For a while he proceeded cautiously enough, as a scout should, watching the enemy's movements without risking his own men; but when he saw scattered parties of Numidians, some of whom he was even lucky enough to surprise and kill, from that moment he was obsessed with the desire for a real fight. Forgotten, now, were the warnings of the dictator, who had ordered him to advance as far as he safely could but always to withdraw before the enemy could see him. Party after party of Numidian horse by feigned attacks and rapid withdrawals drew him almost to the Carthaginian camp, exhausting both his men and his horses in the process; at that moment Carthalo, in command of the Carthaginian cavalry, charged at the gallop, forced Mancinus's men to turn and run even before they were within missile range, and chased them for nearly five miles without a pause. When Mancinus realized that there was no chance of the enemy either desisting from the chase or getting clear away, he rallied his men and turned to face his pursuers, inferior though he was in every arm. He himself and the pick of his mounted troops were surrounded and killed; the remnant straggled back to Cales, whence by almost impassable tracks they found their way safely to Fabius.

That day Minucius rejoined Fabius. He had been sent to garrison the pass – the narrow gorge overhanging the sea, above Tarracina – to prevent the enemy from entering Roman territory by the Appian Way. With their combined forces the dictator and the master of Horse took up a position on the road along which Hannibal was certain to march. 16. Two miles separated them from the enemy. On the next day the Carthaginians occupied the entire stretch of road between the two positions. The Roman troops had taken their stand with the rampart of their camp right at their backs, and undoubtedly had the more favourable position; none the less Hannibal sent his light horse into action, hoping by the usual tactics of alternate advances and withdrawals to provoke his enemy to make a major move. No move was made; it was a slow fight – and more to Fabius's taste than to Hannibal's. Roman losses amounted to 200, Carthaginian to 800.

With the road to Casilinum blocked it now began to look as if Hannibal were penned in. The Roman forces would be able to draw supplies from Capua and Samnium and the rich lands of many other friendly peoples in their rear; but Hannibal, it seemed, would be forced to winter amongst the rocks of Formiae and the desolate sands and swamps of Liternum. He saw all too clearly that he was hoist with his own petard. He could not get out by way of Casilinum but would have to make for the hills and cross Mt Callicula; and there was always the danger of an attack while his troops were enclosed in some valley; accordingly he devised a stratagem, a terrifying ocular illusion designed to baffle his antagonists, and determined to move up to the foot of the mountains just after nightfall. The means by which he produced his ingenious deception were these: he collected wood, bundles of twigs, and all sorts of dry stuff wherever he could find them and had this material tied on to the horns of oxen, of which there were a great number, both tame and wild, amongst the various sorts of plunder he had taken from the countryside. Nearly two thousand of them were treated in this manner, and Hasdrubal was instructed to set fire to the brushwood on their horns as soon as daylight failed and drive the whole herd up the hills, especially, if he could, over the passes held by the enemy.

17. Immediately after dark Hannibal set his men on the move, keeping absolute silence, and the oxen were driven on a little ahead of the column; when the army reached the foothills and entered the narrow passes, the signal was given to light up and drive the oxen up the slopes in front of them. The unfortunate beasts ran like mad things, terrified by the glare of the flames, not to mention the pain which soon burned down to the very root and quick of their horns. They dashed this way and that, and before long all the scrub was burning as if the woods and mountains had been set on fire. Tossing their heads in a vain attempt to shake off the pain, they succeeded only in fanning the flames to greater violence, till the whole scene looked, from a distance, like an army of men rapidly running hither and thither. The Roman garrison guarding the pass, seeing fires high up in the hills and over their own heads, thought they were surrounded; they abandoned their post and made for the heights by what seemed the safest way, in the direction where the fires were fewest, but, even so, fell in with some of the oxen which had become separated from the herd. While they were still some way off, the alarming spectacle of creatures apparently breathing flames brought them to a halt; but it was no miracle, only a human stratagem, and concluding that

they were about to fall into a trap, they took to their heels, more frightened than ever, only to fall in with Hannibal's light-armed troops. Both sides however shrank equally from an engagement in the dark, so no move was made till dawn. Meanwhile Hannibal got his whole column safely through the pass, surprising a few of the enemy in the actual defile, and took up a new position near Allifae.

18. Fabius was aware of these alarms, but continued none the less to keep his men within their fortifications, partly because he feared a trap, partly because he wished especially to avoid a battle by night. When dawn broke, there was an engagement near the summit of the range, and the Romans, who were superior in numbers, might easily have cut off and destroyed the Carthaginian light troops, had not a Spanish contingent, sent back by Hannibal for the purpose, arrived on the scene. The Spaniards were well accustomed to mountain warfare, and well adapted by training and equipment to rapid assaults over craggy and broken ground; so what with their speed of foot, the character of their weapons, and the mobile tactics they adopted, they had little difficulty in foiling a heavily armed enemy, untrained in guerrilla warfare and accustomed to fight on level ground. The combatants separated on by no means equal terms – the Spaniards almost without loss, the Romans with a number of dead – and returned to camp.

Fabius also moved, and after crossing the pass took up a well fortified position on high ground above Allifae. Hannibal then, feigning a march on Rome through Samnium, turned back and entered the territory of the Peligni, devastating the country on his route. Fabius kept his troops on high ground between Rome and the enemy column, keeping constantly in touch but avoiding a collision. Hannibal next changed direction, and returning into Apulia reached Gereonium, a town abandoned as unsafe by its inhabitants, as part of its walls had collapsed. The dictator encamped, in a strongly fortified position, near Larinum.

After these moves Fabius was recalled to Rome to attend to certain religious matters; before he left he spoke with his master of Horse: what he said was not only a command, it was the most earnest advice: nay, he almost begged him with prayers to act prudently instead of trusting to luck, and to imitate himself, Fabius, in his strategy rather than Sempronius or Flaminius. He urged him not to suppose that nothing was accomplished if the whole summer were spent in eluding and frustrating the enemy – even doctors sometimes had greater success by prescribing rest than vigorous exercise – and it was something, at any rate, to have put a stop to the long series of defeats and won a breathing-space from an unbroken succession of disasters. Such was the counsel he offered Minucius before his departure for Rome. It proved to be in vain.

19. At the beginning of this summer, hostilities in Spain, too, were begun both by land and sea. Hasdrubal added ten ships to the fleet he had taken over, ready for sea, from his brother, entrusted the whole fleet of forty vessels to Himilco, and set out from New Carthage, his troops keeping close to the coast and the ships only a short distance off-shore, so that he was ready to engage whichever enemy arm he fell in with. Gnaeus Scipio had the same idea when he first heard that the enemy had moved from his winter quarters; but a rumour of enemy reinforcements on a massive scale making him less confident in the result of an engagement on land, he embarked a picked force of marines and with his fleet of thirty-five vessels sailed to meet his antagonist. On the second day out from Tarraco he found a suitable anchorage ten miles from the mouth of the Ebro, and two reconnaissance vessels from Massilia reported to him that the Carthaginian fleet was lying in the river, with their camp on the bank close by. Scipio promptly weighed anchor and sailed for the Ebro, determined to take them all off their guard by a sudden unexpected attack. There are in Spain a number of towers, built on hills and used by the natives both as look-outs and as defences against brigands. It was from these towers that the Roman fleet was first seen, and the signal was passed to Hasdrubal. Violent activity amongst the troops on shore began before the fleet in the estuary even knew what was happening. Neither the beat of oars nor any other sound of a vessel under way had been heard, and the intervening headlands still concealed the approaching fleet; the ships' crews were either strolling about the beach or resting in their tents, without an idea in their heads of having to fight that

day, when horsemen suddenly came galloping up, one after another, with orders from Hasdrubal to embark immediately and prepare for action, as the Roman fleet was already not far from the harbour. Hasdrubal himself was soon on the spot with his whole army, and a scene of extraordinary confusion followed: crews and soldiers scrambled aboard together – more like men making a dash for safety than an organized force preparing to engage. Hardly were they all aboard, before shore cables were cast off, only to bring the ships up hard against their anchors; on other vessels, to get clear quickly, anchor cables were cut, and, what with the general hurry and lack of order, the soldiers and their gear got in the way of the sailors, while the sailors in their excitement and confusion prevented the soldiers from preparing their weapons and equipment for the coming action.

The Roman fleet was now not only near but actually advancing to the attack. The Carthaginians, who were thrown off their balance less by the prospect of an encounter than by the appalling muddle aboard their own ships, made no real attempt at resistance, but fled. Their fleet was strung out on a broad front, and there were far too many ships to be able to enter the estuary all at once, so the crews ran them ashore where they could, in shallow water or on the beach, and the men aboard them, whether armed or not, sought safety with their comrades who were drawn up in battle order on the shore. Two vessels were, however, captured at the first onslaught of the Romans, and four were sunk.

20. In spite of the fact that the enemy was master of the land, his troops lining the whole stretch of the foreshore, the Romans did not hesitate to pursue the broken fleet, and succeeded in towing into deep water all the ships which were not either stove-in when they ran ashore or stuck too hard to be moved. They took in all twenty-five ships out of the forty. The finest result of this success was, even so, the fact that by one unimportant battle they had made themselves masters of the sea along that whole coast.

They now sailed for Onusa, where they landed, stormed and ransacked the town, and then proceeded to New Carthage. They devastated all the neighbouring countryside, set fire to buildings contiguous with the wall and gates, and sailed on, heavily loaded with plunder, to Longuntica, where they found a quantity of esparto grass collected there by Hasdrubal for the use of the fleet. Of this they took what they needed for their own use and burned the rest. In addition to coasting past the various headlands they also crossed to the island of Ebusus, where they attempted to take the chief town; it proved a laborious operation and ended after two days in failure, so when they found that they were merely wasting their time to no purpose they turned to devastating the crops, pillaged and burned several villages and returned on board their ships with more plunder than they had taken from the mainland. At this juncture envoys from the Baleares came to Scipio with a request for peace.

From Ebusus the fleet turned back and made for the more northerly part of the Spanish coast, whither envoys assembled from all the peoples north of the Ebro and from many, also, in the most distant parts of Spain. More than 120 Spanish tribes formally subjected themselves to the authority and dominion of Rome, and gave hostages. This gave Scipio confidence in his military, as well as his naval, strength, and induced him to advance as far as the pass of Castulo. Hasdrubal withdrew westward into Lusitania.

21. The remainder of the summer looked like being a quiet time, and so it would have been, so far as the Carthaginians were concerned. But two other factors were at work: first the restless Spanish temperament, always hungry for adventure and change, and, secondly, the rising led by Mandonius and a former chieftain of the Ilergetes named Indibilis. These two men, when the Romans left Castulo for the coast, roused their countrymen and raided the peaceful territories of Rome's allies. An officer with a force of light auxiliaries was sent against them by Scipio and had no difficulty in breaking them up, as they were little more than an ill-organized crowd: some were killed or captured, and most of them disarmed. None the less this very minor action was enough to stop Hasdrubal's withdrawal towards the Atlantic and to bring him back to protect his friends north of the Ebro. He had established himself amongst the Ilergetes, and Scipio was at Nova Classis, when unexpected intelligence diverted the campaign elsewhere. The Celtiberians,

who had sent their leading men as envoys to Scipio and given hostages to guarantee their loyalty, suddenly, on receipt of a message from Scipio, invaded Carthaginian Spain with a strong force and took three towns by storm. They then twice engaged Hasdrubal himself, on both occasions fighting magnificently, killing 1,500 and capturing 4,000, together with many military standards.

22. This was the state of affairs in Spain when Publius Scipio entered upon his duties there. His command had been extended after his consulship and he was sent by the Senate with twenty warships, 8,000 men, and a large stock of supplies. The fleet, swollen to a great size by the numerous transport vessels, was descried when still a long way off-shore, and put in at Tarraco to the great joy of Romans and allied peoples alike. The troops were disembarked and Scipio went to link up with his brother, so that thenceforward the direction of the war was under their joint control. Their first move, the Carthaginians being occupied with their campaign against the Celtiberians, was at once to cross the Ebro, after which they proceeded south, without seeing a sign of the enemy, to Saguntum, as they had received intelligence that hostages from all over Spain had been placed in that town by Hannibal for safe-keeping, and that the guard of the fortress where they were imprisoned was a comparatively weak one. Those hostages constituted the only check upon the Spanish tribes who favoured an alliance with Rome, for they knew that if they seceded from Carthage the penalty would be their children's death. One man's wits removed this heavy chain from the necks of the Spanish peoples – and the device he used, though based upon treachery, was certainly an ingenious one. He was a Spanish nobleman named Abelux, living in Saguntum. Previously he had been loyal to Carthage, but change of fortune – as it usually does where foreigners are concerned – had changed his principles. Now as it seemed to him that to come to the Romans as a deserter without bringing anything of real value with him would be merely presenting them with a single worthless and discredited individual, he determined to render his new friends as great a service as he could, and, after exploring every possibility, hit upon the plan of handing over the hostages, as the one thing most likely to

win for Rome the friendship of the Spanish chieftains. He was well aware that the guards would do nothing without being authorized by the governor, Bostar; so to Bostar he applied himself, craftily enough. The governor had his troops stationed outside the city walls, right on the shore, to block the approach from the harbour, and there Abelux took him aside and laid the situation before him, assuming his ignorance of it. His argument was that hitherto the Spaniards had been made to toe the line only by fear, as the Romans had been far away; but now the position was very different, as they were encamped south of the Ebro and could offer, in consequence, a safe refuge for anyone who was dissatisfied with the present state of affairs. Therefore, since fear could no longer guarantee their loyalty, they must be bound to the Carthaginian interest by gratitude for a generous act. Bostar, in surprise, asked what it was, of such value, that could suddenly be given to them – what could the generous act be? 'Send the hostages,' replied Abelux, 'back to their homes. That will be a personal boon to their parents – and their parents are the most influential people in their respective communities; and it will also be acceptable to the people generally. Everyone likes to be trusted, and often enough merely to trust a man will make him trustworthy. The actual business of restoring the hostages to their homes I want for myself, so that I may add to the success of my plan by the trouble I take over it, and increase as much as I can the value of a service in itself eminently acceptable.'

Bostar, by Carthaginian standards, was not a man of much subtlety, and he allowed himself to be persuaded. That night, Abelux went secretly to the enemy guard-posts, where he fell in with some Spanish auxiliaries who took him to Scipio. Having explained what he proposed to do, he returned to Saguntum, after a proper exchange of guarantees and an agreement on the time and place for the transfer of the hostages. The following day he spent with Bostar, receiving his instructions for the transfer. He had arranged to go at night so as not to be seen by the sentries, so when he left Bostar he woke the soldiers who were guarding the hostages at the predetermined time, and, starting on his way, led them – of course to his own great surprise – straight into the trap he had himself prepared. They were taken at once to Roman headquarters. All the other details of their surrender were carried out, as had been arranged with Bostar, in the same order as if the whole thing had been in the name, and under the authority, of the Carthaginians; but the Romans gained much more gratitude by the transaction than the Carthaginians would have done, had it been they who were responsible for it: for it might well have been supposed that the latter, who had shown themselves haughty and oppressive in the days of success, had been somewhat softened by anxiety at the present turn of events; but the Romans, on the contrary, hitherto an unknown quantity, had signalized their very first appearance by an act of liberality and mercy. Abelux was a sensible fellow, and it seemed that he had changed his allegiance to some purpose. The result was that the Spanish peoples began almost unanimously to contemplate a break with Carthage, and they might have taken up arms immediately if they had not been prevented by the coming of winter, which compelled Romans and Carthaginians alike to seek the shelter of their roofs.

23. Such were the events in Spain during the second summer of the Punic War, when in Italy the wise delaying tactics of Fabius had broken the terrible continuity of Roman defeats. These tactics gave Hannibal much cause for anxiety, as he could see that at last the Romans had chosen a war leader who, instead of trusting to luck, was capable of a rational plan of campaign; but in Rome they met with nothing but contempt. Everyone, soldiers or civilians, despised Fabius, especially when, during his absence from the army, the irrepressible Minucius had fought a battle with some success – or which had, at least, a not unhappy ending.

Two things increased the unpopularity of the dictator: deserters had pointed out to Hannibal some land which Fabius owned, and Hannibal had issued the horribly intelligent order that no damage of any kind, by fire or sword, was to be done to it, though everything in the neighbourhood was to be utterly destroyed. The object of the order was, of course, to suggest a secret pact, and that the land had been spared as payment for some service. The other cause of Fabius's growing disrepute was an act of his own: at first it may have looked suspicious, as he did not wait for the Senate's sanction; but ultimately it brought him, without any doubt at all, the highest credit. It concerned the exchange of prisoners. Following the precedent of the first Punic War, an agreement had been reached between the Roman and Carthaginian commanders to the effect that whichever side received in the exchange more prisoners than it gave should pay two and a half pounds of silver for each man. The Romans received 247 more than the Carthaginians, but because Fabius had not consulted the Senate, the money due, though the question was frequently debated, was not forthcoming for a long time. In these circumstances Fabius sent his son Quintus to Rome, sold the estate which Hannibal had spared from devastation, and paid the public debt out of his own pocket.

Hannibal was now in permanent camp outside Gereonium. The town had been captured and burnt, but he had left a few buildings intact to serve as store-houses for grain. From this base it was his practice to send two thirds of his men on foraging expeditions, while the remainder he kept, ready for action and under his own command, to guard the camp, and at the same time remained on the alert for possible enemy action against the foraging parties. 24. The Roman army at that time was near Larinum, under the command, as I have already mentioned, of Minucius, the master of Horse, during the dictator's absence in Rome. Minucius's camp had been in a safe position high up in the hills, but now it was moved down into the plain. Minucius being the man he was, plans of a warmer nature were brewing – an attack either on the foraging parties or, perhaps, on Hannibal's camp, left, as it had been, with a comparatively weak garrison. Hannibal was well aware that the change of commander meant a change of strategy, and that his enemy would throw caution to the winds. Moreover, he now took the almost incredible step of weakening the garrison of his camp, just when the enemy was close at hand, by sending a third of it out to join the foragers. He then moved the camp itself nearer to the enemy's position, to an eminence within sight of them about two miles from Gereonium, so that they might know he was on the look-out to protect his foragers should they be attacked. From his new position a hill could be seen still nearer the Roman lines, and obviously commanding them; this hill he could hardly occupy in daylight, as the Romans having a shorter way to go would certainly have forestalled him, so he sent a party of Numidians to seize it under cover of darkness. Next morning the Numidians, a contemptible little force in Roman eyes, were flung out, and the Roman camp was itself transferred thither.

As a result of these moves the camps of the opposing armies were now very close together, and the intervening space was almost completely filled by the Roman line; and at the same time the Roman cavalry and light infantry were sent out through (as it were) the back door to attack the foragers, whom they caught in scattered bands and handled very roughly. Hannibal could not risk a regular engagement, as with the few men at his disposal he could hardly protect his camp if it were attacked. He was driven, therefore, having only a portion of his army with him, to adopt Fabian tactics, biding his time, refusing to move, postponing the critical encounter. He had, moreover, withdrawn to his previous position outside Gereonium.

According to some historians a pitched battle was actually fought. At the first shock Hannibal's men broke and retired in disorder within their defences; recovering, they made a successful sortie which, in its turn, shook the Romans badly, until they were enabled to recover by the arrival on the scene of Numerius Decimius the Samnite. Decimius, in family and wealth the most distinguished man not only of his native Bovianum but of all Samnium, was bringing up by Fabius's orders a force of 8,000 foot and 500 horse, and when he appeared in Hannibal's rear, both sides imagined that reinforcements were coming with Fabius from Rome. Hannibal accordingly, fearing a trap in addition to this new threat, withdrew, and the Romans, pressing their advantage, took by storm, with Decimius's aid, two strong-points in the course of that day. Enemy losses amounted to 6,000 dead; Roman losses to about 5,000. Nevertheless though the losses were so nearly equal, a report reached Rome, together with a letter full of braggadocio from Minucius, of a great victory.

25. All this was discussed over and over again in the Senate and at public assemblies. The country was delighted at the

news, and the only man to refuse to believe either the report or Minucius's letter was Fabius. Moreover, he declared that even if the whole thing were true, he was himself more afraid of success than of failure. This was too much for Metilius, a people's tribune, who found such an attitude intolerable: the dictator, he said, had not only hampered the proper conduct of the war while he was on the spot, but was opposed to its success now that he was away from the army; he was deliberately dragging out hostilities in order to prolong his period of office and retain sole power in his own hands both at home and in the field – one consul having been killed in action, and the other being well out of the way on the pretext of pursuing a Carthaginian fleet. The two praetors, moreover, were busy in Sicily and Sardinia, though neither province needed a praetor at the moment. As for Minucius, his master of Horse, why – he had been almost kept under guard, simply to prevent him from striking a blow, or even from getting a sight of the enemy. And what was the result? Not Samnium only had been surrendered to Hannibal, as if it had been a bit of territory somewhere south of the Ebro, but fire and sword had brought ruin to Campania, Calenum, and Falernum, while the dictator loitered at Casilinum, protecting his private property with the armed forces of the Roman people. The master of Horse and the army itself, spoiling for an honest fight, were kept almost like gaol-birds within their defences, and deprived of their weapons as if they were prisoners of war. At last, the moment the dictator left them, they took the field, like besieged men liberated, and inflicted a crushing defeat on the enemy. 'And therefore,' cried Metilius in conclusion, 'if only the people of Rome were like their fathers of old, I should have boldly proposed that Quintus Fabius should be deprived of his high office; but, as things are, I shall moderate my demand, asking only that power be equally shared between the dictator and the master of Horse. To this I add one further suggestion: that, even if my demand is accepted, Fabius shall not be sent to rejoin the army till he has seen to the election of a consul in place of Gaius Flaminius.'

Fabius kept away from the popular assemblies, where he was not likely to be heard with favour. Even in the Senate he was listened to with considerable hostility when he praised the enemy, attributed the two years of defeat to the rashness and ignorance of the Roman command, and declared that the master of Horse should be brought to account for having gone into action against orders. 'If,' he said, 'the supreme command, with full direction of affairs, is entrusted to me, I shall soon make everyone realize that to a good commander the shifts of circumstance are never of the first importance. What counts is intelligence combined with a firm grasp of principle. That I saved the army without dishonour, before it was too late, is a better thing than the killing of many thousands of the enemy.'

Speeches in this vein did little to help him, so after the election of Marcus Atilius Regulus to the consulship, Fabius, to avoid having to take part in person in the debates over the division of the command, left Rome by night to rejoin the army on the day before the new measure was to be proposed. Early next morning there was a meeting of the people. The general feeling was one of unexpressed hostility towards the dictator and of strong support for Minucius, but in spite of this there was reluctance to come forward and actively support the measure which the people were known to approve. Feeling in favour of it was very strong, but authoritative sponsors were lacking. One man was, however, found who was willing formally to propose it: this was Gaius Terentius Varro, the praetor of the previous year. Varro was of humble, indeed of mean, origin: his father is said to have been a butcher who retailed his own meat and employed his son in the servile offices of his trade. 26. The son, in early manhood, having inherited his father's savings, began for that reason to set his hopes on better things. He acquired a taste for the forum and the toga, and by making impassioned speeches on behalf of the underdog and against the privileges of the dominant class he became a well-known popular figure and ended by acquiring public office. Having served first as quaestor, then twice as aedile – both plebeian and curule – then as praetor, he began to raise his hopes to the consulship; with this in view he had sufficient acumen to seek the breath of popular favour by maligning the dictator; and when the people's decree was passed, he alone got the credit for it.

Everyone but Fabius himself, both in Rome and in the army, whatever his private feelings were, took the new measure as a deliberate insult to the dictator. Fabius however bore the fury of the mob, undeserved though it was, as calmly as he had borne the accusations which his enemies had brought against him before the people. While he was still on the road a letter was brought him, containing the Senate's decree on the equalization of the command. Convinced, as ever, that that was by no means the same thing as the equalization of tactical or strategic skill, he went on to join his troops – the same Fabius still, for neither Hannibal nor his own countrymen had got the better of him.

27. Even before this, success and popularity had rendered Minucius intolerable enough; but now his behaviour went beyond all bounds of moderation and decency, and he bragged about his defeat of Fabius even more than his so-called defeat of Hannibal. That Fabius, sought out in times of stress as the one and only match for the victorious Hannibal, should now, by popular vote, be made equal to a junior officer – he, a dictator, brought to the level of his master of Horse – and that, too, in a country where mere masters of Horse had been in the habit of cringing like curs before the dictator's terrible rods and axes: why, the thing was unprecedented in all history! Such was the result of his own dazzling valour and success! He was determined, therefore, to follow where his fortune led, if the dictator persisted in the dilatory and do-nothing tactics which gods and men had alike condemned.

Accordingly, on the very day of his meeting with Fabius, he declared that the first question to be decided was the best method of putting into practice the new joint command. Personally, he favoured the plan of their exercising supreme command on alternate days, or perhaps for longer fixed periods, as that would enable each of them to be a match for the enemy in strength as well as in strategy, should a chance of action occur. Fabius strongly disagreed: he pointed out that nobody could possibly count upon the results of his colleague's rashness; that the command had not been taken out of his hands – even for a day – but shared between them; and that he therefore refused ever to give up what contribution he was still able to make towards the proper direction of the war. He was willing to divide the army with Minucius, but not the periods of command, whether it were one day or more; and, since he was not allowed complete control, he was determined to save what he could by following his own policy.

The result was that the two men divided the legions between them, as, in ordinary circumstances, the two consuls do. The first and fourth fell to Minucius, the second and third to Fabius. They also equally divided the cavalry and the auxiliary troops, allied and Latin. Minucius further demanded that the two sections of the army should have separate camps.

28. These arrangements gave Hannibal two reasons for satisfaction, for through the agency of his spies and the frequent reports of deserters nothing that went on in the enemy's camp escaped his knowledge. In the first place, Minucius's recklessness was now free of all restraint, and Hannibal could turn it to his own advantage; secondly, Fabius's tactical wisdom was robbed of one half of its strength.

Between Minucius's camp and that of the enemy there was a hill, the occupation of which by either side would certainly put the other in a disadvantageous position. It would have been worth Hannibal's while to seize this eminence without a fight, and he would have liked to do so; but he wanted still more to use it as a bait for Minucius who, he knew, would be certain to oppose any move he might make. The ground between the opposing forces was, to the casual eye, quite unsuitable for laying a trap in, as it was bare of woodland, and even of scrub; actually, however, it was made for the concealment of troops – perfect terrain for an ambush, especially as no such thing would be suspected in a bare and treeless valley. In its various twists and turns there were rocky recesses, some of them large enough to contain 200 men; and it was in these hide-outs that Hannibal concealed as many men as each could conveniently hold, in all 5,000 horse and foot. As in so open a valley the movement of a soldier thoughtlessly coming out of hiding, or perhaps the gleam of arms, might reveal the trap, Hannibal distracted the enemy's attention by sending a small party at dawn to occupy the hill which I mentioned above. They were only a handful; the sight of them filled the Romans with contempt and they all demanded for themselves the easy task of driving them off and occupying the hill in their turn. Minucius himself was as unwise and impetuous as anyone, calling to arms, and blackguarding the enemy with empty threats. First he sent out his light troops, then the cavalry in close order; lastly, seeing enemy reinforcements also coming up, he marched to meet them with his heavy infantry in battle array. Hannibal, too, as the action grew hotter, by sending reinforcements of horse or foot wherever his men were hard pressed, had brought up his army to full strength, and the engagement was now an all-out struggle. The Roman light infantry, leading the advance from the lower ground up the hill which was already in Carthaginian hands, was flung back, spread panic and confusion amongst the mounted troops behind them, and fled for safety to the legionaries in the rear. It was the legionaries who alone remained unshaken, and if only it had been a straight fight without complications, they might well have proved equal to the situation, their morale being high as a result of their success a few days before. But it was just at this moment that the troops Hannibal had concealed suddenly appeared upon the scene: falling upon the Roman rear and both flanks simultaneously they created such appalling confusion that Minucius's shattered army had neither the stomach to fight on nor any hope of escape.

29. Fabius heard the cries of bewilderment and terror; then, a moment later, he saw, in the distance, the broken lines. 'So!' he exclaimed, 'it has come! Recklessness has met with its deserts just as soon as I feared it would. Now, though equalled with Fabius in command, he sees that Hannibal is his superior in the military virtues and the success that attends them. But this is no time for reproach or indignation. Forward, my men, into the field! Let us wrest victory from the enemy, and make our countrymen confess their fault!'

Many of Minucius's men already lay dead, others were looking desperately for some way of escape, when Fabius's troops suddenly revealed themselves, as if sent from heaven to help them. Before they were within range – long before they actually came to grips – their appearance checked the rout and forced the enemy to caution. Those of Minucius's army who had broken ranks and were scattered over the field all joined up hurriedly with the fresh battle-line; groups of men who had turned tail and fled now faced the enemy again, and in circular formation disputed their ground yard by yard, or in massed order stood firm. Soon the two armies, the beaten and the fresh, were almost united in a single force, and were on the point of advancing to the attack, when Hannibal sounded the retreat – an open admission that though he had beaten Minucius he had had to yield to Fabius.

When towards the end of this eventful day the Roman armies had returned to their camps, Minucius addressed his assembled troops: 'My men,' he said, 'I have often heard that the best man is he who can give good counsel; the next best he who is ready to obey the good counsel of another. Long last comes the fool who is too ignorant to do either. We, alas, have not been granted the first, and highest, quality; so let us hold to the second; let us bethink ourselves of obeying a wise man as the first step in learning to command. We must unite our force with Fabius; when we have carried our standards to his tent, I shall call him Father, the name he deserves by virtue of his exalted rank and the service he has rendered us; and you, soldiers, will salute as your protectors the men whose swords have so lately saved you. This day will prove to have given us one splendid gift at least – the gift of a grateful heart.'

30. The trumpet sounded, and the cry was raised to break camp and move. As they marched in column to Fabius's headquarters, the dictator himself and all who were there to see watched their approach with surprise; when they halted before the tribunal, the master of Horse stepped forward and saluted Fabius by the name of Father, whereupon his soldiers, to a man, hailed as protectors the comrades who were crowding round him. 'Sir,' said Minucius, 'to my parents, to whom just now I equalled you in name – I can express it no better – I owe only my life; to you I owe the preservation of it, and the safety of all my men. Mine, therefore, shall be the first voice to abrogate and annul the decree of the people, which has brought me, indeed, but little honour, and a heavy burden. I have come back to serve again under your auspices and your command;

I restore to you these standards and these legions – and God grant it may prosper both you and me, and these your two armies, the saviour and the saved. One thing I ask: let me, in your generosity, retain my rank as your master of Horse, and these men of mine such rank as befits them.'

The two shook hands, the parade was dismissed, and Minucius's troops were kindly and hospitably entertained by friends and strangers alike. The day, a few hours before so dark, so fraught with horror, ended in rejoicing.

When the news was heard in Rome, and later confirmed by letters from the common soldiers of both armies as well by dispatches from the two commanders, every man in the City praised Fabius Maximus to the skies. Nor did his reputation stand less high with Hannibal and the Carthaginians: at last they felt that it was indeed the Romans they were fighting and that Italy was the seat of war – whereas for the past two years both officers and men in the Roman army had seemed so despicable that they could hardly believe they were at war with the terrible foe of whom their fathers had told them. There is a story, too, of a remark which Hannibal made after the battle: 'The cloud,' he said, 'which used to rest on the mountain tops, has come down at last in a storm of rain.'

31. During these events in Italy the consul Gnaeus Servilius Geminus with a fleet of 120 vessels sailed round Sardinia and Corsica and, after taking hostages from both islands, crossed to Africa. On the route thither he laid waste the island of Menix, allowed the people of Cercina to buy for ten talents of silver the immunity of their territory from the ravage of fire and sword, and then made the African coast, where he disembarked his troops. Plundering raids at once began, the ships' crews roaming the countryside as free-and-easy as if they were out to strip some uninhabited island. Their recklessness soon led them into a trap, and they found themselves surrounded: unlike themselves, their enemies were familiar with the country; compact bands easily rounded up the scattered parties of the invaders, with the result that they were driven back to their ships badly beaten-up and leaving many dead on the field. Something like a thousand men, amongst them the quaestor Sempronius Blaesus, were killed, and the fleet got hurriedly under way

again from a shore crowded with enemy soldiers and made for Sicily, where, at Lilybaeum, it was handed over to the praetor Titus Otacilius, to be taken back to Rome in charge of his lieutenant Publius Sura. Geminus proceeded through Sicily on foot, and crossed the Straits into Italy, in answer to a summons from Fabius ordering him and his colleague Atilius to take over the command of the armies, as his six-months period as commander-in-chief had nearly expired.

We read in the accounts of nearly all the annalists that it was as dictator that Fabius directed the war against Hannibal. Coelius Antipater adds that he was the first dictator to be appointed by the people. But Coelius and the other historians all forget that the right of naming a dictator belonged to Gnaeus Servilius who was the one surviving consul and absent at the time in Gaul.[1] As it was impossible in the national panic following upon a disastrous defeat to face the delay which would have been involved, recourse was had to the election by popular vote of an acting dictator; the subsequent conduct of the war, Fabius's immense reputation as a commander and the addition by his descendants of fresh inscriptions on his portrait-bust, led naturally enough to the general belief that he was appointed dictator, not acting dictator at all.

32. The consuls Marcus Atilius Regulus and Gnaeus Servilius Geminus took over the armies previously commanded by Fabius and Minucius respectively. Though it was only late autumn, they established themselves in strongly fortified winter encampments, and were unanimous in their decision to model their strategy on that of Fabius. If Hannibal sent out foraging parties, they were ready to meet them wherever it might be, harassing their columns and cutting off stragglers; but they steadily refused to risk a general engagement, the one thing Hannibal was doing everything he could to provoke. In consequence Hannibal found himself so short of supplies that but for the fear of an apparent confession of defeat he might well have withdrawn into Gaul, for in his present situation it was hopeless to expect to feed his troops if the consuls of the following year continued the same strategy.

While winter had more or less brought hostilities to a halt in

1. i.e. Cisalpine Gaul, or North Italy.

the neighbourhood of Gereonium, envoys from Naples came to Rome. They brought with them into the Senate-house forty large platters of solid gold and delivered a harangue to the effect that they were well aware of the drain on the Roman treasury in consequence of the war, and that as that war was being fought as much in defence of the cities and lands of her allies as to maintain the sovereignty of Rome herself, the capital city and protectress of Italy, the Neapolitans had felt it their duty to assist the Roman people by a gift of the gold which had been left them by their fathers for the adornment of their temples and their own enrichment. If, they added, they could suppose their military strength to be of any value, they would have offered it no less willingly; and the Senate and people of Rome would be doing them a favour if they considered as their own everything which Naples possessed, and honoured her by accepting a gift the value of which, small enough in itself, was enhanced only by the spirit in which it was freely given. The envoys were thanked for their generosity and thoughtfulness, and the smallest of the forty platters was accepted.

33. About this time a Carthaginian spy who had worked undetected for two years was caught in Rome. His hands were cut off, and he was let go. Twenty-five slaves were crucified for conspiracy in the Campus Martius, and the informer, a slave, was given his liberty and a reward of 20,000 *asses*. A delegation was sent to Philip,[1] King of Macedon, to demand the surrender of Demetrius of Pharus, who had taken refuge at his court after a military reverse. Another delegation was sent to Liguria to complain of the aid given to Hannibal in both money and men, and at the same time to gather direct evidence of what was going on amongst the Boii and Insubres. A third embassy visited Pineus, prince of the Illyrians, to demand payment of the tribute which was overdue, or to accept hostages should he wish to defer payment still longer. The Romans, in short, despite the burden of a major war, still found time to pay attention to all that concerned them anywhere in the world, however remote. Moreover, their conscience was uneasy because the Temple of Concord which the praetor Manlius had vowed two years previously in Gaul on the occasion of a

1. Philip V.

mutiny, had not yet been contracted for; so two officials, Pupius and Flamininus, were specially appointed by Marcus Aemilius the City praetor, to place the contract for the erection of the shrine on the Citadel.[1]

Aemilius also, on the Senate's instructions, wrote to the consuls to ask that one of them, if they thought fit, should come to Rome to preside over the consular elections, adding that he himself would announce the elections for the date they desired. The consuls replied that neither of them could quit his post without putting the country in jeopardy, so it would be more advisable to hold the elections under the presidency of an interrex than to recall either consul from his military duties. The Senate, however, thought it more proper that one of the consuls should nominate a dictator to hold the elections. Lucius Veturius Philo was nominated, and appointed, in his turn, Manlius Pomponius Matho as his master of Horse. As there was some technical fault in the appointment of these two men, they were ordered to resign after fourteen days, and there was once more an *interregnum*. 34. The consul's command was extended for a further year; the Senate named as interrex Gaius Claudius Centho, son of Appius, followed by Publius Cornelius Asina during whose period of office the elections were held.

The elections aroused the bitterest controversy between the senatorial order and the populace. The popular party exerted every effort to raise to the consulship Gaius Terentius Varro, a man of their own sort, who had endeared himself to them by his attacks on leading citizens and general demagogy, and ever since his attempt to undermine the influence of Fabius and the dictatorship had, by maligning others, directed the limelight on himself. The Senate no less vigorously opposed his candidature, as they feared the possibility of anyone coming to rival them in influence by the simple expedient of mud-slinging. Quintus Baebius Herennius, a people's tribune and kinsman of Varro, went further than to hurl abuse at the Senate: he also accused the augurs of preventing the dictator from holding the elections, and by maligning them won support for his own

1. One of the two summits of the Capitoline hill, the other being the Capitol.

candidate. The nobility, he said, had wanted war for years past, and had brought Hannibal into Italy; and now, though the war could be brought to an end, they were prolonging it by underhand means. The fact that Minucius had fought successfully without help from Fabius made it obvious that four legions united would make an entirely adequate fighting force; two legions had been sent to their deaths in action and rescued at the last moment simply in order that the man who had deprived the Romans of victory before he saved them from defeat might be hailed as Father and Protector. Subsequently the consuls had, by the use of Fabian guile, deliberately prolonged the war when they might have brought it to a successful conclusion. It was a pact entered into by every member of the ruling class, and they would never see the end of the war until they had a consul who really belonged to the people – a man who had never before held high office. Plebeians who had taken their place in the senatorial party by virtue of the offices they had held were already initiated into the mysteries, and had begun to despise the people ever since they themselves ceased to be despised by the nobility. Nothing could be plainer than that the deliberate intention had been to engineer an *interregnum*, so that the elections might be controlled by the Senate; that was the purpose of the consuls when they insisted on staying with the army; and that was their object when, a dictator having been appointed against their wishes to hold the elections, they had fought to obtain the augurs' decision that the appointment had been invalid. Well, they had got their *interregnum*. However, there was no doubt that one consulship belonged to the people; and the people would use their unrestricted privilege to give it to the man who would rather win the war than protract his own command.

35. Popular feeling was inflamed by speeches of this kind, and in the ensuing election, though there were three patrician candidates, Merenda, Volso, and Lepidus, and two plebeians, Serranus and Paetus, who had risen in the social scale by previously holding offices of state (one was pontiff, the other an augur), only one consul, Gaius Terentius Varro, was elected, on the understanding that he would preside over a further election for the appointment of a colleague. The patricians had

by now realized that the candidates they had put up were not strong enough, so they induced Lucius Aemilius Paullus, a violent opponent of the popular party, to stand, though very much against his own wishes. Paullus had been consul on a previous occasion with Marcus Livius. Livius had been condemned on some charge,[1] and Paullus himself had come near to it, and only got off with a seriously damaged reputation. On the next election day, with the approval of all Varro's opponents, he was returned – though the relationship of the two men was less like that of colleagues than of a couple of gladiators in the arena. The election of praetors followed, the successful candidates being Manlius Pomponius Matho and Publius Furius Philus, to the latter of whom was assigned the administration of justice in the City, to the former the hearing of disputes between Roman citizens and foreigners. Two praetors were added, Marcus Claudius Marcellus for Sicily, Lucius Postumius Albinus for Gaul. All were elected in their absence, and with the exception of Varro none of them was given a post which he had not previously held. A great many first-rate people were deliberately passed over, as it was felt that in a crisis like the present no one should be entrusted with an office in which he had not had previous experience.

36. The armed forces were also increased. I cannot state exactly the size of the increases in the cavalry and infantry respectively, because both about their number and kind our accounts differ greatly. 10,000 fresh troops were raised as a reinforcement, according to some writers; others say four new legions, to bring the total fighting force to eight legions. It is also said that the complement of a legion was increased by the addition of 1,000 foot and 100 horse, making it consist of 5,000 foot and 300 horse. Allied states were required to supply a double number of mounted troops, but the same number of infantry. Some have put it on record that at the time of the battle of Cannae Rome had 87,200 men in service. Of one thing there is no difference of opinion, namely that the war effort was greater and the forces involved more powerful than in

1. Marcus Livius Salinator, consul in 219, had been condemned for dishonesty in conducting the war against Demetrius of Pharus. In 207 he defeated Hasdrubal at the river Metaurus. See pp. 492ff.

previous years. The change was due to the fact that Fabius had made it possible to hope for victory.

Before the new legions left Rome, the Board of Ten were instructed to consult the Sacred Books. Once again queer things had been happening and superstitious fears had been aroused: on the Aventine in Rome, and simultaneously in Aricia, a rain of stones had been reported; amongst the Sabines statues had exuded blood, and hot water had flowed from springs. The latter phenomenon caused the more alarm in that it had occurred quite often. Again, on the Arched Way near the Campus Martius some men had been struck by lightning and killed. To deal with these prodigies, the appropriate formulae were drawn from the Books. A delegation from Paestum brought some golden platters to Rome. They were thanked, as the Neapolitans were, but the gift was not accepted.

37. About this time a fleet arrived at Ostia from Hiero, with a cargo of supplies. The Syracusan spokesmen said, on their introduction into the Senate, that Hiero had been so much grieved by the news of the death of Flaminius and the destruction of his army, that no calamity to himself or his kingdom could have moved him more deeply. Though he knew very well that Rome was greater and more to be admired in adversity than in success, he had none the less sent her all those things which good and loyal allies were accustomed to contribute towards the expenses of a war, and he earnestly entreated the Senate not to refuse them.

First, as an omen of success, they had brought with them a statue of Victory, in gold, of 220 pounds weight, which they begged the Senate to accept and to keep as their own peculiar possession for ever. Next, they had on shipboard 300,000 measures of wheat and 200,000 of barley, to ensure an adequate supply of food, and would carry as much more as was needed to any port named. They were aware that Rome did not employ as heavy infantry or cavalry any troops except her own and those of the Latin confederacy, though they had observed the presence in the Roman forces of light-armed foreign auxiliaries; Hiero, therefore, had sent a contingent of bowmen and slingers, 1,000 strong, which would be useful against the

Baliares and Moors or any other troops whose national weapons were missile.[1]

The gifts were backed up by a piece of advice: that the praetor who was serving in Sicily should invade Africa; for if he did, Hannibal, too, would have a war on his hands at home, and Carthage would be less free to send him reinforcements.

In reply to Hiero the Senate thanked him for his good will, declaring that he was a much valued ally who, ever since he became the friend of Rome, had remained consistently loyal, and had in all times and places assisted her cause with great munificence. The Roman people were grateful to him, as he deserved. They had not accepted the offer of gold from certain other communities, though they had gratefully recognized the spirit in which the offer had been made. In the present case, they were pleased to accept the Victory, with the good omen it implied, and would solemnly dedicate to that Goddess a home on the Capitol, in the temple of Jupiter Greatest and Best. There, in the citadel of Rome, she would be consecrated, and remain for ever firm and immovable, to bless and prosper the Roman people.

The slingers and bowmen were handed over to the consuls, together with the grain. Twenty-five quinqueremes were added to the fleet under the command of the propraetor Otacilius in Sicily, and he was given permission to cross into Africa, if he should think it advisable.

38. When the recruitment of the forces was complete, the consuls waited a few days for the arrival of the allies from the Latin confederacy. On this occasion, for the first time in history, the men were made to take a formal oath, administered by the general officers, to the effect that they would assemble for service on the consuls' orders and remain in service while those orders lasted. Hitherto the only oath had been the voluntary oath of allegiance to the commander; and further, when the troops met to be posted to their respective decuries (in the case of the cavalry) and centuries (in the case of the infantry) they used to swear voluntarily, within their own units, never to leave the field in order to save their own skins, nor to abandon

1. According to Polybius, the Senate had sent a request to Hiero for help, but Livy prefers to omit this humiliation.

their place in the line for any purpose other than to recover or fetch a weapon, to strike an enemy or to save a friend. Thus a formal and legally binding oath, administered by the military tribunes, was now substituted for what was previously a voluntary engagement amongst the men themselves.

Before the troops left Rome, the consul Varro made a number of extremely arrogant speeches. The nobles, he complained, were directly responsible for the war on Italian soil, and it would continue to prey upon the country's vitals if there were any more commanders on the Fabian model. He himself, on the contrary, would bring it to an end on the day he first caught sight of the enemy. His colleague Paullus spoke only once before the army marched, and in words which though true were hardly popular. His only harsh criticism of Varro was to express his surprise about how any army commander, while still at Rome, in his civilian clothes, could possibly know what his task on the field of battle would be, before he had become acquainted either with his own troops or the enemy's or had any idea of the lie and nature of the country where he was to operate – or how he could prophesy exactly when a pitched battle would occur. As for himself, he refused to recommend any sort of policy prematurely; for policy was moulded by circumstance, not circumstance by policy. He could but hope, he said, that any plan of action sensibly and cautiously carried out would prove successful. Up to the present, recklessness, even apart from its stupidity, had been a failure. It was manifest, in short, that Paullus would play for safety and avoid precipitate action, and to strengthen his determination Fabius (we are told) spoke to him at his departure in the following words.

39. 'If, Lucius Aemilius, you were like your colleague, or if – which I should much prefer – you had a colleague like yourself, anything I could now say would be superfluous. Two good consuls would serve the country well in virtue of their own sense of honour, without any words from me; and two bad consuls would not accept my advice, nor even listen to me. But as things are, I know your colleague's qualities and I know your own, so it is to you alone I address myself, understanding as I do that all your courage and patriotism will be in vain, if our country must limp on one sound leg and one lame one. With

the two of you equal in command, bad counsels will be backed by the same legal authority as good ones; for you are wrong, Paullus, if you think to find less opposition from Varro than from Hannibal. Hannibal is your enemy, Varro your rival, but I hardly know which will prove the more hostile to your designs; with the former you will be contending only on the field of battle, but with the latter everywhere and always. Moreover, against Hannibal and his legions your weapons will be your own cavalry, your own infantry; but these same men of yours will be a weapon in Varro's hand to use against yourself. Maybe it is unlucky to mention Gaius Flaminius, but I must take the risk: he was already consul, remember, commanding his troops in his allotted sphere, when he began to lose his wits; but Varro was a madman before ever he stood for the consulship; his frenzy continued throughout the election campaign, and it continues still, before he has seen anything at all of the tasks that await him. A man who here, amongst civilians, can raise such a storm of popular feeling by his wild talk of massed ranks in battle array – what do you think he will do amongst soldiers in arms, and in circumstances where words are at once followed by deeds?

'If Varro plunges, as he swears he will, straight into action, then (mark my words!) there will in some place be another and yet more terrible Trasimene, or I am no soldier and know nothing of the nature of this war, nor of Hannibal. Indeed this is no time to magnify myself at another man's expense – and I would rather go too far in despising fame than in seeking it. None the less, this is the truth: the only way of fighting the war with Hannibal is *my* way. This is shown not only by the result – that teacher of fools – but by that same process of reasoning which held good before, and will continue to do so without change so long as circumstances remain as they are.

'We are fighting in Italy, in our homeland; we have friends and allies everywhere to help us, now and in the time to come, with arms, men, horses, and supplies. In our peril they gave us that proof of their loyalty. Every day that passes makes us better, wiser, firmer. Hannibal, on the contrary, is on foreign and hostile soil, far from home and country, surrounded by every menace, every danger; for him there is no peace on land or sea; no towns receive him, no protecting walls; nothing he sees can he call his own; he has nothing to live on beyond the plunder of a day. He now has hardly a third of the army with which he crossed the Ebro; more of his men have died of hunger than fallen in battle, and the few that remain have not enough to eat. Can you then doubt that *inactivity* is the way to defeat an enemy who is daily growing more decrepit, and has neither adequate supplies, nor reinforcements, nor money? How long has he remained before the walls of Gereonium, a wretched little fortress in Apulia, as if they were the walls of Carthage . . . but I will not boast in your presence – you need only consider how the last consuls Atilius and Servilius baffled and made a fool of him there. This, Paullus, is the only way to safety: and it is not the enemy who will make it difficult and dangerous for you to tread, but your fellow-countrymen. Your own men will want precisely what the enemy wants; the wishes of Varro, the Roman consul, will play straight into the hands of Hannibal, commander-in-chief of the Carthaginian armies. You will have two generals against you; but you will stand firm against both, if you can steel yourself to ignore the tongues of men who will defame you – if you remain unmoved by the empty glory your colleague seeks and the false infamy he tries to bring upon yourself. Truth, they say, too often comes near to extinction, but is never quite put out. True glory will belong to the man who despises it. Never mind if they call your caution timidity, your wisdom sloth, your generalship weakness; it is better that a wise enemy should fear you than that foolish friends should praise. Hannibal will despise a reckless antagonist, but he will fear a cautious one. Not that I wish you to do nothing – all I want is that your actions should be guided by a reasoned policy, all risks avoided; that the conduct of the war should be controlled by you at all times; that you should neither lay aside your sword nor relax your vigilance but seize the opportunity that offers, while never giving the enemy a chance to take you at a disadvantage. Go slowly, and all will be clear and sure. Haste is always improvident and blind.'

40. Paullus's reply to these words was hardly a cheerful one: the advice, he admitted, was sound and true, but not easy to

carry out. If Fabius – the all-powerful dictator – had found his master of Horse an intolerable subordinate, what compelling authority could a consul expect to have over a reckless and turbulent colleague? He reminded Fabius how he himself in his former consulship had escaped badly scorched from the blaze of popular indignation, and could only hope now that all would be well. 'But in the event of failure,' he ended, 'I should rather face the enemy's spears than the condemnation of my compatriots.'

We are told that Paullus left Rome immediately after this interview, escorted by the leading senators. Varro, the plebeian consul, had an escort drawn from his supporters, more remarkable for numbers than for dignity. When they arrived in camp the fresh troops were incorporated with the old, and two separate divisions formed: the new, and smaller, camp being nearer Hannibal's position, the old camp containing greater numbers and all the best and most experienced troops. Of the two consuls of the previous year, one, Atilius, was sent to Rome as too old for further campaigning, the other, Geminius Servilius, was given command, in the smaller camp, of a Roman legion and 2,000 allied horse and foot.

As for Hannibal, his satisfaction at the arrival of the new consuls was profound, in spite of the fact that he knew the Roman strength had been increased by half. Such supplies as he could take from the country for his immediate needs were exhausted, and there was no place left from where he could get more, as all the grain in the whole district had been stored in fortified towns as soon as the open fields had become unsafe. Indeed he was so pressed that, as was subsequently learned, he had hardly ten days' food remaining, and his Spanish troops had prepared to desert – and would have actually done so if the Romans had waited till the moment was ripe. But it was not to be.

41. Varro's reckless and passionate impatience was further inflamed by a successful piece of luck. In the course of checking the enemy's raiding parties a minor engagement took place. There was nothing organized about it and no orders by either commander were given, but the whole thing started from a casual forward movement of the troops themselves. In the

sequel the Carthaginians had decidedly the worst of it: some 1,700 of them were killed, with a loss of Roman and allied troops of not more than a hundred. The victors, in no sort of order, were following up their success, when Paullus, who was in command that day (the consuls commanded on alternate days) stopped the pursuit because he feared a trap. Varro was furiously angry, exclaiming at the top of his voice that they had let the enemy slip from their grasp, and that if the order to halt had not been given the war could have been won outright. Hannibal was but little concerned over his losses, being more inclined to consider the incident as a bait to lure the more headstrong of the consuls, together with his soldiers – especially the new recruits – to even greater recklessness.

Hannibal had as full and accurate knowledge of the state of things in the Roman army as he had of his own. He was well aware that the command was in the hands of two dissimilar men, who would never agree, and that almost two thirds of the Roman force were raw recruits. He was confident that the time was ripe, and the means at hand, to catch them in a trap.

On the following night, therefore, he led his men out of camp carrying nothing but their weapons, and left the camp itself fully stocked with everything of value, both public and private property. Crossing the neighbouring hills, he concealed his infantry, drawn up in battle order, on one side, and his mounted troops on the other, taking his baggage over along a dip in the hills between the two. His object was to lure the enemy to plunder his apparently deserted camp and to fall suddenly upon them while they were in no fit state to resist. He left numerous fires burning in his camp, to make it appear occupied and to create the impression that he wanted the consuls to stay where they were while he put a good distance between himself and a possible pursuer. He had baffled Fabius the year before by a similar ruse.

42. At dawn, the sentries were gone. Some Roman soldiers moved closer. Everything was strangely silent. Then, when it was apparent that the camp was deserted, there was a rush to headquarters bringing the news that the enemy had fled in such desperate haste that they had even left their tents standing, and that fires had been left burning to disguise their flight. The

men clamoured for the order to march – to plunder the deserted camp instantly and be on the tracks of the fugitives. Varro could control himself no better than the common soldiers, though Paullus repeatedly urged the necessity for foresight and caution. But at last, when he saw there was no other way to stop a mutiny or to deal with its leader, he ordered out Marius Statilius, a cavalry officer, with a troop of Lucanian horse to reconnoitre. Statilius rode up to the gates of the camp, halted his men outside the fortifications, and himself accompanied by two troopers passed inside the rampart; after a careful and thorough survey he returned with the report that the whole thing was undoubtedly a trap: fires had been left burning in that portion of the camp which faced the Roman position; the tents were open, and all valuables exposed to view; he had seen silver scattered about in the camp-lines – clearly a deliberately contrived bait.

This report, intended to curb the soldiers' cupidity, succeeded only in aggravating it. They roared with one voice that if no order were given they would go on their own, leader or no leader. But of course a leader was at hand – it was Varro, who promptly gave the signal to proceed. Paullus, who in any case had no wish to move, was further supported in his judgement by a warning sign – the chickens refused their food. He sent a messenger to Varro to report the omen, and caught him just as he was passing through the gates. Varro was annoyed; nevertheless he was seized by a certain superstitious dread when he remembered the recent fate of Flaminius and the story of the naval defeat of the consul Claudius in the first Punic war. In what followed it looked as if the gods themselves on that day at least postponed, though they could not prevent, the coming disaster; for it so happened that when the mutinous troops refused to obey the consul's order to march back into camp, two slaves suddenly put in an appearance. One belonged to a cavalryman from Formiae, the other to a cavalryman from Sidicinum, and during the previous year they had been caught in a foraging party by the Numidians. They had escaped, and were now returning to their masters. These two men were brought before the consuls and gave the information that Hannibal's entire force was lying in ambush on the other side of the hills. Their opportune arrival restored the consuls' authority – though one of them, by his reckless courting of his men's favour and unworthy compliance with their wishes, had impaired the dignity proper to his position.

43. Hannibal now saw that the Roman move was only a rash venture; they had not been tempted to fling themselves thoughtlessly into a major assault. His trick was discovered, nothing had been accomplished, and he returned to camp. Lack of supplies made it impossible for him to stay there long; every day amongst his men, a mixed lot composed of the sweepings of every nation, some new plan was mooted and discussed, and Hannibal himself was in many minds about the best course to take. The troops had begun by grumbling; then had come loud and open complaints over arrears of pay, insufficient food, and, finally, actual starvation; rumour spread that the mercenaries, especially the Spanish mercenaries, had planned to go over to the Romans, and it is said that even Hannibal himself had sometimes debated the wisdom of retiring into Gaul, leaving his infantry behind and making a dash for safety with his cavalry. However, such being the state of thought and feeling in the camp, he finally decided to move into Apulia; the climate was warmer there and the harvests earlier, and there would be the additional advantage that, the greater the distance between himself and the enemy, the more difficult it would be for his untrustworthy troops to desert.

He set out at night, once again kindling fires and leaving a few tents by way of a blind, hoping that fear of a trap would, as on the previous occasion, stop the Romans from making a move. Statilius the Lucanian was again sent to reconnoitre. Having examined all the ground beyond the Carthaginian camp and on the other side of the hills, he returned with the report that he had seen the enemy column in retreat and already far away. At once discussion began about the advisability of pursuit, and each consul stuck to the opinion he had consistently held in the past. Almost everyone supported Varro, the only man to agree with Paullus being the ex-consul Servilius. So thus, by a majority vote, the army marched on its way to Cannae, to make it famous in history as the scene of a catastrophic Roman defeat. Destiny itself was at its heels.

Near the village of Cannae Hannibal had taken up a position facing away from the prevailing wind from the hills, which drives clouds of dust over that stretch of parched and level ground. This was a great convenience to his men in camp, and it would be especially advantageous once the action began, as his own men would be fighting with their backs to the wind against an enemy blinded by the flying dust.

44. In their pursuit of the Carthaginians the consuls spared no pains in reconnoitring the route. Arrived at Cannae, where they had the Carthaginian position full in view, they fortified two separate camps about the same distance apart as at Gereonium, dividing the forces as before. The river Aufidus, flowing between the two camps, could be reached by watering-parties, as opportunity arose, though not without opposition; but parties from the smaller camp, on the further (or southern) side of the river, could water more freely, as the bank on that side was not guarded. Hannibal hoped that the consuls would offer to engage him on ground peculiarly suited to cavalry, the arm in which he was invincible; and with this in view he formed his line and sent his Numidian horse to provoke the enemy by small-scale, rapid charges. At this, the old trouble broke out again in the Roman lines: the men threatened mutiny; the consuls were at loggerheads. Paullus faced Varro with the reckless conduct of Sempronius and Flaminius; Varro replied by holding up Fabius as a specious example for commanders who wanted to conceal their own timidity and lack of spirit. Varro called gods and men to witness that it was no fault of his that Hannibal now owned Italy by right of possession – his hands had been tied by his colleague; his angry men, spoiling for a fight, were being robbed of their swords. Paullus, in his turn, declared that if the legions were recklessly betrayed into an ill-advised and imprudent battle and suffered a reverse, he would himself be free of all blame for the disaster, though he would share its consequences. It was up to Varro, he added, to see that their readiness to use bold words was matched, when it came to action, by the vigour of their hands.

45. Thus in the Roman camp the time was passed in altercation rather than in planning for the coming fight. Meanwhile Hannibal began to withdraw the main body of his men from

the battle-positions they had occupied during the greater part of the day, and at the same time sent his Numidians across the river to attack the Roman watering-parties from the smaller of their two camps. The watering-parties were mere unorganized groups, and the Numidians sent them flying in much noise and confusion almost before they were over the river, and then continued their advance to a guard-post in front of the Roman defences, carrying on almost to the very gates of the camp. That their camp should be threatened by what was only a small skirmishing force of auxiliary troops was felt by the Romans as an insult; and the only thing that prevented them from immediately crossing the river in force and offering battle was the fact that it was Paullus's day of command. Varro's turn was on the day following, and he used it as was to be expected: without in any way consulting his colleague he gave the order for battle, marshalled the troops, and led them across the river. Paullus followed, for he could not but lend his aid, deeply though he disapproved of what was done.

Once over the river, they joined up with the troops in the smaller camp, forming their line with the Roman cavalry on the right wing, nearer the river, and the Roman legionaries on their left; on the other wing were stationed, first – on the extreme flank – the allied cavalry, then the allied foot extending inwards till they joined the legionaries in the centre. The javelins and other light auxiliaries formed the front line. The consuls commanded the wings, Varro the left, Paullus the right. The task of controlling the centre was assigned to Servilius.

46. At dawn Hannibal first sent his light contingents, including the Baleares, across the river, then followed with his main force, drawing up in their battle positions the various contingents as they reached the other side. On his left, near the river bank, were the Gallic and Spanish horse, facing their Roman counterparts; on his right were the Numidians, and his centre was strongly held by infantry, so disposed as to have Gauls and Spaniards in the centre and African troops on each flank. To look at them, one might have thought the Africans were Roman soldiers – their arms were largely Roman, having been part of the spoils at Trasimene, and some, too, at the

Trebia. The Gallic and Spanish contingents carried shields of similar shape, but their swords were of different pattern, those of the Gauls being very long and not pointed, those of the Spaniards, who were accustomed to use them for piercing rather than cutting, being handily short and sharply pointed. One must admit, too, that the rest of the turn-out of these peoples, combined with their general appearance and great stature, made an awesome spectacle: the Gauls naked from the navel upwards; the Spaniards ranged in line in their dazzling white linen tunics bordered with purple. The total number of infantry in the battle-line was 40,000; of cavalry 10,000. The left wing was commanded by Hasdrubal, the right by Maharbal; Hannibal in person, supported by his brother Mago, held the centre. The Roman line faced south, the Carthaginian north; and luckily for both the early morning sun (whether they had taken up their positions by accident or design) shone obliquely on each of them; but a wind which had got up – called locally the Volturnus – was a disadvantage to the Romans as it carried clouds of dust into their eyes and obscured their vision.

47. The battle-cry rang out; the auxiliaries leapt forward, and with the light troops the action began. Soon the Gallic and Spanish horse on the Carthaginian left were engaged with the Roman right. Lack of space made it an unusual cavalry encounter: the antagonists were compelled to charge head-on, front to front; there was no room for outflanking manoeuvres, as the river on one side and the massed infantry on the other pinned them in, leaving them no option but to go straight ahead. The horses soon found themselves brought to a halt, jammed close together in the inadequate space, and the riders set about dragging their opponents from the saddle, turning the contest more or less into an infantry battle. It was fierce while it lasted, but that was not for long; the Romans were forced to yield and hurriedly withdrew. Towards the end of this preliminary skirmish, the regular infantry became engaged; for a time it was an equal struggle, but at last the Romans, after repeated efforts, maintaining close formation on a broad front, drove in the opposing Gallic and Spanish troops, which were in wedge formation, projecting from the main body, and too

thin to be strong enough to withstand the pressure. As these hurriedly withdrew, the Romans continued their forward thrust, carrying straight on through the broken column of the enemy now flying for their lives, until they reached the Carthaginian centre, after which, with little or no resistance, they penetrated to the position held by the African auxiliaries. These troops held the two Carthaginian wings, drawn back a little, while the centre, held by the Gauls and Spaniards, projected somewhat forward. The forcing back of the projecting wedge soon levelled the Carthaginian front; then, as under increasing pressure the beaten troops still further retired, the front assumed a concave shape, leaving the Africans on, as it were, the two projecting ends of the crescent. Recklessly the Romans charged straight into it, and the Africans on each side closed in. In another minute they had further extended their wings and closed the trap in the Roman rear.

The brief Roman success had been in vain. Now, leaving the Gauls and Spaniards on whom they had done much execution as they fled, they turned to face the Africans. This time the fight was by no means on equal terms: the Romans were surrounded, and – which was worse – they were tired men matched against a fresh and vigorous enemy.

48. Meanwhile the Roman left, where the allied horse confronted the Numidians, was also engaged. For a while things went slowly, owing to a Carthaginian ruse right at the outset. About 500 Numidians pretended to desert: in addition to their regular weapons they concealed swords under their tunics and rode up to the Roman line with their shields slung behind their backs. Suddenly dismounting, and flinging their shields and javelins on the ground, they were taken into the line by the Romans, and then conducted to the rear, where they were ordered to remain. While the general action was developing, they kept quiet enough; but as soon as no one in their vicinity had eyes or thoughts for anything but the progress of the battle, they picked up their shields from where they lay scattered around amongst the heaps of dead, and attacked the Roman line in the rear, striking at the soldiers' backs, hamstringing them, and causing terrible destruction, and even more panic and disorder.

It was at this juncture, when in one part of the field the Romans had little left but to try to save their skins, while in another, though hope was almost gone, they continued to fight with dogged determination, that Hasdrubal withdrew the Numidians from the centre, where they were not being used to much advantage, and sent them in pursuit of the scattered fugitives, at the same time ordering the Spaniards and Gauls to move to the support of the Africans, who by now were almost exhausted by what might be called butchery rather than battle.

49. Paullus, on the other wing, had been severely wounded by a sling-stone right at the start of the fight; none the less, at the head of his men in close order, he continued to make a number of attempts to get at Hannibal, and in several places succeeded in pulling things together. He had with him a guard of Roman cavalry, but the time came when Paullus was too weak even to control his horse, and they were obliged to dismount. Someone, it is said, told Hannibal that the consul had ordered his cavalry to dismount, and Hannibal, knowing they were therefore done for, replied that he might as well have delivered them up to him in chains.

The enemy's victory was now assured, and the dismounted cavalry fought in the full knowledge of defeat; they made no attempt to escape, preferring to die where they stood; and their refusal to budge, by delaying total victory even for a moment, further incensed the triumphant enemy, who unable to drive them from their ground, mercilessly cut them down. Some few survivors did indeed turn and run, wounded and worn out though they were.

The whole force was now broken and dispersed. Those who could, recovered their horses, hoping to escape. Lentulus, the military tribune, as he rode by saw the consul Paullus sitting on a stone and bleeding profusely. 'Lucius Aemilius,' he said, 'you only, in the sight of heaven, are guiltless of this day's disaster; take my horse, while you still have some strength left, and I am here to lift you up and protect you. Do not add to the darkness of our calamity by a consul's death. Without that, we have cause enough for tears.' 'God bless your courage,' Paullus answered, 'but you have little time to escape; do not waste it in useless pity – get you gone, and tell the Senate to look to

Rome and fortify it with strong defences before the victorious enemy can come. And take a personal message too: tell Quintus Fabius that while I lived I did not forget his counsel, and that I remember it still in the hour of death. As for me, let me die here amongst my dead soldiers: I would not a second time stand trial after my consulship, nor would I accuse my colleague, to protect myself by incriminating another.' The two men were still speaking when a crowd of fugitives swept by. The Numidians were close on their heels. Paullus fell under a shower of spears, his killers not even knowing whom they killed. In the confusion Lentulus's horse bolted, and carried him off.

After that, there was nothing but men flying for their lives. 7,000 got away into the smaller camp, 10,000 into the larger; about 2,000 sought refuge in Cannae, but the village had no sort of defences and they were immediately surrounded by Carthalo and his cavalry. Varro, whether by chance or design, managed to keep clear of the fugitives and reached Venusia alive, with some seventy horsemen. The total number of casualties is said to have been 45,500 infantrymen and 2,700 cavalrymen killed[1] – about equally divided between citizens and allies. Amongst the dead were the consuls' two quaestors, Lucius Atilius and Lucius Furius Bibaculus, twenty-nine military tribunes, a number of ex-consuls and of men who had the rank of praetor or aedile – amongst them are numbered Gnaeus Servilius Geminus and Marcus Minucius (who had been master of Horse the previous year and consul some years earlier) – eighty distinguished men who were either members of the Senate, or had held offices which qualified for membership, and had, on this occasion, volunteered for service in the legions. The number of prisoners amounted to 3,000 infantry and 1,500 cavalry.

50. Such is the story of Cannae, a defeat no less famous than the defeat on the Allia;[2] for the enormous losses involved, it was the more dreadful of the two, though less serious in its results, as Hannibal did not follow up his victory. The rout at

1. On p. 300 Livy gives the round figure as 50,000 killed and so do Appian and Plutarch. Quintilian puts it at 60,000 and Polybius at 70,000.

2. The victory of the Gauls over the Romans in 390 B.C.

the Allia lost Rome, but it left the army still in existence; at Cannae hardly seventy men got away with Varro, and almost the whole army shared the fate of Paullus.

In the two camps the men were now leaderless, and most of their weapons were gone. Those in the larger camp sent a message to their comrades in the smaller, asking them to join them, and suggesting that they could probably get across during the night while the enemy troops were asleep after their exertions in the battle and the subsequent feasting and rejoicing over their victory. They could then go in a body to Canusium. By some, however, the message was very ill received: why (it was asked) didn't they come themselves, which would be just as good a way of effecting a junction? Obviously, because the intervening ground was full of enemy troops, and the senders of the message preferred to risk other people's lives to risking their own. Others approved the plan but lacked heart to carry it out. It was a military tribune named Publius Sempronius Tuditanus who roused them to act: 'So,' he cried, 'you would rather be taken prisoner by a brutal and avaricious enemy – have a price put on your heads – be asked if you are a Roman citizen or a member of the Latin Confederacy and have the ransom demanded accordingly, that another may be exalted by your misery and shame! No, no! Not at least if you belong to the same country as the consul Paullus who preferred a noble death to a life of dishonour, or as all those brave men whose bodies lie heaped around him. Come then: before daylight is upon us and more of the enemy troops block our way, let us get out – and quickly – and fight our way through that howling and undisciplined mob around our gates. However dense an enemy's line, boldness and a good sword can find a way to pierce it; as for that loose and disorderly mob, you can drive through it as easily as if there were nothing to stop you. Come with me then – if you want to save yourselves, and your country.'

With these words he drew his sword and led his comrades, in wedge formation, straight through what opposition there was. Some Numidians on their right, and exposed, flank discharged their javelins at them, but they shifted their shields over and forced their way, some 600 of them, to the larger camp. From there, without further delay and with a great accession of numbers, they reached Canusium in safety. This was in no sense a planned action; nobody gave orders or took command; it arose, amongst this remnant of a beaten army, from sheer impulse dictated by the individual temperaments, such as they happened to be, of the men concerned.

51. Meanwhile the victorious Hannibal was surrounded by his officers offering their congratulations and urging him to take some rest during the remainder of the day and the ensuing night, and to allow his tired troops to do the same; Maharbal, however, the commander of his cavalry, was convinced that there was not a moment to be lost. 'Sir,' he said, 'if you want to know the true significance of this battle, let me tell you that within five days you will take your dinner, in triumph, on the Capitol. I will go first with my horsemen. The first knowledge of our coming will be the sight of us at the gates of Rome. You have but to follow.'

To Hannibal this seemed too sanguine a hope, a project too great to be, in the circumstances, wholly conceivable. 'I commend your zeal,' he said to Maharbal; 'but I need time to weigh the plan which you propose.' 'Assuredly,' Maharbal replied, 'no one man has been blessed with all God's gifts. You know, Hannibal, how to win a fight; you do not know how to use your victory.'

It is generally believed that that day's delay was the salvation of the City and of the Empire.

At dawn next morning the Carthaginians applied themselves to collecting the spoils and viewing the carnage, which even to an enemy's eyes was a shocking spectacle. All over the field Roman soldiers lay dead in their thousands, horse and foot mingled, as the shifting phases of the battle, or the attempt to escape, had brought them together. Here and there wounded men, covered with blood, who had been roused to consciousness by the morning cold, were dispatched by a quick blow as they struggled to rise from amongst the corpses; others were found still alive with the sinews in their thighs and behind their knees sliced through, baring their throats and necks and begging who would to spill what little blood they had left. Some had their heads buried in the ground, having apparently dug themselves holes and by smothering their faces with earth had choked themselves to death. Most strange of all was a Numidian soldier, still living, and lying, with nose and ears horribly lacerated, underneath the body of a Roman who, when his useless hands had no longer been able to grasp his sword, had died in the act of tearing his enemy, in bestial fury, with his teeth.

52. Much of the day was spent in collecting the spoils. Hannibal then moved against the smaller camp and, preparatory to an assault, constructed a barrier-wall to cut it off from access to the river. However, the place was surrendered sooner than he expected, as all the men in it were either wounded or worn out through lack of sleep and the hardships they had undergone. By the terms of surrender they were to hand over their horses and weapons; the ransom for Romans was to be fixed at 300 *denarii* a head, for allies at 200, for slaves at 100; and when the money was paid they were to be allowed to go free with not more than a single garment apiece. The terms settled, the gates were opened to the enemy. Every man was delivered into custody, Roman and allied troops being kept separate.

Meanwhile all the men in the larger camp who had strength or heart for the undertaking – in all about 4,000, together with 200 cavalrymen – escaped to Canusium, some marching in column, others, which was no more dangerous, making their way individually over the countryside. The camp itself was surrendered by the wounded or faint-hearted who remained, on the same conditions as the other.

An enormous quantity of valuable material was taken: Hannibal's men were given the free run of all of it with the exception of horses, men, and what silver there was – most of it was in the trappings of the horses, for the Romans used very little silver plate for their tables, especially on active service.

Hannibal then gave orders for the bodies of his men to be collected for burial. There are said to have been about 8,000, all from his best troops. According to some writers Paullus's body, too, was searched for and given burial.

The fugitives who went to Canusium were given protection by the people of the town and the shelter of a roof, but no more. But a wealthy Apulian woman of good family, named Busa, further provided them with food, clothing, and money for the road, a munificent act for which she was formally honoured by the Senate after the war.

53. With the fugitives were four military tribunes: Fabius Maximus, son of the dictator, of the First Legion, Lucius Publicius Bibulus and Publius Cornelius Scipio of the Second, and Appius Claudius Pulcher who had lately held the office of aedile of the Third. By universal consent command was offered to Appius Claudius and Scipio, who was still a very young man.[1] The four tribunes were discussing with a few friends what measures to adopt, when Philus, the son of an ex-consul, broke in upon them with startling news: to cherish hope was useless, for all was lost – the future had nothing to offer but misery and despair. A number of men of patrician blood, led by Lucius Caecilius Metellus, were turning their eyes to the sea and planning to abandon Italy and find refuge with some foreign prince. This news, dreadful enough in itself and coming as a new sort of horror on top of all their previous calamities, struck them into a kind of numbed stupor of incredulity. Those who had been listening to the tribunes' discussion proposed to call a general conference, but young Scipio – the man who was destined to command the Roman armies in this war – said that this was no matter for debate: the crisis had come, and what was needed was not words, but bold action. 'Come with me,' he cried, 'instantly, sword in hand, if you wish to save our country. The enemy's camp is nowhere more truly than in the place where such thoughts can rise!' With a few followers he went straight to where Metellus was staying. Assembled in the house were the men of whom Philus had spoken, still discussing their plans. Scipio burst in, and holding his bared sword over their heads, 'I swear,' he cried, 'with all the passion of my heart that I shall never desert our country, or permit any other citizen of Rome to leave her in the lurch. If I wilfully break my oath, may Jupiter, Greatest and Best, bring me to a shameful death, with my house, my family and all I possess! Swear the same oath, Caecilius; and, all the rest of you, swear it too. If anyone refuse, against him this sword is drawn.' They could not have been more scared had they been looking in the

1. He was about nineteen.

face of their conqueror Hannibal. Every man of them took the oath, and gave himself into Scipio's custody.

54. During these events at Canusium some 4,000 fugitives, foot and horse, who had been making their way across country, joined Varro at Venusia. The townspeople billeted them on various families where they were welcomed and hospitably looked after, and presented every cavalryman with a toga, a tunic, and twenty-five denarii, and every infantryman with ten, with a further gift of arms to those who had none. By these and other acts of hospitality both individual and at the public expense, they showed their determination not to let the people of Venusia be outdone in the duties of a host by a woman of Canusium. Busa, however, had the heavier burden: for the number of fugitives was increasing and there were now nearly 10,000 of them.

When Appius and Scipio learned that Varro was safe, they at once sent to inform him of the number of troops, horse and foot, which they had with them, and to ask whether he wished them to be brought to Venusia or to remain in Canusium. Varro replied by bringing his own force to Canusium, and its arrival made something at any rate resembling a consular army, so that all now felt that they would be capable of defending themselves within their fortified walls at least, though hardly in the open field.

No news had reached Rome of the survival even of this remnant of the national and allied armies, but it was still believed that both consuls had perished with all their men and that the entire military force had been wiped out. Never, without an enemy actually within the gates, had there been such terror and confusion in the city. To write of it is beyond my strength, so I shall not attempt to describe what any words of mine would only make less than the truth. In the previous year a consul and his army had been lost at Trasimene, and now there was news not merely of another similar blow, but of a multiple calamity – two consular armies annihilated, both consuls dead, Rome left without a force in the field, without a commander, without a single soldier, Apulia and Samnium in Hannibal's hands, and now nearly the whole of Italy overrun. No other nation in the world could have suffered so tremendous a series of disasters, and not been overwhelmed. It was unparalleled in history: the naval defeat off the Aegates islands,[1] a defeat which forced the Carthaginians to abandon Sicily and Sardinia and suffer themselves to pay taxes and tribute to Rome; the final defeat in Africa to which Hannibal himself afterwards succumbed – neither the one nor the other was in any way comparable to what Rome had now to face, except in the fact that they were not borne with so high a courage.

55. The praetors Philus and Pomponius summoned the Senate to meet in the Curia Hostilia to consider the defence of the City, as nobody doubted that Hannibal, now that the armies were destroyed, would attack Rome – the final operation to crown his victory. It was not easy to work out a plan: their troubles, already great enough, were made worse by the lack of firm news; the streets were loud with the wailing and weeping of women, and nothing yet being clearly known, living and dead alike were being mourned in nearly every house in the city. In these circumstances, Quintus Fabius Maximus put forward some proposals: riders, he suggested, lightly equipped, should be sent out along the Appian and Latin Ways to question any survivors they might meet roaming the countryside, and report any tidings they could get from them of what had happened to the consuls and the armies. If the gods, in pity for the empire, had suffered any of the Roman name to survive, they should inquire where they were, where Hannibal went after the battle, what his plans were, what he was doing, and what he was likely to do next. The task of collecting this information should be entrusted to vigorous and active men. There was also a task, Fabius suggested, for the Senate itself to perform, as there was a lack of public officers: this was, to get rid of the general confusion in the city and restore some sort of order. Women must be forbidden to appear out of doors, and compelled to stay in their homes; family mourning should be checked, and silence imposed everywhere; anyone with news to report should be taken to the praetors, and all individuals should await in their homes the news which personally concerned them. Furthermore, guards should be posted at the gates to prevent anyone from

1. The end of the First Punic war in 241 B.C.

leaving the city, and every man and woman should be made to believe that there was no hope of safety except within the walls of Rome. Once, he ended, the present noise and disorder were under control, then would be the proper time to recall the Senate and debate measures for defence.

56. The proposals of Fabius won unanimous support. The city magistrates cleared the crowds out of the forum and the senators went off to restore some sort of order in the streets. It was at this juncture that a letter from Varro arrived, with the information that the consul Paullus had perished with his army, and that he himself was at Canusium engaged in salvaging what he could from the wreck. He had with him about 10,000 men – bits and pieces from various units, and nothing like a coherent force. Hannibal was still at Cannae, bargaining over his prisoners' ransom and the rest of his booty – by no means what one would expect of a great and victorious commander.

Families were then informed of their personal losses, and the city in consequence was so filled with mourners that the annual festival of Ceres was cancelled.[1] Religion did not allow the rites to be celebrated by people in mourning, and there was no married woman at the time who was not. To prevent the abandonment of any other religious celebration, national or private, for a similar reason, the Senate issued a decree limiting the period of mourning to thirty days. But there was more bad news to come; for as soon as things in the city were quiet again and the Senate had been recalled, another dispatch arrived. This time it was from Titus Otacilius the propraetor in Sicily, who reported that a Carthaginian fleet was doing serious damage to the dominions of Hiero. Otacilius was preparing to answer his request for assistance, when a message had arrived that a second fleet was lying, fully equipped and ready for action, at the Aegates islands, the obvious intention being to attack Lilybaeum and the rest of the Roman territory there as soon as it was seen that Otacilius had turned his attention to protecting the Syracusan coast. A fleet was therefore needed if Sicily and their ally King Hiero were to be given protection.

57. When the two despatches had been read, it was decided

1. Not the Cerealia, the chief festival, which was celebrated in April: Cannae was fought on 2 August.

to send Marcus Claudius Marcellus[1] who was in command of the fleet at Ostia to the army at Canusium, and to send written instructions to Varro to repair to Rome at the earliest moment consistent with public safety after handing over the troops to the praetor.

In addition to this dreadful series of disasters, there was yet another cause for alarm in the occurrence of certain events of evil omen. Of these the chief was the conviction for sexual incontinence of two Vestal Virgins, Opimia and Floronia. One of them was buried alive at the Colline Gate, the traditional punishment for this offence; the other killed herself. The man who had debauched Floronia, Lucius Cantilius, secretary of the Pontiffs – an office now known as that of the Lesser Pontiffs – was beaten to death by the *pontifex maximus* in the place of assembly. The act of impiety coming, as it did, as one of a succession of calamities, was not unnaturally looked upon in a superstitious light, and orders were given to the Board of Ten to consult the Sacred Books. Quintus Fabius Pictor was also sent to inquire of the oracle at Delphi about the forms of prayer and supplication necessary for placating the wrath of heaven and to ask what end to their overwhelming disasters they might expect. Meanwhile on the authority of the Sacred Books some unusual rites were performed: one of them consisted in burying alive in the cattle market a pair of Gauls, male and female, and a pair of Greeks. The burial was in a walled enclosure, which had been stained before with the blood of human sacrifice – a most un-Roman rite.

The gods being now, it was supposed, adequately appeased, Marcus Claudius Marcellus sent to help garrison Rome the 1,500 men which he had with him for naval duty at Ostia, and himself hurried to Canusium, having a few days previously sent on a marine legion – the third – with the military tribunes to Teanum Sidicinum, and handed over command of the fleet to his colleague Philus. Marcus Junius, who had been appointed dictator on the Senate's authority, and Tiberius Sempronius his master of Horse, proclaimed a levy and enlisted for service men from the age of seventeen, and some still younger not

1. Already distinguished for his victory over the Gauls in 222 B.C. Marcellus was one of the outstanding generals of the war.

yet out of their boys' togas. From these four legions were raised and 1,000 cavalrymen. They sent also to the allied communities and the Latin Confederacy to receive reinforcements according to the agreement. Orders were issued for the preparation of arms, weapons, and other equipment; the spoils of former wars were removed from temples and porticoes. There was also another, and unprecedented, form of recruitment, rendered necessary by the pressure of circumstances and the shortage of free citizens: this was the arming of 8,000 slaves, healthy and in the prime of life. They were bought from their owners at the public expense, having first been asked individually if they were willing to serve. This type of recruit was preferred in spite of the fact that it would have been possible to ransom the prisoners for less cost.

58. After his great victory at Cannae Hannibal was temporarily occupied with the cares of a conqueror rather than of a general with a war still on his hands. When the prisoners had been brought out and the Romans separated from the rest, he spoke kindly to the non-Romans and set them free without ransom, as he had done before at the Trebia and at Trasimene. This time, however, he went on to do what he had never anywhere done before: he had the Roman prisoners, too, called before him and addressed them in comparatively mild terms. He was not, he said, engaged in a war to the death with Rome; he was fighting only for honour and empire. His forebears had yielded to the valour of Roman arms, and the object for which he strove was to force others to yield in their turn to his own valour combined with his good fortune. He therefore offered his prisoners the chance of ransoming themselves, at the price of 500 *denarii* for a cavalryman, 300 for a foot soldier, and 100 for a slave. The price for a cavalryman was somewhat higher than had been agreed upon at the time of their surrender; nevertheless they were glad to accept an agreement now upon any terms, and decided to select, by their own votes, a delegation of ten men to go to Rome and lay their case before the Senate. No further guarantee was required of them beyond an oath that they would return. Carthalo, a Carthaginian nobleman, was instructed to accompany them, and to propose terms should Rome be inclined towards a peace.

After the delegation had left camp, one of the members – no Roman he! – pretended to have forgotten something and went back to fetch it, his object, of course, being to free himself from the obligation of his oath. Before night he caught up his companions again. As soon as it was known that they were approaching the City, a lictor was dispatched to meet Carthalo and to tell him, as from the dictator, to leave Roman territory before nightfall. 59. The dictator then granted the delegation an audience in the Senate, and its leader spoke as follows:

'Marcus Junius and gentlemen of the Senate, we all know that no country in the world has held its own prisoners of war in greater contempt than ours. Nevertheless – if I may say so without incurring the charge of undue egotism – no prisoners have ever fallen into an enemy's hands who less deserve your neglect than we do. It was not fear which drove us to surrender: on the contrary, we continued the struggle almost to nightfall, standing over the heaped bodies of our dead comrades, and only then withdrew to our camp. For the rest of that day and throughout the following night, despite exhaustion and wounds, we defended the rampart; next morning enemy troops were all round us; we were cut off from access to the river; there was no longer a hope of breaking through the dense lines of the besiegers. In such circumstances we thought it no crime that a handful of Roman soldiers should survive Cannae, when fifty thousand had been killed. So then it was, and only then, that we agreed upon terms for our ransom and surrendered our now useless swords.

'History, moreover, had told us that Romans once bought their freedom from the Gauls with gold; and your own fathers, for all their unrelenting temper in negotiating a peace, yet sent a delegation to Tarentum to arrange for the prisoners' ransom. Yet – note this! – in both those battles, at the Allia with the Gauls, at Heraclea against Pyrrhus, what made defeat shameful was not our losses but the panic-stricken flight of our troops. How different was Cannae! The dead lie in heaps on the field; we ourselves survive only because the weary enemy had no longer steel or strength to cut us down. Some of us moreover did not even seek to save themselves during the actual battle: they were left to guard the camp and were taken when it was surrendered.

'I, for my part, do not envy any Roman or fellow-soldier his luck, or what his luck has brought him: I should never wish to exalt myself by denigrating another; yet let me say that not even the men who left their swords on the field and fled without stopping till they reached Venusia or Canusium, can justly claim to be better soldiers than we are or boast that our country can better look to them for protection than to us – unless, indeed, there is some special prize reserved for running races and speed of foot. None the less you will find those men good and brave soldiers; and you will find us even more zealous in our country's cause, in that your generosity will have secured our ransom and restored us to our homes.

'You are enlisting for service men of all ages and all conditions. Eight thousand slaves, I hear, are being armed. We prisoners are no fewer, and we could be ransomed for a sum less than the purchase-money of the slaves: but I should be insulting the Roman name if I compared ourselves with *them*.

'Gentlemen of the Senate, in deciding this question there is a further point for you to consider, should you incline to the harsher view, little though we deserve that you should do so: to what sort of an enemy do you propose to abandon us? Is it, for instance, to a Pyrrhus, who treated our prisoners like guests – or is it to a barbarian, a Carthaginian, in whom rapacity and savagery struggle for pre-eminence? Could you but see your countrymen lying in their chains and hideous squalor, the sight would surely move you no less than the spectacle of your legions lying dead on the field of Cannae. One thing at least is before your eyes – the anxiety, the tears, of our kinsmen out there in the vestibule, waiting for your answer. If they suffer that agony of suspense for us and for the other prisoners who are far away, how do you think *we* feel, whose life and liberty are in the balance? If Hannibal – God help us – were to deny his own nature and be kind to us, would our lives be worth living? No, not when, in your eyes, we were not worth a ransom. Time was when Pyrrhus let Roman prisoners return home before a penny was paid: they came with ambassadors, distinguished citizens entrusted with the task of fixing the ransom. And shall I come home as a citizen not valued at three hundred coins? A man has his feelings, gentlemen. I know my body – indeed my life – to be in peril; but I care more for the threat to my good name, should it be that we must leave here disowned and condemned. For assuredly no one will suppose you found the price too high to pay.'

60. The crowd in the place of assembly burst into tears on the conclusion of this speech; everyone held out his arms towards the Senate-house, begging for the restoration of children, or brothers, or kinsmen. By now women, too, had mingled with the crowd, in anxious fear for the fate of their kinsfolk. In the Senate, the house was cleared and the debate began. Various opinions were put forward: that the ransom money should be paid from the public funds; that no public outlay was justifiable, though individual prisoners ought not to be prevented from paying from their own pockets; again, if any were short of ready money, they should be granted a loan from the treasury on proper security. After these views had been expressed, Titus Manlius Torquatus was asked his opinion; he was a man of the stern old school – too stern, most people thought – and he is said to have spoken to the following effect:

'If the prisoners' representatives had confined themselves to a request for ransoming those of our troops who are in enemy hands, I could have given them a short answer. I would have had no need to waste words in invective. I should simply have advised you to follow the ancient custom of our country, a precedent indispensable for military discipline. But as it is, they have made their surrender almost a cause for self-congratulation; they have claimed to be better men than their comrades who were taken prisoner during the battle, better than those who reached Venusia and Canusium, and even than the consul Varro himself. Now, gentlemen, I will not suffer you to be ignorant of any detail of what happened on this occasion; and I can only wish that what I am about to say could be said in the presence of our troops in Canusium, who are the best witnesses of the courage or cowardice of their fellow-soldiers. I wish at least that Sempronius were here, if no one else – Sempronius, by following whose gallant leadership these so-called soldiers might today have been soldiers indeed, in a Roman camp, not prisoners in the hands of the enemy. But, when most of Hannibal's forces had withdrawn, unopposed, into their camp, and all of them were weary with fighting and joyfully celebrating their victory, these men of ours, though they could have used the darkness to aid their escape and were numerous enough – 7,000 strong – to force their way through an enemy line however dense, yet made no attempt on their own initiative to do so, nor had the will to follow another's lead. Sempronius spent almost the whole night trying to bolster up their courage, urging them to follow him, while enemy forces around the camp were still few, while all was hushed and silent and darkness might still conceal their design, and telling them that before dawn broke they would be safe in some friendly town. Remember Publius Decius, the military tribune in Samnium some two generations ago – remember Calpurnius Flamma, in our own youth during the last war with Carthage, and how he said to the three hundred volunteers he was about to lead to the capture of a hill in the enemy's lines: "Men, let us die, and save by our death the surrounded legions!" If Sempronius had spoken like that, and not one of you had offered to share with him in so great an act of courage, he would have thought you neither soldiers nor Romans. The way he showed you led not to glory only but to safety; he was giving you the chance to return home to your parents, to your wives and children. Haven't you the courage even to save your lives? What would you do, then, if you had to die for your country? On that day 50,000 of your fellow-citizens and allies lay dead around you; if so many examples of valour cannot move you, nothing ever will. What will make you hold life cheap if losses on such a terrible scale have not already done so?

'While you are safe and free – that is the time to long to see your country again: nay rather, while she *is* your country, and you her sons. Now it is too late: disgraced, disfranchised, made slaves of Carthage, you long in vain. Do you think to buy yourselves back to the place you lost by cowardice and crime? You turned a deaf ear to your fellow-countryman Sempronius when he bade you take arms and follow him; but you listened soon after, when Hannibal called for the betrayal of the camp and the surrender of your swords.

'But why should I accuse these fellows of cowardice, when I

might accuse them of villainy? For they not only refused to follow Sempronius, good though his counsel was: they tried to obstruct him and hold him back – and might have succeeded, had not some brave men drawn their swords and cleared the wretches out of the way. Sempronius, gentlemen, had first to fight his way through a line of *Roman* soldiers, before ever he got to the enemy. Is that the sort of citizen our country would miss? If all had been like them, Rome would not now possess a single citizen out of all who fought at Cannae. Of seven thousand soldiers six hundred were found with the courage to escape, and to return free men, sword in hand, to their country; and forty thousand enemies did not stop them. Don't you think the passage would have been safer for nearly two legions? Then you would have had today twenty thousand men in arms at Canusium, brave and loyal soldiers. But it was not to be: how can these men be called good and loyal soldiers (for not even they themselves claim courage) unless anyone can suppose that they were trying to help their comrades to break out when in fact they stopped the escape: or suppose that they do not envy their comrades their safety and the honour their courage won them, knowing as they do that timidity and cowardice led, in their own case, to ignominious servitude? They might have escaped while all was dark and silent, but they chose to skulk in their tents and wait for the enemy to come with the dawn. No doubt one would like to say that though they lacked the courage to make their escape, they did, at least, courageously defend the camp. Surrounded as they were, for several days and nights they defended the rampart with their swords and themselves with the rampart; then at last, having reached the end of their tether, with nothing to support life left, when weakened by hunger they had not strength any longer to bear the weight of their weapons, they admitted defeat – rather by the pressure of human need than the strength of enemy arms. But how different is the truth! At dawn the enemy moved up; less than an hour later, without any attempt at resistance, they laid down their arms and surrendered.

'Just let me remind you again of their two days' campaigning: they fled to the camp when it was their duty to stand firm and fight; when honour called for the defence of the rampart, they surrendered. What service did they do either in the field or afterwards in the camp? None whatever.

'So you want me to ransom you! When duty demands that you force your way out to freedom, you do not budge an inch; when military necessity calls for you to stay firm and defend your camp by force of arms, you surrender – everything, your camp, your swords, and yourselves!

'In my opinion, gentlemen of the Senate, these fellows no more deserve to be ransomed than their brave comrades, who fought their way through the enemy and by their heroic courage restored themselves to their country's service, deserve to be handed over to Hannibal.'

61. Blood relationship counts, and most, even of the senators, had kinsmen amongst the prisoners; nevertheless, when Manlius ended, such sentiments had to give way. Nor was it only the ancient Roman tradition of showing little tenderness towards prisoners which now influenced the Senate's decision; there was also the question of the money involved. A large sum had already been earmarked for the purchase, and equipment for service, of the slaves, and they neither wished to drain the treasury nor to enrich Hannibal who, it was said, was more in need of money than of anything else. So the harsh answer was given that the prisoners would not be ransomed. At the loss of so many fellow-citizens a fresh outburst of lamentation followed; crowds, weeping bitterly, accompanied the delegation to the city gate. One delegate went home, having, by his dishonest return to the camp, absolved himself from his oath. When his conduct became known and was reported to the Senate, it was unanimously resolved to arrest him and to take him to Hannibal under a public guard.

There is an alternative version of the story of the prisoners. According to this, ten representatives originally came to Rome. After a discussion in the Senate on the question of their admission into the City, they were allowed in but not granted an audience. Later, as they stayed in Rome longer than anyone expected, three more representatives came, Lucius Scribonius, Gaius Calpurnius, and Lucius Manlius. Only then was a motion on the ransom of the prisoners at last brought before the Senate, the mover being a relative of Scribonius and a people's tribune.

The Senate voted against the ransom, and the three representatives who had been the last to come returned to Hannibal. The ten original ones remained behind, giving as their excuse that after leaving Hannibal's headquarters they had already gone back once, in order to make a list of the prisoners' names, and were thus absolved from the guilt of perjury. The question of handing over these men to Hannibal was passionately debated in the Senate, and those who voted in favour of it were narrowly defeated. However, under the next censors, they were so overwhelmed by every conceivable brand of ignominy that some of them committed suicide and the remainder did not dare for the rest of their lives to enter the forum, or, indeed, to appear at all in the streets during daylight. It is easier to be surprised at the discrepancy between authorities than to decide which story is true.

How much more serious was the defeat at Cannae than those which had preceded it can be seen by the behaviour of Rome's allies: before that fatal day their loyalty had remained unshaken; now it began to waver, for the simple reason that they despaired of the survival of Roman power. The following peoples went over to the Carthaginian cause: the Atellani, Calatini, Hirpini, some of the Apulians, all the Samnites except the Pentri, the Bruttii, the Lucanians, the Uzentini, and nearly all the Greek settlements on the coast, namely Tarentum, Metapontum, Croton, and Locri, and all the Gauls on the Italian side of the Alps.

But neither the defeats they had suffered nor the subsequent defection of all these allied peoples moved the Romans ever to breathe a word about peace, either before Varro's arrival in Rome or when his presence in the city had brought home to them afresh the fearful calamity which had befallen them. So great, in this grim time, was the nation's heart, that the consul, fresh from a defeat of which he had himself been the principal cause, was met on his return to Rome by men of all conditions, who came in crowds to participate in the thanks, publicly bestowed upon him, for not having 'despaired of the commonwealth'. A Carthaginian general in such circumstances would have been punished with the utmost rigour of the law.

# BOOK XXIII

1. After the battle of Cannae and the capture and looting of the two Roman camps, Hannibal hastily left Apulia and moved into the territory of the Hirpini in Samnium, on the invitation of one Statius Trebius who promised to deliver Compsa into his hands.

Trebius was a native of Compsa and by birth a man of some local importance, but he was kept down by the party of the Mopsii, a family which owed its influence to the favour of Rome. The supporters of the Mopsii left the town when the news of Cannae was received and Trebius began to spread talk of the imminent arrival of Hannibal; so it was handed over without opposition and garrisoned by Carthaginian troops. All baggage and captured material were left there; the army was then divided, Mago being instructed to take over all the towns of that part of Italy as they seceded from Rome and to compel the secession of any which showed signs of resistance, while Hannibal himself proceeded through Campania to the southern coast with the intention of attacking Naples, which would give him a base on the sea.

Once within Neapolitan territory, he took advantage of the numerous sunken tracks and blind corners in the vicinity to conceal, at strategic points, some of his Numidian horsemen, and ordered others to round up cattle and ride to the city gates ostentatiously driving the captured animals before them. A squadron of Neapolitan horse galloped out to meet this latter party, as they looked a scratch lot and were few in number; whereupon the Numidians withdrew according to plan and led their adversaries into the prepared trap, where they were surrounded. Not one would have escaped but for the fact that the sea was so near, and that some boats, mostly fishing-craft, full in view just off-shore, offered a refuge to those who could swim. None the less a number of men of good birth were captured or killed; amongst the dead was Hegeas who was in command of the Neapolitan cavalry and had too recklessly pressed his pursuit of the retreating Numidians. Hannibal was deterred from an attempt on the city itself when he saw its walls, which presented a most formidable obstacle.

2. From Naples he marched to Capua. Capua was a city of great wealth and luxury, and had long prospered as the favourite of fortune; but there was general corruption there, due, more than to anything else, to the licence of the common people, who enjoyed unlimited freedom. A certain Pacuvius Calavius, a noble who supported the popular party and had gained power by chicanery, had made the senate a tool to serve his personal interests and those of the commons. It so happened that this man held the highest state office in the year of the defeat at Trasimene; he knew the commons had long hated the senate, and he thought it possible that the chance of a political revolution might spur them to risk a desperate stroke: this was, in effect, to murder the senators and deliver Capua to the Carthaginians if Hannibal and his victorious army should come anywhere near. Calavius was a scoundrel certainly, though not absolutely of the worst sort, as he preferred to exercise power in a state which had not politically disintegrated, and believed that no state could be politically intact if it was deprived of its deliberative council; so for this reason he devised a plan by which he could preserve the senate and at the same time make it the servant of the commons and himself.

Having summoned the senate, he began by saying that, unless it proved necessary, the policy of secession from Rome would by no means have his support. He had children by a daughter of Appius Claudius, and had married a daughter of his own to Marcus Livius in Rome. However, they were faced at the moment by an imminent peril much greater and more alarming: the commons (he declared) were not considering getting rid of the senate by changing their allegiance from Rome to Carthage; rather they were planning to cut the senators' throats and deliver the city, helpless and stripped of all control, into Hannibal's hands. He went on to say that he could free them from that danger if they would leave everything to him and trust him, forgetting their past political differences.

Sheer terror made the senators consent, whereupon, 'I will

shut you up,' Calavius said, 'in the senate-house, and pretend to be a party to the crime. By appearing to approve a plan which I should try in vain to oppose, I shall find the means of saving you. Accept the pledge you desire for the performance of my promise.'

The pledge given, Calavius left the chamber and ordered the senate-house to be locked, and posted a guard in the courtyard to prevent anyone approaching without his orders, or leaving the chamber. 3. He then called a meeting of the people, and addressed them in the following terms: 'Men of Campania, you have often wished for a chance of wreaking your revenge on the senate, that criminal and detested body of men. Well, you have got it, safely and freely in your hands – with no need for a popular rising and a perilous series of attacks on senators' houses, guarded as they are by their dependants and slaves. The senators are all locked up in the senate-house unarmed and alone: you may take the lot. But don't be in a hurry – do nothing reckless or rash; I propose to bring them before you one at a time for trial and offer you the opportunity to give your verdict so that each may be punished as he deserves.

'Now above all things you must remember that, however much you give rein to your resentment, your safety and advantage are of even greater importance to you. It is these senators, I imagine, whom you hate; but you do not wish to have no senate at all. There are, after all, but two alternatives: you must either have a king – God help you! – or the only possible deliberative body for a free community: namely, a senate. So there are two things for you to do: get rid of the present senate, and elect a new one. I shall have the senators called out one by one, and ask your advice as to their fate. In each case your recommendation will be carried out. But before a guilty senator is punished, you will yourselves select some active and vigorous candidate to take his place.'

Calavius sat down; the senators' names were put into the bowl to be drawn for, and when the first was drawn Calavius ordered the bearer of it to be brought from the senate-house. As soon as the crowd heard whose name it was, there was not one but shouted that he was a vile brute and ought to have his head cut off, to which Calavius replied: 'Your opinion about this gentleman is clear enough. He is a brute. Very good: now choose an honest and upright man to succeed him.' For a minute there was silence, and nobody seemed able to suggest a better candidate. Then, when a member of the crowd, taking the bull by the horns, mentioned the name of some ridiculous nobody, there was immediately a tremendous outcry – much louder than before, some shouting that they had never heard of him, others howling insults and accusing him of low birth, criminal conduct, beggary, or of earning his living by an indecent trade. The same thing happened – only worse – in the case of the second and third senators to be cited: it was plain, that is, that though everyone was sick to death of the man in question, nobody could propose a satisfactory substitute; nor did there seem much point in bringing forward a second time names which had already been mentioned only to be abused, while any others that might remain were even closer to the gutter than the ones first thought of. The meeting, in consequence, melted away, people telling each other that, after all, familiar evils are the most tolerable, and asking that the senators should be released from custody.

4. When by this ruse Calavius, having apparently saved the senators' lives, had made the senate subservient to himself personally even more than to the commons, he began to exercise power by universal consent and without resort to force. A change in the senate's attitude quickly followed: senators forgot their former dignities and liberties and began to court the favour of the commons; they would bid them good morning, invite them politely to call, entertain them to rich dinners; in the law-courts they undertook cases, or appeared as counsel, or gave their verdict as jurors, always in the popular interest and with an eye to conciliating popular favour. In the senate things were conducted precisely as if that body were a people's council. Life in Capua had always been soft and luxurious; this was the result partly of defects of character in the population, though the chief reason was the superabundance in the city of all that can delight the senses, of every charm of sea and land which can tempt men to indulgence; now, however, what with the unbridled licence of the commons and the obsequiousness of the ruling class, all control went to the winds: no extrava-

gance was spared, no sensual pleasure unindulged. Add to all this the fact that the Capuans, besides their contempt for the law and its representatives, now, after the defeat at Cannae, began to despise the power of Rome for which they had previously felt a certain respect. The one thing which delayed their immediate secession was the fact that the old-established right of intermarriage had linked many powerful and distinguished Capuan families with Rome; moreover, though a number of Capuans was serving with the Roman army, a yet stronger tie was the 300 horsemen, all of the noblest Campanian blood, who had been selected by the Romans and sent to join the garrisons of the towns in Sicily.[1]

5. The parents and other relatives of these men succeeded, with difficulty, in forcing a decision to send representatives to the Roman consul. He – Varro – had not yet started for Canusium, and they found him still at Venusia with a few half-armed troops – a spectacle which from a loyal ally would deserve the deepest sympathy, but from the false and arrogant Campanians earned nothing but contempt. Moreover, Varro did anything but mollify their contemptuous attitude towards his troubles and himself personally by his excessive frankness in speaking of the recent defeat. The envoys had begun by saying that the senate and people of Campania were distressed to hear of any reverse to Roman arms, and went on to promise all such military aid as might be required; to which Varro replied that in telling him to ask them for what he needed they did, indeed, preserve the conventional form of speech amongst allies, though what they said was hardly relevant to the present state of his fortunes. 'To want an ally,' he went on, 'to supply one's deficiencies surely involves the possession of *something*, to start with. But at Cannae we lost everything we had: do you expect us to ask you for a reinforcement of foot-soldiers – as if we were, of course, well enough off for cavalry? Or to say we are short of money – just *money*, as if that were all? Allies reinforce – but fortune has left us nothing which can *be* reinforced. Our legions, our cavalry, our arms, standards, horses, men, money, supplies – everything went, either in the battle or in the loss of the two camps next day. It is your duty, men of Campania,

1. i.e. as hostages to ensure the loyalty of Capua.

not merely to aid us in the war, but rather to fight it yourselves on our behalf.

'Remember the past – how once your ancestors were driven in confusion within their walls, facing the menace not only of the Samnites but of the men of Sidicinum too; and how we took them under our protection and defended them at Saticula. Remember how on your account we declared war upon Samnium, and continued to wage it with varying fortunes for nearly a hundred years. Remember too that when you submitted we granted you just terms, allowed you to keep your own laws, and finally – this, before the disaster at Cannae, was assuredly the greatest privilege – gave many of you a share in Roman citizenship. In consequence, men of Campania, you ought to feel that you have a share in the calamity which has befallen us; that it is your country as well as ours which calls for protection. It is not with Samnites or Etruscans we are dealing now, so that power, lost by us, might yet remain in Italy; our enemy is the Carthaginian, and he drags behind him a barbarous soldiery – not natives even of Africa, but savages from the world's end, from the Straits of Ocean and the Pillars of Hercules, who know nothing of civilization under law and can hardly even speak like human beings. These creatures, by nature and habit cruel and bestial enough, their leader has himself yet further brutalized by his building of bridges and embankments out of corpses and by teaching them – can I say it without a shudder? – to eat human flesh. To see them here – fed fat with their unspeakable meat, monsters it would be impious even to touch – to have them as our masters, to look for our laws to Africa and Carthage, to let Italy be a province of Numidians and Moors: is there anyone born, if nothing else, in Italy to whom this would not be an abomination?

'Men of Campania, the power of Rome is brought low; it will be a glorious thing if your loyalty, your strength, shall have kept it alive and restored it to what it was. 30,000 foot, 4,000 horse can, I believe, be enrolled in Campania; of money and grain you have enough. If your loyalty is as great as your prosperity, then, for all that has happened, Hannibal will not feel his victory nor the Romans their defeat.'

6. With these words of Varro the envoys were dismissed, and

on their way home one of their number, Vibius Virrius, remarked that the time had come for the Campanians not only to recover the territory wrongfully taken from them in former days by Rome, but to assume the dominant position throughout Italy. They could, he suggested, make a treaty with Hannibal on any terms they pleased, and there would be nothing to prevent the control of all Italy being left in their hands, when, after the war, the victorious Hannibal left the country for Africa and took his army with him. The other delegates agreed and they so reported the result of their mission that it seemed to all who heard them that the Roman name had ceased to exist.

In consequence of this report the commons in Capua and the majority of the senate at once began to consider the abandonment of the Roman alliance, though a decision was postponed for a few days by the authority of the older senators. Finally it was determined by a majority vote to send to Hannibal the same representatives as they had sent to Varro.

I have read in some accounts that before the envoys started or the question of revolt had been decided, a delegation was sent to Rome with a demand that, if the Romans wanted assistance, one of the two consuls should be a Campanian. The demand was met with indignation; the delegates were turned out of the Senate-house, and a lictor was sent to escort them out of the city and convey to them the order to remain that day outside Roman territory. I have hesitated to record this as a fact, because a suspiciously similar demand was once made by the Latins, and because Coelius and other writers, not without good reason, made no mention of it.

7. The envoys went to Hannibal and the following terms were agreed between them: first, that no Carthaginian military or civil officer should have jurisdiction over any Campanian citizen; secondly, that no Campanian should serve in the army or in any other capacity against his will; thirdly, that Capua should have her own laws and her own magistrates; fourthly, that Hannibal should hand over to the Campanians three hundred selected Roman prisoners, for whom they would exchange the Campanian cavalrymen serving in Sicily. So much for the terms; but the Campanians, not content with a

formal pact only, followed it by an abominable crime: the mob suddenly arrested the Roman officials known as Prefects of the Allies, and other Roman citizens – some engaged in war service, others busy about their personal affairs – and had them shut up in the baths, as if for safe custody. They were all choked by the heat and steam and died a horrible death.

One man, Decius Magius – he lacked nothing but the goodwill of a healthy community to have attained the highest office – had strained every nerve to prevent these criminal acts and to stop the legation from being sent to Hannibal. When he learned that Hannibal was sending a garrison to Capua, he proclaimed openly and in the strongest terms that it should not be admitted, telling his fellow-townsmen to take warning from the haughty tyranny of Pyrrhus and the miserable servitude of the Tarentines; then, when the garrison had been admitted, he pressed for its ejection, and finally urged that if they were willing to atone by a bold and memorable stroke for the crime of deserting their ancient allies and kinsmen, they should kill the intruders and restore their allegiance to the Romans.

No secret was made of all this, and Hannibal, when he was told of it, sent men to summon Magius to appear before him at his headquarters. Magius, nothing daunted, refused to go, asserting that Hannibal had no legal authority over a Campanian citizen, whereupon Hannibal, in a rage, ordered him to be seized and dragged before him in chains. Later, however, fearing that if force were used and passions roused some unpleasant incident might occur or a riot break out, he dispatched a messenger to the praetor Marius Blossius, saying he would be in Capua on the following day. He then left camp with a small escort of troops.

Marius called a meeting of the people and ordered them to go in a body with their wives and children to meet Hannibal. So enthusiastic was the crowd, and so eager to go and see a general famous for so many victories, that the order was obeyed by everyone with the greatest good will. Decius Magius neither joined the crowd nor shut himself up at home, as that might have indicated an uneasy conscience; he strolled in the forum at his ease with his son and a few dependants, while the rest of the town was going mad with excitement at the prospect of seeing and entertaining the great Carthaginian. Hannibal on his arrival immediately asked for an audience of the senate; but the leading senators begged him to consent to honour in the proper holiday spirit the day which his visit had made a festive one, and not to mar it by serious business. Hannibal, though constitutionally quick-tempered, did not wish to begin by a refusal, so he spent much of the day in seeing the sights of the town.

8. He lodged with Sthenius and Pacuvius, two brothers of the noble and wealthy family of the Ninnii Celeres. Pacuvius Calavius, whom I have already mentioned[1] as leader of the party which befriended Carthage, brought his son to the house, having got him away from Decius Magius. The young man had confidently supported Magius in his advocacy of the Roman alliance, and against a treaty with Carthage, and neither the fact that the government took the opposite view nor his father's eminent position had made him change his mind. Calavius had won Hannibal's indulgence for this son of his; not that he actually cleared him of guilt, but Hannibal was sufficiently worked upon by the father's earnest prayers and tearful entreaties to have the young fellow invited to dinner, together with his father. This was a marked favour, as no Campanians were to be asked to attend apart from the hosts and a certain distinguished soldier named Vibellius Taurea.

The banquet began early. There was nothing Carthaginian about it, nothing to suggest the severities of a military regimen. On the contrary, it was a very splendid affair, typical of a wealthy household in a luxurious city, and provided with every allurement to every pleasure. Calavius's son was the one guest who could not be induced to drink: his hosts, sometimes even Hannibal himself, invited him, but to no purpose; he continued to plead indisposition, while his father suggested as a further excuse his mental agitation which, in the circumstances, was hardly surprising.

Just before sunset Calavius left the banqueting-hall. His son followed him, and when they found themselves alone in a garden behind the house, 'Father,' he said, 'I have a plan by which we can not only obtain pardon from the Romans for our

1. p. 168.

treacherous desertion of their cause, but also win for our fellow Campanians much greater dignity and favour than we have ever before enjoyed.'

Calavius asked in surprise what the plan could be, whereupon the young man flung back his toga and revealed a sword hanging at his side.

'This very night,' he said, 'I shall ratify our pact with Rome in Hannibal's blood. You, father, I have warned of my purpose, as you may prefer not to be present when the deed is done.'

9. Seeing the sword and hearing these words, the old father was as mad with terror as if he had been actually present at the doing of the fatal deed. 'My son,' he cried, 'I implore you by all the sacred ties between parents and children not to commit this unspeakable crime before your father's eyes or suffer its dreadful consequences. A few hours ago, swearing by all the gods and putting our hands in his, we bound ourselves to loyalty: was it only that now – coming straight from our meeting with him – we should arm against his life the hands we pledged by a solemn and sacred oath? Did you rise from a hospitable board, one of three Campanians honoured by Hannibal's invitation, only to stain it with your host's blood? Did I win Hannibal's regard for my son, yet cannot win my son's loyalty to Hannibal?

'But, if you will, let us away with honour and truth, with the fear of God, with a son's duty to his father. Let the hideous crime be dared and done, provided only that it does not involve us in ruin. Do you propose, single-handed, to attack Hannibal? My son, remember all those freedmen and slaves – all the eyes that will be turned upon you, friendless and alone – all the drawn swords! No hand will be slow to avenge so frantic a deed; and Hannibal's face, the terror of armies, the face which the Roman people shudders to look on, will *you* have the strength to see it and not fail? There will be no help for you, none – yet will you endure, even so, to strike your father when he defends Hannibal's body with his own? For do not doubt that only through *my* heart will a sword be able to find and pierce his breast.

'Better to repent here and now than to be ruined *there*. Let my prayers prevail with you now, even as they prevailed *for* you this day!'

The young man was moved to tears by this appeal. Calavius embraced and kissed him, continuing his entreaties until he finally induced him to lay the sword aside and promise not to do the dreadful deed. With his eyes on his father, 'The duty,' he said, 'which I owe to my country, I will pay to you. For you I am sorry, for you will have to bear the charge of thrice betraying your country: once when you made her secede from Rome, a second time when you caused her to make peace with Hannibal, a third time today, when because of you the restitution of Capua to the Romans is hindered and delayed.

'Take back, my country, the sword I have brought into this citadel of our enemies – my father forces it from my grasp.' With these words he flung the sword over the garden wall into the street; then, to allay suspicion, he returned to the banquet.

10. Next day there was a crowded senate to give audience to Hannibal. The opening of his speech was nothing if not bland and benignant; he thanked the people of Campania for preferring his friendship to alliance with Rome, and, amongst other magnificent promises, declared that Capua would soon be the capital city of Italy, whence Rome, like every other Italian community, would seek her laws. He went on to say that there was one man who had no share in the friendship of Carthage or in the treaty with himself – one man who deserved neither to be nor to be called a Campanian: and his name was Decius Magius. 'I require,' he ended, 'that he should be delivered into my hands. His case must be discussed, and the senate's decree pronounced, in my presence.'

To this demand the senate unanimously assented, in spite of the fact that many members felt that Decius did not deserve so fearful a punishment, and also that their liberties were being significantly infringed at the very start.

Hannibal left the senate-house, took his seat on the magistrates' official chair, and ordered the arrest of Decius Magius, who was to plead his cause before him. Magius, his spirit by no means crushed, was still vigorously asserting that there was nothing in the terms of the treaty to justify this act of violence, when chains were thrown upon him and the order was given to take him, followed by a lictor, to Hannibal's headquarters. Large crowds gathered and he harangued them in loud and bitter words as he was marched off: 'So you've got the liberty you wanted,' he shouted. 'Here am I – in the forum, in daylight, before your eyes – I, second to none in this city of ours – dragged off in chains to my death. Could an enemy do worse if Capua had fallen? Go to meet Hannibal, put out more flags, make his coming a holiday, that you may enjoy the spectacle of this triumph over your fellow-citizen!' Till now, Magius was bare-headed; but when it seemed that his words were not without effect on the crowd, his guards covered his head and face and he was hurried more quickly out through the city gate. In this condition he was taken to headquarters, where he was immediately put on board ship and sent to Carthage. The object of this was to forestall any disturbance which might have occurred in Capua as a result of this high-handed act. Had there been a rising, the senate, too, might have had second thoughts about the surrender of a distinguished Capuan; and then, if a delegation had been sent to ask for his release, Hannibal would have found himself in a dilemma: either he would have had to antagonize his new allies by refusing their first request, or, if he granted it, he would have been forced to keep in Capua an instigator of rebellion against his authority.

The ship in which Magius sailed was driven by bad weather to Cyrenae, which at that time was subject to the Egyptian monarchy. Magius fled for refuge to Ptolemy's statue, whence he was taken by guards to Alexandria to the court of the reigning monarch, Ptolemy Philopator, who on being told that he had been bound by Hannibal in violation of the treaty, had him released and gave him the choice of either going to Rome or returning to Capua. Magius said that Capua would be unsafe for him, and his position in Rome, if he settled there while she was at war with the Campanians, would be that of a deserter rather than of a guest; consequently there was nowhere he would rather live than in the realm of a king who had given him his liberty and was willing to defend it.

11. Meanwhile Quintus Fabius Pictor[1] returned to Rome from his mission to Delphi. He read from a written paper the answer of the oracle, which contained the names of the gods to whom prayer was to be offered, and in what form, and ended

1. See p. 157.

thus: 'If, Romans, you do these things, your fortunes will be better and your burdens lighter; your country will go forward more as you wish her to go, and the Roman people will have victory. When you have well ordered your affairs and preserved your commonwealth, send to Pythian Apollo a gift from your gains, and do him honour with a portion of your booty and profits and spoils. Do not be puffed up by your victory.' Pictor translated this from the original Greek verses, and then went on to say that as soon as he left the shrine of the oracle he offered sacrifice of wine and incense to all the divinities mentioned, and was told by the temple priest to return on shipboard still wearing the wreath of laurel which he had worn when he came and when he sacrificed, and not to take it off until he was back in Rome. All the priest's instructions he had carried out with the most scrupulous care, and had deposited the wreath on the altar of Apollo in Rome. The Senate then decreed that the prescribed rites and ceremonies should be exactly performed at the first available opportunity.

During these events in Italy and Rome, Hamilcar's son Mago had arrived in Carthage with the news of the victory at Cannae. His brother Hannibal had not sent him direct from the battlefield, but had kept him for some days to take over the Bruttian communities and others which were throwing off their allegiance to Rome. At a session of the Carthaginian senate he reported, in his account of the successes in Italy, that his brother had fought major engagements with six commanders-in-chief – four consuls, a dictator, and his master of Horse – and six consular armies; that he had killed over 200,000 of the enemy and taken more than 50,000 prisoners; of the four consuls two had been killed, another had got away wounded, and the fourth had escaped with barely fifty men after the loss of his entire army. The master of Horse, whose power is equivalent to a consul's, had been utterly defeated; the only man to deserve, in Roman eyes, the name of general had been the dictator – because he had never risked a battle. The Bruttians and Apulians, some of the Samnites and Lucanians had joined the Carthaginian cause. Capua, the capital not only of Campania but, since the crippling defeat of Rome at Cannae, of all Italy, had surrendered to Hannibal. For all these splendid victories it was only right, Mago added, to be grateful to the gods and to express that gratitude. 12. Then, as evidence of the success of the campaign, he had the captured gold rings poured out in the courtyard of the senate-house.[1] The rings made such a heap that, according to some writers, they were found when measured to amount to three and a half measures – though it is generally and more credibly held that there was not more than a measure of them. Further to indicate the magnitude of the defeat, Mago went on to explain that gold rings of that sort were worn only by knights – and only by the most distinguished in that Order. The chief point in his speech was, however, this: that the nearer Hannibal came to his hope of bringing the war to a successful conclusion, the more necessary it was to give him every possible assistance and support. He was fighting in enemy country, far from home; money and grain were being consumed in large quantities; the numerous engagements, besides destroying the enemy forces, had also to some extent diminished the manpower of the victor. Accordingly, reinforcements must be sent; grain must be supplied, and money for the pay of the troops who had served Carthage so well.

Everyone was delighted with what Mago had to say, and Himilco, a supporter of the Barcine faction, seeing a chance of a shrewd thrust at Hanno, remarked: 'Well, Hanno, what about it now? Are you still sorry we undertook the war against Rome? Shall we order Hannibal home? Would you like to forbid our public thanksgiving for victory? Suppose we listen to a Roman senator here in the senate-house at Carthage!'

'Gentlemen,' Hanno replied, 'I should have liked to hold my tongue today for fear of saying something disagreeable which might mar the general rejoicing. But I cannot: a member of the senate asks if I still regret the war with Rome; if I refuse to answer, I must either seem too proud – like a man who ignores another's liberty, or too subservient – like a man who forgets

1. ... and that long war
Whose spoil was heaped so high with rings of gold,
As Livy tells, who errs not:
(Dante, *Inferno* XXVIII, 10, transl. D. Sayers).

his own. Let me therefore in reply to Himilco declare that I have not ceased to regret the war, and shall never cease to accuse that invincible general of yours until I see the war brought to a conclusion on tolerable terms. A new peace is the only thing which will end my longing for the old peace which is gone.

'Those things which Mago has just been boasting about already give pleasure to Himilco and to Hannibal's other yes-men; to me they may perhaps give pleasure too, as success in war, if we are willing to make good use of it, will procure us a better peace. Now is the moment when we are in a position to *grant* terms of peace rather than to accept them; and if we let it slip, I fear that our joys, too, may perish of their own excess.

'Even as things are, what, precisely, have we to rejoice over? Hannibal says he has killed whole enemy armies – and then asks for reinforcements. What else would he have asked for if he had been defeated? He says he captured two Roman camps, both (of course) full of valuable material and supplies – and then asks us to give him money and grain. Is that not what he would have wanted if he had lost his own camp and been stripped of everything?

'Now, not to keep all the astonishment to myself, I should like to ask some questions – I have every right to do so, since I have answered Himilco. Very well, then, here are two questions which I should wish either Himilco or Mago to answer: first, in spite of the fact that the Roman power was utterly destroyed at Cannae, and the knowledge that the whole of Italy is in revolt, has any single member of the Latin Confederacy come over to us? Secondly, has any man belonging to the five and thirty tribes of Rome deserted to Hannibal?'

When Mago had answered both questions in the negative, 'So therefore,' Hanno continued, 'all too many of the enemy are still left. I should now like to know what is the morale, and what the hopes, of those thousands of men still ranged against us.' 13. Mago said he had no idea; so Hanno went on: 'The answer is perfectly obvious: tell me – have the Romans sent Hannibal any envoys to treat for peace? Indeed, so far as your information goes, has the word "peace" ever been breathed in Rome at all?'

'No,' said Mago.

'Very well then,' replied Hanno; 'in the conduct of the war we have not advanced one inch: the situation is precisely the same as when Hannibal first crossed into Italy. Most of us here remember the former war with Rome and its fluctuating fortunes; both by land and sea never, it seemed, had we been in such a strong position as we were before Lutatius and Postumius assumed the consulship; yet, after their election, we suffered a crushing defeat off the Aegates islands. Now if – which God forbid – our luck should again change as it did then, can you hope in defeat for the same sort of peace terms as no one even offers you now, in the hour of our victory?

'For my part, if I were asked whether we should offer terms to the enemy now, or be forced to accept them from him later, I know what my answer would be; if you are bringing Mago's demands before the House, then I say that, in my view, to send those reinforcements and supplies to a victorious army is unnecessary and irrelevant – and far less do I think they should be sent to men who are cheating us with false and empty hopes.'

Few were affected by Hanno's speech, partly because his feud with the Barcine faction rendered his views less influential, and partly because it is only human nature to refuse, in a time of rejoicing, to listen to arguments which would turn the substance of it to a shadow. They all thought that, with a little further effort, the war would soon be won and, in consequence, passed an almost unanimous decree to send Hannibal a reinforcement of 4,000 Numidian horse, forty elephants, and a large sum of money in silver.[1] An officer was sent with Mago to Spain for the purpose of enlisting mercenaries to the number of 20,000 foot and 4,000 horse, to be added to the forces already in Spain itself and in Italy.

14. These measures, as often happens when things are going well, were carried out in a slow and dilatory manner – very different from that of the Romans who, even apart from their characteristically active temperament, were forced to move quickly by the serious position of their affairs. The consul promptly carried out all his necessary duties; the dictator, Marcus Junius Pera, having first satisfied the demands of

1. The Latin text is defective here.

religion and obtained from the commons the customary bill authorizing him (for by tradition the dictator commanded the infantry) to appear on horseback, set about the difficult task of recruitment. There were already the two City legions which had been enrolled at the beginning of the year by the consuls, the slave-levy and the cohorts raised in Picenum and Gaul; but to find more he was driven to the last resource of a country almost at the end of its tether – in that desperate situation where honour must give way to expedience – and issued a proclamation to the effect that, on condition of their serving under him in the army, he would remit the punishment of all criminals detained on capital charges and cancel the debts of all imprisoned debtors. There were 6,000 of these men, and he armed them with Gallic weapons, spoils of war which had been carried in the triumph of Gaius Flaminius.[1] With these forces, amounting in all to 25,000 men, the dictator then marched from Rome.

After taking over Capua Hannibal made a second attempt on the Neapolitans; but finding that he could neither tempt nor frighten them into surrender he moved on to the territory of Nola. As he had some hopes that the town would come over to him voluntarily, his first approach was not a hostile one, though he had every intention, if the townspeople should disappoint him, of sparing them none of the horrors of war. The senate, especially its leading members, remained loyal to the Roman alliance; the people, on the other hand, were, characteristically, all for Hannibal and a change of régime, picturing in their minds, as they did, the ruin of their crops and the terrible sufferings they would have to endure if the town were besieged. Nor was there any lack of voices to propose defection. Accordingly the senate, hesitating to take overt action lest they should not be strong enough to resist the excited mob, feigned concurrence with its wishes in order to gain time. They declared they were quite willing to go over to Hannibal, but had not yet reached full agreement on what the terms of a treaty with their new friends should be. This gave them a breathing space, which they instantly used to send representatives to the Roman praetor Claudius Marcellus, who was with the army at Casilinum, to inform him of the perilous

1. After his victory in the Po valley in 223 B.C.

situation. The countryside, they told him, was already in Carthaginian hands, and any day the town would be so too, if help did not come. The senate had prevented an immediate revolt of the people only by telling them that they were themselves willing to secede whenever the commons wished.

Marcellus commended the Nolan senators and told them to continue the deception in order to keep matters as they were until his own arrival at the town; meanwhile they were to say nothing either of their interview with him or of any hopes of assistance from Rome. He then left Casilinum and made for Calatia, proceeding thence by a roundabout route over the Volturnus, through the territory of Saticula and Trebia, above Suessula and across the mountains, to Nola.

15. On his approach, Hannibal withdrew from the vicinity of Nola and went down to the coast near Naples. He was eager to acquire a naval base, to enable his ships to cross safely from Africa; but when he learned that Naples was held by a Roman prefect, Marcus Junius Silanus, who had been called in by the Neapolitans themselves, he abandoned the project, as he had done at Nola, and moved on to Nuceria. He besieged the town for some time, during which he made various efforts, sometimes by force, sometimes by trying to win over either the commons or the ruling class, to bring it to surrender; but the efforts failed and it was hunger which finally reduced it. The inhabitants he allowed by the terms of the surrender to leave the place with one garment apiece, and then, to maintain his character of mildness towards all Italians except the Romans, he offered rewards and promotion to any of the townspeople who stayed behind and were willing to serve in his army. Not a man of them took the bait; they all dispersed, going where impulse took them, or where they knew they could find hospitality, to this or that town in Campania, especially to Nola and Naples. About thirty leading members of the senate went to Capua, and, being refused admission there as they had opened their gates to Hannibal, went on to Cumae. Nuceria was sacked and burnt, and everything of value in it was turned over to the troops.

As for Nola, Marcellus held it less by any confidence in his force than by the goodwill of the leading citizens. The commons were a source of anxiety, and in particular one Lucius Bantius, whom the guilty knowledge of an attempted rebellion combined with fear of the Roman praetor was driving either to betray his native town or, should luck be against him, to desert to Hannibal. Bantius was a young man of spirit and of the greatest distinction amongst the knights of the allied communities. At Cannae he had been found half dead amongst a heap of bodies and Hannibal had not only had him tended with all kindness, but had sent him home with a present. It was in gratitude for that kindly act that he wanted to surrender Nola to Carthaginian control. Marcellus saw that the young man was uneasy and anxious for a change of allegiance, and that left two courses open to him: he could execute him for treason, or win his friendship by kindness. Preferring therefore to gain a brave and active friend for himself rather than merely to deprive Hannibal of one, he sent for him and addressed him in courteous terms. 'It is easy,' he said, 'to understand that many of your countrymen hate you, as not a man in Nola has said a word to me about your many acts of courage on the battlefield. But your soldierly qualities cannot be hidden from anyone who has served in the Roman forces. Many a man who has served with you has often told me what you are like and recounted the perils you have again and again faced to preserve the life and dignity of the Roman people. I have heard above all how at Cannae you did not cease to fight until life was almost crushed out of you by the heaped weapons and corpses – horses and men together – under which you lay. So good luck to your courage, I say! Under my command, you will have all advancement and every reward you wish for; and the more you are with me, the more you will feel it is both for your dignity and your advantage.' Bantius was delighted. Marcellus gave him a splendid horse and instructed the quaestor to pay him 500 denarii. The lictors were ordered to allow him free access to the praetor as often as he wished. 16. By this considerate treatment Bantius's hostility was so successfully mollified that no one amongst Rome's allies thereafter defended her cause with more courage and loyalty.

Hannibal had left Nuceria and was soon at the gates of Nola again. The mob, as before, were turning their eyes towards abandoning the Roman alliance, when Marcellus, at the approach of the enemy, withdrew his troops within the walls of the town. The move was dictated not by fear for the safety of his camp but by his wish not to give an opportunity of betraying the town to any of the large number of people who were looking for the chance of doing so. Preparations were soon made for battle, the Romans now marshalling their force before the walls, the Carthaginians in front of their camp. This resulted in a number of minor and inconclusive skirmishes on the ground between the town and the Carthaginian position, the two commanders being unwilling to order a general engagement, though neither objected to small parties of their men putting out feelers and risking a clash.

While the two armies remained, as it were, on daily guard in this way, the leading men of the town reported to Marcellus that the commons were holding secret talks with the enemy at night; it had been arranged, they told him, to seize the baggage and personal belongings of the Roman soldiers when they marched out, to shut the gates upon them, and man the town walls: then, having gained full control and with the town in their hands, they would be rid of the Romans and able to admit Hannibal in their stead.

Marcellus thanked the senators for this intelligence, and at once determined to try his fortune in the field before any hostile move could begin inside the town. He stationed his men in three divisions, one at each of the three gates which faced the Carthaginian camp, and ordered the baggage-trains to follow when they moved forward; the sutlers, camp-followers, and soldiers on the sick-list had orders to carry stakes for entrenchments. At the centre gate were posted the Roman cavalry and the finest units of the Roman foot, at the other two the recruits, the light-armed divisions, and the allied horse. No citizen of Nola was allowed to approach the walls or the gates; supporting units were told off to guard the baggage, to prevent an attack upon it while the legions were engaged. In this order, the army stood ready, inside the town-gates.

As for several days past, Hannibal was still keeping his men in their battle positions well on into the evening, and he could not at first understand why it was that the Roman forces did not leave the town or why no soldiers were posted on the walls; but coming to the conclusion that the secret talks had become known to Marcellus and that fear of their consequences had discouraged the Romans from action, he sent a portion of his force back into camp with orders to bring up immediately into the front line all the gear needed for an assault on the town; for he was confident that, if he pressed his advantage while the enemy hesitated, the mob would almost certainly rise in his support. His men were busy executing their orders and hurriedly bringing the gear up to the front line, and the actual advance towards the walls had begun, when suddenly the middle gate was flung open and Marcellus had the trumpet sounded for attack. The war-cry was raised, and the infantry, followed by the mounted troops, came pouring from the town with all the weight they could muster behind their thrust. Hannibal's centre reeled under the shock, and at that moment Flaccus and Aurelius, from the other two gates, delivered a vigorous attack on the Carthaginian wings. The clamour was increased by a simultaneous roar from the odds and ends of non-combatants detailed to guard the baggage, thus giving the appearance of a very large force – an unpleasant surprise for the enemy, who had supposed it to be small and had little respect for it in consequence. I hesitate to adopt the statement of some historians, that 2,800 of the enemy were killed, with a loss on the Roman side of not more than 500; none the less, whether that is an exaggerated estimate or not, that day's achievement was a splendid one, perhaps the greatest in that phase of the war, when it was still a harder task to avoid defeat by Hannibal than it was to defeat him later on.

17. Having lost his hopes of getting possession of Nola, Hannibal withdrew to Acerrae. Marcellus immediately shut the gates of Nola, set guards to prevent egress, and held a public inquiry into the conduct of the traitors who had held the secret talks with the enemy. More than seventy men were condemned and executed, and their property confiscated; full control of the town's affairs was entrusted to the senate, and Marcellus then left the town with his whole force and took up a position above Suessula. Hannibal tried to induce Acerrae to surrender voluntarily, but finding the inhabitants firm in

their refusal made his preparations for a siege and an assault. However, the men of the town had not the strength to match their courage, and soon despaired of defending themselves; watching the gradual circumvallation of their walls, they seized the chance while it lasted, and, before the works were complete, slipped away through the unguarded gaps during the silence of the night and by devious paths or over trackless country, where their feet led them or they thought to find a way, made their escape to such Campanian towns as they knew had remained loyal to Rome.

Hannibal sacked and burned Acerrae and then moved to Casilinum; for news had reached him from there that the Roman dictator and the freshly raised legions were being summoned, and he was afraid, with enemy troops so near, of a rising in Capua. Casilinum at that time was in the hands of 500 men from Praeneste together with a few Romans and Latins who had been brought there by the news of the defeat at Cannae. The levy at Praeneste had not been punctually completed, and these men had started too late; they reached Casilinum before they had heard about the battle, joined up there with other troops, Roman and allied, and marched from the town; they were a considerable body of men, and the news of Cannae, reaching them on the march, turned them back to Casilinum again. For some days they remained there in an uncomfortable atmosphere of mutual suspicion, plotted against by the Campanians and plotting in their turn, until they had pretty definite information of the impending revolt of Capua and the admission of Hannibal; then, one night, they murdered the townspeople and seized the part of the town on the north bank of the Volturnus (the river divides it in two). That, then, was the garrison which the Romans had at Casilinum; it was increased by a cohort from Perusia, 460 strong, which had been brought there by the same news as the men from Praeneste a few days previously. The force was quite adequate to protect so small a place, especially as the river formed one portion of the defence; but they were short of food – so short indeed as to make them feel that their numbers were too great.

18. As soon as Hannibal was in the neighbourhood of

Casilinum he sent an advance-party of Gaetulians under an officer named Isalcas, with orders to seek a parley and by a friendly approach to try to persuade the defenders to open their gates and admit a Carthaginian garrison; but if they persisted in an obstinate refusal, Isalcas was to take action and attempt an entry by force. On reaching the walls they found everything as silent as a deserted town, and Isalcas, supposing that the garrison had taken fright and gone away, was about to smash the bars and force the gates open, when they were suddenly flung wide and two cohorts, which had been drawn up inside for the purpose, charged out with a tremendous roar and cut the enemy to pieces. The first attempt having failed, Maharbal was ordered forward with a more powerful force, but had no better success; finally Hannibal himself moved right up to the walls and prepared an assault on the town, small though it was and weakly defended, with all the forces at his disposal.

While he was pressing the attack, the defences having already been completely surrounded, he lost a few of his most active men by missiles thrown from turrets on the wall. On one occasion a sortie was attempted; Hannibal sent elephants[1] and almost cut off the men's retreat, driving them hurriedly back into the town with considerable losses for so small a force. More would have been killed, had not darkness intervened. Next day Hannibal was determined to fire all ranks with enthusiasm for the assault: the 'mural crown' – the golden crown for the first man over the wall – was offered for competition; Hannibal in person reproached the men who had stormed Saguntum with their feeble efforts against a mere fortress which was not even on a hill, reminding them individually and collectively of Cannae, Trasimene, and the Trebia. Activity began: mantlets were brought up, saps dug. Rome's allies, for their part, were equal to the occasion, countering by force or ingenuity every attempt to circumvent them: against the mantlets they set up defence-blocks, dug cross-saps to intercept the enemy's mines, countered his every strategy above ground or below, until shame, not to mention frustration, drove Hannibal to abandon his attempt. He completed the fortification of his camp, left a fair-sized garrison to

1. Evidently those mentioned on p. 182 had reached Hannibal.

hold it in order to give the impression that the operation was only postponed, and withdrew into winter quarters at Capua.

He kept his army, properly housed, in Capua during most of the winter – with unexpected results. His men in many vicissitudes over a long period had been hardened to all the ills that flesh is heir to; to comfort they were complete strangers. And so it was that though they had risen superior to the most overwhelming hardship, they were an easy prey to luxury and pleasure, both of which lay superabundantly to hand. The more eagerly sheer inexperience led them to plunge into sensuality, the more utterly were they ruined. Sleep and wine, rich dinners and prostitutes, baths and the habit of idleness which each day made more seductive, so weakened the fibres of both body and mind that from that time forward it was their past victories that protected them rather than their present strength. Military critics have held that Hannibal here made a greater tactical error than when he failed after Cannae to march directly upon Rome;[1] his hesitating then might seem to have merely postponed his victory: his mistake at Capua robbed his army of the strength needed to conquer at all. Indeed, when he left Capua, it was with a different army – all trace of the old morale was gone. Many of the men were tied up with prostitutes and went back, and as soon as the army began to live under canvas again and had to resume its marching and other military labours, they all lost heart, or gave out physically, like raw recruits. Moreover, throughout the summer's campaigning any number of men kept going off without leave – and the den where such deserters hid was invariably Capua.

19. With the warmer weather towards the end of winter Hannibal returned from Capua to Casilinum. The direct assault upon that town had not been repeated, but the continuous blockade had reduced the people and defenders of the town to extreme want. The Roman force outside was commanded by Tiberius Sempronius Gracchus, the dictator having gone to Rome to take the auspices afresh. Marcellus at Nola was anxious to assist the besieged garrison, but was held back by

1. See pp. 223–4: 'Capua was Hannibal's Cannae'. Livy is too anxious to bring home this moral lesson. Polybius says Hannibal kept his men in open camps throughout the winter.

the fact that the Volturnus had flooded and also by the entreaties of the people of Nola and of the men from Acerrae who had taken refuge there, all of whom had reason to fear the Campanians if the Roman garrison left the town. Gracchus was no more than on the watch outside Casilinum, as the dictator had left orders that he should take no action during his absence in Rome; so, though the reports which reached him from the town were of a nature to try his patience to the utmost, he could make no move. Men there, it was said, desperate from hunger, had flung themselves from the battlements; others would stand unarmed on the walls offering their bared bodies as a mark for the enemy's missiles. For Gracchus it was an intolerable situation; but as he could not risk a clash against the dictator's orders – and it was clear he would have to fight if he openly conveyed food into the town – and as there seemed little hope of getting it in unobserved, he hit on the plan of collecting grain from the surrounding fields, packing it into jars, and sending word to the officials in the town to look out for them as they floated down on the river. Next night all eyes were on the river, all thoughts on the new hope that Gracchus's message had inspired. The jars, which had been set upon their course in mid-stream, came duly floating down, and the grain was served out, fair shares for all. On the two following days the process was repeated – the jars starting and ending their journey after dark, thus escaping the notice of the enemy's guards. The night after that, however, continuous rain having increased the force of the current, the jars were caught in an eddy and carried to the enemy's side of the river. There they stuck amongst the shallows along the bank, and were of course seen. Hannibal was informed, and a closer watch was kept to ensure that nothing else, by means of the river, got through to the town. Nevertheless, Gracchus's men did succeed in getting some nuts through; they were tipped into the river, carried by the current into the town, and there caught by hurdles placed across the stream.

Ultimately the shortage of food became so serious that they were reduced to chewing leather thongs and the hides from their shields, softened in hot water; they ate mice and other creatures, and dug up every sort of root and green-stuff they could find in the bank under the walls. When the Carthaginians ploughed up all the ground outside the wall with a blade of grass in it, they sowed turnip seed – as a gesture, making Hannibal exclaim: 'What? Am I to sit here till *that* comes up?' And finally, this man who never before had listened to terms, permitted negotiations to be held for the ransom of the free men in the besieged town. A price was agreed of seven-twelfths of a pound of gold a head.[1] The bargain made, the men surrendered and were kept in chains till the full sum was paid, when they were sent back to Cumae in fulfilment of the agreed terms. This account is more likely to be the true one – another says they were attacked and killed by mounted troops as they were leaving Casilinum. Most of them were Praenestines. Of the 570 who had formed the garrison less than half perished by the sword or starvation; the remainder returned safely to Praeneste with their praetor, Marcus Anicius. Anicius had formerly been a clerk, and as evidence of his part in this affair there was a statue of him in the forum at Praeneste; it represented him in a corselet and toga, with his head covered, and bore an inscription on a bronze plate: *Marcus Anicius has redeemed his vow on behalf of the garrison at Casilinum.* The same inscription was placed under three statues in the temple of Fortune.

20. Casilinum was given back to the Campanians and defended by a garrison of 700 men from Hannibal's army, to guard against an attack by the Romans when the Carthaginians withdrew. The Senate in Rome passed a decree doubling the pay of the soldiers from Praeneste and exempting them from military service for five years. They were offered Roman citizenship as a reward for their courage, but preferred to remain as they were. What happened to the men from Perusia is more obscure; no decree of the Senate and no record of their own throws any light on the matter.

Petelia at this time, the only Bruttian town which had remained faithful to the Roman alliance, was under attack not only by the Carthaginians in control of the country around but also by the other Bruttian communities which resented

1. A very high price: 200 silver denarii was the demand for an ally after Cannae, about a quarter of this figure. See p. 152.

the fact that Petelia had not followed their lead. When the pressure became too great, the Petelini sent to Rome for military assistance. Their representatives, being told that they would have to shoulder their own burden, burst into tears in the vestibule of the Senate-house, and that, together with their pitiful entreaties, excited great compassion amongst both senators and people. Their case was brought a second time before the House by the praetor Manlius Pomponius; but the senators, after examining all the resources of the empire, were forced to confess that they no longer had the means of assisting distant allies. They advised them accordingly to go home, and, having preserved their loyalty to the last, to consider only their own interests in future, as circumstances should dictate.

When the result of this mission was known, the senate in Petelia was seized with such panic and misery that some of its members proposed abandoning the town and letting every man fend for himself and take what road he could, while others urged that, as they were deserted by their old allies, they should join the other Bruttian communities and, through them, go over to Hannibal. The party, however, which opposed hasty action in the heat of the moment and asked for further deliberation, carried its point, so that when on the following day, in a less hectic atmosphere, the question was again raised, the nobles obtained a decision to bring in all moveable property from the countryside and strengthen the town's defences.

21. About this time dispatches reached Rome from Sicily and Sardinia. The first to be read in the Senate were those from Otacilius the pro-praetor in Sicily. He reported that the praetor Publius Furius had arrived in Lilybaeum from Africa with the fleet; he had been badly wounded and was in grave danger of his life. Neither the soldiers nor the ships' crews were being punctually paid; nor were supplies arriving on time. Indeed, there was no source from which money or grain could be obtained. It was of the first importance that both should be sent as soon as possible. He further asked that if the Senate saw fit, one of the new praetors should be sent out to succeed him. Cornelius Mammula, the pro-praetor in Sardinia, had much the same to report about the men's pay and supplies. In both cases the reply was that there was nothing available

to send, and they were instructed to do the best they could on their own initiative for the forces, naval and military, under their command. Otacilius sent a mission to Hiero, Rome's solitary stand-by in the hour of need,[1] and received from him the money he needed and six months' supply of grain. In Sardinia the allied communities sent a generous contribution to Mammula.

In Rome, too, money was short. On a motion by Marcus Minucius, a people's tribune, three finance commissioners were appointed – Lucius Aemilius Papus who had served as consul and as censor, Marcus Atilius Regulus, who had been consul twice, and Lucius Scribonius Libo, at that time a people's tribune. Two other officials, Marcus and Gaius Atilius, were appointed and dedicated the temple of Concord, which the praetor Lucius Manlius had previously vowed. Lastly, Quintus Caecilius Metellus, Quintus Fabius Maximus and Quintus Fulvius Flaccus were appointed pontiffs in succession to Publius Scantinius, deceased, and the consul Paullus and Quintus Aelius Paetus, both of whom had been killed at Cannae.

22. When the Senate, so far as human wisdom was equal to the task, had made good the losses inflicted by a long series of disasters, they turned their attention to themselves – to the now almost empty Senate-house, where so few were left to attend the Council of State. In spite of the fact that in the past five years death by natural causes and on the field of battle had carried off so many senators, the list had not been revised since the censorship of Lucius Aemilius and Gaius Flaminius. In view of this a motion in accordance with a general request was brought forward by the praetor Pomponius, the dictator having left Rome after the loss of Casilinum to join his troops; and in reply to the motion Spurius Carvilius made a long speech in which he lamented not only the small numbers to which the Senate was reduced but also the lack of suitable candidates for election, and went on to say that, in order to recruit the Senate and at the same time to strengthen the bond between Rome and the Latin confederacy, he earnestly advised

1. See p. 135. He ruled Syracuse from 270 to 215 B.C. and was a loyal ally of Rome from 263 onwards.

the granting of Roman citizenship to two selected senators from each of the Latin communities; then, from their number, the Roman Senate should elect new members to fill the vacancies left by death.

This proposal was no better received than the similar demand once made by the Latins themselves. There was a roar of indignation from the whole House, not least from Manlius, who cried that there still lived a man sprung from the same stock as that consul of old, who threatened on the Capitol to kill with his own hand any Latin he saw in the Senate-house; and Quintus Fabius Maximus followed by declaring that never had a question on any subject been mooted in the Senate at a more inappropriate moment than this proposal to discuss, at a time when the attitude of the allies was so uncertain and their loyalty so much in doubt, a subject which could not but aggravate their unsettled state of mind. 'Our unanimous silence,' he said, 'must muffle the sound of that one, rash, dissentient voice. If ever in this House there has been a solemn secret to be veiled in silence, this, of all others, is that secret. Cover it up, gentlemen, hide it, forget it – pretend that the words were never spoken.' No further mention was made of Carvilius's proposal.

It was then decided to appoint as dictator to draw up the list of senators a man who had previously been censor and was the senior of all living ex-censors, and an order was issued to summon the consul Varro to Rome for the purpose of naming him. Varro left a garrison in Apulia and hastened to Rome, where on the night after his arrival, as custom demanded, he named Marcus Fabius Buteo as dictator 'according to the decree of the Senate, without a master of Horse, for a period of six months.'

23. When Buteo mounted the rostra with his lictors he said that two dictators holding office simultaneously was an unprecedented thing, and he did not approve of it; secondly, he objected to being appointed dictator without a master of Horse; thirdly, to the power of the censorship being entrusted to one man, who had, moreover, held the office before; and fourthly, to the granting of the full power of the dictatorship for six months for any purpose other than that of directing

operations in the field. He declared his intention of setting a limit to any irregularities due to the pressures of the immediate situation: for instance, he would not remove from the Senate any member who had been enrolled by the censors Gaius Flaminius and Lucius Aemilius: he would merely have a new list made of the existing senators, and publicly read, a proceeding which would remove the onus of passing a judgement on the reputation and character of a senator from the shoulders of a single individual. Finally, in filling the gaps left by death in the ranks of the senators he would give preference not to individuals but to rank and position.

Then, when the list of the old Senate had been read, Buteo first chose in succession to the deceased members men who, after the censorship of Aemilius and Flaminius, had held curule office but had not previously been senators. These were chosen in the order of seniority. Next came men who had been people's aediles or people's tribunes or quaestors; lastly, men who had held no public office but either had spoils taken from the enemy hung up on their houses or had won the 'civic crown'. On this principle he elected to the Senate with universal and enthusiastic approval 170 new members, and, his object gained, at once resigned office, dismissed his lictors, and walked down from the rostra a private citizen again. There he mixed with the crowd busy with its own affairs, deliberately killing time so as not to draw people away from the forum for the purpose of escorting him home. None the less many did so, as the waiting about had by no means taken the edge off public interest in him. On the following night the consul rejoined his troops; he left Rome without informing the Senate, to avoid being detained to preside at the elections.

24. Next day, on a motion by the praetor Pomponius, the Senate decreed that the dictator[1] should be invited by letter to come, if he thought it in the public interest, to Rome together with the master of Horse and the praetor Marcellus for the purpose of holding the elections. This would give the Senate an opportunity of learning from them at first hand how things were going and of laying their plans accordingly. All three men answered the summons, leaving senior officers in

1. M. Junius Pera. See p. 157.

command of the troops. The dictator addressed the Senate in modest terms, saying little of himself and attributing much of the credit to his master of Horse, Tiberius Sempronius Gracchus; he then proclaimed the elections. Lucius Postumius – in absence, for he was commanding at the time in Gaul – was elected consul (for the third time) together with Tiberius Sempronius Gracchus, the master of Horse and curule aedile. Marcus Valerius Laevinus, Appius Claudius Pulcher, Quintus Fulvius Flaccus and Quintus Mucius Scaevola were appointed praetors. The dictator, the elections over, rejoined his troops in winter quarters at Teanum; the master of Horse, who in a few days would be entering upon his new office, he left in Rome to consult with the Senate on the raising of fresh troops for the coming year.

That year, it seemed, fortune was piling one disaster upon another; for while these proceedings were still going on, more bad news arrived. The consul-elect, Lucius Postumius, had been killed in Gaul and his army wiped out. He was about to march by way of a desolate stretch of forest, known to the Gauls as Litana. On both sides of the track the Gauls had cut the trees in such a way that they still remained standing but were ready to fall at the slightest impulse. Postumius had two Roman legions, and had also enlisted such a number of allied troops from the Adriatic coast that he was entering enemy territory with a total force of 25,000 men. The Gauls were lying in wait for him on the edge of the forest, and as soon as he entered the stretch of road prepared for the trap, they pushed over the trees at the end of the line. Down they came – all were nearly cut through at the base and only precariously keeping upright – each tree bringing to earth its tottering neighbour, and all overwhelming, from both sides of the track at once, arms, horses, and men beneath. Scarcely ten escaped alive. The greater number were killed by the falling trunks and broken branches, and the rest, bewildered by the unexpectedness of the horror, were dispatched by the Gauls who were waiting, sword in hand, all round the fatal spot. A few only out of so large a force were taken prisoner: they had made for a bridge over the river, but found it already occupied, and were cut off. Postumius, who was with them, fought to the end to avoid capture and was killed. The Boii stripped his body, cut off the head, and carried their spoils in triumph to the most hallowed of their temples. There they cleaned out the head, as their custom is, and gilded the skull, which thereafter served them as a holy vessel to pour libations from and as a drinking-cup for the priest and the temple attendants. The spoils from this battle were hardly less valuable to the Gauls than the fact of their victory: most of the horses and pack-animals had perished under the falling timber, but as there had been no attempt to escape and consequently no dispersal of military gear and equipment, everything else was found lying in place along the whole length of the column of dead men.

25. For many days after the news of this catastrophe the alarm in Rome was so great that all shops were closed and the streets were as silent and deserted as if it were midnight. The Senate instructed the aediles to go round the city and order the shops to be opened again to remove the appearance of public mourning, and, when this had been done, Gracchus called a meeting of the Senate and said what he could by way of consolation, urging the senators not to let lesser calamities unduly depress them, when they had refused to succumb to the appalling disaster of Cannae. As for Hannibal and the Carthaginians, he went on to say that if things went well, as he hoped they would, then the war in Gaul could be safely played down till some later time, while revenge for that treacherous attack would be in the hands of God and the Roman people. The one thing which demanded serious consideration was the threat from Hannibal, and the armies by means of which the war with Hannibal must be waged. At this point in his speech Gracchus gave details of the strength of the dictator's force, stating the numbers of horse and foot, of Roman and of allied troops. Marcellus followed with a statement of the forces under his own command, and information was sought from the appropriate persons about the strength of the consul Varro's force in Apulia. No satisfactory means could be found of bringing the consular armies up to a strength sufficient for the tasks before them, so it was decided to abandon the Gallic campaign during that year, despite the goad of righteous indignation. The dictator's army was assigned by decree to the

consul, and a decision was arrived at to send to Sicily all men in Marcellus's force who were survivors of the rout at Cannae, and to let them serve there as long as the war lasted in Italy; also to remove to that island any sick or inferior troops from the dictator's legions without fixing their term of service except for men who should already have served the statutory number of campaigns. The two City legions were assigned to the consul who was to succeed Postumius, and who was to be elected to office as soon as the auspices were favourable. Two legions were to be summoned as soon as possible from Sicily, where the consul to whose command the City legions fell was to raise what troops were needed. Varro's command was to be continued for another year, and the force with which he was garrisoning Apulia was not in any way to be weakened.

26. Meanwhile the fighting in Spain was no less active than in Italy, and up to that time, at any rate, more in favour of the Romans. Publius and Gnaeus Scipio had divided the command between them, the former conducting operations at sea, the latter on land. The Carthaginian commander Hasdrubal was not confident of the adequacy of either his naval or his military forces, so he continued to avoid the risk of finding himself anywhere near the Roman armies until, in answer to his frequent and urgent requests, reinforcements of 4,000 foot and 500 horse were sent him from Africa. Their arrival after a long delay encouraged him to take up a position nearer to the enemy, and to order his fleet to be put in proper condition to defend the coast and off-shore islands. However, in the first flush of getting things on the move again, he received a setback in the desertion of his naval captains. These men had been severely reprimanded after the incident on the Ebro, when the fleet had been abandoned in panic, and they had never since been really loyal either to their commander or to the Carthaginian cause. They had caused trouble amongst the Tartesii, and a number of towns had followed their lead and thrown off their allegiance; one town they had actually stormed and captured. As a result, it was against the Tartesii that Hasdrubal had now to direct his operations: he invaded their territory and determined to attack a certain Chalbus, a Tartesian chieftain, who was in position with a powerful force in front of the walls of

a town which had been taken a few days previously. Hoping to draw the enemy to engage, Hasdrubal sent his light troops against them and at the same time ordered out some of his infantry to do what damage they could to their crops over a wide area and to cut off stragglers. The immediate result was confusion in Chalbus's camp and panic and slaughter over the countryside; soon, however, the scattered warriors found their way by various routes back into camp, with the result that alarm and confusion vanished as suddenly as they had come: now, the Tartesian warriors found heart not only to defend their fortifications but even to take the offensive in their turn. Out they poured, dancing their native war-dance, and the unexpected change from timidity to reckless daring was a severe shock to the Carthaginians, who so short a time before had been eager to provoke a battle.

Hasdrubal withdrew to a hill, quite steep and further protected by an intervening stream, and then ordered his light troops, previously sent in advance, and his scattered cavalrymen to join him. Doubtful as to whether either the hill or the stream would prove an adequate defence, he then strongly fortified his position. In this state of affairs, when now one side, now the other felt conscious of inferiority, a few skirmishes took place, in which it appeared that the Numidian horsemen were not a match for the Spanish, nor the Moorish javelin-men for the Spaniards with their little round shields – troops who were their equals in speed and their superiors in strength and daring. 27. Continued threats to Hasdrubal's position failed to draw him out to an encounter, and the position itself was not an easy one to rush; consequently the Spaniards changed their tactics, seized the town of Ascua, where Hasdrubal on entering the territory had stored his grain and other supplies, and made themselves masters of the surrounding country.

After this action the Spanish fighting men lost all sense of discipline, whether on the march or in camp. Nothing could control their reckless behaviour, which sprang, as it often does, from success, and Hasdrubal, as soon as he was aware of this, urged his own troops to attack the scattered and disorderly groups wherever they found them, and, leaving his position on the hill, marched in regular formation upon their camp.

Guards and look-outs hurriedly abandoned their posts to announce his approach, and the call to arms rang out. Men snatched their weapons and without waiting for the signal or any word of command rushed in a disorderly rabble to the fray. The first out were already engaged while other groups of men were still hurrying from the camp, and some had not yet even started; none the less, the very recklessness of the attack was, in the first few moments, something of a shock to the enemy. Soon however discipline began to tell: small parties of the Spaniards found themselves up against massed enemy ranks, and, too weak to defend themselves, began to look back for support from other groups, until under pressure from every side they were driven inward upon each other; at last they were completely surrounded and packed so close, body to body, weapon to weapon, that they scarcely had room enough to raise their swords for a blow. Till late in the day the slaughter went on, only a few of them managing to break through and escape to the woods and hills. In their camp the panic was no less: it was abandoned and on the following day the whole tribe surrendered.

The terms of surrender were not observed very long; for Hasdrubal soon received orders from Carthage to march for Italy at the earliest possible moment. The news once known diverted the allegiance of nearly all the Spanish tribes to the Roman interest. Hasdrubal wrote immediately to Carthage, pointing out the seriousness of the loss which had been caused by the news of his imminent departure, and adding that if he did have to leave Spain the whole country would be in Roman hands before he was across the Ebro. He went on to say that he had no troops and no adequate commander to leave in his place, not to mention the fact that the Roman commanders in Spain were men whom it would be hard to resist even on equal terms. Consequently, if the Carthaginian government were interested in Spain at all, they must send someone with a powerful army to take over from him – and whoever it was (he ended), even if everything went well, would certainly not find the assignment a leisurely one.

28. The immediate effect of Hasdrubal's letter upon the Carthaginian senate was considerable; nevertheless, as their

chief concern was really with Italy, no change was made with regard to Hasdrubal or his forces. Himilco was sent with a fully equipped force and an enlarged fleet to hold and protect Spain by land and sea, and his first act after getting his army and fleet across was to fortify a strong position, haul his ships ashore, and build a rampart to protect them from attack; he then with a select cavalry escort hurried with all possible speed to Hasdrubal, passing on the way with equal alertness through tribes which were either suspect or frankly hostile. Having informed Hasdrubal of the senate's decree and the orders he had received, and having been instructed, in his turn, how best to carry on operations in Spain, he returned to his camp. It was a dangerous journey, but speed saved him, as he never stayed long enough in one place to allow the natives time to agree upon action.

Before marching for Italy, Hasdrubal took the precaution of forcing a contribution of money from all the tribes under his control; for he was well aware that Hannibal had on more than one occasion bought the right of passage, and also that no Gallic auxiliary forces had served him except for pay. Had he started on that long march unprovided with money he knew he would hardly have got as far as the Alps, and it was for that reason that he made his hurried requisition of cash before proceeding to the Ebro.

As soon as the two Roman commanders knew of the Carthaginian decrees and of Hasdrubal's proposed march, they joined forces and prepared, to the exclusion of everything else, to thwart his intentions, convinced as they were that if he and his troops from Spain once succeeded in joining Hannibal, who even by himself was an enemy that Italy could hardly bear, it would mean the end of Roman imperial power. So it was with this anxiety uppermost in their minds that they proceeded to concentrate on the Ebro; they then crossed the river, and after long deliberation upon whether they should advance directly upon Hasdrubal's camp or content themselves with delaying his proposed march by attacking tribes or settlements allied to Carthage, they made preparations to attack Ibera, a town which took its name from its proximity to the Ebro and was at that period the most flourishing in the neighbourhood. Hasdrubal did not attempt to assist his allies; instead, he himself, in his turn, moved to the assault of a town which had recently gone over to the Romans, with the result that the Romans abandoned the siege of Ibera and turned their attention directly against Hasdrubal.

29. For a few days the opposing armies lay some five miles apart; there were a few skirmishes but no move towards a general engagement. Then suddenly, as if by mutual agreement, the signal for battle was given simultaneously in both camps, and the antagonists took the field in full strength. The Roman line was drawn up in three divisions; some of the light troops were posted in advance of the standards, amongst the pick of the infantry, others in the rear with the veteran reserves. The cavalry were stationed on the wings. Hasdrubal's centre was strongly held by his Spanish contingents; on his right wing he posted the Carthaginians, on his left the African units with the hired auxiliaries, the latter supported by all the mounted troops except the Numidian, which were sent to cover the Carthaginian infantry on the right. Actually, not all the Numidians were on the right, but only those of them which had been trained to ride into battle leading a spare horse: such was the quickness of these men, and so highly trained were their mounts that often in the heat of an engagement when the horse they were riding tired, they would leap, like circus riders, fully armed upon the back of the fresh one.

While the two armies faced each other in this order, their respective commanders might well have felt equal confidence, for neither side had much superiority either in the number or the type of its soldiers. But in the spirit of the men there was a vast difference: the Roman commanders had easily persuaded their troops that, far though they were from home, they were fighting in defence of Rome and Italy; every man knew that his return to his country depended upon the issue of the coming battle, and was therefore determined to conquer or die. On the Carthaginian side there was much less resolution: most of the men were Spaniards, and naturally preferred defeat in their own country to being dragged off to victory in Italy, so at the very first onset, almost before the javelins were thrown, Hasdrubal's centre gave, and, on a vigorous charge by the Roman infantry, turned their backs and fled. On the wings the fighting was, none the less, pretty hot: there was strong pressure from the Carthaginians on the one side and the Africans on the other, and they had the Romans almost surrounded and fighting in two directions simultaneously. But once the Roman infantry had been driven inward into a solid mass, they found themselves strong enough to force apart the encircling enemy wings, and in the double thrust which resulted the Romans had unquestionably the best of it, as, once the enemy centre had been routed, they were superior both in numbers and in fighting quality.

Casualties were very heavy: indeed, if the Spaniards had not broken and fled almost before the action began, few of the whole infantry force would have survived. There was no cavalry fighting at all, for as soon as the Numidians and Moors saw the centre giving way, they turned tail and fled, leaving the wings exposed and driving the elephants off in front of them. Hasdrubal waited till the end, and then made his escape from the carnage with a few followers. His camp was taken and stripped of all it contained.

This battle brought to the Roman side all the Spanish peoples who still wavered in their allegiance, and not only robbed Hasdrubal of any hope of getting his army into Italy but made it perilous for him even to remain any longer in Spain. When despatches from the two Scipios arrived in Rome with the news, there was less satisfaction in the victory than in the knowledge that Hasdrubal's march to Italy had been prevented.[1]

30. It was during the course of these events in Spain that the Bruttian town Petelia fell to Hannibal's officer Himilco after a siege of several months. For the Carthaginians it was an expensive victory in blood and wounds. It was famine rather than force which finally ended the siege: all vegetable and animal food of every kind – however strange – had been consumed, and the inhabitants reduced to living upon hides, grass, roots, soft bark and leaves stripped from trees; and they had continued to hold out until they no longer had the strength to carry their weapons or stand on the walls.

1. It was nine years before he succeeded in carrying out this march. See p. 480.

After taking Petelia the Carthaginians moved to Consentia, which was less obstinately defended and surrendered within a day or two. About the same time a Bruttian force laid siege to the Greek town of Croton, once a strong and populous community but now so greatly reduced by a long series of disasters that it contained less than 2,000 citizens, including the boys and the aged. Bereft, therefore, of defenders, it fell an easy prey to the enemy; only the inner fortress was held, in which a few had found refuge from the blood and confusion when the town was stormed. Locri, too, went over to the Bruttians and Carthage, its people having been betrayed by their leaders. Rhegium was the only town in that part of the country to remain loyal to Rome and independent to the end.

The same shift of feeling away from Rome spread as far as Sicily, where not even the house of Hiero was wholly free from disloyalty. Gelo, the eldest son, contemptuous, after Cannae, of the Roman alliance and despising his father as a dotard, went over to the Carthaginian interest; and his action would have led to a rising, if, in the very act of arming the populace and trying to get support, he had not been carried off by a death so opportune that even his father did not escape suspicion.

Such, then, is the history of this eventful year in Italy, Africa, Sicily, and Spain.

At the end of the year Quintus Fabius Maximus asked for the Senate's permission to dedicate the shrine of Venus of Eryx which he had vowed during his dictatorship. A decree was passed to the effect that Gracchus, the consul elect, should upon entering office bring a bill before the people asking them to sanction the appointment of Fabius as one of the two officials responsible for the dedication. In honour of Marcus Aemilius Lepidus who had been augur and twice consul, his three sons, Lucius, Marcus, and Quintus organized funeral games lasting three days, including the exhibition in the forum of twenty-two pairs of gladiators. The curule aediles, Gaius Laetorius and Gracchus the consul elect, who during his aedileship had served as master of Horse, held the Roman Games, celebrated on three consecutive days. The Plebeian Games of the aediles Cotta and Marcellus were thrice repeated.

Gracchus entered upon his consulship on the Ides of March

at the end of the third year of the war. The praetors were Quintus Fulvius Flaccus, Marcus Valerius Laevinus, Appius Claudius Pulcher, and Quintus Mucius Scaevola; of these, Flaccus, who had been consul (twice) and censor, obtained by lot the 'City' jurisdiction – the duty, that is, of hearing cases between Roman citizens – and Laevinus the 'foreign', or the hearing of cases in which non-Romans were involved; to Pulcher was allotted Sicily, to Scaevola Sardinia. It was the people's will that Marcellus should have full military authority as proconsul, in recognition of the fact that after Cannae he had been the only Roman commander to fight a successful action in Italy.

31. During its first session on the Capitol the Senate decreed that the tax for the current year should be doubled; the normal tax was to be collected immediately and the proceeds used to pay in cash all the soldiers except those who had fought at Cannae. As for the armies, the Senate's instructions were that the consul Gracchus should name a date for the mobilization of the two City legions at Cales, and that those legions should then be moved to the Claudian camp above Suessula. The troops already there, mostly survivors of Cannae, were to be taken to Sicily by the praetor Pulcher, and the troops in Sicily brought back to Rome. Marcellus was sent to the army which had been ordered to assemble at Cales, and he had instructions to take the City legions to the Claudian Camp. Appius Claudius entrusted to his officer Titus Metilius Croto the duty of taking over the veteran troops, the survivors of Cannae, and transporting them to Sicily.

People had been expecting that the consul would hold an election for the appointment of his colleague; nothing at first was actually said about this, but when it looked as if Marcellus, the man they most wanted as consul for the coming year because of the fine service he had done as praetor, had been deliberately sent out of the way, murmurs of dissatisfaction began to be heard in the Senate. Aware of this, the consul remarked: 'It was in the public interest, gentlemen, both that Marcellus should leave for Campania to make the exchange of troops, and also that no election should be proclaimed until he returned to Rome after completing the mission with which he was entrusted – as in that way you could have the consul whom you prefer and the situation demands.' Nothing more, in consequence, was said about the election before Marcellus's return.

Meanwhile Quintus Fabius Maximus and Titus Otacilius Crassus were appointed *duumviri* for dedicating shrines – the former for that of the Erycine Venus, the latter, for one to Mens. Both shrines stand on the Capitol, separated by a single water-channel. A motion was brought before the people offering Roman citizenship to the 300 Campanian horsemen who had come to Rome after loyal service in Sicily,[1] with the further provision that they should be citizens of Cumae dating from the day before the Campanian secession. The main reason for this proposal was a remark of the men themselves, who said they did not know where they belonged, as they had left their original home and were not yet admitted to municipal privileges in the town they had come back to.

On Marcellus's return to Rome an election was ordered by edict to name a consul to succeed Postumius. Marcellus was elected almost unanimously, and required to enter office at once. He was in the act of doing so when there was a clap of thunder; the augurs were summoned and gave it as their opinion that there had been something amiss with his election; and the Senate followed by spreading the rumour that the gods were displeased at the election of two plebeians to the consulship – a thing which had never happened before. Marcellus resigned and Fabius Maximus was chosen in his place. It was Fabius's third consulship. That year the sea caught fire. At Sinuessa a cow dropped a colt; at Lanuvium statues in the temple of Juno Sospita oozed blood, and it rained stones outside. Because of this ominous shower there were the customary nine days of religious observance; the other prodigies were expiated in the appropriate manner.

32. In the division of the forces the army at Teanum, formerly commanded by Pera the dictator, was assigned to Fabius; Gracchus, the other consul, took over the slave volunteers[2] at Teanum together with 25,000 of the allies; the praetor Valerius was given command of the legions which had been recalled

1. See p. 171.
2. See p. 158. They were the volunteers after Cannae.

from Sicily, and the proconsul Marcellus was sent to the army above Suessula, to guard Nola. The praetors left for Sicily and Sardinia. The consuls issued an order to the effect that whenever they called a meeting of the Senate, the senators and all entitled to speak in the Senate should meet at the Porta Capena. The praetors who had judicial duties held their tribunals at the Piscina Publica, where they ordered all private suits to be brought for hearing and where justice was administered during that year.

Meanwhile news reached Carthage of the defeat in Spain and the revolt to Rome of nearly all the Spanish tribes. Hannibal's brother Mago was on the point of leaving Carthage for Italy with reinforcements of 12,000 foot, 1,500 horse, twenty elephants, and 1,000 talents of silver, under an escort of sixty warships; but it was now suggested in certain quarters that he should be diverted with all these forces, naval and military, from Italy to Spain. Suddenly however there appeared to be good hopes of recovering Sardinia: the Roman garrison in the island was small; the former praetor Aulus Cornelius, who was familiar with the situation there, had gone and a new governor was expected; the people of the island were, moreover, growing sick of their long subservience to Rome, and in the past year had been the victims of considerable harshness and greed from their rulers in the form of oppressive tribute and immoderate requisitioning of grain. In short, all they needed was a leader, and they would go over to him at once. This information had been conveyed to Carthage by leading Sardinians, of whom the prime mover was a certain Hampsicora, at that period the wealthiest and most influential person in the island, and the effect of it was at the same time disturbing and encouraging. In the end, Mago with his ships and land forces was sent to Spain, and Hasdrubal was chosen to conduct operations in Sardinia with a force of approximately the same strength.

In Rome the consuls had completed what had to be done at home and were now busying themselves with the coming campaign. Gracchus set the date for the mobilization of his allied contingents and slave-volunteers at Sinuessa, and Fabius issued an order on the Senate's authority for all grain to be got in before June 1st and conveyed into fortified towns; anyone failing to comply was to have his farmlands ravaged, his slaves sold by auction, and his farmhouses burned down. Not even the praetors elected for judicial duties were allowed exemption from military service: it was decided to send the praetor Valerius to Apulia to take over the army there from Varro, to use the legions from Sicily chiefly for the defence of that region, and to send Varro's force to Tarentum under the command of one of its officers. Twenty-five ships were assigned to this officer for the protection of the coast between Tarentum and Brundisium. An equal number of ships was assigned to the City praetor Fulvius to defend the coast in the neighbourhood of the Tiber. The proconsul Varro was instructed to raise troops in Picenum and see to the defence of that part of the country. Titus Otacilius Crassus, after dedicating the temple of Mens on the Capitol, was sent with full powers to command the fleet in Sicily.

33. This war, a struggle between the two wealthiest peoples in the world, had attracted the attention of all kings and all nations elsewhere. Philip, King of Macedon, was particularly concerned in its progress because of his proximity to Italy and the fact that he was separated from it only by the Ionian sea. His first reaction to the news that Hannibal had crossed the Alps was not a simple one: he was glad that war had broken out between Rome and Carthage, but still doubtful, while the resources of the two nations were as yet unknown, as to which he hoped would prove victorious. But when there had been three battles and three Carthaginian victories, he sided with success and sent a deputation to Hannibal. His envoys avoided the ports of Brundisium and Tarentum which were guarded by Roman ships, and landed at the temple of Lacinian Juno, near Croton, whence, proceeding through Apulia towards Capua, they fell in with the Roman garrison forces and were taken to the praetor Laevinus, who was encamped near Luceria. Xenophanes, the leader to the delegation, boldly asserted that they had been sent by King Philip to arrange a pact of friendship between him and Rome and that they had communications to make to the consuls, the Senate, and the Roman people. Laevinus, at a time like this when old allies were falling

away, was delighted at the prospect of a new alliance with so eminent a monarch, and, taking his enemies for friends, gave them a hospitable welcome. He provided men to escort them, to give them careful information about routes, to indicate what passes and localities were in Roman hands and what in the hands of the enemy. Xenophanes, accordingly, made his way through the Roman forces into Campania and thence by the shortest route to Hannibal's camp, where he made a treaty of friendship with him. The terms of the treaty were these: King Philip was to cross to Italy with the largest fleet he could raise (perhaps 200 ships), harry the coast, and carry on offensive operations by land and sea to the best of his ability; at the end of the war, Rome and all Italy were to pass into the possession of Hannibal and the Carthaginians, and all captured material was to be ceded to Hannibal; Italy once crushed, the Carthaginians were to sail for Greece and make war upon any states the King might choose. The mainland states and offshore islands in the general vicinity of Macedonia should become the property of Philip and be incorporated in his kingdom.

34. These, approximately, were the terms of the agreement between Hannibal and Philip's envoys. When the envoys left, three Carthaginian representatives, Gisgo, Bostar, and Mago, were sent with them to confirm the pact by getting Philip himself to swear to it. They joined the ship in the concealed anchorage near the temple of Juno Lacinia and put to sea; but some distance offshore they were seen by the Roman fleet patrolling the Calabrian coast, and Valerius Flaccus ordered out some light vessels to chase them and bring them back. The king's envoys tried for a time to get clear away, but soon found they were being overtaken, and gave themselves up. They were brought before the commander of the fleet, and when he asked their names and destination and where they had come from Xenophanes repeated the lie which had once already proved so successful and said he had been sent by Philip to make contact with the Romans; he had reached Laevinus, to whom alone he was able to get in safety, but had been unable to pass through Campania because it was blocked by enemy troops. As the dress and appearance of Hannibal's envoys aroused suspicion, they were questioned, and their accent

betrayed them, whereupon their attendants were taken aside and, under threats, revealed the truth. Letters were found from Hannibal to Philip containing agreements between the King of Macedon and the Carthaginian commander. It was decided, in these circumstances, to send the prisoners and their attendants without delay to the Senate in Rome, or to the consuls wherever they might be, and for this purpose five fast ships were chosen and put under the command of Lucius Valerius Antias. His instructions were to distribute the envoys amongst the ships, to be separately guarded, and to see to it that they had no chance of talking to each other or of putting their heads together.

To return to events in Rome: Aulus Cornelius Mammula, the retiring governor of Sardinia, in his report on the state of things in the island, said that war and revolt were universally expected. Quintus Mucius, his successor, had fallen a victim, as soon as he arrived, to the damp and unwholesome climate; his indisposition, though not dangerous, was likely to be protracted and he would not for a long time be fit for active service. The army in the island, though adequate for the defence of a province in peacetime, was not sufficient for the war which was expected to break out at any moment. In view of this report the Senate instructed Quintus Fulvius Flaccus to raise 5,000 foot and 400 horse, to have them despatched to Sardinia at the earliest possible moment, and to send, with full military powers, the best man he could find to carry on until Mucius recovered. The man selected was Titus Manlius Torquatus, who had been censor and twice consul, and during his first consulship had subdued the Sardinians.

About this time a fleet from Carthage was also sent to Sardinia; it was commanded by Hasdrubal – surnamed the Bald – and was caught by bad weather and forced to run for the Balearic islands. Not only was the ships' gear damaged but the hulls were badly strained; they were hauled ashore, and a considerable time was spent in repairs.

35. After Cannae military operations had slowed down, the morale of one side having suffered[1] and the fighting strength of

1. Presumably as a result of the winter spent at Capua: though Livy exaggerates this. (A. de S.)

the other having been seriously impaired. In these circumstances the Campanians attempted on their own initiative to get control of Cumae. Their first move was to try to persuade the town to revolt from Rome, and when that failed they had recourse to trickery. All the Campanian communities used to observe a regular religious ceremony at Hamae, and to this ceremony they told the people of Cumae that the Campanian senate would come, and asked the Cumaean senate to be there too in order to consult together and ensure that both peoples should have the same friends and the same enemies. They added that they would have an armed force there to guard against any danger from either the Romans or the Carthaginians. The people of Cumae suspected a trick, but none the less made no objection, as they thought that this would be the best way of hiding a little scheme of their own.

Meanwhile at Sinuessa, where his troops had been ordered to report, the consul Gracchus had held a review and then crossed the Volturnus to the neighbourhood of Liternum, where he encamped. As there was little for his men to do there, he kept them occupied with frequent manoeuvres to accustom the recruits – most of them slave-volunteers – to follow the standards and get to know their proper places in the line. He was aware that the stigma of some of the men's origin and background might well cause ill-feeling between the different classes of soldiers, and this he was himself particularly anxious to avoid and had given all his officers instructions to the same effect; he wanted veterans and recruits, free citizens and slave-volunteers, all to feel themselves equals, and to believe that anyone to whom the Roman people had entrusted its arms and standards was for that reason a man of good enough station and good enough blood. The fortune of war, he said, had put them into their present situation, and the same fortune compelled them to maintain it now. The troops were as eager to accept this view of things as their officers had been to inculcate it, and soon they became so united and harmonious a body of men that the social standing of individuals was hardly even remembered.

It was while Gracchus was thus employed that envoys from Cumae informed him of the proposal made to them a few days previously by the Campanians, and of their reply to it. They went on to say that in three days' time the festival would take place and not only would the whole senate be present but a Campanian army, too, encamped on the spot. Gracchus, in reply, ordered the people of Cumae to convey all moveable property from their farms to the town and to stay with it inside their defences, and himself, on the eve of the Campanian festival, marched with his force to Cumae.

Hamae is three miles away. Already the Campanians had gathered there in large numbers according to the agreement; and not far away Marius Alfius, their *medix tuticus* (as the chief Campanian magistrate was called) lay secretly encamped with 14,000 armed men, though considerably more intent upon preparing for the festival and under cover of it laying his treacherous plot than upon any soldierly duty such as fortifying his camp. The ceremony at Hamae took place at night, but was designed to be over before midnight; this was the moment, therefore, that Gracchus was on the watch for: he posted guards at the camp gates to prevent any leakage of information, got all his men together early in the evening and ordered them to rest and sleep so as to be ready to parade as soon as it was dark. Then, during the first watch, he gave the word to move. The column marched without a sound and reached Hamae at midnight. The vigil had made the Campanians careless, and their camp was ill-guarded: Gracchus burst in through every gate simultaneously, and the men as they lay asleep, or came strolling back unarmed from the ceremony, were butchered. In that brief nocturnal fray more than 2,000 were killed, including Marius Alfius, the Campanian leader. Thirty-four military standards were captured.

36. Gracchus, who had lost fewer than a hundred men in the action, now hurriedly withdrew to Cumae, as he suspected a move by Hannibal, who lay at Tifata above Capua. And he guessed right, for no sooner had the report of the slaughter of the Campanians reached Capua, than Hannibal, supposing that the army, mostly of recruits and slaves, would be crowing over their unexpected success and that he would find them stripping the bodies of the dead and driving the captured animals off to Hamae, marched with all possible speed past Capua, giving orders that any fugitive Campanians met on the way were to

be taken to that town under the protection of an escort, and any wounded men conveyed thither in carts. At Hamae he found the enemy's camp deserted, and there was nothing to be seen but the dead bodies of his allies lying all over the place, as evidence of the recent slaughter. There were some who urged him to march immediately on Cumae and attack it, and he would have dearly liked to do so in order to have it as a maritime base instead of Naples, which he had failed to get control of; but he had no option but to return to his camp above Tifata, simply because his march had been such a scramble that his men had brought nothing with them except their weapons. On the following day, unable to resist the entreaties of the Campanians, he returned to Cumae with all the necessary gear for an assault, devastated the countryside, and took up a position a mile from the town. Gracchus was still there, as, though he was far from confident in the men under his command, he was ashamed to desert in their need allies who implored his aid and that of the Roman people. Nor did the other consul, Fabius, who was encamped at Cales, venture to cross the Volturnus, engaged, as he was, first in taking fresh auspices and then with a succession of ominous events which were being reported to him. He took the usual steps to neutralize these portents, but the soothsayers continued to announce that the entrails of the sacrificial victims indicated nothing but ill luck.

37. While Fabius was thus kept inactive, Gracchus was in a state of siege. Siege-engines were already being brought into position against him, amongst them an immense wooden tower, close to the town wall. He countered this by raising another tower – actually on the wall – and because of the additional height of the wall itself, which he had shored up with heavy timbers and used as a foundation, it considerably overtopped the enemy one. From this tower they kept the attackers at bay for a time by flinging stones and stakes and anything else they could find down upon them, until they saw that the enemy's tower had been moved farther forward and was now hard up against the wall, when they changed their tactics and threw fire – hundreds of blazing brands. The effect was immediate: armed men – hordes of them – lost their heads and leapt down from the tower, and at the same time a sally from the

town by two gates simultaneously drove the enemy guards in headlong flight back to their camp, so that the Carthaginian besiegers changed their role and rather resembled the besieged. The Carthaginian losses were some 1,300 killed and fifty-nine taken prisoner – the latter, men who had been picketed around the walls but had been paying little attention to their duties: a sortie was the last thing they expected, and they were caught almost before they knew what was happening. Gracchus sounded the retreat and withdrew his troops into the town before the enemy could rally from the unexpected shock, and on the following day Hannibal, who was sure Gracchus would be encouraged by his success to risk a major action, drew up his force in battle order between his camp and the town. However, there was no movement of troops; the usual guard over the town was maintained, and it was clear that Gracchus had no intention of gambling on his chances. Hannibal accordingly withdrew to Tifata, no better off than before.

About the same time as the siege of Cumae was raised Tiberius Sempronius, surnamed Longus,[1] fought a successful action near Grumentum in Lucania against the Carthaginian commander Hanno. He killed over 2,000 of the enemy with a loss to himself of 280 men, and captured 41 military standards. Hanno, forced out of Lucania, withdrew into Bruttium.

Vercellium, Viscellium, and Sicilinum, three towns of the Hirpini which had revolted from Rome, were stormed and retaken by the praetor Valerius, and the leaders of the revolt executed. More than 5,000 prisoners were sold at auction; other captured material was turned over to the troops, and the army was marched back to Luceria.

38. During these operations, the five ships carrying the Macedonian and Carthaginian envoys to Rome had cruised along most of the Italian coast from the Adriatic to the southern sea, and were now passing Cumae under sail. Gracchus, uncertain whether they were friends or enemies, sent some vessels from his own fleet to meet them, and when inquiry had revealed that the consul was at Cumae, the five ships put in there, the prisoners were conducted to the consul, and the letters handed over to him. Gracchus read the letters of Philip and

1. The commander defeated at the Trebia in 218 B.C.

Hannibal and sent them all under seal overland to the Senate, and gave orders for the envoys to be conveyed by sea. They reached Rome almost at the same moment as the letters; there they were questioned, and when it was found that what they said was in agreement with the letters, the Senate was at first gravely perturbed at the prospect of having to face a large-scale war with Macedon when the burden of the war with Carthage was already almost more than the country could bear. None the less, far from sinking under this new menace, they promptly initiated discussions upon how best to keep the enemy out of Italy by themselves taking the offensive.

The prisoners were put in chains and their attendants sold as slaves; that done, a decree was issued to the effect that twenty-five new ships should be added to the twenty-five already under the command of Valerius Flaccus. The vessels were got ready and launched, the five which had brought the captured envoys were added to their number, and the fleet of thirty sailed from Ostia for Tarentum. Flaccus received orders to put on board at Tarentum the troops commanded there by Lucius Apustius – they had previously been Varro's men – and with his fleet of fifty sail not only to patrol the Italian coast but also to go in search of information about the hostile intentions of Macedon. If Philip's plans agreed with the captured letters and with the information supplied by the envoys, Flaccus was to inform the praetor Valerius by letter, and Valerius, in his turn, after placing his lieutenant Apustius in command of the army, was to proceed to the fleet at Tarentum and cross at the first possible moment to Macedonia and do what he could to keep Philip inside his own dominions. The money which had been sent to Appius Claudius in Sicily to repay King Hiero's loan, was assigned by the Senate to the maintenance of the fleet and the prosecution of the war with Macedon. It was conveyed to Tarentum in charge of Lucius Antistius, and at the same time 200,000 measures of wheat and 100,000 of barley were sent by Hiero.

39. In the course of these active preparations the one ship which had been captured out of the squadron sent to Rome made her escape while under way and returned to Philip. Thus it became known in Macedon that the envoys and their letters

had fallen into Roman hands. As Philip could not know if any agreement had been made between his envoys and Hannibal, or what answer the former were to have brought him, he sent a second delegation with the same instructions as before. The members of the delegation were Heraclitus, surnamed Scotinus, Crito, a Boeotian, and Sositheus of Magnesia, and they were wholly successful; but before Philip could make any active preparations, the summer was over. The war which menaced Rome was postponed – and all because of the capture of a single ship in which Philip's envoys were sailing.

Meanwhile both consuls were active in the neighbourhood of Capua, Fabius having at last finished the rites of appeasement in connexion with the various prodigies, and crossed the Volturnus. He assaulted and captured the towns of Compulteria, Trebula, and Austicula, which had all gone over to Hannibal, and their Carthaginian garrisons together with many Campanians were taken prisoner. At Nola, as in the previous year, the senate remained pro-Roman while the commons sided with Hannibal; there were conspiracies to murder the leading citizens and betray the city, and Fabius, to nip them in the bud, marched his troops between Capua and Hannibal's camp at Tifata and took up a fresh position in Marcellus's old camp; from there he sent Marcellus, the pro-praetor, to garrison Nola with the forces under his command.

40. There was activity in Sardinia too. Operations which had been abandoned when the praetor Mucius fell sick were now resumed under the direction of Titus Manlius. Manlius, who had beached his warships at Carales and armed their crews to serve as infantrymen, had taken over the army from Mucius and controlled, in all, a force of 22,000 foot and 1,200 horse. With this force he marched into enemy territory and encamped not far from the position held by Hampsicora, who happened at the moment to have gone off to the mountain districts to find recruits for his army amongst the wild 'Goatskins', as they were called. A son of his named Hostus was in command of the camp – a young man who with the over-confidence of youth flung himself into battle and was utterly defeated. About 3,000 Sardinians were killed and some 800 taken alive; the rest took to their heels at random through farmland and forest, until

word came that their leader had fled for refuge to a town called Cornus, the chief settlement of the district, whereupon they followed him thither.

This battle would have finished hostilities in Sardinia, had not hopes of further resistance been raised by the opportune arrival of Hasdrubal with the Carthaginian fleet which had been driven by bad weather to the Balearic Islands.

When Manlius learned that the fleet had come in, he withdrew to Carales and thus enabled Hampsicora to effect a junction with Hasdrubal, who disembarked his troops, sent the ships back to Carthage, and proceeded, with Hampsicora as his guide, to lay waste the farms belonging to Rome's allies; he would, indeed, have got as far as Carales, if Manlius had not marched to meet him and checked the widespread and indiscriminate devastation. For a time the two armies lay facing one another, not far apart; then minor probing movements took place and a few indecisive skirmishes; finally on both sides line of battle was formed, the antagonists met and for four hours there was a full-scale engagement. The Sardinians were well used to being easily beaten, but for a long time the Carthaginians kept the issue in doubt, until at last when the battleground was thick with Sardinian fugitives and Sardinian dead, they too were routed. As they turned and ran, the wing of the Roman army, which had crushed the Sardinians, enveloped them and cut off their retreat. From that moment the fight was a mere butchery: 12,000 of the enemy, Sardinian and Carthaginian, were killed, and nearly 3,700 taken alive; twenty-seven military standards were captured. 41. What made the battle a famous and memorable one was, more than anything else, the capture of the Carthaginian commander Hasdrubal together with Hanno and Mago, both of noble blood and the latter a member of the family of Barca and closely related to Hannibal. Hanno had been responsible for the revolt of Sardinia and was undoubtedly the instigator of the war. Nor was less lustre shed upon this battle by the fate of the Sardinian leaders: Hampsicora's son Hostus fell in action; Hampsicora himself fled with few horsemen attending him, and then, when he learned that the ruin of his fortunes had been crowned by the death of his son, he waited for darkness lest anyone should find and prevent him, and killed himself. The other fugitives fled as before to Cornus; Manlius attacked the town with his victorious army and captured it a few days later. That was the signal for the other communities which had gone over to Hampsicora and the Carthaginians to give hostages and surrender; from all of them tribute and contributions of grain were exacted in proportion to their resources or to their guilt. Manlius then returned to Carales; he launched his warships, embarked the troops he had brought with him, and sailed for Rome, where he reported to the Senate the complete subjugation of Sardinia. The tribute-money he handed over to the quaestors, the grain to the aediles, the prisoners to the praetor Quintus Fulvius.

While all this was going on, Titus Otacilius had crossed from Lilybaeum to the African coast and inflicted severe damage upon the country around Carthage; he then sailed for Sardinia, in pursuit of the rumour that Hasdrubal had recently gone there from the Balearics, and on the way fell in with Hasdrubal's fleet as it was returning to Africa. There was an action of sorts, and seven Carthaginian ships were captured with their crews. The rest broke formation and fled; last time it was bad weather that scattered them: this time it was panic.

During this same period Bomilcar happened to arrive at Locri with the troops, elephants, and supplies which had been sent as reinforcements from Carthage. Appius Claudius hoped to catch him off his guard, and with this in view hurriedly marched to Messana, pretending to be making the round of his province, and sailed from there with a fair wind and current to Locri. But Bomilcar had already left to join Hanno in Bruttium, and the people of Locri shut their gates against the Romans. So Appius returned to Messana with nothing to show for the very considerable effort he had made.

The same summer Marcellus, who was still holding Nola, frequently raided the territory of the Hirpini and the Samnites of Caudium. The raids were so destructive that they seemed like a repetition of the horrors the Samnites had suffered in former times; 42. a delegation, accordingly, was sent by both peoples jointly to Hannibal. 'We' (said the spokesman) 'first fought our battles against Rome alone, so long as our own swords and our own resources were enough to protect us. When we lost confidence in their power to do so, we allied ourselves with king Pyrrhus; he left us in the lurch, and we were forced to accept terms of peace, by which we abode nearly fifty years – until you, Hannibal, came to Italy. So closely were we bound to you by your valour and success, and even more by the unparalleled kindliness and courtesy which led you to restore to us those of our people whom you took prisoner in battle, that so long as we kept you safe and sound as our friend we had nothing to fear from Rome – nay, if I dare say so – nothing to fear even from the anger of the gods. Yet despite your continued safety, despite your victorious career, despite your presence amongst us – so near that you might almost hear the weeping of our wives and children and watch our houses burn – we have repeatedly this summer suffered such terrible losses that one might fancy it was Marcellus, not Hannibal, who won the battle of Cannae, while the Romans are boasting that you had strength for one stroke only and are now as harmless as a bee which has spent its sting.

'For nearly a hundred years we were at war with Rome, unaided by foreign armies or foreign generals. Pyrrhus, indeed, fought for two years at our side; but Pyrrhus was not using his strength to defend us – he was using *us* to increase his own resources. I will not boast of our victories – of two consuls and two consular armies sent by us "under the yoke", or of any other splendid achievements of ours; as to the reverses we suffered in those days, we can recall them with less shame than what is happening to us now. In those days great dictators with their masters of Horse, two consuls, each with his consular army, used to invade us: their scouts preceded them, their reserves stood ready, they marched with their standards to devastate our land; but now we are the prey of one pro-praetor – of a contemptible little army assigned to the defence of Nola. They do not even come like soldiers, in companies: they roam like brigands here, there, and everywhere – as much at their ease as if they were at home. And why is this? Because you do not protect us, because all our own men, who would defend us were they with us, are away serving in your army.

'I should be ignorant indeed of you and of your soldiers, if I did not think it would be an easy task for a man who, I know, has routed and laid low so many Roman armies, to crush these casual raiders, who go where they please, without order or discipline, over our countryside, in pursuit even of the flimsiest hope of plunder. A few Numidians will suffice to round them up – you will have sent help to us and at the same time robbed Nola of its garrison, if only you deign to afford protection to men whom you thought worthy to be your friends.'

43. Hannibal replied that one thing at a time might have been better – for, as it was, the envoys had reported their losses, asked for aid, and complained of abandonment and neglect all in a breath. They ought to have reported first, asked for help next, and lastly, if they did not get it, they might justly have complained that they had begged in vain. He did not intend, he told them, to bring troops into the territory of the Hirpini or the Samnites, for that would be only an added burden; he preferred to invade the nearest territory belonging to the allies of Rome, as that would serve the double purpose of satisfying his own men's appetite for plunder and of providing sufficient cause of anxiety elsewhere to keep the Romans away from Samnium. As to the war itself, Trasimene had indeed been a nobler fight than Trebia, and Cannae than Trasimene – but the summit was not yet: he would, he declared, dim the memory even of Cannae by a still greater and more brilliant victory.

The envoys having been dismissed with this answer and with the addition of generous presents, Hannibal left a fair-sized force at Tifata and proceeded with the rest of his army to Nola, where he was joined by Hanno, who came from Bruttium with the reinforcements from Carthage, including the elephants. He encamped not far from the town and found on inquiry that everything was very different from what his allies' representatives had told him: Marcellus had done nothing which could in any sense be described as a blind risk; nor had he underrated the enemy: on the contrary, his raids had been preceded by careful reconnoitring, and carried out by strong forces, with a safe position to retire on should need arise; every precaution had in fact been taken, as though Hannibal in person had confronted him.

And now, on learning of the enemy's approach, he kept his

troops within the town's defences, and ordered the Nolan senators to walk up and down on the walls and keep a sharp eye upon what was going on amongst the Carthaginians. Hanno rode up close to the wall and called to two of the senators, Herennius Bassus and Herius Pettius, to meet him for a colloquy, and when both men, with Marcellus's permission, came out to him, he addressed them through an interpreter. He began by lauding Hannibal's valour and success, and belittling Rome, whose former majesty was, he said, following her power into senility. Even if her majesty equalled her might, as once it did, anyone who knew by experience how burdensome was her rule and how great had been Hannibal's indulgence even to all prisoners of war of Italian blood, would be bound to prefer friendship and alliance with Carthage to friendship and alliance with Rome. Moreover, if both consuls were at Nola with their armies, they would no more be a match for Hannibal than they had been at Cannae – and how much less could one praetor with a small and inexperienced force be expected to defend the town? It affected Hannibal, he pointed out, less than it did them whether he took over Nola by force or upon terms. Take it he would, just as he had taken Capua and Nuceria; and the people of Nola, situated as it was between them, knew very well how differently Capua and Nuceria had fared. What would happen if their town were taken by force, he did not care to prophesy; he would guarantee, however, that if they surrendered the town together with Marcellus and his troops, no one but themselves would dictate the terms upon which they would enter into friendship and alliance with Hannibal.

44. To these proposals Bassus replied that for many years past there had been friendship between the people of Rome and the people of Nola, and that neither yet saw reason to regret it; moreover, if the men of Nola ought to have changed their allegiance with their fortunes, it was now too late. Had they meant to surrender to Hannibal, what call was there to ask for Roman aid? In every respect they were, and would remain to the last, bound in friendship to the men who had come to protect them.

After this conversation Hannibal could no longer hope that Nola might be betrayed into his hands. Accordingly he surrounded the town in preparation for a simultaneous assault upon its defences from every side. Marcellus replied by forming his men into line of battle inside the town gate, ready for a sortie. Out they came, with a rush and a roar, and not a few wavered or fell before them; but soon more enemy troops rallied to the point where the fighting was, so that they were no longer numerically inferior, and a savage struggle began which might have proved one of the great battles of the war if a violent storm of wind and rain had not parted the combatants. As it was, after a comparatively minor engagement, only enough to inflame their passions, both sides withdrew, the Romans into the town, the Carthaginians to their camp. In the first sortie the Carthaginians had lost not more than thirty men, the Romans fifty. The rain continued all night, till the third hour of the next day; so both armies, though eager for a fight, remained within their fortifications. On the day after that Hannibal sent a party to raid Nolan territory, and Marcellus promptly replied by forming for battle outside the town. Hannibal accepted the challenge.

There was about a mile between the town and the enemy's camp; and it was there, on the level ground – all the country round Nola is flat – that the fighting began. On both sides the battle-cry was raised: those of Hannibal's men who had gone raiding and were not yet too far away, heard it and hurried back to join the struggle which had already begun. The men of Nola reinforced the Roman line – they had instructions from Marcellus, who thanked them for their support, to remain in reserve and carry back the wounded, but not to take part in the fighting without a direct order from himself. 45. The battle was hard fought; leaders and led spared themselves nothing, the latter in deeds, the former in exhortation and encouragement. 'You beat them,' cried Marcellus, 'two days ago; before that you drove them from Cumae; last year another army under my command forced them back from Nola – so have at them again! Why, they are not even at full strength – some of them have gone off for a walk, looking for loot! Even those who face you have lost their sap in luxury and Campanian vice – worn out by a winter of drinking and whoring and every other excess! Gone is that once-famed dash and vigour, melted away that strength of limb and staunchness of heart, which brought them over the Alps and Pyrenees! Those were men – these but their relics and shadows, hardly strong enough to stand or wield their swords. Capua was Hannibal's Cannae: in Capua was put out the flame of their valour, their discipline, their former fame, their hope of things to come.'

While Marcellus sought to encourage his men by denigrating the enemy in this sort of way, Hannibal was flinging much more serious reproaches at his own. He recognized (so he put it) the arms and the standards he had once been familiar with at the Trebia, at Trasimene, at Cannae; but it was too true that he had led one army into winter quarters at Capua, and led out a different one. 'What?' he exclaimed, 'can you not, for all your efforts, hold up against a mere Roman brigade-officer with one legion and its paltry auxiliaries – you, whom once two consular armies could never resist? Marcellus with an army of recruits and Nolan reserves is now for the second time attacking us unavenged! Where is that soldier of mine who dragged the consul Flaminius from his horse and cut off his head?[1] Where the man who killed Paullus at Cannae?[2] What strange curse has fallen upon you, that swords have lost their edge and hands their strength? Once, though few, you could conquer many; now you are many and can scarcely stand against a few. Your words, at least, were bold enough when you boasted you would storm the walls of Rome could you but find a leader. Look then – here is a lesser task: here and now I wish you to make trial of your strength and courage; storm the walls of Nola – see how low it lies, there in the plain, behind no barrier of river or sea! And how rich it is! Take it, load yourselves with plunder and spoils, and I will lead you whither you will, or follow you.'

46. But neither praise nor blame could put heart into Hannibal's men. Everywhere they were forced back, while the fighting spirit of the Romans rose under Marcellus's exhortations and their ardour was fanned to a hotter flame by the men of Nola who cheered them on. Overpowered, the Carthaginians broke, and were driven to seek refuge in their camp; the Roman rank

1. See p. 100; a slightly different version.
2. See p. 149.

and file were eager to attack it, but Marcellus ordered a withdrawal to Nola, where he was received with joyful congratulations even by the commons who had previously supported the Carthaginians.

The enemy that day had more than 5,000 killed, 600 captured, with nineteen standards and two elephants. Four elephants had been killed in the action. The Roman losses were less than 1,000 killed. Next day both sides observed an unspoken truce for burying the dead, and Marcellus burned the spoils as an offering to Vulcan. Three days later 272 cavalrymen, Spanish and Numidian, deserted to Marcellus; maybe they had some private grudge to satisfy, or perhaps they expected service under more liberal conditions. Often in the course of the war the Romans found them loyal and courageous soldiers, and when the war was over they gave them land in their home countries as a reward for good service.

Hannibal sent Hanno back into Bruttium from Nola with the forces he had brought with him, and himself made for winter quarters in Apulia, taking up his position near Arpi. Fabius, on learning that Hannibal had started for Apulia, conveyed grain from Nola and Naples to the camp above Suessula, strengthened the defences there, and put in a garrison strong enough to hold it through the winter; he then moved his camp nearer Capua and carried on a systematic devastation of the Campanian farmlands, until the Campanian owners in the town, though they had no confidence in their resources, were compelled to take the field and fortify a position in the open outside the town walls. They had 6,000 men under arms – infantrymen, and poor stuff at that; in cavalry they were more effective, and began, in consequence, a series of minor cavalry skirmishes.

Amongst the many distinguished Campanian horsemen was a certain Cerrinus Vibellius, surnamed Taurea; a Campanian by birth, he had been granted Roman citizenship, and he was by so much the finest cavalryman of all the Campanians that, when he was serving in the Roman army, the only Roman to equal him in reputation was Claudius Asellus. On this occasion, then, Taurea came riding up to the Roman squadrons, and for several minutes ran his eye along the ranks. A silence fell, and 'Where is Asellus?' he asked. 'He used to dispute with me about our valour, so why does he not offer to fight it out and give or receive the "spoils of honour" according to the issue?'

47. Asellus was in camp when he was told of this challenge; waiting only to ask the consul's permission to answer to it and leave the ranks to fight in single combat, he immediately armed himself, rode out in front of the guards, and called upon Taurea by name to meet him wherever he pleased. Crowds of Romans had soon left camp to watch the duel, and the Campanians made a dense line of spectators along the rampart of their camp and even along the town walls. Haughty words from each of the combatants cast a glamour on the scene; then, with spears at the ready, they spurred their horses to the charge. For some time it was an exhibition only, as the two men wheeled and eluded one another on the open ground as if in sport, and no blood was shed; but at last the Campanian cried, 'Come now what of the fight? This will be only a test of horses, not of men, unless' – and he pointed to a sunken track between high banks on the edge of the plain – 'unless we ride down into *that*. Then, with no room to dodge each other, we shall be compelled to fight it out.'

Almost before the words were out of his mouth Claudius jumped his horse down into the track, but Taurea, when deeds were called for instead of words, found his heart fail him. 'What?' he muttered; 'a gelding in a ditch? I think not!' The remark has since become a country proverb.[1]

Claudius rode a long way round along the sunken track, emerged from it into the open plain again without meeting an enemy, and, pouring scorn upon his antagonist's cowardice, returned victoriously to camp amidst the joy and congratulations of his friends. Some annals include in their account of this affair a further detail which is certainly remarkable, though how true it is we may judge for ourselves: Claudius, it is said, in his pursuit of Taurea rode straight through one of the town gates which happened to be open, and, while the enemy stood fixed in helpless astonishment, galloped out through the opposite gate without receiving a scratch.

1. Apparently with reference to the disposal of a useless animal.

48. After this little happened; the consul moved his camp further back to allow the Campanians to sow their fields. He left the growing grain untouched until the green was high enough to serve as fodder, which he then conveyed to the Claudian camp above Suessula, where he constructed permanent quarters for the winter. He gave the proconsul Marcellus orders to leave in Nola a garrison adequate for its defence and to dismiss the rest of his troops to Rome, to save the country expense and the allies the burden of their maintenance. After Gracchus had moved his legions from Cumae to Luceria in Apulia, the praetor Valerius was sent to Brundisium with the troops he had had at Luceria, with orders to defend the Sallentine coast and to take any necessary measures for a war with Philip and the Macedonians.

At the end of the summer I have been describing dispatches reached Rome from Publius and Gnaeus Scipio; they contained a report of their important and successful campaigns in Spain,[1] and went on to state that there was no money left for the soldiers' pay, and no clothing or other supplies either for the army or the ships' crews. As for the pay, the two commanders suggested that if the treasury were empty they might find means of raising the money in Spain, though the other things would all have to be sent from Rome if there was to be any chance of keeping either the army or the province.

When the dispatches had been read, the Senate unanimously admitted both the truth of the statement and the reasonableness of the demand; none the less they could not but remember the immense forces, both military and naval, which they were already maintaining, and the great new fleet which would soon have to be put into commission if war started with Macedon. They knew all too well that Sicily and Sardinia, which before the war paid tribute in kind, were now scarcely able even to feed the troops which garrisoned them; that expenses could be met only by the property tax on individuals, while the number of people paying that tax had been reduced by the enormous losses at Trasimene and Cannae, and the few who survived would merely be involved in a different sort of ruin if they were called upon to bear the weight of a greatly increased

1. See pp. 120 ff. and 199 ff.

contribution. The fact was, that the country could not exist on its assets; if it was to survive, it would have to borrow.

It was decided therefore that the praetor Fulvius should go before the assembly with a public statement of the country's difficulties, and urge all those who had increased their property by government contracts to allow the government – which was the source of their wealth – time for payment, and in their contracts for the supply of what was needed for the army in Spain to admit a clause to the effect that, when there was money in the treasury, they should be the first to be paid. The praetor further announced the date on which he proposed to place the contracts for food and clothing for the army in Spain and whatever else was required for the ships' crews. 49. On the appointed day three companies of nineteen persons in all came forward to undertake the contracts, making at the same time two stipulations: first, that they should be excused military service during their term as government contractors; secondly, that the state should accept all risks from tempest or enemy action to goods sent by sea. Both demands were allowed, and the contracts were accepted. Thus public business was carried on by means of private funds – so deep was patriotic sentiment in all classes of society almost without exception. The honesty with which the contracts were carried out was no less remarkable than the generosity with which they were undertaken, so that the fighting forces were supplied no less well than they used to be when there were ample funds in the public treasury.

It was at this moment, when the fresh supplies were arriving, that the town of Iliturgi, which had gone over to Rome, was being besieged by Hasdrubal, Mago, and Hamilcar the son of Bomilcar. Grain was short in the town – which was now an ally – and the Scipios, bringing a new supply, forced their way into it between the three armies which beset it, not without hard fighting and heavy losses to their opponents. They then urged the inhabitants to defend themselves with the same courage with which they had seen the Roman army fighting on their behalf, and proceeded to the assault of the main enemy position under Hasdrubal. Hasdrubal was soon joined by the other two Carthaginian armies, as their commanders realized it was there that the immediate issue would be decided. The battle began by a sortie from the camp; and though the Romans on that day had only 16,000 men in the field against 60,000 of the enemy, the undisputed nature of their victory is evident from the losses they inflicted: the enemy lost in killed more than the total strength of the Roman army; over 3,000 were taken prisoner together with just under 1,000 horses, fifty-nine standards, and seven elephants – five other elephants having been killed in the fighting. The three camps were also captured.

After the relief of Iliturgi the Carthaginian armies moved to the attack of Intibili, having made good their losses by drawing recruits from a province which was full at that time of likely young men and passionately devoted to war, provided that pay was to be earned or plunder picked up. Here there was a second engagement, and each side fared as before: more than 13,000 of the enemy were killed, over 2,000 taken prisoner, forty-two standards captured and nine elephants.

After this second victory nearly all the Spanish tribes came over to the Romans. Much more was achieved in Spain during that summer than in Italy.

# BOOK XXIV

1. Hanno returned to Bruttium from Campania,[1] and with the assistance of the Bruttians, who also acted as his guides, began to move against the Greek communities there. These towns were the more inclined to remain loyal to Rome in that they saw that the Bruttians, whom they feared and hated, had gone over to Carthage. Rhegium was the first to be attacked, but without success and several days were wasted in the attempt. Meanwhile the people of Locri were hurriedly bringing in grain and timber and other necessities from the farms and fields, both to supply their own needs and to prevent anything of value from falling into enemy hands; every day an increasing stream of them poured out of the town in every direction, until only some 600 were left for the essential duty of repairing the walls and gates and collecting a store of weapons on the battlements. The others, a motley crowd of all ages and classes, most of them unarmed, were scattered all over the countryside, when Hamilcar sent out some mounted troops against them with orders not to hurt anyone but merely to block the way if they attempted to escape back into the town. Hamilcar himself occupied some high ground which gave him a good view of the town and the surrounding country, and ordered a cohort of Bruttians to move close up to the walls and invite the leading men to come out and parley, and by promising Hannibal's friendship to persuade them to put the town into his hands. The parley took place, but nobody believed a word the Bruttians said; but when the Carthaginians were seen on the high ground and a few fugitives began to come in with the report that the whole population out there in the fields were in the enemy's power, the Locrian leaders were sufficiently alarmed to say that they would lay the proposal before the people. An assembly was immediately called. In the course of it the light-weights expressed the usual frivolous preference for change and the new alliance; those who had relatives cut off and prevented from

1. See p. 225.

getting back to the town felt they had given hostages to the enemy and had no freedom of choice in consequence; while a few, though in their hearts they approved of remaining loyal to Rome, did not venture openly to recommend it. The result was that there was apparent unanimity for surrender to Carthage. They secretly escorted Atilius, the commander of the Roman garrison, and his troops down to the harbour, put them aboard ship for Rhegium, and admitted Hamilcar and the Carthaginians into the town on the condition that an equitable treaty should immediately be drawn up between them. The promise of fair terms was given but very nearly not kept, when the Carthaginians accused the Locrians of having treacherously allowed Atilius to slip away, while the Locrians, in their turn, tried to make out that he had escaped on his own initiative. Some horsemen went after him, on the chance that the current in the Straits might hold up his ships or force them ashore, but they failed to catch their quarry. They did however see some other vessels crossing the Straits from Messana and making for Rhegium: they were the Roman troops sent by the praetor Claudius to hold the town. The siege of Rhegium was in consequence at once abandoned.

By Hannibal's orders peace was granted to the Locrians, with the promise of complete independence: it was agreed that Carthaginians should have the right of entry into the town and that the harbour should be controlled by the Locrians; further, that the alliance should include the obligation upon each party to assist the other in peace and war.

2. These were the circumstances which led to the withdrawal of the Carthaginians from the Straits – to the extreme annoyance of the Bruttians, who had looked forward to looting Rhegium and Locri, now left untouched by the Carthaginians' departure. To make up for their disappointment they enrolled and equipped 15,000 of their compatriots and went off on their own to attack Croton, another Greek town on the coast, in the confident hope that their resources would be enormously increased if they got possession of a coastal town with a good harbour and strong defences. One thing worried them, however: namely, that they did not quite dare not to ask for Carthaginian help, lest they should seem to have acted improperly towards

an ally, whereas if the Carthaginians once again appeared as arbiters of peace rather than helpers in war, the attempt to 'liberate' Croton would prove a failure, as at Locri. They decided therefore to send a delegation to Hannibal and to obtain his assurance that Croton, if it were recovered, should belong to the Bruttians. Hannibal replied that that was a matter to be determined by the men on the spot, so the envoys were referred back to Hanno, from whom they obtained no definite promise. Hanno did not want a famous and wealthy city like Croton to be sacked, and he hoped that its people would come over to him all the more readily when they found the Bruttians attacking them and the Carthaginians obviously neither aiding nor approving the attempt.

Amongst the people of Croton there was no common purpose or unanimity of feeling. All the Italian communities were sick of the same disease – the split between the lower orders and the nobility, the senate supporting Rome, the commons working in the Carthaginian interest.[1] The existence of this division in Croton was reported to the Bruttians by a deserter, who told them that the leader of the populace, and the man who urged turning the city over to Hannibal, was a certain Aristomachus; much of the city, he said, was uninhabited; the walls covered a large area and ran in many directions; the senators had placed guards only at wide intervals, and there would be easy entrance at any point where the guards belonged to the popular party. The Bruttians acted on the deserter's information, and taking him as a guide they surrounded the town. They were admitted by the commons and without opposition gained possession of the whole town except for the citadel, which was held by the aristocrats who had previously prepared it as a refuge in an emergency of this kind. Aristomachus also fled for refuge there, pretending that he had advised the surrender of the city not to the Bruttians but to the Carthaginians.

3. Before Pyrrhus's invasion of Italy Croton had a wall twelve miles in circumference; but after the devastation caused by that war hardly half of it remained inhabited.[2] The river

1. Livy exaggerates this.
2. Less than 2,000 inhabitants: see p. 205.

which had formerly flowed through the centre of the town was then beyond the thickly inhabited area, and that area was itself far removed from the citadel. Six miles from this famous place there was a temple dedicated to Lacinian Juno, a building more famous even than the city itself and held in reverence by all the peoples of the neighbourhood.[1] It had an enclosure surrounded by dense woodland, with lofty firs, and, in the centre, rich grassland where cattle of all kinds, sacred to the goddess, grazed without any shepherd to attend them. At night the various flocks and herds used to return each to their own stalls, unharmed by lurking beasts of prey or marauding men. Thus a great deal of money was made out of these cattle, and from the profits a column of solid gold was dedicated to the goddess. The temple, too, was as famous for its wealth as for its sanctity, and, as often happens with well-known places, stories of supernatural things are connected with it: for instance, it is said that in the entrance court there is an altar on which the ashes are never stirred by wind.

The citadel of Croton falls sheer to the sea on one side, and on the other, landward, side slopes down more gently; formerly its strength was in its natural situation only, but in later times it was given the additional protection of a wall covering the section where, along the cliffs on the further side, Dionysius, the tyrant of Sicily, had treacherously attacked and captured it. It was in this stronghold, then, that the governing class of Croton were maintaining themselves, and it seemed safe enough even though they were beleaguered by their own people as well as by the Bruttians.

As time went on and the Bruttians realized that they had not the resources to take the citadel by storm, they were compelled to ask Hanno for assistance. In reply, Hanno tried to induce the Crotonians to surrender on condition of their allowing Bruttian settlers into the town, by which means they might make good the ravages of former wars and restore the population to its old numbers. Nobody, however, but Aristomachus would listen to the proposal; the rest repeatedly declared that they would rather die than permit an admixture of Bruttian

1. Here Polybius saw Hannibal's inscription in Latin and Punic recording his achievements. Polybius III: 33: 18. See p. 12 and p. 564.

blood to bring about the gradual adoption of rites, customs, laws, and ultimately even the language of an alien people. Aristomachus, therefore, having failed by persuasion to bring about surrender, and unable to find means of betraying the citadel as he had betrayed the city, went over to Hanno by himself. Soon afterwards envoys from Locri entered the citadel with Hanno's consent, and persuaded the people not to hang on to the bitter end but to allow themselves to be transferred to Locri. The Locrians had already sent a delegation to Hannibal and obtained his permission for this proceeding. Thus Croton was evacuated. The governing class were escorted down from the citadel to the sea, where they went aboard ship, and the entire population, commons included, migrated to Locri.

In Apulia even the winter was not wholly without activity. The consul Gracchus was wintering at Luceria, Hannibal near Arpi, and skirmishes took place between them as occasion offered, and as one side or the other seemed to see an advantage. The Romans' efficiency improved in consequence; they became progressively more cautious and less liable to be caught off their guard.

4. In Sicily the situation had been fundamentally changed by the death of Hiero and the transference of power to his grandson Hieronymus, who was hardly yet of an age to bear with any sort of decency even the ordinary responsibilities of an adult, let alone the burden of absolute monarchy. Such as he was, guardians and friends had taken him over only to tumble him headlong into a sink of iniquity. Hiero towards the end of his long life had foreseen the danger, and he is said to have wished to leave Syracuse a free community, to prevent his kingdom, won and built up over the years by honest means and sound government, from falling to pieces in the hands of a boy and becoming a mere mockery. His intention was, however, violently opposed by his daughters, who looked forward to a time when the boy would be nominally king but the actual power would be wholly in their own hands and in the hands of their husbands, Adranodorus and Zoippus, who were being left the principal guardians. It had not been easy for a man in his ninetieth year, surrounded, as Hiero was, day and night by feminine blandishments, to free his mind from its

concern with the personal and turn it to public affairs. So it was for this reason that he left the boy fifteen guardians, begging them on his death-bed to maintain inviolate the loyalty which for fifty years he had preserved towards Rome and to persuade his young successor to follow in his footsteps and continue for him the moral and intellectual training in which he had been brought up.

After his death the guardians produced the will and had the boy (then about fifteen years old) brought before an assembly of the people. A few men who had been specially placed here and there amongst the crowd to lead the applause expressed approval of the will, but the general feeling was fear for what the future might bring now that the father of them all was dead and the country orphaned. In these circumstances the guardians assumed their duties and the royal funeral took place – more remarkable for the love of Hiero's subjects than for the grief of his own family. Soon afterwards Adranodorus got rid of the other guardians, professing to believe that Hieronymus was now old enough to assume power, then by resigning his own guardianship, which he had shared with a number of others, he got, in effect, the power of all of them into his own hands.

5. It would not have been easy for any king, even for one who ruled well and justly, to find favour with the Syracusans after Hiero, who had been so well beloved. But Hieronymus on his very first appearance showed how sadly things had changed. It was as if he were deliberately vicious in order to make people wish his grandfather back again. For many years the Syracusans had known Hiero and his son Gelo dressed like themselves and distinguished by no outward mark of royalty, and now they saw the royal purple, the diadem, the armed attendants – even, at times, the young king driving from the palace behind four white horses, like Dionysius the tyrant of old. All this outward show of regal dress and appurtenances was soon followed by behaviour to match: contemptuous treatment of everybody, haughty refusal to listen to advice or complaint, insolent speech, denial of access not only to outsiders but even to his former guardians, strange forms of lust, inhuman cruelty. The result was such universal terror that some of the guardians anticipated the punishment they expected by either flight or suicide. There

were three, however, Adranodorus, Zoippus, Hiero's son-in-law, and Thraso, who had access to the palace on more or less familiar terms; these men were not, indeed, much listened to in the ordinary course of things, but as two of them were inclined to the Carthaginian interest while Thraso supported the Roman alliance, the clash of their political interests and the disputes between them occasionally drew the attention of the young king. Then, one day, information of a plot against the king's life was brought by one Callo, a boy of the same age as Hieronymus and already for most of his life on the most intimate terms with him. The informer was able to name only one of the conspirators, Theodotus, by whom he had himself been approached. Theodotus was immediately arrested and handed over for torture to Adranodorus, but, though he quickly admitted his own guilt he refused to reveal his accomplices. Finally, subjected to torments beyond human endurance, he pretended to succumb to his suffering and to give the information required: none the less he still concealed the names of his actual accomplices and named innocent men instead, falsely declaring that the instigator of the plot was Thraso and that they would never have risked such an undertaking without the support of so powerful a leader. He added the names of some of the tyrant's attendants, men of no importance whom he picked upon almost at random, as they occurred to him in his agony. The mention of Thraso, more than anything, induced the tyrant to believe the information; he was at once handed over to the executioner and the others, equally innocent, suffered the same punishment. Not one of the actual conspirators, though their associate was for a long time in the torturer's hands, either hid or fled – so great was their confidence in the courage and loyalty of Theodotus, and so great Theodotus's own determination to keep their secret.

6. With the removal of Thraso the one remaining link with the Roman alliance was broken, and from that moment there could be little doubt that revolt would come. Envoys were sent to Hannibal, who, in his turn, sent back in company with a young nobleman, his namesake, two representatives, Hippocrates and Epicydes, both born in Carthage and Carthaginian on their mothers' side, though Syracusan in origin, their

grandfather being an exile. These men negotiated an alliance between Hannibal and Hieronymus, and with Hannibal's permission remained in Syracuse.

Appius Claudius, the praetor in charge of Sicilian affairs, at once sent envoys to Hieronymus when he heard this news; they were openly laughed at when they said they had come to renew the alliance which had existed with his grandfather; and Hieronymus dismissed them with the ironic question of how they had fared at the battle of Cannae – as the story told by Hannibal's envoys was difficult to believe. 'For I should like,' he added, 'to know the truth, as only so can I determine which side to base my hopes upon.' The Romans said they would visit him again when he began to listen seriously to embassies, and left him with what was a warning rather than a request not to change his allegiance too lightly. Hieronymus then sent a delegation to Carthage to negotiate the terms of the alliance, and it was agreed that when they had driven the Romans from Sicily – which would be quickly done if Carthage sent the men and the ships – the river Himera which divides the island more or less into two should form the boundary between the Syracusan kingdom and the Carthaginian dominion. Hieronymus later sent a second delegation, blown up as he was by the windy flattery of men who urged him to remember not only Hiero but also King Pyrrhus, his maternal grandfather. This time his envoys were instructed to say that he thought it fair that the whole of Sicily should pass into his hands, leaving Carthage to acquire her own empire in Italy. The Carthaginians felt no surprise at such frivolity and conceit in a wild young man; nor did they wish to censure his attitude provided they could make him break with Rome.

7. But the gulf was already yawning before Hieronymus's feet. He had sent Hippocrates and Epicydes, each with a force 2,000 strong, to attack the towns held by the Romans, and had himself with the rest of his army – in all some 15,000 foot and horse – proceeded to Leontini. Here the men who had plotted to kill him – they were all serving with the forces – took possession of an empty house overlooking a narrow street by which the king used to go down to the forum. The plan was that the rest should wait in the house, armed and ready, for the

king to pass, while to one of them as a member of the king's bodyguard – his name was Dinomenes – was assigned the task of finding some means of holding up the crowds of people walking behind the king just as, in the narrow street, he was approaching the door. All went according to plan: Dinomenes pretended his shoe was tied too tightly and raised his foot to loosen the knot; this stopped the crowd and enabled the king to go so far in front of them that as he passed the house without any guards the attack was made on him, and he was stabbed in several places before help could arrive. There were cries of alarm, and a moment later it was obvious that Dinomenes was deliberately blocking the way. Spears were hurled at him, but, though wounded in two places, he escaped. The king's attendants, seeing him prostrate on the ground, fled; of the conspirators, some made their way to where the crowds in the forum were rejoicing over their liberty, others hurried to Syracuse to forestall any steps which might be taken by Adranodorus and the other supporters of the king.

In this confused situation Appius Claudius, who being on the spot could see that war was coming, informed the Senate by letter that Sicily was going over to Hannibal and Carthage; at the same time, as a precaution against any move by the Syracusans, he concentrated all his forces at the boundary between the Syracusan kingdom and the Roman-held portion of the island.

At the end of this year Quintus Fabius, on the Senate's authority, fortified and garrisoned Puteoli, a town which had grown populous during the war as a centre of exchange. On his way from there to Rome for the elections he announced them for the first date on which they could legally be held, and on his arrival proceeded direct to the Campus Martius without entering the city. On election day the right to vote first fell to the junior section of the Aniensis tribe; they named for the consulship Titus Otacilius and Marcus Aemilius Regillus, whereupon Fabius called for silence and addressed the people in the following terms. 8. 'Anyone who attempted to check the genuine enthusiasm with which you come here to confer office upon the men of your choice, would, in my view, be paying too little regard to your liberties, if Italy were at peace, or if the nature of the war we were involved in admitted any sort of carelessness. But that is not so: such is the enemy with whom we are at grips, that not once has a mistake been made by any general commanding our armies without involving us in terrible losses; and, that being so, it is your duty in the election of your consuls to vote with the same sense of responsibility as that with which you march to battle, and to say, each one of you, to himself, "I name as consul a man who is as fine a general as Hannibal."

'Earlier this year at Capua a Campanian knight of high distinction, Vibellius Taurea, issued a challenge; it was answered by a Roman knight of equal quality, Claudius Asellus. Time was when a Gaul sent us a challenge on the Anio bridge; to take it up, our fathers sent Titus Manlius, in all the confidence of his courage and strength. It was for the same knowledge of his worth, I doubt not, that, not many years later, Marcus Valerius found himself trusted when he took arms in answer to a similar challenge from a Gaul.[1] Just as we wish to have infantry and cavalry stronger than the enemy, or, at least, equal to him, so we should seek a commander who is a match for his commander.

'When we have chosen the best military officer we have, he will, immediately upon his appointment – and that for a single year only – be matched against an experienced general who holds his command indefinitely, not prevented at every turn by legal restrictions upon his period of office from conducting all operations as occasion shall demand. We, on the contrary, are always *preparing* – always starting things afresh – as the annual period comes round again.

'Very good, then: I have told you what qualities you must look for in the consuls you choose; it remains to say a few words about the men towards whom the favour of the initial vote has inclined. Marcus Aemilius Regillus is the priest of Quirinus, and we cannot either take him from his duties or keep him at home without neglecting our responsibility either for religion or for the conduct of the war. Otacilius is the husband of my niece, and there are children of the marriage; but the generosity you have shown to me and to my ancestors is too great to allow

1. These stories are told by Livy in Book VII, ch. 10 and ch. 26.

me to put the ties of kinship before my duty to the country. Anyone – sailor or passenger – can steer a ship when the sea is calm; but when it starts to blow and the waves rise and the vessel drives before the storm, a helmsman is needed who is a man indeed. It is on no tranquil sea that we are sailing now; already in more than one tempest we have come near to sinking; therefore we must use all possible diligence and foresight in deciding who shall sit at the helm.

'In certain minor enterprises, Otacilius, we have already given you a trial, but you have certainly not offered any obvious reason why we should trust you in greater things. The fleet you commanded this year was put into commission for three purposes: to raid the African coast, to protect the coast of Italy, and, most particularly, to prevent reinforcements, together with money and provisions, from reaching Hannibal from Carthage.

'Men of Rome, if Otacilius has rendered his country I will not say all, but any single one, of these services, then elect him consul; but if, Otacilius, during your command even such things as Hannibal did not need reached him as safe and sound as if he had cleared the sea of his enemies; if the Italian coast has had more dangers for us this year than the coast of Africa; can you then give any reason why we should choose you, of all men, to lead us against such a foe as Hannibal? If you were consul, we should follow precedent and propose the appointment of a dictator; nor would you have any right to be angry because someone in Rome was considered a better soldier than yourself. That a burden too heavy to bear should not be laid upon your shoulders is to no one's advantage more than to your own.

'Citizens of Rome, my most earnest advice to you is this: imagine you are standing armed for battle, and have suddenly to choose two men under whose command, with heaven's help, you are to fight; then, in the spirit with which you would choose them, choose now the consuls to whom your sons shall swear the oath, by whose edict they shall assemble, under whose care and protection they shall serve. It is a bitter thing to remember Trasimene and Cannae; but they are a warning to beware of similar disasters in the future.

'Herald, call the Junior Century of Aniensis to vote again.'

9. Otacilius did his best to make a scene, shouting at the top of his voice that Fabius only wanted to continue his own consulship for another term, and Fabius, in reply, ordered up his lictors and warned him that, as he had not entered the city but had proceeded straight to the Campus Martius, the consular *fasces* still had their axes.[1] Then the leading century voted again, with the result that the successful candidates were Quintus Fabius Maximus (for the fourth time) and Marcus Marcellus (for the third). The other centuries unanimously followed the lead and named the same two men. One praetor, Fulvius Flaccus, was re-elected and three new ones appointed – Titus Otacilius Crassus (for the second time), Quintus Fabius, the consul's son, who was then a curule aedile, and Publius Cornelius Lentulus.

The election of praetors completed, the Senate decreed that Flaccus, without recourse to the usual drawing of lots, should assume the duties of City praetor and be in charge of the city when the consuls were away on active service.

There were two bad floods that year, when the Tiber overflowed its banks and caused much damage to farm buildings and serious loss of life amongst men and cattle.

In the fifth year, then, of the Second Punic War, Quintus Fabius Maximus entered upon his fourth consulship and Marcus Claudius Marcellus upon his third. Both men had won for themselves unusual respect and affection, and indeed for many years past so distinguished a pair had not held office. To older men they recalled the appointment of Maximus Rullus and Publius Decius for the Gallic war, and later of Papirius and Carvilius for the wars with Samnium, Bruttium, Lucania, and Tarentum. Marcellus was elected in his absence, as he was with his army; Fabius, when re-appointed for a further year, was of course present and actually presiding at the elections. In view of the critical situation and the pressing needs of the war nobody felt bound to seek a precedent for his re-election or suspected him of a dangerous lust for power; on the contrary, people praised the greatness of spirit which allowed him, knowing as he did that the country needed a supreme soldier

1. The removal of the axes from the 'rods' when a consul entered the City indicated that his sentence was subject to appeal. (A. de S.)

and that he himself was undoubtedly the man, to rate his own unpopularity, if there were any, as of less importance than the public advantage.

10. On the day when the new consuls took office, the Senate met on the Capitol. Their first act was to issue an order that the consuls should decide, either by lot or by mutual agreement, which of them should preside at the election of censors before leaving to join his troops. It was then determined to continue the commands of all army-commanders then with their troops, and orders were given them to remain in their various stations, or theatres of operation – Gracchus at Luceria with his force of slave-volunteers, Varro in Picenum, Pomponius in Gaul. Next, of the praetors of the previous year, now pro-praetors, Quintus Mucius was to hold Sardinia, and Marcus Valerius to take command of the coast at Brundisium keeping a careful watch for any move by Philip King of Macedon. Sicily was assigned to the praetor Publius Cornelius Lentulus, and Otacilius was entrusted with the fleet he had commanded against the Carthaginians the previous year.

During the course of this year there were many reports of prodigies – and the stories of them grew in number the more they were believed in by simple and superstitious people. At Lanuvium crows nested in the shrine of Juno Sospita; a young green vineshoot burst into flames in Apulia; at Mantua a swamp where the river Mincius had overflowed was seen to be coloured with blood; it rained chalk at Cales and in the cattle-market of Rome it rained blood; a subterranean spring on the Vicus Insteius welled up with such a volume of water that it overturned, as with the force of a torrent, and swept away some jars which were standing there; the Atrium Publicum on the Capitol was struck by lightning, as were the shrine of Vulcan in the Campus Martius, the temple of Vacuna and a public road in the Sabine district, a wall, and a gate at Gabii. There was also talk of other unnatural phenomena: the spear belonging to the statue of Mars at Praeneste was said to have moved forward of its own accord; an ox in Sicily talked; amongst the Marrucini a child in the womb shouted 'Hurrah!'; at Spoletium a woman changed her sex; at Hadria an altar appeared in the sky with men in white robes standing round it. In Rome too, actually in the city, after a swarm of bees had been noticed in the forum, there were people who were so sure that they saw soldiers in arms on the Janiculum that they gave the alarm, though all who were actually on the Janiculum denied that anyone had been seen there except the regular occupants. On the advice of the soothsayers propitiatory rites, with full-grown sacrificial victims, were performed, and an edict was issued for a period of prayer to all the gods who had festal couches in Rome.

11. With the gods propitiated, and the needs of religion satisfied, the consuls proceeded to business and laid before the Senate their proposals for the strength and location of the various forces needed for the conduct of the war. It was decided to put a total of eighteen legions into the field;[1] each consul was to take two; two each were to be detailed for the defence of Gaul, Sicily, and Sardinia; the praetor Fabius was to command two in Apulia, and Gracchus his two slave-volunteer legions at Luceria; one was to be assigned to the proconsul Varro in Picenum, one to Valerius for service with the fleet at Brundisium, and two to be left in Rome for home defence. To make up this number of legions six new ones were to be enrolled. The consuls were instructed to enrol them at the first available moment and to bring the fleet, including the vessels stationed for the defence of the Calabrian litoral, to a total number of 150 ships of war. When the levy had been held and 100 new ships launched, Fabius presided at the election of censors. The successful candidates were Marcus Atilius Regulus and Publius Furius Philus.

As more news kept coming in of hostilities in Sicily, Otacilius was ordered to the island with the vessels under his command. In view of the shortage of crews, the consuls on the Senate's authority issued an edict to the effect that anyone whose property, or whose father's property, had been assessed during the censorship of Aemilius and Flaminius at anything between 50,000 and 100,000 *asses*, or whose assets had subsequently increased to that figure, should furnish one sailor with six months' pay; those assessed at over 100,000 and up to 300,000 were to furnish three sailors with a year's pay; those whose

1. Not counting those in Spain.

assets were between 300,000 and 1,000,000 were to make themselves responsible for five sailors, and those with more than a million, for seven.[1] Senators were to furnish eight sailors with a year's pay. The additional crews thus raised joined their ships armed and equipped by their masters and with cooked rations for thirty days. This was the first occasion on which a Roman fleet was provided with crews at the expense of private individuals.

12. Preparations on this unwonted scale especially alarmed the Campanians, who were afraid the Romans might begin the year's campaigning by a siege of Capua. Accordingly they sent a delegation to Hannibal with an earnest request that he should move troops up to the town; fresh troops, they declared, were being raised for the express purpose of attacking it, and its defection had been a worse blow to the Romans than that of any other allied community. All this was said in such a flurry of excitement and alarm that Hannibal felt that no time was to be lost if the Romans were not to forestall him; so he left Arpi and took up a position in his old camp at Tifata, above Capua. There he left his Numidian and Spanish contingents to guard the camp and the town, and himself proceeded with the rest of his force down to the lake of Avernus, ostensibly to offer sacrifice there but with the actual intention of attacking Puteoli and its garrison. When Fabius learned that Hannibal had left Arpi and was on his way back into Campania, he rejoined his troops immediately, travelling day and night, sent orders to Gracchus to bring his force to Beneventum, and instructed his son to relieve Gracchus at Luceria. At the same time the two praetors left for Sicily, Publius Cornelius to the army and Otacilius to take command of the coast and to direct naval operations. The other officers also left for their several theatres of war, and all whose command had been continued for a further period kept control of the same regions as in the previous year.

13. While Hannibal was at the lake of Avernus five young noblemen from Tarentum sought an interview with him. Some of them had been taken prisoner at Trasimene, some at Cannae,

1. The value of the *as* may be taken, very roughly, as rather less than one penny. (A. de S.)

and all had been sent home with the consideration which Hannibal had consistently shown towards the communities allied to Rome. They told Hannibal that they had not forgotten his kindness and that in return for it they had prevailed upon most of the younger men in Tarentum to agree that friendship and alliance with him would be a better thing for them than to remain dependent upon Rome. They had, they said, a commission from their people to ask Hannibal to move troops nearer Tarentum; for if his camp and his standards were visible from the town it would be promptly surrendered. The government, they added, was in the hands of the common people, who, in their turn, submitted to the direction of the younger men. Hannibal expressed his thanks, loaded his visitors with splendid promises, and told them to return home to hasten the execution of their design, assuring them that he would be there when the time was ripe. With these high hopes the five Tarentines were dismissed.

Hannibal himself was passionately eager to get possession of Tarentum. Not only was it a wealthy and famous town, but it was also a seaport and conveniently situated, facing Macedonia; King Philip would certainly use it if he crossed into Italy, as the Romans held Brundisium.

Meanwhile having performed the sacrifice which was the ostensible reason for his visit, and having devastated, while he was in the neighbourhood, the territory of Cumae as far as Cape Misenum, Hannibal made a sudden dash for Puteoli, hoping to surprise the Roman garrison. The garrison was 6,000 strong, and the place was well defended, having fortifications as well as a good natural position. Hannibal spent three days before it, probing the defences from every side, but without any success; then, in sheer irritation rather than with any hope of taking the town, he proceeded to devastate the country around Naples.

His arrival in the neighbourhood roused to action the commons of Nola who had long been averse to the Roman alliance and hostile to their own government. Representatives accordingly came with an invitation to Hannibal and a firm promise that the town would be surrendered to him. The consul Marcellus, however, was called in by the leading men and forestalled the attempt; he had covered the distance from Cales to Suessula in one day in spite of the delay caused by the crossing of the Volturnus, and from there he sent 6,000 foot and 300 horse the same night into Nola to support the senatorial party. The vigour and promptitude which enabled Marcellus to be first into the town was as marked as the dilatoriness of Hannibal, whom two previous failures had made less ready to believe what the people of Nola told him.

14. Meanwhile the consul Fabius was planning an attack on Casilinum, then in Carthaginian hands, and at Beneventum, too, events were moving. As if by pre-arrangement, Hanno from Bruttium with a strong force of infantry and cavalry, and Gracchus from Luceria converged upon the town. Gracchus, on his arrival, entered the town, but then, when he learned that Hanno was in position about three miles away on the river Calor and from that base was devastating the countryside, he marched out again and encamped a mile or so from the enemy, and delivered an address to his men. His troops consisted largely of slave-volunteers, men who for two years past had preferred silently to earn their liberty rather than openly to demand it; nevertheless, on leaving winter quarters, he had been aware of dissatisfaction and of the muttered question when, if ever, they were to serve as free citizens. He had written to the Senate, stressing not so much what the men wanted as what their conduct deserved, and saying that up to that time he had had consistently good service from them, and that all they now lacked to make them real soldiers of their country was liberty. The Senate replied that he might deal with the situation in any way he thought advantageous to the common interest. On the present occasion, therefore, before engaging with the enemy, he announced that the moment had come for his troops to win the freedom they had so long hoped for. 'Tomorrow,' he said, 'I shall be fighting a battle hand to hand, on clear and open ground; there will be no fear of hidden traps, and mere valour will decide the issue. My order now is that any man who brings from the field an enemy's head shall at once be given his freedom; whoever abandons his post will be punished like a slave. Each of you therefore has his future in his own hands. The granting of your liberty will be due not to me only, but to the consul

Marcellus and the unanimous consent of the Senate, who upon my request have authorized me to act in this way.'

With this, he read to the troops the consul's letter and the Senate's decree, which were greeted with a cheer and the most enthusiastic approval. All demanded action and with high hearts urged that the signal should be given forthwith, and Gracchus, announcing that tomorrow would be the day, dismissed them. The soldiers were happy men, especially those for whom freedom would be the reward of one day's good work, and spent what remained of that day in seeing that their arms and equipment were in order.

15. Next morning when the trumpets began to sound, these men were the first to assemble, all prepared and in formation, at headquarters. After sunrise Gracchus drew up his battle-line in the open ground outside the camp, and the enemy were not slow to accept the challenge. They had 17,000 infantrymen, mostly Bruttians and Lucanians, and 1,200 cavalry, of whom only a few were Italian and the rest nearly all either Numidian or Moorish. The struggle was fierce and prolonged, and for four hours neither side had the advantage. What more than anything told against the Romans was the fact of the severed heads having been made the price of liberty; for whenever a Roman soldier had, with a vigorous thrust, killed his man, he wasted time in the task, awkward enough in the seething mass around him, of cutting off the head; and then, too, his right hand was out of action through having to carry it, so that the finest soldiers were incapacitated for further fighting, which was left to their more laggard and timid comrades. The military tribunes reported this state of affairs to Gracchus; how the men were so much occupied in chopping up the dead that they were making no attempt upon any of the enemy who were still on their feet, and how human heads had taken the place of swords in the soldiers' hands; whereupon Gracchus instantly gave the order to drop the heads and attack, for the men's valour had already been clearly proved and if they did not slacken their efforts their liberty was assured.

On this the fighting once again flared up. The Roman cavalry was ordered forward; and as it met with spirited resistance from the Numidians, and the cavalry of both sides became as hotly engaged as the infantry, the issue was once more uncertain. Both the rival commanders tried to drive their men to greater effort, Gracchus taunting the Bruttians and Lucanians who had so often been beaten to their knees by the Romans of old, Hanno pouring abuse upon the Roman gaolbirds and slaves masquerading as soldiers, until at last Gracchus proclaimed that not a man of his could hope for freedom unless the enemy that day were utterly defeated. 16. Those words were the torch which finally set them on fire: the battle-cry rang out afresh, they were different men, and attacked with such fury that the shock was irresistible. The Carthaginian van shivered and broke, then the support-lines around the standards, and finally their whole front was driven in. After that it was a clean rout: they fled for their lives to their camp in such alarm and confusion that not a single man turned to resist at the gates or on the rampart, and the Romans following hard on their heels found themselves engaged in a second struggle inside the Carthaginian defences. There, jammed as they were in a confined space without room to manoeuvre, the slaughter was yet more savage than before. The Romans were, moreover, helped by the prisoners, who took advantage of the confusion to seize weapons and, advancing in a solid mass, cut the Carthaginians down from behind and prevented the rest from getting away. Out of Hanno's large force fewer than two thousand escaped alive; most of them were cavalry and included the commander. All the others were either killed or captured. Thirty-eight standards were taken. The victors' losses amounted to about 2,000. All captured material was turned over to the troops, except prisoners of war and such cattle as might be identified by the owners within thirty days.

When the army had returned to camp loaded with its spoils, some 4,000 of the slave-volunteers who had done less than their duty in the fight and had not followed their comrades into the Carthaginian camp, went off, in fear of punishment, to a near-by hill. Next day they were brought down by the military tribunes and arrived in camp after a parade had been ordered by Gracchus. At the parade the proconsul began by decorating the veteran soldiers, each according to his valour and service in the battle, and then turned to the volunteers: as to them, he said, he would prefer to thank them all, whether they deserved it or not, rather than have any man punished that day. 'By my orders,' he declared 'every one of you is now a free man – and may it bring blessings and prosperity and happiness upon our country, and upon yourselves.'

A burst of enthusiastic cheering followed these words; the men embraced, they congratulated one another, they raised their hands to heaven in prayer for Rome and for their beloved general. But soon Gracchus intervened: 'Before I made you equal,' he said, 'by giving you the privileges of freedom, I did not wish to mark any man amongst you as a good soldier or a bad; but now that I have kept the promise made you in our country's name, it is not right that all distinction between courage and cowardice should be lost. My orders therefore are that the names should be reported to me of all those who were driven just now to leave us by their guilty consciousness of duty shirked. I shall then call out each man in turn and make him swear that, short of sickness as an excuse, he will never, so long as his service lasts, sit down to his supper, but take his food and drink standing. You will hardly object to this punishment, if you reflect that, as a mark of cowardice, it could not have been less severe.' He then gave the signal to pack the gear in preparation for marching, and the soldiers, carrying their booty and driving before them such captured cattle as they were allowed to keep, returned to Beneventum laughing and joking and so full of high spirits that they might have been going home after a banquet at some national holiday rather than from the field of battle.

The people of Beneventum came flocking out to meet them at the gates, embraced them, congratulated them, and offered them hospitality. Meals had been laid out in the open courts of every house, and the townsfolk invited the soldiers to partake of them, begging Gracchus to give them permission to make a regular feast of it. Gracchus consented, but stipulated that the feasts should take place outside, before the doors of the houses. So everything was brought out, and the slave-volunteers – slaves no longer, but all now wearing the cap of liberty or white woollen headbands – began to regale themselves, some reclining, others on their feet serving and eating at the same time.

Gracchus thought the occasion deserved permanent record, and when he was back in Rome he ordered a picture to be painted of that festal day; the picture was housed in the temple of Liberty, which his father had dedicated on the Aventine, having had it built with money collected from fines.

17. During these events at Beneventum Hannibal moved up to Nola after causing great destruction to the country around Naples. As soon as Marcellus was aware of his approach he sent for the pro-praetor Pomponius and the troops in the camp above Suessula and prepared to encounter the enemy and force an engagement. He ordered Gaius Claudius Nero to take a picked detachment of cavalry in the dead of night through the gate furthest from the enemy position, ride round in a wide detour, taking care not to be seen, to the enemy's rear, and to follow cautiously in his tracks; then, when the two armies were engaged, to block his retreat. This order Nero failed to carry out, though for what reason is not clear; perhaps he lost his way, or it may be that he had insufficient time. In any case, the fight began without him, and there was no doubt that the advantage lay with the Romans; nevertheless the failure of the cavalry contingent to arrive in time upset the prearranged plan. Though the enemy were forced back, Marcellus did not like to press the pursuit, but gave his victorious troops the order to retire. Even so, the enemy casualties are said to have amounted to 2,000 dead, the Romans losing less than 400. Nero returned to camp round about sunset; by riding all day and the previous night he had exhausted his men and horses to no purpose, and had not even glimpsed the enemy. The consul censured him in the strongest terms, even going so far as to say that, but for his failure, the enemy might have been paid in full for the disaster at Cannae.

Next day Marcellus again took up position for battle, but Hannibal remained in camp – a tacit admission of defeat. On the day after that he abandoned hope of taking Nola, an enterprise never yet attended with success, and in the dead of night set off on his march to Tarentum, where his hopes of having the town betrayed into his hands were better founded.

18. Meanwhile the vigour of military operations was matched in Rome by the attention to domestic affairs. As the treasury

was empty and the censors, in consequence, freed from the duty of placing contracts for public building, they turned instead to the regulation of morals and the punishment of vicious practices which had been produced by the war, much as physical defects are produced in a man's body by chronic disease. Their first act was to summon those who, after Cannae, were said to have considered abandoning their country and going abroad. The chief of them, Lucius Caecilius Metellus, was quaestor at the time; he and the others charged with the same crime were ordered to defend themselves; they failed to establish their innocence, and the censors gave as their verdict that they had spoken, both in public and private, against the interests of the state, with the object of forming a conspiracy to abandon Italy. Next to be summoned were the men who had put an over-subtle interpretation upon the meaning of an oath – the prisoners, namely, who after leaving Hannibal's camp secretly went back again and pretended to think that by so doing they had kept their oath to return. These men and those mentioned above were deprived of their horses – if they had them provided by the state – and were removed from their tribes and degraded to the *aerarii* – the lowest class of citizens without the right of voting or holding office. Nor did the censors confine their scrutiny to members of the Senate or the order of knights: from the lists of the younger men they took the names of all those who had not served in the army during the past four years and had no regular exemption or were not disqualified by sickness. Of these more than 2,000 were degraded to the class of *aerarii*, and all were expelled from their tribes. On top of this cruel stigma inflicted by the censors came a decree of the Senate, no less harsh, to the effect that all the men made an example of by the censors should serve as foot-soldiers and be sent to Sicily to join the survivors of Cannae. These troops were not due to be released from service until the enemy had been driven from Italy.

In these circumstances, when lack of funds was preventing the censors from contracting for the upkeep of sacred buildings, for the provision of horses used in public religious processions, and for other things of the kind, numbers of men who were in the habit of accepting such contracts came in a body to the censors and urged them to carry on with the normal financial arrangements just as if there were funds in the treasury, and undertook that not one of them would seek payment until the war was over. They were followed by the owners of the slaves whom Gracchus had freed at Beneventum: these, in their turn, said they had been called upon by the bank commissioners to accept payment for the slaves, but refused to do so before the end of the war. Such being the general inclination towards relieving the financial difficulties of the state, the next thing was that funds held for the benefit of wards and of widows began to be brought in, those who deposited them believing that they could nowhere find better or more inviolable security than under the guarantee of the state. Thereafter, when anything was purchased or acquired for a ward or a widow, it was paid for by a note of hand from a quaestor. This generous behaviour, begun by private individuals, spread to the army in the field: no cavalryman or centurion accepted pay – and if any did, he was contemptuously called a mercenary.

19. The consul Fabius was lying at Casilinum, which was held by 2,000 Campanians and 700 of Hannibal's soldiers. Statius Metius was in command there; he had been sent by the *medix tuticus*[1] of that year, Gnaeus Magius of Atella, and he was arming everybody, populace and slaves alike, with the intention of attacking the Roman camp while the consul was occupied with the siege. Fabius, who was fully aware of the position, sent word to his colleague at Nola that, while the siege was in progress, he had need of another army to deal with the Campanians. Either, therefore, Marcellus must leave an adequate garrison at Nola and come in person, or, if that were impracticable and there were still a threat to Nola from Hannibal, he would send for the proconsul Gracchus from Beneventum. Marcellus, on receiving the message, left a garrison of 2,000 men in Nola and proceeded with the rest of his force to Casilinum, where his arrival put a stop to the movements already begun by the Campanians.

The siege of Casilinum by the two consuls had now begun. The Romans by approaching the walls of the town without due caution were soon suffering numerous casualties, so, as the

1. The chief magistrate. cf. p. 213.

operation was not progressing satisfactorily, Fabius judged that it would be best to abandon it. It was, he argued, a small affair in itself, though as difficult as any, and the wisest course would be to leave the place, as matters of greater moment were impending. Marcellus disagreed. Maintaining that though there were plenty of things a good general ought not to attempt, nevertheless once the attempt was made it ought not to be abandoned – as reputation moved quickly, up or down, according to a man's failure or success – he succeeded in persuading Fabius not to break off the operation before anything had been achieved. Mantlets, accordingly, and all the other kinds of siege apparatus were moved into position: the Campanians begged Fabius to let them go to Capua without molestation, but Marcellus, after a few had left the town, occupied the gate by which they were coming out, and an indiscriminate slaughter began, first around the gate itself and then inside the town as the troops poured in. About fifty of the Campanians who were the first out sought protection from Fabius and reached Capua under escort. Casilinum was taken during the delay caused by the application of these men for a promise of protection. All prisoners, Campanian or Carthaginian, were sent to Rome and locked up; the bulk of the population was distributed for safe keeping amongst the neighbouring communities.

20. At the time of the withdrawal of the troops from Casilinum after their successful operation, Gracchus sent certain cohorts, which had been raised in Lucania, under the command of a Prefect of the Allies to raid enemy territory. Hanno caught them off their guard, when they were in no sort of formation, and so severely mauled them that he came near to repaying the Romans for the losses they had inflicted upon him at Beneventum; after which he hurriedly withdrew into Bruttium before Gracchus could come up with him. Of the two consuls, Marcellus returned to Nola, while Fabius proceeded into Samnium to devastate the countryside and to recover the towns which had seceded from the Roman alliance. The country about Caudium received the severest treatment: farmlands were burnt over a wide area, cattle were driven off and men taken prisoner, and the settlements of Compulteria, Telesia, Compsa, Fugifulae, and Orbitanium were attacked and

captured. The Lucanian settlement of Blandae was also taken, and the Apulian town of Aecae. In these places a total of 25,000 men were either captured or killed, and 370 deserters were caught: they were sent to Rome by the consul, where they were publicly scourged in the Place of Assembly and then thrown from the Tarpeian Rock. A few days sufficed Fabius for these operations. While ill health kept Marcellus inactive at Nola, the town of Acuca was stormed and taken by the pro-praetor Fabius, who was on duty in the neighbourhood of Luceria, and a permanent camp was constructed and fortified at Ardoneae.

While the Romans were thus occupied elsewhere, Hannibal had already reached Tarentum, spreading destruction in his path; only when he arrived in Tarentine territory did he check his troops in their depredations. There, no damage was done, and the marching column was kept strictly to the road – not, indeed, from any sense of restraint either in the soldiers or in their leader, but for the obvious purpose of securing the good will of the Tarentines. However, when he was quite near the town's defences and found, contrary to his expectation, that no rising of the people greeted the sight of his approaching column, he came to a halt and pitched camp about a mile away. The fact was that, three days before his coming, the pro-praetor Valerius who commanded the fleet at Brundisium had sent Marcus Livius to organize the town's defence; Livius had enrolled all men of military age, posted guards at every gate and, wherever necessary, around the walls, and by exercising the greatest vigilance day and night left no loophole for a hostile move either by the enemy or by the possible treachery of friends. Hannibal, in consequence, was merely wasting his time, and after a few days during which not one of the men who had visited him at Lake Avernus either came to him in person or communicated with him by messenger or letter, he left the neighbourhood, realizing that he had been led, all too easily, to follow a mere empty promise. Even then he refrained from doing any damage to crops or farms, for though his pretence of lenity had produced no results as yet, he still clung to the hope of undermining the loyalty of the Tarentines to Rome.

When he reached Salapia, he had the grain brought in from the country around Metapontum and Heraclea, for summer was over and the place seemed to him a good one for wintering in. With that as his base he sent raiding parties of Numidians and Moors over Sallentine territory and into the nearest woodlands of Apulia; the raids produced little except horses: herds of them were rounded up, and some 4,000 were distributed amongst the mounted troops to be broken in.

21. Meanwhile Marcellus, one of the consuls, had been entrusted with the task of dealing with the situation in Sicily, for a war of by no means negligible importance was clearly on the way, and the murder of Hieronymus had made no difference to the attitude of the Syracusans, but had merely given them leaders ready and willing to act. The assassination had been followed by demonstrations amongst the troops in Leontini and the impassioned cry that the blood of the conspirators must be shed in atonement for the king's death. Soon, however, the delightful phrase 'liberty restored' began to be heard more and more often, and hopes grew of substantial benefits out of the dead king's money and of the chance of service under better commanders. This, added to stories of the tyrant's abominable crimes and still more abominable sexual excesses, so altered the soldiers' feelings that they allowed the body of the king they had so recently mourned to lie unburied.

All the conspirators except two had remained in Leontini to keep control of the army; the two remaining ones, Theodotus and Sosis, rode off, on the king's horses, with all possible speed to Syracuse, intending to surprise the king's supporters there before they had got wind of what had occurred. But they were too late, for not only had rumour, swiftest of all travellers in circumstances like these, outstripped them, but a slave of the king's had already arrived with the news. Adranodorus had, in consequence, already garrisoned the Island and Citadel, together with such other advantageous positions as he was able to strengthen.

Theodotus and Sosis entered the city by the Hexapylon. It was after sunset and already growing dark. They displayed the king's bloodstained mantle and his diadem, and rode on through Tyche calling the populace to arms and liberty, and bidding them assemble in Achradina.[1] People ran out into the streets, or stood staring in their doorways, or looked down from roofs and windows, asking what the excitement was about. There were lights everywhere, and confused noise and shouting. Those who had arms collected in open spaces; those who had none snatched down weapons from the temple of Olympian Jupiter – spoils taken from Gauls and Illyrians which had been presented by the Roman people to Hiero and hung by him in the building – with a prayer that Jupiter would graciously consent to give the sacred weapons into hands that were arming themselves in defence of liberty, of their country, and of the shrines of their gods. All these people were sent to strengthen the guard-posts stationed in the chief quarters of the city. In the Island Adranodorus had garrisoned, amongst other places, the public granaries; it was a place walled with squared stone and strongly fortified like a citadel, and it was taken control of by the men assigned to its defence, who then sent word into Achradina that the grain and granaries were in the council's hands.

22. At dawn next morning all the people, armed and unarmed, gathered at the council house in Achradina. There, standing in front of the Altar of Concord, Polyaenus, one of the leading citizens, delivered a speech which, though frank, was none the less moderate in tone. Men, he declared, who had experienced the terrors and humiliations of slavery had felt anger against an evil with which they were familiar; but the horrors consequent upon civil strife were known by the people of Syracuse only at second hand from their fathers, not at all from the evidence of their own eyes. 'I approve,' he went on, 'the readiness with which you took up arms; and I shall be even better pleased if you use them only under the compulsion of absolute necessity. For the moment my advice is that we send representatives to Adranodorus, demanding that he put himself in the hands of the council and people, open the gates of the Island, and surrender the citadel. Then, if Adranodorus wishes to exchange his regency for a throne of

1. The Island, Tyche, and Achradina were quarters of Syracuse. The Hexapylon was the great northern gate of the wall of Dionysius. (A. de S.). See plan, p. 684.

his own, my view is that you should fight more fiercely to regain your liberty from him than ever you fought to regain it from Hieronymus.'

The representatives were sent at once. The council then sat – during the reign of Hiero it had remained in being as a consultative body, but since his death this was the first occasion on which the councillors had been summoned or consulted upon any subject. Adranodorus, after his interview with the envoys, was not unaffected by the unanimity of feeling in the city, as well as by the fact that parts of it had already been seized, and above all by the betrayal into his enemies' hands of the most strongly fortified part of the Island. But his wife Damarata, a proud woman, who was Hiero's daughter and still very much the princess in her general attitude, drew him aside and bade him remember the often repeated saying of the tyrant Dionysius: 'There is only one way,' it ran, 'for a monarch to leave his throne: not on horseback, but dragged feet first.' It was easy, she said, at any moment to give up a great position; the hard thing – the laborious thing – was to attain to it. What he should do was to gain time from the envoys for deliberation, and use it in fetching the troops from Leontini; then, if he promised them money from the king's treasury, everything would be under his control.

So much for a woman's advice: Adranodorus neither wholly rejected nor immediately accepted it, feeling, as he did, that a safer way to power lay through a temporary submission to circumstances. Accordingly he instructed the envoys to report on their return that he was willing to put himself in the hands of the council and people. At dawn next day he had the gates of the Island opened and entered the forum in Achradina; there he mounted the Altar of Concord, from which Polyaenus had spoken the previous day, and began his speech by asking pardon for his hesitation. 'I kept the gates closed,' he continued, 'not for my own privacy but because once swords were drawn I was apprehensive about where the bloodshed would stop; I did not know if you were content with the death of the tyrant – enough, in itself, to set us free – or if all those connected with the court either by blood or marriage or the official positions they hold were to be killed too, as being involved in another's guilt. But when I saw that the liberators of our country wished also to keep her free and that thoughts everywhere were concentrated upon the general good, I had no hesitation in surrendering not only this body of mine but everything which has been entrusted for safe-keeping to my care, since the man who laid on me that trust has perished of his own excesses.'

Then, turning to the assassins of the king, and mentioning Theodotus and Sosis by name, 'You have done,' he said, 'a memorable deed. But believe me, the first step only has been taken towards the fulfilment of your noble purpose. There is still the terrible danger that, if you fail to take measures for peace and harmony, our country's freedom may prove her grave.'

23. With these words he laid at their feet the keys of the gates and the royal treasury, with the result that, for that day at least, people dispersed from the assembly in high spirits and offered prayers of thanksgiving with their wives and children at every shrine in the city. Next day elections were held. First to be elected to office was Adranodorus, and most of the others were those who had been involved in the assassination of the king. Two men were elected in their absence: these were Sopater and Dinomenes, who on hearing of events in Syracuse transferred thither the royal treasure in Leontini and placed it in the care of officials specially appointed for the purpose. The treasure in the Island was moved into Achradina, and by general consent the section of the wall which made an unnecessarily strong barrier between the Island and the rest of the city was taken down. This and the other measures were all in accordance with the trend towards free institutions.

When Hippocrates and Epicydes learned of the assassination – which Hippocrates had tried to conceal by the extreme measure of killing the messenger who brought the news – they were deserted by their troops. They then returned to Syracuse, as this seemed, in the circumstances, the safest plan. Once in the city, to avoid suspicion of looking for a chance to seize power, they approached the magistrates and, through them, the council, where they declared that they had been sent by Hannibal to Hieronymus, as to a friend and ally, and had obeyed the order of the man whom their own commander wished them to obey. They now wanted to return to Hannibal; but since with Roman troops all over the island the roads were not safe, they would be glad of a guard to escort them to Locri in Italy. They assured the council that this small service would procure them great favour with Hannibal.

The request was readily granted, for the council was glad to have the two men out of the way – generals as they were of the king's army and experienced soldiers, not to mention the fact that they were bold fellows and temporarily out of a job. None the less, though the council wanted their departure, no steps were taken to expedite it. Meanwhile both men used their familiarity with the common soldier's temper to approach the troops with whispered accusations against the council and nobility; for the same purpose they got into touch with deserters, mostly from the crews of Roman ships, and even with the lowest dregs of the populace, persuading them that there was a secret plan afoot to put Syracuse, under cover of renewing the alliance, into Roman hands, and to enable a small clique – the men, namely, who favoured the renewal of the treaty – to exercise power.

24. Every day more and more people were flocking into Syracuse, all of them prepared to listen to and believe these charges. In these circumstances hopes of a successful *coup* were raised not only in Epicydes but also in Adranodorus, who had at long last given way to his wife's admonitions. She had repeatedly urged that now was the time to seize power, while the situation was still confused and the recently liberated state still at sixes and sevens, while the troops were still going around fat and prosperous on the king's money and experienced generals sent by Hannibal were at hand to assist the design. Adranodorus, accordingly, had formed a plot with Themistus, husband of one of Gelo's daughters, and a few days later he was rash enough to speak of it to an actor named Aristo, with whom he had been accustomed to share his secrets. Aristo was a man of good family and position and in no way adversely affected by his profession, as in Greek eyes the pursuit of the arts is never discreditable; so, in the belief that the loyalty he owed the community took precedence of everything else, he informed the magistrates of the plot. They, once they had sufficient evidence to assure them of the truth of the story, conferred

with the senior councillors and with their authority placed a guard at the doors of the council house, and, when Themistus and Adranodorus came in, had them both assassinated. As nobody else knew why this was done, it seemed a more atrocious crime than it actually was, and for a while confusion reigned; then, when at last there was silence, the magistrates brought the informer into the Chamber. Point by point he went through the whole story: the conspiracy, he declared, had begun with Themistus's marriage to Gelo's daughter Harmonia, and he went on to describe how African and Spanish auxiliaries had been primed for the murder of the magistrates and other leading citizens and an announcement made that their property should pass to the murderers; already a mercenary force accustomed to obey Adranodorus was all prepared for the seizure of the Island. Finally, enumerating every detail and all the agents to be employed, he laid before them a picture of the whole conspiracy, complete with the men and the weapons with which it was to be carried out.

The effect on the council was to make them feel that the assassination of Themistus and Adranodorus was as well justified as that of Hieronymus, but the mass of the populace was more doubtful; bewildered crowds assembled in front of the council house and there was much noise and shouting. Indeed, they looked like becoming dangerous, until the bodies of the two conspirators were exposed in the courtyard; this frightened them so much that they at once fell silent and followed to the assembly the rest of the populace who had not yet yielded to the excitement. 25. There Sopater, by the request of the council and his fellow-magistrates, delivered a harangue, which, beginning with the past lives of the accused, he conducted like a prosecution in a court of law. 'Every foul and criminal act,' he said, 'committed since Hiero's death, has been the work of Adranodorus and Themistus. Hieronymus was a mere boy who had scarcely reached puberty – what, then, could he have done on his own initiative? His officials and his guardians were the real kings – sheltering under the hatred directed against another. They should have been killed at the same time as Hieronymus – nay, before him. But, owed to death though they were, and marked out for the grave, they planned fresh crimes after the king's assassination – at first openly, when Adranodorus closed the gates of the Island and called himself heir to the throne, entering as master into possession of what previously he had held in trust; next, when betrayed by those in the Island, beset by the whole body of citizens holding Achradina, he tried by trickery and stealth to win the power he had failed to win by overt means. Not even advancement or the good will of his fellows availed to check him – this man who, a plotter against liberty, was chosen to hold office amongst the liberators of his country.

'These men thought themselves kings – but it was their royal wives, Hiero's daughter and Gelo's daughter, who inspired them to think so.'

At the mention of the princesses there was a shout from all parts of the assembly that neither of them deserved to live, and that no member of the family of the tyrants ought to survive. Indeed, that is the nature of crowds: the mob is either a humble slave or a cruel master. As for the middle way of liberty, the mob can neither take it nor keep it with any respect for moderation or law. Moreover, there is seldom a lack of men to minister to its savage passions and drive to bloodshed those who already are all too eager to inflict torture and death. Thus, in the present instance, the magistrates immediately put forward a bill, asking for the death of every member of the royal family. The bill was adopted almost before it was proposed, and on the magistrates' authority the assassins proceeded to their task. Damarata, daughter of Hiero and wife of Adranodorus, and Harmonia, daughter of Gelo and wife of Themistus, were both killed.

26. There was another daughter of Hiero, Heraclia, whose husband Zoippus had been sent by Hieronymus on a mission to King Ptolemy and had remained in Egypt in voluntary exile. This woman, learning that the assassins were on the way to her too, took refuge with her two young daughters in the private chapel of her house. There they were found with their hair loosened and their dress and bearing all making a dumb appeal for pity – to which Heraclia added her prayers, by the memory of her father Hiero and her brother Gelo, not to let her innocent self be consumed in the fire of hatred against Hieronymus.

'What have I gained,' she cried, 'from his reign but my husband's exile? When the tyrant was alive I never enjoyed the same high place as my sister; and now he is dead, why should I be linked with her? If Adranodorus had succeeded, my sister would have sat upon the throne at his side, while I, with everyone else, would have been her slave. If Zoippus were told that Hieronymus was dead and Syracuse free, who can doubt that he would embark at once and return to his native country? Alas for human hopes! Here, in his city now set free, his wife and children, guiltless of any offence against liberty or law, are fighting for their lives. What danger could anyone fear from me – a lonely woman with no husband at my side – or from these fatherless girls? Perhaps you will say that, though we are personally harmless enough, it is the royal family you hate. Very well, then: send us away, far from Syracuse, far from Sicily. Have us exiled to Alexandria, where I may join my husband and my children their father.'

Heraclia's appeal fell upon deaf ears and stony hearts. There was an exclamation that time was short, and the unhappy woman saw men drawing their swords. Forgetful of herself at the sight, she besought the assassins at any rate to spare the girls – children too young even for an enemy in the heat of battle to harm – and not, in their revenge upon tyrants, themselves to commit the very crimes they hated. The assassins, while the prayer for mercy was still on her lips, dragged her from the inner chapel and cut her throat. The two girls were spattered with their mother's blood, and, when the assassins turned upon them, they ran out of the chapel like mad things in the desperation of their fear and grief. If they could have escaped into the streets, their wild rush for safety might have well caused a riot; even as it was, in the confined space within the house, surrounded as they were by armed men out for their blood, they more than once escaped unharmed from the fatal blow and tore themselves free from clutching hands – so many and so strong. At last, exhausted by wounds and loss of blood, they collapsed and died.

Their death was pitiful enough, but it was rendered even more so by the chance that a message arrived soon afterwards to the effect that, owing to a sudden change in feeling from anger to pity, the children were not to be killed after all. The result was a fresh outburst of wrath at the over-hastiness of the punishment, which had left no room for a change of mind or a cooling of the moment's passion. The mob was in a dangerous mood, and clamoured for an election to fill the now vacant magistracies previously held by Adranodorus and Themistus. The demand was by no means likely to be welcomed by the existing magistrates.

27. A day was fixed for the election, and to everyone's surprise a man right out on the fringe of the crowd nominated Epicydes; then somebody else nominated Hippocrates. The two names were taken up and repeated more and more frequently, with the evident approval of the crowd. It was a confused sort of assembly, as amongst the populace there were a great many soldiers, and a good sprinkling even of deserters, all eager for an upheaval of some kind. The magistrates at first ignored them, and played for time; but, forced in the end to yield to the general will, and fearing a popular rising, they declared the two men magistrates. Once elected, they, in their turn, did not immediately disclose their intentions, angry though they were that envoys had gone to Appius Claudius to ask for a ten days' truce, and that this being secured a second delegation had been sent to negotiate the renewal of the old treaty. The Romans at this time had a fleet of 100 ships at Murgantia, and were keeping an eye on the progress of things in Syracuse after the disturbance caused by the assassinations, and on the direction in which their new and unaccustomed freedom would drive the populace.

It was at this moment that Marcellus arrived in Sicily, and the Syracusan envoys were accordingly sent on to him by Appius. When he heard the conditions, Marcellus thought an agreement might be reached, and himself sent representatives to Syracuse with instructions to discuss the renewal of the treaty personally with the magistrates there. By now, however, things in Syracuse were on the boil again and fresh troubles brewing: news of a Carthaginian fleet off Cape Pachynum emboldened Hippocrates and Epicydes to come out into the open and spread the story amongst the mercenaries and deserters that Syracuse was being betrayed to the Romans. Then when

Appius began to keep ships lying off the harbour entrance, to encourage the pro-Roman party in the city, considerable substance was apparently added to what might have been mere empty charges – so much so that at first there had been an excited and disorderly scramble down to the waterside to prevent any attempt at a landing.

28. In this confused situation it was decided to call an assembly. Various opinions were expressed, and an outbreak of violence seemed not far away, when Apollonides, one of the leading citizens, made a speech which, in the circumstances, was a salutary one. He said that no state had ever been confronted with a better hope of salvation or a more immediate prospect of ruin: for if only they could agree unanimously to take either the Roman or the Carthaginian side, their position would be happier and more prosperous than that of any community in the world. But if the present internal dissension continued, then the war between Rome and Carthage would be nothing in savagery compared with the civil war which was bound to come in Syracuse, where within the same walls each side would have its own army, its own weapons, its own leaders. The essential thing, therefore, was to make every effort to secure unanimity; merely to decide on the comparative advantages of an alliance with Rome or with Carthage was a minor matter and of far less importance. None the less, he added, it was better in the choice of allies to follow the authority of Hiero than of Hieronymus, and wiser to prefer a well-tried friendship of fifty years to one which once proved faithless and was at the moment an unknown quantity. Moreover, there was a further point which should influence their decision: it was possible to refuse peace with Carthage without immediately declaring war upon her, whereas with the Romans it would be necessarily, from the outset, either peace or war.

As the speech was free both from personal ambition and party spirit, it was proportionately the more effective. In addition to the magistrates and the committee of councillors a military council was also formed, and commanders of the various units and the captains of auxiliaries were ordered to take part in the deliberations. The debate was long and violent, and at last, forced to realize that they had not the resources for a war with Rome, they decided upon peace and the despatch of a delegation to renew and ratify the treaty.

29. Not many days had passed when envoys from Leontini arrived in Syracuse with a request for troops to protect their territory. The request provided a perfect opportunity for unloading the city of its explosive and disorderly rabble and of getting rid of the mob leaders. Hippocrates was instructed to take the deserters to Leontini, and they were followed by many of the mercenary auxiliaries, making a total of 4,000 armed men. The arrangement was apparently an excellent one for everybody: the troops sent were given the opportunity they had long desired of causing an upheaval, and the men who sent them were delighted to have had the bilges – if one may so put it – properly pumped out and the city relieved of offensive matter. Unfortunately, however, it was only a temporary alleviation; the city was sick, and was soon to relapse into a worse sickness than before.

Hippocrates began by making stealthy raids on the territory bordering Roman-occupied Sicily; then when aid was sent by Appius to protect the farmlands of Rome's allies, he made a full-scale attack upon the Roman unit which faced him on guard-duty, inflicting heavy casualties. Marcellus, when this was reported to him, promptly sent envoys to Syracuse to say that the promise of peace had been broken and that the prospect of war could never be ruled out unless Hippocrates and Epicydes were not only ejected from Syracuse but banished once and for all to some distant country. Epicydes had no wish either to remain in Syracuse to face an accusation directed against his absent brother, or to fail in playing his part in fanning the flames of war; accordingly he, too, went to Leontini, where, finding the people already sufficiently hostile to Rome, he began to embitter their relations with Syracuse as well. He claimed that the agreement between Rome and Syracuse had contained the provision that all communities which had been in the power of the tyrants should pass into Syracusan control, and complained that Syracuse was no longer content with her own liberty unless she could use it to dominate others. He therefore urged that the Syracusans should be told that the men of Leontini also thought liberty to be their due, either because it was in their city that the tyrant was killed, or because it was there that the cry for liberty had first been raised, at the time of a general movement to Syracuse after abandoning the king's generals. Either, therefore, the offensive clause must be removed from the treaty, or the treaty as it stood declared unacceptable. Epicydes had no difficulty in carrying the people with him; and when the envoys from Syracuse complained of the murderous attack on the Roman guard-post and demanded the departure of Hippocrates and Epicydes either to Locri or anywhere else they preferred, provided they left Sicily, they received the haughty reply that the people of Leontini had not asked the Syracusans to make peace for them with Rome, and did not consider themselves bound by other people's treaties. This was reported to the Romans by the Syracusans, with a denial of any control over Leontini: for that reason, they claimed, the Romans could make war upon the town without violating their treaty with Syracuse, and they themselves would lend their aid on condition that Leontini, after defeat, should again be under Syracusan control, according to the terms of the agreement.

30. Marcellus, who had marched for Leontini with his whole force and also called upon Appius to attack simultaneously from the opposite direction, found that anger at the attack on the guard-post while negotiations were still in progress had inspired his men with such ardour that they carried the town at the first assault. Hippocrates and Epicydes, seeing the gates forced and the walls in enemy hands, withdrew with a few supporters to the inner fortress, whence later, under cover of darkness, they slipped away to Herbesus.

A Syracusan column, 8,000 strong, on its way to Leontini was met at the river Mylas with the report of the capture of the town. The report also contained a number of fabrications: for instance, that soldiers and civilians had been butchered indiscriminately and that probably not a single adult was left alive; that the town had been looted and the property of the rich turned over to the troops. The news of these atrocities brought the column to a halt; alarm rapidly spread, and the leaders – they were Sosis and Dinomenes – anxiously considered their next move. The false report of terrorism in the town had received apparent confirmation from the scourging and beheading of some 2,000 deserters; though in point of fact no other soldier, and no citizen, had been touched after the town was taken, and all property except what had been lost in the first confusion of the assault was being restored to its owners. The Syracusan contingent, however, complaining that their comrades had been betrayed to their deaths, could neither be induced to proceed to Leontini nor to wait where they were for more certain news. So when their officers saw they were inclined to mutiny but that the trouble would soon be over once the leaders of such folly were removed, they marched the army to Megara and themselves with a handful of mounted troops started for Herbesus in the hope that the town, amidst the general alarm, might be betrayed into their hands. Disappointed in this, they determined upon vigorous action and on the following day brought the army from Megara in order to attack Herbesus in force. Hippocrates and Epicydes rode out to meet the column: to entrust themselves to troops largely accustomed to their command but inflamed, at the moment, by the report of the slaughter of their comrades, was clearly a risky thing to do; however, in the present desperate circumstances, there seemed to be no alternative. It so happened that the leading troops in the column were 600 Cretans, who had served under them in Hieronymus's army and were under an obligation to Hannibal for their liberation, with other Roman auxiliaries, after being taken prisoner at Lake Trasimene. As soon as Hippocrates and Epicydes recognized these men by their standards and accoutrements, they implored their protection; holding out olive branches and displaying fillets such as suppliants wear, they begged them to give them asylum and not betray them to the Syracusans, only to be themselves handed over to the Romans for execution. 31. The Cretan soldiers, in reply, told them to keep their courage up and promised to stand by them whatever might happen.

While these exchanges were taking place, the column had halted, but the officers in command were not yet aware of the reason for the delay; however, as soon as word reached them that Epicydes and Hippocrates had made their appearance, and it was evident from the rumble of satisfaction which spread through all ranks that their arrival was welcome, they at once galloped to the head of the column and angrily asked what the Cretans supposed they were up to, and what sort of discipline it was to enter into conversation with an enemy and without orders to admit him into their ranks. Then, having ordered that both brothers should be arrested and put in chains, they were met by such an outcry, first from the Cretans and then from the other units that there could be little doubt that, if they proceeded farther, they would have to look to their own safety. It was an anxious moment, and, as their position was by no means clear, they ordered a return to Megara, where they had come from, and sent messengers to Syracuse to report on the situation.

Hippocrates took advantage of the general state of mutual suspicion to play a further trick of his own: he sent some of the Cretans to watch the roads, and read out a letter, which he pretended to have intercepted but had actually written himself, from the Syracusan commanders to the consul Marcellus. After the customary greeting, the letter went on to say that Marcellus had acted with perfect propriety in sparing no lives in Leontini. The position of all mercenary troops was the same, and Syracuse would never enjoy tranquillity while there remained any foreign soldiers either in the city or in the army. Therefore Marcellus should take steps to lay his hands upon the men who, with their officers, were in camp at Megara, and, by having them executed, at last set Syracuse free.

When this letter was read, there was a rush to arms accompanied by such a roar of indignation that the commanders, in the general confusion, galloped off to Syracuse. But the mutiny was not checked even by their flight; a number of attacks were made on the Syracusan soldiers, and not a man of them would have been spared, had not Epicydes and Hippocrates made a move to quell the angry mob – not, indeed, out of pity or from any considerations of humanity, but merely in order to leave the way open for their own return; for this would be feasible only if they kept the men loyal to them and at the same time in the position of hostages, and won the goodwill of their relatives and friends first by gratitude for their apparent clemency and, secondly, by the more practical compulsion of the fact that the men *were* hostages. Then, well aware of how easily the crowd is swayed by the lightest and most empty breath, they bribed one of the soldiers who had been besieged in Leontini to go to Syracuse with a story similar to the pack of lies which had been reported at the Mylas, and by personally vouching for its accuracy and relating all the unlikely incidents as if he had seen them with his own eyes, to arouse general indignation. 32. Not only was this fellow believed by the mob, but when he was brought into the council chamber his tale had great effect on the councillors too: a number of men – and no fools either – openly said that the affair at Leontini had been a perfect revelation of Roman savagery and greed, and that if Roman troops had entered Syracuse they would have done the same, or even worse, as there was more in Syracuse to satisfy their avarice. The council accordingly unanimously determined to close the gates and have the city guarded.

Unfortunately, however, the objects of their fear or their hatred were not in every case the same: by all the military and a large part of the populace the Roman name was held in abhorrence; the magistrates and a few of the leading class of citizens, inflamed though they were by the false report, were none the less inclined to greater caution in view of the more immediate danger from Epicydes and Hippocrates, who by now were actually at the Hexapylon, while talks were going on through relatives of citizens in the army with a view to opening the gates and allowing the defence of their common home against attack by the Romans.

One gate of the Hexapylon had already been opened, and the troops had begun to be admitted, when the magistrates – now in the position of military commanders – intervened. They issued their orders; they resorted to threats; they exerted their personal authority to try to stop the proceeding, but all in vain. Finally they forgot their dignity and besought their compatriots not to betray their native city to scoundrels who had once served the tyrant and were now seducing the army from its allegiance. But the ears of the excited mob remained deaf to all their pleas, and soon the gates were being torn down as violently from within as from without, until all of them were forced and the column was admitted through the whole span of the Hexapylon. The commanders and all citizens of military age fled for refuge to Achradina; the mercenary troops and deserters, together with such remnants of the king's army as were still in the city, went to swell the forces of the enemy. Achradina fell at the first assault, and all the magistrates and officers were killed, except for a few who escaped in the confusion. Night put an end to the slaughter; next day slaves were granted freedom, criminals were released from prison, and the whole mob, such as it was, elected Hippocrates and Epicydes generals. Thus Syracuse, having enjoyed for a brief hour the light of liberty, fell back into her former servitude.

33. When these events were reported to the Romans, they immediately left Leontini and moved to Syracuse. As it happened, a quinquereme bearing envoys had been sent by Appius by way of the harbour; and as a quadrireme previously sent had been captured just inside the harbour entrance, the envoys were lucky to escape. Thus normal relations even between countries at war – not to mention peace – were already severed, when the Roman army took up its position about a mile from the city, near the temple of Olympian Jupiter. None the less it was decided to send a delegation from here too, but it was met outside the gate by Hippocrates and Epicydes with their troops, to prevent it from entering the city. The Roman spokesman said he was not bringing war to the people of Syracuse; on the contrary, he was offering assistance and protection, both to those who had escaped the slaughter and sought refuge with the Roman army, and to those who had been terrified into enduring a slavery worse than exile or death. 'Nor,' he continued, 'shall we allow the brutal slaughter of our allies to go unavenged. If, therefore, the men who have found refuge with us are suffered to return home in safety; if those responsible for the bloodshed are surrendered to us, and liberty and law restored to the people of Syracuse, there will be no need to resort to arms. If this is not done, we shall use force against anyone who stands in the way.'

Epicydes replied that if the Roman mission had been addressed to him and his brother, they would have given an answer; but, as things were, the envoys had better come again when the control of Syracuse was in the hands of those to whom they really wished to address themselves. 'And if you attack us,' he added, 'experience will soon show you that an attempt upon Syracuse is by no means the same thing as an attempt upon Leontini.' This said, he walked off and had the city gates shut behind him.

From that moment the attack upon Syracuse was begun simultaneously by land at the Hexapylon and by water on Achradina, the wall of which runs down into the sea. The Romans, inspired by their success in taking Leontini at the first overwhelming thrust, were confident of their ability to penetrate, at one point or another, into a vast and sprawling town like Syracuse, and accordingly moved into position all the assault artillery they possessed.

34. An operation launched with such strength behind it might well have proved successful, had it not been for the presence in Syracuse at that time of one particular individual – Archimedes. Archimedes, unrivalled in his knowledge of astronomy, was even more remarkable as the inventor and constructor of types of artillery and military devices of various kinds, by the aid of which he was able by one finger, as it were, to frustrate the most laborious operations of the enemy. The city wall ran over ground of varying altitude: in most places it was high and difficult of access, but here and there were level stretches which could be approached along low, flat ground; and along the whole extent of it Archimedes had moved into position the type of artillery which he thought suitable for the various sections. Marcellus, for his part, began the attack on the defences of Achradina, which, as I have said, run down to the water, from sixty quinquiremes. On most of the ships archers and slingers – and also light troops armed with a special javelin which anyone not used to it finds difficult to hurl back – made it almost impossible for any defender to stand on the wall without being hit. These troops kept their vessels somewhat away from the wall, as they needed range for their missiles; other quinquiremes were lashed together in pairs, one

close alongside the other with the inner banks of oars removed; each pair was propelled, like a single vessel, by the outer banks of oars, and they were employed to carry towers, several storeys high, and other devices for breaching defences. This elaborate sea-borne attack Archimedes countered by moving into position on the walls pieces of artillery of varying size; at the ships off-shore he hurled stones of enormous weight, assailing those closer in with missiles which, though lighter, could for that reason be discharged more frequently. Then, to enable his own men to discharge their missiles at the enemy without danger to themselves, he made rows of loopholes, ranging from top to bottom of the wall and some eighteen inches wide, through which, themselves unseen, they could shoot at the enemy either with arrows or with smallish catapults. Some of the enemy ships came close in-shore, too close for the artillery to touch them; and these he dealt with by using a swing-beam and grapnel. The method was this: the swing-beam projected over the wall and an iron grapnel was attached to it on a heavy chain; the grapnel was lowered on to a vessel's bows, and the beam was then swung up, the other arm being brought to the ground by the shifting of a leaden weight; the result was to stand the ship, so to speak, on her tail, bows in air, Then the whole contraption was suddenly let go, and the ship, falling smash as it were from the wall into the water (to the great alarm of the crew), was more or less swamped even if it happened to come down on an even keel.

By these devices the attack from the sea was frustrated, and all available strength was diverted to an assault by land. Even there, however, every section of the defences had been equipped with various missile-throwing machines, all at the expense and by the forethought of Hiero over many years, aided by the unique engineering skill of Archimedes. Moreover, the nature of the ground helped the defence, in that the rocky cliff on which the foundations of the wall are built is mostly so steep that not only missiles hurled from catapults but even such as were allowed to roll down the cliff by their own weight, took deadly effect on the enemy below. The same reason rendered an approach to the walls difficult and gave but an insecure foothold to the attacker. Thus it was that at a council of war the decision was reached to abandon the assault, as all attempts were baffled, and to confine operations to a blockade by sea and land.

35. Meanwhile Marcellus marched with about a third of the army to recover the towns which, in the disturbed state of affairs, had gone over to Carthage. Helorus and Herbesus surrendered to him without a blow; Megara he took by assault, then sacked and devastated it as an object lesson to others, especially the Syracusans. At just about the same time Himilco, who for a long while past had kept his fleet lying off Cape Pachynum, landed at Heraclea (known as Minoa) 25,000 foot-soldiers, 3,000 cavalry, and twelve elephants. This was a much greater force than he had previously kept with his fleet at Pachynum; and the reason was that after Hippocrates' seizure of Syracuse, he, Himilco, had crossed to Carthage, where he found strong support from Hippocrates's envoys and also from Hannibal, who had written to say that the time had come to win back Sicily as the national honour demanded. In addition, Himilco's own influence, together with his actual presence in Carthage, all tended to the same result: the decision to dispatch the strongest possible force of both horse and foot to Sicily. On arrival he quickly recovered Heraclea and Agrigentum; and in the other communities which supported the Carthaginian interest, such hopes were aroused of driving the Romans out of the island that eventually even the men who were blocked up in Syracuse took courage, and changed their tactics accordingly. Believing that a part of their forces would be adequate for the defence of the city, they allotted separate spheres of action to their two commanders, entrusting Epicydes with defence, while Hippocrates was to join forces with Himilco and oppose the Roman consul, Marcellus. Hippocrates with 10,000 foot and 500 horse left the city during the night through parts of the wall which were unwatched by the enemy and started to encamp near Acrillae; but was surprised while the work of fortification was still incomplete by Marcellus who was on his way back from Agrigentum, which was already occupied as he had failed, in spite of his haste, to forestall the enemy there. To encounter a Syracusan army at that time and in that place was the last thing Marcellus expected;

nevertheless from fear of Himilco and the Carthaginians, for whom with his present forces he was by no means a match, he was taking all possible precautions and had his column so organized as to be ready for any emergency. 36. These measures, though taken against the Carthaginians, were, as it turned out, of use to him against the Sicilians: coming upon them as they were in the act of pitching camp and consequently in no sort of order or formation, and mostly unarmed, he surrounded all the infantry, while their mounted troops after slight resistance fled with Hippocrates to Acrae.

The action was some check upon the Sicilians who were inclined to desert the Roman cause, and Marcellus then returned to Syracuse. A few days later Himilco, joined by Hippocrates, took up his position at the river Anapus, some eight miles from the city. About the same time fifty-five Carthaginian warships under the command of Bomilcar ran into the Great Harbour; and a Roman fleet of thirty quinquiremes disembarked the first legion at Panormus, so that it might well have seemed that the seat of war had now shifted from Italy altogether, so intent were both antagonists upon Sicily. Himilco thought that the Roman legion which had landed at Panormus would certainly fall a prey to him on its march to Syracuse; but he was disappointed as it took a different route from what he had expected: Himilco himself marched by an inland route, but the Romans kept to the coast, escorted by the fleet, till they joined Appius Claudius, who had advanced with part of his forces to meet them at Pachynum. After that the Carthaginians did not remain at Syracuse; and Bomilcar, partly because he had insufficient confidence in his fleet, as the Roman fleet was at least double the size, and partly because he realized it would be useless to wait longer and merely to intensify, by the presence of his men, the shortage of supplies from which his allies were already suffering, set sail again and crossed to Africa. As for Himilco, he followed Marcellus to Syracuse, hoping to find a chance to engage him before he was joined by larger forces; but it was to no purpose: the opportunity did not present itself, so when he saw the enemy in a safe position near Syracuse, with strong defences and adequate numbers, he preferred not to waste time in laying useless siege to him and watching the blockade of his allies. So he cleared out, intending to move his force to wherever a hope of a revolt from Rome might call him and by his presence to encourage any of the Sicilian communities who supported the Carthaginian cause. Murgantia was the first town recovered, the inhabitants having betrayed the Roman garrison. In the town a large quantity of grain and supplies of all kinds had been accumulated for the Romans.

37. The revolt of Murgantia aroused sympathetic feelings in other communities, and Roman garrisons were in various places either driven from their strongholds or betrayed by treachery and overwhelmed. The case of Henna was a remarkable one: built on a high hill with the ground falling almost sheer on every side, the town was not only impregnable but also had a powerful Roman garrison commanded by a man who was by no means apt to be caught out by treachery. He was Lucius Pinarius, an active soldier who found it better worth while to guard against deception than to trust the honour of Sicilians. Moreover, he had been urged at this time to take every possible precaution by the news of so many acts of betrayal elsewhere, of the revolt of so many towns and the murder of their garrisons. So day and night he had kept everything in Henna in a state of readiness, with guards and sentries always on duty; not a man was allowed to leave his post or go unarmed. When the leading citizens of the place, who had already arranged with Himilco to betray the garrison, saw that this constant preparedness precluded all chance of a treacherous attack, they came to the conclusion that they must act openly. They declared, accordingly, that the town and its citadel ought to be under their own control, if they had entered the Roman alliance as free men, and not – as it now appeared – been handed over to the Romans as slaves for safe-keeping. It was only right that the keys of the town gates should be surrendered to them. 'Loyalty,' they added, 'is the strongest bond of an honest ally; and the Roman people and Senate will be grateful to us for the very reason that we remain their friends willingly and not by compulsion.' Pinarius in reply pointed out that he had been placed in his present position by his own superior officer, from whom he had received the keys of the gates and the duty of

defending the citadel; he held them not at his own discretion or that of the people of Henna but of the man who had placed them in his charge. 'We Romans,' he ended, 'believe that to abandon one's post is a capital offence: even fathers have put their sons to death as punishment for that crime. The man you should approach is the consul Marcellus. He is not far away; and it is he who has the power to decide the matter. So send him a deputation.'

However, they refused to do so and vowed that if words availed them nothing they would seek some more practical means of recovering their liberty; whereupon Pinarius said that if they disliked the idea of applying to the consul they might at least oblige him by holding an assembly of the people, which would make it plain whether their demand was merely a personal matter or an expression of the general will. They agreed to call an assembly on the following day.

38. After this conversation Pinarius returned to the citadel, called together his troops, and addressed them as follows: 'Soldiers, no doubt you are aware of how Roman garrisons have latterly been beset and murdered by the Sicilians. Till now you have avoided a similar treacherous attack, first by the favour of the gods, secondly by your own soldierly qualities, standing watch continuously day and night under arms. I only wish that we might get through the days to come without being either the victims or the perpetrators of an act of horror. While the Sicilians plotted in secret, we had our own method of frustrating them; but since their guile has met with no success, they are now openly demanding the keys of the gates. If we give them up, Henna will immediately be in Carthaginian hands, and we shall be butchered where we stand even more foully than the garrison at Murgantia. I have managed to gain one night in which to inform you of the impending danger; at daybreak they are to hold an assembly in order to incriminate me and incite the populace against you. Tomorrow, therefore, Henna will be drenched with blood – their blood, or your own. Let them make the first move, and your case is hopeless; make it yourselves, and you will be safe. Victory will be with him who first draws the sword.

'Every one of you, therefore, armed and alert, will await

my signal. I shall be at the assembly, and by talking and arguing I shall keep things going until everything is ready. When I give the signal with my toga, you are to raise the battle-cry, hurl yourselves upon the mob, and cut them down. See that none survive from whom force or fraud may be feared. And you, O mother Ceres and Proserpina, and all you upper and nether gods who dwell in this city, in these sacred lakes and groves, be with us with your kindly favour, if indeed we have planned this act not for treachery's sake, but to frustrate a treacherous attack from our foes!

'Now if, my men, you were about to fight with an armed enemy, I should have for you further words of exhortation; but they will be unarmed and off their guard. You will butcher them to your hearts' content. Moreover, the consul's camp is not far off: so you will have nothing to fear from Himilco and the Carthaginians.'

39. The troops were then dismissed, to eat and sleep. Next day parties were posted to watch the roads and close all means of egress. The majority of them took their position above and around the theatre – they had often watched assemblies there before, so this caused no surprise. The Roman commandant, brought by the magistrates before the people, repeated much of what he had said the previous day, to the effect that the power of decision in the matter lay not with him but with the consul. One or two voices were heard to call out, 'Give up the keys!'; then more took up the cry, and soon it was on the lips of every man in the theatre. Pinarius temporized and pretended to put them off, and was met by savage threats; then, when at last it was evident that they were on the point of resorting to violence, he gave the prearranged signal with his toga. His men, who throughout the proceedings had been on the alert, rushed down with a yell upon the mob from behind, while others stood massed at the exits to bar the way out. Penned in the auditorium, the people of Henna were cut down. Panic increased the hideous confusion: the victims desperate to escape came tearing down over each other's heads, and the heap of bodies rose higher and higher as those still unscathed fell upon the wounded, the living upon the dead. The troops then scattered, and in every corner of the town

there was nothing but blood and terror, as if it had been taken by assault; that the victims were an unarmed mob no more mitigated the soldiers' lust for blood than if they had been driven on by a shared danger and the ardour of battle. Thus Henna was held – by a criminal act or a necessary one, call it which you will.

Marcellus expressed no disapproval, and allowed the troops to plunder the town in the belief that the Sicilians had now been frightened into stopping their betrayal of Roman garrisons. In fact, however, the story of the massacre at Henna, a city in the middle of Sicily and famous both for its almost impregnable site and for the wealth of its sacred associations with the rape of Proserpine, was all over the island within a single day; and because of the feeling that a place where gods had dwelt as well as men had been polluted by this shocking act, even those communities whose allegiance had hitherto been doubtful now went over to Carthage.

After this Hippocrates withdrew to Murgantia and Himilco to Agrigentum, having marched to Henna to no purpose at the call of the would-be betrayers of the garrison there. Marcellus returned to Leontini, and after stocking the camp with grain and other supplies, left an adequate force to defend it and himself proceeded to the blockade of Syracuse. Appius Claudius left for Rome to stand for the consulship, and Titus Quinctius Crispinus was appointed by Marcellus to succeed him in command of the camp and fleet. Marcellus himself constructed and fortified a winter camp at a place called Leon, five miles from the Hexapylon. This concludes the operations in Sicily up to the beginning of winter.

40. The same summer also saw the outbreak of the anticipated war with King Philip. Envoys from Oricum came to the praetor Marcus Valerius Laevinus, who was watching Brundisium and the neighbouring coast of Calabria with his fleet; they reported that Philip had begun with an attempt upon Apollonia, sailing up the river with 120 light triremes, and that finding things progressed more slowly than he hoped, had moved his army secretly by night to Oricum, which, lying as it did on level ground and having neither fortifications nor adequate manpower, was taken by assault. The envoys begged

Valerius to send aid and by land and sea to keep a declared enemy of Rome away from the coastal towns, which were being attacked only because their position made them a likely base for an attack on Italy. Marcus Valerius left his second-in-command Publius Valerius in charge of a garrison of 2,000 men and himself with the fleet fully prepared for action sailed for Oricum, the troops for which there was no room on the warships being embarked in transports. He reached the town on the second day; it was held by only a weak garrison which the king had left there on his departure, and was recaptured after slight resistance. Envoys then arrived from Apollonia to report that their town was under siege because they refused to desert the Roman alliance, and added that they could not hold out any longer against the Macedonians without Roman assistance. Valerius promised to accede to their wishes, and sent 2,000 picked men in warships to the mouth of the river, under the command of Quintus Naevius Crista, a Prefect of the Allies and an active and experienced soldier. Crista landed the troops, sent back the ships to rejoin the fleet at Oricum, and began his march. Taking a route well away from the river and inadequately watched by the king's forces, he entered the city under cover of darkness and unperceived by any of the enemy. The following day no action was taken, as Crista wanted time to inspect such men of military age as Apollonia contained, together with the arms and other resources of the city; the inspection proved encouraging, and when at the same time he learned from scouts of the general slackness and negligence in the Macedonian army, he decided to act. In the silence of night he marched his force very quietly out of the city, and entered the enemy's camp. Sheer carelessness had left it completely open, and it is said that a thousand of his men were past the rampart before anyone noticed them, and that they could have reached the king's tent if only they had refrained a little longer from shedding blood. As it was, the slaughter of the men nearest the gate raised the alarm, whereupon such was the universal panic and confusion that not a man attempted to arm himself or drive the enemy from the camp, and even the king himself, half-naked and straight from his bed, in an outfit – such as it was – hardly seemly for a common soldier, not to mention a king, took to his heels and fled to his ships in the river. The rest of his people followed him in a disorderly rabble.

In the camp nearly 3,000 men were captured or killed, the prisoners somewhat outnumbering the dead. The camp was sacked; the Apollonians removed the catapults and other artillery provided for a siege to their own city, to protect their walls should a similar danger arise; everything else of value in the camp was turned over to the Romans.

When news of this operation reached Oricum, Marcus Valerius at once sailed to the mouth of the river to prevent the king's escape by sea. And so Philip, now convinced that he would not be equal to a battle either on sea or land, beached and burned his ships and returned overland to Macedonia with an army for the most part disarmed and despoiled. Marcus Valerius and the Roman fleet wintered at Oricum.

41. During this year in Spain, too, the war continued with varying success. Mago and Hasdrubal inflicted a heavy defeat on a very large Spanish force before the Romans could cross the Ebro, and all Spain south of the river would have been lost to Rome but for the prompt action of Publius Cornelius Scipio, who crossed over with all speed and was on the spot while the tribes allied to Rome were still hesitating which way to go. The Romans first encamped at White Fort, famous as the place where the great Hamilcar was killed in action; it was a well fortified stronghold and supplies of grain had previously been stored there. However, as the surrounding country was heavily occupied by enemy troops, and the Roman column had been attacked – though without loss – by enemy cavalry, while some 2,000 stragglers in various places had been caught and killed, Publius Scipio decided to shift his position nearer the regions where there was less activity, and fortified a camp at Mount Victory. Here he was joined by his brother Gnaeus Scipio, just as Hasdrubal, the son of Gisgo, arrived on the scene with an army at full strength. Three Carthaginian generals were now present, and all three took up their position on the other side of the river, opposite the Roman camp. Publius Scipio, going out to reconnoitre with a party marching light, failed to escape the enemy's vigilance, and had he not succeeded in occupying an adjacent hill, the whole party might have

been overwhelmed, as the ground was open and without cover. Even as it was, he was surrounded, until the arrival of his brother got him out of difficulties.

Castulo, a famous and important Spanish town, went over to the Romans: its ties with Carthage had been very close, Hannibal's wife being a native of the place.

The Carthaginians tried to take Iliturgi, where there was a Roman garrison; it seemed likely that the place would be starved into surrender, but Gnaeus Scipio came promptly to its aid. Marching with one legion, unencumbered by baggage, he passed between the two enemy camps and entered the town after inflicting heavy casualties, and again on the following day made a sudden sortie with equally successful results. More than 12,000 men were killed in the two engagements, and over 1,000 taken prisoner together with thirty-six military standards. The next town to be attacked was Bigerra, which was also within the Roman alliance; it was beset by Carthaginian troops but relieved without a battle by the arrival of Gnaeus Scipio.
42. After that the Carthaginians moved to Munda and the Romans followed them with all speed. The opposing forces met and after four hours of fighting, in which the Roman troops were conspicuously superior, the retreat was sounded because Gnaeus Scipio had been wounded by a javelin through his thigh and the men near him had had a moment of panic lest the wound should prove fatal. But there was no doubt that the enemy camp could have been taken that day, but for this unlucky check. Already not only men but elephants were right back against the rampart, and thirty-nine elephants were killed with pikes as they were actually crossing the trenches. In this battle too nearly 12,000 men are said to have been killed and 3,000 taken prisoner together with fifty-seven standards. The Carthaginians then withdrew to Aurinx, followed by the Romans, who were determined to press their advantage. There Scipio fought another battle, having himself carried into the line on a stretcher. It was a decisive victory, though the enemy losses were only half what they had been before, as there were fewer of them left to take the field. However, the family of the Barcae were born fighters and it was in their blood to set a tottering cause on its feet again: Mago was sent to raise

fresh troops, and soon the army was once more at full strength and the spirit of the men ready for a renewed effort. Most of the soldiers were Gauls, and they fought no worse than their predecessors for a side which had suffered so many defeats within a few days, and with the same result: more than 8,000 were killed, nearly 1,000 captured, with fifty-eight standards. Most of the spoils, too, were taken from Gallic soldiers, golden collars and bracelets in large numbers. Two distinguished Gallic chieftains, named Moenicaptus and Vismarus, were killed in the action. Eight elephants were captured and three killed.

These successes in Spain at last shamed the Romans into remembering that Saguntum, the immediate cause of the war, had now been seven years[1] in Carthaginian hands. They expelled the garrison there, recovered the town and gave it back to such of the former inhabitants as the war had spared. As for the Turdetani, who had brought on the war between Saguntum and Carthage, they reduced them to subjection, sold them as slaves, and destroyed their capital city.

43. Such were the events in Spain during the consulship of Quintus Fabius and Marcus Claudius. In Rome, as soon as the new people's tribunes had entered office, a summons to appear before the people was issued by the tribune Marcus Metellus against the censors Publius Furius and Marcus Atilius. Metellus had been quaestor the previous year and the censors had deprived him of his horse, removed his name from his tribe, and reduced him to the lowest citizen class as a punishment for conspiring, after Cannae, to abandon Italy. However by the support of nine tribunes the censors were excused from standing trial while they were still in office, and were consequently released. They did not complete their term, as Furius died and Atilius resigned.

The consular elections were conducted by Quintus Fabius Maximus. Both the successful candidates, Quintus Fabius Maximus the consul's son and Tiberius Sempronius Gracchus (for the second time), were elected in absence. The new praetors were Marcus Atilius, Marcus Aemilius Lepidus, and two men who at the time were curule aediles, Publius Sempronius

1. Only four, according to Livy's chronology. (A. de S.)

Tuditanus and Gnaeus Fulvius Centumalus. It is generally believed that on four days of the festival organized that year by the curule aediles stage plays were exhibited for the first time. The aedile Tuditanus was the same who made the breakthrough at Cannae when the horror of their position had paralysed others and prevented their escape.

After the elections the in-coming consuls, on the proposal of Fabius, were summoned to Rome and entered upon office They then consulted the Senate upon the conduct of the war the spheres of action which they and the praetors should severally assume, and the troops which each should command

44. To the consuls were entrusted operations against Hannibal with two armies – one which Gracchus himself had commanded and the other which Fabius had commanded during his term as consul. These armies were of two legions each. The praetor Aemilius, to whom fell jurisdiction in cases where foreigners were involved, was instructed to surrender his judicial duties to his colleague Atilius, the City praetor, and himself to operate in Luceria with the two legions which the new consul Fabius had commanded when he was praetor. Ariminum was assigned to Tuditanus and Centumalus got Suessula – each with two legions, the latter having the City legions, the former taking over from Marcus Pomponius. Other commands and assignments were continued for a further term: for Marcellus, Sicily within the boundaries of Hiero's former kingdom; for the pro-praetor Lentulus, the old province, and command of the fleet for Otacilius. In these cases no new troops were added. Marcus Valerius was to continue to operate in Greece and Macedonia with the legion and the ships already at his disposal; Quintus Mucius with his old army of two legions was to continue in Sardinia; Varro was to keep Picenum and the one legion he already commanded. Orders were further issued for the enrolment of two City legions and 20,000 allied troops. These, then, were the forces and these the generals with which the Roman dominion was to be defended against many simultaneous aggressors, actual or potential.

At this time further ominous events were reported, and the consuls, when the two City legions had been enrolled and other legions brought up to strength, performed the customary rites of expiation before leaving Rome. The wall and gates had been struck by lightning; also the temple of Jupiter at Aricia. Various ocular and aural illusions had been taken for reality: for instance, non-existent warships were seen on the river at Tarracina; in the temple of Jupiter Vicilinus in the territory of Compsa the clash of arms was heard; in the river at Amiternum the water looked like blood. The expiatory rites were performed according to the instructions of the pontiffs, and the consuls left the city, Gracchus for Lucania and Fabius for Apulia. The elder Fabius joined the camp at Suessula as second-in-command to his son. While the two were advancing to meet each other, the lictors out of respect for the old man's dignity preceded the consul in silence; he rode on past eleven of the twelve *fasces*, and not until the consul ordered the last lictor to give the admonition and the lictor, in his turn, called out the order to dismount, did the old man leap from his horse, with the words: 'My son, I wished to find out if you really knew that you were a consul.'

45. A man from Arpi, named Dasius Altinius, presented himself at the camp secretly by night, accompanied by three slaves, and promised to betray his town, if it were made worth his while. Fabius brought the matter up for discussion, and the general view was that the fellow ought to be scourged and executed as a deserter whose honour neither side could trust. After the defeat at Cannae he had gone over to Hannibal – on the principle, apparently, that success should determine a man's loyalties – and dragged Arpi into revolt. Now that, contrary to what he wished and expected, he was witnessing the resurgence of Roman hopes, he was offering to pay his debt to the betrayed by a new betrayal – a scoundrel with an ever-divided mind, as worthless as an enemy as he was treacherous as a friend. Such a man, it was felt, was a model for deserters and should be classed with the betrayers of Falerii and Pyrrhus. But Fabius, the consul's father, took a different view: everyone, he said, was forgetting the realities of the situation; in the heat of war they were trying to exercise free judgement, as they would in peace time. The result was that, when all their efforts and thoughts ought to be directed upon preventing, in any

possible way, the secession of allies, they were in fact thinking of something quite different. They were saying they ought to make an awful example of a man who had come to his senses and turned to look once more upon his former friends. If then anyone was at liberty to leave the Romans but was not allowed to come back to them, who could doubt that the cause of Rome would soon be despaired of by her allies and that the whole of Italy would be united by treaties with Carthage? 'I for my part,' he went on, 'by no means imagine that we ought to trust Altinius. But I should follow a middle course, and propose for the moment to consider him neither as enemy or friend. Let him be put under free arrest in some town we can rely upon, not too far away, and kept there while the war lasts. After the war we can discuss the question whether or not his return to our cause outweighs the crime of his previous treachery.'

The view of the elder Fabius was adopted, and the man together with his companions was turned over to representatives from Cales, and orders were given that the considerable quantity of gold which he had brought with him should be kept for him. At Cales he was permitted to go free during the day time, though followed by guards; at night he was shut up and closely watched. In Arpi he was first missed in his own house, and a search began; then the story of his disappearance spread through the town, causing the sort of uproar one expects when a conspicuous figure is suddenly missing. Fear of a rising caused the townspeople at once to send messengers to Hannibal, who was not in the least troubled by the news, as he had long been doubtful of Altinius's loyalty; moreover, Altinius was a wealthy man, and there was now a good excuse for seizing and selling his property. None the less, as he wanted people to think that his motive was not avarice but anger, he had the traitor's wife and children brought to his headquarters and questioned first about his flight, then about how much gold and silver had been left in his house. When he had learned all the facts he had them burnt alive. This was indeed an act of supererogation – cruelty added to greed.

46. Marching from Suessula the consul Fabius began operations first against Arpi. Establishing himself about half a mile

from the town, he decided, after a close look at its situation and defences, to deliver his attack at the point where the latter were strongest and, consequently, least carefully guarded. When all the various engines of assault had been brought into position, he selected the best centurions the army possessed, put them in charge of brave and capable officers, and assigned them a force of 600 men. This he judged an adequate number, and his orders were that, when the trumpets sounded for the fourth watch, they should carry ladders to the spot indicated. There was a low, narrow gate there, leading to an unfrequented street through a more or less deserted part of the town. Their task was first to get over the wall by means of the ladders and open the gate from inside, or to break it down; then, when part of the town was already theirs, to give the signal on a trumpet for the rest of the troops to move up. He himself would have everything in order and ready for the signal. His instructions were carried out with vigour and promptness; and now what might have hampered the men's action in fact greatly assisted them to avoid attracting the enemy's attention; about midnight it began to rain hard, and the guards and sentries left their posts and ran for shelter; then it rained harder still, and the sound of it drowned the noise the enemy made as they were forcing the gate; finally, when the rain eased off, its gentle and monotonous whispering falling upon the sentries' ears sent many of them to sleep. Once in possession of the gate, the advanced party ordered the trumpeters, posted at equal intervals along the street, to give their signal to summon the consul. This done according to plan, the consul ordered his men to march, and a little before daybreak he entered the town by the broken gate.

47. Only then did the enemy awake to the situation, dawn being now at hand and the rain becoming lighter. There was a garrison of Hannibal's in the town about 5,000 strong, and the townspeople themselves had armed a force of 3,000 men, which the Carthaginians put in the front line, to avoid possible treachery from their rear. The fight began in narrow streets, still dark before the dawn. The Romans were soon in possession not only of the streets but of the houses near the gate, which they had seized to prevent casualties from missiles flung from

above them. This led to mutual recognition between some of the soldiers in the opposing forces, and to an exchange of talk between them. The Romans asked the people of Arpi what on earth they were about – for what fault in Rome or merit in Carthage were they, an Italian people, fighting against old allies for a foreign and barbarous nation, and trying to make Italy a tributary to Africa. The others in reply excused themselves by saying that they had been sold to Carthage, in absolute ignorance, by their government – that they, the people, had been caught and overpowered by their leaders, few though they were. Once started, the talk spread to larger and larger groups, until finally the chief magistrate of the town was brought by his own people before the consul; promises were exchanged in the very midst of hostilities, and the Arpini, with a rapid right-about-turn, fought for the Romans against the Carthaginians. The Spanish contingent as well, nearly 1,000 strong, came over to Fabius, having demanded, as a condition for doing so, only that the Carthaginian garrison should be allowed to leave the town without molestation. The condition was fulfilled; the gates were opened and the garrison was permitted to go, finally rejoining Hannibal, safe and sound, at Salapia. Arpi was thus restored to Rome; there had been no casualties beyond one man – once a traitor and recently a deserter. The Spaniards were ordered double rations, and the country was frequently benefited by their brave and loyal service.

While one consul was in Apulia and the other in Lucania, 112 Campanian noblemen rode to the Roman camp above Suessula. They had been allowed by the magistrates of Capua to leave the town on the pretext of plundering enemy territory. Arrived at the camp, they told the sentries who they were and said they wished to speak with the praetor, Gnaeus Fulvius, who was in command there. Fulvius gave orders for ten of them to be brought to him, without arms, and when he learned what they wanted – it was simply that when Capua was recovered their property should be restored to them – he took them all under his protection.

The other praetor, Sempronius Tuditanus, took by storm the town of Atrinum: more than 7,000 prisoners were taken, and a quantity of coined copper and silver. In Rome there was a terrible fire which raged for two nights and a day: everything between the Salinae and the Porta Carmentalis was burnt to the ground, including the Aequimalium, the Vicus Jugarius, and the temples of Fortune and Mater Matuta. The fire also spread to a great distance beyond the gate and destroyed many houses and sacred buildings.

48. During this year the two Scipios were led by their successes in Spain, with the recovery of many former allies and the acquisition of new ones, to extend their hopes to Africa as well. There was, for instance, the Numidian prince Syphax, who had suddenly turned against Carthage: to him they sent three centurions, charged with the mission of forming a pact of friendship and promising that, if he continued to press hostilities against Carthage, he would earn the gratitude of the Senate and people of Rome, who in their turn would endeavour, when the opportunity came, to repay the debt with interest. This communication delighted the barbarian prince; he discussed military tactics with the three centurions, and when he heard what those experienced soldiers had to say, he became aware, by contrast with the regular Roman system of training, of the extent of his own ignorance. Thereupon he begged them to behave as good and faithful allies by allowing two of their number to report to their commanding officers, while the third stayed behind with him as instructor in the art of war. He admitted that the Numidians had no experience of infantry warfare and were useless except on horseback – a kind of fighting used by the Numidian people ever since their earliest history, and to which they had themselves been trained from boyhood. They were now faced with an enemy who relied chiefly upon his infantry, and it was evident that he must himself train an infantry force, if he wanted to fight upon equal terms. He added moreover that his kingdom had plenty of men for the purpose; his only trouble was ignorance of how to arm, equip, and train them. As things were, his fighting force was quite shapeless and haphazard, a mere casual mob.

The centurions replied that they would do what Syphax asked, but only on condition that he guaranteed immediately to send the man back, if their superior officers disapproved of their decision. The name of the man who stayed with Syphax was Quintus Statorius.

With the two centurions Syphax sent three Numidian envoys to Spain to confirm the pact with the Roman commanders, giving them further instructions at once to approach any Numidians serving as auxiliaries with the Carthaginian army and to try to persuade them to desert. Statorius found ample material from which to enrol infantry soldiers for Syphax; he organized them very much after the Roman pattern, gave them instruction in forming up, manoeuvring, following the standards, and keeping formation, and accustomed them to the various regular military duties, including fortification, and all so successfully that the prince soon came to trust his infantry no less than his cavalry, and that when an engagement took place on open ground he defeated his Carthaginian foe. The Romans too derived great advantage from the arrival of Syphax's envoys, for as soon as their presence was known Numidians began to desert in increasing numbers. This, then, was how the pact of friendship came to be made between Syphax and the Romans.

At the news of the pact the Carthaginians lost no time in communicating with Gala, who ruled over the other – Maesulian – section of Numidia. 49. Gala had a seventeen-year-old son,[1] Masinissa, a young man whose ability even then left little doubt that he would add to the wealth and size of the kingdom he inherited. The Carthaginian envoys pointed out that, as Syphax had joined the Romans in order by alliance with them to increase his power against the kings and peoples of Africa, it would be no less advantageous for Gala, too, immediately to join the Carthaginians, before Syphax could cross to Spain or the Romans to Africa. Syphax, they urged, could be crushed before his alliance with Rome had brought him any solid or practical advantage. Gala was easily persuaded to send an army, as his son begged for the command, and Masinissa, reinforced by Carthaginian troops, encountered Syphax in a great battle and defeated him. Thirty thousand men are said to have been killed; Syphax himself escaped with a small

1. More likely twenty-seven: he was ninety-two when he died in 149 B.C.

company of horse to the Maurusian Numidians – the tribe far away to the West, near the Atlantic coast opposite Gades. There native warriors, hearing of his presence, came flocking to him from all sides so that he was soon able to equip a huge fighting force with which to cross the narrow strait into Spain. But Masinissa arrived with his victorious army, and, this time without any help from Carthage, carried on the war with Syphax with great gallantry and success.

In Spain nothing worth mentioning occurred except that the Roman commanders obtained the services of the fighting men of the Celtiberians, at the same rate of pay as had been previously offered by the Carthaginians; and over 300 Spaniards of noble blood were sent to Italy to try to induce their fellow-countrymen serving as auxiliaries in Hannibal's army to desert. This is the only occurrence of that year in Spain which is worth recording, as those Celtiberians were the first mercenary troops which the Romans had ever employed.

# BOOK XXV

1. During these operations in Africa and Spain Hannibal spent the summer in the neighbourhood of Tarentum, hoping that the town might be betrayed into his hands. Meanwhile certain unimportant Calabrian communities went over to him. At the same time in Bruttium two of the twelve communities, Consentia and Taurianum, which in the previous year had joined the Carthaginians, now returned to their allegiance to Rome. More would have followed their example had it not been for one Titus Pomponius Veientanus, a Prefect of the Allies: this man carried out a number of successful raids in Bruttium, on the strength of which he was able to pass himself off as a recognized military commander; which done, he scraped together some sort of an army and engaged Hanno. A great many men were killed or captured in this engagement, all of them an ill-trained mob of slaves and peasants. The least part of the loss was the capture of the prefect himself, for he was not only responsible for the whole reckless venture, but had previously been a notably dishonest tax-farmer, whose untrustworthiness had been as ruinous to his own profession as to the country. The consul Gracchus fought a number of minor engagements in Lucania, but none of them worth recording; he also stormed and captured a few unimportant towns.

As the war dragged on, the alternations of success and failure seemed to affect men's minds hardly less than they did the general situation: an instance of this was the flooding of the country by a wave of superstition, drawn mostly from foreign cults and so overwhelming that one might have thought that either the gods or their worshippers had suddenly changed their nature. It was no longer only in the privacy of individual homes that Roman forms of worship ceased to be observed; in public too, actually in the forum and on the Capitol, crowds of women were to be seen praying and offering sacrifice in accordance with unaccustomed rites. Prophets and priestlings had come into their own; and their number was increased by the rude peasantry driven into the city by fear of famine from the farms which the long years of war had made dangerous or left uncultivated, and by the prospect of easy gain from others' ignorance, a trade they followed with the assumed confidence of recognized professionals. At first nothing was heard beyond private expressions of indignation amongst decent people; but soon complaints of the scandal were voiced in public and reached the ears of the Senate, which passed a serious vote of censure on the aediles and the police magistrates for their failure to check it, and when these officials tried to clear the crowds from the forum and break up the apparatus of their unholy rites, they narrowly escaped rough handling. When it became evident that the evil had grown beyond the power of minor officials to control. Marcus Atilius, the City praetor, was instructed by the Senate to take steps to free the masses from these superstitions. Accordingly he read the Senate's decree at a mass meeting and issued the order that anyone who possessed books of prophecies or prayers, or copies of sacrificial ritual set down in writing was to bring all such written matter to him before the first of April, and that nobody henceforward should offer sacrifice according to foreign or unfamiliar rites in any public or consecrated place.

2. Several men holding official priesthoods died that year: Lucius Cornelius Lentulus, the *pontifex maximus*; Gaius Papirius Maso, son of Gaius, another priest; Publius Furius Philus, an augur; and Gaius Papirius Maso, son of Lucius, a decemvir in charge of sacrifices. Marcus Cornelius Cethegus was appointed to succeed Lentulus, and Gnaeus Servilius Caepio to succeed Papirius; Lucius Quinctius Flamininus was elected augur and Lucius Cornelius Lentulus decemvir.

The date of the consular elections was now at hand; but as it was judged unwise to call the consuls away from their preoccupation with military duties, the consul Gracchus named Gaius Claudius Centho dictator, to conduct the elections. Centho made Quintus Fulvius Flaccus his master of Horse, and on the first day available for the elections announced the appointment to the consulship of Flaccus, his master of Horse, and Appius Claudius Pulcher, who had been praetor in Sicily.

New praetors elected were Gnaeus Fulvius Flaccus, Gaius Claudius Nero, Marcus Junius Silanus, and Publius Cornelius Sulla. The elections over, the dictator resigned his office. Publius Cornelius Scipio, who was later to win the title of Africanus, was curule aedile that year together with Marcus Cornelius Cethegus; when the people's tribunes opposed Scipio's candidature, saying that it ought not to be considered as he had not yet reached the legal age which qualified him to stand, he said: 'If all Rome wants to make me aedile, well then – I am old enough.' Thereupon everybody hurried with such enthusiasm to join his tribe for the purpose of voting that the tribunes promptly abandoned their hostile position. The aediles' public benefactions that year consisted in staging the Roman Games in a style which, for the resources of that time, was sumptuous, and in repeating them for a second day; they also distributed measures of oil[1] to each quarter of the city. The plebeian aediles Tappulus and Fundulus brought several married women before the people on charges of immorality; some were convicted and exiled. The Plebeian Games were held on two successive days, and a Banquet for Jupiter was held to mark the festival.

3. Appius Claudius and Quintus Fulvius Flaccus (for the third time) now entered upon the consulship. The praetors drew lots for their respective spheres, Publius Cornelius Sulla getting the double duty of City and Foreign praetor – formerly two separate offices; Gnaeus Fulvius Flaccus, Apulia; Gaius Claudius Nero, Suessula, and Marcus Junius Silanus, Etruria. The consuls were formally entrusted with operations against Hannibal and assigned two legions each. One was to take over from Fabius, the consul of the previous year, the other from Fulvius Centumalus. Of the praetors, Flaccus was to have the legions which had been with Aemilius at Luceria, and Nero those which had been with Varro in Picenum. They were to take steps themselves to bring them up to strength again. Silanus was given the City legions of the previous year for service in Etruria. Gracchus and Tuditanus had their commands, in Lucania and Gaul respectively, continued for a further term, together with their armies; the same was done

1. The text is defective here.

for Lentulus, who was to continue to act within the 'old province' in Sicily, and for Marcellus, commanding at Syracuse and within the former boundaries of Hiero's kingdom. The fleet was entrusted to Otacilius; Marcus Valerius was to command in Greece, Quintus Mucius Scaevola in Sardinia, Publius and Gnaeus Scipio in the two provinces of Spain. In addition to the existing forces the consuls enlisted two fresh City legions, bringing the total strength for that year up to twenty-three legions.

The enlistment of fresh troops was hampered by a certain Marcus Postumius, of Pyrgi, whose behaviour came near to causing a serious disturbance. Postumius was a tax-farmer who for avarice and fraudulent dealing had had no equal in the country for many years past except Titus Pomponius Veientanus – the man who had been taken prisoner the year before by Hanno's troops during one of his ill-considered raids in Lucania. These two scoundrels, taking advantage of the assumption by the state of all risks from tempest in the case of goods carried by sea to armies in the field, had been reporting imaginary shipwrecks, while even such losses as actually occurred were often due not to accident but to deliberate sabotage. Their method was to load small and more or less worthless cargoes into old, rotten vessels, sink them at sea after taking off the crews in boats standing by for the purpose, and then, in reporting the loss, enormously to exaggerate the value of the cargoes. The swindle had been brought to the attention of the praetor Atilius the previous year and by him reported to the Senate, but it had received no official condemnation as the Senate did not wish at a time of such national danger to make enemies of the tax-farmers. The people however proved sterner judges, and two people's tribunes, Spurius and Lucius Carvilius, recognizing that the scandal was a serious one, were at length aroused to action and proposed to fine Postumius 200,000 *asses*. When the day came for his appeal, the people attended the assembly in such numbers that the open space on the Capitol was packed to capacity; the case was heard to the end, and it seemed that the one hope for the accused was that Casca, the tribune and a blood relative of Postumius, should interpose his veto before the tribes were called upon to vote. The other tribunes produced witnesses to watch the balloting, and cleared the crowd; then an urn was brought for the lots which should determine the tribe with which any Latins present should vote. Meanwhile the tax-farmers were pressing Casca to veto the continuation of proceedings. The people protested. Casca, as it happened, was in the front seat, over to one side, feeling very uncomfortable – half frightened, half ashamed; and the tax-farmers, seeing they would get little support from him, determined to wreck proceedings themselves. Shoulder to shoulder, like troops breaking through the enemy's line, they thrust their way into the space left by the crowd when it was ordered to stand back, hurling insults as they went at people and tribunes alike. It had nearly come to blows, when the consul Fulvius called out to the tribunes: 'I suppose you know you are deposed from office, and that unless you dismiss the assembly at once there will be an insurrection.'

4. The assembly was dismissed and a meeting of the Senate called. The consuls brought forward the matter of the lawless violence of the tax-farmers which had led to the break-up of the assembly. They recalled how Marcus Furius Camillus, whose exile would have been followed by his country's ruin, allowed himself to be condemned by his angry fellow-citizens, and how before him the decemvirs, whose code of laws was still the foundation of Roman society, and after him many distinguished national leaders had submitted to popular condemnation. Postumius of Pyrgi, far from submitting, had robbed the people of their right to vote, wrecked the assembly, degraded the tribunes, threatened his countrymen with battle, forced himself and his friends in between the tribunes and the crowd deliberately to prevent the tribes being called on to vote. Nothing, they went on, had stopped a bloody struggle from developing but the forbearance of the magistrates who had temporarily yielded to the outrageous self-assertion of a small group, allowed themselves and the populace to be worsted, and, to deprive those who wanted it of an excuse for bloodshed, had of their own free will broken up an assembly which Postumius and his gang were prepared to wreck by armed force.

These remarks were accepted by all right-thinking senators

as fully justified by the atrocious nature of Postumius's behaviour, which was formally declared to be an act of violence against the State and a most dangerous precedent. The two Carvilii, as tribunes, promptly dropped proceedings for the fine and brought a capital charge instead, adding an order that if Postumius failed to furnish sureties he was to be arrested and taken to prison. Postumius did provide sureties but did not appear in person. The question was put to the people, who returned a decision to the following effect: 'If Postumius fails to appear before the first of May, and, being summoned on that day, does not reply and is not excused, then it shall be understood that he is an exile; his property shall be sold and he shall be refused water and fire.' The tribunes then began to bring capital charges against all the men who had helped to stir up riot and sedition, ordering them to produce sureties. Those who failed to do so were imprisoned at once; then others who were in a position to do so were imprisoned too; the majority avoided the risk by going into exile. 5. So ends the story of the tax-farmers – a story first of dishonesty, then of the audacious means by which they hoped to get away with it.

An election was now held for the appointment of a *pontifex maximus*. Cethegus, himself newly appointed a pontiff, presided. There was strong rivalry for the post between three candidates – the consul Flaccus, who had twice before been consul and once censor, Manlius Torquatus, also distinguished by a censorship and two previous consulships, and Publius Licinius Crassus who had not yet stood even for the office of curule aedile. Young Crassus was the successful candidate, defeating his rivals, both of them old men and distinguished by high office. For a hundred and twenty years no one else except Publius Cornelius Calussa had been made *pontifex maximus* without having previously held a curule magistracy.

The consuls were having difficulty in raising enough recruits for the army, as the number of young men was hardly adequate for the new City legions as well as for bringing the old legions up to strength. None the less the Senate forbade them to abandon their efforts, and ordered the appointment of six commissioners, three to work within fifty miles of Rome, and three beyond those limits. Their duty was to inspect all free-born males in every country district, market town and local centre, and to enlist for service any who seemed fit to bear arms even though not yet of military age. The people's tribunes were to be asked to bring forward a proposal to the effect that, in the case of boys under seventeen who took the military oath, their period of service should be reckoned just as if they had been enlisted at seventeen or over.[1] In accordance with this decree the commissioners were appointed and proceeded to comb the country for free-born males fit for service.

It was about this time that a dispatch from Marcellus in Sicily about the demands of the troops serving under Publius Lentulus was read in the Senate. The troops were the remnant of the army destroyed at Cannae, and, as has already been said, they had been relegated to Sicily and forbidden to return to Italy until the war with Carthage was over. 6. With Lentulus's permission they chose representatives from their chief cavalrymen and centurions, including the best of the legionaries, and sent them to Marcellus at his winter quarters. When they were asked to state their case, a member of the delegation spoke as follows. 'In your consulship, Marcellus, and while we were still in Italy, we should have approached you, when first the Senate passed the decree against us – severe indeed, though not, perhaps, unjust – had we not hoped that we were being sent to a place of danger, to a country in turmoil after the death of its kings, there to fight a hard campaign simultaneously against Sicilians and Carthaginians, and by our blood and wounds to make reparation to the Senate, as once those who were taken prisoner by Pyrrhus at Heraclea afterwards fought him and justified themselves.

'For what fault of ours, gentlemen of the Senate – for looking at you, Marcellus, I seem to have both consuls and all the Senate before my eyes – were you angry with us then, or are you angry

1. Men were liable to service between the ages of seventeen and forty-six. Within this period a foot-soldier could be called upon for twenty campaigns. Livy apparently means here that any campaigns fought by boys of sixteen or less would be included in the statutory twenty and would thus, if circumstances permitted, shorten the total period in which they were liable to service. (A. de S.)

now? If we had had you, Marcellus, as our consul and commander at Cannae, our fortune, and our country's fortune, would be better than it is. Before I complain of our sorry plight, allow us to acquit ourselves of the charge against us. If the loss of our army at Cannae was due to some fault and not to the anger of the gods, or to Fate, by whose law event is linked unalterably to event in human affairs, then whose was that fault? Was it ours or our commanders'? I am a soldier, and I shall never say anything about my commander, especially as I know that he was thanked by the Senate for "not despairing of the commonwealth", and ever since Cannae, year by year, has been retained in his command. Other survivors of that disaster, men who served as legionary officers, seek election – we are told – to offices of state, and hold them too, and govern provinces. Can it be, gentlemen, that you readily pardon yourselves and your sons, but remain cruelly obdurate to us poor fellows who count for nothing? Did you send the common soldiers into battle to a certain death, though it was no disgrace to the consul and his distinguished friends to save their skins, when all other hope had gone? On the Allia nearly the whole army fled; at the Caudine Forks they surrendered without even striking a blow – and there have been other shameful defeats which I pass over in silence. But so far were men from seeking to brand those beaten armies with any mark of ignominy, that Rome was actually recovered by the very troops which had escaped from the Allia to Veii, while the Caudine legions which had returned disarmed to the city were there re-armed and ordered back to Samnium, where they utterly crushed the enemy who had gloried in their shame and now felt it to be his own.

'Can anyone accuse the army which fought at Cannae of panic or cowardice, on that field where more than fifty thousand perished, whence the consul fled with seventy horsemen, and of which the only survivors are those the enemy was too weary with killing to kill? When it was first decided not to ransom the prisoners, people praised us because we had saved ourselves for further service, because we had joined the consul at Venusia and there made up something, at any rate, which resembled an army. But now we are in a worse plight than ex-prisoners used to be in the old days: in their case only their weapons and the unit in which they served were changed, and the place which their tents might occupy when in camp; and all these they could recover by a single act of good service or by a single victory. Not one of them was driven into exile, or robbed of the hope of serving his full term: on the contrary they were given an enemy in battle with whom they might once for all end either their life or their shame.

'But we, who can be charged with nothing but our responsibility for the survival of a few Roman soldiers from the battle of Cannae, have been relegated to a spot not only far from Italy and home, but from the enemy too, where we are condemned to grow old in exile with neither hope nor opportunity of wiping out the stain of guilt, of appeasing the anger of our countrymen, or even of dying an honourable death. We do not expect our disgrace to be forgotten; we seek no reward for valour: all we ask is a chance to prove our courage and to act, once more, like men. We ask for toil and danger, for leave to play a man's, and a soldier's, part. The war in Sicily is now in its second year; it is a war of bitterest rivalry; to each of the combatants in turn cities are falling; armies of horse and foot are meeting in conflict; at Syracuse operations go on by land and sea; the cries of battle and the clash of arms come to our ears where we sit as idle and useless as if we had neither swords nor hands to grasp them. The consul Gracchus with his slave legions has fought many a pitched battle against the enemy: their service has been rewarded with freedom and citizenship. Can you not think of us, too, as slaves bought to fight this war? Allow us to meet the enemy and seek our liberty in battle; test our courage as you will, by sea, by land, in the line, in the assault of cities: we ask only for the worst dangers, the most exacting toil, in order that what ought to have been done at Cannae may now be done as quickly as possible, as all our life since that day has been marked out for ignominy.'

7. At the end of this speech they fell at Marcellus's knees. Marcellus told them that the matter was not within his competence to decide, but that he would write to the Senate and act upon its instructions. The letter was delivered to the new consuls and read by them to the Senate, where it was discussed. The Senate's decision was that they saw no reason why the

national safety should be entrusted to men who at Cannae had deserted their comrades in battle. If, however, the proconsul Marcellus had other views, he was at liberty to do what he felt to accord with the public welfare and his own duty, provided that none of the men in question should be excused fatigues, or decorated for valour, or allowed to return to Italy while the enemy was still on Italian soil.

In accordance with a decision of the Senate and the expressed will of the people, an assembly was now called by the City praetor for the appointment of five commissioners for the repair of the walls and defence-towers, and of two other commissions, each of three members, one for examining the sacred vessels and making a record of temple gifts, the other for repairing the temples of Fortune and Mater Matuta inside the Porta Carmentalis, and also of the temple of Hope outside the gate, all of which had been destroyed by fire in the previous year. The weather was exceedingly bad: on the Alban Mount it rained stones for two days without stopping; many buildings were struck by lightning, including two shrines on the Capitol and numerous sections of the rampart round the camp above Suessula. Two sentries were killed. The wall and several defence-turrets at Cumae were actually demolished by lightning; at Reate a big rock was seen to fly through the air and the sun looked redder than usual, like blood. To meet these portents there was a day of public prayer and the consuls for several days following busied themselves with the demands of religion. About the same time there was a nine-day festival of religious observance.

The revolt of Tarentum, which the Romans had long suspected to be imminent and Hannibal had long desired, was now hastened by an event from outside. Phileas, a native of the town, had spent a considerable time in Rome, nominally as an ambassador, and being a man of restless temperament, quite unable to endure the inactivity in which he had felt himself to be rotting for so long, now procured access to the hostages from Tarentum and Thurii. The hostages were confined in the Atrium Libertatis, but under somewhat casual guard, as any sort of sharp practice would have been of no advantage either to themselves or their governments. In the course of frequent conversations Phileas worked on their sympathies, and one night, soon after dark, having bribed two temple attendants, he induced them to escape from custody and himself joined the party on its secret journey. Early next morning everyone knew of the escape; men were sent in pursuit of the fugitives, all of whom were caught at Tarracina and brought back to Rome. With the approval of the people they were taken into the Comitium, scourged, and then hurled from the Rock.

8. The extreme severity of the punishment caused bitter resentment in the two most famous of the Greek settlements in Italy – resentment both public and personal, in so far as the friends and relatives of the murdered men were concerned. Some thirteen of these, all young men of Tarentum of noble birth, accordingly formed a conspiracy. The leaders were Nico and Philemenus, and these two, convinced that a necessary preliminary was to obtain a personal interview with Hannibal, left the city one night on the pretext of a hunting expedition and made their way to his headquarters. When they were near his camp, eleven of them hid in a wood close to the road while Nico and Philemenus approached the sentries, who arrested them and, at their own request, took them to Hannibal. They laid before him the reasons for their plan and explained what they had in mind; in return they were warmly thanked, loaded with promises and instructed to round up some of the Carthaginian cattle that were out at pasture and drive them to the city, in order to make their compatriots think that they had gone out on a raid. A guarantee was added that they should not be in any way interfered with in the process. Back in the city such a fine haul attracted attention; but when the feat was constantly repeated it was greeted with less and less surprise. At a second interview with Hannibal the conspirators obtained an assurance that the Tarentines, once liberated, should enjoy their own laws, keep all their possessions, pay no tribute to Carthage, and not be forced against their will to admit a Carthaginian garrison. The Roman garrison, together with all houses occupied by Romans, was to be left at Hannibal's disposal.

Once these terms were agreed on, Philemenus made a much more regular habit of passing in and out of the city during the hours of darkness. He was, as it happened, well known as a keen huntsman; he was followed on his expeditions by his dogs and so on, and he usually came home with something he had caught, or which had been brought him by arrangement with the enemy, and made a present of it to the prefect or the guard. That his comings and goings were nearly always at night was put down to his fear of the Carthaginians. When the thing had become so much of a habit that the gate was opened for him at any time of the night simply in answer to his whistle, Hannibal knew that the time for action had come. His camp was three days' march away; he had been feigning sickness there, to make his keeping of his permanent quarters for so long in the same place look less odd, and the Romans on garrison duty in Tarentum had, in fact, ceased to see anything suspicious in his protracted inactivity. 9. But now, having determined to move to Tarentum, he picked a force of 10,000 horse and foot – all of them men who, with their light equipment and exceptional physical agility, he knew would be best suited for the task – and left camp during the fourth watch of the night. He sent in advance a party of about eighty Numidian horsemen, with orders to cover all the ground in the neighbourhood of the roads, keeping everywhere a sharp look-out for anyone who might catch a glimpse of the column without himself being seen. Any men moving ahead of them they were to bring back, and those they met they were to kill, in order to give the local peasantry the impression of a raiding-party rather than an army on the march. Hannibal himself lost no time on the way and pitched camp about fifteen miles from Tarentum; even then he did not declare his objective, but simply called his men together and warned them to keep strictly to the road and not to let anyone leave his place in the column; above all they were to be on the alert for orders, and to do nothing except on direct instruction from their officers. His own instructions would all be issued in due time.

It was just at this moment that a report reached Tarentum of a small force of Numidian cavalry out on a raid and spreading alarm all over the countryside. The Roman garrison-commander took the report lightly enough, and merely gave orders for some of his mounted troops to go out at dawn next morning to check the raiders; indeed, so far was he from being disturbed by the reality of the threat that he took the raid to be a proof that Hannibal and his army had not left camp.

At the hour of the first sleep Hannibal was on the move again. Philemenus, carrying his usual load of game, acted as his guide; the other traitors waited to play their parts according to the arrangement by which Philemenus was to admit armed men by the postern-gate he always used as he brought in his game, while Hannibal on the other side of the town approached the Temenitis Gate, in the quarter facing east, away from the sea – inside the walls at that point a good deal of space is occupied by tombs.

As he drew near the gate, Hannibal showed the agreed signal, a blazing torch. The signal was answered in the same way by Nico. Then both torches were smothered and Hannibal silently led his men up to the gate, which was opened by Nico, who had fallen upon the sleeping sentries and murdered them in their beds. Hannibal entered with his infantry, having ordered his mounted troops to stay where they were, ready for action in the open ground wherever they might be wanted. Meanwhile Philemenus, on the other side, was approaching the postern-gate he regularly used; the guard's attention was attracted by the well-known voice and the now familiar whistle, and the gate was opened just as Philemenus was saying that the beast they had killed was almost too heavy for them to carry. It was a boar, and two men lugged it in, followed by Philemenus with another huntsman whose hands were free; then, as the sentry, astonished by the creature's size, turned all too rashly towards the men who were carrying it, Philemenus stabbed him with a hunting-spear. Some thirty soldiers then passed in through the postern, cut down the other guards, and broke open the nearest gate. Immediately the Carthaginian column poured in, and proceeded quietly to the forum where they joined Hannibal. Hannibal sent 2,000 Gallic troops, in three divisions, all over the town, attaching two Tarentines as guides to each. His orders were that the busiest streets were to be occupied and, once real trouble began, all Romans were to be killed and all Tarentines spared. To make this possible he instructed Philemenus and his fellow-conspirators to urge any of their people they saw in the streets to do and say nothing, and keep their spirits up.

10. Soon there was all the noise and confusion to be expected in a captured city, but nobody had any clear idea of what was actually happening. The Tarentines thought the Romans had made a sudden attack and were all out for plunder; the Romans supposed it was some sort of treacherous move by the people of the town. The garrison commander at the first sign of the disturbance made his way hurriedly to the harbour, where he was picked up by a boat and towed round to the citadel. A further cause of confusion was a trumpet-blast from the theatre: it was a Roman trumpet, furnished by the traitors for the purpose, and the fact that it was blown by a Greek who was naturally unfamiliar with the instrument made it impossible to tell either the origin or the purpose of the signal. With dawn came clearer knowledge: the Romans' doubts were removed as they recognized the Carthaginian and Gallic arms, and the sight of the Roman dead told the Greeks that it was Hannibal who had seized the town.

As daylight grew stronger and the uproar began to die down, the Roman survivors having fled for refuge to the citadel, Hannibal ordered the townspeople to assemble, bringing no weapons with them; and all obeyed the order except those who had gone with the Romans to the citadel, determined to share with them whatever fortune might bring. Hannibal addressed the assembled citizens in friendly terms, reminding them what he had done for their compatriots whom he had taken prisoner at Trasimene and Cannae, and inveighing against the pride and tyranny of Rome. He then told them to go home and each write his name on his door, adding that he would at once order the plundering of all houses not so marked. If anyone wrote his name on a Roman's lodging (Romans were occupying vacant houses), he would consider him an enemy. The assembly was then dismissed, and as soon as the houses of friends and enemies had been distinguished by the names written on the doors, the order was given and Hannibal's men scattered through the town to strip all lodgings occupied by Romans. Property of considerable value was found and taken.

11. Next day Hannibal proceeded to an attempt on the citadel. He soon saw that it would be impossible to take it either by

assault or by siege-works, as on the side of the sea, which turns it into a sort of peninsula, it was defended by high cliffs, and on the city side by a wall and very deep fosse. Accordingly, not wishing to be kept from more important enterprises by the need for protecting the Tarentines, or to allow the Romans at any moment to attack them from the citadel if they were left without a strong garrison, he determined to construct an earthwork as a barrier between the citadel and the rest of the city. He felt moreover that by doing this he might well have an opportunity of a clash with Roman troops if they tried to obstruct the progress of the work, while if they should make a real attack in full strength their losses might diminish their man-power to such an extent that the Tarentines would have little difficulty in defending the town by their own unaided efforts.

As soon as the construction began, a gate was flung open and the Romans attacked the men engaged upon it. An advanced post of the Carthaginians allowed itself to be driven back, hoping to induce the enemy, reckless with apparent success, to follow up his advantage in greater numbers and to a greater distance; then at the given signal the main Carthaginian force, which Hannibal had kept ready for the purpose, suddenly made its appearance all round the Roman contingent. The weight of the attack was too much for the Romans, who were prevented from a precipitate retreat only by lack of room to move freely, all the ground being cluttered up either by the building work actually in progress or by the gear and equipment of the builders. Many of them leapt into the fosse and fewer were killed in combat than in trying to escape. After that the work of building was able to proceed without hindrance. A fosse was dug, very deep and broad, and a rampart on the inner side of it; Hannibal also made preparations to add a stone wall at a short distance from the rampart and running parallel with it, to enable the Tarentines to defend themselves against the Romans even without Carthaginian support, though he did, in fact, leave a small garrison, partly to assist in the construction of the wall. He then withdrew with the rest of his force and took up a position five miles away on the river Galaesus.

Returning later from this camp on the river to inspect the progress of the work, and finding they had got on with it a good deal more quickly than he expected, he thought it possible that the citadel itself might be taken by storm. Unlike most citadels, that of Tarentum is not rendered safe from attack by its height; it is situated on flat ground and divided from the rest of the town only by a wall and fosse. When the assault, supported by all sorts of artillery and siege-engines, was already under way, the arrival of a contingent from Metapontum encouraged the Romans to make a surprise attack under cover of darkness and they succeeded in smashing up some of the enemy's gear and material, and destroyed some of it by fire, thus putting an end to Hannibal's attempt, at any rate in that quarter. All his hopes now lay in a blockade; but that was unlikely to succeed, as the Romans in the citadel – built as it is on a peninsula and commanding the entrance to the harbour – had free use of the sea, whereas the town itself was cut off from seaborne supplies. It was the besiegers, in consequence, who were more likely to go short than the besieged. Hannibal called the leading Tarentines to a conference and laid before them all the difficulties with which they were faced: he saw no way, he said, of taking a citadel with such strong defences by assault, and had no faith in the efficacy of a blockade so long as the enemy had command of the sea. If, however, he had ships with which to prevent the landing of supplies, the enemy would very quickly either abandon the citadel or surrender.

The Tarentines accepted this, but expressed the opinion that to give advice was not enough: means must also be provided to carry it out. Carthaginian ships, they said, might be sent for from Sicily to do the job; as for their own, they were bottled up in the harbour, and since the enemy controlled the entrance, how could they possibly get out into the open sea? 'Ah, but they will,' Hannibal replied. 'Many problems naturally difficult are solved by a little brainwork. Look: your town is situated on open ground; you have broad and level streets running in all directions. I can quite easily have your ships transported on wagons by the road which runs from the harbour through the centre of the town and down to the sea. Then the sea, now controlled by the enemy, will be ours; and we shall invest the citadel on both sides, by land and water. Or, rather, we shall take it in no time – with or without its defenders.'

Hannibal's words not only produced hopes of success, but filled his hearers with unbounded admiration of their leader. Immediately the town was ransacked for wagons; they were lashed together, tackles were brought for hauling the ships out of water, and the road was freshly paved to lighten the labour of getting the loaded wagons along. Men and mules were then assembled and set to work with such vigour that a few days later the fleet, fully equipped for service, sailed round the citadel and came to anchor right at the harbour mouth.

Such was the position at Tarentum when Hannibal returned to his winter quarters. Writers differ as to whether the revolt of Tarentum took place this, or the previous, year; that it was this year is stated by the greater number and by those who lived nearer in time to the actual events.[1]

12. The consuls and praetors were kept in Rome until 26 April by the Latin Festival: then after performing the sacred rite on the Alban Mount they left for their various military duties.

The discovery at this time of the prophecies of Marcius stirred religious feelings and caused some fresh anxiety. Marcius had been a celebrated seer, and when, the year before this, the Senate had ordered a search for books of prophecies, Marcius's prophecies had come into the hands of Marcus Atilius, the City praetor, who was organizing the search. Atilius had at once passed them to the new praetor, Sulla. Of the two prophecies of Marcius, one was confirmed by the course of events, though it did not come to light until later, and this naturally inclined people to believe the other, which concerned what had not yet occurred. The earlier prophecy had predicted the defeat at Cannae, more or less in the following terms: 'Flee the river Canna, O child of Troy, and let not foreign men compel you to fight in the plain of Diomed. But you will not believe me until you have filled the plain with blood and the river carries from the fruitful land down to the great sea many thousands of your dead. Your flesh shall be food for the fishes and birds and beasts that dwell in the land. For thus Jupiter has spoken to me.' The men who had fought there recognized the reference to the 'plain of Diomed' and 'the river Canna' no less than the

1. See p. 462, which suggests that the earlier date is correct.

actual disaster. Then the second prophecy was read – a more obscure one, not only because the future cannot be as clear as the past, but also because it was couched in a more perplexing style. 'If, Romans,' it ran, 'you wish to drive out the enemy, that ulcer which comes from afar, I propose you vow games to Apollo, which each year shall be celebrated with graciousness in Apollo's honour. When the people shall have given a part out of the public purse, then let each privately contribute for himself and his own. Presiding over this festival shall be the praetor who metes out the highest justice to the people and commons. Let the decemvirs perform the rites with victims in the Grecian manner. If you duly do these things, you will rejoice always and your fortune will grow better: for that God who peacefully nurtures your fields, will extinguish your foes.'

A day was spent in disentangling the meaning of this prophecy, and on the day after the Senate passed a decree authorizing the decemvirs to consult the Sibylline Books on the matter of the festival and the religious rites in honour of Apollo. When the results of their consultation were reported, the Senate decided to vow and celebrate the festival, and when it was over to give the praetor 12,000 *asses* towards the expenses, and two full-grown sacrificial victims. A second decree was passed to the effect that the decemvirs should conduct the ceremonies according to the Greek ritual and that the animals sacrificed should be, for Apollo, an ox with gilded horns and two white goats with gilded horns, and, for Latona, a cow similarly gilded. When the praetor was about to open proceedings in the Circus Maximus, he issued an edict ordering the people to make their contribution to Apollo, during the festival, according to their means.

This is how the Festival of Apollo originated: it was vowed and celebrated not, as most people suppose, to secure health, but victory in the war. To watch it the people wore wreaths; married women offered the prayers; meals were eaten with open doors in the courtyards of houses, and the day was marked with every sort of observance.

13. Hannibal, meanwhile, was still in the neighbourhood of Tarentum. The consuls, though they were both in Samnium, seemed on the point of investing Capua, and the Campanians,

as Roman troops had prevented them from sowing their land, were already feeling the pinch of hunger, the inevitable accompaniment of a long blockade. They accordingly sent a delegation to Hannibal begging him to have grain brought into Capua from neighbouring localities before the consuls arrived on the scene and all roads were blocked by enemy forces. Hannibal sent Hanno from Bruttium with orders to cross with his troops into Campania and to organize the supply of grain to the Campanians. Marching from Bruttium, Hanno was careful to avoid enemy-held positions and the two consuls in Samnium, and on approaching Beneventum encamped on high ground three miles short of the town; from there he issued an order for the collection of grain from allied peoples in the neighbourhood who had had supplies stored the previous summer, and provided an escort of troops to protect it in transit. He then sent to Capua, naming a day for people to present themselves in his camp to take over their supplies, after previously collecting from all the farms in the district every sort of vehicle and draught-animal they could find. His instructions were carried out by the Campanians, with characteristic feebleness and negligence: little more than 400 vehicles were sent, and a few draught-animals. For this Hanno gave them the rough side of his tongue: they were worse, he grumbled, than dumb brutes, for not even hunger could stir them to take a little trouble. However, he gave them another date, a little later, for collecting the grain – this time with more adequate transport.

This was all reported in detail to the people of Beneventum, and they at once sent ten representatives to the consuls in their camp near Bovianum. The news of events at Capua induced the consuls to agree that one of them should proceed with his army to Campania, and Fulvius, to whom the duty fell, started off at night and entered Beneventum. Once on the spot, he learned that Hanno had gone off with his troops to collect grain, that his supply-officer had organized the allocation of grain to the Campanians, and that 2,000 wagons had arrived together with a motley crowd of people, all of them unarmed. Everything moreover was being done in a confused and scrambling manner and the arrangement of the camp and proper military procedure had been wrecked by the influx of peasants, some of them not even Campanians. Once assured of the truth of this the consul gave orders for his men to prepare to move next night, taking nothing with them but their weapons and the standards, as the Carthaginian camp was to be attacked. At the fourth watch the army marched: packs and baggage were all left in Beneventum, and a little before daybreak they reached Hanno's camp. So great was the alarm at their appearance that the camp would certainly have fallen to a single determined rush if it had been on level ground; but its situation afforded powerful protection – the height of the eminence on which it stood and the fortifications which nowhere admitted approach except by a steep and arduous climb. As soon as dawn broke a violent battle flared up: the Carthaginians not only defended the rampart but from their superior position on the higher ground flung back the attackers as they came struggling up the steep slope. 14. None the less the determination and valour of the Roman troops was equal to everything, and in several places simultaneously they pushed forward up to the rampart and fosse, though not without heavy loss in wounded and killed. Perturbed by the losses, the consul called his officers together and told them that the operation was too risky and must be abandoned. The safer course, he thought, would be to withdraw to Beneventum and then on the following day to take up a position close to the enemy's camp so as to prevent the Campanians from getting out and Hanno from re-entering it. The better to assure the success of this move, he proposed to summon his colleague so that their combined forces might concentrate on this one objective.

But the consul's plan, just as the bugles were sounding the retreat, was frustrated by a roar of disgust from the men, who were contemptuous of so unsoldierly an order. It so happened that a Pelignian cohort was at the moment in the van, and its officer, Vibius Accaus, seized a banner and flung it over the rampart; then with a prayer that he and his cohort might be damned if the enemy got it, he led the way over the fosse and rampart and burst into the camp. His Pelignian were already engaged inside the defences when in another section Valerius Flaccus, an officer of the third legion, began to reproach the Romans with cowardice for yielding to allies the honour of taking the enemy's camp; whereupon Titus Pedanius, leading centurion of the *principes*, snatched a standard from its bearer and cried out: 'In one moment this standard and I who carry it will be over the rampart. Whoever wants to prevent the enemy getting it, follow me.' As he crossed the fosse, his own company followed him, then the whole legion.

Now at last even the consul had second thoughts, when he saw his men swarming over the rampart. He no longer wished to hold the others back, but urged them to fresh efforts, pointing to the imminent and terrible danger which threatened a valiant cohort of their allies and a whole Roman legion. The response was immediate: through a hail of missiles, past enemy swords, and through packed ranks which tried to bar their way, every man, to the best of his strength and regardless of the difficulties of the ground, thrust forward, till the whole army had won its way in. Many wounded men, even though faint from loss of blood, struggled to get inside before they fell.

It was all over in a moment. The camp was taken almost as easily as if it had been on level ground and unfortified. What remained could not be called a fight; it was mere butchery in the hopeless confusion. More than 6,000 of the enemy were killed and over 7,000 taken prisoner, including the Campanians who had come for their grain and the entire outfit of wagons and draught-animals. A great deal else of value was captured, livestock and material which Hanno had taken during his raids from farms belonging to Rome's allies. Then the camp was completely dismantled and the troops returned to Beneventum, where the two consuls (for Appius Claudius had arrived on the scene a few days later) disposed of the booty partly by sale, partly by distribution. The men whose services had led most directly to the capture of the camp were rewarded, in particular Accaus the Pelignian and Pedanius, leading centurion of the third legion. Hanno was at Cominium Ocritum when he learned of the disaster; he left with the small foraging party he happened to have with him and returned – more or less a fugitive – to Bruttium.

15. The Campanians, at the news of what was as serious a blow to themselves as to their friends, sent a delegation to Hannibal to report the presence of both consuls at Beneventum,

one day's march from Capua, which meant that the war was right at their gates. Unless, they said, he came speedily to their aid, Capua would pass into enemy hands sooner even than Arpi had done. Not even Tarentum – not to mention its citadel – ought to be important enough to let Capua, a city he liked to compare with Carthage itself, pass abandoned and defenceless into the hands of the Roman people. Hannibal in reply promised to keep the Campanian situation in mind, and sent back with the delegation a force of 2,000 cavalry which would enable them for the time being to protect their lands from devastation.

The attention of the Romans, meanwhile, was occupied amongst other things by the citadel in Tarentum and its besieged garrison. Gaius Servilius, whom the Senate had authorized the praetor Cornelius to send into Etruria to purchase grain, succeeded in slipping through the enemy patrols and bringing a number of laden ships into the harbour. The position of the besieged had previously been almost hopeless, and the enemy had often parleyed with them and urged them to desert to Hannibal; but now with the arrival of the food-ships it was the besiegers who found themselves being badgered to change their allegiance. The garrison was, in fact, pretty strong now that the troops from Metapontum had been brought in to aid the defence. The Metapontines themselves, relieved of their fears by this transfer of troops, went over to Hannibal, and their example was followed by Thurii, another town on that coast. The people of Thurii were induced to make this move not so much by the revolt of Tarentum and Metapontum – to the Metapontines they were also related by blood, both having come originally from Achaea – as by indignation against the Romans for the recent murder of the hostages. The friends and relatives of these men got into communication with Hanno and Mago,[1] who were not far off in Bruttium, and undertook to betray the town into their hands if they would move an army up to the walls. Marcus Atinius controlled Thurii with a garrison of moderate strength, and they believed that because of his confidence, not so much in his own small force as in the fighting men of Thurii itself, whom he had drilled and equipped

1. Not Hannibal's brother.

on purpose to deal with such an emergency, he could easily be drawn into an action without taking proper precautions.

The two Carthaginian commanders entered the territory of Thurii, Hanno proceeding with the infantry, all equipped for action, to the town, while Mago and the cavalry took up a position behind some hills conveniently situated to conceal an ambush. Atinius's scouts had informed him only of Hanno's column of foot, so when he marched out to offer battle he knew nothing either of the treachery within the town or of the trap which awaited him. The infantry engagement which followed was a half-hearted affair, the small Roman force fighting in the van while the Thurians awaited events rather than did anything to precipitate them. The Carthaginian line continued deliberately to give ground in order to draw the unsuspecting enemy to the farther side of the hill where Mago's cavalry lay in wait. The stratagem succeeded: with a yell Mago's men charged and promptly put to flight the mob of Thurians, almost undisciplined as they were and of doubtful loyalty to the side on which they were supposed to be fighting. The Romans, though caught between the enemy horse and foot, continued for a time to resist, but in the end turned tail like the rest and hurriedly retreated to the town. There the traitors were waiting, massed together: they had opened the gates to admit their fellow-townsmen, but when they saw the routed Romans approaching they cried out that the Carthaginians were upon them and would get into the town at the same time unless they immediately closed the gates. So the Romans were shut out and left at the enemy's mercy, only Atinius and a few others being admitted. Inside the town there was dissension for a time, as the party opposed to Atinius proposed to yield to circumstances and surrender to the victors; however, bad luck and bad counsels, as usual, prevailed, though Atinius was spared. He and his men were taken down to the sea where ships were waiting, and the Carthaginians were admitted into the town. The indulgence shown to Atinius was due rather to their wish to save him in return for his mild and just rule than to any consideration for the Romans.

The consuls marched into Campania from Beneventum. Their object was not only to destroy the crops, which had just begun to show above ground, but to attack Capua. Both felt that their consulship would be made famous by the destruction of this wealthy city, while at the same time they would be freeing the Roman name from the deep disgrace of having allowed the defection of so close a neighbour to go unpunished for over two years.

None the less they took the precaution of ordering Tiberius Gracchus to leave Lucania and join them at Beneventum with his cavalry and light infantry – partly that Beneventum might not be left without a garrison, and partly to give their cavalry force sufficient strength to meet emergencies if Hannibal should come, as they had no doubt he would, to the aid of Capua. Gracchus was further instructed to appoint some officer to take charge of the camp and heavy infantry in Lucania, to maintain the situation there.

16. While Gracchus was offering sacrifice before starting on his march, something occurred which portended disaster: when the victim had been killed, two snakes came gliding from nowhere and began to eat the liver, and on being seen as suddenly vanished. The soothsayers advised that the sacrifice should be performed afresh; this time the entrails of the victim were more carefully watched, but again – and again after that – the snakes (so they say) came gliding up, tasted the liver, and disappeared unharmed. The soothsayers gave warning that it was the general himself who was threatened by this omen, and urged him to beware of hidden men and veiled plots; but no foresight was able to avert the fate which hung over him.

There was a Lucanian named Flavus, leader of the party in Lucania which had stood by Rome when the other party had gone over to Hannibal. His party had elected him praetor and he was now in his second year of office. This person, to curry favour with Hannibal, suddenly swung round, and, which was worse, was not content to change sides himself and to draw the Lucanians after him, without ratifying his pact with the enemy by the betrayal and death of the Roman commander, who was also bound to him by the ties of hospitality. Obtaining a secret interview with Mago, who commanded in Bruttium, he was promised that, if he delivered the Roman general into Carthaginian hands, the Lucanians would be received into the

Carthaginian alliance as a free people with their own laws; whereupon he conducted Mago to a place whither he undertook to bring Gracchus with only a handful of men. Mago was to conceal there an armed force of horse and foot – and it was a spot, he added, where a large number could lie hidden. The spot was then carefully examined by the two of them and the surrounding country thoroughly gone over, after which a day was fixed upon for carrying out the plan.

Flavus went to the Roman commander and told him that he had on hand an important scheme for the completion of which Gracchus's help was necessary. He said he had persuaded the magistrates of all the Lucanian peoples who had gone over to Carthage in the general upheaval to resume friendly relations with Rome now that her prospects, which had looked so desperate after the defeat at Cannae, were daily becoming better and more promising, while Hannibal's strength was on the wane and had indeed been reduced almost to nothing. 'We have erred,' he continued, 'in the past, but the Romans will not be implacable. No nation has ever been more easily moved by repentance than they, or more prompt to pardon. Think how often in the past they have forgiven a rebellion even of their own people. All this I said to the Lucanian magistrates; but they would prefer to hear it from your own lips and themselves to grasp your hand as a pledge of your good faith. I have arranged a place for them to meet you – a place well out of sight and not far from your camp. There a few words will settle the matter and all the peoples of Lucania will once more be the allies of Rome and under Roman protection.'

Gracchus saw nothing to suspect either in the matter or the manner of what Flavus said. The plausibility of it took him in completely; so accompanied by his lictors and a squadron of horse he left camp and, led by the man who had once been his guest, fell straight into the trap. In a moment the enemy were upon him and Flavus, to leave no doubt of his treachery, joined in the attack. Missiles flew from every side. Gracchus leapt from his horse and ordered his men to do the same, urging them to ennoble by their courage the one thing that fate had left them to do. 'For what is there but death,' he cried, 'for a few men penned by an army in a ravine whence forest and mountain admit no escape? All that matters now is how we die: shall we offer our bodies helplessly, like cattle, to the knife, or, refusing passively to await the end shall we turn the strength of our anger to one last battle, till, daring and doing, we fall, drenched with their blood, amongst the heaped bodies and weapons of our dying enemies? Seek him out, the Lucanian traitor, the deserter! Seek and kill him! The man who before he dies sends Flavus as a victim down into Hell, will have great honour and a supreme consolation for his own death.'

As he spoke Gracchus wrapped his cloak – for they had not even brought their shields – round his left arm and advanced to the attack. His men were few, but the fight which followed was out of all proportion to their numbers. It was to missiles that the Romans were most exposed; from every side they showered down into the gully, until they had found a mark in every man except Gracchus himself, who now stood alone. The Carthaginians did all they could to take him alive; but at that moment he caught sight of his Lucanian guest in the enemy's ranks, and rushed forward with such furious energy through the press that any attempt to spare his life would have proved too costly. He fell; and Mago at once sent his dead body to Hannibal with orders to lay it with the captured fasces in front of the commander's tribunal.

If this is the true account of Gracchus's death, he perished in Lucania, at the place known as Old Plains. 17. Some have maintained that he died near Beneventum, not far from the river Calor: according to this account, he had left camp with his lictors and three slaves to wash in the river, when he was surprised, stripped of his clothes, and unarmed, by enemy soldiers who chanced to be concealed amongst the willows on the bank. He defended himself with stones from the river-bed until he was killed. Others say that by the advice of the soothsayers he had gone about half a mile from the camp to find an uncontaminated spot where he might perform the rites to expiate the evil omens I mentioned above, and that there he was surrounded by two squadrons of Numidians which were lurking in the neighbourhood. In the case of a man of such very great eminence, these discrepancies about the place and manner of his death are indeed remarkable.

The accounts of his funeral also vary. Some say he was buried in camp by his own troops; others – and this is the account more widely accepted – that Hannibal erected a funeral pyre outside the gate of the Carthaginian camp; his troops in full armour marched past, the Spanish contingents performing dances, each tribe going through its national movements of the body and weapon-drill, while Hannibal in person paid honour to the obsequies in all due acts and words. This is the version of those who maintain that Gracchus was killed in Lucania; if you prefer to believe that he was killed at the river Calor, then you must also accept the rest of the story: that the enemy got possession only of his head; that the head was taken to Hannibal, who immediately instructed Carthalo to carry it to the quaestor Gnaeus Cornelius in the Roman camp. Cornelius then conducted the funeral there in the camp, the people of Beneventum joining with the soldiers in doing honour to the dead commander.

18. When the consuls had entered Campanian territory and had begun to devastate the crops over a wide area, troops from Capua supported by Mago's cavalry made a sortie against them. At this sudden alarm the consuls hurriedly recalled their scattered troops, and they scarcely had time to assume battle formation before they were overwhelmed, with the loss of more than 1,500 men. This success increased the confidence of a naturally proud people, and they continued to take every opportunity of harassing the Romans; but the result of that first encounter in which they had been caught off their guard had made the consuls very much more wary. An incident, however, occurred which served at the same time to restore Roman morale and to check the audacity of their enemy. It was a small matter in itself, but in war the slightest thing may often have important results. Titus Quinctius Crispinus had a Campanian friend, named Badius, and the two men were linked by the most intimate ties of hospitality. Their friendship had grown because before the Campanian revolt Badius had been in Rome, where he fell ill and was nursed with much liberality and kindness in Crispinus's house. This Badius rode out in front of the guards before the gate and asked them to call Crispinus. Crispinus, informed of the request, supposed that

all that was wanted was a friendly talk, the memory of personal ties remaining, naturally enough, even though the public relationship between their respective communities had broken down. So he pressed on a little in front of his companions, and, as soon as the two men were in sight of each other, Badius called out: 'I challenge you to fight, Crispinus. Let us mount our horses and in single combat see which of us is the better man.' 'But surely,' Crispinus replied, 'both you and I have enemies enough on whom to show our valour. Why, even if I met you in the thick of battle, I should turn aside and refuse to stain my hands with an old friend's blood.' He turned and was about to go, when the Campanian in yet haughtier terms began to call him a coward and a weakling, hurling at his innocent friend reproaches he himself deserved, reviling him as a 'guest-enemy' rather than a 'guest-friend', who was pretending mercy towards one he knew that he dared not fight. 'If you imagine,' he cried, 'that personal ties can remain when treaties are broken, then I, Badius the Campanian, here in the presence of both our armies, openly renounce my bond of hospitality with Quinctius Crispinus the Roman. You and I have nothing left to share; no pact unites us now; I am your enemy and you are mine, since you have come to attack my homeland, the gods of my city, and the gods of my hearth. If you are a man, lay on!'

For a long time Crispinus hesitated, but was finally induced by the others in his troop not to let the Campanian insult him with impunity. So without further delay than was needed to ask, and obtain, the permission of his commanding officers to accept an individual and personal challenge, he armed himself, mounted his horse, and called Badius to come out and fight. The call was promptly answered and the antagonists rode at one another. Crispinus ran his spear through Badius's left shoulder, above his shield, and, when he fell wounded, leapt from his horse to despatch him as he lay on the ground; but before the fatal blow could be dealt the wounded man managed to get away and rejoin his friends, leaving his shield and his horse behind him. Crispinus proudly displaying his spoils – the horse, the captured arms, and his own bloody spear – amidst the admiring congratulations of the troops was escorted to the consuls, where he was praised in the highest terms and richly rewarded.

19. Three days after his move to Capua from Beneventum Hannibal offered battle. He was confident that as the Campanians a few days previously had fought a successful engagement without his assistance, the Romans would be still less able to stand up against himself and his army which had already won so many victories. When the action began, the Romans' line was hard pressed, especially by the Carthaginian cavalry and the weight and number of missiles, until the order was given to their own cavalry to advance to the attack. It was during the struggle between the mounted troops of each side that another body of men was seen in the distance to be approaching: they were in fact Gracchus's army, now commanded by the quaestor Gnaeus Cornelius, but both sides were equally alarmed by the thought that they might be a reinforcement for the enemy. Accordingly, almost as if by agreement, both had the order to break off the engagement and returned to camp with the honours more or less equal, though in the first cavalry charge the Roman losses were the greater.

The consuls were anxious to draw Hannibal away from Capua; so on the following night Fulvius marched away in the direction of Cumae, while Appius Claudius made for Lucania. In the morning, when Hannibal was informed that the Roman camp was deserted and that the two divisions of the army had gone off in different directions, he determined after a moment of hesitation to follow Appius, who, having led his pursuers in circles at his pleasure, returned to Capua by another route. But Hannibal had another opportunity for a success in this neighbourhood, as a result of the ambition of a certain Marcus Centennius, surnamed Paenula. He was a leading centurion, an immensely tall man and renowned for his courage; though he had completed his military service, he obtained through the praetor Sulla an interview with the Senate, at which he asked to be given a force of 5,000 men, saying that his familiarity with the country and the enemy's tactics would soon enable him to do something worth while, and promising to employ against their inventor the very stratagems by which our own armies and generals had hitherto been caught off their guard. It was a stupid promise, and it was no less stupidly believed – as if the qualities which make a good soldier also make a good commanding officer. Centennius was given not 5,000 but 8,000 men, half of them Roman, half from allied communities; and he himself raised a large additional number of volunteers in the course of his march, so that when he reached Lucania, where Hannibal had stopped after his vain pursuit of Claudius, his force was nearly doubled. The issue, of course, was never in doubt, as between Hannibal and a mere centurion, and between armies one of which had a long tale of victories behind it, and the other was entirely raw and composed chiefly of irregular and ill-equipped troops. Upon sighting each other, neither side declined combat; each immediately formed for battle. Things went as might be expected from the disparity between the combatants; they fought for over two hours, hope inspiring the Romans so long as their leader stood; but when, like the brave soldier he had always been known to be, and dreading the disgrace of surviving a defeat for which his own temerity had been responsible, he deliberately exposed himself to the enemies' missiles and was killed, the result was utter and immediate rout. All roads were blocked by Carthaginian cavalry; escape was impossible, and scarcely a thousand out of that large force got away alive. The rest, scattered over the countryside, were all, in one way or another, killed.

20. Both consuls now resumed the siege of Capua with all their available strength, and the necessary equipment and supplies were brought in and got ready for action. Grain was stored in Casilinum; a strong-post was constructed at the mouth of the Volturnus, where the town now stands, and there and at Puteoli, which Fabius Maximus had previously fortified, a garrison was stationed to control the river and the coastal waters. The grain which had recently been sent from Sardinia together with what the praetor Marcus Junius had purchased in Etruria was brought from Ostia and stored in these two coastal strongholds, to supply the army through the winter. Another reverse was, however, to be added to the recent defeat in Lucania: this was the dispersal of the force of slave-volunteers who while Gracchus was alive had served with the utmost loyalty. They took the death of their general as the equivalent of a discharge, and all deserted.

Hannibal did not want Capua neglected nor his allies abandoned in their dangerous situation; nevertheless the success which had been offered him by the reckless conduct of one Roman leader kept him eagerly on the look-out for an opportunity of some sudden stroke elsewhere, against another commander and another army. News was reaching him that the praetor Gnaeus Fulvius, during operations against certain towns in Apulia which had joined the Carthaginian cause, had at first given full attention to his military duties, but as time went on and he was uniformly successful, both he and his men, loaded as they were with plunder, had grown so slack and careless that there was no longer any discipline in the army at all. Hannibal accordingly, having had frequent experience in the past – not to mention the events of a few days ago – of what happens to an army under incompetent leadership, moved into Apulia.

21. The Roman legions with the praetor Fulvius were in the vicinity of Herdonea. On the news of the enemy's approach the men came near to wrenching their standards from the ground and forming for battle without any orders from their commanding officer; and indeed they were held back only by the conviction that they could behave in that arbitrary and undisciplined manner whenever they pleased. Hannibal knew that everything in the Roman camp was at sixes and sevens, with most of the soldiers demanding action and recklessly urging their commander to order them forward; and the knowledge convinced him that an opportunity for a successful stroke was in his hands. That night, therefore, he concealed a force of 3,000 men, lightly equipped, in the neighbouring farms and amongst the woodlands and scrub with orders to be ready, on the given signal, for a concerted surprise attack. Mago with some 2,000 horse was instructed to hold all roads by which he thought the enemy might try to escape. These dispositions made, he formed his main army into line of battle at dawn next morning.

Fulvius, for his part, accepted the challenge – not that he had any confidence of success, but simply because he was dragged into it by the chance impulse of his men. The same irresponsible spirit with which they had taken the field governed the actual formation of the line: discipline gave place to the moment's whim; men scrambled to take their places wherever their fancy prompted, and no less irresponsibly, when they found them too dangerous, hurriedly shifted to others. The first legion with the allied auxiliary contingent of the Left were stationed up in front, the whole line being shallow and much extended. The officers loudly objected that it was hopelessly weak from lack of depth and would be broken at any point where the enemy might attack, but the men refused even to listen to salutary advice, let alone pay attention to it. And there, facing them, was Hannibal, a very different commander with a very different army, drawn up, moreover, in by no means so haphazard a fashion.

The result was that the Romans failed to withstand the first onset – indeed, the mere battle-cry of the enemy was too much for them. The officer in command, no less stupid, no less foolhardy than Centennius, proved far from his equal in courage, for as soon as he saw things going against him and his army in confusion, he made a dash for his horse and galloped off for his life with some 200 troopers. All the rest, driven in by the frontal attack and surrounded in flank and rear, were so badly cut to pieces that of 18,000 men not more than 2,000 escaped alive. The camp was taken.

22. The news of these successive disasters was received in Rome with very great distress and alarm; none the less the anxiety was less than it might have been because the consuls, who held the supreme command, had hitherto been successful. Laetorius and Metilius were sent to the consuls with the Senate's instructions to round up with all diligence the remnants of the two armies and to do all they could to prevent the men from surrendering in fear or desperation to the enemy, as had occurred after the defeat at Cannae; at the same time they were to start a search for the deserters from the army of slave-volunteers. The same task was assigned to Publius Cornelius, who was also in charge of recruiting, and he issued orders in the market towns and local centres for a search to begin and for the recall of the men to the colours. All these measures were conscientiously carried out.

The consul Appius Claudius put Decimus Junius in charge

at the mouth of the Volturnus and Marcus Aurelius Cotta at Puteoli, both with orders to send all grain cargoes immediately to the camp as ships came in from Etruria and Sardinia; he himself then returned to Capua, where he found his colleague Fulvius bringing in all necessary material from Casilinum and urging forward preparations for the siege. Both consular armies then invested the town, and at the same time the praetor Claudius Nero was summoned from the Claudian camp at Suessula. Accordingly, he too left an adequate garrison to hold the camp, and marched down to Capua with all the rest of his forces. Thus three army-headquarters were stationed around Capua, and three armies set to work, each in its own sector, and prepared to construct a fosse and rampart all round the town. At convenient intervals strong-points were built, and in many places local engagements were fought with the Campanian troops who attempted to interfere with the work – and so successfully that the enemy was at last driven to remain inside his defences. But before the work of circumvallation was complete, a delegation from the town was sent to Hannibal to complain that he had abandoned Capua, which was as good as given over to the Romans, and to beg him to bring help, now if ever, as their situation had deteriorated from a mere siege to a complete blockade.

The Senate sent written orders to the consuls by the praetor Cornelius to allow any Campanian who wished to do so to leave the town before the circumvallation was complete, and to take all his possessions with him: any who left before 15 March were to be free and to remain in possession of their property; after that date both those who left and those who remained would be held to be enemies. The offer was received by the Campanians not only with contempt but with the addition of insults and threats.

Hannibal meanwhile had marched from Herdonea to Tarentum in the hope of taking the citadel by any means he could, open or underhand; but, making no progress there, he moved to Brundisium, convinced that it would be betrayed into his hands. Here too he was disappointed, and while he was still in the neighbourhood the delegation from Capua arrived with complaints and entreaties. 'Once before,' was Hannibal's regal reply, 'I raised the siege, and this time too the consuls will not withstand my coming.' With this the delegation had to be content. They were dismissed, and had great difficulty in getting back into Capua, as it was now surrounded by a double fosse and wall.

23. It was just about this time that the siege of Syracuse came to an end; the successful issue was due not only to the brave and active soldiership of the army and its commander, but also in part to domestic treachery. At the beginning of spring Marcellus had hesitated between turning his attention to Himilco and Harpocrates at Agrigentum or continuing to press the siege despite his knowledge that the inexpugnable defences of the city both by land and sea put any attempt to take it by storm out of the question, while to starve it into surrender was equally impossible, as supplies from Carthage could not be intercepted. Now the Romans chanced to have with them certain Syracusan aristocrats who at the time of the revolt had been exiled because of their dislike of the changes in policy; so Marcellus, determined to leave nothing untried, told these men to arrange a conference with, and to put pressure upon, others of their party in the city, and to promise that, if Syracuse were surrendered, they should have their freedom and the right to live under their own laws. To arrange a conference turned out to be impossible, as so many were suspected of treachery that everybody was on the look-out to prevent anything of this kind passing without notice. However, one slave belonging to the exiles got admission as a deserter into the city, and by meeting a few men started discussion of this momentous affair. Some of them then hid under the nets in a fishing-boat and had themselves rowed round to the Roman camp, where they talked with the exiles. Others, and again others, followed their example, until there were eighty of them. At last, when all plans were complete for the betrayal of the city, a certain Attalus (out of pique because he had not been let into the secret) turned informer and told Epicydes. All eighty were put to death under torture.

This having come to nothing, another hope soon dawned. A Lacedaemonian named Damippus was captured by Roman ships while on a mission from Syracuse to King Philip. Epicydes was desperately anxious to ransom him at any cost, nor was Marcellus averse from letting him do so, as the Romans just then were angling for the friendship of the Aetolians, who were in alliance with Lacedaemon. Representatives were sent to discuss the ransom and they had decided to meet at the Trogili Harbour, near the tower known as Galeagra, as being a half-way point and most convenient for both parties. They came here a number of times and on one occasion a member of the Roman party, having had a close look at the wall, counted the courses in it, and by estimating the height of the stone slabs which composed them arrived, by a reasonable inference, at the total height of the wall. Since it turned out to be considerably lower than either he or anyone else had previously supposed, and consequently scaleable, in his opinion, by means of ladders of quite moderate length, he reported his discovery to Marcellus, who took it seriously enough. Since, however, this section of the wall, for the reason mentioned, was guarded with special care, it could not readily be approached, unless some favourable opportunity were found. This was provided by the information, brought by a deserter, that a three-day festival of Diana was in progress, and that because other things were in short supply owing to the siege, wine, provided by Epicydes for the whole population and distributed amongst the tribes by leading citizens, was being drunk at the festal banquets in more lavish quantities than usual. Marcellus at once conferred with some of his legionary officers; they chose such centurions and men as were fit for the difficult and dangerous enterprise and had the ladders secretly got ready, while Marcellus ordered the rest of his troops to eat and sleep early, as during the night they would be going out on a raid. Then, when he judged it late enough for men who had been at table since long before dusk to have drunk all they could hold and to be feeling sleepy, he gave the order to a single company to bring the ladders. After them came about 1,000 armed men marching silently in single file. The leading company climbed without a sound or a slip to the top of the wall; one by one the others followed, some not without trepidation, though the boldness of those first up could not but be infectious. 24. A section of the wall was already in the hands of the first thousand when the rest of the forces were moved up. More ladders were brought, and on a signal from the Hexapylon they began to climb. The advanced troops had already reached the Hexapylon through streets absolutely deserted, as most of the Syracusans after their festal banquet in the turrets had either drunk themselves to sleep or were well on the way to doing so. A few were caught in their beds and killed.

Near the Hexapylon there is a postern-gate; the Romans were soon at work breaking this in, and once the agreed signal had been given by trumpet from the troops on the wall, all stealth was abandoned and violent fighting broke out on every side; for they had now reached Epipolae, a strongly guarded locality, and their object was no longer to conceal their movements but to strike terror into the enemy – as indeed they did. For as soon as the trumpet-call was heard and the shout of the men already in possession of the wall and a part of the city, the guards fled for their lives along the wall, in the belief that the whole city had fallen, or leapt from it to the ground, or were pushed over in the general panic. Nevertheless, terrible though the situation was, many of the people were entirely unaware of it: they had drunk themselves into insensibility – and in any case in an immense city like Syracuse knowledge of what is happening in one quarter may well not extend to the whole.

Just before dawn the Hexapylon was forced and Marcellus entered the city with his whole army. This at last roused the people from their stupor and drove them to arm themselves and defend, if defence were possible, the city which was already all but lost. Epicydes hurried out with a column of troops from the Island (locally known as Nasos), convinced that only a small party had got in over the wall through the negligence of the guards and that he would soon drive them out again. Met by panic-stricken citizens, he at first told them that their exaggerated reports were false alarms and only added to the confusion; but when he saw for himself that armed men were all over Epipolae, he contented himself with the discharge of a few missiles, faced about, and withdrew to Achradina. It was not so much the strength and numbers of the enemy he feared as the possibility of domestic treachery and the danger of finding that in the general confusion the gates of Achradina and the Island had been shut against him.

When Marcellus stood on the heights of Epipolae and looked down at the city below him – in those days the most beautiful, perhaps, in all the world – he is said to have wept, partly for joy in the accomplishment of so great an enterprise, partly in grief for the city's ancient glory. He remembered the sinking, long ago, of the Athenian fleets, the two great armies wiped out with their two famous commanders, and the perils she had passed through in all her wars with Carthage. He saw again in fancy her rich tyrants and kings, Hiero above all, still vivid in men's thoughts, and glorious for his generosity to the people of Rome before everything which his own valour and success had achieved. As all these memories thronged into his mind, and the thought came that within an hour everything he saw might be in flames and reduced to ashes, he determined on a last effort to save the city. Before moving up to Achradina, he sent forward the Syracusan exiles – who had been, as I have said, with the Roman army – to parley with the enemy in mild terms and try to induce them to surrender.

25. The gates and walls of Achradina were held mostly by deserters who, if terms were made, had no hope of pardon. They refused to allow the men to approach the walls or to speak to anyone. So Marcellus, having failed in his purpose, ordered his troops back to Euryalus, a hill on the extreme edge of the city's territory, facing away from the sea, dominating the road which leads to the country and the interior, and admirably situated for receiving supplies. In command of this stronghold was Philodemus, an Argive, posted there by Epicydes; Marcellus sent Sosis, one of the assassins of Hieronymus, to him to negotiate, but Philodemus put him off with a lengthy and inconclusive speech, which Sosis interpreted to Marcellus by saying he wanted time to think things over. In fact Philodemus was deliberately postponing an answer because he was waiting for the arrival of Hippocrates and Himilco with their army and was sure that, once he could get them inside his defences, the Roman army, penned within the city walls, could be destroyed. Marcellus, therefore, seeing that Euryalus would not be surrendered and could not be taken by force,

encamped between the two city districts (virtually towns in themselves) called Neapolis and Tyche. This was because he feared that if he entered a densely populated area it might not be possible to keep his men, in their greed for plunder, under proper control. He was visited there by a delegation from Tyche and Neapolis, the members of it dressed like suppliants, begging him to spare them fire and slaughter. He thereupon held a council to discuss their entreaties (they could not be called demands) and it was unanimously agreed that no free man should receive bodily injury, but that everything else should be at the disposal of the troops. Marcellus accordingly issued this order.

The camp was defended by a wall constructed of bricks taken from the walls of houses. Marcellus posted guards at the gates which opened on to the streets to prevent a possible attack while his men were scattered in search of plunder; then the signal was given, and off they went. Doors were smashed in, terror and confusion reigned; but in all the uproar no blood was shed. The plundering continued until the soldiers had carried from the houses all valuable objects which had been accumulated through the long years of prosperity. Philodemus, despairing of assistance, removed his garrison from Euryalus and let the Romans in, on condition of being allowed to return unmolested to Epicydes.

While attention was concentrated on the tumult and uproar of the capture of part of the city, Bomilcar sailed for Carthage. The weather helped him, for it blew so hard that night that the Roman fleet could not ride at their anchors in the open; so with thirty-five ships he slipped out of the harbour without opposition and set his course for the south, leaving behind fifty-five ships for Epicydes and the Syracusans. Arrived at Carthage, he reported the critical situation of Syracuse and returned a few days later with a hundred ships. He was rewarded, we are told, by Epicydes with valuable presents from the royal treasure of Hiero.

26. With Euryalus in his possession and now defended by a Roman garrison, Marcellus was freed at any rate from the anxiety that enemy troops might be admitted into the fortress in his rear and thus make things difficult for his own men shut

up without freedom of movement within the city walls. He then proceeded to invest Achradina, establishing three tactically advantageous positions in the hope of cutting off all supplies and reducing it to starvation. For several days the outposts of both armies remained inactive, but the situation was suddenly changed by the arrival of Hippocrates and Himilco. The Romans now found themselves attacked from all sides, for Hippocrates, having fortified a position on the Great Harbour and given the signal to the troops in Achradina, attacked the old Roman camp where Crispinus was in command, and at the same time Epicydes made a sortie against Marcellus's outposts, while the Carthaginian fleet, anchoring off the shore between the city and the Roman camp, threatened to stop Marcellus from sending reinforcements to Crispinus. However, the result of these moves could hardly be called a battle – it was a mere momentary disturbance. Crispinus not only repelled Hippocrates' attack but drove off his men helter-skelter and chased them as they ran; and Marcellus soon forced Epicydes back into the town. It was clear enough from this easy success that Marcellus would have little danger in future from surprise attacks.

At this point plague broke out – a disaster for both armies, turning their thoughts, inevitably, from the prosecution of the war. It was autumn, and the locality a naturally unhealthy one; the intolerable heat affected nearly everybody in both armies, though the distress was worse outside the city than in it. At first it was climate and locality only that caused sickness and death; but soon the disease spread by contagion and the mere act of nursing the sufferers, until those who caught it were either left to die alone or took with them to the grave whoever sat by their bedside and tried to tend them. Death grew familiar, funerals were a daily spectacle, and everywhere, night and day, was the sound of lamentation. As time went on, from sheer habituation to the dreadful thing all natural sentiment was lost; people no longer followed the funeral train with the tears and lamentation due to the dead; indeed, they did not even remove them from the houses where they died or bury them. Corpses lay everywhere and anywhere, in sight of men who only awaited a similar death; and, through fear combined with the pestilent stench of putrefaction, the horrible thing was passed on from the dead to the sick, and from the sick to the whole. Some preferred death by the sword and flung themselves alone amongst the enemy soldiers on guard.

The epidemic had attacked the Carthaginian camp in a much more virulent form even than the Roman, for the Romans in the course of their long blockade had grown more accustomed to the moist and steaming climate. The Sicilians in the Carthaginian army all dispersed to their various towns near by, as soon as they saw that the epidemic had got a serious hold; but the Carthaginians themselves, having nowhere to go, perished to the last man, Hippocrates and Himilco included. Marcellus had moved his troops inside the city when things began to get intolerably bad, and many sufferers were helped to recovery by having shade and a roof over their heads. But even so the deaths in the Roman army were numerous.

27. After the destruction of the Carthaginian land-force, the Sicilians who had been serving under Hippocrates took possession of two small towns,[1] one of them three miles from Syracuse, the other five. Both lay on defensible sites and were fortified, and to both of them the Sicilians set about bringing supplies from their own communities and sending for reinforcements. Meanwhile Bomilcar again sailed for Carthage, where his account of the situation of their allies in Syracuse was designed to persuade his government not only that effective help could still be sent to them but also that the tables might be turned on the Romans, who at the moment virtually held the city. He thus induced the authorities to send with him as many merchant vessels, laden with supplies of all sorts, as they could raise, and to reinforce his fleet. Accordingly he sailed from Carthage with 130 ships of war and 700 transports. For his passage to Sicily he had fair enough winds, but, being easterly, they did not allow him to round Pachynum. The news of his arrival, and then of his being unexpectedly held up west of Pachynum brought joy and alarm in succession to Romans and Syracusans alike. Epicydes feared that if the wind continued many more days in the east, the Carthaginian fleet would return to Africa, passed the command in Achradina to the

1. The names are missing from the text.

generals of his mercenary troops, and sailed to meet Bomilcar, who was keeping his fleet in an anchorage open only to the south. Bomilcar shrank from a naval engagement, not because he was inferior in strength or numbers – actually he was superior – but because the easterly wind was more favourable to the Roman ships than to his own. Nevertheless Epicydes succeeded in overcoming his reluctance and persuaded him to risk an action.

Marcellus had no wish to be shut up in the enemy's city and subjected to simultaneous pressure from land and sea; so as soon as he was aware that a native army was being assembled from every part of Sicily, while at the same time a Carthaginian fleet was at hand with a huge cargo of supplies, he determined in spite of the numerical inferiority of his fleet to prevent Bomilcar from reaching Syracuse. The two opposing fleets lay one on each side of the promontory of Pachynum, ready to engage as soon as the weather allowed them to get out to sea; so when the easterly wind, which for several days had blown very hard, began to subside, Bomilcar was the first to move. For a time it looked as if he were putting out to sea in order the more readily to round the promontory; but later, seeing the Roman ships making towards him, he was assailed by some sudden misgiving and carried on straight out to sea, then rounded Sicily and steered for Tarentum, having previously sent orders to Heraclea for the transports to return to Africa. Epicydes' hopes of powerful assistance were thus suddenly dashed; rather than return to the city already largely in Roman hands and there endure the perils of a siege, he sailed to Agrigentum, not so much to plan any further move as simply to await events.

28. When the Sicilian troops received the news that Epicydes had gone and that the island, abandoned by the Carthaginians, had once again been as good as handed over to the Romans, they sent envoys to Marcellus to discuss terms for surrender, having first had talks with the besieged to ascertain their wishes. It was agreed with little dissension that everything which had belonged to the kings should pass into Roman hands and that everything else should be secured for the Sicilians, who should also keep their liberty and their own laws. The envoys then

invited to a conference the men whom Epicydes had entrusted with power, and told them they had been sent by the Sicilian army on a mission both to them and to Marcellus, in order to ensure that everybody, whether blockaded in the city or not, might receive the same treatment and neither section make any terms for its own individual advantage. They were admitted, and allowed to speak with their relatives and friends, to whom they explained the terms they had made with Marcellus; then, by holding out to them the hope of safety, they managed to induce them to join in an attack upon Epicydes' nominees – the three officers Polyclitus, Philistio, and another Epicydes, surnamed Sindon. The men were killed, and the populace summoned to an assembly. Addressing the crowd, one of the envoys began by complaining of the various troubles which everyone had been privately grumbling about, especially the food shortage, and then went on to declare that it was absurd to blame fortune for all the miseries they were forced to endure. 'It is in our own power,' he said, 'to determine how long we have to bear them. The reason why the Romans attacked Syracuse was not hatred for us, but concern; for it was when they learned that power had been seized by Hippocrates and Epicydes, the satellites first of Hannibal and then of Hieronymus, that they moved against us and began the siege. It was not Syracuse they wanted to lay their hands upon, but its cruel tyrants. But now Hippocrates is dead; Epicydes is excluded from the city and his officers have been killed; the Carthaginians, driven back by land and sea, have no foothold left in Sicily. So what remains to prevent the Romans from wishing to see Syracuse unharmed, just as if Hiero himself, who above all men cultivated friendly relations with Rome, were still alive? Neither we nor the city now face any danger except from ourselves: and that danger will come if, now that we are free from the insolent tyranny which oppressed us, we let slip our chance of a reconciliation with Rome.[1] We shall never have such a chance again as we have at this moment.'

29. The speech was received with great approval and without a dissentient voice. But it was decided to appoint magistrates before naming the members of a delegation to Marcellus. This

1. A conjectural rendering of a gap in the text.

was done, and then some of the newly elected magistrates were sent to put the case to the Roman general. Their leader spoke in the following terms.

'It was never we, the citizens of Syracuse, who severed relations with Rome: it was Hieronymus, and in doing so he sinned against us far more than against you. And later, when peace had been concluded after the assassination of the tyrant, it was no Syracusan who broke it, but the tyrant's satellites Hippocrates and Epicydes, having crushed us first by terror and treason. No one can say there has ever been a time of freedom for us except when we were at peace with you. So now that the oppressors of Syracuse are dead and we are beginning to be our own masters again, we come to you without hesitation to surrender our arms, to give up to you our city, our defences, and ourselves, and to refuse nothing which it may be your pleasure to impose upon us. The gods, Marcellus, have granted you the glory of taking the most famous and beautiful of Greek cities; everything worthy of record that we have ever achieved by land or sea is added to the renown of your triumph. Would you trust to mere report the splendour of the city you have captured, rather than let generations to come see it for themselves? Let Syracuse show to all who may visit her in after days by land or sea the trophies we have won from the Athenians and Carthaginians, and which you have won from us! Let her pass unravaged to your family, to be kept under the patronage and protection of the name of the Marcelli! Do not, we beg, let the memory of Hieronymus move you more than the memory of Hiero, who was your friend for many more years than Hieronymus was your enemy. Of the services of the one you have had practical experience; the folly of the other has effected nothing but his own destruction.'

From the Romans who were ready to grant all that was asked, they had nothing to fear; it was amongst the Sicilians themselves that the dangers of violence lay. The deserters, sure of being handed over to the Romans, persuaded the mercenaries that they too were threatened by the same fate, with the result that the latter flew to arms, murdered the magistrates, and then turned to massacre the Syracusans wherever they found them. In rage and terror they killed whoever came in their way and carried off everything of value they could lay their hands on. Then, not to be without leaders, they chose six prefects, three to take charge of Achradina and three of the Island. When the tumult at length subsided and they made inquiries about the terms agreed upon with the Romans, the truth began to dawn on them that their position was altogether different from that of the deserters, (30.) for the envoys returned from Marcellus with the opportune information that their fears were unfounded, the Romans having no reason for wishing to punish them.

One of the three prefects put in charge of Achradina was a Spaniard named Moericus. The idea was conceived of sending to him, amongst the envoys' retinue, a Spanish soldier belonging to the auxiliaries; this man obtained a private interview with Moericus, during which he gave a full account of the conditions in Spain, from which he had recently come. The whole country, he said, was held by Roman arms, and added that Moericus, should he want to do something really worth while, might become a person of great influence amongst his countrymen if he chose to serve under the Romans, or to return to his native place. On the other hand, if he continued to prefer to endure the siege, shut in by land and sea, what hopes had the future to offer him?

This suggestion was not without effect, and Moericus, when it was decided to send envoys to Marcellus, included his brother amongst them. The latter was taken privately to Marcellus by the same Spanish soldier as before; promises were exchanged and a scheme of action was drawn up, after which he returned to Achradina. Then Moericus, to divert attention from any suspicion of treachery, announced that he disapproved of the constant coming and going of delegations, and would in future neither receive nor send any at all; and further, that guard might be better kept, he ordered that separate sections, where attack was likely, should be assigned to each prefect, who would thus be responsible for his own section. To this proposal there was no opposition, and to Moericus himself fell the section from the Fountain of Arethusa round to the mouth of the Great Harbour. He was careful to let the Romans know of this.

That night, accordingly, Marcellus ordered a merchant vessel with troops aboard to be towed by a quadrireme to the Island, where the troops were to be landed near the gate by the Spring of Arethusa. This was done in the hours before dawn, and when the men had been landed and Moericus had admitted them according to plan, Marcellus at first light made a general assault on the defences of Achradina, the result of which was to occupy the attention not only of the garrison which held it but also to bring a column of troops from the Island, who abandoned their posts and came hurrying on the scene to help beat off the Roman attack. During the confused fighting which followed, a number of light vessels which had previously been got ready came round to the Island and landed their men. These made a surprise attack on the half-manned guard-posts and the gate which the troops there in their hurried exit had just left open; and thus with but slight opposition they got possession of the Island, stripped as it was of its proper defences by the hasty flight of the guards. None showed less determination to stay at their posts than the deserters, who, not trusting even their own leaders, made their escape while the fighting was still going on.

Marcellus did not wish the royal treasure (which was reported to be greater than it actually was) to be plundered; so when he learned that the Island had been taken and one part of Achradina occupied, and that Moericus had come over to him with his troops, he gave the signal for withdrawal.

31. The assault checked, and the deserters in Achradina having been given time and opportunity to get away, the Syracusans at last had nothing more to fear: they opened the gates of Achradina and sent representatives to Marcellus with a request for nothing more than the preservation of their own and their children's lives. Marcellus called a conference and invited the exiled Syracusans who had been with the Roman army to attend it; then, in reply to the envoys' request, he said that the services of Hiero to Rome during half a century had not been more numerous than the disservices of the rulers of Syracuse during the past few years. However, most of the crimes had, very properly, recoiled upon their authors, and they had punished themselves for breaking the treaties far more

severely than the Romans would have wished. For himself, he had spent nearly three years in the siege of Syracuse, not to make it the slave of the Roman people but to prevent the leaders of foreigners and deserters from holding it in subjection. What, he added, the Syracusans might have done was clear from the example of the exiles in the Roman army; or that of the Spanish leader Moericus, who surrendered his garrison; or even of the decision, brave but belated, of the Syracusans themselves. The fact, he ended, that he had been able to take Syracuse was by no means an adequate recompense for the labours and perils he had for so long endured around her walls.

A quaestor was then sent with a party of men to take over and guard the royal treasure. The city was turned over to the troops to pillage as they pleased, after guards had been set at the houses of the exiles who had been in the Roman lines. Many brutalities were committed in hot blood and the greed of gain, and it is on record that Archimedes, while intent upon figures which he had traced in the dust, and regardless of the hideous uproar of an army let loose to ravage and despoil a captured city, was killed by a soldier who did not know who he was. Marcellus was distressed by this; he had him properly buried and his relatives inquired for – to whom the name and memory of Archimedes were an honour and protection.

This, then, is the story of the capture of Syracuse. The booty taken was almost as great as if it had been Carthage herself, Rome's rival in power, which had fallen.

A few days before the capture of Syracuse, Titus Otacilius crossed with eighty quinqueremes from Lilybaeum to Utica. He entered the harbour before dawn, took possession of the laden transports lying there, and then landed his men. After laying waste a stretch of country round the town he returned to his ships with all sorts of captured material. Three days after leaving he was back in Lilybaeum with a prize of 130 merchant vessels loaded with grain and other things. He dispatched the grain forthwith to Syracuse, and its timely arrival saved victors and vanquished alike from the very real threat of a serious famine.

32. In Spain little worth recording had been done during the

past two years,[1] ways and means rather than actual fighting having occupied the attention for the antagonists. But this summer the Roman commanders on leaving their permanent quarters united their forces. A council was held and it was unanimously agreed that it was time for action: hitherto all that had been done was to prevent Hasdrubal marching into Italy; now steps must be taken to bring the Spanish war to a conclusion. They believed that they had adequate forces for the purpose, as they had been reinforced that winter by 20,000 Celtiberian troops. The Carthaginians had three armies: Hasdrubal son of Gisgo held in conjunction with Mago a position some five days' march from the Romans; Hasdrubal son of Hamilcar (the general who for so long had commanded in Spain) was nearer, at a town called Amtorgis. It was the intention of the Roman leaders to crush him first, and though they had full confidence in the strength at their disposal, the anxiety remained lest, if he were defeated, Mago and the other Hasdrubal might be sufficiently shaken to withdraw into the wilds of forest and mountain and so prolong the war indefinitely. They determined therefore to include the whole of Spain in their plan of campaign, and for this purpose divided their forces into two parts, Publius Scipio taking two thirds of the total strength of Roman and allied troops for action against Mago and Hasdrubal, and Gnaeus Scipio one third of the original army together with the Celtiberians for action against Hasdrubal son of Hamilcar. The two commanders with their armies set out together, the Celtiberians marching at the head of the column, and took up their position near Amtorgis in sight of the enemy but separated from him by a river.[2] There Gnaeus Scipio remained with the force already mentioned, while his brother Publius proceeded to his agreed assignment.

33. Hasdrubal was soon aware that the Roman force was small and that they were pinning their hopes on the Celtiberian auxiliaries. Accordingly, familiar as he was with the perfidy of barbarian peoples, especially of those amongst whom he had been campaigning for so many years, he arranged secret conversations with the Celtiberian leaders. As there were numerous

1. From a source which dated the death of the Scipios in 211.
2. Probably the Baetis.

Spaniards both in his army and theirs, there was no language difficulty, and he succeeded in concluding a bargain with them at a high price, for the withdrawal of their troops. This was not, in his view, an outrageous thing to do, as there was no question of the Celtiberians turning their arms against the Romans; and the reward offered for abstaining from action would have been quite big enough to purchase their active support. Moreover, most of the rank and file were only too pleased with the prospect of peace and of returning home to see their families and belongings again. So there was no more difficulty in persuading the men to accept the bargain than their leaders. Nor was there anything to fear from the Romans, few as they were, should they attempt to retain them by force. Here, then, is something which Roman commanders will always have to be careful about: this incident should be taken as a solemn warning not to trust in foreign auxiliaries without the presence in the army of a numerically superior force of native Roman troops.

The Celtiberians took up their standards and suddenly departed; and when the Romans asked why they were going and besought them to remain, their only reply was that a war in their own part of the country demanded their presence. Scipio, now that there was no hope of retaining them either by force or entreaty, was fully aware that without them he was no match for the enemy and would also be unable to rejoin his brother; accordingly, since there was nothing else he could do to better his situation, he determined to withdraw as far as he could, taking every possible care not to risk an engagement on open ground. As he moved off, the enemy crossed the river and followed close on his heels.

34. About the same time an equally alarming situation and an even greater danger from a new enemy threatened his brother Publius. This was the young Masinissa, at that time in alliance with Carthage, and later to be made famous and powerful by his friendship with Rome. On the present occasion, at the head of his Numidian cavalry, he happened to fall in with Publius Scipio's advancing column; he hung on to it assiduously night and day, cutting off parties of men in search of wood or fodder at a distance from the camp; often he would ride right up to the camp itself and charge at the gallop through

the outposts guarding it, causing the greatest confusion. There was much trouble, too, at the gates and on the rampart owing to his frequent and unexpected attacks at night. The Romans, in short, were kept always and everywhere in a state of nervous apprehension and compelled to remain inside their defences with no chance of getting fresh supplies. It was already something like a blockade, and that blockade would clearly become stricter if the Carthaginians were joined by Indibilis, who was said to be on the way with 7,500 Suessetani. In these circumstances the usually cautious and provident Scipio yielded to necessity and determined upon the rash move of marching by night to meet Indibilis and of engaging him wherever the encounter might be.

Leaving in camp a garrison of moderate strength under his lieutenant Tiberius Fonteius, he started at midnight, met the enemy, and joined battle. As neither column stopped to form into line, it was something of a running fight, and disorderly at that; and, all things considered, the Romans had the advantage. But it was not to last, for suddenly the Numidian cavalry, to whom Scipio thought he had given the slip, appeared on both flanks; this, in itself, was alarming enough, but no sooner had they entered upon a fresh struggle with the Numidians than a third enemy appeared upon the scene – the Carthaginian generals, who had come up on their rear while they were already engaged. Thus the Romans, subjected to pressure from two directions at once, found themselves in doubt against which enemy, in front or in the rear, it would be best to attempt a breakthrough. Scipio, in the thick of things, fighting, encouraging his men, exposing himself wherever they were hardest pressed, was pierced through the right side by a lance. A section of enemy troops, in wedge formation, had been trying to break through the Roman soldiers massed around him, and when they saw him fall dying from his horse, they ran off shouting and wild with joy to spread the news all along the line that the Roman commander had been killed. That alone, once it was generally known, really decided the issue. Their leader lost, the Romans immediately began to take to flight. It seemed at first not impossible to break out through the Numidians and other light-armed auxiliaries, but they were unable to escape mounted men in such numbers, together with infantry nearly as quick on their feet as the horses were. Rather more were killed while trying to escape than in the actual fighting, and there might well have been no survivors had not darkness, the hour being already late, intervened to stop the slaughter.

35. The Carthaginian commanders were quick to follow up their success. Immediately after the battle, having scarcely allowed their men the rest they needed, they hastened with all possible speed to join Hasdrubal son of Hamilcar, confident that once the junction had been effected the war could be brought to a triumphant end. There was much rejoicing when they arrived over the recent victory, and fervid mutual congratulations between the armies and their commanders, while satisfaction in the destruction of an entire army together with its famous commander was matched by unshakeable confidence in a second victory no less decisive. The Romans as yet had no news of the terrible disaster; but a sort of silent gloom weighed upon them, the wordless foreboding and presentiment of coming doom. Gnaeus Scipio himself, in addition to the knowledge of his allies' desertion and the immense increase in the enemy's forces, was inclined by the evidence of the facts to suspect a disaster rather than to hope that all might yet be well; for how could Hasdrubal and Mago have brought up their armies unopposed, unless they had already fought a successful battle? How was it that Publius had neither prevented their advance nor yet followed them, so that even if he failed to prevent the junction of the two enemy forces, he might at least have joined his brother? Tormented by these anxieties, he judged that the only safe course for the moment was to move as far away from his present position as he could. In the course of the following night he got well away before the enemy were aware of his departure or could make any move to stop it; but at dawn they saw he had gone and started in pursuit at their utmost speed, having sent the Numidians in advance. Before dark the Numidians were up with them. Harassing the rear and flanks of the marching column, they compelled it to halt and stand on the defensive. Scipio kept urging his men, as far as was possible with safety, to keep moving and to fight at the

same time, before the Carthaginian foot could overtake them. 36. For some time, what with orders to press on and orders to halt, little progress was made, and night was approaching; so Scipio broke off the action and withdrew his troops to a near-by hill. It was by no means a safe position, least of all for a body of men already badly shaken, but it was at any rate higher than the ground around it. There he formed his infantry in a circle round the baggage and the cavalry, and for a time they were able without difficulty to beat off the assaults of the Numidians; but later, when the three enemy commanders with their three fully equipped armies arrived upon the scene, it was plain that without proper defences arms alone would be quite inadequate to hold the hill. Scipio therefore began to look about him in the hope that it might be feasible to construct some sort of earthwork. But the hill was bare and the soil so stony that no timber could be found for stakes, no turves could be cut, no trench could be dug: for any work of fortification whatever it was useless. At no point was the ascent rough enough or steep enough to cause the enemy any serious difficulty: on all sides there was no more than a gentle slope. None the less, to make something at any rate resembling a rampart, they piled their pack-saddles, with the loads still attached, all round in a circle, building them up to the normal height of a rampart, and heaping on top of them, where there were not enough, any sort of baggage and gear they could get hold of.

The Carthaginians arrived, and their column had not the smallest difficulty in climbing the hill. On top they were checked for a moment in a sort of astonished incredulity at the odd appearance of the 'fortifications'; but their officers loudly and angrily demanded what they were waiting for and why they did not pull to pieces such a ridiculous affair, hardly strong enough to stop women and boys. The enemy, they added contemptuously, trying to hide there behind his bundles of clothes was already a prisoner in their hands. Nevertheless it was not so easy to get over the barrier, or to clear away that mass of gear and hack a passage through the closely-packed saddles buried under all the other stuff. But once they had set to work with poles to demolish the erection they cleared a way for the soldiers; and the same being done at various points in the ring, the whole position was soon in the enemy's hands. Then the blood began to flow, for the Romans were few and already shaken, their enemies many and with victory in their grasp. None the less a considerable portion of the Roman force succeeded in escaping into the neighbouring woods, whence they made their way to Publius Scipio's camp, now commanded by his lieutenant Fonteius.

According to some accounts Gnaeus Scipio was killed on the hill during the first attack; others say that he escaped with a few men to a look-out tower near by and that a fire was kindled round it; the doors, which they had failed to force, were thus burned away, the tower was captured and all inside, including the commander, were killed. It was in the eighth year[1] after his coming into Spain that Gnaeus Scipio was killed, and twenty-nine days after the death of his brother Publius.

Grief for the death of the two brothers was as great throughout Spain as it was in Rome. To the citizens of Rome the destruction of the armies, the loss of the province, and the national disaster all brought their share of sorrow; and Spain mourned for her personal loss in the death of the two commanders, of Gnaeus especially as he had held the command longer and was the first to win their favour, and the first of all men to show them an example of Roman justice and moderation.

37. In this situation, with all Spain apparently lost and both armies wiped out, one man restored the shattered fortunes of Rome. Serving in the army was a certain Lucius Marcius, son of Septimius and by rank a knight; he was a young man physically active and with more dash and intelligence than might be expected from his station in life. In addition to his excellent natural qualities he had benefited by the training of Gnaeus Scipio, under whom he had acquired over the course of many years all the knowledge a good soldier should possess. This, then, was the man who had got together a fresh and by no means comtemptible army out of fugitives rounded up after the recent defeat, strengthened by certain units withdrawn from garrisons, and joined up with Scipio's lieutenant Fonteius. The two forces, after fortifying a position north of the Ebro, wanted to elect a commander by military vote; and so great

1. Correct if he died in 211: the seventh year if he died in 212.

amongst the rank and file was the authority and respect enjoyed by a mere Roman knight, that when, by a system of regular reliefs for duty on the defences and outposts every man had cast his vote, the supreme command was unanimously offered to Lucius Marcius. He at once proceeded to spend all the time he had – and it was not much – on strengthening his fortifications and laying in supplies; all his orders were carried out by the men with a vigour very unlike the dejection of a beaten army. When, however, news came that Hasdrubal son of Gisgo had crossed the Ebro and was already close at hand to wipe out what remained of the Roman power of resistance, and the troops saw the battle signal raised by their new commander, all their newly found courage ebbed away: it was then they remembered the men who had recently led them, the two great generals, the fine armies which had given them confidence in the hour of battle; and they suddenly began to weep, to beat their heads, to raise hands in prayer to heaven, blaming the gods, or flinging themselves prone on the ground and pitifully invoking the name of the dead commander under whom they had served. Nothing could stop their lamentations, though the centurions tried to rouse the men in their sections and Marcius himself, when the attempt at consolation failed, chid them for abandoning themselves to womanish and useless tears instead of steeling their hearts to defend themselves and their country, and refusing to allow their commanders to lie in their graves unavenged.

Suddenly, at that moment, a shout rang out and trumpets blared. The enemy was near. In an instant grief was changed to rage: every man ran for his weapons, and all, fired with a sort of madness, rushed to the camp gates and hurled themselves upon the enemy. The Carthaginians were coming up in disorder and with no precautions against surprise, and the unexpected assault was a severe shock to them. They could not understand where so large an enemy force had so suddenly sprung from, since the Roman army had been almost annihilated, or how beaten men could have such audacity and self-confidence. Who, they asked themselves, had come forward to take command after the death of the Scipios? Who was in charge now? Who had given the signal for action? Bewildered, almost stunned, by all these surprises, they first gave ground, then, under the weight of the Roman attack, broke and fled. They might have been terribly cut up if the Romans had pressed their pursuit; on the other hand, to press it might well have proved both rash and dangerous; so, to avoid this, Marcius sounded the recall, actually holding back with his own hands some of the leading men as the line surged on in wild excitement. He then led them back to camp, still hungering for blood and slaughter. When the Carthaginians after their first repulse in confusion from the rampart saw that the pursuit had ceased, they supposed that the Romans were afraid to come on; so once again they were as contemptuous as before and returned to camp, marching at ease.

They were no less negligent in guarding their camp; for though the enemy was near, they could not get out of their heads the idea that the Roman force was merely the remnant of the two armies so nearly annihilated a few days previously. Because of this carelessness throughout the Carthaginian lines, Marcius, after carefully gathering information, determined on a plan which on the face of it was reckless rather than merely audacious. This was to take the initiative and attack the Carthaginian camp, on the grounds that the camp of *one* Hasdrubal could be taken more easily than his own could be defended, should the three armies, under their three respective generals, again unite. He was also well aware that in the event of success he would restore the broken fortunes of the Roman army, while if he failed the mere fact of having assumed the offensive would save him from the enemy's contempt. 38. He was anxious, however, to avoid upsetting his men by an unexpected and alarming night attack – indeed by a plan of action hardly consistent with their present situation. So he thought it wise to give them some preliminary words of encouragement. For this purpose he called a parade, and delivered the following address:

'Anyone, my men, who knows my devotion to our generals, living or dead, anyone who considers the critical situation in which we all now are, will surely understand that the command I hold, however much you honoured me by conferring it, is in itself a heavy burden and an anxious care. At the very moment when, if danger did not deaden grief, I should be too little master of myself to find any comfort for my sorrow, I am compelled, alone, to plan and think for you all – a difficult task for one who mourns. Even when I must consider how to save these remnants of the two armies for our country, I may not put aside the grief which dwells within my heart. Here with me always is a cruel memory; day and night the two Scipios vex my thoughts and haunt my dreams, often waking me from sleep and bidding me avenge them – and avenge our country, too, and your comrades, their soldiers, who for eight years were undefeated here in Spain. They urge me to follow what they taught, the lines they laid down, and, just as no one while they lived was readier than I to obey their commands, so after their death they would have me think that course the best which I believe, in any circumstance, they would themselves have adopted. And you too, my men, must honour them, though not with the lamentations and tears with which we follow a body to the grave – for indeed they still live a vivid life in the fame of their deeds – but, whenever you think of them, you must march to battle as if you heard their voices and saw them giving you the signal. Surely it was that very image which yesterday helped you to fight that good fight, by which you proved to the enemy that the Roman name did not die with the Scipios and that the nation whose strength and manhood was not overwhelmed by Cannae would rise again from any blow which fate might deal, however cruel.

'And now, since you have dared so much on your own initiative, I want to make trial of your courage when I, your leader, give the command. Yesterday, when I called you back from your wild pursuit of the routed enemy, it was not that I wished to damp your ardour; what I wanted was to save it for a better moment, when greater glory could be won, to give you later the chance for a surprise attack when, well prepared and armed, you could fall upon them when they were unarmed or even, may be, asleep. And the hope, my men, that this chance will come is no mere fancy of mine: it is justified by the facts. If anyone asked you how it was that you, so few in number, defended your camp against a superior and victorious force, your obvious answer would be that it was just this – the fear of their superiority – which made you keep all the defences strong and yourselves ready and on the alert. Precisely: for men are always least safe against the danger which their situation happens to conceal; one takes no precautions against a chance that one feels is negligible. Now the enemy fears nothing at this moment less than our turning the tables on them – that we, so recently the object of their attack, should ourselves take the offensive. Let us then venture this bold and, to them, inconceivable stroke. Its apparent difficulty is the very thing which will make it easier. In the third watch of the night I shall give the order to march, and you will march in silence. My scouts have told me their sentries are not properly relieved, their outposts not properly posted: one cry from you at the gates, and at the first assault the camp will be ours. Then amongst those torpid sleepers, those wretches trembling at the unexpected din and caught defenceless in their beds, you may enjoy the blood-letting of which, to your chagrin, you were yesterday deprived.

'I know the plan sounds over-bold; but for men in danger and almost without hope the way of courage is the safest; the moment of opportunity is a fleeting moment – delay only a little and you may look in vain for its return. One army lies near; two others are not far away. If we attack now, there is hope; you have already made trial of your strength and theirs. If we postpone the attempt, and the report of yesterday's action makes the enemy take us seriously again, there is danger that all the commanders may unite their forces against us. Shall we then be able to stand against three generals and three armies, when Gnaeus Scipio himself, with his forces still intact, was not strong enough to face them? It was by dividing their forces that our leaders perished: the enemy, too, if his three armies are not suffered to unite, can be overwhelmed. That is the only way of fighting this war. Let us then wait for nothing beyond the chance this night holds out to us. With the gods' help, go; take your rest, so that fresh and strong you may rush the enemy's camp as bravely as you defended your own.'

The troops heard with joy their new commander propose his unexpected plan, and it pleased them the more for its audacity. What remained of the day was spent in preparing equipment and attending to personal needs, and the greater part of the night was given over to rest. At the fourth watch they moved.

39. Beyond the nearest enemy camp, at a distance of six miles, lay other Carthaginian forces. Between them was a deep and thickly wooded valley. In about the middle of this wood a Roman cohort, supported by cavalry, was concealed – a Punic stratagem. The way between the enemy camps being thus blocked, the rest of the troops marched silently on towards their nearest objective. There were no outposts before the camp gates, no sentries on the rampart; the Romans walked in, with no opposition whatever, as if the camp were their own. Then the trumpets blared, the battle-cry rang out: men's throats were cut as they lay half asleep, the dry thatch on huts was set ablaze, and the gates were seized to prevent escape. The enemy were stunned: what with the fire, the noise, and the blood they could hear no orders, do nothing for their own defence. Unarmed they were caught in a ring of swords. Some made a dash for the gates; others, finding the ways blocked, leapt over the rampart. All who managed to get out made straight for the other camp and were surrounded and killed to a man by the cohort and mounted men who sprang from their place of concealment to intercept them. Even if any had escaped, so swiftly did the Romans move from the nearer camp to the other that no one could have brought the news of its capture before their arrival. There, in the second camp, they found even greater neglect and lack of discipline, partly because it was farther from the enemy's position, partly because a number of men had gone off before dawn to collect wood and fodder, and anything else they might find worth taking. At the neglected outposts weapons were piled; unarmed men were sitting about or lying on the ground, or strolling in front of the rampart and gates; and this was the enemy, men without a thought or care in the world, whom the Romans, hot from their recent exploit and elated by victory, first attacked. Inevitably there was no stopping them at the gates; but inside a savage struggle began, when throughout the camp the noise and confusion brought a general and immediate rush to arms. The fight might have been a long one, if the sight of the blood on the Roman shields had not told the Carthaginians of their other disaster. Then their

nerve was broken – they were beaten men, seeking only escape. All who were not caught and killed poured out wherever they could find a way, and the camp was lost.

Thus in a night and a day two enemy camps were taken, under the leadership of Lucius Marcius. Claudius, who translated the annals of Acilius from Greek into Latin, records that the Carthaginian losses amounted to 37,000 killed, 1,830 captured, together with a mass of valuable material. Amongst it was a silver shield weighing 137 pounds and bearing a portrait of Hasdrubal son of Hamilcar. According to Valerius Antias, one camp, Mago's, was taken, and 7,000 of the enemy killed; there was then a second battle with Hasdrubal in which 10,000 were killed and 4,330 taken prisoner. Piso writes that 5,000 were ambushed and killed when Mago was conducting a disorderly pursuit of our troops as they withdrew. All these writers pay high tribute to Marcius; not content with his real claim to honour they add the miraculous, too: for instance, as he was delivering his harangue a flame burst from the top of his head, without his feeling it but to the great alarm of the troops on parade. It is further recorded that as a memorial of his victory a shield, known as the Marcian Shield and bearing a likeness of Hasdrubal, hung in the Capitoline temple until the year of the Great Fire.[1]

Things were then quiet in Spain for a considerable time, both sides hesitating to risk a decisive engagement after successive victories and defeats on such a scale.

40. Meanwhile, after the capture of Syracuse, Marcellus had made a general settlement of affairs in Sicily, and that, too, with such honourable integrity as could not but enhance the dignity of the Roman people as much as it added to his own reputation. This is undeniable: but at the same time he removed to Rome the beautiful statues and paintings which Syracuse possessed in such abundance. These were, one must admit, legitimate spoils, acquired by right of war; none the less their removal to Rome was the origin of our admiration of Greek art and started the universal and reckless spoliation of all buildings sacred and profane which prevails today, and which ultimately turned against our own Roman gods, beginning

1. In 84 B.C.

with the very temple which Marcellus so splendidly adorned. For time was when foreigners used to visit the temples dedicated by Marcellus at the Porta Capena, drawn thither by the magnificent examples of Greek art which they contained; but hardly any of them are to be seen today.

Delegations from almost all the Sicilian communities kept waiting upon Marcellus; the terms they were granted varied according to what they had to say for themselves. Those who before the capture of Syracuse had either not gone over to Carthage or had returned to friendly relations with Rome were gladly accepted as loyal allies; those whom the fall of Syracuse had frightened into surrender were treated as defeated enemies and given terms accordingly.

In spite of the general settlement, the Romans still had to deal with a considerable remnant of opposition around Agrigentum. Epicydes and Hanno, commanders in the previous campaign and still active, were both there, and a third new general had been sent by Hannibal to replace Hippocrates. This was a man known as Muttines in his own country; he was of Libyphoenician blood, a native of Hippacra,[1] and an active soldier who had been thoroughly trained under Hannibal in the whole science of war. He was given the command by Epicydes and Hanno of a force of Numidian auxiliaries with which he so successfully overrode the enemy's territory, losing no opportunity to approach friends and keep them loyal by the offer of timely assistance, that in a short time he filled Sicily with his name and was the chief hope of all who favoured the Carthaginian cause. Consequently the Carthaginian and Syracusan generals, who until then had been shut up within the walls of Agrigentum, were emboldened by their confidence in Muttines, even more than by his advice, to make a move. So they left the protection of the city walls and took up a position on the river Himera.

When news of this reached Marcellus he marched immediately and took up a new position about four miles away, in order to wait and see what were the enemy's intentions. But Muttines gave him no time for waiting and no opportunity to lay his plans: he promptly crossed the river and attacked the Roman outposts with devastating effect. Next day, in a more or

1. i.e. Hippo Diarrhytus.

less regular engagement, he forced his enemy to withdraw within their fortifications. He was then recalled by a mutiny of the Numidians at headquarters, some 300 of them having gone off to Heraclea Minoa. He set off at once to try to pacify them and get them back, and before starting he is said to have strongly advised the two commanders not to engage the enemy during his absence. Both of them were much offended by this, especially Hanno, who had already begun to resent Muttines' growing reputation. It was preposterous, he thought, that he, Hanno, a commander of the Carthaginian armies, commissioned by the government and people, should be taught his business by a half-breed African. And so he prevailed upon Epicydes to agree to their crossing the river and offering battle; for if they waited for Muttines and were then successful, the credit would undoubtedly go to him. 41. Marcellus, remembering how he had driven Hannibal from Nola with all the weight of his victory at Cannae behind him, was ashamed to give ground before an enemy he had already beaten by land and sea; so he gave orders to his men to arm instantly and march out to accept the challenge. As he was marshalling his ranks, ten Numidians from the enemy force galloped up to him and declared that the rest of their countrymen were not unaffected by the mutiny in which 300 of them had deserted to Heraclea, and that they also resented the fact that their commander had been sent away on the eve of battle by two generals who cried down his triumphs out of envy. For these reasons, they said, when the fight started they would hold aloof. The Numidians are liars, but this time they kept their promise. Roman spirits rose as word went swiftly through the lines that the enemy had been deserted by his cavalry, which they had specially feared; and the enemy were correspondingly nervous, not only because they had lost the support of the major part of their forces but also because they dreaded an attack upon themselves by the treacherous Numidians. The fight, in consequence, was a minor affair: a shout and a charge, and all was over. The Numidians had at first remained inactive on the wings; then, when they saw their comrades in retreat, they took part at any rate in their flight, though not for long; for, once it was evident that the whole force was making headlong for Agrigentum, they scattered and sought refuge in neighbouring communities to avoid at all costs the miseries of a siege. Many thousands of men were killed or captured, and eight elephants. This was Marcellus's last battle in Sicily; he then returned victorious to Syracuse.

The year was now drawing to a close. The Senate in Rome instructed the praetor Cornelius to send their orders by letter to the consuls at Capua: these were that, while Hannibal was far away and no very important operations were in progress, one of them, if they approved, should come to Rome for the election of new magistrates. On receipt of the letter the consuls agreed between them that Claudius should preside at the elections, while Fulvius remained at Capua. For the new consulships Claudius announced the election of Gnaeus Fulvius Centumalus and Publius Sulpicius Galba, the son of Servius. The latter had not previously held any curule office. The new praetors were Lucius Cornelius Lentulus, Marcus Cornelius Cethegus, Gaius Sulpicius, and Gaius Calpurnius Piso; the duties of City praetor fell to Piso; Sulpicius was assigned Sicily, Cethegus Apulia, and Lentulus Sardinia. The consuls had their military commands extended for a year.

# BOOK XXVI

1. The new consuls Gnaeus Fulvius Centumalus and Publius Sulpicius Galba entered office on 15 March. They called a meeting of the Senate on the Capitol and initiated a discussion on the state of the country, the conduct of the war, and the strength and distribution of the armed forces. The consuls of the previous year, Fulvius and Claudius, had their commands continued, with the troops they already controlled, and were further instructed not to abandon the siege of Capua until the city fell. Capua, at this time, took precedence over almost everything else in the minds of the Romans, less from resentment against her, though that was better justified than against any other community at any period, than because the recovery of so famous and powerful a city, whose defection had drawn a number of other communities to take the same course, would, they believed, turn the general feeling once again towards respect for the old alignment of power. The praetors, also, of the previous year had their commands extended, Junius in Etruria and Sempronius in Gaul, each with the same two legions. The same was done for Marcellus, to allow him as proconsul to complete his Sicilian campaigns with the army already under his command. If he needed reinforcements, he was to get them from the legions in the island which were commanded by the pro-praetor Cornelius, with the further provision that he took none of the men to whom the Senate had refused either discharge or permission to return to Italy before the end of the war.

To Sulpicius in Sicily were assigned the two legions which Publius Cornelius had commanded, together with reinforcements from the army of Gnaeus Fulvius, who had suffered the disgraceful defeat of the previous year in Apulia. On these latter troops the Senate imposed the same limit of service as on those who were beaten at Cannae. A further mark of disgrace was that both these units were forbidden to winter in towns or to establish their winter camps less than ten miles from any city.

To Cornelius in Sardinia were assigned the two legions formerly commanded by Quintus Mucius; the consuls were instructed to raise any necessary reinforcements. To Otacilius and Valerius was given control of the seaboard of Sicily and Greece, with the troops and ships already under their command, Greece having fifty ships and one legion, Sicily a hundred ships and two legions. The total number of troops on service that year by land and sea was twenty-five legions.

2. It was at the beginning of this year that the dispatch from Lucius Marcius[1] was brought up for discussion in the Senate. The Senate recognized the magnificent nature of his achievement, but widespread offence was caused by the formal title he had assumed in writing his dispatch; for he had referred to himself as 'pro-praetor' in spite of the fact that his command had not been given him by the people of Rome nor by the authority of the Senate. It was taken as a bad precedent that army-commanders should be chosen by the troops or that the ceremony of an official appointment, with all due auspices, should be removed from the proper sanction of law and official control and abandoned to soldiers' whims in their camps abroad. Some people thought the matter should be brought before the Senate, but it seemed better to postpone discussion of it until the departure of the riders who had brought the dispatch. As to the food and clothes for his men, it was decided to write in answer that the Senate would see to both, but they refrained from addressing their letter 'to the pro-praetor', lest Marcius should take as already determined what they had left for discussion later.

Directly the riders had been sent off with the Senate's answer, the consuls brought the matter forward, and it was unanimously agreed to ask the tribunes to put before the people at the earliest possible moment the question of whom they wished to send with full military authority to take over the army in Spain which Gnaeus Scipio had commanded. This was arranged with the tribunes, and notice was given. By now, however, another dispute had arisen. The tribune Sempronius Blaesus had issued a summons against Gnaeus Fulvius, charging him with the loss of his army in Apulia. He continually attacked him in public

1. cf p. 344.

speeches, saying that though many generals through rashness or incompetence had brought their troops into a position of danger not one except Fulvius had ever ruined the morale of his men by encouraging them to every vice before actually betraying them. It would be no exaggeration, he declared, to say they were dead before they even saw the enemy, beaten not by Hannibal but by their own commander. No one going to record his vote really understood as yet to what sort of man he was entrusting the command of an army. Let them just consider the difference between Fulvius and, say, Gracchus. Gracchus was given an army of slaves, and his authority and discipline soon made every man of them, once battle was joined, forget his lowly origin, and act as a tower of defence for his friends and as a terror to his enemies. This army of slaves snatched Cumae, Beneventum, and other towns from the very jaws of Hannibal and restored them to Rome. Fulvius, on the contrary, with an army of Roman citizens, well-born, brought up in the tradition of freedom, had imbued them with vices fit only for slaves. Thus they had become insolent and uncontrollable amongst friends, unwarlike and cowardly amongst enemies, so that one shout from the Carthaginian ranks, let alone a charge, was more than they could stand. 'Nor, God help me,' he went on, 'is it surprising that the rank and file should yield, when their general is the first man to run for his life. I wonder rather that there were some, at least, who died at their posts, and that they did not all join Fulvius in his terrified scamper for safety. Flaminius, Paullus, Postumius, Gnaeus and Publius Scipio chose to die in action rather than desert their men when the enemy had hemmed them in; but Fulvius was almost the only man to bring back to Rome the news of the annihilation of his army. The troops who fled from the field of Cannae have been removed to Sicily and refused permission to leave it while the enemy remains on Italian soil, and the same punishment has recently been decreed against the legions of Fulvius. But surely it is grossly unfair that Fulvius's own flight from a battle which his own recklessness provoked should go unpunished, leaving him free to pass his old age in the brothels and cookshops of his youth, while his men, whose only crime is their resemblance to their general, are forced to serve for the rest of the war under shameful conditions and almost in exile. So different a thing is liberty in Rome for the rich and for the poor, for the man in office and the ordinary citizen!'

3. The accused tried to shift the blame on to his troops. They, he maintained, had been clamouring for battle, and were led out into line not on the day they wished, as it was then too late, but on the day following. They had been drawn up at a favourable hour and in a good position, and had failed to stand up to the enemy's strength, or even to his reputation. When they were all in precipitate flight, he too had been carried along with the crowd, like Varro at Cannae and many other commanders. How, he asked, could he have helped his country by remaining at his post all by himself, unless, indeed, his death was likely to prove a remedy for national disasters? He had not run short of supplies and let himself be lured into a trap; he had not been caught in an ambush on the march through any failure to reconnoitre; he had been worsted in a straight and open fight. His men's feelings were not for him to control, nor the enemy's either: courage or cowardice were matters of individual character.

He was twice accused, each time with the proposed penalty of a fine. At the third hearing witnesses were produced, and in addition to loading him with every sort of reproach, a large number declared on oath that it was Fulvius himself who started the panic, and that the soldiers, abandoned by their leader and supposing that his fear was not without foundation, had then turned tail. At this, indignation was fanned to so hot a flame that the assembly loudly demanded the death penalty. This gave rise to a further dispute; for since the tribune Blaesus had twice proposed a fine and now, at the third hearing, declared that he was making the charge a capital one, the defendant, Fulvius, appealed to the other tribunes; and they, in their turn, said they would not try to prevent their colleague from doing what tradition allowed, that is from demanding either the strict legal penalty of death or the customary mitigation of a fine, until he should get a judgement on the accused one way or the other.

Blaesus then said that he accused Fulvius of treason, and asked the City praetor Calpurnius to appoint a day for the hearing before the people. This suggested to Fulvius another possible loophole, namely, the hope that his brother Quintus Fulvius, then in high favour both for his past successes and for the near prospect of the capture of Capua, might be able to attend the hearing. He accordingly wrote Quintus a letter, piteously begging him to save a brother's life. The Senate, however, declared that it was not in the national interest for him to leave Capua, whereupon Gnaeus, the accused, went into exile at Tarquinii just before the day fixed for the hearing. By his exile the people judged that the law was satisfied.

4. Meanwhile the whole effort of the war was concentrated on Capua. There were few serious attempts to storm it, but the siege was pressed with great vigour; so close were the guard-posts surrounding it that the populace and the slaves were suffering from acute starvation and were unable to send messengers to Hannibal. Finally a Numidian was found who declared he would get through with a letter. He kept his promise, and slipping out one night through the middle of the Roman lines raised hopes of the possibility of a general break-through while they still had some strength left. There were a number of minor engagements in which the Campanians usually proved their superiority in cavalry, though their infantry was regularly worsted. For the Romans, on the other hand, the bitterness of defeat in any arm by a besieged enemy almost at the end of his tether was by no means compensated by their successes. At length, however, a means was found to make up by ingenuity what they lacked in strength. From all the legions special men were selected, all vigorous fellows, lightly built and quick on their feet; they were furnished with smaller shields than the cavalry, and each man carried seven lances, four feet long, tipped with iron like the spears of the light infantry. Each cavalryman took one of them on his horse and trained him to ride behind him and dismount rapidly at a given signal. Daily practice soon showed that this could be done smartly, and, once sure of this, the new combination moved forward into the open ground between the Roman camp and the city wall against the formations of Campanian cavalry. Then, as soon as they were within range, the signal was given and the lancers dismounted. The line of cavalry was transformed into a line of infantry, which immediately charged,

hurling its lances in rapid succession and with great force. A great number were flung all along the line against both horses and men, inflicting many casualties; but an even greater shock was caused by the strange and unexpected mode of attack. The enemy were badly shaken and the Roman cavalry at once followed up the first assault, pursuing them to the city gates with great slaughter. From that moment the Romans had the upper hand in both arms, and the custom was established of including light infantry in the heavy-armed legions. It is on record that it was the centurion Quintus Navius who first thought of combining infantry and cavalry, and he was honoured for it by the commander-in-chief.

5. This being the position at Capua, Hannibal found himself in two minds, hesitating between the capture of the citadel at Tarentum and the attempt to save Capua. Capua prevailed. He realized that it was upon Capua that the thoughts of both his allies and his enemies were all concentrated, and that the city, whichever way its secession from Rome might end, would provide a warning and a precedent. Accordingly he left most of his baggage and all his heavier armament in Bruttium, and, equipped for speed to the best of his ability, marched for Campania with a select force of infantry and cavalry. However, in spite of his haste, he took with him thirty-three elephants. He established himself in a valley, hidden from sight, behind Tifata, the mountain close to Capua. On the way he took the fort of Calatia, after driving out the garrison, and then turned to threaten the forces besieging Capua. By sending messengers in advance to say when he proposed to attack the Roman position and thus ensure that his own assault should coincide with a sally in strength from every gate of the city, he caused very great alarm to the Romans. For while his own attack came from one direction, from the other came the Campanians, horse and foot, pouring in mass from the city and supported by the Carthaginian garrison under Bostar and Hanno.

It was a difficult situation for the Romans. Not to leave gaps in their defence by concentrating upon a single section, they divided the forces at their disposal, Appius Claudius opposing the Campanians, and Fulvius dealing with Hannibal, while the pro-praetor Gaius Nero took up a position with the cavalry of six legions on the Suessula road, and the lieutenant Gaius Fulvius Flaccus established himself with the allied cavalry in the direction of the Volturnus.

The fight began not only with the usual wild battle-cry. In addition to the shouts of men, the neighing of horses, and the clash of arms, the Campanian non-combatants on the city wall uttered a great cry which, with the clattering of brazen pans such as is often heard in the silence of the night during an eclipse of the moon, was enough to distract the attention even of men in the heat of battle. Appius kept the Campanians from the rampart without difficulty; Fulvius, on the other side, had to deal with a more powerful thrust from Hannibal and the Carthaginians. In that sector the sixth legion was driven back, and a cohort of Spaniards with three elephants penetrated right up to the rampart; the Spaniards had actually broken through the enemy line, and found themselves torn between hope of forcing a way into the Roman camp and fear of being cut off from their friends. When Fulvius was aware of the alarming condition of the sixth legion and the consequent threat to the camp, he urged Quintus Navius and other leading centurions to attack the enemy cohort in action under the rampart. The position, he said, was highly critical; either the Spaniards must be let through – and it would cost them less effort to break into the camp than it had to penetrate the solid line which opposed them – or they must be cut to pieces where they stood. It could hardly be a difficult undertaking, for they were few in number and out of contact with their friends, and the Roman line, which in the temporary panic seemed to have been broken, could, if the two parts wheeled inward upon the enemy, catch him between two fires. Navius no sooner heard his commander's words than, snatching from its bearer a standard of the second company of *hastati*,[1] carried it towards the enemy, and threatened to fling it amongst them if his men did not follow him with all speed and bear their part in the fight. He was a big man, and his armour graced his strength; as he held the standard high above his head, the eyes of friend and enemy alike were turned upon him. When he reached the Spaniards'

1. *Hastati*, *principes*, *triarii* were the three divisions of the Roman infantry – van, main body, supports. (A. de S.)

van, missiles came flying from every side and the whole line seemed to make him the one object of attack. But neither the enemy's numbers nor the hail of spears could stop the onset of this splendid soldier.

6. Now Marcus Atilius, a legionary officer, began to carry a standard of the first company of the *principes* against the Spaniards; and the officers in charge of the camp, Licinus and Popillius, fought a vigorous action in defence of the rampart and killed the elephants as they were trying to get across it. Their bodies completely filled the trench, forming a sort of embankment or bridge by which the enemy could come over; they tried to do so, and a terrible slaughter took place on top of the dead beasts.

On the other side the Campanians and the Carthaginian garrison had already been thrust back and fighting was going on close to the city gate leading to Volturnum.[1] The Romans as they tried to break in were kept off less by actual armed resistance than by missiles from catapults and 'scorpions' in position at the gate. Moreover, their attack was held up by the fact that Appius Claudius was wounded – he was in the van encouraging his men when he was hit by a javelin under the left shoulder, high up on his breast. But despite these setbacks a great number of the enemy were killed in front of the gate, and the rest driven in confusion back into the town.

When Hannibal saw that the Spanish cohort had been cut up and that the Roman camp was being defended with the greatest possible vigour, he broke off the assault and began to withdraw, wheeling about and covering the infantry's rear with his cavalry, to prevent pursuit. The Roman legionaries were hot to give chase, but Flaccus ordered the retreat to be sounded, convinced that enough had been achieved to show the Campanians how little they could count upon Hannibal to protect them, and to make Hannibal, too, aware of his failure.

Historians have recorded that in this battle 8,000 men of Hannibal's army were killed, and 3,000 of the Campanians; fifteen Carthaginian and eighteen Campanian standards were captured. In other accounts I have found it said that the actual fighting was on a much smaller scale: indeed, that the salient

1. A fortified post at the mouth of the Volturnus.

fact was not the fighting at all, but the panic caused when Numidians and Spaniards unexpectedly burst into the Roman camp with their elephants, which, as they passed through, knocked over the tents, making a fearful din and terrifying the pack-animals, which broke their tethers in the effort to escape. An underhand ruse added to the confusion. Men in Italian clothes and able to speak Latin were sent in by Hannibal to order the troops, in the name of the consuls, to escape as best they could to the neighbouring hills, as the camp was lost. The trick, however, was soon exposed and measures taken to stop its effect, and many of the enemy were killed. The elephants were scared off by fire.

Whatever the facts about its beginning and end, this was the last battle before Capua surrendered. The chief Campanian magistrate – the *medix tuticus* – that year was a certain Seppius Loesius, a man of obscure birth and slender means. The story goes that when he was a minor, his mother, on one occasion, was expiating by sacrifice an omen which had some special reference to the family, and the diviner said to her in his reply that the highest office in Capua would one day come to her boy. Seeing no reason to justify such a hope, 'You mean,' she said, 'that it will be a bad look out for the Campanians when the chief honour in the state falls to my son.' The words were meant as a mockery of the truth – but they came true all the same, for when the city was hard pressed by famine and the sword and there was no hope left that either could be stayed; when those whose birth entitled them to hope for office were refusing to accept it, then Loesius, complaining that Capua had been abandoned and betrayed by her leaders, himself assumed the magistracy. He was the last Campanian ever to do so.

7. Hannibal now saw that the Romans could not be drawn to risk a further engagement, and that there was no chance of breaking through their lines and reaching Capua. He therefore gave up the fruitless attempt and determined to withdraw for fear that the new consuls might intercept his own supplies as well as those intended for the city. He was much exercised in mind as to where he should go next, when the impulse seized him to make straight for the centre of things and march on Rome. He had always wanted to do this, but after Cannae he

had let the opportunity slip, as others often complained and he himself was ready to admit. It was not, he felt, beyond hope that in the unexpected panic and confusion some part of the city might be seized; and if Rome were in peril, either one or both of the Roman commanders would immediately let Capua go. If they divided their forces, then the consequent weakening of the two parts would offer a chance of success either to him or to the Campanians. His one anxiety was lest his departure should mean the immediate surrender of the Campanians, so he bribed a Numidian, a bold fellow, ready for anything, to take a letter, enter the Roman camp in the guise of a deserter, and then slip secretly out on the other side and make his way into Capua. The letter was full of exhortations: in it Hannibal declared that his departure would be a good thing for the city, as it would draw the Roman commanders and their armies away from the siege to the defence of Rome. There was no need to despair: let them but endure a few days longer, and the siege would be raised. He then gave orders for the boats on the Volturnus to be seized and brought to the fort which he had previously built there as a guard-post. When he was informed that there were enough boats for his troops to be ferried across in a single night, he had food prepared for ten days, marched his men down to the river under cover of darkness, and got them across before daylight.

8. Fulvius Flaccus had had previous information of this move from deserters, and when he wrote to report it to the Senate in Rome, it was received with diverse feelings. In view of the alarming nature of the situation the Senate was immediately convened. Publius Cornelius (surnamed Asina) put Capua and everything else right out of his head and urged the recall of every general and every man from the whole of Italy for the defence of the city. Fabius Maximus, on the contrary, declared that it would be criminal to abandon Capua, or to be scared by Hannibal's threats and pushed around at his beck and call. 'What?' he cried, 'when he did not dare to come near Rome after his victory at Cannae, is it likely that he hopes to capture it after his repulse from Capua? He is on his way now merely to relieve Capua, and with no intention of besieging Rome. With the troops we already have, Jupiter, the witness of the treaties

Hannibal has broken, and the other gods will defend our city.'

These two extreme views gave way to a compromise. Valerius Flaccus, forgetting neither Capua nor the situation in Rome, proposed writing to the commanders on the spot, informing them of the strength of the present garrison in Rome and adding that they themselves would know both what troops Hannibal was taking with him and how large a force was needed to maintain the blockade of Capua. Then, if one commander and a part of the army could be spared for Rome without detracting from the efficient prosecution of the siege by the other, they were to agree between themselves which was to remain to continue the siege and which was to come to Rome to prevent the beleaguering of their native city. When this decree of the Senate reached Capua, the proconsul Quintus Fulvius, who had to return to Rome as his colleague was disabled, picked troops from the three armies and crossed the Volturnus with a force of about 15,000 foot and 1,000 horse. On learning that Hannibal was to march by the Latin Way, he sent word in advance to the towns along the Appian Way, or not far from it, such as Setia, Cora, and Lavinium, to have supplies ready within their own walls and also to bring them down to the road from the outlying farms, adding, further, that they were to collect men for the defence of their communities to ensure that each had its own welfare under its control.

9. The day Hannibal crossed the Volturnus he encamped not far from the river and on the following day passed Cales and entered the territory of the Sidicini. After a day spent there in raiding the countryside he proceeded along the Latin Way through the territory of Suessa, Allifae, and Casinum. Under Casinum he remained in camp for two days, making extensive raids; then, passing Interamna and Aquinum, he reached the river Liris in the territory of Fregellae, where he found that the people of the town had destroyed the bridge in order to delay his progress.

Fulvius too had been held up by the Volturnus, for Hannibal had burnt the boats, and he had difficulty, owing to the great scarcity of timber, in procuring rafts for ferrying his men across. However he succeeded in doing so, and the rest of his march went smoothly enough, supplies having been generously put out for him in the towns and by the side of the road. Moreover, the men were keen, and kept urging each other to step out smartly and remember that they were on the way to defend their native city. A messenger from Fregellae, riding night and day, brought the news to Rome. Panic ensued; the first reception of the news was bad enough, but worse confusion was caused when it was spread everywhere by exaggerated rumours, adding fiction to fact, till the whole city was in turmoil. In private houses women could be heard weeping and wailing; they also poured out into the streets and ran aimlessly amongst the shrines of the gods, sweeping the altars with their loosened hair, or kneeling, or raising their palms to the gods in heaven with prayers that they might save the City from the enemy's hands and keep inviolate Roman mothers and their little children. The Senate sat in the forum, to be available to the magistrates, should they want advice. Orders were issued; men hurried off to the tasks assigned them, while others offered their services wherever they might be of use. Guards were posted on the Citadel, on the Capitol, on the walls, and around the city, even on the Alban Mount and the citadel of Aefula. In the midst of all this bustle news came that the proconsul Fulvius with a contingent of troops had started from Capua. To prevent his losing his military command if he entered the city, the Senate decreed that his authority should be on a par with that of the consuls.

Hannibal meanwhile had revenged the destruction of the bridges by a more savage devastation of the farmlands of Fregellae, and had now reached Labici by way of Frusino, Ferentinum, and Anagnia; then he made for Tusculum over Mt Algidus; refused admission there, he bore right and descended to Gabii below. Then, marching down into the region called Pupinia, he encamped eight miles from Rome. The nearer the Carthaginians approached, with the Numidian horsemen leading the column, the greater the number of fugitives that were caught and killed, and more of every age and class were taken prisoner.

10. Such was the state of things when Fulvius entered Rome with his army by the Porta Capena; passing through the centre

of the city by way of the Carinae he made for the Esquiline, then, going out, encamped between the Porta Esquilina and the Porta Collina. The people's aediles saw to the bringing of supplies; the consuls and members of the Senate came to the camp, and high policy was discussed. It was decided that the consuls should take their positions near the two gates, the Colline and Esquiline; the City praetor Gaius Calpurnius was to assume control of the Capitol and Citadel, and the Senate in full numbers was to continue to sit in the forum, to be ready for consultation in the emergency.

Meanwhile Hannibal moved up to the river Anio, three miles from Rome. There he established his army, and himself with 2,000 horsemen rode up to the Porta Collina as far as the temple of Hercules, and personally surveyed the defences and siting of the city from the nearest possible point. That he should do so in so apparently free and easy a manner Fulvius felt to be an outrage, so he sent his cavalry against him with orders to clear away the enemy horse and drive them back to their camp. When the two forces were already engaged, the consuls ordered the 1,200 Numidian deserters then on the Aventine to pass through the city across the Esquiline, in the belief that no troops would be better fitted for fighting in narrow valleys, or round buildings in gardens, or amongst tombs and in a maze of sunken lanes. Some men on the citadel and Capitol saw these troops riding down the Clivus Publicius, and cried out that the Aventine was in enemy hands. This caused such confusion and panic that the entire non-combatant population, desperate to escape, would have poured out of the city if there had not been the Carthaginian camp outside to stop them. As it was, they fled to their homes or under any roof they could find, and assailed these supposed enemies with stones and missiles as they rode this way and that through the streets. It was impossible to make them see their mistake or to quell the uproar, because the roads were blocked by a mob of peasants and cattle which the sudden alarm had driven to seek refuge in the city.

The cavalry engagement proved successful and the enemy force was driven off. Then, to control outbreaks of panic or excitement which for one reason or another kept occurring all over the place, the Senate decreed that all who had held the office of dictator, consul, or censor should be invested with full military authority until the enemy withdrew. During the remainder of the day and the following night many such outbreaks occurred and were successfully checked.

11. On the next day Hannibal crossed the Anio and formed his whole army into line of battle. Flavius and the consuls did not refuse the challenge. As the opposing armies faced one another for a fight in which the prize of victory would be the city of Rome, a torrential downpour of rain and hail caused such confusion that both returned to camp, hardly able to hold their weapons and almost without a thought of the enemy who, for the moment, had lost all his terrors. On the day after, the two lines were drawn up in the same positions, and again a similar storm kept them apart; then, when they had returned to camp, the sky, as before, miraculously cleared and there was perfect calm. The Carthaginians took this as an intervention of providence, and there is a story that Hannibal was heard to say he had twice missed capturing Rome, once because he lacked the will, then because he had missed his chance. His hope of doing so was, moreover, now diminished by two other things, one trivial, the other important. The latter was the fact that, while his army was lying at the very walls of Rome, he learned that reinforcements of Roman troops, with their colours, had started for Spain. The minor incident was that the piece of land where he was encamped happened about that time to be on the market and was sold without any reduction in price. He was told of this by a prisoner. That a purchaser should have been found in Rome for the land he had taken by force of arms and of which he was now the occupier and owner seemed to him evidence of such outrageous conceit that he promptly called a crier and ordered the sale of the bankers' shops in the forum.

In these circumstances he withdrew to the river Tutia, six miles from the city, going on from there to the Grove of Feronia, where the temple in those days was famous for its treasures. The people of Capena and others in the neighbourhood used to bring their first fruits to it and anything else they could afford, and kept it adorned with much gold and silver. On this occasion it was stripped of all its gifts; large heaps of bronze were found after Hannibal's departure – crude bronze money which the soldiers' religious feelings had led them to deposit there. The robbing of this temple is not in doubt in the various records: Coelius states that Hannibal turned off at Eretum to visit it while on his way to Rome, and traces his route from Reate, Cutiliae, and Amiternum; from Campania he passed into Samnium, thence to Paelignian territory, and crossed to the Marrucini by way of Sulmo; thence by way of Alba to the Marsi, and on to Amiternum and the village of Foruli. Traces of so famous a leader and so large an army could not have been so quickly effaced from men's memory: so it is not about the actual route that there is uncertainty, for all agree on that point; the only difference is whether he followed that route on his way to Rome or on his return from Rome into Campania.

12. Hannibal proved by no means so determined to defend Capua as the Romans were to press the siege. On the contrary, he marched through Samnium, Apulia, and Lucania, and on to Bruttium and the town of Rhegium on the Straits so swiftly that his unexpected arrival almost took people unawares. In Capua, though there had been no relaxation of the siege, people were aware of the arrival of Flaccus, and there was general surprise that Hannibal had not returned at the same time. Soon, however, talks with the enemy revealed that they had been abandoned and deserted, and that the Carthaginians had despaired of holding the city. Added to this was an edict of the proconsuls, put out on the Senate's authority and made public throughout the city, to the effect that any Campanian citizen who came over to Rome before a certain day should suffer no harm. Not one took advantage of the offer: it was not loyalty that stopped them, rather it was fear, because in seceding from Rome they had committed crimes too great for pardon. But the fact that no one took matters into his own hands and deserted to the enemy was balanced by their inability to find a common policy of any sort of worth. The nobility had been doing nothing whatever to serve the state and could not be induced to attend the council; while the man who did hold office could hardly be said to have brought himself honour. He was a low fellow who by his worthlessness had robbed the

office he held of its power and authority. No aristocrat was any longer to be seen in any public place, not even in the forum; they all shut themselves up in their houses, awaiting from one day to the next the fall of their native city and their own deaths.

The whole burden of responsibility had fallen upon Bostar and Hanno, who commanded the Carthaginian garrison, and it was their own danger, not that of their allies, that troubled them. They had written to Hannibal accusing him roundly and bitterly not only of having betrayed Capua into the enemy's hands but also of having abandoned themselves and their men to be tortured to death. He had gone off to Bruttium they declared, simply to spare himself the disagreeable experience of having Capua taken before his eyes. How different were the Romans! Not even a threat to Rome had been able to draw them from the siege of Capua, so constant an enemy were they, compared with Hannibal so inconstant a friend! If he returned to Capua and concentrated all his efforts upon it, then, they assured him, both they and the Campanians would be ready for an attempt to break the blockade. 'We,' they ended, 'did not cross the Alps to fight against Rhegium or Tarentum; the armies of Carthage should be where the Roman legions are. It was by meeting them face to face, by pitching our camps where they pitched theirs, by risking the luck of the day that we were victorious at Cannae and Trasimene.' The letter, written in these or similar terms, was handed to some Numidians who, for a price, offered to deliver it. Pretending to be deserters, they presented themselves to Flaccus in the Roman lines, with the intention of slipping away when an opportunity offered – and the famine from which Capua had so long suffered gave anyone a plausible excuse for deserting. Suddenly, however, a Campanian woman, kept by one of the Numidians, appeared on the scene and informed the Roman commander that the story of desertion was a hoax and the Numidians were taking a letter to Hannibal. She was prepared, she said, to prove her charge against the one who had told her of the plan. The man was summoned and at first pretty steadily kept up the pretence that he did not know the woman; but gradually the facts proved too much for him, and when he saw the instruments of torture being got ready, he admitted the truth and the letter was produced. In addition to the woman's information a further secret was brought to light, namely, that other Numidians, also pretending to be deserters, were at large in the Roman lines. More than seventy of them were seized, and together with the ones who had recently arrived they were scourged and sent back to Capua with their hands cut off.[1]

13. The sight of so harsh a punishment broke the spirit of the Campanians. The populace mobbed the council house and compelled Loesius to call the council; they threatened the leading citizens, who for a long time past had taken no part in state affairs, that unless they attended the council they would go round to all their houses and drag them out into the streets by force. The threat scared them, and provided Loesius with a full house. At the meeting various people proposed sending representatives to the Roman commanders, but Vibius Virrius, who had been responsible for the secession, on being asked his opinion, gave a very different answer. He declared that those who talked about delegations and surrender and peace-terms had forgotten what was in store for them and what they would themselves have done had they had the Romans in their power. 'What?' he cried, 'do you really imagine that surrender now will be like it was when we put ourselves and all we possessed into the hands of Rome in order to get their help against the Samnites? Have you already forgotten *when* we rebelled; in what a critical position Rome then was; or how we put the Roman garrison to an ignominious death by torture, when we might easily have been content with expelling it; or how often and with what savagery we have assailed their besieging army, attacked their camp, called upon Hannibal to crush them; or – most recent of all – our direct responsibility for Hannibal's march on Rome? No, no! If you want to know what lies in store for you, call to mind what the Romans have *done*, and that will reveal how much they hate us. With a foreign enemy in Italy, and that enemy Hannibal, with the country aflame with war, they have sent both consuls and two consular armies to attack Capua, neglecting everything else, even Hannibal himself. For the second year now they are wasting us with famine, blocked in and beset within their siege-works, and they

1. The usual punishment for spies.

themselves, like us, are willing to face deadly danger and gruelling work, suffering casualties around the rampart and trenches, and now at last almost deprived of their camp. But I pass over this. There is nothing new or strange in having to face toil and danger in a siege, and I come to what really does reveal the truly frightful nature of their anger and hatred. Hannibal with a vast army of horse and foot attacked their camp and partly took it. The danger was acute, but it had no effect whatever in moving them to give up the siege. Hannibal crossed the Volturnus and burnt the farms round Cales: it was a serious loss to their friends, but it never called them away. Hannibal ordered a direct threat against Rome itself; they took lightly the menace even of such a storm as that. He crossed the Anio and encamped within three miles of the City; he moved right up to the walls and gates, making it clear that he would take Rome from them unless they let Capua go. They did not let it go. Wild beasts, which are roused to action only by blind instinct and rage, can be diverted to protect their young if you go near the whelps in their lairs, but the Romans could not be turned from Capua even by the siege of Rome, not by their wives and children, whose weeping we could almost hear all those miles away, nor by their altars and hearths, the shrines of their gods, the tombs of their ancestors desecrated and despoiled. So rabid is their hunger to punish us, so fierce their thirst to drink our blood.

'Ah well – perhaps they are right: we should have done the same, if we had had the chance. And therefore, since the immortal gods have ordained otherwise, and I may not shrink from death, I am able, while I am still free and master of myself, to escape the ignominy and the tortures which the enemy are preparing for us by a death not only honourable, but easy. Never shall I see Claudius and Fulvius on their throne of insolent victory; never shall I be dragged in chains through Rome to grace their triumph and then to be flung into prison, or, bound to the stake, to be beaten bloody by rods and to offer my neck to a Roman axe. Not for me the sight of my city devastated and in flames, or of Capuan women and girls and free-born boys haled off to serve the conquerors' lust.

'Even Alba, whence they sprang, the Romans utterly destroyed, to leave no memory of their stock and origins; far less, I fancy, are they likely to spare Capua, which they hate more bitterly than Carthage. Therefore, for any of you who intend to yield to destiny before they can see all these cruel sights, there is in my house today a dinner ready and prepared. When you have eaten and drunk your fill, the same cup as is given to me shall be brought to each in turn; that draught will save your bodies from torment, your minds from insult, your eyes and ears from seeing and hearing the bitter sights, the shameful sounds, which await the vanquished. Men will be ready and willing to light a great pyre in the courtyard of the house and to fling our bodies into the flames. This is the only way for us to die, as free and honourable men. The Romans, too, will admire our courage, and Hannibal will know that the friends he deserted and betrayed were brave.'

14. Many agreed with what Virrius said, but not so many had the fortitude to carry out in practice what they approved in principle. The greater part of the council, confident of Roman clemency from their experience in many wars, that they, too, would find their enemy not implacable, voted the dispatch of representatives to surrender Capua to the Romans. This was accordingly done. About twenty-seven senators accompanied Virrius to his house; there they dined with him and, after drinking to dull their minds as much as they could to the realization of what was hanging over them, they all took the poison. Then the party broke up; they shook hands, they gave each other the last embrace; and with tears for their city's downfall and their own they parted, some staying to be burned on the common pyre, others going to their homes. The surfeit of food and wine which they had taken rendered the poison less efficacious in causing a speedy death. Most of the men throughout that night and for part of the following day continued to breathe, though all were dead before the city gates were opened to the Romans.

Next day the Jupiter Gate, facing the Roman camp, was opened by order of the proconsuls. One legion marched in and two squadrons of horse, with Gaius Fulvius the commander. His first act was to have all weapons of any kind in the city collected and brought to him; then, after placing guards at all the gates to prevent anyone from either getting out or being sent out, he seized the Carthaginian garrison and ordered the Capuan senators to present themselves before the Roman commanders in their camp. On their arrival they were immediately put in chains and ordered to have all the gold and silver they possessed brought to the quaestors. The gold amounted to 2,070 pounds, the silver to 31,200 pounds. Twenty-five of the senators were sent into custody at Cales, twenty-eight at Teanum – all of them men known to have particularly supported the revolt from Rome.

15. About the punishment of the Capuan senators Fulvius and Claudius saw by no means eye to eye. Claudius took a lenient view; Fulvius was in favour of much greater severity. Claudius would have liked to refer the whole decision to the Senate in Rome, for he felt it was only fair to give the Senate a chance of making an inquiry into whether the Capuans had had an understanding with any of the peoples of the Latin Confederacy, or had received help from them in the war. Fulvius, on the other hand, maintained that the last thing they ought to do was to let faithful allies be upset by vague and unproven accusations, or to make them the target of informers who had never had any scruple about either what they said or did. He would, therefore, strongly oppose such an inquiry and do what he could to quash it. After the two men had talked it over, Claudius was fairly sure that his colleague, in spite of his fierce words, would wait for a letter from Rome in a matter of such importance. But that was just what Fulvius wished to avoid, as it would stop his doing what he wanted to do. So he dismissed the conference and ordered the military tribunes and Prefects of the Allies to issue instructions for a picked force of 2,000 cavalry to parade at the bugle-call in the third watch.

With this force he left camp during the night and at dawn entered Teanum and proceeded to the forum. A crowd gathered as soon as the horsemen rode in, and Fulvius, having sent for the chief magistrate, ordered him to produce the Capuan senators whom he was keeping under guard. All of them were scourged and beheaded. Fulvius then rode with all speed to Cales; he took his seat on the tribunal, and the Capuan senators were brought before him. As they were being bound to the stake, an express rider from Rome delivered to Fulvius a letter from the praetor

Gaius Calpurnius containing a decree of the Senate. A murmur spread from the tribunal through the assembly that the whole question of the Capuans was being held up for decision by the Senate. Fulvius thought so too: so taking the letter and putting it unopened in the fold of his cloak, he ordered a herald to tell the lictor to proceed according to the law. Thus the Capuans at Cales too were executed. The letter and the Senate's decree were then read, but too late to stop the executions, which had indeed been carried out in haste with the deliberate purpose of forestalling intervention.

As Fulvius was getting up from his seat, a Campanian named Vibellius Taurea pushed through the crowd and called out to him. Wondering what he wanted of him, Fulvius resumed his seat, and Taurea said: 'Order my execution too, so that you may boast of killing a much braver man than yourself.' Fulvius remarked that the fellow must be off his head, adding that he was prevented by the Senate's decree from killing him, even if he wished to do so; whereupon Taurea cried: 'My native city taken, my friends and kinsmen lost, with my own hand I have killed my wife and children to save them from shame. But it is not given to me even to share the death of these my fellow citizens. Therefore I call upon my own courage to find release from this hateful life.' With these words he drove through his breast the sword he had concealed under his clothes, and fell dying at Fulvius's feet.

16. To explain the fact that most things, including everything connected with the executions, had been done on the decision of Fulvius alone, some historians have said that Claudius died just before Capua surrended. Taurea too, according to this account, did not come to Cales of his own accord, nor kill himself; but while he was being bound to the stake with the others, Fulvius called for silence because he was shouting something which could not be heard in all the noise that was going on. It was then that Taurea spoke the words I have already recorded to the effect, that is, that he was a brave man being put to death by one who was by no means his equal in courage. As soon as he had said it, a herald, by Fulvius's orders, pronounced the sentence: 'Lictor, scourge the brave man: on him first let the law take its course.' Again, according to some

writers, Fulvius read the Senate's decree before the executions, but because it contained the clause that he might 'if he saw fit'[1] refer the matter to the Senate for decision, he took that to mean that he was permitted to use his own judgement about what he thought to be the better course to take.

Fulvius returned from Cales to Capua. Atella and Calatia also surrendered, and in both towns the political leaders were executed. Altogether some seventy leading senators were put to death, and about 300 Campanian aristocrats imprisoned, while others were put under guard in towns of the Latin confederacy and perished in various ways. The rest of the citizens were sold as slaves. In Rome discussion continued about Capua and the land belonging to it. Some expressed the opinion that complete destruction was the only policy in the case of a city so powerful, so close, and so hostile; but this extreme view gave way to considerations of immediate practical advantage, and for the sake of its land, which was generally recognized as the most productive in Italy, the city was saved to provide homes for the farmers. To fill it up, the resident aliens, freedmen, small traders, and artisans were allowed to remain; all the land and buildings became the public property of the Roman people. The decision was that Capua should remain a city only in the sense of a place of residence; it was to have no political organization, no senate, no people's council, no magistrates; for it was felt that the populace, without any controlling political body or military authority, and sharing no common interest, would be incapable of any sort of combined action. An officer to administer justice would be sent out annually from Rome.

The settlement of Capuan affairs was thus in every respect admirable: the most guilty were promptly and severely punished; the mass of free citizens was dispersed and had no hope of return; innocent buildings and city-walls were spared the useless savagery of fire and demolition; and Rome, besides profiting by the city's preservation, was able to appear before her allies in the guise of a merciful conqueror – Capua had been a rich and famous city, and all Campania would have wept over her ruins, and all the neighbouring peoples. The enemy were compelled to admit the power of Rome to exact punishment

1. Intended only as a polite formula.

from treacherous allies, and the helplessness of Hannibal to defend those whom he had taken under his protection.

17. After settling all business that concerned Capua, the Roman Senate passed a decree assigning to Gaius Nero a force of 6,000 foot and 300 horse, to be chosen by himself from the two legions he had had at Capua, and an equal number of infantry together with 800 cavalry from the allies of the Latin Confederacy. Nero embarked these troops at Puteoli for Spain. Arrived at Tarraco he landed his men, beached the ships and, having armed the crews as well to increase his numbers, started for the Ebro, where he took over the army from Fonteius and Marcius. He then proceeded against the enemy.

Hasdrubal, son of Hamilcar, was encamped at the Black Stones, a place in the country of the Ausetani between Iliturgi and Mentissa. It was in a valley, or pass, and Nero occupied the entrance to it, thus catching Hasdrubal in a trap. Hasdrubal sent him a herald with a promise that, if he were allowed to get out, he would evacuate Spain completely. Nero was delighted, and Hasdrubal asked for a conference on the following day to agree, in the course of personal discussion, on terms for the surrender of strongholds in the various towns and on a date for the evacuation of garrisons and the removal, without molestation, of all property belonging to the Carthaginians. His request was granted, whereupon he immediately gave orders that his heaviest troops should get out of the pass in any way they could, beginning as soon as it was dark and continuing throughout the night. He took great care to avoid getting large numbers out that night; for he knew that small numbers would be better able to move silently and so avoid detection, as well as to pick a way along the narrow and awkward tracks. On the following day the conference took place; Hasdrubal talked a great deal, and by wasting time in writing down a lot of deliberately irrelevant details managed to obtain a day's postponement. The following night gave him a further opportunity for evacuating more of his men, and still, on the day after that, no conclusion was reached. In this way a number of days were spent in arguing about terms, and as many nights in secretly evacuating the Carthaginian camp. Once most of the troops were out, Hasdrubal ceased even to stand by his own original proposals: there was less and less agreement. Hasdrubal, with less to lose had less reason to keep his word. Then one dawn, when nearly all the infantry were safely out, a thick mist covered the pass and the surrounding country, and Hasdrubal took advantage of it to send a messenger to Nero with a request for another day's postponement. That day, he asserted, was, for certain religious reasons, banned for the transaction of any important business. Not even then was treachery suspected: the day's grace was granted and Hasdrubal promptly and silently slipped out of camp with his cavalry and elephants to a place of safety. Some three hours after sunrise the mist dispersed and in clear daylight the Romans saw that the enemy's camp was deserted. Only then did Nero realize that the Carthaginians had tricked him; he hastened to give chase, prepared for a full-scale engagement, but Hasdrubal refused the challenge. All that happened was some skirmishes between the Carthaginian rear and the Roman advanced guard.

18. Meanwhile the Spanish peoples who had revolted from Rome after the defeat of the Scipios were not returning to their allegiance, nor were any new ones coming to join her. In Rome, moreover, now Capua was recovered, both Senate and people were as much concerned about Spain as about Italy. It was the intention that the army should be reinforced and a commander-in-chief sent out; but there was less agreement upon whom to send than upon the obvious fact that, where two most eminent generals had perished within thirty days, their successor needed to be chosen with extraordinary care. Various names were put forward and rejected, until the Senate finally had recourse to holding an election for a proconsul to take over Spanish affairs, and the consuls announced the date.

Up to now people had been waiting for anyone who thought himself good enough for so important a command to hand in his name; and when nobody did so, the loss of the two dead generals seemed to make itself felt afresh, together with distress at the defeat of their armies. The City was in mourning, and had no clear idea of the next step to take. Nevertheless, on election day, everyone went down to the Campus. People turned towards the magistrates and watched the faces of the leading citizens, the likely candidates: they were exchanging glances with one another. A murmur arose that things were desperate, that hope of saving the country had been so utterly lost that no one dared accept the Spanish command. Such was the general feeling when suddenly Publius Cornelius Scipio, son of the Publius Scipio who had been killed in Spain and still a young man of about twenty-four, announced his candidature for the command. He then moved to a spot where the ground rose a little, and stood there, visible to the whole assembly. All eyes were turned upon him, and the crowd by their roar of approval unanimously predicted good luck for him and every success. Bidden to record their votes, not only all the centuries, but every individual man, supported him for the Spanish command. However, once that was done and the first sudden impulse had had time to cool, there was an awkward silence and people began to ask themselves if what they had done had not been prompted by personal feeling rather than by common sense. It was Scipio's youth which, more than anything, gave them pause, though some were chilled by the evil destiny of his house and dreaded the name of this man who belonged to two mourning families and was about to leave for a field of action where he would be forced to fight by the graves of his father and his uncle.

19. Scipio was quick to observe the anxious concern which followed that over-impulsive vote. He called an assembly, and discoursed of his youth, of his appointment to the command, and of the coming war in such lofty and magnanimous terms that he kindled afresh the cooling ardour of the populace, and filled everybody with a more confident hope than is usually inspired by trust in a mere promise or even by a reasoned deduction from facts. For Scipio was a remarkable man not only by virtue of his actual attainments; he had also from his early youth practised their display by certain deliberate devices. For instance, he used to present most of his public actions as inspired by nocturnal visions or by warnings from heaven, perhaps because he was himself of a superstitious turn of mind, perhaps to get his orders carried out promptly in the belief that they came from some sort of oracular response. Moreover, to prepare men's minds, from the earliest days when he first came

of age he never on any day performed any public or private business until he had first gone to the Capitol, where, taking his seat in the temple, he watched and waited, apart and usually alone. This habit, continued throughout his life, confirmed in some men the belief (which may or may not have been deliberately spread) that he was a man of divine race, and revived the old tale once told of Alexander the Great, and equally empty and absurd, that his conception came from the embraces of a huge snake, a monster that was often seen in his mother's bedroom, only to glide away and vanish when anyone came in. Scipio himself never said a word to diminish belief in these marvels; on the contrary, he tended to strengthen it by skilfully and deliberately refusing either to deny or openly to affirm their truth. Many other similar things, some true, some fictitious, had set the young Scipio on a sort of pinnacle, above the heads of mere men; and that was the reason why the citizens of Rome entrusted the heavy burden of this important command to a man who had by no means reached full maturity.

To the old army in Spain and the forces which sailed with Nero from Puteoli were added 10,000 foot and 1,000 horse, and the pro-praetor Marcus Junius Silanus was appointed as an assistant in the conduct of operations. So with a fleet of thirty ships, all quinqueremes, Scipio sailed from Ostia at the mouth of the Tiber along the Etruscan coast, past the Alps, and across the Gallic gulf, and thence round the promontory of the Pyrenees, finally disembarking his troops at Emporiae, a Greek settlement originally founded by men from Phocaea. Then, after ordering the fleet to follow, he proceeded by land to Tarraco, where he summoned representatives of all the allies to meet him, for at the news of his approach delegations had come thronging from everywhere in the province to attend upon him. There he had the ships beached after sending back four triremes from Massilia which had escorted him from their home-port to show their respect. That done he proceeded to answer the delegations, who were in great anxiety owing to the recent ups-and-downs of fortune in the war. Supremely confident in his own abilities, he spoke with a studied and lofty pride, yet without allowing a single arrogant word to escape his lips, and informing all he said with overwhelming authority and sincerity.

20. From Tarraco he went on to visit the allied communities and the army's winter quarters. He congratulated the troops on having held the province in spite of their two successive and disastrous defeats, and praised them for not allowing the enemy to profit by his victories, for keeping him out of the country north of the Ebro, and for loyally protecting their allies. He kept Marcius with him, treating him with such respect that it was obvious he had not the least fear of anyone stealing his limelight. Silanus then took over from Nero, and the new troops were marched into winter quarters. Scipio lost no time in doing all that had to be done and making the necessary tour of inspection, after which he retired to Tarraco.

Scipio's reputation was as great amongst the enemy as it was with the Romans and their allies; it was accompanied in the former by a certain foreboding, all the more alarming in that their fears were apparently causeless and could not be rationally accounted for. They, the Carthaginians, had retired to their respective quarters for the winter, Hasdrubal son of Gisgo to Gades on the Atlantic, Mago into the interior beyond the Forest of Castulo. Hasdrubal, son of Hamilcar, wintered nearest to the Ebro, in the neighbourhood of Saguntum.

At the end of the summer which saw the taking of Capua and Scipio's arrival in Spain, a Carthaginian fleet had been summoned from Sicily to stop the inflow of supplies to the Roman garrison in the citadel of Tarentum. But, though it succeeded in closing every approach from the sea, its continued presence rendered the question of supply even more difficult for friends than for enemies. The protection of the Carthaginian fleet did, indeed, keep the shore and the harbours open, but it was not possible, even so, to get as much grain through to the people in the town as the ships' crews, a mixed mob of all nationalities, themselves consumed. The result was that the small Roman garrison in the citadel was able to support itself on what it already had, without the need to import, while not even what they did import was sufficient to feed the people of Tarentum and the Carthaginian seamen. In the end the departure of the fleet caused much greater satisfaction than its arrival. Nevertheless, its going did not much relieve the situation, as without naval protection no supplies at all could be brought in.

21. At the end of the summer Marcellus returned to Rome from Sicily, and the praetor Calpurnius granted him an audience in the Senate, sitting in the temple of Bellona. After giving an account of his campaigns, Marcellus, more on his men's account than on his own, mildly protested against the decision not to allow him, now that his task in Sicily was accomplished, to bring his army home, and then went on to ask leave to enter the City in triumph. His request was refused. A long argument ensued about which of two courses would be less in accordance with precedent. Should a man in whose name, during his absence, a thanksgiving had been decreed to celebrate his victories and honour had been paid to the gods be refused a triumph now that he was present in Rome; or ought a commander whom the Senate had ordered to hand over to a successor (an order which would not have been given unless fighting had still been going on) be allowed to celebrate a triumph as if the war had been successfully concluded, while his army was not present to witness the ceremony, whether deserved or not deserved? A compromise was finally reached and Marcellus was permitted to enter the City with the minor ceremony of an 'ovation'.[1] The people's tribunes were authorized by the Senate to bring before the people the formal proposal 'that Marcus Marcellus, when he entered the City in his ovation, should keep full military powers.' On the day before he did so he celebrated a triumph on the Alban Mount; then, in 'ovation', he entered Rome, preceded by his spoils of war. Amongst them was a representation of captured Syracuse, with catapults, artillery, and specimens of all other engines of war, besides beautiful objects with which royal opulence had adorned the long years of peace – vessels of wrought silver and bronze in quantities, furnishings, precious fabrics, and many noble statues such as had put the glory of Syracuse above that of any other Greek city. Then, to represent the victory over the Carthaginians, eight elephants were led in the procession, and not the least impressive spectacle was afforded by Sosis of Syracuse and

1. i.e. on horseback or on foot instead of in a triumphal chariot.

the Spaniard Moericus,[1] riding in front with golden wreaths on their heads. One of them, it will be remembered, had served as guide when Syracuse was entered by night, and the other had betrayed the Island and its garrison to the Romans. To both these men Roman citizenship was granted, together with 500 *iugera* of land – to Sosis such land in Syracusan territory as had belonged either to the king or to enemies of Rome, with a house in Syracuse which he was himself to choose from houses owned by men who had been punished according to the laws of war; and to Moericus and the Spaniards who with him had joined the Roman cause a town and land in Sicily previously belonging to those who had abandoned their allegiance to Rome. The duty of making over to them such property wherever he thought fit was entrusted to Marcus Cornelius Cethegus. In the same part of the island 400 *iugera* of land were assigned to Belligenes, the man who had persuaded Moericus to come over to the Romans.

After the departure of Marcellus from Sicily a Carthaginian fleet landed a force of 8,000 infantry and 3,000 Numidian cavalry. The towns of Murgantia and Ergetium joined their cause, and their revolt was followed by the towns of Hybla and Macella and a number of smaller communities. The Numidians under their leader Muttines began to wreak widespread havoc throughout Sicily upon agricultural land owned by allies of Rome. In addition to this the Roman troops, incensed at not being allowed to leave the province with Marcellus, and also at the order which forbade them to winter in towns, were growing slack in their duties and might have been ready to mutiny, had they had a leader to follow. The situation was not without its dangers, but the praetor Cornelius succeeded in bringing the men to heel again by a judicious mixture of sympathy and severity, and in regaining control over all the communities which had revolted. One of them, Murgantia, he made over to the Spaniards to whom the Senate had decreed the gift of a town and its territory.

22. Both consuls were at the moment on duty in Apulia, but, as there was now less danger expected from Hannibal and the Carthaginians, the Senate issued instructions that one of them

1. cf. p. 336.

should assume control in Macedonia. They accordingly drew lots and Macedonia fell to Sulpicius, who therefore took over from Laevinus. Fulvius was called to Rome for the consular elections, and when they were being held, the century of the younger men of the Voturia tribe (on this occasion the 'prerogative' century, entitled by lot to vote first) voted for Titus Manlius Torquatus and Titus Otacilius. Manlius was there in person, and when a crowd gathered to congratulate him and there was no question of the popular approval, he made his way, surrounded by hundreds of people, to the consul's tribunal and begged him to listen to a few words he wished to say, and to have the century which had already voted called back. Excitement was intense, and everyone was wondering what it was he was going to ask, when he pleaded to be excused from the position offered him because of the weakness of his eyes. Impudent indeed, he said, would be the pilot of a ship or the commander of an army who, though he had to depend on other men's eyes in all he did, nevertheless expected their lives and fortunes to be committed to his charge. So he would like the consul, if he saw fit, to order the younger men of Voturia to vote again and to remember, as they voted, the sort of war in which Italy was engaged and the circumstances in which the country was involved. Their ears, he added, had scarcely yet been relieved of the din and tumult of a hostile army, which only a few months ago had almost set Rome ablaze. In answer the entire century loudly insisted that they would never change their minds, but would name the same men again for the consulship; whereupon Torquatus said: 'If I am consul I shall be no more able to endure the way you behave than you will be able to endure my authority. Go and vote again, and remember that we have a war with Carthage on our hands and that the enemy commander is Hannibal.' The century was so much impressed by the man's authoritative manner and the applause of his supporters that it asked the consul to call the century of the older men of its tribe, as the younger ones wished to talk with their seniors and to vote according to their authority. The seniors were accordingly summoned, and an opportunity was granted for a private discussion in that part of the Campus known as the Sheepfold. The seniors suggested that their deliberations should be confined to three candidates, two of them, Quintus Fabius and Marcus Marcellus, already full of honours, and, if they were determined to elect a new man to face the Carthaginians, Marcus Valerius Laevinus, who had fought a brilliant campaign against King Philip by land and sea. So when the claims of these three had been debated, the seniors were allowed to go and the younger men voted. The two they elected were Marcellus, then at the height of his reputation for the subjugation of Sicily, and Laevinus, both men being absent. All the centuries followed the lead of the 'prerogative' century.

Who, after this, will dare to jeer at those who praise the olden times? If there were a city composed of sages such as philosophers have imagined in some ideal, but surely not actual, world, I for my part cannot think that it could contain leaders with greater dignity of mind and less lust for personal power, or a populace more admirably conducted. That a century of juniors should have wished to consult their seniors on the question of whom to entrust with power may seem almost incredible; if it does so, that is due to the fact that in our day even the authority of parents over their children is held cheap and of slight account.

23. Elections for the praetorship were held next. The successful candidates were Publius Manlius Volso, Lucius Manlius Acidinus, Gaius Laetorius, and Lucius Cincius Alimentus. It so happened that after the elections were over news came of the death in Sicily of Otacilius, whom the people had seemed likely to elect in his absence as colleague to Torquatus, had not the order of proceedings been interrupted. The Games of Apollo had been celebrated the previous year, and to ensure their repetition this year the Senate, on a motion put by the praetor Calpurnius, decreed that they should be vowed in perpetuity. A number of prodigies were seen and reported: in the Temple of Concord an image of Victory on the gable was struck by lightning, but the little ornaments along the guttering caught it as it came down, so that it fell no farther; it was reported that at Anagnia and Fregellae the wall and gates had been struck; at Forum Subertanum streams of blood flowed all day long; at Eretum it rained stones, and at Reate a mule had a foal. These signs and wonders were expiated by the sacrifice of full-grown

victims, a day of public prayer was ordered and nine days were devoted to religious ceremonies. The same year several men holding state priesthoods died and new priests were appointed: Manlius Aemilius Numida, a member of the board for controlling ceremonial, was succeeded by Marcus Aemilius Lepidus; Pomponius Matho, a priest, by Gaius Livius; and the augur Spurius Carvilius Maximus by Marcus Servilius. The priest Titus Otacilius Crassus died at the end of the year, so no successor was nominated. Gaius Claudius, priest of Jupiter, resigned because of a fault in his arrangement of the victim's entrails during a sacrifice.

24. It was about this time that Laevinus went with a fast-sailing fleet to Aetolia. He had already held secret conversations with the leading men to test their attitude and it was now his object to attend a conference which had already been announced for the purpose. He began by referring to the capture of Syracuse and Capua as examples of Roman successes in Italy and Sicily, and went on to say that the Romans had inherited from their forebears the tradition of treating their allies with consideration, conferring upon some of them equal citizen rights with themselves and keeping others so prosperous that they preferred the status of ally even to that of Roman citizenship. The Aetolians, he added, would be held in the greater honour in that they would be the first oversea people to have made ties of friendship with Rome. Philip and the Macedonians were oppressive neighbours, whose power and pride he himself had already broken and whom he would soon so far humiliate that they would not only have to leave the towns they had forcibly taken from the Aetolians but would find Macedonia itself too hot for them. The Acarnanians, moreover, whose separation from the Aetolian federation they resented, he promised to restore to them on the old terms, to be subject to Aetolian control.

All this was confirmed by the authority of Scopas, the Aetolian chief magistrate, and of Dorimachus, a leading citizen, both men extolling the power and majesty of the Roman people with more loyalty than restraint. What moved them most was the hope of getting possession of Acarnania; so the terms under which they were to enter into friendship and alliance with

Rome were agreed and reduced to writing, with the following additional clauses: (i) Should they so wish it, the Eleans, the Lacedaemonians, Attalus King of Asia, Pleuratus King of Thrace, and Scerdilaedus King of Illyria, should enjoy the same rights of friendship; (ii) the Aetolians should immediately declare war on Philip by land, the Romans supporting them with a fleet of not less than twenty-five quinqueremes; (iii) of the towns from Aetolia northwards as far as Corcyra, the soil, buildings, walls, and farmlands should belong to the Aetolians, while all other captured material should belong to the Romans, who should make it their object that Acarnania should go to the Aetolians; (iv) if the Aetolians should make peace with Philip, the treaty should contain the provision that peace would be valid only if Philip abstained from attacking the Romans or their allies or those who were under their control; similarly, if the Roman people made a pact with the king, they should add a clause denying him the right of making war on the Aetolians or their allies.

These terms were agreed to, but written copies were not deposited till two years afterwards, at Olympia by the Aetolians and on the Capitol by the Romans, to invest the record with sanctity. The reason for the delay had been the unexpectedly long detention of the Aetolian envoys in Rome, which did not, however, prove any impediment to action. The Aetolians promptly moved against Philip, and Laevinus captured Zacynthus, a small island close to Aetolia, containing a single town of the same name. He took the town, though not its citadel, by storm; Oeniadae and Nassus, two Acarnanian towns, he also took and annexed to the Aetolians. Then, thinking that Philip was sufficiently involved in a war near home not to be able to spare a thought for Italy or the Carthaginians or pacts with Hannibal, he withdrew to Corcyra.

25. News of the revolt of the Aetolians was brought to Philip at Pella, where he was wintering. He intended to march into Greece at the beginning of spring; and so, to ensure that Macedonia should have the Illyrians and the neighbouring communities frightened into inactivity in his rear, he made a sudden raid on the territories of Oricum and Apollonia. The men of the latter town came out to meet him but were driven back in

terror and confusion within their walls. After devastating the nearer parts of Illyricum he turned with equal swiftness into Pelagonia, and then captured the Dardanian town of Sintia, which might have been useful to the Dardanians as a base from which to invade Macedonia. These rapid movements completed, the thought of the Aetolian war and a Roman war combined with it brought him down into Thessaly by way of Pelagonia, Lyncus, and Bottiaea, believing, as he did, that men could be induced to join him against the Aetolians. Leaving Perseus at the pass into Thessaly with 4,000 troops to hold off the Aetolians, he then marched into Macedonia before he could become involved in more serious matters, and thence into Thrace against the Maedi. This latter people had made a habit of raiding Macedonia whenever they knew that the king was occupied with a foreign war and the kingdom, in consequence, inadequately defended. So in order to break them he set about the devastation of their land and, simultaneously, the siege of their capital town, Iamphorynna.

When Scopas learned that Philip had gone to Thrace and was engaged in operations there, he armed all the Aetolians of military age in preparation for the invasion of Acarnania. The Acarnanians were inferior in strength; Oeniadae and Nassus were already lost to them and they saw that war with Rome was impending; none the less they prepared to resist, though more out of anger than with any clear plan of campaign. They sent their women and children and everyone over sixty over the border into Epirus, and all the men between fifteen and sixty swore an oath never to come home except as victors; against any man who owned defeat and left the line they composed a frightful curse – a most solemn adjuration addressed to the Epirotes, begging that none of them should admit the dastard to his city, or his house, or his board, or his hearth. At the same time they besought the Epirotes to bury in a common grave all of their men who might fall in battle, and to place this inscription over their bodies: 'Here lie the Acarnanians who died fighting for their country against the unprovoked violence of the Aetolians.' Their courage raised by these patriotic professions, they took up a position right on their frontier, facing the enemy. A message was sent to Philip informing him of the dangerous turn events had taken, and he was compelled to give up the war in which he was engaged, though Iamphorynna had already surrendered and other successes had been won. The Aetolians' attack had first been held up by the report of the oath that the Acarnanians had sworn, and then news of Philip's approach had caused them to retire right back into the interior. Philip, too, although he had made all possible speed to save the Acarnanians from being crushed, did not advance beyond Dium; then, when he learned that the Aetolians had moved out of Acarnania, he returned to Pella.

26. At the beginning of spring Laevinus left Corcyra and sailed round Cape Leucata to Naupactus, where he issued orders for Scopas and the Aetolians to join him at Anticyra, the place he intended to make for next. Anticyra is in Locris, on the left hand as one enters the Gulf of Corinth; it is only a short way from Naupactus either by land or water. Some two days later the siege of the town began simultaneously by sea and land, the pressure from the sea being the heavier because it was the Romans who were applying it, and because they had siege artillery of all kinds on board their vessels. In a few days the town surrendered and was handed over to the Aetolians; all captured material, according to the terms of the treaty, passed into Roman hands. Laevinus was informed by letter that he had been made consul in his absence and that Publius Sulpicius was coming to relieve him; but in fact he returned to Rome later than was generally expected, as he fell sick and was a long time recovering.

Marcellus entered upon his consulship on the Ides of March. On the same day, as a matter of custom merely, he held a meeting of the Senate, declaring that he would propose no business concerning the country or the provinces while his colleague was absent. He was aware, he said, that large numbers of Sicilians were just outside Rome, staying in the country houses of his detractors; it was, however, far from the truth that it was he who refused to allow them openly to make known in Rome the charges which his enemies had trumped up against him. On the contrary, he would have given them a hearing in the Senate immediately, if they did not pretend some reluctance to speak of a consul in his colleague's absence. But as soon as his colleague came, he would not, he declared, allow anything to be discussed before the question of bringing the Sicilians into the Senate. He went on to complain that Cornelius had more or less combed the whole of Sicily to have as many people as possible come to Rome to lay complaints against him; moreover, he had filled the city with dispatches falsely stating that war was still continuing in the island, in order to diminish his credit.

That day Marcellus won a reputation for restraint; he dismissed the Senate, and it almost seemed as if public business was to come to a complete standstill until the other consul should arrive. Lack of occupation, as it usually does, started people talking. There were grumblings about the length of the war, the devastated farms near the city in the track of Hannibal's column, and the election of two consuls both of whom were by nature fighters, fiercer and more proud-spirited than they should be, men only too likely even in peace-time to start a war, and certainly not the sort to give the country a breathing-space when a war was actually in progress. 27. Talk of this sort was interrupted by a fire which broke out simultaneously in several places around the forum on the eve of the festival of Quinquatrus. At the same time the Seven Shops (afterwards five) and the bankers' premises now known as the Novae Tabernae, burst into flames; later private houses caught fire – there were no basilicas there in those days – then the Quarries, the Fish Market, and the House of the Vestals. The shrine of Vesta was with difficulty saved by the good service of thirteen slaves, who were afterwards bought by the state and freed. The fire continued to burn night and day, and everyone was convinced that it was due to a deliberate criminal act, since it had broken out in several, and not continuous, places simultaneously. Accordingly the consul on the Senate's authority announced at a mass meeting of the people that anyone giving information on who started the fire would be rewarded: if the informer were free, the reward would be money; if a slave, his liberty. The offer of the reward led a slave, Manus by name, belonging to the Capuan family of the Calavii to declare that the fire was the work of his masters and of five other young Capuan noblemen whose fathers had been executed on Fulvius's orders. He added that they would start other fires all over the place unless they were arrested. So arrested they were, and their slaves with them. At first they tried to counter the evidence by disparaging the informer as a runaway slave who had received a beating the previous day, and was now taking advantage of an accident to trump up a charge against his masters simply out of rage, like the frivolous creature he was. But later, when they were accused in the presence of the informer, and the examination of their slave accomplices began in the forum, they all confessed, and masters and slaves alike were punished. Manus the informer was given his liberty and 20,000 *asses* in money.

As the consul Laevinus was passing Capua, great crowds from the city came swarming round him, begging him with tears for permission to go to Rome to implore the Senate, if now at last any pity could touch them, not to persist in ruining Capua utterly or to let the Capuans' name be blotted out for ever by Fulvius. Fulvius denied that he had any personal quarrel with the Capuans: his enmity, he declared, had a purely patriotic motive, and it would continue as long as he knew that their attitude to Rome was unchanged, for there was no nation or people in the world who more bitterly hated the Roman name. That was why he kept them shut up within their walls, for any who got out roamed the country like wild beasts tearing and killing whatever was thrown in their way. Some of them had deserted to Hannibal, others had gone to Rome meaning to burn it to the ground; in the charred ruins of the forum the consul would find the record of the Capuans' crime; an attempt had been made on the temple of Vesta, on the Undying Fire, on the Palladium, that most solemn pledge of Roman sway, laid up there in the temple's inmost shrine. For his own part, he ended, he by no means thought it a safe thing that Capuans should be allowed to enter the walls of Rome.

Laevinus got Fulvius to make the Capuans swear an oath to return to Capua five days after receiving the Senate's answer, and then told them to follow him to Rome. Surrounded by the crowd of them, with Sicilians too coming out to meet him and following him on the road, Laevinus gave the impression of a man cut to the quick by the ruin of two famous cities, and bringing the vanquished to Rome to accuse her leading statesmen. However, it was on the state of the country and the various theatres of war that both consuls first opened discussion in the Senate. 28. Laevinus began by giving an account of the position in Macedonia and Greece and of the Aetolians, Acarnanians, and Locrians, and of his own operations in that region by land and sea. Philip, he said, while making war on the Aetolians had been driven back into Macedonia and had retired deep into his own territory; the Roman legion there could therefore be withdrawn, as the fleet was enough to keep Philip out of Italy. This was the extent of what Laevinus had to report about his own actions and the province of which he had been in charge. Both consuls then introduced the question of the distribution of spheres of command, and the Senate decreed that one consul should assume responsibility for Italy and the war with Hannibal, while the other had the fleet previously commanded by Otacilius, and the control of Sicily, assisted by the praetor Lucius Cincius. The consuls were assigned the two armies which were in Etruria and Gaul, consisting of four legions; the two City legions of the previous year were to be sent to Etruria, and the two which had been commanded by the consul Sulpicius to Gaul. Gaul and the legions there were to be under the command of whoever was appointed by the consul in charge of operations in Italy; Calpurnius was sent to Etruria after his praetorship, his command being continued for a further year. Capua was assigned to Quintus Fulvius, and his command continued; an order was made for the diminution of the army of citizens and allies, the two legions to be combined as a single unit containing 5,000 foot and 300 horse, the men with the longest service being discharged; of the allies, 7,000 foot and 300 horse were to be retained, old soldiers being discharged on the same principle of length of service. As for Gnaeus Fulvius, the previous year's consul, no change was made either in his province, Apulia, or in the force under his command: his command was merely extended for another year. His colleague Sulpicius was instructed to discharge all his forces with the exception of the naval crews. In Sicily the army which had been commanded by Cornelius was to be discharged when the consul arrived in the island. The praetor Cincius was given the survivors of Cannae, equivalent to about two legions, to hold Sicily; for Sardinia the same number of legions were assigned to the praetor Volso as Cornelius had commanded there in the previous year. The consuls were instructed to raise the City legions, but not to include in them any veteran who had served under Marcus Claudius, Marcus Valerius, or Quintus Fulvius. Finally the total number of Roman legions for that year was not to exceed twenty-one.

29. After the Senate had thus completed its instructions, the consuls drew lots for their respective spheres of action; Sicily and the fleet went to Marcellus, Italy and operations against Hannibal to Laevinus. The Sicilians who were standing in sight of the consuls while they waited for the draw, were dumbfounded by its result. For them, it was the capture of Syracuse over again, and their lamentations and tears made everyone turn to look at them and soon became the subject of talk. For they started visiting senators' houses, dressed in mourning, and declaring that if Marcellus returned for a second period of command they would not only leave their respective towns but abandon Sicily altogether. For no fault of theirs, they said, Marcellus had already treated them without mercy; so what would he do in anger, now that he knew that Sicilians had come to Rome to complain of him? Better for that island to be overwhelmed by the fires of Etna or sunk in the sea than to be given over for punishment to an enemy who hated it.

Complaints of this sort, which began by circulating round the houses of the nobility and aroused much talk, instigated partly by pity for the Sicilians, partly by dislike of Marcellus, finally reached the Senate. The consuls were asked to propose to the Senate that the allocation of provinces should be changed. Marcellus said that if the Sicilians had already been given a hearing in the Senate, his own opinion might have been different; but as it was, to prevent anyone from saying that the Sicilians were afraid to express freely their complaints against the man in whose power they would soon be, he was prepared, if it did not inconvenience his colleague, to change his province. At the same time he deprecated any prejudgement of the case by the Senate, for since it would have been contrary to law for his colleague to be given the choice of a province without the usual drawing of lots, how much greater would the injustice, nay, the insult be if the province which had fallen by lot to himself were transferred to his colleague?

The Senate, having indicated its feeling in the matter but passed no formal decree, was then adjourned and the consuls made the exchange by private agreement between themselves. Fate had a hand in it – it was already hurrying Marcellus towards Hannibal. Marcellus had been the first to win from Hannibal, after many defeats, the distinction of some sort of success, and he was now destined to bring glory to Hannibal by his own death in the hour of victory, the last Roman general to fall on the battlefield.

30. After the exchange of provinces had been made, the Sicilian envoys were brought into the Senate. They tried to reflect credit upon Syracuse by making a long speech about the unvarying loyalty to Rome of King Hiero; Hieronymus, they said, and then Hippocrates and Epicydes had been hateful to them for various reasons, but especially because they had abandoned the Romans and gone over to Hannibal. For that reason Hieronymus had been assassinated by a group of young aristocrats almost as an act of state policy, and for that reason too seventy young men of the very highest rank had formed a conspiracy to kill Epicydes and Hippocrates. They had been disappointed by Marcellus's delay – he had not moved his army to Syracuse at the time he had named: information had been laid, and all the conspirators had been executed. Moreover, the tyrannical government of Epicydes and Hippocrates had been provoked by the brutal way in which Marcellus had plundered Leontini. After that, they declared, leading Syracusans never ceased going over to Marcellus with promises to betray the city to him whenever he wished. But he had preferred to take it by force, at any rate until all his efforts to do so by land and sea had failed, and then he had deliberately rejected the assistance of the Syracusan nobility, who had again and again vainly offered it of their own free will, and had found Sosis the coppersmith and the Spaniard Moericus more to his taste, as offering him a better excuse for robbing and murdering the oldest allies of the Roman people. If it had not been Hieronymus who had gone over to Hannibal, but the people and senate of Syracuse;

if it had been the Syracusans themselves, as an act of stated policy, who shut their gates against Marcellus instead of their tyrannical rulers Hippocrates and Epicydes, after first crushing their resistance; if, lastly, they had fought Rome with true Carthaginian bitterness, what, short of destroying Syracuse utterly, could Marcellus have done against them worse than what he did do? In any case nothing was left in Syracuse except the walls, the houses stripped of all they contained, and the shrines of the gods broken open and despoiled, their images and adornments stolen. Many had been robbed of their land, so that even from the bare soil they could no longer support themselves and their families with the remnants of their possessions. Could not the Senate, they begged, order the restoration, if not of everything, at least of such property as could be definitely identified?

Laevinus requested the envoys to leave the Senate-house to enable the members to discuss their demands, but Marcellus at once objected. 'No,' he said; 'let them stay so that they can hear my answer to their complaints – for it seems, gentlemen, that we generals, in waging war on your behalf, are expected to accept as our accusers the men we have beaten in battle, and that the two cities captured this year are each to have a prisoner in the dock – Capua Fulvius and Syracuse myself.' 31. So the envoys were brought back and Marcellus spoke as follows:

'I have not, gentlemen of the Senate, so far forgotten the dignity of the Roman people and of the office I hold as to be willing to defend myself against Greeks if there were any question of a charge against me personally. But the subject of inquiry is not what I have done – the law of war is my defence for whatever I did against an enemy of our country – but what these men have deserved to suffer. If they have not been enemies of our country, it makes no difference if it was today or in Hiero's time that I brought force to bear on Syracuse. But if, on the contrary, they rebelled against Rome, if they made a murderous attack upon Roman envoys, if they closed their city against us and defended their walls with the help of a Carthaginian army, who can think it unjust that they should be done by as they did? When leading men in Syracuse offered to put the city in my hands, I rejected the offer and preferred to entrust so important a matter to Sosis and the Spaniard Moericus: very well – but what about yourselves? You are hardly the *lowest* members of Syracusan society, or you would not jeer at others for their humble birth; but which of you ever promised to open the gates to me or to admit my troops into the city? Far from it: you hate and curse the men who did so, and even here in the Senate cannot refrain from insulting them. Clearly, it is the very last thing you would ever have done yourselves. No, gentlemen; the very obscurity of those two, which our friends the envoys cast in their teeth, is the best proof that I rejected the help of nobody who was willing to serve our country's interest. Moreover, before I began the siege I made efforts for peace: I sent a delegation, I went in person to a conference; and when they shamelessly mishandled my envoys and refused an answer even to me in person when I met their chief men at the gates, then, and only then, after enduring many hardships on land and sea, did I at last take Syracuse by force of arms. What happened to them then they should more justly complain of to Hannibal and his beaten Carthaginians than here in the Senate of their conquerors. For myself, gentlemen, if I wanted to deny that Syracuse was stripped of its treasures, I should not now be adorning Rome with her spoils; and as for individuals and what I took from them or gave them by right of victory, I am satisfied that I did so in accordance both with the laws of war and with each man's desert. Whether you, gentlemen, ratify these acts of mine or not is less my personal concern than the country's; my task has been faithfully discharged, and it is now in the national interest that you should not by refusing to ratify my acts make other commanders in future less anxious to do their duty.

'Well, gentlemen, you have now heard what both the Sicilians and I have had to say: we will therefore all leave the House together, so that my presence amongst you may not hamper your deliberations.' The Sicilian envoys were thus dismissed and Marcellus left for the Capitol, where he was to attend to the raising of troops.

32. The other consul then formally opened the discussion of the Sicilians' demands. Different views were expressed and the debate was a protracted one. A large part of the Senate, led by

Titus Manlius Torquatus, was of the opinion that it was the tyrants, who were enemies both of Rome and of the Syracusan people, against whom war should have been waged; then, the tyrants defeated, the city ought not to have been taken by force but received back into the Roman alliance and restored to stability with its ancient laws and liberty, not crushed by hostile action when it was already exhausted by its miserable servitude. In the conflicts between the tyrants and the Roman commander the prize of victory, the most famous and beautiful city in the world, had been destroyed, in the city which had once been the granary and the treasury of the Roman people, by whose munificent gifts the state on many occasions, and lastly in this very war against Carthage, had been aided and enriched. If Hiero, Rome's most faithful friend, could come back from the dead, how could they show him without shame either Syracuse or Rome, since on entering Rome after a glance at his native city half-ruined and despoiled he would see its stolen treasures in the very vestibule of the city, nay, almost at the gates?

Views of this sort were expressed, partly to arouse pity for the Sicilians, partly to discredit Marcellus. The Senate, however, passed a decree in milder terms: the acts of Marcellus, both during the campaign and after his victory, were to be ratified; the Senate, for the future, was to attend to the interests of the Syracusan state, and would instruct the consul Laevinus to assist it in any way he could without loss or injury to Rome. Two senators were then sent to the Capitol to recall Marcellus to the House, the Sicilian envoys were brought in, and the decree was read. The envoys, courteously dismissed, threw themselves at Marcellus's feet and begged him to pardon what they had said in lamenting their lot and in the hope of lightening it, and prayed to be taken, with Syracuse their city, under his patronage and protection. Marcellus promised to do so, spoke to them kindly, and let them go.

33. Next the Capuans were given a hearing in the Senate. Their plea was the more pathetic as their case was a harsher one. They could not deny that their punishment was deserved and they had no tyrants on whom to shift the blame; they did believe, none the less, that what with so many of their senators executed and so many who had poisoned themselves, they had

been already punished enough. There were a few nobles, they said, still alive who had neither been driven to suicide by their own consciences nor condemned to death by the anger of their conqueror. These men, as Roman citizens and in most cases linked to Rome, through the ancient right of intermarriage, by marriage ties and, in consequence, by the closest ties of blood, were asking for liberty for themselves and their families, and for some portion of their property.

The delegates were then removed from the House and there was a moment of doubt as to whether Quintus Fulvius should be sent for from Capua (the consul Claudius had died after the city's capture), to allow the question to be discussed in the presence of the officer who had commanded on the spot, just as had been done between the Sicilian envoys and Marcellus. But then they noticed the presence in the House of Marcus Atilius Regulus and Gaius Fulvius, Quintus Fulvius's brother, both of whom had served under Fulvius at Capua, and also of Quintus Minucius and Lucius Veturius Philo, officers who had served under Claudius, and all of them men who had been present during the whole course of the operations. This, combined with the Senate's unwillingness to call Fulvius away from Capua or to postpone the hearing of the Capuan envoys, induced them to turn to Marcus Atilius Regulus, who of all the officers who had been at Capua had the greatest influence. Asked his opinion, Regulus replied: 'I testify that after Capua was taken I attended the conference with the consuls when the question was raised whether anyone in the city had done anything to serve us. It was found that there were two women, Vestia Oppia of Atella but then living in Capua, and an ex-prostitute named Pacula Cluvia, the former of whom had sacrificed every day with prayers for the safety and victory of Rome, while the latter had secretly supplied needy prisoners with food. The attitude towards us of all the rest of the Campanians was no different from that of the Carthaginians, and it was not the most guilty of them so much as the most influential who were selected by Fulvius for execution. The Campanians are Roman citizens, and I do not see how their case can be discussed in the Senate without reference to the people's will. Long ago, when the people of Satricum revolted, what we did was to see that the tribune Antistius should first bring forward a formal proposal; and as a result the people voted that the Senate should be empowered to decide the case. My view therefore is that we ought now to approach the people's tribunes, in order to get one or more of them to bring a bill before the people by virtue of which we may have the right of deciding the case of the Campanians.'

The tribune Atilius, on the Senate's authority, accordingly put the question to the people in the following terms: 'All the Campanians, including the Atellani, Calatini, and Sabatini, who have surrendered themselves to the will and power of the Roman people and to the proconsul Fulvius; all the non-citizens they have surrendered with themselves; all the property – the city, the land, things human and things divine, implements and whatsoever else they have surrendered together with themselves – concerning these things I ask you, citizens of Rome, what you wish to be done.' The people expressed their wishes in these words: 'What the Senate on oath, a majority of those present, may deem fit, that is our will and command.'

34. In accordance with this expression of the popular will the Senate, after consultation, first restored to Oppia and Cluvia their liberty and possessions, with the further provision that if they wished to ask the Senate for other rewards they were to come to Rome. Decrees were passed against individual Capuan families which need not be recorded in detail; some were to have their property confiscated and themselves, their children, and their wives sold into slavery, except for daughters who had married abroad before the city fell into Roman hands; some were to be imprisoned and their case reserved for future judgement; in other cases a distinction was made in the rating of their property before determining whether or not it was to be confiscated; cattle, not including horses, and slaves, not including adult males, and everything not attached to the soil was to be restored to the owners. All Campanians – Atellani, Calatini, and Sabatini – except those who, themselves or their parents, had served in the Carthaginian army were to be free men but without the right of Roman citizenship or membership of the Latin confederacy, and with the provision that none of them who

had been in Capua while the gates were closed should remain beyond a certain date either in the city or its territory. A place to live in was to be assigned to them beyond the Tiber but not contiguous with its banks. Those who during the war had not been in Capua, or in any other Campanian town which had revolted from Rome, were to be removed to a spot on the Roman side of the river Liris; and those who had come over to the Romans before Hannibal reached Capua, to territory on the Roman side of the Volturnus, none of them to possess land or buildings less than fifteen miles from the sea. Those removed across the Tiber, themselves and their descendants, were forbidden to acquire or hold property anywhere except in the territory of Veii, Sutrium, and Nepete, with the further provision that no one was to own more than fifty *jugera* of land. The property of all who had been senators or magistrates in Capua, Atella, or Calatia was to be sold in Capua. Free persons whose sale had been ordered were to be sent to Rome and offered for sale in the market there. Bronze statues and busts said to have been captured from the enemy were referred to the College of pontiffs for decision as to whether they were sacred or profane.

The Capuans were then dismissed; much sadder men on account of these decrees than they had been when they came. No longer did they blame the severity of Fulvius; rather they accused the injustice of the gods and their own execrable fortune.

35. After the hearing of the Sicilian and Capuan envoys recruiting began. When the troops were enrolled, the question of additional oarsmen was taken up. At the moment there was not only an insufficiency of men for this purpose, but no money in the treasury for finding or paying them; so the consuls issued an edict ordering private individuals, according to their class and property-rating, to provide oarsmen, as had been done on a previous occasion, together with pay and rations for thirty days. The edict was greeted with a roar of protest, and so great was the indignation that there was little lacking for a popular rising but someone to lead it. Next after Syracuse and Capua, it was the Roman people, it seemed, that the consuls had set about ruining and tearing to pieces. For years the people had

been drained dry by taxation; they had nothing left but the land, and that was stripped bare. The enemy had burnt their houses, the state had stolen the slave-labour from their farms, either impressing the slaves as oarsmen for the fleet, or buying them cheap for military service; any silver or copper money a man might have had been taken from him either for the oarsmen's pay or for the annual tax. They could not be compelled by any force or any authority to give what they had not got. Let their property be sold and their naked bodies, all they had left, be subjected to insult: there was nothing left for them even to buy their ransom. Angry complaints of this sort, far from being whispered in secret, were openly expressed in the forum by crowds of people pressing round the consuls without any attempt at concealment, and nothing the consuls could do, either by reprimand or by attempted consolation, was able to quiet them. They accordingly announced that they gave the populace three days to think the matter over, and then proceeded to use the interval themselves in an effort to examine and resolve the problem.

Next day the consuls called a meeting of the Senate to discuss the recruiting of oarsmen. During the session they began by speaking at length on the justice of the people's objection, and then went on to shift their ground. The burden, they declared, whether just or unjust, ought to be laid upon private citizens, for, as the treasury was empty, where could they get crews? And how without fleets could Sicily be held, or Philip be kept out of Italy, or the Italian coast be protected?

36. So difficult was the situation that policy seemed to have come to a standstill. Brains refused to work and there was not a thought in anyone's head until the consul Laevinus came to the rescue. 'As the magistrates,' he said, 'are superior in dignity to the Senate, and the Senate superior to the people, so it is the Senate's duty to give the lead in shouldering all heavy and disagreeable burdens. If you want to make a demand on an inferior, assume the same responsibility for yourself and your family and you will find that all will obey you. The expense to each of the commons will not be heavy once they see every leading man assuming more than his single share in it. So if we want Rome to have fleets, and to fit them out, and individual citizens

to provide crews willingly, let us first lay the obligation to do so on ourselves. I suggest that we senators bring into the treasury tomorrow all our gold, silver, and coined bronze, each man leaving only a ring for himself, his wife, and his children, a *bulla*[1] for his son, and an ounce of gold each for his wife and daughters, if he has any. Men who have held a curule magistracy may, I suggest, keep a pound of silver and the ornaments on their horses' harness, to provide them with a salt-cellar and dish for religious purposes; other senators should keep a pound of silver only. Let us leave each head of a family 5,000 *asses* in coined bronze; all other gold, silver, and coined bronze we should deposit at once with the commissioners in charge of banking, and not wait for a decree of the Senate before we do so, in order that a voluntary contribution and rivalry in public service may rouse the order of knights first, and then the rest of the people, to emulate us.

'My colleague and I have discussed the matter thoroughly, and this is the one solution we have found. With the gods' good help, let us act upon it. When the country is sound, it preserves private property easily enough; betray what belongs to the commonwealth, and you will seek in vain to keep safe what is your own.'

This proposal met with such enthusiastic acceptance that the consuls were actually thanked for making it. The Senate was adjourned, and everybody proceeded to bring his silver and gold and his bronze money to the treasury; and such was the competition to be entered first, or amongst the first, on the books, that the commissioners were hardly able to receive the contributions or the clerks to list them. The Senate's unanimous response was followed by that of the knights, and that of the knights by the commons; and thus, with no government order or official compulsion, the state found itself in want neither of crews to make up the necessary complement nor of money to pay them with.[2] And so, all preparations made, the consuls left Rome to take up their respective duties.

1. The amulet worn round the neck by free-born Roman children.

2. This voluntary loan was repaid in the last years of the war. See p. 586.

37. At no other period of the war were both Romans and Carthaginians less sure of what the future might bring, or more involved in rapid alternations of failure and success. Outside Italy, distress at the Spanish reverses had been balanced for the Romans by joy at the victory in Sicily; in Italy itself the capture of Tarentum, a bitter blow and a serious loss, was offset by the unexpected satisfaction of continuing to hold the citadel, while the sudden and dreadful alarm caused by Hannibal at the gates of Rome was turned a few days later into rejoicing at the fall of Capua. Operations overseas also had their corresponding ups and downs: the hostility of Philip, at an inopportune moment, and to balance it, the making of a new alliance with the Aetolians and Attalus, King of Asia, like a promise from fortune of Roman power in the East. The Carthaginians, similarly, had the capture of Tarentum to set against the loss of Capua; the glory they enjoyed in having reached the walls of Rome without opposition was matched by their disappointment in failure to complete the undertaking, and in shame at finding themselves so lightly thought of that while they lay encamped at the walls a Roman army had marched out by another gate on its way to Spain. As for the Spanish provinces themselves, the nearer the Carthaginians had come to hope that with the destruction of two great armies and the deaths of their famous commanders the war in that country was over and the Romans driven out, the greater in proportion was their indignation that their victory had been brought to nothing by Lucius Marcius, who had taken command merely as a stop-gap in an emergency. So it was that Fortune held her scales; for both sides everything hung in the balance: it was as if, with all still to win and all to lose, they were only then beginning the war.

38. Nothing was more distressing to Hannibal than the fact that the Roman attack upon Capua, so much more determined than his own defence, had alienated many of the Italian peoples. He could not hold all of them by garrisons without cutting up his army into numerous small parts, at the moment a far from expedient proceeding; nor could he withdraw the garrisons he already had, and so leave his allies, so far as their loyalty was concerned, either free to see which way the cat would jump, or the prey of mere uncertainty. The avarice and cruelty of his

temperament inclined him to despoil where he could not protect, so that only ruins might be left to the enemy. This was a policy shameful in its inception and no less so in the event, as not only were those alienated who suffered undeservedly at his hands, but everyone else as well; the precedent had repercussions beyond the places that actually suffered, nor did the Roman consul fail to exert pressure wherever he saw any hope of success.

In the town of Salapia the two leading men were Dasius and Blattius. Dasius was friendly to Hannibal, Blattius, so far as he could with safety, favoured the Roman interest and through secret messages had given Marcellus hopes of betraying the town into his hands. This could not be effected without Dasius's support, so after long and anxious hesitation he began to make approaches to Dasius on the subject, not that he had much hope of success, but simply because he could think of nothing better to do. Dasius, however, who was opposed to the step and was also no friend of his rival for power, disclosed the plot to Hannibal. Both men were sent for, and whilst Hannibal was engaged in some business or other in front of his tribunal, intending soon to hear Blattius's case, and accuser and accused, the crowd having been cleared away, were standing there waiting, Blattius reopened to Dasius the question of betraying the town. The latter cried out that he was being urged under Hannibal's very eyes to turn traitor – as if nothing could be more obvious. But Hannibal and his assistants were inclined to feel that such an act was too audacious to be probable, and that it was nothing more than jealousy and hatred between the two rivals; the accusation was of a sort all the more easy to invent in that it did not admit of proof. The men were accordingly dismissed. Blattius, none the less, did not give up his bold design until by continual repetition and persistent harping upon the admirable results it would bring both for themselves and for their native town, he succeeded in persuading Dasius to surrender the place to Marcellus together with the Carthaginian garrison of 500 Numidians. As these troops were much the best cavalry in the Carthaginian army the surrender proved impossible without serious bloodshed. Unexpected though the move was and in spite of the fact that cavalry tactics were impracticable inside the town, the Numidians none the less armed themselves in the confusion and attempted to break out. Unable to do so, they fell fighting to the last and not more than fifty of them were taken alive. The loss of this squadron was more serious to Hannibal than the loss of Salapia; never after that was he superior to the Romans in cavalry, the arm in which by far his greatest strength had lain.

39. About this time the shortage of supplies in the citadel of Tarentum had become almost intolerable; the Roman garrison there and its commander Livius placed all their hopes in supplies from Sicily, and a fleet of some twenty ships was lying at Rhegium to ensure their safe passage along the Italian coast. In command of the provision-fleet was Decimus Quinctius, a man of obscure birth but high military reputation, won by much fine service. Originally Marcellus had given him five vessels, the two largest of which were triremes; later, when he had often shown great vigour in action, three quinqueremes were added to his force, and finally he himself, by demanding from the allies, and from Rhegium, Velia, and Paestum, the vessels due under the terms of the treaty, made up his fleet to the number of twenty, which I mentioned above. This fleet had sailed from Rhegium, when Democrates fell in with it at Sapriportis, about fifteen miles from Tarentum, with an equal number of Tarentine ships. Quinctius was under sail, as he did not expect an engagement; he had, however, while in the neighbourhood of Croton and Sybaris,[1] taken on board a full complement of oarsmen, so that his fleet was admirably armed and equipped for the size of the vessels it contained. Now just at this moment, when the enemy were in sight, it so happened that the wind fell away, which gave him time to stow his sails and rigging, get the men to the oars, and prepare his soldiers for the fight now clearly imminent. Seldom had regular fleets engaged with such determination, for they were fighting with more at stake than their own lives: on the one side the Tarentines, having recovered their city from the Romans, after nearly a hundred years,[2] fought to free the citadel as well, if only they could succeed in cutting off supplies by depriving the enemy of

1. i.e. Thurii. This is the only time Livy uses the older name.
2. In fact, sixty-two years since its capture by the Romans in 272 B.C.

the command of the sea; while the Romans, on the other side, were fighting to prove, by keeping possession of the citadel, that Tarentum had not been taken by superior strength or courage but stolen from them by treachery.

In both fleets the signal for action was given. They met head-on, beak to beak. Once engaged, they made no attempt to back-water, no enemy ship was allowed to cast loose; every vessel rammed was promptly grappled and fighting began at such close quarters that it was almost hand to hand, swords being used as much as missiles. The bows of opposing vessels were interlocked, while enemy oarsmen tried to free them by swinging the sterns this way and that; all were packed so closely together that hardly a weapon fell without effect into the sea; like two lines of infantry the opposing fleets tried to force each other back, and fighting men could step without difficulty from one ship to another. Most notable was the struggle between the two ships which had led their respective columns and had been the first to encounter one another. In the Roman ship was Quinctius himself; in command of the Tarentine was Nico, surnamed Percon, a man who belonged to the party which had betrayed Tarentum to Hannibal and so both on national and personal grounds was as much hated by the Romans as he, in his turn, hated them. Quinctius was fighting hard himself and cheering on his men, when Nico caught him off his guard and ran him through with a spear. Weapons in hand, he fell forward over the ship's bows, and the victorious Tarentine leapt across on to his ship and thrust back the enemy, who were already dismayed by the loss of their commander. The fore part of the vessel being thus in Tarentine hands, while the Romans were huddled together trying to protect her after-part, another trireme suddenly made its appearance astern of her thus hemming her completely in. The Roman ship was captured and the rest of the fleet, seeing the flagship in enemy hands, fled in alarm in all directions. Some were sunk in open water, some were run ashore and soon became the prey of men from Thurii and Metapontum. Of the merchant vessels which were following with the supplies very few fell into enemy hands; others, by continually trimming their sails to the variable breeze, managed to make their escape out to the sea.

Meanwhile at Tarentum itself the fortune of war was very different. Some 4,000 men had left the town on a foraging expedition and were scattered about all over the countryside. Livius, who commanded the Roman garrison in the citadel and was always on the look-out for an opportunity of action, now saw his chance: Gaius Persius, no laggard soldier, was promptly ordered out with 2,500 men. Falling upon the straggling groups of foragers all over the neighbouring farms, he cut them down here, there, and everywhere, and at last drove back into the town the small remnant of them, who, desperate to escape, flung themselves through the half-opened gates. Indeed, such was the vigour of his onslaught that he was not far from taking the town. Thus the honours were equal, with a Roman victory on land and a Carthaginian at sea. Both sides were equally disappointed in their hope of fresh supplies, a hope which had seemed certain enough.

40. It was about this time, when the year was already drawing to a close, that the consul Laevinus arrived in Sicily, where the old and new allies were both expecting him. The peace at Syracuse was still very recent and there was much disorder there in consequence; so he thought that his first and most important duty was to achieve a settlement, after which he proceeded with his troops to Agrigentum where fighting was still going on, as the town was held by a strong Carthaginian garrison. As it happened, luck was on his side. The Carthaginian commander there was Hanno, but it was still upon Muttines and his Numidians that all hopes were centred. Muttines was out on raids all over Sicily; he was plundering Rome's allies at will; neither force nor stratagem could cut him off from Agrigentum and nothing could stop his coming out on a foray whenever he wished to do so. His continued success had for some time been casting a shadow upon Hanno's reputation as a commander-in-chief, and it ended in producing jealousy and dislike, so that Hanno no longer took pleasure even in a victory, because it was Muttines who won it. In the end he deprived Muttines of his cavalry command and transferred it to his son, in the belief that the loss of the command would involve the loss of his influence with the Numidians. The result was far otherwise; for Hanno was himself disliked, and by his

unpopularity he only increased the favour which Muttines already enjoyed. Moreover, Muttines himself had no intention of putting up with the insult; on the contrary, he promptly sent a secret message to Laevinus proposing to put Agrigentum into his hands. Through the men who brought the message guarantees were given and a plan of action agreed upon: the Numidians after killing or driving off the guards seized the gate of the town leading to the sea, and let in a party of Romans who had been sent for the purpose. As the Roman contingent marched towards the forum in the centre of the town, there was much noise and confusion, which Hanno supposed to be nothing more serious than another mutiny of the Numidians. He proceeded to the spot to check it; but when he saw in front of him a much greater number of men than he expected and heard the roar of Roman voices, which he knew all too well, he took to flight before coming within range of missiles. Passing through the gate on the far side of the town he made his way with Epicydes and a small company of men to the sea, where they were lucky enough to find a small vessel in which they crossed to Africa, abandoning Sicily, the prize of so many years of warfare, to the enemy. The remaining rank and file of Carthaginians and Sicilians did not even attempt resistance; trying blindly to save themselves by flight and finding all means of exit closed, they were cut down at the gates.

On gaining possession of the town Laevinus scourged and beheaded the leading citizens of Agrigentum; the rest he sold along with other captured material. All the money he sent to Rome. News of the fall of Agrigentum spreading through Sicily produced an immediate shift in favour of Rome: within a brief time twenty towns were betrayed and six taken by force. Some forty others surrendered voluntarily and accepted Roman protection. Laevinus punished or rewarded the leading men of these various communities according to their deserts, and compelled the Sicilians at last to lay down their arms and turn their attention to agriculture. His object in this was not only that the island should produce enough to support its inhabitants but that it should once again, as often before, be able to relieve the market in Rome and Italy. This done, he returned to Italy taking with him a mob of down-and-outs from Agathyrna. These men, 4,000 of them, were a mixed and unsavoury lot – exiles and bankrupts, most of whom had committed capital offences, while they lived under the law in their own communities, and now, when their common misery had, for one reason or another, brought them together at Agathyrna, they were living as best they could on highway robbery and brigandage. Laevinus felt it would be unwise to leave them in the island, where unity and any sort of settled conditions were still so recent, as they might well be a cause of serious disturbances; they would, moreover, be of service to the people of Rhegium, who were on the look-out for experienced cut-throats to help them in their raids on Bruttium. So far as Sicily was concerned, the war was finished that year.

41. In Spain at the beginning of spring Scipio got his ships afloat again; then, having summoned the allied auxiliaries to Tarraco, he ordered the fleet, warships and transports, to the mouth of the Ebro. The legions were ordered to leave their winter quarters and assemble at the same point, and Scipio himself with 5,000 allied troops marched from Tarraco to join them. On his arrival, wishing particularly to speak a word to the veterans who had survived such grave defeats, he had them paraded and delivered the following address: 'I am the first newly appointed commander-in-chief who has been in a position to express deserved and justifiable thanks to his men before he has experienced what they can do for him. Even before I saw the camp or the country in which my duties were to lie, Fortune had made a bond between you and me: I was grateful, first for the devotion you showed to my father and my uncle both before and after their deaths; and secondly, for your soldierly qualities in holding intact for me, their successor, and for the Roman people the possession of this province which had been so disastrously lost. But since now, by God's blessing, the object before us is not to stay in Spain ourselves but to push the Carthaginians out of it – not to stand in front of the Ebro and keep the enemy from crossing it, but to cross it ourselves and take the initiative on the other side – I fear that some of you may feel that such a plan is beyond the capacity of a commander so young as I am, and too bold when we remember those recent defeats. No one could be

less able than I am to forget our defeats in Spain: within thirty days my father and my uncle were killed, two grievous losses in succession for my family to bear. But though, as an individual, to be all but orphaned and left desolate is enough to break my spirit, yet the Fortune of our country and her valour forbid me to despair of the final issue. The destiny granted us by some inscrutable providence is, that in all our great wars we have emerged victorious from defeat.

'I will not speak of the distant past, of Porsenna, the Gauls, the Samnites – let me begin with Carthage. How many fleets, generals, armies were lost in the first Punic war? And what of the present one? I was present myself at all our defeats, or if I was not, they touched me more closely than anyone else. Trebia, Trasimene, Cannae, what are those names but records of the destruction of Roman armies and the deaths of consuls? Then think of the defection of a large part of Italy and Sicily and of Sardinia, and then of that moment of ultimate horror when the Carthaginians lay in camp between the Anio and Rome, and victorious Hannibal was seen almost within the gates. When everything, it seemed, was falling about us in ruin, one thing alone stood firm – the inviolable, the unshakeable courage of the Roman people. This it was that raised up again the scattered fragments of our fallen fortunes. You, soldiers, under the auspices of your general my father, were the first to check the advance of Hasdrubal to the Alps and Italy, after the defeat at Cannae; and if Hasdrubal had joined forces with his brother, the Roman name would now have ceased to exist. This success of yours was the prop to sustain us in our reverses; and now, by the favour of the gods, all our affairs in Italy and Sicily are prospering, and the news is more cheerful and better every day. In Sicily, Syracuse and Agrigentum have been taken, the enemy has been expelled from the island, the province is restored to the control of Rome. In Italy Arpi has been recovered, Capua has fallen. Hannibal has been sent scurrying back along the road from Rome and driven into the remotest corner of Bruttium, where now he prays for nothing better than leave to escape with his life from his enemies' territory. What then, my soldiers, could be more unreasonable than that you should be faint-hearted now, when everything in Italy smiles upon our triumphs, you, who with my parents – let them share that honourable name – upheld the tottering fortunes of the Roman people when disaster after disaster was being heaped upon them and the gods themselves, it seemed, fought on Hannibal's side?. . . .[1]

'And now the immortal gods, guardians of our empire, who at the elections inspired the people to vote unanimously for my appointment to the command, are by auguries and auspices and visions in the night foreshowing nothing but prosperity and success. My own mind too, always my most trusted seer, foresees that Spain is ours and that every Carthaginian will soon be gone, their fleeing armies covering the land as their ships the sea. What the mind of itself divines is suggested no less by sound reasoning: their allies are weary of their burdens and are beginning to beg for our protection; their three army-commanders are so much at odds that each is almost a traitor to his colleagues, and the three divisions of their force are widely separated. The ill fortune which so short a time ago crushed us is now gathering its strength against them: they are being deserted by their friends, as we were by the Celtiberians; they have divided their forces, the very thing that brought disaster upon my father and uncle; their private differences will not let them unite, while separately none of them will be able to stand against us. All I ask you, my men, is that you give your loyalty to the name of Scipio, to the scion of your lost commanders, growing again from the lopped branch. Come, my veterans, take with you across the Ebro a new army and a new commander; take them into territory you have so often trod, fighting like the brave men you are. Already you recognize in me something of my father and uncle, in my face, my look, the turn of my body; soon I shall strive to give you back an image of their hearts as well, of their loyalty and courage, so that each of you may say that Scipio, his beloved general, has risen from the dead or been born again.'

42. After these heartening words Scipio left Silanus on guard with 3,000 foot and 300 horse and crossed the Ebro with the rest of the army, 25,000 infantry and 2,500 mounted

1. There is a break in the Latin text here.

troops. Some of his officers tried to persuade him to move at once against the nearest of the three widely separated Carthaginian contingents; but fearing that, if he were to do so, he might invite a junction of all three against him and prove no match for so powerful a combined force, he decided instead to employ the interval by an attack upon New Carthage, a town not only with great resources of its own but also the repository of a mass of enemy equipment of all kinds. Weapons, money, hostages from all over Spain were kept there; its site, moreover, was a convenient one for the passage to Africa, and it lay on a harbour big enough for any number of ships and probably the only one facing the Mediterranean on the Spanish coast.

No one except Laelius knew what their objective was. He had received instructions to bring the fleet round, but to go slow so as to enter the harbour of New Carthage at the same time as Scipio's troops made their appearance on the landward side. Seven days[1] after leaving the Ebro the two forces, naval and military, arrived and a position was taken up northward of the town; a rampart was thrown up to protect its rear, the nature of the ground being sufficient protection in front.

A word on the site of New Carthage: about half-way down the east coast of Spain there is a bay, open to the south-west; it runs about two and a half miles inland and in breadth is some three hundred yards less. At the mouth of the inlet a small island protects the anchorage from all winds except the south-west. From the head of the bay a peninsula runs out, high land, on which the town was built. Thus the town has sea to the east and south of it, while on its western and part of its northern sides it is surrounded by a lagoon in which the depth of water varies with the ebb and flow of the tide. It is connected with the mainland by a ridge about 250 yards wide. Fortification on this side would have involved little labour, but Scipio none the less had no earthwork constructed, perhaps out of ostentation, to show the enemy his confidence, perhaps to leave the way back unobstructed every time he had need to approach the walls. 43. When he had completed such other

1. An impossible figure: Polybius gives the distance as 2,600 *stades* (325 miles).

works of fortification as were necessary, he ordered the fleet to take stations in the harbour, thus making it clear to the townspeople that they were blockaded simultaneously by land and sea. He then visited each ship in turn and warned the captains to keep the closest possible look-out during the night, as an enemy on first finding himself blockaded was always sure to try everything at any likely point. That done, he returned to camp and called a meeting of his troops to explain to them his reason for beginning operations with the siege of a town and to encourage them to look forward to its capture.

'If anyone,' he said, 'imagines that you have been brought here just to attack one town, he has made a better reckoning of your labour than of your profit. It is indeed true that you are about to assault the walls of one town, but in that one town you will have taken the whole of Spain. In it are the hostages of all the great princes and peoples, and once they are in your hands they will immediately surrender everything which is now subject to the Carthaginians; in it is all the enemy's money, the capture of which would be a crippling loss to them because they employ mercenaries and cannot carry on without it, to us a great gain, as we can use it to buy the support of the Spanish tribes. Here too catapults, weapons, and war-material of all kinds are stored; these will add to your equipment and at the same time strip the enemy bare. We shall be taking, moreover, a town which is not only wealthy and beautiful, but one with a splendid harbour, from which all material we need can be supplied either by land or by sea. All these will be great gains for us, and yet greater losses for the enemy; for this is their citadel, their granary, their treasury, their arsenal – a storehouse for everything they need. Hither lies the direct course from Africa; it is the only safe anchorage between Gades and the Pyrenees. From this point all Spain is under threat from Africa....'[1]

44.... Mago had armed all available men, and he made the following dispositions when he saw that the attack was developing from land and sea simultaneously. He stationed 2,000 of the townspeople on the side nearest the Roman camp,

1. The rest of Scipio's speech and part of the following paragraph describing the beginning of the attack are lost. (A. de S.)

garrisoned the citadel with 500 men, and put another 500 on the hill in the eastern part of the town. All the rest were ordered to keep their eyes and ears open and to give assistance wherever the shouts of the combatants or any sudden emergency seemed to require it. He then opened the gate and ordered out the troops he had drawn up on the road leading to the Roman camp. The Romans, by Scipio's orders, began by giving ground a little, to be nearer the supports which were to be sent up during the actual fighting; and at first the two opposing lines seemed not unfairly matched. Soon, however, the supporting troops from the Roman camp began coming up in frequent relays, with the result that the defenders were forced to retreat: indeed the Romans pressed so hard on their broken and disorderly ranks that if Scipio had not sounded the recall they might well have broken into the town along with the fugitives.

The alarm throughout the town was no less than on the actual battlefield; many men on guard duty abandoned their posts and fled in panic; the walls were left unmanned as the defenders came scrambling down by the nearest way they could find. Scipio had gone up what is locally known as Mercury's Hill, and when he saw that many sections of the town wall were now undefended, he gave orders for his whole force to leave camp in preparation for the attack and for ladders to be brought. He himself moved up to the town, protected against the hail of missiles from the walls by the shields which three strong young soldiers held over him. There he heartened his men, issued the necessary orders and, most valuable of all for fanning the flame of their courage, was present to witness with his own eyes the prowess, or the lack of it, which every man displayed. So they surged forward, regardless of missiles, careless of wounds; neither the walls nor the soldiers on guard there could stop their ascent or their eager rivalry to be the first up. At the same moment the assault began from the fleet on the seaward side of the town, but resulted, on the whole, in more smoke than fire; for in course of making the ships fast, landing the ladders and men in a hurry, all being eager to get ashore the quickest way, the race to be first led not to speed but to mutual impediment and confusion.

45. Meanwhile Mago had re-manned the walls and had no shortage of missiles from the vast stores collected in the town. None the less in the defence of the walls neither men nor missiles were as effective as the walls themselves, for few ladders were long enough to reach the top, and the longer the ladders the less secure they were. The first man up would find himself unable to get over, others would be mounting behind him, and the ladder would break under their weight. Sometimes the ladders stood the strain, but the height made the climbers giddy, and they fell. When everywhere ladders were breaking and men falling, and success was bringing added keenness and courage to the enemy, the recall was sounded, and thus the besieged were given the hope of an immediate respite from trouble and strife. They could also hope that it would prove impossible in the future for the town to be taken by means of ladders and encirclement. Such an operation was clearly a difficult one, and if it was attempted again it would give time for the other Carthaginian commanders to bring help.

But scarcely had the din and confusion of the first assault died down when Scipio ordered fresh troops to take over the ladders from their exhausted or wounded comrades and to make a yet more vigorous attempt to storm the town. He had already been told by fishermen from Tarraco who had been all over the lagoon in boats, or wading when there was not enough water to float them, that he could easily get across to the wall of the town on foot. So now, when a message came to him that the tide was ebbing, he started for the lagoon with a party of 500 men. It was about midday, and a brisk northerly wind which had got up was helping to drive the water in the lagoon in the same direction as the natural fall of the tide, uncovering the shoal patches and leaving depths in some places up to a man's navel, in others scarcely up to his knees. What Scipio had found out by careful inquiry he now proceeded to attribute to the miraculous intervention of the gods, who, he declared, to let the Romans cross, were turning the sea, draining the lagoon, and opening ways never before trodden by the foot of man. He ordered his men accordingly to follow Neptune their guide and make their way across the lagoon to the walls of the town.

46. On the landward side the task of the attacking troops was a very severe one. The sheer height of the walls was by no means their only difficulty, for, in addition to that, the defenders had the men between two fires as they climbed up and in greater danger from both flanks than from in front. But the 500 with Scipio had little trouble either in crossing the lagoon or in getting over the wall, as in that sector, where the lie of the ground and the presence of the lagoon seemed sufficient protection, it had not been constructed with any sort of elaboration. No guards had been posted, and the attackers found no pickets to dispute their passage, all enemy troops being on the alert to move at once to any spot where there was obvious danger. Scipio, therefore, entered the town unopposed, and proceeded with his men at all speed to the gate around which the fighting was concentrated. It was this struggle that absorbed everybody's attention and energy. The eyes and ears not only of the men actually fighting but of all who watched and encouraged them in their efforts were so intent upon it that no one noticed that the town had been captured, as it were, behind their backs, until the hail of missiles from the rear told them they were indeed caught between two fires. Panic ensued; the walls were taken, and from inside and outside the work of forcing the gate began. Soon it was hacked to pieces and the fragments flung aside to leave a clear passage; then the armed men charged. Thousands were by now swarming over the walls and scattering all over the town to butcher the inhabitants, while the regular formation which had entered through the gate marched in proper order under its officers straight to the forum. From the forum Scipio saw the enemy trying to make their escape in two directions, some to the hill facing east, which was held by a party of 500 soldiers, and others to the citadel, to which Mago himself had withdrawn together with nearly all the men who had been driven from the walls. Accordingly he sent a part of his force to storm the hill and himself led another section to the citadel. The hill was taken at the first assault; Mago attempted to defend the citadel, but when he saw the enemy in possession everywhere he knew there was no hope and surrendered. Up to the moment when the citadel was surrendered the work of butchery had con-

tinued throughout the town, no adult encountered being spared; but then the signal was given to halt the bloodshed and the victorious troops turned their attention to plunder, which was immense and of every kind.

47. Of free males about 10,000 were captured: all of these who were citizens of New Carthage Scipio released and allowed to keep possession of the town and of such of their property as the fighting had left them. The artisans numbered about 2,000: these he made by decree state-slaves of the Roman people, with the hope of freedom in the near future if they worked hard to provide necessary war materials. Male non-citizens and able-bodied slaves he sent to the fleet (which was increased by eight[1] captured ships) as supplementary oarsmen. In addition to all these there were the Spanish hostages, who were treated with as much consideration as if they had been children of allies.

The amount of captured war material was very great: 120 catapults of the largest sort, 281 smaller ones; twenty-three large, fifty-two smaller *ballistae*; countless 'scorpions'[2] large and small, and a great quantity of equipment and missiles, and, finally, seventy-four military standards. In addition, much gold and silver was brought to Scipio; it included 276 gold platters, nearly all of them a pound in weight; 18,300 pounds of silver, either coined or in ingots; and a great many silver vessels. All this was handed over, weighed and counted, to the quaestor Flaminius. There were 400,000 measures of wheat and 270,000 of barley; sixty-three merchant vessels were attacked and taken in the harbour, some of them with their cargoes of grain and arms, besides bronze, iron, sail-cloth, esparto for rope-making, and timber for shipbuilding. In fact, of the vast quantity of captured war material the town itself was the least important item.

48. On the day of the victory Scipio ordered Laelius and the marines to guard the town and himself withdrew his weary troops into camp, to rest as they deserved. In the course of a single day they had been through all the operations of war:

1. Eighteen in Polybius.
2. Both types of catapult, used in siege warfare to project stones or darts.

they had fought a regular engagement; in taking the town they had faced extremes of peril and labour; and after its capture they had fought, and on unfavourable ground, with those of the enemy who had fled for refuge to the citadel. On the next day he called an assembly of his regulars and marines, and offered thanks and praise to the gods who had not only made him master in one day of the richest city in Spain but had previously amassed within it all the wealth of Spain and Africa, with the result that the enemy were left with nothing, while he and his men could revel in abundance. He went on to thank his men for their fine service. Nothing, he said, not the enemy's sally, nor the height of the walls, nor the unknown depths of the lagoon nor the fortress on its hill, nor the strongly fortified citadel itself had prevented them from breaking through and surmounting every obstacle. He was in debt for the whole success to every one of them; but he owed the special honour of the mural crown to the man who had been first over the wall. The man who claimed to have earned that decoration was then asked to come forward, and there were two rival claimants, Trebellius, a centurion of the fourth legion, and a marine named Digitius. The personal rivalry between the two was hardly less fierce than the passions each aroused in the men of his own unit. Laelius, who commanded the fleet, supported the marines, and Tuditanus the legionaries. The dispute had almost reached the dimensions of a mutiny, when Scipio announced that he would appoint three adjudicators to hear the case and decide who the first man over the wall had been; and then, in addition to Laelius and Tuditanus, representing the opposing parties, he called upon Publius Cornelius Caudinus, as a neutral third, and ordered the three to sit and hear the evidence. These men being out of the way (they had acted not so much as advocates for the award of this important honour as moderators of the passions aroused), the contention between the parties rose to even greater heat, and Laelius, in consequence, left the other adjudicators, went to Scipio, and told him that the whole affair was getting completely out of hand and that the rival factions were on the point of coming to blows. He added, moreover, that even if there were no violence such behaviour set a most abominable precedent, allowing a decoration for valour to be competed for by lying and dishonesty. There stood the rival parties, legionaries on one side, marines on the other, both ready to swear by all the gods not what they knew, but what they wished, to be true, and to involve in the guilt of perjury not only themselves and their own lives but the honour of their profession, the military standards, the eagles, and their solemn oath of allegiance. Cornelius and Sempronius, he said, both supported his decision to make this report.

Scipio thanked Laelius and called the troops once more on parade. Then he announced that he was satisfied that Quintus Trebellius and Sextus Digitius had been *equal* in getting over the wall first, and that he therefore presented both of them with a mural crown 'for valour'. After that he distributed other rewards such as he judged suitable to the good service or courage of the rest; in particular he distinguished Laelius, commander of the fleet, putting him on a level with himself, praising him in every way, and presenting him with a gold wreath and thirty cows.

49. His next act was to send for the hostages from the Spanish communities – I hardly like to state the number of them, as I find in one record that it was about 300, in another that it was 3,724. There is a similar discrepancy amongst the historians on other points: for instance, the Carthaginian garrison is variously stated as being 10,000, 7,000, and not more than 2,000 strong; prisoners are reckoned to number 10,000 and over 25,000. Again, if I followed the Greek writer Silenus,[1] I should put the larger and smaller 'scorpions' captured at sixty; if Valerius Antias, at 6,000 large ones and 13,000 small. There is really no limit to historians' lies. Even about the officers in command there is no agreement: most records state that Laelius commanded the fleet, but in some we are told that it was Marcus Junius Silanus. Again, Valerius writes that the officer who commanded the Carthaginian garrison and surrendered to the Romans was Arines, others that it was Mago; nor is there any consistency in the records of the number of ships captured, or of the weight of gold and silver, or of the

1. He was actually with Hannibal: Coelius and Polybius both use him as a source.

amount of money. If one is to accept any of the estimates, then some mean between the extremes is likely to be nearest the truth.[1]

Having sent for the hostages, Scipio urged everybody, hostages and prisoners, to keep a good heart, reminding them that they had fallen into the hands of the Romans, a people who preferred to bind men by gratitude rather than by fear, and to have foreign nations linked with them by the ties of loyalty and a common purpose, not kept, like slaves, in cruel subjection. Then he learned the names of the various communities, drew up a list of the prisoners under the several tribes to which each belonged, and sent messengers to their homes with instructions for them to be fetched by some member of the family. In cases where envoys from any community happened to be present, the hostages or prisoners were restored to them at once; the duty of properly looking after the rest was assigned to the quaestor Flaminius.

During these proceedings an old woman, the wife of Mandonius, who was a brother of Indibilis, prince of the Ilergetes, stepped from the crowd of hostages, threw herself weeping at Scipio's feet, and began to beseech him to tell the guards to give particular care and attention to the women in their charge. Scipio at once replied that they would lack nothing in that respect, whereupon the woman resumed: 'It is not such things as that which much concern us – for what is not enough for people in our condition? It is a different sort of anxiety I feel when I look at these young girls, for I myself am too old to suffer what a woman may suffer.' Around her were standing Indibilis's daughters, in the flower of their youth and beauty, and other girls of equally noble rank, all of whom treated her with filial respect. 'My own training,' said Scipio, 'and that of the Roman people has taught me to strive to keep inviolate amongst us anything which is anywhere sacred; and now I am helped to pay yet stricter attention to that lesson by the courage and dignity of all of you, who have not forgotten the grace of true womanhood even in misfortune.' He then put them in charge of a man of proved integrity, whom he

1. Livy's task is complicated by his inability to discriminate between sources of varying reliability.

told to care for them with the decency and consideration he would show to the wives or mothers of his friends.

50. At this point another prisoner was brought him by some soldiers. She was a young girl and so beautiful that everyone turned to look at her wherever she went. Scipio asked where she came from and who her parents were, and was told amongst other things that she was betrothed to a Celtiberian chieftain, a young man named Allucius. He at once sent for the girl's parents and her lover, and as soon as the latter arrived he spoke to him, choosing his words with more care than in what he said to the father and mother, simply because he had learned meanwhile of the man's passionate love for his betrothed. 'I address you,' he said, 'as one young man talking to another, so that what I have to say may cause neither of us embarrassment. The woman whom you are to marry was taken prisoner and brought to me by our soldiers, and I now learn that you care for her deeply – and indeed her beauty makes it easy to believe that this is so. Now as I myself, if I were at liberty to enjoy the pleasures of youth, especially in an upright and legitimate love, instead of being, as I am, wholly caught up in the service of my country, should wish to find indulgence for loving my bride too ardently, I give my blessing where I may – namely, to this love of yours. Your bride has been treated under my protection with all the delicacy she would have found in the house of her parents, your own parents-to-be; she has been kept for you, an inviolate gift, worthy of myself and of you. The only payment I would ask in return is that you should be a friend of the Roman people. If you think I am a good man, as the peoples of Spain have already found my father and uncle to be, then I would have you know that in the Roman state there are many like us and that there is no nation in the world today which you could less wish to be the enemy of you and yours, or more wish to be your friend.'

Despite the sense of his unworthiness the young man was overcome with joy. He grasped Scipio's hand and prayed heaven to reward his benefactor, since he himself had not wealth enough to do so as his heart prompted and Scipio's generosity deserved. Then the parents and relatives of the girl were sent for. They had brought with them a weight of gold sufficient for her ransom, and when they found she was being restored to them for nothing, they begged Scipio to take the treasure as a gift, declaring that they would be as grateful for his acceptance as they were for the restoration of the girl in her virgin innocence. In reply to their urgent entreaties Scipio agreed to take it; then, having asked for it to be laid at his feet, he called Allucius and told him to take the gold and keep it for his own, saying, 'This is my wedding present, to be added to the dowry you will receive from your bride's father.'

Happy in the honour done to him and the gift he had received, Allucius was then sent home, where he filled the ears of his compatriots with the well-deserved praises of Scipio, telling them that a godlike young warrior had come, who carried all before him not only with arms but with generosity and kindliness. After holding a levy of his dependents he returned a few days later with a brigade of picked cavalry 1,400 strong.

51. Scipio kept Laelius with him to benefit by his advice in the disposal of the prisoners, hostages and captured material. That done, he furnished him with a quinquereme, embarked the prisoners in six ships, together with Mago and some fifteen senators who had been taken prisoner at the same time, and sent him to Rome to report the victory. He himself spent the few days he had decided to remain at New Carthage in exercising his troops, naval and military. On the first day the legionaries manoeuvred under arms over a distance of four miles; on the second their orders were to parade in front of their tents and attend to the maintenance and cleaning of their weapons; on the third they had a mock battle all in proper form with wooden swords and foiled missiles; on the fourth they rested, and on the fifth there were more manoeuvres in full equipment. In the same alternation of work and rest they spent all the time they remained in New Carthage. The oarsmen and marines, in good weather, were sent to sea to test in mock battles the capability of their vessels in rapid manoeuvre. All this activity on shore and afloat not only provided good physical exercise but strengthened the men's morale as well, while the city itself, with the smiths and artisans of all trades shut up in the

state workshops, rang continuously with the sound of warlike preparations. There was nothing on which the commander did not keep a careful eye, now with the fleet or at the docks, now attending the infantry manoeuvres, now watching all the work which was going on in the shops, in the armoury, in the docks under the hands of the multitude of workmen labouring with the intensest rivalry as day succeeded day.

With all this for a beginning, the damaged sections of the wall were then rebuilt, a garrison was posted to guard the town, and Scipio set out for Tarraco. Numerous delegations approached him in the course of his march, some of which he answered and dismissed on the spot, postponing his reply to others till he should reach Tarraco, where he had issued orders to all allies, new and old, to meet. The Carthaginian leaders at first deliberately suppressed the news of the capture of New Carthage; later, when the fact was becoming too obvious to conceal or pretend to deny, they tried to make light of it, saying that it was only a single Spanish town that had been surprised by the unexpected, and indeed stealthy appearance of the enemy on one particular day; and that an arrogant young officer, carried away by exaggerated delight at this minor success, had given it the appearance of a great victory. But when he learned that three generals, with three victorious hostile armies were on the way, then, they declared, he would soon enough remember the deaths which had already occurred in his family. Such was their report of the matter for public consumption, but they knew very well themselves how serious a drain on all their resources the loss of New Carthage was.

# BOOK XXVII

1. This, then, was the state of affairs in Spain. Meanwhile in Italy the consul Marcellus, after Salapia had been betrayed into his hands, stormed and captured from the Samnites the towns of Marmoreae and Meles. Some 3,000 of Hannibal's troops, left there on garrison duty, were caught and destroyed; the plunder, of which there was a considerable amount, was turned over to the soldiers. In addition to other material 240,000 measures of wheat were found in these places and 110,000 of barley. However, the satisfaction caused by this success was more than outweighed by a defeat which occurred a few days later near the town of Herdonea. The proconsul Gnaeus Fulvius was encamped near by, hoping to recover the town, which had gone over to Carthage after Cannae. The position he held was not a naturally strong one and was inadequately defended; and his characteristic negligence was increased by hopes of success based on the report that the people of the town had begun to weaken in their support of Carthage when news reached them of Hannibal's departure into Bruttium after the loss of Salapia. Secret messengers from Herdonea reported all this to Hannibal, with the result that he was anxious to keep control of the allied town and at the same time hopeful of catching the enemy there off his guard. So he set out with a force marching light, and such was his speed of movement that he was on the spot before anyone even knew he was coming; and, to cause the greater alarm and confusion, he approached the town in battle order. His Roman antagonist, though inferior in skill and strength, was his equal in audacity; hurriedly leading his men from their quarters, he offered battle. The fifth legion and the left *ala* went into action with great determination, but Hannibal was ready for them. Once the struggle between the opposing infantry forces had become the centre of effort and attention, he ordered his cavalry round the flanks, partly for an assault on the Roman camp, partly to cause confusion in the Roman infantry by an attack

on their rear. At the same time he made contemptuous play with the Roman commander's name: he had defeated the praetor Gnaeus Fulvius two years before in this part of the country, and now, he declared, he would beat his namesake too – the same name, the same result. And he was not wrong; for though in the hand-to-hand infantry struggle the Romans, despite heavy losses, had yet managed to keep their standards in place and their ranks unbroken, the sudden cavalry charge in their rear brought a shocking change. This, together with the enemy's battle-cry heard simultaneously from the camp, first broke the sixth legion, which in the second line had been the first to suffer from the Numidians' attack, and then the fifth too and the troops in the van. Some tried to save themselves by flight, others were killed where they stood, including Fulvius himself and eleven military tribunes.

How many thousands of Roman and allied troops perished in this battle, who will venture to say with certainty, as I find in one authority the number put at 13,000, in another at not more than 7,000? The victor took possession of the camp and all it contained; Herdonea, Hannibal having learned that it would have gone over to the Romans and abandoned the Carthaginian alliance if he had left the neighbourhood, was burnt to the ground, and its population removed to Thurii and Metapontum; the leading men found to have had secret conversations with Fulvius were executed. The Roman survivors of this disaster lost half their equipment and made their escape by various routes into Samnium, where they joined the consul Marcellus.

2. Marcellus was not at all disturbed by this serious defeat; he reported the loss of the army and its commander in a letter to the Senate in Rome and went on to say that, as he was still the same man who had crushed Hannibal in the pride of his victory at Cannae, he was now marching against him, determined to bring his exultant joy to a rapid end. In Rome itself there was less confidence – indeed there was fear for what the future might bring, as well as grief for what had just occurred. Marcellus, however, crossed from Samnium into Lucania and took up a position near Numistro, on level ground and in sight of Hannibal, who was encamped on a hill. Moreover, as

a further indication of his confidence, he was the first to take up battle positions, and Hannibal, on seeing the standards carried out from the camp gates, accepted the challenge. The Carthaginian right extended some way up the hill, while the Roman left rested on the town. First to engage were the Roman first legion and right *ala* against Hannibal's Spaniards and Balearic slingers, his elephants being driven into the line after fighting had begun. For a long time neither side had the advantage. From early morning to nightfall the struggle went on, and then, when the front lines were exhausted, the first legion was relieved by the third and the right *ala* by the left, while on the Carthaginian side fresh troops took over from their weary comrades, and immediately, by this accession of men in the full vigour of body and mind, the fighting which had begun to languish blazed up again in new fury. Darkness, however, separated the antagonists with the issue still undecided. Next day the Romans stood formed for battle from sunrise until late in the morning, and when none of the enemy came forward against them they set about gathering the spoils at their leisure, and collecting and burning their dead. The following night Hannibal got silently on the move and went off into Apulia. When daylight revealed that the enemy had gone, Marcellus at once followed in their tracks, leaving the wounded at Numistro with a small garrison in charge of an officer named Purpurio. Near Venusia he came up with Hannibal, and for several days there was spasmodic fighting, minor attacks being made by outposts, cavalry and infantry together engaging in what would more properly be called skirmishes than battles, and almost invariably to the advantage of the Romans. From there the armies passed through Apulia, but still without any major engagement, as Hannibal always moved at night looking for a place to trap his antagonist, and Marcellus never followed except in daylight and after careful reconnaissance.

3. Meanwhile at Capua, while Fulvius Flaccus was occupied in selling the property of the leading citizens and leasing the confiscated land (in every case taking grain by way of rent), a new crime, fomented in secret, was brought to his notice by informers. He was not, it seems, to lack occasion for severity

towards that city. Some time previously he had turned his troops out of the houses where they were quartered, partly to be able to let the houses together with the land, and partly because he was afraid that his own men, like Hannibal's, might be adversely affected by the excessive amenities of the place. So he had made them put up their own quarters, of a more military sort, at the gates and along the walls. Most of these erections were of wattle and plank, some of plaited reed, and all thatched – about the most inflammable materials one could possibly think of. A group of a hundred and seventy Capuans, led by the Blossius brothers, had planned to set fire one night to the whole lot together. Information of the plot was laid by some slaves belonging to the brothers; by the proconsul's orders the gates were immediately closed and the Roman troops called to arms; all the guilty men were arrested, a rigorous inquiry was held, and they were condemned and executed. The informers were given their liberty and a reward of 10,000 *asses*. The people of Nuceria and Acerrae, who complained of having nowhere to live, as Acerrae had been partly burned down and Nuceria completely destroyed, were sent by Fulvius to the Senate in Rome. The men of Acerrae were granted permission to rebuild what had been destroyed by fire, and those of Nuceria were transferred, in accordance with their expressed preference, to Atella. The Atellines were ordered to move to Calatia.

Amongst all these stirring events, adverse or favourable, which occupied the thoughts of men, the citadel at Tarentum was not forgotten. Marcus Ogulnius and Publius Aquilius were sent as commissioners into Etruria to purchase grain for Tarentum, and a thousand men from the City army, half Roman and half allied troops, were sent there at the same time on garrison duty.

4. Summer was now drawing to a close and the consular elections were approaching; but a dispatch from Marcellus raised a difficulty, as he reported that he was following hard on the tracks of Hannibal, who was steadily retreating and refusing combat, and that to lose touch with him by a single yard would be the worst possible policy. This left the Senate with two alternatives, both bad: either to recall from the field

a consul actively engaged, or to have no consuls elected for the coming year. It seemed best in the circumstances to ignore precedent and recall the consul Valerius Laevinus from Sicily. Accordingly on the Senate's instructions the City praetor Lucius Manlius wrote to him, sending Marcellus's dispatch with his letter, in order that he might understand why the Senate was recalling him from his province instead of his colleague.

About the same time a delegation came to Rome from King Syphax to report his successes against the Carthaginians. The king, the envoys declared, was the Carthaginians' worst enemy and the Romans' closest friend; he had previously sent envoys to the Roman commanders Gnaeus and Publius Scipio in Spain, and his desire now was to ask for the friendship of Rome at the fountain-head. The Senate replied graciously, and as a further token of favour sent three men, Genucius, Poetelius, and Popillius, to attend upon him with gifts. The gifts consisted of a toga and purple tunic, an ivory chair, and a golden goblet weighing five pounds. The three ambassadors had instructions to go on to other African princes, to whom they were to take as presents fringed togas and golden goblets of three pounds weight. Envoys, Marcus Atilius and Manius Acilius, were also sent to Ptolemy and Cleopatra in Alexandria, to remind those monarchs of the friendship between the two countries and to strengthen old ties. These also took presents with them, a toga and purple tunic and an ivory chair for the King, and for the Queen an embroidered mantle and a purple cloak.

In the course of this summer many prodigies were reported from neighbouring towns and farms. At Tusculum a lamb was born with milk in its udders, and the top of the temple of Jupiter was struck by lightning and nearly all the roof stripped off; at Anagnia about the same time ground in front of the gate was struck and burned for a day and a night without anything to feed the flames, and birds near the cross-roads by the town in the grove of Diana left their nests in the trees; at Tarracina not far from the harbour huge snakes jumped about in the sea like fish disporting themselves; at Tarquinii a pig was born with a human face, and in the country near Capena, at the grove of Feronia, four statues profusely sweated blood during a day and a night. All these alarming phenomena were, by decree of the pontiffs, duly expiated by the sacrifice of full-grown victims, and a day of prayer at all the 'couches' was proclaimed in Rome and also at Capena in the grove of Feronia.

5. The letter from Rome set the consul Laevinus on the move. He handed over control of Sicily and his army to the praetor Cincius; sent Messalla, his fleet commander, with a squadron of ships to Africa to raid the coast and gather information about the activities and preparations of the Carthaginians; and himself started with ten ships for Rome. Safely arrived there, he at once held a meeting of the Senate and reported his achievements, pointing out that Sicily, which had endured nearly sixty years of warfare by land and sea, including many disasters, had been finally settled by him. No Carthaginian remained in the island; no Sicilian was out of it; all refugees had been brought back and resettled in their towns and on their farms, and were ploughing and sowing once more; neglected land was again under cultivation and in production at last for the benefit of its owners, and as a constant source of additional supply for Rome in peace or war. After this Muttines[1] and others who had rendered valuable services to Rome were brought into the Senate and honoured by the consul in fulfilment of his promise; Muttines himself was granted Roman citizenship, a bill for the purpose having been presented by the tribunes, on the Senate's authority, to the people.

Meanwhile Messalla with a fleet of fifty ships had reached the African coast before daylight. He made an unexpected landing near Utica, raided a considerable extent of the surrounding country, took a number of prisoners together with valuable material of all kinds, and got safely back to his ships. He then crossed to Sicily, returning to Lilybaeum thirteen days after he had left it. The prisoners were interrogated and the following facts about the position in Africa were carefully written down for the benefit of the consul Laevinus: 5,000 Numidians were at Carthage with Masinissa, son of Gala and a keen and active soldier, and other troops were being hired from all over Africa for the purpose of joining Hasdrubal in Spain in order that at the earliest possible moment and with

1. The betrayer of Agrigentum. See p. 351.

the largest possible army he might cross into Italy and effect a junction with Hannibal. The Carthaginians were convinced that victory depended upon this junction. In addition, a powerful fleet was being fitted out with the object of recovering Sicily, and it was thought that it would not be long before it made the crossing. The reading of this report so profoundly disturbed the Senate that it was judged to be unwise for the consul to wait in Rome for the elections: instead, he was to return immediately to his province, after the appointment of a dictator to preside at the elections. One point, however, remained at issue: the consul insisted that he would name as dictator in Sicily Valerius Messalla who was then commanding the fleet, while the Senate refused to admit that a dictator could legally be appointed outside Roman territory, that is, outside the boundaries of Italy. Lucretius, a people's tribune, put the question formally to the House, and the Senate decreed that the consul, before leaving the City, should ask the people whom they wished to be named dictator, and should name him accordingly. If the consul refused, then the praetor was to put the question to the people; if he, too, refused, the duty was to be carried out by the tribunes. Laevinus declared that he would not ask the people's will in a matter which rested within his own authority, and forbade the praetor to do so either; so the tribunes put the question and the people expressed it as their pleasure that Quintus Fulvius, then at Capua, should be appointed.

On the day for which the meeting of the people had been fixed, Laevinus slipped away for Sicily under cover of darkness, and the Senate, left in the lurch, decided to write to Marcellus, asking him to come to the rescue of his country, which his colleague had abandoned, and to name as dictator the man the people had voted for. Fulvius was in consequence named by Marcellus, and, by the authority of the same plebiscite, he in his turn named Publius Licinius Crassus, the *pontifex maximus*, as his master of Horse.

6. The dictator on coming to Rome sent Blaesus, who had been his second-in-command at Capua, to the army in Etruria to relieve the praetor Calpurnius, whom he sent for by letter to take over Capua and the troops stationed there. He then

announced the elections, to take place on the nearest possible date. However, a serious hitch arose owing to a dispute between himself and the tribunes. The Galeria century of the younger men, which had obtained by lot the right to vote first, named as consuls Quintus Fulvius and Quintus Fabius, and the other centuries, if duly called to vote, would have followed their lead, had not the people's tribunes, Gaius and Lucius Arrenius, intervened and insisted not only that to prolong an office for a further term was unconstitutional, but also that to allow the appointment of the man who was presiding over the elections would be to set an even more dangerous precedent. Accordingly they declared their intention of vetoing the proceedings if the dictator, Fulvius, allowed his own name to stand. If other candidates were considered instead of Fulvius, they would raise no objection. The dictator in reply defended the position and to support his argument adduced senatorial authority, the people's expressed will, and precedent. He pointed out that in the consulship of Servilius, after the death of his colleague Flaminius at Trasimene, a bill was brought before the people by the authority of the Senate, and that the people had in consequence expressed it as their pleasure that, so long as the war lasted in Italy, they should have the right of re-appointing as consuls as often as they wished any of the men who had previously held that office. As for precedents, there was, in the past, the case of Lucius Postumius Megellus who, as *interrex*, had been elected consul with Gaius Junius Bubulcus at the elections over which he himself presided, while a recent instance was that of Quintus Fabius who would never have allowed his consulship to be continued for a further term unless it had been for the public advantage. The argument went on for a long time, but finally the dictator and the tribunes agreed to abide by the Senate's decision. This was that the elections should proceed, as it was only proper in view of the situation that control should be in the hands of old and thoroughly experienced soldiers. The tribunes gave way, the elections were accordingly held, and Quintus Fabius Maximus (for the fifth time) and Quintus Fulvius Flaccus (for the fourth time) were returned as consuls. Philo, Crispinus, Tubulus, and Aurunculeius were then appointed praetors, and, the election of officers for the coming year being complete, Fulvius laid down his dictatorship.

At the end of this summer a Carthaginian fleet of forty vessels under the command of Hamilcar crossed to Sardinia and raided the territory of Olbia; then, when the praetor Volso appeared with his army, the fleet sailed round to the other side of the island and raided the territory of Carales,[1] returning to Africa with captured material of all kinds.

A number of Roman priests died in the course of this year and successors were appointed. Cn. Servilius took the place of Titus Otacilius Crassus as pontiff, and Tiberius Sempronius Longus (son of Tiberius) was made augur in place of Titus Otacilius Crassus. As decemvir for the performance of religious rites Tiberius Sempronius Longus (son of Tiberius) took the place of Tiberius Sempronius Longus, son of Gaius. Marcus Marcius, the *rex sacrorum*, and Marcus Aemilius Papus, the chief *curio*,[2] died, and no priests were appointed this year to fill the vacancies they left. The censorship this year was held by Lucius Veturius Philo and Publius Licinius Crassus, the *pontifex maximus*. Crassus had not previously held the office either of consul or praetor, but passed straight to the censorship from the office of aedile. These censors however did not revise the list of senators nor do any public business: their term of office was ended by Philo's death, whereupon his colleague resigned. The curule aediles continued the Roman Games for an additional day, and the people's aediles, Quintus Catius and Lucius Porcius Licinus, presented to the temple of Ceres some bronze statues, paid for out of the money from fines, and celebrated the Plebeian Games with what was, for the resources of those days, great magnificence.

7. At the end of the year Laelius, Scipio's second in command, arrived in Rome thirty-four days after leaving Tarraco, and great crowds assembled to watch his entry into the city with his prisoners. The day after his arrival he made his report to the Senate of the capture, in a single day's fighting, of New Carthage, the Spanish capital, the recovery of a number of

1. Cagliari.

2. Each of the thirty divisions (*curiae*) into which the Roman tribes were divided had its presiding priest (*curio*).

towns which had gone over to the enemy, and the inclusion of fresh ones in the Roman alliance. From the prisoners information was obtained which agreed in the main with the account Messalla had sent in his dispatch. What most disturbed the Senate was Hasdrubal's imminent arrival in Italy, where it was already difficult enough to withstand the armed might of Hannibal alone. At an assembly of the people Laelius repeated his account of the activities in Spain; the Senate decreed one day of public thanksgiving in honour of Scipio's successes and ordered Laelius to return to Spain, with the ships he had come in, at the earliest moment possible.

I have followed the authority of many annalists in placing the fall of New Carthage in this year, though I am aware that some writers have stated that it was captured in the year following. My reason is that I feel it is less likely to be true that Scipio spent a whole year in Spain doing nothing.

The new consuls, Quintus Fabius Maximus (for the fifth time) and Quintus Fulvius Flaccus (for the fourth), entered office on the Ides of March. Both had Italy assigned them as their sphere of action, though their commands were divided geographically, Fabius acting in the region of Tarentum, Fulvius in Lucania and Bruttium. Marcellus's command was prolonged for a further year. Provinces assigned by lot to the praetors were as follows: the City jurisdiction to Tubulus, Gaul and cases where foreigners were involved to Philo, Capua to Crispinus, Sardinia to Aurunculeius. As to the division of troops, Fulvius had the two legions which had been in Sicily with Laevinus, and Fabius the legions which Calpurnius had commanded in Etruria; the City army was to take over in Etruria with Calpurnius in command; Titus Quinctius took over Capua and the troops formerly commanded there by Fulvius; Hostilius was to succeed to the control of the forces then at Ariminum with the pro-praetor Laetorius. Marcellus was to keep the legions he had commanded during his consulship; Laevinus and Cincius (for their commands, too, in Sicily were extended) were given the troops which had survived from Cannae, with instructions to recruit them from the survivors of Gnaeus Fulvius's legions; these were rounded up and sent by the consuls to Sicily, and were forced to serve under the same conditions of ignominy as the survivors of Cannae and the remnants of Fulvius's army which had been sent there by the Senate as punishment for the same sort of disgraceful conduct on the field. Aurunculeius in Sardinia was given the legions with which Manlius Volso had previously held the island, and Sulpicius had his command extended for another year with orders to hold Macedonia with the same legion and fleet as before. Thirty quinqueremes were ordered to be sent from Sicily to the consul Fabius at Tarentum, and it was decided to employ the rest of the fleet in raiding the African coast; Laevinus was either to conduct the raids himself or to send Cincius or Messalla, as he pleased. As regards Spain no change was made, except that the commands of Scipio and Silanus were extended not for one year but until the Senate might choose to recall them. Such, then, was the distribution of the various spheres of action and the division of the forces for the year.

8. Though everybody was occupied with more important matters, the election of a chief *curio* when a priest was being chosen to succeed Marcus Aemilius stirred up an old dispute, for the patricians insisted that the candidacy of the one plebeian who was standing for election, Gaius Mamilius Atellus, should be ignored, because previously no one but a patrician had ever held that priesthood. The tribunes were appealed to and referred the question to the Senate, which, in its turn, gave the right of decision to the people. Thus Atellus came to be the first plebeian to be appointed to the office of chief *curio*.

Publius Licinius, the *pontifex maximus*, compelled Gaius Valerius Flaccus, against his wishes, to be installed as *flamen* of Jupiter. In place of Mucius Scaevola, who had died, Gaius Laetorius was made a decemvir for the performance of rites and sacrifices.

I should gladly have passed over in silence the case where a *flamen* was installed against his own wishes, had it not been for the change in his character from bad to good. Gaius Flaccus as a young man had lived an irregular and dissipated life and was disliked for his vices by his brother Lucius and his other relatives; and it was for this reason that Licinius, the *pontifex maximus*, seized upon him for the office of *flamen*. And indeed, as soon as he found himself absorbed in religious rites and ceremonies, he suddenly became a different man: gone were all his former habits, and nobody amongst the younger men in Rome stood higher in the estimation of the leading senators, whether related to him or not. This general recognition of his reformed life gave him the well merited confidence to revive the privilege of admission to the Senate, a privilege which for many years had been in abeyance because of the bad character of previous *flamines*. When he entered the Senate-house, he was escorted out of it by the praetor Licinius, whereupon he appealed to the tribunes, claiming as *flamen* an ancient right belonging to his priesthood, and declaring that it had been granted to holders of his office together with the *toga praetexta* and the curule chair. The praetor rejoined that a right or privilege was based not upon musty precedents dug out of old chronicles but, in each case, upon recent usage or custom, and that no *flamen* of Jupiter had enjoyed that particular privilege within the last two generations. The tribunes expressed the opinion that the obsolescence of a practice due to the inadequacy of the *flamines* was a reflection not upon the office they held but upon themselves as individuals; whereupon, without further opposition even from the praetor, Senate and people found themselves in unanimous agreement and the *flamen* was escorted into the House, in the universal belief that he had won the privilege rather by the purity of his life than by the rights of his office.

Before the consuls left Rome to take up their duties in the field, they enrolled two City legions to supplement the other armies as far as was necessary. The consul Fulvius instructed his brother Gaius, his second-in-command, to take the old City army into Etruria and bring back the legions already there to Rome; his colleague Fabius, after rounding up the remnants of the defeated Fulvian army (there were 4,344 of them), ordered his son Quintus Maximus to take them to the proconsul Messalla in Sicily and to take over from him two legions and thirty quinqueremes. The withdrawal of those forces did not reduce the defences of the island either in actual or in apparent strength; for Messalla, in addition to the satisfactory recruitment of the two old legions, had at his disposal a large number of Numidian deserters, cavalry and infantry, and had also enrolled in his army the Sicilians, skilled fighting men, who had served under Epicydes or the Carthaginians. By including these foreign troops in each of his two legions he preserved the appearance of two armies, with one of which he ordered Cincius to hold the part of the island which had formerly been Hiero's kingdom, while with the other he himself defended the rest – once divided by the boundaries between the Roman and Carthaginian spheres of influence.[1] The fleet, too, of seventy vessels, was so divided as to protect the entire circuit of the coast. Messalla himself regularly toured the island with Muttines' cavalry to visit the farms, to note their state of cultivation or neglect and to praise or castigate their owners accordingly. His attention was rewarded by so good a harvest that he was able to send grain to Rome and also to Catana, from where supplies could be conveyed to the troops who would be encamped during summer near Tarentum.

9. The movement of great events often hangs upon trivial incidents, and so it was that the transfer of troops to Sicily, most of them from the Latin Confederacy or allied communities, came near to causing a serious rising. At local meetings of Latins and allies complaints began to be heard: for nine years now levies of money and men had been draining them dry; almost every year they suffered a grave defeat; some were killed in battle, others carried off by disease. Their friends who were drafted into the Roman army were more completely lost to them than prisoners of war in Carthaginian hands; for the enemy sent prisoners home without a ransom, but the Romans dragged them off to fight outside Italy in what was more like exile than war. For seven years now the survivors of Cannae were growing old abroad, and they would be dead before the Carthaginians, now stronger than ever before, were forced to leave Italy. If old soldiers did not come home and new ones were always conscripted, soon there would not be a man left. For these reasons, they declared, before they were reduced to absolute desolation and want, they had better refuse the Romans

1. An unexplained statement of Livy's. Possibly 'Roman' is a mistake for 'Greek'.

what circumstances themselves would in any case soon prevent them from supplying. If the Romans saw that their allies all felt alike in this, they would lose no time in turning their thoughts towards a treaty of peace. Otherwise Italy would never be free from war while Hannibal lived. These were the arguments heard at the meetings.

There were at this period thirty Latin colonies which had been sent out by Rome; twelve of these (delegations from all thirty being present in Rome) told the consuls that they had not the resources to supply either men or money. The twelve were Ardea, Nepete, Sutrium, Alba, Carseoli, Sora, Suessa, Circeii, Setia, Cales, Narnia, and Interamna. It was a totally unexpected shock; the consuls, hoping to deter them from this monstrous decision, and supposing they could more readily do so by severity and reproof than by any more gentle means, declared that they had had the insolence to say to them what they, the consuls, could never bring themselves to repeat in the Senate; for their words implied not merely refusal of military duties but open rebellion. They advised them accordingly to hurry back to their respective homes and discuss the whole position afresh with their fellow-townsmen, before their abominable crime could grow from mere words to deeds. They must remind their people that they were not Campanians or Tarentines but Romans, sprung from Roman stock and sent out from Rome to found on soil captured by force of arms new settlements to increase the Roman race. If they still remembered the old country and were bound to it by any bonds of duty or affection, they owed to Rome what children owed to their parents. So let them think again, for the reckless decision they had just made would mean the betrayal of the Roman empire and the yielding of victory to Hannibal.

For a long time first one consul then the other continued to argue in this strain, but the envoys were unmoved. They merely said that they had gained nothing to take home with them and nothing new to lay before their governments, for they had not a single soldier to conscript or any money to pay him with. Once the consuls were convinced that they really meant what they said, they informed the Senate, where such panic ensued that many members said that the Roman dominion was done for; the other colonies would follow suit, so would the allies; all had conspired to betray Rome to Hannibal.

10. The consuls endeavoured to encourage and console the Senate, saying that the other colonies would remember their duty and remain loyal to Rome; indeed, even those which had behaved so treacherously would feel respect for Roman rule if representatives were sent to speak to them with proper severity and without any yielding to entreaty. Having obtained permission to take such action as they thought to be in the national interest, the consuls, after a preliminary sounding of the other colonies to discover their attitude, sent for their representatives and asked them if they had troops ready according to the formal agreement. Marcus Sextilius of Fregellae replied on behalf of eighteen of the colonies that the troops were there, that if more were needed more would be supplied, and that they would use their utmost endeavours to do anything else that the Roman people might desire or command. For that purpose, he added, they had sufficient resources and more than sufficient determination. The consuls in reply said that their own personal thanks were quite inadequate to the occasion, unless the whole Senate, in formal session, had first expressed its gratitude. They asked them accordingly to come with them into the House, where they were addressed in the most honourable terms; and the consuls were then instructed to take them before the people and declare in public the service they had just rendered to the State, one of the many they had so nobly rendered during past and present years.

All this was long ago; but even so I must not pass over in silence the names of the communities which remained loyal, nor rob them of their praise. They were these: Signia, Norba, Saticula, Fregellae, Luceria, Venusia, Brundisium, Hadria, Firmum, Ariminum; on the southern sea, Pontiae, Paestum, Cosa; and inland, Beneventum, Aesernia, Spoletum, Placentia, and Cremona.

By the support of these colonies at this time the empire of the Roman people was enabled to stand firm, and thanks were duly tendered to them in the Senate and before the people. The Senate forbade mention to be made of the twelve communities which refused to obey; the consuls were not permitted to speak to their envoys or to dismiss or retain them. They were punished by silence – a silence which was felt to be most in accord with the dignity of Rome.

While the consuls were making all necessary preparations for the war, it was decided to draw out the reserve of gold (the produce of the five-per-cent tax on manumitted slaves) which was kept in the 'more sacred' treasury for use in extreme emergencies. Four thousand pounds' weight of gold was brought out, of which five hundred pounds were given to each consul, to each of the proconsuls Marcellus and Sulpicius, and to the praetor Veturius in command of operations in Gaul; the consul Fabius was given in addition a special sum of one hundred pounds' weight of gold to be taken to the citadel of Tarentum. The rest of it was employed for ready-money contracts to buy clothing for the army which was earning a good reputation for itself and its commander by its activities in Spain.

11. Another senatorial decree provided for the atonement by sacrifice of certain prodigies before the departure of the consuls for Rome. On the Alban Mount a statue of Jupiter had been struck by lightning, also a tree near the temple; at Ostia a fountain had been struck, at Capua the wall and the temple of Fortune, and the wall and a gate at Sinuessa. In addition to this it was reported by some that the Alban Lake had flowed red, like blood, and in Rome, inside the shrine of the temple of Fors Fortuna, a figure fixed to the wreath round the head of a statue fell without apparent cause into the statue's hand. It was common knowledge that at Privernum an ox talked and a vulture, while the forum was full of people, flew down on to a shop, and that at Sinuessa a child of ambiguous sex was born, half male half female – an *androgynous* child, to use, as often, the popular term, Greek being better adapted than Latin for the formation of compound words. At Sinuessa it also rained milk and a male baby was born with an elephant's head. These odd phenomena were atoned for by sacrifices of full-grown victims, and a decree was issued for prayer at all the 'couches' and for one day of special entreaties; it was also decreed that the praetor Hostilius should vow and celebrate the Games in honour of Apollo according to the procedure of that period.

About this time the consul Fulvius held the election for censors. The men elected, Marcus Cornelius Cethegus and Publius Sempronius Tuditanus, had neither of them previously held the consulship. On the Senate's authority a bill was brought before the people, proposing that the new censors should lease the agricultural land around Capua for cultivation. The bill was passed.

The revision of the list of senators was delayed by a dispute between the censors on the appointment of a leader of the House. The choice lay with Sempronius, but his colleague Cornelius insisted that the tradition should be preserved according to which they should elect as leader the ex-censor who had first held that office. This was Titus Manlius Torquatus. Sempronius declared that the gods who had given him by lot the right of making a choice had also given him a free hand as to whom he should choose; he was determined, he said, to use his own judgement and would appoint Quintus Fabius Maximus, a man whose claim to be the chief citizen of Rome at that time he could prove, even before Hannibal himself, to be indisputable. The argument was long drawn out, but at last Cornelius gave way and Fabius the consul was appointed leader by Sempronius. After that the rest of the senators were listed, eight men being passed over, amongst them Caecilius Metellus who had made the infamous proposal after the defeat at Cannae to abandon Italy. A similar procedure was followed in the case of knights deserving censure, though there were very few of them guilty of that particular infamy. All those (and they were many) who as survivors of Cannae were serving as cavalrymen in Sicily were deprived of their horses. The severity of their punishment was increased by an addition to their length of service: the campaigns on which they had served with horses provided by the State were not to be reckoned in the total to which they were liable, but they were all to serve ten campaigns with horses provided at their own expense. The censors also rounded up a large number of men who ought to have served in the cavalry, and reduced to the status of *aerarius*, the lowest citizen rank, all of them who at the beginning of the war had been seventeen years old but had avoided service. They then contracted for the rebuilding of what the fire had destroyed round the forum – the seven shops, the provision market, and the *atrium regium*.

12. When all necessary business in Rome had been completed the consuls left for the seat of war. Fulvius left first, on his way to Capua, and a few days later was followed by Fabius. Fabius had urged his colleague by word of mouth, and Marcellus by letter, to engage Hannibal with all possible vigour while he himself was operating against Tarentum, pointing out that once that city was lost, the enemy, beaten on every side and without anywhere to make a stand or any place they could trust to in their rear, would have no further reason even for remaining in Italy. He then sent a message to the commander of the garrison stationed by the consul Laevinus at Rhegium to deal with the Bruttians. This garrison consisted of the 8,000 men, robbers and brigands (mostly, as I mentioned before, from Agathyrna) sent over from Sicily; Bruttian deserters had been added to the number, men whom the buffets of the world had rendered equally reckless and careless of consequence. Fabius's orders were that this crowd should first be marched to Bruttium to do what damage they could to farms and crops, and then to make an assault on the town of Caulonia. They carried out their orders with more than vigour – indeed, with eager delight. Having plundered and scattered the Bruttian farmers to the winds, they proceeded to the attack on the town with all their might.

Marcellus, partly in consequence of Fabius's letter and partly because he had come to feel that there was no Roman general who was a better match for Hannibal than himself, left his winter quarters as soon as there was sufficient forage to be found in the countryside and fell in with Hannibal near Canusium. Hannibal was trying to persuade Canusium to renounce its allegiance to Rome, but he moved off when he learned of Marcellus's approach. As the country round about was open and had no suitable spot for laying a trap, he began to withdraw, directing his march through country which was thickly wooded. Marcellus kept at his heels, encamped always close to where Hannibal did and, as soon as his defences were in order, promptly marshalled his men for battle. Hannibal continued to believe that a general engagement might be avoided and contented himself with minor clashes, sending out his light spearmen or his cavalry a squadron at a time; but he was none the less drawn into the struggle he was trying to avoid. He had moved forward under cover of darkness, when Marcellus started in pursuit; the ground was level and open, and as Hannibal was fortifying his camp, Marcellus by attacks from every direction prevented the men from continuing their work. This began it: the opposing armies met, the engagement became general, and continued till near nightfall, when it was broken off without a decision. The two camps were quite close to each other and were hurriedly fortified before total darkness. At dawn next day Marcellus again took the field and Hannibal did not refuse the challenge, having urged his men at considerable length to remember Trasimene and Cannae and crush their enemy's pride into the dust. The Romans, he said, were continually pressing on their rear, never letting them move a step without a threat of battle, nor giving them a chance to pitch a camp, or draw breath, or look around them; every day, punctually at sunrise, there was the Roman army drawn up for battle. Let the challenge once be accepted, let the enemy come out of a single battle with some bloodshed, and they would wage war more calmly and quietly in future. Hannibal's men were not unaffected by his exhortations; moreover, they were sick of the confident spirit shown by the Romans in their unrelenting pursuit and daily provocation. They advanced eagerly to the attack, and for over two hours the struggle continued. Then, on the Roman side, the right *ala* and the picked allied troops began to weaken, and Marcellus brought the eighteenth legion up into the front line, but without avail: half his army was hastily withdrawing, half moving up, though slowly, into the line, with the result that all were soon flung into confusion. Confusion turned to rout, duty was forgotten in panic, and they fled for their lives. In this action, before and during the rout, some 2,700 men, citizens and allies, were killed; amongst them were four Roman centurions and two military tribunes, Licinius and Helvius. Four military standards belonging to the *ala* which was first to turn tail were lost, and two from the legion which had come to relieve the allies when they began to break.

13. Back in camp Marcellus addressed his men in such bitter

and angry terms that a whole day's fighting followed by defeat was a lighter burden to bear than the words of their enraged commander. 'Thanks and praise be to God,' he said, ' – if such words make sense in this situation – that the victorious enemy did not actually attack our camp while you were hurling yourselves in panic on to the rampart and through the gates. You would assuredly have abandoned it as chicken-heartedly as you refused to stand up to him in the field. What is the meaning of this terror and fear? Of this sudden oblivion of who you are and with whom you are fighting? They are the same enemy as you spent last summer in thrashing on the field and in chasing off it, the same whom in these last few days you have day and night pursued in their efforts to escape you, whom you have skirmished with till they are sick of it, whom yesterday you would not allow either to keep going or to pitch a camp without molestation. Of the achievements you may be proud of I say nothing: I shall speak only of what you should be ashamed of and sorry for – that yesterday, in fair and equal fight, you broke off the battle. That was yesterday, but now, what have last night and today brought us? Have your forces been weakened or Hannibal's increased in those few hours? I can hardly believe I am speaking to my army, to Roman soldiers; only your bodies and your weapons are recognizable as the same. If in those bodies you had had the same hearts, would the enemy have seen your backs? or taken the standards from a cohort or company? Till now he could boast only about the destruction of Roman legions; today you have given him for the first time the distinction of routing an army.'

From the ranks arose a cry for pardon for that day's sorry work, and Marcellus was besought to put his men's courage once more to the test whenever he might wish. 'Yes,' he said, 'I shall do so, my soldiers; tomorrow I shall lead you into battle, so that as victors rather than as vanquished you may win the pardon for which you ask.'

Marcellus ordered an issue of barley for the cohorts which had lost their standards, and the centurions of the maniples whose standards had been taken were told to fall out with drawn swords and no belts. The order was then given for all mounted and unmounted troops to parade under arms on the following day. With this the men were dismissed, all admitting that they had fully deserved censure and that in the day's fighting there had been not a single real man in the Roman line except their commander, to whom they owed the reparation either of death or of glorious victory.

Next day they presented themselves in full equipment according to orders. Marcellus congratulated them and announced his intention of bringing up to the front line the troops which had started the rout on the previous day and the cohorts which had lost their standards. Every man, he declared, must fight and conquer, doing his utmost as an individual and in concert with his fellows to prevent the news of yesterday's defeat from reaching Rome before that of today's victory. The troops were ordered to eat and rest, to give them a reserve of strength should the battle be a long one; then, when all was said and done for arousing in them a spirit of offence, they moved forward into line.

14. 'How very odd!' was Hannibal's comment on receiving a report of all this. 'We have an enemy to deal with who seems unable to endure either success or failure. If he wins, he can't keep his hands off the vanquished; if he loses, he renews the struggle with the men who beat him.' He then ordered the trumpets to sound and took the field. The battle which ensued was fought on both sides with much greater vigour than on the previous day, the Carthaginians striving to keep the honours they had already won, the Romans to get rid of their disgrace. On the Roman side, the left *ala* and the cohorts which had lost their standards were fighting in the van, and the eighteenth legion was drawn up on the right wing; the military tribunes Lentulus and Nero commanded the wings; the presence of Marcellus, as witness of its work, strengthened and encouraged the centre. On Hannibal's side the Spaniards, the best troops in the army, held the front line. After much indecisive fighting Hannibal ordered the elephants up to the front line on the chance that this might cause panic and confusion, and at first it did so: ranks and standards were thrown into turmoil; some of the men within reach were trampled to death, others broke and fled, and a section of the line was stripped bare. The rout would have spread farther if a military tribune named Gaius Decimius

Flavus had not seized a standard of the first maniple of the *hastati* and called to the men to follow him. He led them in to the very thick of the turmoil caused by the solid mass of the elephants and ordered them to let fly with their javelins. Every weapon found a mark – and indeed beasts of such size and packed so closely together presented no difficult target; but not all were hit, and those which had spears sticking in their backs turned and ran, like the untrustworthy creatures they are, and in their efforts to escape carried with them the others who were still untouched. After that it was not one maniple only which hurled their spears but every man for himself who managed to come up with the running elephants. The poor brutes charged their own masters and caused even greater carnage amongst them than they had caused amongst the enemy – inevitably, because a frightened beast is driven more fiercely by terror than when he is under the control of his rider. The Roman infantry advanced to the attack of the enemy line, already flung off its balance by the passage through it of the elephants, broke it up with little effort and forced it into a hasty retreat. Then Marcellus ordered his cavalry to ride them down, and the pursuit of the fugitives was continued until they were driven to seek refuge in their camp. Even this the routed army did not accomplish too easily: the enemy on their heels was bad enough, but in addition to that the corpses of two elephants lay right in the gateway, so that the men were compelled to tumble into the camp as best they could across the ditch and rampart. It was there that the worst slaughter took place: they lost about 8,000 men, and five elephants. But the Romans' victory was not a bloodless one: approximately 1,700 men from the two legions were killed, and more than 1,300 of the allies. A large number of both citizens and allies were wounded. That night Hannibal got on the march again; Marcellus was eager to follow him but was prevented by the number of his wounded. 15. Scouts sent out to keep track of the column reported next day that Hannibal was making for Bruttium.

About this time the Hirpini, the Lucanians, and the people of Volceii surrendered to the consul Fulvius after handing over Hannibal's garrisons which they had in their towns. Fulvius received them kindly, contenting himself with a reproof for their past errors; and the Bruttians, too, were led to expect similar clemency when the brothers Vibius and Paccius, men of the noblest Bruttian blood, arrived with a request for the same terms of surrender as had been granted to the Lucanians.

The consul Fabius took by storm Manduria, a town in Sallentinian territory. About 4,000 men were captured in it and a considerable quantity of material. From there he marched to Tarentum and took up a position right at the entrance to the harbour. Some of the ships which Laevinus had used to safeguard supplies he equipped with artillery and other gear for assaulting fortifications, others with catapults, stones, and every variety of missile weapon. He similarly equipped the merchant vessels – not only the light ones which depended only on oars – so that some crews could carry artillery and ladders close up to the walls and others harass the defenders at long range. These ships were all put in order for an assault on the city from the open sea. This was clear of enemy forces, as the Carthaginian fleet had been sent over to Corcyra when Philip was preparing to attack the Aetolians. Meanwhile in Bruttium the troops besieging Caulonia, in order to avoid being caught, had retired, just before Hannibal's arrival, to some high ground where, though they had no other advantages, they were safe from immediate attack.

During his siege of Tarentum Fabius was helped to attain his resounding success by an incident almost too trivial to mention. In the garrison provided by Hannibal there was a contingent of Bruttians, commanded by a man who happened to be desperately in love with some woman or other who had a brother serving in Fabius's army. The woman wrote to her brother about this new connexion with a wealthy stranger much respected by his people, and the news aroused in him the hope that through his sister's influence the love-sick captain might be induced to do pretty well anything they wanted. He informed Fabius of his hopes, and, as they seemed by no means without foundation, he received instructions to enter Tarentum in the guise of a deserter. This he did, and obtained, through his sister, an introduction to the captain; he then began to put out cautious feelers, until, having satisfied himself about the fellow's lack of character, he was able, by the help of the woman's blandishments, to get him to betray his trust. Time and method were agreed upon between them, and a soldier was sent out of the town under cover of darkness, through the gaps between the guard-posts, to report to the consul what had been done and the arrangements for what remained to be done.

During the first watch Fabius gave the signal to the troops in the citadel and those guarding the harbour, and himself moved round the harbour to a concealed position on the eastern side of the city. The trumpets sounded simultaneously from the citadel, the harbour, and the ships which had moved in from the open sea, and a great shouting and uproar was raised as a deliberate blind at every point except the one from which real danger threatened. Fabius meanwhile kept his own contingent absolutely silent. Democrates, who had previously commanded the fleet, happened to be in charge of that section of the defences, and when he saw that all was quiet there while in other sections a fearful uproar was going on, interspersed with what sounded like the cries of men in a captured city, he was not slow to act. Fearing that Fabius was taking advantage of his delay to make a direct assault, he moved his men to the citadel whence, it seemed, the most alarming noises were coming. Fabius waited till sufficient time had passed and he could tell, by the silence which had succeeded to the uproar of men calling their comrades to arms, that the guard had been moved from its post, and then gave orders for ladders to be brought to the section of wall where the man who had organized the betrayal had told him that the Bruttian cohort was on guard. The wall was taken in that section first, the Bruttians giving their help and letting in the Romans, who thus got over into the city; the adjoining gate was then broken open to admit a strong detachment of troops. Just about dawn the battle-cry was raised, and they penetrated to the forum without meeting any armed resistance; there they drew the attack of all the troops who were engaged at the citadel and harbour.

16. The action at the entrance to the forum was begun by the Tarentines not without spirit; but they had no staying-power, being inferior to the Romans both in weapons and tactical skill, not to mention determination and sheer physical strength. So

after merely throwing javelins they turned tail almost before coming to grips at all, and slipped away along the familiar streets to their own or their friends' houses. Two of their leaders, Nico and Democrates, fell fighting bravely; Philemenus, who had been responsible for betraying the city to Hannibal, made his escape from battle on horseback and, though his horse was recognized soon after, wandering loose about the city, his body was nowhere found. It was generally believed that he threw himself off its back into an open well. Carthalo, the commander of the Carthaginian garrison, had laid down his arms and was coming to Fabius to recall to his memory the family tie of hospitality between them, when he was met by a soldier and killed. Elsewhere there was indiscriminate slaughter, Roman troops butchering armed and unarmed, Carthaginians or Tarentines alike. Many Bruttians were also killed in various parts of the city, either by mistake or because of the inveterate hatred the Romans felt for them, or perhaps to prevent the story that Tarentum had been betrayed from getting out and to make it seem that it had been taken simply by force of arms.

From the work of butchery the troops turned to plunder. It is said that 30,000 slaves were taken, an immense quantity of wrought silver and silver coins, 3,080 pounds weight of gold, and almost as many statues and pictures as had adorned Syracuse. Fabius, however, showed a nobler restraint than Marcellus in dealing with this sort of prize: when asked by a clerk what he wanted done with some enormous statues representing gods as warriors, each in his own characteristic dress and bearing, he replied that the Tarentines could keep their gods, who were clearly angry with them. The wall dividing the city from the citadel was then pulled down and completely destroyed.

During these operations Hannibal received the surrender of the force besieging Caulonia. When he learned of the attack upon Tarentum he started with all possible speed, marching day and night, to go to its assistance, and hearing on the road that it had already fallen, he said: 'The Romans, too, have their Hannibal; we have lost Tarentum by the same strategy as won it for us.' None the less, to avoid the appearance of returning on his tracks like a beaten enemy, he halted and took up a position some five miles from the city; he remained there a few days and then withdrew to Metapontum. From Metapontum he sent two natives of the place to Fabius with a letter from the leading men, in the hope that they would secure the consul's promise that, if they betrayed the town together with its Carthaginian garrison, he would let bygones be bygones. Fabius took the communication at its face value and fixed a day for his arrival, giving the messengers a letter for their masters. The letter was put into Hannibal's hands, whereupon, delighted with the success of his ruse and the discovery that not even Fabius was proof against trickery, he proceeded to lay a trap in the neighbourhood of the town. When Fabius was taking the auspices before leaving Tarentum, the birds repeatedly failed to give the favourable sign; and again, when by offering sacrifice he was seeking to find the will of heaven, the priest warned him to beware of a trap and of the enemy's guile. When he did not appear on the agreed date, the two Metapontines were sent back to urge him to cut short his delay; they were immediately arrested and, fearing they might be subjected to a more painful sort of inquiry, they revealed the existence of Hannibal's trap.

17. At the beginning of the summer in which these events took place Scipio was visited in Spain by a distinguished Spanish leader named Edesco. (The whole of the previous winter he had spent conciliating the Spaniards, either by giving them presents or by freeing prisoners of war and hostages.) Edesco's wife and children were with the Romans, but that was not the only reason for his coming, for he was also influenced by the feeling which had arisen, it seemed, almost spontaneously and was drawing the whole of Spain away from Carthage to the support of the Roman power. Indibilis and Mandonius, indubitably the most important men in Spain, had the same reason for leaving Hasdrubal, taking themselves and all their countrymen off to the heights above his camp, from which there was a safe line of retreat along continuous ridges to the Roman position.

Hasdrubal, aware of the increase of his enemy's strength by all these important additions and of the proportionate diminution of his own, knew well enough that unless he ventured on some bold stroke, what had begun as a trickle would end as a landslide; so he determined to offer battle at the first opportunity. Scipio was even more eager for action, not only by reason of the increasing confidence which success had given him, but also because he preferred not to wait for the junction of the Carthaginian armies: it would clearly be better to engage one of the three only, before the junction could take place. However, on the supposition that he might have to deal with more than one at the same time, he had increased his forces by a sensible move. Seeing that his fleet had no active employment, as the whole Spanish coast was clear of Carthaginian ships, he beached his own vessels at Tarraco and took over the crews to reinforce his army. He had moreover a very large reserve of weapons, which included those taken at New Carthage and all he had had made after the capture of the town by the numerous workmen he had kept shut up for the purpose.

With these forces Scipio left Tarraco at the beginning of spring and made for Hasdrubal's position. Laelius had already returned to Rome, and he did not wish to undertake any major action without him. His route lay through country where all was quiet, and he was welcomed and escorted by friendly peoples as he passed the boundaries of the various tribes. It was in the course of this march that he was met by Indibilis and Mandonius together with their forces. Indibilis acted as spokesman; what he said was by no means as stupid or ill-considered as one might expect from a wild Spaniard; on the contrary, he spoke modestly and seriously, not bragging about their change of sides as if they had seized the first chance to come over, but excusing it, rather, as something forced upon them by necessity. He was well aware, he said, that the name of deserter was hated by old allies and held in suspicion by new; nor had he any fault to find with this universal attitude, provided that it was not the word but the motive which caused the mutual dislike. He went on to mention his services to the Carthaginian generals, services ill rewarded by their avarice and arrogance and every sort of injustice to him and his friend, and to their fellow-countrymen. For these reasons it was his body only which had remained with them hitherto: his mind for a long time past had dwelt where they both believed that justice and right were held in honour. Those who cannot endure the violence and brutalities of men take refuge, as suppliants, with the gods; and as for themselves, they begged Scipio to accept their change of sides without prejudice, counting it neither criminal nor creditable. Then he could value their service according to the qualities which, by putting them to the test thereafter, he found them to possess.

The Roman replied that he would do as they asked, adding that he could not give the name of deserter to men who believed that no association was valid in which nothing human or divine was held sacred. Their wives and children were then brought into their presence and restored to them while they wept tears of joy. For that day they were taken to guest-quarters; on the day following, their promise of friendship was formally accepted and they were dismissed to fetch their troops. From then on, until under their guidance contact was made with the enemy, they were quartered in the same camp.

18. The nearest of the three Carthaginian armies was Hasdrubal's, in a position near Baecula. His camp was guarded by cavalry outposts; these were promptly attacked by the Roman light troops and those at the head of the column – they went for them as they came up, straight from the march, without waiting to choose a site for their camp, and with such contemptuous confidence as to leave no doubt about the respective morale of the two armies. The cavalry pickets were driven helter-skelter back into camp and the Roman standards were all but carried through the gates. Passions were up, but for that day there was no further fighting. The Romans encamped, and during the night Hasdrubal withdrew his forces to a hill which had a wide area of level ground at its summit; behind him was the river, in front and on both sides the whole position was encircled by a sort of steep bank. Below him was another stretch of open ground, on a slight slope, and this too was surrounded by a wall-like rim, no easier to get over. It was into this lower area that Hasdrubal on the following day, when he saw the Roman line in position in front of his camp, sent his Numidian cavalry together with his light-armed Balearic and African troops.

Scipio rode round the various units of his force and pointed out to his men how the enemy had already lost hope of a successful action on open ground and were clinging to the hills. There they were in full view, but where was their confidence? Not, surely, in their courage or their swords, but merely in the strength of their position. 'But New Carthage,' he said, 'had higher walls, and Roman soldiers climbed them; neither hills, nor citadel, nor even the sea withstood our arms. Those heights the enemy have occupied will do them no good, unless to tempt them to escape us by tumbling down precipices or jumping amongst the crags. But I shall see to it that even that way of escape is closed.' He then ordered forward two cohorts, one to hold the mouth of the gully down which the river ran, the other to block the track which led from the town down across the hill into open country. He himself led the troops (leaving behind their heavy gear), which on the previous day had routed the enemy pickets, towards Hasdrubal's light-armed units on the lower slope. The going was very rough, but at first there was nothing else to check them; soon, however, they came within range, and were subjected to an exceedingly heavy attack by missile weapons of all kinds. They replied with a hail of stones, picked up from the ground, where they lay in abundance, and nearly all of convenient size. The camp-servants mixed with the troops also took a hand in the work.

The ascent was a difficult one and the men were all but overwhelmed with missiles and stones; none the less, determination and the training they had received in scaling walls enabled the leaders to reach the top. Once on level ground which gave them a firm foothold, they had little trouble from Hasdrubal's light troops, which were accustomed to skirmishing and fighting only with missiles at long range, avoiding close encounter, and were not to be relied on for hand-to-hand combat. These they quickly dislodged and drove back with great slaughter on to the line of their comrades above them on the higher plateau of the hill. Following this success, Scipio ordered a continued advance against the centre of Hasdrubal's line; then, dividing the rest of his force with Laelius, he sent Laelius's party round the hill towards the right to look for an easier way up, while he himself turned left, found a suitable place after a brief circuit, and attacked the enemy in the flank. The result was great confusion in Hasdrubal's line; his men attempted to change the direction of their front to meet the shouts of the Romans which rang out on every side, and right in the midst of the hurly-burly Laelius arrived. At once the Carthaginians gave ground to avoid an attack in their rear, and the consequence was a break-up of their front line so that the Romans in the centre too, those who had led the first attack, were enabled to reach the plateau where the fight was going on. This they could never have done over such difficult ground if the enemy line had remained intact, with the elephants in the van. All over the field enemy troops were being cut down, and Scipio, having advanced against Hasdrubal's right with his own left, was fighting mainly against his exposed flank. Now, moreover, all ways of escape were closed: on both sides Roman pickets were blocking the tracks; the gate of the camp had been shut, the commander and chief officers having fled; and there was panic amongst the elephants which, in that state, were as great a cause of fear as the enemy himself. About 8,000 of Hasdrubal's men were killed.

19. Before the battle Hasdrubal had already hastily got his money together and sent on the elephants in advance; now he rounded up as many of his fugitive troops as he could and set off along the Tagus for the Pyrenees.[1] Scipio took possession of the camp, and except for free male persons, turned all articles of value over to his men. Counting the prisoners, he found them to number 10,000 foot and 2,000 horse; of these he let all Spaniards return to their homes without ransom, and instructed his quaestor to sell the Africans. The Spaniards, both those previously surrendered and those taken prisoner the day before, all came thronging about him and with a single voice hailed him as king. At this, Scipio told his herald to call for silence and said that the noblest title he bore was the one his own men had conferred upon him, that of *Imperator*, or Commander-in-Chief.[2] The name of king, elsewhere great, was not to be tolerated in Rome. 'If you think,' he added, 'that I have the spirit of a king, and that a royal mind is the greatest of

1. This must have been in Autumn 208: he crossed the Alps the following Spring. Appian *Hisp.* 28 says he crossed the Pyrenees near the Atlantic.

2. The first recorded use of the army's saluting a general in this way.

human qualities, let the judgement be a silent one. The word must never pass your lips.' Barbarians though they were, they were not insensible of the magnanimity which could so loftily despise a title at whose wonderful power other men were struck dumb. Gifts were then distributed amongst the Spanish chieftains and princes, and from the immense number of captured horses, Indibilis, by Scipio's orders, was allowed to choose 300 for his own.

While the quaestor was carrying out his orders about the sale of the Africans, he found among them a handsome youth who, he was told, was of royal blood. He sent the lad to Scipio, who asked him who he was, where he came from, and why he was serving in the army so young. 'I am a Numidian,' the boy replied; 'and my countrymen call me Massiva. My father died, I was brought up by my maternal grandfather Gala, King of the Numidians, and I came over to Spain with my uncle Masinissa, who arrived not long ago with cavalry reinforcements for the Carthaginians. I have never before been in a battle – Masinissa forbade it as I was too young. The day we fought the Romans I stole a horse and armour without my uncle knowing, and went into the line. My horse fell and I was thrown, and the Romans took me prisoner.'

Scipio ordered the boy to be carefully protected, finished what official business he had still to do, and then retired to his headquarters, where he sent for him again and asked him if he would like to go back to Masinissa. With tears of pleasure the boy replied that that was, indeed, what he wanted; whereupon Scipio presented him with a gold ring, a broad-banded tunic, a Spanish cloak, a gold brooch, and a horse with full trappings, and sent him off with a cavalry escort which had orders to accompany him as far as he wished.

20. After this there was a council of war. Some of Scipio's officers suggested the immediate pursuit of Hasdrubal, but Scipio disagreed, thinking that there might well be a danger of Hasdrubal's being joined by Mago and the other Hasdrubal; he therefore sent a small force only to hold the Pyrenees and himself spent the rest of the summer receiving the Spanish tribes back into the Roman alliance.

A few days after the fight at Baecula, when Scipio on his way back to Tarraco had got clear of the forest of Castulo, Hasdrubal son of Gisgo, and Mago marched from Further Spain and joined the other Hasdrubal. The latter having been already defeated, their arrival was too late for practical assistance, though opportune enough for the discussion of future plans. They compared notes on the attitude of the Spaniards in the various parts of the country where each of them had been operating, and Hasdrubal son of Gisgo was the only one of the three to maintain that the extreme west towards Gades and the Atlantic still knew nothing of the Romans and was, in consequence, sufficiently loyal to Carthage. Mago and the other Hasdrubal were both convinced that the entire Spanish population had been deeply affected, individually and collectively, by Scipio's generosity and that there would be no end to the Spaniards' going over to the Roman cause until all their soldiers were either moved to the remotest parts of the country or carried into Gaul. Consequently, even without official instructions from the Carthaginian government, Hasdrubal would still have had to go to Italy, for Italy was the main theatre of the war and his going there would take all the Spanish troops out of Spain and at the same time far away from the sound of Scipio's name. They proposed therefore that his army, weakened by desertions and by the losses incurred in the recent defeat, should be made up with Spanish troops and that Mago should hand over his forces to Hasdrubal son of Gisgo and cross to the Balearics with a supply of money to hire auxiliary troops. Further, that Hasdrubal son of Gisgo should take his army deep into Lusitania and avoid action against the Romans; that Masinissa should have 3,000 of the best available cavalry for a roving commission through Hither Spain, helping allies and raiding enemy towns and farms. Having made these decisions the three generals separated and proceeded to implement them.

Such, then, were the events of that year in Spain. In Rome meanwhile Scipio's reputation was growing daily; the capture of Tarentum was counted to Fabius's credit despite the fact that it was due to a trick rather than to military prowess. The reputation of Fulvius was, on the contrary, declining, and Marcellus was even becoming the target of malicious gossip.

This was due not only to his defeat in the first of his two battles, but also to his having billeted his troops in Venusia in spite of the fact that it was midsummer and that Hannibal was ranging through Italy. The people's tribune, Gaius Publicius Bibulus, was doing all he could to discredit Marcellus; he had been constantly blackening Marcellus's name in public speeches and trying to rouse the commons against him ever since his first, unsuccessful, battle, and he was now beginning to urge the abrogation of his command. However, Marcellus's relatives persuaded the authorities to allow him to leave an officer in charge at Venusia and return to Rome to defend himself against his enemies' accusations; they also got proceedings about suspending his command dropped during his absence. It so happened that Marcellus arrived in Rome to clear the stain on his character at the same time as the consul Fulvius, who came to preside at the elections. 21. The question of the former's command was heard in the Circus Flaminius before an immense crowd of people of every rank and station; the tribune accused not Marcellus only but the nobility as a whole, maintaining that it was owing to their dishonesty and dilatoriness that Hannibal for the past nine years had been treating Italy as his province – a longer time than he had lived in Carthage. The Roman people, he said, were reaping the fruits of the prolongation of Marcellus's command: his army after two defeats was now spending the summer in comfortable quarters at Venusia!

Marcellus replied by giving an account of his actions, and what he said made the tribune's speech look so utterly absurd that not only was the bill to abrogate his command annulled, but he was elected consul on the following day by the unanimous vote of all the centuries. Titus Quinctius Crispinus, who was then praetor, was elected as his colleague. Next day the praetors were elected: they were Publius Licinius Crassus Dives, the *pontifex maximus*, Publius Licinius Varus, Sextus Julius Caesar, and Quintus Claudius.

During the elections news of a revolt in Etruria brought a fresh cause of anxiety. Gaius Calpurnius, in charge of affairs as pro-praetor there, had written to say that the trouble had started in Arretium, and Marcellus the consul designate was accordingly sent there at once to look into the matter and, if he thought it called for such strong measures, to send for an army and transfer the seat of war from Apulia to Etruria. The threat proved sufficient and the Etruscans made no further move. Envoys from Tarentum came to Rome to discuss peace terms; they asked to keep their liberty and their own laws, but were told in reply by the Senate to come back when the consul Fabius had returned to Rome.

That year the Roman and Plebeian Games were both repeated for an additional day. The curule aediles were Lucius Cornelius Caudinus and Servius Sulpicius Galba, the plebeian aediles Gaius Servilius and Quintus Caecilius Metellus. It was said that Servilius had not been legally tribune and was not now legally aedile, because his father, who for nine years had been supposed dead – killed by the Boii near Mutina when he was one of the three land-commissioners[1] – was now generally believed to be alive and a prisoner of war.

22. In the eleventh year of the war with Carthage, Crispinus and Marcellus entered upon the consulship – Marcellus, if one includes the consulship he did not actually hold because of a technical fault in the election, for the fifth time. Both consuls were instructed to operate in Italy and were given the two consular armies of the previous year – there was a third army, previously commanded by Marcellus, at Venusia – the arrangement being that of the three they should choose the two they preferred, and that the remaining one should be entrusted to whoever was chosen to operate in the area around Tarentum. Other duties were distributed as follows: the City praetorship to Varus; jurisdiction involving foreigners to Crassus, the *pontifex maximus*, together with a command wherever the Senate should decide; Sicily to Caesar, and Tarentum to Claudius. Flaccus had his command continued for a further year with instructions to take over from the praetor Quinctius the charge of operations at Capua, with one legion. Two other men also had their commands extended: Tubulus, who was to take over Calpurnius's two legions in Etruria as pro-praetor; and Veturius Philo, who as pro-praetor was to be in control of

1. cf. p. 48. So long as a patrician father was alive, his son was not eligible for plebeian offices without his permission.

Gaul. This was the same assignment he had had as praetor, and he was to keep the same two legions. A similar decision was made by the Senate in the case of Gaius Aurunculeius, who as praetor had been in control of Sardinia with two legions, and a bill was brought before the people for continuing his command; he was also given for the defence of his province the fifty warships which Scipio had sent from Spain. Scipio and Silanus were entrusted for a further year with their own provinces of Spain, with the armies they already commanded; and Scipio was ordered to send to Sardinia fifty of the eighty ships which he had with him (either brought from Italy or captured at New Carthage) because it was believed that great naval preparations were going on that year at Carthage and that the enemy intended to cover the coasts of Italy, Sicily, and Sardinia with a fleet 200 strong.

The arrangements for Sicily were that Caesar should take over the army of Cannae, and that Laevinus (who also had his command extended) should have the fleet of seventy ships already stationed at the island and should add to it thirty other vessels which had been at Tarentum the year before. With the fleet of a hundred vessels thus formed he was to raid the African coast, if he judged it advisable. Sulpicius's command was extended for another year, and his instructions were to hold Macedonia and Greece with the same fleet as before. With regard to the two legions which had been quartered in Rome, no change was made. The consuls were empowered to recruit additional troops as necessary. That year there were, in all, twenty-one legions under arms for the defence of the Roman dominion.

Varus, the City praetor, received instructions to refit thirty old warships lying at Ostia and to find crews for twenty new ones, to give him a fleet of fifty vessels for the protection of the coast in the vicinity of Rome. Calpurnius was ordered not to move from Arretium until he was relieved; similar orders were given to Tubulus, to be specially on the alert against any seditious movements there.

23. The praetors then left for their spheres of action, but the consuls were detained in Rome by certain religious difficulties – a number of prodigies had been reported and they were having

trouble in getting good results from sacrifice. From Campania reports had come that the temples of Fortune and of Mars had been struck by lightning, also several tombs; at Cumae (superstition sees the finger of God even in trivialities) mice had gnawed the gold in the temple of Jupiter; at Casinum a large swarm of bees had settled in the forum; at Ostia the wall and a gate had been struck by lightning; at Caere a vulture had flown into the temple of Jupiter, and the lake at Volsinii had had its water discoloured with blood. Because of these ominous events one day of public prayer was held, and for several days full-grown victims were offered in sacrifice but without success, and for a long time the favour and forgiveness of the gods was not obtained. In the event, the ruin these prodigies foretold was to fall upon the consuls, while Rome herself was to receive no hurt.

The Games of Apollo had first been celebrated by the City praetor Cornelius Sulla in the consulship of Quintus Fulvius and Appius Claudius; subsequently all the City praetors had celebrated them, though vowing them for one year only and not fixing a regular date. This year a serious epidemic broke out in Rome and the surrounding country. Though serious, it was seldom fatal, but left its victims weak and ailing for a long period; and because of it prayers were offered at all cross-roads in the city, and the praetor Varus was ordered to bring before the people a bill to make the Apolline Games a permanent institution to take place on a fixed date. It was Varus who was the first praetor to vow them on these terms, and the date was 5 July. That day was henceforward observed as a holiday.

24. The news from Arretium continued to grow more serious, and anxiety in the Senate increased accordingly. Written instructions were sent to Tubulus to take hostages from the Arretines immediately, and Varro was dispatched, with full military authority, to receive them and bring them to Rome. On Varro's arrival Tubulus promptly ordered the one legion which was encamped in front of the town to march in, and posted his guards wherever he thought fit; then he summoned the town's senators to the forum and demanded hostages. The senate asked for two days to consider their answer, but were told by Tubulus that they must themselves provide the hostages

immediately, or, if they refused, that he would take all the children of the senators on the following day. The military tribunes, the Prefects of the Allies, and the centurions were then ordered to guard the gates and prevent anyone from leaving the town during the night; but the order was carried out slackly and carelessly, and seven leading senators got away with their children during daylight before the guards could be posted at the gates. Next day at dawn their absence was noticed when the senators were being summoned to the forum, and their property was sold. From the remaining senators 120 hostages, all children of their own, were taken and handed over to Varro for removal to Rome. In the Roman Senate Varro's report made the whole situation seem more alarming than it had been originally, and he was ordered in consequence to march to Arretium himself with one of the two City legions and to garrison the town with it, on the supposition that an Etrurian revolt was imminent. It was decided at the same time that Tubulus, with the rest of the forces available, was to cover the whole province and take precautions to nip in the bud any movement towards a revolutionary outbreak. When Varro arrived with his legion at the town, he demanded the keys of the gates from the magistrates; they replied that they could not be found, whereupon Varro, convinced that they had not really been lost but had been deliberately, and dishonestly, removed, had other keys provided for all the gates and took all precautions to have everything under his control. Tubulus he warned with great emphasis that the only ground for supposing that the Etruscans would make no movement was to take precautions which would render any such move impossible.

25. On the subject of the Tarentines, strongly opposing views were put forward in the Senate. Fabius, who was present at the debate, defended those whom he had taken by force of arms, but others were hostile, the majority putting their guilt, and consequent liability to punishment, on a level with that of the Capuans. A decree was passed on the lines of a proposal by Manius Acilius to the effect that Tarentum should be occupied by a military force and all Tarentines kept within the walls; the whole question was to come up for discussion again later, when things in Italy were quieter. There was no less conflict

of opinion on the subject of Marcus Livius, the officer in command of the citadel. Some wanted him officially disgraced by a senatorial decree on the ground that it was his failure to act with vigour that put Tarentum into the enemy's hands; others were for rewarding him because he had defended the citadel for five years and had contributed more than anyone else to the recovery of the city. Between these extremes were others who maintained that the hearing of his case belonged, not to the Senate, but to the censors. With this view Fabius agreed; however, he added that he was prepared to admit that the recovery of Tarentum was due to Livius, as his friends had urged in the Senate, for it could not have been recovered if it had not first been lost.

Of the two consuls one, Crispinus, left for Lucania with reinforcements for the army previously commanded by Flaccus; Marcellus, however, was detained in Rome by a succession of religious scruples which kept occurring to his mind. One of them was the fact that at Clastidium in the war with Gaul he had vowed a temple to Honour and Courage, but had been prevented by the priests from dedicating it. They had maintained that a single shrine could not properly be dedicated to more than one deity, the reason being that if it were struck by lightning, or some other evil omen occurred in connexion with it, the act of propitiation would cause difficulty, as it could not be known which of the two deities should receive the sacrifice. Moreover, a single victim could not properly be sacrificed to two gods simultaneously except in certain recognized cases. Consequently a shrine to Courage was also erected in a great hurry; though even so the two shrines were not dedicated by Marcellus. But at last he managed to get away, and went with reinforcements to join the army he had left at Venusia the year before.

Crispinus, in the belief that Tarentum had greatly enhanced the reputation of Fabius, was making an attempt on Locri in Bruttium, and had sent for all sorts of artillery and siege-engines from Sicily; ships also had been brought over from there to aid in the attack on the seaward side of the town. But the attempt was broken off, as Hannibal had moved his forces to Lacinium, and a report had come in that Marcellus had already left Venusia. Crispinus wanted to join his colleague and returned in consequence from Bruttium to Apulia. The two consuls encamped, less than three miles apart, between Venusia and Bantia. Hannibal also returned to this part of the country once he had averted the attempt on Locri. There, then, lay the two consuls: in both the offensive spirit was high; almost every day they formed their troops for battle, fully confident that if the enemy engaged the combined force of their two consular armies a final decision would be the inevitable result.

26. Hannibal had twice fought Marcellus the previous year, once successfully, once unsuccessfully; consequently if he had had to meet him again now his confidence, or the lack of it, would at least have been founded upon experience; but as he did not feel himself to be a match for two consular armies combined, he had recourse to his by now familiar strategy and began to look round for a suitable place for a trap. Minor skirmishes did however take place between the camps, with varying success. The consuls, though they were of opinion that engagements of this sort might last out the summer, felt none the less that an attempt might be made on Locri, and sent a written order to Lucius Cincius to bring over a fleet from Sicily for the purpose; at the same time they ordered the transference to Locri of a part of the force garrisoning Tarentum, to enable an assault upon the defences to be made from the land as well. Hannibal was informed by some men of Thurii that these moves were about to take place, and he sent troops to invest the road from Tarentum. Three thousand cavalry and 2,000 infantry were stationed in hiding under the hill of Petelia, and the Romans, marching with no scouts out, ran straight into them with the result that 2,000 were killed, about 1,500 taken prisoner. The remainder scattered, and made their way back over farmlands and through woods to Tarentum.

Between the Carthaginian and Roman camps near Venusia there was a hill, covered with trees. Neither side had yet occupied it, for the Romans did not know what it was like on the farther side towards the enemy's position, while in Hannibal's judgement it was better suited to an ambush than to a camp. Hannibal accordingly had sent up under cover of darkness some squadrons of Numidian cavalry with orders to conceal themselves deep in the woods; and there they remained, not a man moving from his post while daylight lasted, lest they or the flash of their arms should be seen from below. In the Roman camp the men were uneasy: the hill, they grumbled, ought to be occupied and held by a fort, for if Hannibal got there first they would have the enemy, so to speak, on top of them. This roused Marcellus to take action. 'Why not go ourselves,' he said to his colleague, 'with a few mounted men, and take a look? Once we have seen the hill we shall be in a better position to make a decision.' Crispinus agreed, and they set off with a party of 220 cavalrymen, forty of them from Fregellae, the rest Etruscans. Two military tribunes, Marcellus the consul's son and Aulus Manlius, went with them, and two Prefects of the Allies, Lucius Arrenius and Manius Aulius. Some writers have left it on record that when Marcellus offered sacrifice that day, the liver of the first victim was found to have no head; in the next victim everything was seen to be normal; indeed, the head of the liver was somewhat enlarged. The soothsayers did not find altogether promising the appearance of entrails which were almost too favourable immediately after others which were malformed and truncated. 27. But so great was Marcellus's eagerness to engage Hannibal that he kept saying that the two camps had never been close enough together; and now, too, as he passed through the fortifications, he gave orders for the men to be ready at their posts, so that they could pack up their traps and follow him if the result of his reconnaissance proved satisfactory.

In front of the Roman camp was a small area of level ground from which a track, open on both sides and without any cover, led up the hill. An enemy scout, who was lying thereabouts on the chance of cutting off a few men who might have gone some distance from their camp in search of wood or fodder, but assuredly not in expectation of such a prize as this, signalled to the Numidians to emerge simultaneously from their hiding-places. Those who had to show themselves on the top of the hill fronting the Romans as they came up, remained hidden until their comrades had moved round to the Roman rear and cut off their retreat; then the whole lot, front and rear, sprang from concealment, raised the battle-cry, and charged. The consuls had no room to manoeuvre; they could not get out on to the summit of the hill because the enemy held it, and they could not retreat because the enemy were also in their rear; nevertheless, they might well have held out longer than they did if the Etruscans had not started to run and thus infected the rest with their own panic. In spite of this the men of Fregellae, though deserted by the Etruscan party, fought on as long as the two consuls were unhurt and could keep things going with their cries of encouragement and personal participation in the fighting. But when they saw that both consuls had been hit, Marcellus, indeed, run through with a lance and falling at his last gasp from his horse, then they too, the few who survived, took to their heels with the consul Crispinus, who himself had two javelin wounds, and the young Marcellus, who was also wounded. Manlius the military tribune was killed, and of the two Prefects of Allies, Aulius was killed and Arrenius was taken prisoner. Of the consuls' lictors, five were captured and the rest were either killed or got away with Crispinus. Forty-three of the mounted troops were killed either in the fight or while trying to escape, and eighteen were taken alive. In the camp something like a demonstration had already taken place to hurry to the support of the consuls, when Crispinus and Marcellus's son, both wounded, and the pitiful remnant of this unlucky venture were seen approaching. The death of Marcellus, distressing from any point of view, was made more so by the circumstances in which it occurred; for, in spite of his age (he was over sixty), and in spite of the caution he had learned as a veteran commander, he had thoughtlessly hazarded his own life and that of his colleague, and also, one might say, the safety of the country as a whole.

If I were willing to follow all the differing accounts of Marcellus's death, I should have to deal with this single event in much too discursive a manner. Coelius, not to mention other writers, gives three separate versions: one generally accepted by tradition; another given in the eulogy written by his son, who was an eye-witness; and a third which he adduces as the result of his own researches. But in spite of individual variations, most writers state that Marcellus's object in leaving the camp was to reconnoitre, and all agree that he fell into Hannibal's trap.

28. Hannibal knew that the death of one consul and the wounding of the other would have had a shattering effect upon the enemy. Determined therefore to let no advantage slip through his fingers, he immediately transferred his position to the hill where the fight had taken place. He found Marcellus's body and gave it burial. Crispinus, badly shaken by his colleague's death and his own wounds, in the silence of the following night made for the nearest mountains and took up a new position on high ground, where he was well protected from every side. Then began a battle of wits between the rival generals, the one hoping to play a trick, the other trying to circumvent him. When Hannibal found Marcellus's body he took his signet-ring, and Crispinus, who saw the danger that Hannibal might cause serious trouble and confusion by the fraudulent use of it, sent messengers to the neighbouring communities to report the fact that his colleague was dead and that the enemy were in possession of his ring, and to warn them not to trust letters purporting to come from Marcellus. The message reached Salapia just before the arrival of a letter from Hannibal written in the name of Marcellus, saying that he (supposedly Marcellus) would be at Salapia on the following night, and giving instructions for the men on garrison duty to be ready in case their services were needed. The people of the town were not deceived: thinking that Hannibal wanted to punish them for their revolt, and particularly for their murder of his cavalrymen, they sent back the man who had brought the letter (he was a Roman deserter), so that they might make their preparations unobserved, and then proceeded to establish guard-posts along the walls and at convenient places in the town. For the ensuing night they took special care in the posting of sentries and guards, and stationed their best troops near the gate by which they thought the enemy would attempt an entry. About the fourth watch Hannibal arrived. The leading files of his army were composed of Roman deserters carrying Roman arms, and when they reached the gate they called to the guards, all speaking Latin, and told them to open it, as the consul was coming. The guards pretended to have been roused by the

summons, and in great apparent excitement hurried to the task of forcing the gate open. The portcullis was down, and they went to work on it with crowbars and tackles, hauling it up high enough to let a man pass under without stooping. The deserters, directly there was room enough, went scrambling through, and as soon as some 600 had got in, the lifting-tackle was cast loose and down came the portcullis again with a crash. The townspeople then went for the deserters, who had expected a friendly reception and, having come straight from the road, still had their weapons slung casually over their shoulders; others from the walls and gate-turrets drove them off with a shower of stones, stakes, and javelins.

Hannibal was thus caught in his own trap. He withdrew from Salapia and went off to relieve the siege of Locri, which was beset by Lucius Cincius and threatened with siege-works on a great scale and all sorts of artillery which he had had brought over from Sicily. Mago no longer trusted his ability to hold and defend the town, and his first ray of renewed hope came with the news of Marcellus's death. Next came the message that Hannibal had sent on his Numidian cavalry and was himself following with his infantry force at all possible speed so the moment he knew from the look-outs' signal that the Numidians were at hand, he opened the gate and marched boldly out against the besiegers. For a while the battle was indecisive – not that Mago was a match for the Romans, but his sudden sortie had caught them unawares; but soon, when the Numidians appeared on the scene, the spirit of the Romans broke; abandoning their siege-works and artillery, they scattered in a wild scramble for the beach and the comparative safety of their ships. Thus Hannibal's arrival effectively raised the siege of Locri.

29. When Crispinus learned that Hannibal had started for Bruttium, he ordered the young Marcellus to take the army previously commanded by his colleague to Venusia, and himself left for Capua with his own troops. His wounds were very painful, and finding the jolting of his litter almost intolerable he wrote to Rome to inform the Senate of the danger to his life and of his colleague's death. He would not, he wrote, be able to come to Rome for the elections, partly because he did not

think he could bear the fatigue of the journey, and partly because of his anxiety lest Hannibal should leave Bruttium and march on Tarentum. He therefore requested the Senate to send representatives to him, good, sound men with whom he could discuss policy. His letter caused as much grief for the death of one consul as fear for the safety of the other, and led to the dispatch of the younger Fabius to the army at Venusia and of three representatives to Crispinus. The men chosen were Sextus Julius Caesar, Lucius Licinius Pollio, and Lucius Cincius Alimentus, the last of whom had returned a few days before from Sicily. Their orders were to instruct the consul, if he should not be able to come to Rome himself, to name, on Roman soil, a dictator to preside at the elections. If he had already left for Tarentum, it was the Senate's pleasure that the praetor Claudius should move his legions into that part of the country where he could best use them for the protection of the greatest number of allied towns.

In the course of this summer Marcus Valerius crossed from Sicily to Africa with a fleet of 100 ships, landed near Clupea, and caused widespread devastation with hardly any opposition. The raiding-party was hurriedly re-embarked on receipt of a report that a Carthaginian fleet of eighty-three warships was approaching. This fleet was successfully engaged not far from Clupea; eighteen enemy vessels were captured and the remainder driven off. Valerius then returned to Lilybaeum with his prizes and much valuable material taken during the raid on shore.

It was also during this summer that Philip, at their urgent request, went to the help of the Achaeans, whom Machanidas, tyrant of Lacedaemon, was harassing with a war on their borders; the Aetolians, too, had crossed the strait between Naupactus and Patrae (Rhion, as the people in the neighbourhood call it) and ravaged their country. Further, there was a report that Attalus, King of Asia, upon whom the Aetolians at their last council had conferred the highest magistracy of their nation, was about to cross into Europe. 30. It was these reasons which brought Philip down into Greece, and the Aetolians, led by Pyrrhias, who had been appointed to the command for that year in conjunction with the absent Attalus, met him near the town of Lamia. The Aetolians had some of Attalus's troops to reinforce them and also about a thousand men sent by Sulpicius from the Roman fleet. Philip fought two successful battles against Pyrrhias and his forces, on each occasion killing at least a thousand of the enemy; then, as the Aetolians, discouraged by their defeats, shut themselves up within the walls of Lamia, he led his army to Phalara, on the Malian gulf, a place which in the old days was densely populated because of its excellent harbour and well-protected roadsteads and other advantages both maritime and otherwise. Here at Phalara Philip was visited by envoys from Ptolemy, King of Egypt, and from the Athenians, Rhodians, and Chians, with the object of stopping hostilities between him and the Aetolians; Amynander also, King of the Athamanians, was brought in from their neighbours by the Aetolians as an intermediary. In point of fact none of the states thus represented had much at heart the welfare of the Aetolians, who were a more warlike people than Greeks tend in general to be; their real object was to keep Philip and his kingdom out of Greek affairs and thus to avoid a threat to their liberty. The discussion of terms was put off till the Achaean Council met, and a place and date for its meeting were fixed; meanwhile a thirty days' truce was obtained. Philip then left Phalara and went by way of Thessaly and Boeotia to Chalcis in Euboea, as he had learned that Attalus intended to make for that port and he wished to prevent him from landing or entering the harbours. Then, leaving a force behind to deal with Attalus, should he meanwhile make the crossing, he proceeded with a few of his cavalry and light troops to Argos, where the presidency of the Festival of Hera and the Nemean Games (the kings of Macedon claiming Argos as the city of their origin) was conferred upon him by popular vote. The festival over, he went on, immediately after the Games, to Aegium to attend the council of his allies, which had long since been fixed. At the council the termination of the Aetolian war was discussed, the object being to leave no reason either for Attalus or for the Romans to enter Greece; but almost before the end of the truce everything was wrecked by the action of the Aetolians, when they heard that Attalus had come to Aegina and that a Roman fleet was lying at Naupactus.

Summoned to the conference, which was also attended by the legations which had discussed terms of peace at Phalara, the Aetolians began by complaining of certain minor breaches of the agreement during the truce, and went on to declare that there could be no cessation of hostilities unless the Achaeans restored Pylus to the Messenians, and Atintania were given back to the Romans, and the Ardiaei to Scerdilaedus and Pleuratus. Philip was highly indignant that men whom he had defeated in battle should actually presume to offer him terms, and said that even on the former occasion, when he had listened to a plea for peace and had consented to a truce, he had never expected that the Aetolians would keep quiet: on the contrary, his object had been to have all his allies witness the fact that, while he himself wanted peace, the Aetolians wanted war. Thus the conference achieved nothing; Philip dismissed it, leaving a force 4,000 strong to protect the Achaeans and receiving five warships from them. He had already decided, if he could add these to the Carthaginian fleet lately sent to him and to the ships which were on their way from King Prusias in Bithynia, to challenge the Romans at sea in spite of their long-established naval superiority in that area. He himself returned to Argos, as the Nemean Games would shortly be taking place and he wished to grace their celebration by his presence.

31. While he was occupied with the preparations for the Games and indulging, during the days of festivity, in more of a holiday spirit than was possible in war-time, Publius Sulpicius sailed from Naupactus to a point on the coast between Sicyon and Corinth and did widespread damage to an area of country famous for its fertility. The report of the raid roused Philip from the Games, and hurriedly setting out with his mounted troops and ordering his infantry to follow, he attacked and drove back to their ships the Roman soldiers whom he found scattered about the countryside loaded with their spoils and entirely oblivious of any such danger. The Roman squadron returned to Naupactus, by no means pleased with its work; for Philip, on the contrary, the news of a victory, not perhaps important in itself, but over Roman troops, had shed an additional lustre on what remained of the Games. Throughout the holiday there was unbounded rejoicing, still further

increased by the fact that in deference to popular sentiment Philip stopped wearing his diadem and purple and other marks of royalty, and made himself look like everybody else – there is nothing the citizens of a free community like better than that. Indeed, he would by this action have given them a confident hope of their own liberty, if only he had not turned everything to dirt and ugliness by his insufferably libidinous behaviour. He used to walk about the town day and night with one or two companions, visiting the houses of married people, and by lowering himself to the status of an ordinary citizen made himself less conspicuous and therefore freer from restraint, while he employed for himself the liberty which he had shown to others as no better than a shadow merely to satisfy his appetites. Some of his pleasures he did not even pay for, or win by soft words. He used force to gain his criminal ends; and it was at their peril that husbands or fathers disobliged him and by exercising strict control put obstacles in the way of the royal lust. A leading Achaean named Aratus had his wife, Polycratia, stolen from him: she was carried off to Macedonia with the prospect of sharing the royal bed.

Such was the reprehensible conduct of Philip at the Nemean Games. He added a few extra days and then left for Dymae, to expel the Aetolian garrison which had been sent for and received into the town by the Eleans. Cycliadas, who held the chief command, and the Achaeans met the king near Dymae: they hated the Eleans because they would not make common cause with the other Achaeans, and were hostile to the Aetolians because they believed them responsible for the war with Rome. Uniting their forces they left Dymae and crossed the river Larisus which separates its territory from that of Elis. 32. After crossing into enemy territory, they spent the first day devastating the countryside, and on the next moved on the town in battle order. Their cavalry had been sent in advance to ride up to the gates as a provocation to the Aetolians, a people always quick to respond to such a challenge.

Meanwhile Sulpicius had crossed from Naupactus to Cyllene with fifteen ships of war, landed 4,000 men in the dead of night to elude observation, and already entered Elis. Philip and the Achaeans were quite unaware of this, and the shock of discovery was very great when they recognized Roman standards and Roman arms amongst the Aetolians and Eleans. Philip's first thought was to withdraw; but fighting had already started between the Aetolians and the Tralles (an Illyrian people), and when he saw his own troops hard pressed he himself led a cavalry charge against a Roman cohort. His horse was run through with a javelin and he was thrown violently over its head, and this kindled a furious struggle around him, the Romans trying to get at him, while the royal guards strove to protect their master. He too fought with conspicuous gallantry, in spite of the fact that he was now on foot in the midst of mounted men. Soon, however, when things had begun to go against him and many were falling dead or wounded all around, he was picked up by his men and put on another horse, and so made his escape. He took up a new position five miles from Elis, and on the following day marched with his whole force to Pyrgus (as it was called), a near-by fortress belonging to Eleans, as he had been told that a crowd of peasants had been driven by fear of losing their possessions to take refuge in it with their cattle. They were a mere mob and of course unarmed, and the panic inspired by his approach was enough to make them fall into his hands; so he got something, at any rate, to compensate him for the shame of his defeat at Elis. While he was dividing the spoils and the prisoners – there were 4,000 of them and nearly 20,000 head of cattle of all kinds – news came from Macedonia that a certain Aeropus had bribed the officer commanding the garrison in the citadel of Lychnidus and had taken the town; he was also holding some villages belonging to the Dassaretii, and inciting the Dardani to rebellion. In view of this Philip abandoned the war between the Achaeans and Aetolians and set out from Dymae for Demetrias in Thessaly, which he reached in ten days by way of Achaea, Boeotia, and Euboea. He did, however, leave behind him 2,500 troops of all sorts under the command of Menippus and Polyphantas to protect his allies.

33. At Demetrias he was met by news of more serious trouble: the Dardani, pouring into Macedonia, were already in possession of Orestis and had descended into the Argestaean plain. Further, there was a widespread rumour amongst the

wild tribes in those parts that Philip had been killed. The origin of the rumour was that during his fight with the Roman raiders near Sicyon his horse had carried him with some violence against a tree and one horn of his helmet had been broken off by a projecting branch; the fragment had been found by an Aetolian, who took it back to Scerdilaedus, who, in his turn, was familiar with the distinctive marks of the king's helmet.

After Philip had left Achaea, Sulpicius sailed to Aegina, where he joined Attalus. The Achaeans fought a successful action against the Aetolians and Eleans not far from Messene. Attalus and Sulpicius wintered in Aegina.

At the end of this year the consul Crispinus died of his wounds. Before his death he had named Titus Manlius Torquatus as dictator, to preside at the elections and the Games. Some say Crispinus died at Tarentum, others in Campania. There had been no memorable battle; both consuls were dead, and the State was left fatherless. Such a thing had never before happened in war-time.

The dictator Manlius named Gaius Servilius as his master of Horse – he was curule aedile at the time. The Senate at its first meeting instructed the dictator to hold the Great Games which the City praetor Aemilius had celebrated in the consulship of Gaius Flaminius and Gnaeus Servilius, and had vowed as a quinquennial festival. On this occasion the dictator held the Games and also vowed their repetition after another five years. Games, however, were by no means the first thought in men's minds: two consular armies were in close proximity to the enemy, and they were leaderless. Thus the chief, and indeed only, concern of both Senate and people was to elect consuls at the earliest possible moment, and to elect, moreover, men who were good enough soldiers to be proof against Carthaginian wiles. Throughout the war the over-hasty and perfervid temperament of the military commanders had had disastrous consequences, and this year, too, the consuls by their excessive eagerness for action had allowed themselves to be caught in a trap. None the less, men said, the immortal gods in pity for the Roman name had spared the innocent armies, though they had punished the recklessness of their commanders with death.

34. The Senate now began to look round for the best men to

appoint to the consulship. There was one, Gaius Claudius Nero, who was head and shoulders above everyone else, but he needed a colleague. He was, in the Senate's opinion, a man of outstanding ability, but of too quick and fiery a temperament to deal with the present situation, and especially with Hannibal. It was felt that a nature as impulsive as his ought to be tempered by the collaboration of a more cautious and prudent colleague. A possible candidate was Marcus Livius, who a number of years previously had been condemned, after his consulship, by a popular verdict,[1] and had taken the disgrace so hard that he went to live in the country and for years absented himself from the city and the society of his fellows. Some seven or eight years after his condemnation, the consuls Marcellus and Laevinus had induced him to revisit Rome; but he still kept his old clothes and his long hair and beard, and clearly showed both by his dress and his countenance that he had never forgotten his disgrace. The censors Veturius and Licinius made him shave and get rid of his rags, and forced him to attend the Senate and do his duty as a public servant; but even so he confined himself to one word of assent or a silent vote in support of a motion, until a case came up which concerned a relative of his, Marcus Livius Macatus. His relative's reputation was at stake, and this compelled him to rise to his feet and declare his opinion before the House. His voice, heard again after so long an interval, made every senator turn to look at him, and the result was that they were soon saying that here was a man whom the people had undeservedly wronged, and that the country had suffered a great loss in not having made use in so serious a war of the services and counsel of this distinguished citizen. It was pointed out that neither Fabius nor Laevinus could be appointed as Nero's colleague, because it was illegal to have two patrician consuls; there was the same objection to appointing Torquatus, in addition to the fact that he had refused the offer and would continue to do so. So why not give Livius to Nero as his colleague? They would indeed make a notable pair. The idea, first mooted in the Senate, was received without disfavour by the people, and the only man in the country who showed any objection was he to whom the post of honour was offered,

1. See p. 134.

Livius himself. His fellow-citizens, he declared, did not know their own minds: when he was on trial, dressed in mourning, they had shown him no pity; now they were offering him the white toga of a candidate when he did not want it. Honours and ignominy, it seemed, were being heaped on the same head. If they thought him a good man, why had they condemned him for a bad and guilty one? If they had found he was a criminal, why, when his first consulship had been so unjustifiably given him, did they now want to trust him with another? But complaints and arguments of this sort were of no avail; the Senate told him severely to be done with them, and reminded him of Camillus, who, recalled from exile, had saved his country when Rome was occupied by the Gauls. One's country, like an angry parent, must, they said, be mollified by submission and endurance. In the end their united efforts succeeded, and Livius was elected consul as Nero's colleague.

35. Three days later the election for praetors was held, and Lucius Porcius Licinus, Gaius Mamilius, Gaius and Aulus Hostilius Cato were appointed. After the elections and the Games the dictator and his master of Horse laid down their office. Varro was sent to Etruria as pro-praetor to enable Gaius Cato to go to Tarentum and take over the army previously commanded by the consul Crispinus. Lucius Manlius was ordered to Greece, as an emissary, to inform himself of conditions there. The Olympic Festival was to take place that summer and would be attended as usual by vast crowds from all over the country, and Manlius had further instructions to attend it if he safely could, and to encourage any Sicilian refugees who might be there or any Tarentines banished by Hannibal to return home. If they did, they would find that the Roman people was restoring to them everything they had possessed before the war.

As Nero and Livius had not yet actually entered office, the country was without consuls and obviously facing a period of the very greatest peril. Everyone was therefore anxious that the consuls elect should not waste a moment in settling their respective spheres of action, the part of the country that each would control, and the enemy each would have to deal with. Moreover, at the instance of Quintus Fabius Maximus, there was a discussion in the Senate about reconciling their differences. That differences existed between the two men was well known, and on Livius's side the quarrel was all the more bitter and all the harder to bear as he felt that he was despised by his colleague because of his former misfortune. This made him the more implacable of the two: there was no need, he maintained, for a reconciliation; on the contrary, both of them would pay all the more attention to duty if they were afraid that a lapse might give the advantage to an unfriendly colleague. However, the authority of the Senate prevailed; they were induced to bury the hatchet and carry on the government of the country in genuine partnership.

In previous years the consuls had not had their spheres of action geographically divided. But this year they were to operate at opposite ends of the Italian peninsula: the task of facing Hannibal in Bruttium and Lucania was assigned to one, while the other was to operate in Gaul against Hasdrubal, who was reported to be already approaching the Alps. The latter was to choose, as he pleased, either the army in Gaul or the army in Etruria, with the addition of the troops then at Rome; his colleague in the South was to enrol fresh City legions and take over either of the armies commanded by the consuls of the previous year; the proconsul Fulvius was to have whichever army the new consul did not choose, and his command was to run for a year. Gaius Cato, who had been transferred from Etruria to Tarentum, was now transferred to Capua. One legion, commanded last year by Fulvius, was assigned to him.

36. Every day anxiety was growing about Hasdrubal's arrival in Italy. The first news had come from Massilia: envoys reported that he had crossed into Gaul, with a load of gold for hiring mercenaries, and that his coming had roused the natives to a high pitch of excitement. The envoys from Massilia were sent back in company with two representatives from Rome, Sextus Antistius and Marcus Raecius, with instructions to look into things: their report was that they had sent men, with Massilian guides, to collect all the information they could through the agency of such Gallic chieftains as were the guides' friends, and that they were now assured, by the consequent report, that Hasdrubal had already got together an immense

army and intended to cross the Alps next spring. The only thing which prevented him from doing so immediately was the fact that the winter's snow made them impassable.

Publius Aelius Paetus was elected and installed as augur in place of Marcus Marcellus, and Gnaeus Cornelius Dolabella was installed as *rex sacrorum* in succession to Marcus Marcius who had died two years previously. In this same year the five-year lustral period was formally brought to an end by the censors Tuditanus and Cethegus. The census revealed the number of citizens to be 137,108, considerably fewer than before the war. It is on record that for the first time since Hannibal's invasion the Comitium this year was covered over with awnings and the Roman Games were repeated for a second day by the curule aediles Quintus Metellus and Servilius. The Plebeian Games were repeated for two days by the plebeian aediles Mamilius and Marcus Caecilius Metellus, who also presented three statues to the temple of Ceres. In honour of the Games a Banquet for Jupiter was celebrated.

Nero and Livius, the latter for the second time, now entered upon their consulship. Because as consuls designate they had already drawn lots for their provinces, they ordered the praetors to draw for theirs. The City jurisdiction fell to Gaius Cato; he was given control of cases involving foreigners as well, to enable three praetors to be away on service. Aulus Cato obtained Sardinia; Mamilius, Sicily; Porcius, Gaul. The total strength of twenty-five legions was divided as follows: two for each consul; four for Spain; two for each of the three praetors in Sicily, Sardinia, and Gaul respectively; two for Varro in Etruria; two for Fulvius in Bruttium; two for Quintus Claudius in the region of Tarentum and the Sallentini; one for Tubulus at Capua. Orders were issued for the enrolment of two City legions. For the four legions assigned to the consuls military tribunes were elected by the people; the consuls themselves sent tribunes to serve with the rest.

37. Before the consuls left Rome it rained stones at Veii, a portent which occasioned a nine-day period of religious observance. As always happens, the troubles did not stop there: other prodigies were reported. At Minturnae the temple of Jupiter and the Grove of Marica were struck by lightning; the

wall at Atella, and one gate, were also struck. The people of Minturnae added to the horror by telling of a river of blood at the town gate. At Capua a wolf had got in through the gate one night and mauled a sentry. These ominous events were atoned for by the sacrifice of full-grown victims and a day of prayer was decreed by the pontiffs. The nine days of observance were then repeated because stones were seen to fall like rain in the Armilustrum.[1] Consciences were thus quieted, but they were disturbed afresh by news from Frusino of the birth of a baby as big as a child of four, and its size was not the strangest thing about it, for it was also of indeterminate sex, like the baby born at Sinuessa two years before. Soothsayers called in from Etruria pronounced it to be a portent of a repulsive and horrible kind which must be removed from Roman territory and sunk in the sea, away from all contact with the land. It was accordingly put in a box alive, taken off-shore, and thrown overboard. The priests further decreed that twenty-seven virgins should go in procession through Rome, singing a hymn; they were learning the words – composed by the poet Livius Andronicus[2] – in the temple of Jupiter Stator, when the shrine of Queen Juno on the Aventine was struck by lightning. In the opinion of the soothsayers this omen had reference to the married women, and the goddess would have to be propitiated by a gift; so by an edict of the curule aediles all married women living in Rome or within ten miles of it were summoned to the Capitol. These women then chose twenty-five of their number to collect contributions from the dowries of them all, and out of the sum thus raised a golden bowl was made and taken to the Aventine as a gift to Juno. There, after due rites of purification, the women offered sacrifice.

A day was immediately proclaimed by the decemvirs for another sacrifice to the same goddess. The order of the ceremony was as follows: from the temple of Apollo two white cows were led into the city through the Porta Carmentalis; behind them were carried two images, in cypress wood, of

1. The place where the ceremony was held for purification of military arms.

2. *c.* 284–*c.*204 B.C. One of the earliest Roman poets and translator of the Odyssey into Latin.

Queen Juno; then twenty-seven virgins in long robes followed, singing a hymn to Juno. The words of the hymn were no doubt good enough for those rude and uncultivated days, but if I were to quote them now they would sound unpleasing and graceless.[1] The virgins were followed by the decemvirs wearing laurel wreaths and togas with a purple border. The procession passed from the gate by way of the Vicus Jugarius to the forum; there it halted, and the virgins, all taking hold of a rope, moved forward again keeping time with the rhythm of their hymn. From the forum the procession went along the Vicus Tuscus, past the Velabrum and through the cattle-market, and up the Publician hill to the temple of Queen Juno, where the two cows were offered in sacrifice by the decemvirs and the cypress images were taken inside.

38. The gods duly propitiated, the consuls set about raising fresh troops. The levy was carried out with greater care and strictness than anyone could remember in former years, for with the advent of a new enemy, added to the fact that there were fewer men of military age available for service, there was now a double menace to be faced. For this reason they tried to compel even the coast settlements to furnish troops, in spite of the fact that they were supposed to enjoy absolute exemption from military service. When they objected, the consuls fixed a day for each settlement to state before the Senate the grounds on which its claim to exemption was based, and representatives from Ostia, Alsium, Antium, Anxur, Minturnae, Sinuessa, and (from the Adriatic coast) Sena attended the Senate to read the statement of their claims. Except in the case of Antium and Ostia none of the claims was allowed so long as the enemy was on Italian soil; the men of military age from all the others were made to swear that, while the enemy remained in Italy, they would not spend more than thirty nights away from their home-towns.

The whole Senate was convinced that the consuls ought to take the field without a moment's delay. Hasdrubal had to be met as he came down from the Alps to prevent him from raising the Cisalpine Gauls or Etruria, which was already on tiptoe for rebellion; and Hannibal had to be separately engaged, to stop

1. A regrettable decision: they would be of very great interest.

him from leaving Bruttium and joining forces with his brother. But in spite of everything Livius continued to postpone his departure, having little confidence in the armies at his disposal, and aware that his colleague had the choice between two first-rate consular armies and a third which Claudius commanded at Tarentum. He had also brought up the question of recalling the slave-volunteers to the standards. The Senate gave the consuls a completely free hand to supplement their forces from any source they pleased, to choose what troops they wanted from all the armies, and to effect such transfers from one area to another as they believed to be advantageous. All this was done with the greatest harmony between them. The slave-volunteers were attached to the 19th and 20th legions; according to some chroniclers, powerful auxiliaries were sent by Scipio from Spain to join Livius – 8,000 Spanish and Gallic troops, 2,000 Roman legionaries, 1,800 mounted troops, part Numidian, part Spanish. These were brought over by sea by Marcus Lucretius. Some 3,000 archers and slingers were also sent by Gaius Mamilius from Sicily.

39. The anxiety and excitement in Rome were increased by a dispatch from the praetor Porcius in Gaul: Hasdrubal had left his winter quarters and was already on his way across the Alps. Eight thousand Ligurians had been conscripted and armed and would join him in Italy, unless someone were sent in time to keep them occupied with the defence of their own territory. He himself proposed to advance against them, so far as he considered safe with his inadequate force. The effect of this dispatch was to make the consuls complete the levy with all possible speed and leave for their provinces earlier than they had intended, their object being that each of them should contain the enemy in his own area and thus prevent a junction of the two hostile armies. They were greatly assisted in this purpose by an error of Hannibal's, who, though he had expected his brother's arrival in Italy that summer, had never thought, when he remembered his own five months of exhausting struggle to cross first the Rhône, then the Alps, opposed both by hostile tribesmen and the forces of nature, that Hasdrubal would cross over as quickly and easily as in fact he did. In consequence he was slower than he should have been in leaving his winter

quarters. For Hasdrubal on the other hand, everything went more rapidly and expeditiously than he or anyone else had hoped. Not only did the Arverni and, in succession, other Gallic and Alpine tribes allow him to cross their borders, but they actually joined forces with him. Moreover the formerly trackless mountain country through which his route lay had been, in most places, rendered practicable by Hannibal's crossing, in addition to which, as the Alps had by now been opened up by twelve years of constant use, the native tribes along the route had lost some of their wildness and savagery.[1] In former times no one from the outside world had ever set eyes on these people, or they upon a stranger; with the rest of the human race they had no contact whatever. In Hannibal's case they did not know the destination of the Carthaginian army, but supposed that their own strongholds and native crags were the object of its attack, that their cattle would be taken from them and their friends dragged off to slavery. But as time went on stories of the war which for more than eleven years had been desolating Italy brought them to understand that the Alps were not an end but only the means to it, and that two mighty cities at opposite ends of the earth were fighting each other for wealth and dominion.

For these reasons the route over the Alps lay open to Hasdrubal. Nevertheless what he had gained by speed was lost by his delay at Placentia, which he did not directly attack but attempted in vain to starve into surrender. He had thought that to storm a town situated in open country would be an easy matter; moreover the fame of Placentia had led him on, and he felt that its destruction would spread terror amongst the rest. His subsequent siege of it not only held up his own advance but also acted as a check on Hannibal, who on learning that his brother had passed the Alps so much sooner than he expected was on the point of leaving his winter quarters. Now, however, he began to remember how tedious a business it was to besiege a town, and also how he himself had made a fruitless attempt upon that same town of Placentia on the way back from his victory at the Trebia.

40. The departure of the consuls from Rome in opposite

1. More probably, Hasdrubal came by a different and easier route.

directions for two simultaneous campaigns brought with it a double anxiety. Men could not but remember the disasters which Hannibal's first coming had brought upon Italy, and at the same time they were tormented by anxiety. What gods could look with such favour upon Rome and her empire as to allow success simultaneously in both theatres of the war? So far, they had managed to balance loss with gain, and had thus postponed a decision for so long. In Italy Roman hopes had come near to ruin at Trasimene and Cannae, but victories in Spain had raised them up again; later, when in Spain two outstanding generals had been killed and defeat after defeat had partially destroyed two armies, many successful campaigns in Italy and Sicily had buttressed the tottering fabric of the State; mere distance, moreover, since one of the campaigns was being fought almost at the ends of the earth, had given them a breathing-space. But now they had two wars on their hands actually in Italy, two famous military leaders stood one on each side of Rome, and the whole massive weight of the Carthaginian menace was concentrated upon one single point. Whichever of the enemy commanders won the first victory would within a few days join forces with his colleague. A further cause of alarm was the gloom cast over the previous year by the death of both consuls.

So when Nero and Livius parted, each for the scene of his coming activity, their fellow-citizens accompanied them along their way, but with anxious hearts. There is a story that Livius, when he left Rome, was still burning with resentment, and when Quintus Fabius advised him not to be in a hurry to engage before he had learned the quality of his enemy, he replied that he would fight the instant he saw them coming. 'And what,' asked Fabius, 'are your reasons for such precipitancy?' 'Either,' answered Livius, 'I shall win great glory by victory, or pleasure by the defeat of my fellow-citizens – a pleasure which, if not to my credit, I have at least earned.'

Before the consul Nero arrived in his province, Hannibal suffered a reverse. He was taking his men, in no proper or regular order, along the borders of Tarentine territory into the country of the Sallentini, when Tubulus with some cohorts marching light attacked him and caused appalling confusion, killing some 4,000 men and capturing nine standards. Quintus Claudius, who was holding various posts in the Sallentine area, had moved from winter quarters on hearing of the enemy's approach, and so Hannibal, to avoid a conflict with two hostile armies simultaneously, left the neighbourhood of Tarentum under cover of darkness and withdrew into Bruttium. Quintus Claudius then made for the Sallentini, and Tubulus, marching towards Capua, met Nero at Venusia. From the two forces 40,000 infantry and 2,500 cavalry were chosen for Nero to use against Hannibal; the rest Tubulus was ordered to take to Capua and hand over to the proconsul Fulvius.

41. Hannibal now brought together all the troops which he had had either in his winter quarters or on garrison duty in Bruttium, and proceeded to Grumentum in Lucania, hoping to recover the towns which fear had driven to seek Roman protection. Nero followed him from Venusia, carefully reconnoitring his route, and took up a position a mile and a half from the enemy. The defences of the Carthaginian camp seemed almost to touch the walls of Grumentum – only 500 yards separated the two. Between Nero's camp and Hannibal's the ground was level and open; on the Carthaginian left and the Roman right rose bare hills which each side could safely ignore as they had neither trees nor anything else which could provide cover for troops. From time to time a few minor skirmishes, hardly worth mentioning, took place on the open area between the camps, and it was evident that Nero's sole object was to prevent his enemy from getting away, while Hannibal, on the contrary, was so anxious to do so that again and again he brought down his entire force into battle-line. Realizing his intention, Nero, taking a leaf from his enemy's book, prepared a trap: on those open and treeless hills an ambush was not likely to be suspected, so he ordered five cohorts, supported by five maniples, to cross the crest during the night and take up a position on the reverse slopes; the military tribune Asellus and the Prefect of Allies Publius Claudius, in command of the party, were given the exact time when they were to leave their ambush and attack. Nero himself at dawn led out his whole force, mounted and unmounted, into line. A little later Hannibal too gave the order for action and the shouts of his men in camp

broke out as they ran to arm themselves; horse and foot in eager rivalry came pouring through the camp gates, and in loose order made for the enemy with all the speed they could muster. Seeing their straggling and disorderly advance, Nero ordered Aurunculeius, commanding the third legion, to send his cavalry at once into action. 'Let them charge,' he said, 'with the utmost vigour, as a mob like that, scattered all over the place more like grazing cattle than an army, could be overwhelmed and cut to pieces before it has time to form into order of battle.'

42. Hannibal had not yet left camp when he was surprised by the noise of fighting and hurriedly brought his main force into action. Already those first out of the camp had been flung into confusion by the Roman cavalry charge, and the Roman first legion and right *ala* were moving up into the fight. Hannibal's men engaged at haphazard, going for whoever came in their way, horse or foot; supports came up, more and more men pressed forward to join the scrimmage, the fighting spread; and Hannibal, engaged though his men were in a confused and losing battle, would have brought them into some sort of order – a difficult task, in the circumstances, for any but a veteran commander with an experienced army – had not the battle-cry of the Roman cohorts and maniples charging down from the hills rung out at that moment in their rear. The threat of being cut off from their camp broke the spirit of the Carthaginian soldiers; everywhere they turned and ran. If their camp had not been so near, their losses would have been much heavier than they were, for the Roman cavalry were hard on their heels, and on their flanks were the Roman cohorts who had charged over open and easy ground down the slope of the hills. Even as it was, their losses were more than 8,000 men killed and 700 taken prisoner; nine standards fell into Roman hands and of the elephants – in the sort of disorderly free-for-all which the battle had been there was no use for them whatever – four were killed and two captured. The cost of victory to the Romans was about 500 men, citizens, and allies.

Next day Hannibal made no move; Nero brought his men from camp and formed them for battle, but seeing that no opposition was offered he gave orders for the enemy dead to be stripped of their arms and the bodies of his own men to be collected and buried. On several successive days after that he moved close up to the gates of the Carthaginian camp, so close that he seemed almost to be breaking in, until Hannibal one night during the third watch slipped away and made for Apulia, leaving fires burning and a lot of tents in the part of his camp nearest the Roman lines, and a few Numidians with orders to show themselves on the rampart and at the gates. At dawn next morning the Romans moved up again to the rampart and the Numidians let themselves be seen for a while, as ordered; the deception worked, and soon after they galloped away to overtake the retreating Carthaginian column. The camp was now silent; even the few men who at dawn had been walking about in it were nowhere to be seen, so Nero sent two horsemen to enter it and reconnoitre. Then, having received the report that all was safe, he ordered his troops to move in. Giving them time only to scatter for plunder, he then sounded the retreat and was back in his own camp well before dark. Next day he marched at dawn. Making all possible speed in pursuit of Hannibal, where report or the army's tracks indicated the route, he overtook him near Venusia. There was another running fight in which over 2,000 Carthaginians were killed; after which Hannibal, to avoid another conflict, made for Metapontum by night marches across the mountains. Hanno, who commanded the garrison there, was then sent with a small party into Bruttium to raise fresh troops, and his force was taken over by Hannibal, who returned on his tracks to Venusia, and thence proceeded to Canusium. Throughout these movements Nero had maintained a close pursuit, and when he was starting for Metapontum he had sent for Quintus Fulvius to take over in Lucania so as not to leave that district without troops to protect it.

43. Meanwhile Hasdrubal, after abandoning the siege of Placentia, had sent four Gallic and two Numidian horsemen with a letter to Hannibal. These men had ridden through enemy-occupied country along almost the entire length of Italy, but while they were following Hannibal on his retreat to Metapontum they mistook the route and found themselves at Tarentum, where they were picked up by a Roman foraging party and brought to the pro-praetor Quintus Claudius. On

first being questioned they tried to put him off by vague answers, but the threat of torture soon compelled them to confess the truth and they admitted that they were carrying a letter to Hannibal from Hasdrubal. Together with the letter, its seal unbroken, they were handed over to the military tribune Lucius Verginius to be taken to Nero with two troops of Samnite cavalry as an escort. The letter was read by an interpreter, the prisoners were questioned, and Nero was at once convinced that the situation no longer justified the conventional arrangement whereby each consul should fight only within his prescribed area, using only his own troops against an enemy assigned to him by order of the Senate. On the contrary, he felt that this was the moment for a new, bold, and unprecedented stroke, which at first sight might alarm Rome no less than it alarmed the enemy, but would, if it succeeded, turn the worst terrors of his country into rejoicing. He sent Hasdrubal's letter to the Senate in Rome, himself writing at the same time to inform the senators of his intentions; he advised them, in view of the fact that Hasdrubal had informed his brother that he would meet him in Umbria, to transfer a legion from Capua to Rome, raise fresh troops in Rome itself, and send the City army to face the enemy at Narnia. He sent messengers along the line of his proposed march through the territories of Larinum, the Marrucini, Frentani, and Praetutii, with instructions to collect provisions from farms and towns and have them ready on the road for the use of his troops, and to bring horses and mules for additional transport should any of his men fall out from fatigue. From his whole force, Roman and allied, he selected the best men, 6,000 foot and 1,000 horse, announced that his intention was to seize the nearest Lucanian town and its Carthaginian garrison, and gave orders for all to be ready to march. He started south during the night, and then turned north in the direction of Picenum.[1]

Nero had now started on his long forced march to join his colleague. His second-in-command, Quintus Catius, was left behind in command at Canusium. 44. In Rome there was as great alarm and confusion as four years before when Hannibal

1. The distance was nearly 250 miles, and was covered in seven days. See p. 508.

had encamped close outside the walls and gates. Nobody knew whether to praise or blame Nero's bold decision: it would be judged by the event, than which nothing can be more unjust. The more obvious facts were that a camp in proximity to the enemy, and that enemy Hannibal himself, had been left without its general and with an army robbed of its finest troops, and that the consul, having declared his objective to be Lucania, was in fact making for Picenum and Gaul, his camp at Canusium being left with no better protection than the enemy's ignorance that a part of the army together with its commander was no longer there. What would happen if the truth were known and Hannibal decided either to pursue Nero and his paltry 6,000 with his whole force, or to attack the abandoned camp – an easy prey, having no proper troops to defend it, no regular command? Former defeats, the loss last year of both consuls, were alarming enough; and all those disasters had occurred when there was only one enemy army, and one enemy commander in Italy. Now there were two simultaneous wars, two vast armies, almost one might say two Hannibals. For was not Hasdrubal also Hamilcar's son, as active a leader as his brother, trained by years of warfare in Spain against Roman troops, and famous for a double victory in the destruction of two armies and the death of two of Rome's finest generals? In the rapidity of his march from Spain and success in calling the Gallic tribes to arms, he had much more even than Hannibal to boast of; for he had gathered an army where Hannibal had lost one, or most of one, through the miseries of hunger and cold. In addition to all this, those who knew the history of the Spanish campaigns pointed out that when he met Nero it would not be for the first time: he would meet a man whom once, when caught in an awkward spot, he had made an utter fool of, putting him off like a child by pretending to draw up terms of peace.[1] Fear, in short, looks always on the darker side, and everyone believed the enemy's strength to be greater, and their own less, than in fact they were.

45. When Nero had put a sufficient distance between himself and his enemy to be able without risk to reveal his intentions, he briefly addressed his men. 'No commander,' he said, 'has

1. See p. 377.

ever adopted a plan apparently more reckless, but actually more sure of success, than this of mine. I am leading you to certain victory. My colleague Livius did not leave for his field of action until forces sufficient to satisfy him had been granted him by the Senate, forces greater and better equipped than he would have needed against Hannibal himself. Our task now is to add a weight to the scale, never mind how small, to tip it in our favour. I shall see to it that the enemy gets no news of our approach; but once he knows, when the time of action has come, that another consul and another army have arrived, that knowledge will make our victory sure. Even a whispered word may settle a war – it doesn't take much to push a man towards hope or fear. It is we who shall reap the harvest of glory if this enterprise succeeds – for everyone forgets the water in the bucket and imagines it is the last drop that makes it overflow. You can see for yourselves how we are being acclaimed from the crowds of admiring faces along the road as we march by.'

Nero did not exaggerate the truth: every road they traversed was lined with men and women who had come pouring from the farms; vows and prayers and praises met them from every side. They were hailed as their country's defenders, as champions of the City and imperial power of Rome; men cried out as they passed that the safety and freedom of themselves and their children depended upon their swords; they prayed all the gods and goddesses to grant them fair fortune on the march, a successful fight, and a speedy victory; what they had vowed on their heroes' behalf, that they prayed to be obliged to pay, if only a few days hence they might come to meet them in the exultation of their victory with hearts as joyous as they were anxious now. Then came invitations, offers, importunate requests to the troops to take what they needed for themselves or their animals, each man competing with the rest to be the giver. With the utmost generosity everything was heaped upon them. As for the soldiers, they showed the greatest possible restraint, taking nothing beyond their needs; there was no loitering – they ate where the column halted, without leaving ranks or standards; they marched night and day, resting hardly long enough for their physical needs.

Nero had sent riders in advance to his colleague Livius to tell him of his approach and to ask if he would prefer his actual arrival to be open or secret, by daylight or in darkness, and whether he was to join his camp or encamp separately. Livius thought it best that Nero and his men should enter his camp unobserved, under cover of darkness.

46. Livius had sent round an order that Nero's troops were to be quartered in tents according to their rank, each with their opposite numbers, officer with officer, centurion with centurion, private with private, and so on. It would be better, he thought, not to enlarge the camp, for if he did, Hasdrubal might guess that Nero had joined him; and as to lack of space and overcrowding, that was to prove less of a problem than it might have done, because Nero's men had brought with them almost nothing except their weapons. His numbers had, indeed, been increased during his march by volunteers; old soldiers who had served their time offered to join him; young men eagerly gave in their names, and, if they were well set up, physically sound, and looked fit for service, were enrolled.

Livius's camp was at Sena, and Hasdrubal's was only about five hundred yards away. Nero, now rapidly approaching, came to a halt under cover of the hills, to wait for dark; then his men marched silently in. They were given a joyous and generous welcome and taken to their tents, each by his opposite number of equivalent rank. Next day a council of war was held, which the praetor Porcius Licinus also attended. Licinus's camp adjoined Livius's, and before Hasdrubal's arrival he had used every manoeuvre known to warfare in the attempt to hold him up, keeping to high ground, blocking narrow passes to stop his getting through, and harassing his column by attacks on flank or rear. When the situation was discussed, many were opposed to immediate action: the long march and lack of sleep had told heavily on Nero's men; they needed rest, and Nero himself ought to have a few days to get acquainted with the enemy. Nero, however, was against any delay; with the utmost urgency he besought his colleagues not to render the bold step he had taken nugatory – speed, and speed alone, had made his move sure of success; delay now would turn it into a mere reckless adventure. He pointed out that it was only through ignorance, which would all too soon be dispelled, that Hannibal was for the moment inactive and was not attacking the camp at Canusium which was left without its commander, and had not started in pursuit of him. Before he moved they could destroy Hasdrubal's army and return to Apulia. To delay action – to give the enemy time – was to betray the camp at Canusium to Hannibal and to open the road to Gaul so that he could join Hasdrubal at his leisure whenever he pleased. No: the signal for battle must be given immediately; they must take advantage of the fact that both their opponents were unaware of the real situation, that Hannibal still did not know that the army opposed to him had been diminished, or Hasdrubal that he was faced with stronger and more numerous forces than before.

That decided it. The council was dismissed, orders for action were given, and the army moved out immediately and formed into line.

47. Hasdrubal's army was already drawn up in front of his camp. Fighting might have begun sooner but for the fact that Hasdrubal, riding forward with a small cavalry escort, noticed some old shields which he had not seen before in the enemy's ranks, and some horses which looked unusually stringy. Their numbers, too, seemed larger than usual. This led him to suspect the truth, so he hurriedly had the retreat sounded and sent a party of men to the river where Roman troops were watering, on the chance of taking some prisoners and seeing whether any of them had a specially weather-beaten look such as might be expected after their recent march. At the same time he sent another party round the camp, at a safe distance, to see if the rampart had been anywhere extended and to listen for the trumpet-call, whether it was sounded once or twice. The information he wanted was brought back and the fact that the camps had not been enlarged misled him: there were still two of them, as before Nero's arrival, one commanded by Livius, one by Licinus. In neither had the fortifications been extended to give room for additional quarters. The only thing which worried him, experienced general as he was and familiar with Roman practice in the field, was the report that the trumpet had sounded once only in the praetor's camp, but twice in the consul's. This undoubtedly meant that there were two consuls present, and

the question how the second had got away from Hannibal tortured him with anxiety. Not for a moment did he guess the truth, that Hannibal was the victim of such an enormous deception that he did not know the whereabouts of the army and its general with whom he had been in such close contact. It looked very much as if he must have been deterred by a serious setback and had not dared to pursue. If this were so, then all was lost, and he, Hasdrubal, had come too late: the Romans must have triumphed in Italy just as they had triumphed in Spain. It had also occurred to him that his letter to Hannibal might have been intercepted and that Nero in consequence had strained every nerve to take him by surprise. Under the weight of these anxieties he had the camp fires extinguished and at the first watch ordered his men to pack their gear in silence. Then the army got on the move; but in the hurry and confusion of the night march the guides were not properly watched and one of them ran off and hid (he had already picked his hiding-place) while the other escaped across the Metaurus by a ford he was familiar with. Left without guides the column went astray from the track; many men who were heavy from lack of sleep flung themselves on the ground anywhere, and only a few remained with the standards. Hasdrubal gave orders to follow the river bank till it was light enough to see the way; little progress was made, the twists and turns of the tortuous river bringing them continually back upon their tracks; so he called a halt, intending to cross as soon as daylight revealed a suitable place. But the farther up-river he went the higher became the banks, and he was unable to find a ford. The day was wasted, and the enemy was given time to overtake him.

48. Nero with the cavalry contingent was the first to appear; then, hard on his heels, came Licinus with the light troops. They at once began to harass Hasdrubal's weary column with rapid multiple attacks on various points. The Carthaginian commander had already abandoned his march, or rather his attempt to escape, and was hoping to be able to lay out a fortified camp on high ground above the river bank, when Livius arrived with the heavy infantry, not in marching order but formed and equipped for instant action. All the Roman forces were now united and the battle-line drawn up: on the right was

Nero, on the left Livius; the command of the centre was entrusted to the praetor Licinus.

Hasdrubal, seeing that he must fight, broke off the work on his fortified camp and made his dispositions. In the van, in front of the standards, he stationed his elephants; on the left wing, flanking them and facing Nero, he posted his Gallic contingent – not so much because he trusted them as because he thought the Romans were afraid of them. He himself took the right with his Spaniards, veteran soldiers in whom he felt more confidence than in any others. The Ligurians were posted in the centre behind the elephants. These dispositions gave his line more depth than breadth; the flank of the Gallic contingent was protected by a spur of the hills; the Spaniards on the right faced the Roman left, and the whole right wing of the Roman line, prevented as it was by the spur of high ground from making either a frontal or a flank attack, was left, for the time being, idle.

Between Livius and Hasdrubal there now began a violent and bloody conflict. There, in that sector, were the two commanders-in-chief, the greater part of the Roman foot and Roman horse; there were the veteran Spaniards, wise in the ways of Roman warfare, and the tough fighters of Liguria. To that sector, too, came the elephants, which already with their first charge had made havoc in the van and had now forced the standards back; but soon as the din increased and the fighting grew hotter, the brutes got out of control, charging this way and that like rudderless ships between the two lines as if they did not know to whom they belonged. 'Men,' cried Nero, 'for what purpose have we marched so fast and so far?' and tried to press forward up the hill in front of him, but in vain. Then, seeing it was impossible to get through to the enemy in that direction, he detached several cohorts from the right wing (where he knew they would be able to take no active part in the fighting), led them round behind the Roman line, and charged the Carthaginian right wing before they, or even the Roman troops themselves, were aware that the movement had been made. So quickly was it done that the Romans were round in the Carthaginian rear almost as soon as they had appeared on the flank. Hasdrubal's Spaniards and Ligurians were now encircled, and suffering terribly in front, flank, and rear; even the Gauls on the left were beginning to fall, though in that sector there was less actual fighting than elsewhere; for many of the Gauls had deserted during the night and wandered off to find a comfortable spot to sleep in, while those who remained at their posts were so worn out with marching and lack of sleep that they could hardly bear the weight of their equipment. Gauls, to be sure, always lack stamina. It was now midday, and the poor fellows, gasping with thirst and heat, were killed or captured by the hundred.

49. More of the elephants were killed by their own riders than by the enemy. The riders used to carry a mallet and a carpenter's chisel and when one of the creatures began to run amuck and attack its own people, the keeper would put the chisel between its ears at the junction between head and neck and drive it in with a heavy blow. It was the quickest way that had been found to kill an animal of such size once it was out of control; and it was Hasdrubal who first introduced it, Hasdrubal whose fame rests upon many exploits but more than all upon his conduct in this last battle. It was he who kept his men going with words of encouragement, sharing their perils; he who rekindled the courage of the weary and faint-hearted, cursing their slackness or entreating them to rally; he who called back the fugitives to the colours and again and again forced them to fight on. When at last no doubt remained that the day was lost, he refused to survive the great army which had followed his fame, and setting spurs to his horse galloped straight into the midst of a Roman cohort. There, still fighting, he found a death worthy of his father Hamilcar and his brother Hannibal.

Never in the course of the war had so many of the enemy been killed in a single action. By the destruction of an army and the death of its general Cannae was avenged. The Carthaginian dead amounted to 57,000, the prisoners to 5,400;[1] the captured material was very great, especially the silver and gold; 4,000 Romans who had been prisoners in enemy hands were also recovered. Such were the gains to offset the losses in this battle, for the victory was by no means bloodless. About 8,000 men, Romans and allies, were killed, and even the victors were

1. Polybius (XI: 3: 3) puts their losses at 10,000 killed, 2,000 captured.

too sick of bloodshed and slaughter to strike the final stroke; for when on the next day Livius was told that the Cisalpine Gauls and Ligurians who had either not been in the fight or had escaped the carnage were moving off together without guides or standards, a rabble with no officer to control them, and could be wiped out to a man by a single troop of cavalry, he replied: 'No! Let there be some survivors. They can spread the news of our valour and of the enemy's defeat.'

50. On the night after the battle Nero started back for Apulia. He returned even more quickly than he had come, and in less than six days he reached his camp, close to Hannibal's lines. No messenger had preceded him, so there were fewer people along the road to give him greeting, but all who saw him were nearly mad with joy. As for the state of feeling in Rome, it is impossible adequately to describe what it was like while men were still waiting to hear the result of the battle, and then when the news of victory came. Once it was known that Nero had begun his march, never on any day from sunrise to sunset did a single senator leave the Senate-house and the City officials, or the people leave the forum. The women of Rome, helpless as they were for any practical purpose, turned themselves to passionate prayer, wandering from shrine to shrine and giving the gods no rest from their vows and supplications. In the midst of the suspense and anxiety the first news was a rumour that two horsemen of Narnia, who had taken part in the battle, had reached the camp at the gateway to Umbria[1] with a report that the Carthaginians had been cut to pieces. Such news at first seemed hardly more than words to incredulous ears – it was too great, too wonderful, to be grasped or believed. Moreover, as the battle was said to have taken place only two days previously, the very speed with which the news had come made it the harder to trust. Then came a letter from Lucius Manlius Acidinus, written from the camp, about the arrival of the horsemen of Narnia; the letter, taken through the forum to the praetor's tribunal, brought the senators out of the Senate-house, and caused something like a riot in the streets. The messenger could not move for the crowds which struggled and fought their way to the doors of the House, and was almost torn

1. The pass of Furli.

to pieces by people trying to question him and shouting that the letter should be read from the rostra before it was read in the Senate. Finally the magistrates got the people under control, and the joy, the overwhelming joy, could be shared amongst them. The letter was read first in the Senate, then at a mass meeting of the people. Some took it as an assurance that all was well, others, less sanguine, refused to believe it until they had heard the news from the lips of the official envoys or from the consuls' own dispatch.

51. When word came that the envoys were actually on the way, then indeed there was no holding the crowds; old and young flocked to meet them, impatient to see their faces and to drink in the joyful tidings. There was a continuous line of people as far as the Mulvian bridge. The envoys (they were Lucius Veturius Philo, Publius Licinius Varus, and Quintus Caecilius Metellus) were mobbed by high and low as they made their way into the forum; they, or their escort, were pressed with questions about what had happened, and whenever a man heard the glad news – the enemy's army destroyed, its general killed, the Roman legions intact, both consuls safe – he hastened to pass it on to others and so share his delight with them. With difficulty the envoys pushed through to the Senate-house, and it was still harder to disperse the crowd and keep them from mingling with the senators; but it was done, and the dispatch was read. Then they were taken to the assembly, where Lucius Veturius Philo read the dispatch again, and added a fuller and clearer account of his own, which was received with unanimous enthusiasm, the whole assembly finally breaking into uncontrolled and uncontrollable shouts of joy. There was a rush to the temples to render thanks to the gods, and to homes, to share the great news with wives and children. The Senate decreed three days of public thanksgiving to mark the achievement of the consuls Livius and Nero, the destruction, with small loss to themselves, of the enemy legions and the death of the Carthaginian commander. The praetor Hostilius proclaimed the ceremony before an assembly of the people, and it was observed by both men and women. Throughout the three days all temples were equally crowded; married women in their best clothes, accompanied by their children, thanked the gods with

hearts as carefree as if the war were already won. In business, too, the whole attitude of the state was changed by the victory: men ventured again, as if it were peacetime, to carry on commercial affairs, to buy and sell, lend money, and pay off debts.

Nero on his return to Canusium had Hasdrubal's head, which he had carefully preserved during his march, flung on the ground in front of Hannibal's outposts; he also ordered his African prisoners to be paraded in their chains, and had two of them released and sent to Hannibal to tell him all that had happened. The story is that Hannibal under the double blow of so great a public and personal distress exclaimed: 'Now, at last, I see the destiny of Carthage plain!' He moved his camp, intending to concentrate in Bruttium, in the farthest corner of Italy, all the forces he could not protect while they were still dispersed; and he transferred to Bruttian territory the entire population of Metapontum, together with all Lucanians who were subject to him.

# BOOK XXVIII

1. Though Hasdrubal's crossing of the Alps had relieved the pressure in Spain as much as it had increased it in Italy, it was not long before fresh hostilities in Spain broke out on as large a scale as before. At this period Spain was divided between the rival powers as follows: Hasdrubal son of Gisgo had withdrawn to Gades and the western Ocean, while the Mediterranean coast and nearly all the eastern part of the country were controlled by Scipio and under Roman rule. A new commander, Hanno, had crossed from Africa with fresh troops to succeed Hasdrubal Barca, and after joining Mago had lost no time in arming large numbers of men in Celtiberia, which lies between the Atlantic and the Mediterranean. Against him Scipio sent Marcus Silanus with a force of not more than 10,000 foot and 500 horse. Silanus marched with the greatest possible speed; and in spite of being frequently held up by rough going and the narrow passes between wooded hills which are typical of Spain, he outstripped even the rumour of his approach, not to mention any definite report of it, and reached the enemy with the assistance of Celtiberian deserters who acted as his guides. He learned from the guides, when he was about ten miles from the enemy position, that it consisted of two camps, one on each side of the road he was using – the raw Celtiberian troops, over 9,000 strong, on the left; and the Carthaginians on the right. The Carthaginian camp was properly defended by outposts, sentries and all the normal military dispositions, unlike that of the Celtiberians, where everything was casual and all precautions were neglected in the usual manner of barbarians and raw recruits, who were less apprehensive than they would have been in a strange country.

As the latter position was to be Silanus's first objective, he kept as far to the left as possible, to avoid being seen during his approach by any of the Carthaginian outposts. Scouts had been sent ahead, and he followed with the main body of his troops, marching fast. 2. The ground was much broken, and as hills grown over with scrub also provided good cover he got within three miles of his objective without being seen. There, well concealed in a deep valley, he called a halt, and his men took a meal, during which his scouts came back with a report confirming what the guides had told him. Piling their baggage and taking up their arms, the Romans then advanced in battle order, ready to engage. When they were a mile off, the enemy saw them, and at once there were signs of activity; Mago too, at the first sounds of the coming battle, left his camp and rode up at the gallop. In the Celtiberian army there were 4,000 foot equipped with long shields and 200 horse, in numbers a full legion, and the best of his troops; these he posted in the front line, with the light troops as reserves. In this order Mago marched them out of camp, and they were scarcely clear of the rampart when the Romans discharged their javelins. The Spaniards crouched to meet the hail of missiles, then rose to their feet to reply; the Romans received the volley, as their custom is, on their serried shields, and a hand to hand struggle began, Roman swords coming into action. The Celtiberians normally fight by a series of rapid skirmishing attacks, but their speed of movement was rendered useless by the rough and broken ground, a condition which was not unfavourable to the Romans, who are trained to stand-up fighting, though it is true that in this case lack of room and patches of scrub broke the continuity of their ranks so that they were forced to engage singly or in pairs, like gladiators. The enemy, used to rapid movement, might have had chains on their legs: unable to run, they were butchered where they stood. The shield-men were nearly all killed, and soon the light troops and Carthaginians who had come to their help from the other camp were yielding to pressure and suffering heavy casualties. Right at the beginning of the battle Mago made his escape with all the mounted troops and not more than 2,000 infantry; Hanno, the other commander, and the men who had arrived last upon the scene, when the day was almost lost, were taken prisoner. Nearly all the cavalry and such old soldiers as were serving with the infantry followed Mago in his flight and nine days later reached Hasdrubal son of Gisgo near Gades. The Celtiberian recruits scattered in the neighbouring woods and thence made their way to their various homes.

The victory was a timely one. It was not, indeed, decisive, but it checked the build-up of resources for further campaigns such as would certainly have taken place if the Carthaginians had been permitted to persuade other tribes in addition to the Celtiberians to take up arms. Scipio warmly congratulated Silanus on his success, and, confident that rapid action could now bring the war to an end, marched against Hasdrubal, far away in the west, for the final stroke. Hasdrubal had set up his camp in Baetica, to ensure the loyalty of the tribes under his control; none the less on Scipio's approach he got on the move immediately, and with a rapidity which suggested flight withdrew towards Gades on the Atlantic coast. He did not, however, actually cross the bay to Gades; instead, believing that so long as he kept his army together he would be the object of attack, he divided it piecemeal amongst the southern communities, which the various sections could thus help to protect, while at the same time enjoying the comparative safety of walled towns.

3. Aware of this new situation Scipio turned back, for he knew that to attack the towns one by one would be a long task, even if not a difficult one. But not wishing to leave this whole area in enemy hands, he sent his brother Lucius Scipio with 10,000 foot and 1,000 horse to attack Orongis (as the natives call it), the wealthiest town in that part of the country. It lies in the territory of the Maesesses, a branch of the Bastetani; its land is productive, and silver is mined by the inhabitants. Hasdrubal had used it as a base for raids against the tribes of the interior. Lucius took up a position close by and before beginning the work of circumvallation sent a party of men to the town gates to get into talk with the inhabitants and try to persuade them that Roman friendship would be a pleasanter thing to experience than Roman strength. The response was not a friendly one, so Lucius ringed the town with a fosse and double earthwork and divided his force into three sections, so that two could always be off duty while the third carried on offensive operations. At the first assault by the section on duty there was a violent and indecisive struggle; the hail of missiles made it no easy task to come near the walls or bring ladders into position

and those who succeeded in doing so were constantly pushed off them by specially constructed forked poles, or caught by grappling hooks lowered from above so that they were in danger of being lifted off their feet and dragged up on to the wall. It was clear to Scipio that his men were too few to get the upper hand, while the enemy had the additional advantage of their strong position on the walls; so he withdrew the assault-party and sent the other two divisions of his army simultaneously to relieve it. This move so greatly alarmed the defenders, upon whom the fighting had already begun to tell, that the townspeople incontinently abandoned the defence of the walls, and the Carthaginian garrison, thinking the town might have been betrayed, left their stations and concentrated in a single body.

A new fear now presented itself to the men of the town: this was that if the Romans forced an entry they would butcher indiscriminately everyone they met, Spaniard and Carthaginian alike. Accordingly they flung open the gate and hundreds of them rushed out through it, keeping their shields in front of them as a protection against missiles and at the same time holding up their right hands to show that they were not carrying swords. Possibly the Romans were too far off to see precisely what their intention was, or they may, perhaps, have suspected treachery; but for one reason or another they attacked, and the unfortunate natives who were hoping for their protection were cut down just as if they were offering battle. The Roman troops then marched in through the open gate. Meanwhile in others parts of the town axes and mattocks were at work battering in and hacking down gates, and Roman cavalrymen, as soon as they could get through, were galloping, according to orders, to occupy the forum. In the forum the cavalry had the additional support of a company of veteran *triarii*, while the legionaries spread through the rest of the town. There was no looting, and no one was killed who did not carry arms. All the Carthaginians were put under guard together with some 300 of the townspeople who had closed the gates; the others had their property restored and were allowed to remain in possession. The enemy lost in the course of the action about 2,000 men, the Romans not more than ninety.

4. The men responsible for this success were naturally delighted, as were the commander-in-chief and the rest of the army. The victorious troops made a fine sight as they arrived at headquarters driving before them their innumerable prisoners. Scipio congratulated his brother in the most generous terms, putting the capture of Orongis on a level with his own capture of New Carthage. Then, as winter was approaching, and it was not feasible to attack Gades or follow up Hasdrubal's widely dispersed forces, he withdrew into Hither Spain. The legions were dismissed to winter quarters; Lucius was sent to Rome with the Carthaginian general Hanno and the other prisoners of noble rank, and Scipio himself retired to Tarraco.

In the course of this year a Roman fleet commanded by the proconsul Laevinus crossed to Africa from Sicily and caused widespread damage by raids in the neighbourhood of Utica and Carthage. Valuable property was carried off from under the very walls of Utica and along the boundaries of Carthaginian territory. On the return voyage the fleet fell in with a Carthaginian squadron of seventy ships of war; seventeen of them were captured, four sunk; the rest of the squadron though roughly handled made its escape. Victorious on land and sea, Laevinus returned to Lilybaeum with a fine cargo of captured material of all kinds. As a result of the naval victory the sea was safe, and large quantities of grain could be shipped to Rome.

5. At the beginning of the summer in which these events occurred the proconsul Sulpicius and King Attalus, who, as I mentioned above, had wintered in Aegina, combined their fleets and sailed to Lemnos. The Roman contingent consisted of twenty-five quinqueremes, the king's of thirty-five. Philip himself, to be ready to meet any threat either by land or sea, came down to the coast at Demetrias and appointed a day for the army to assemble at Larisa. The report of his coming brought to Demetrias delegations from Philip's allies all over the country, with requests for aid against the dangers which were threatening their respective communities either by land or sea. The Aetolians, they said, had taken heart from their alliance with Rome, especially after Attalus's coming, and were raiding their neighbours' territory; not only had the Acarnanians and

Boeotians and the inhabitants of Euboea great cause for alarm, but the Achaeans too, for these in addition to having the Aetolian war on their hands were under a grave threat from Machanidas, the tyrant of the Lacedaemonians, who had taken up a position near the Argive frontier. Even from Macedon reports were hardly of a peaceful nature: Scerdilaedus and Pleuratus were up in arms; Thrace was restless, and the Maedi in particular were likely to invade Macedonia if Philip were kept employed by a distant campaign. The Boeotians moreover and the peoples of the interior declared that the Aetolians had closed the narrow pass of Thermopylae with a ditch and earthwork to prevent Philip's passing through to bring assistance to his allies.

Even the least active general would have been roused to action by so many simultaneous alarms and excursions. Philip dismissed the delegations with a promise to bring help in every case, as opportunity and circumstances allowed. As the most pressing need of the moment, he sent a force to Peparethus to garrison the chief town of the island in response to a message that Attalus had crossed from Lemnos and devastated the country around it; Polyphantas was sent with a moderate force into Boeotia; and Menippus, one of Philip's own generals, was sent to Chalcis in Euboea with a thousand peltasts (the *pelta* is a shield not unlike the Spanish *caetra*); and 500 Agrianes were attached to the force to help Menippus to protect all parts of the island. Philip himself proceeded to Scotussa and gave orders for the Macedonian troops from Larisa to join him there. News then came that the Aetolians were to hold a council at Heraclea, which Attalus proposed to attend for consultation on the conduct of the war; and Philip at once marched thither with all possible speed, to break up the meeting. In point of fact he arrived after it had already been dismissed; but he destroyed crops, then almost ripe, along the Malian Gulf before returning to Scotussa, where he left his army and withdrew with his bodyguard to Demetrias. Thence, to meet any move the enemy might make, he sent men to Phocis, Euboea, and Peparethus to select suitable heights for signal-fires, and himself had a watch-tower constructed on the lofty summit of Mount Tisaeus to enable him to receive instant information by fire-signal of where his enemies were active.

The Roman general and King Attalus crossed from Peparethus to Nicaea and from there sent a fleet to Oreus, the first Euboean town on the left-hand side as one sails south from Demetrias across the gulf towards Chalcis on the Euripus. Attalus and Sulpicius agreed that the Romans should attack by sea, the king's forces from the land. 6. Four days after the arrival of the fleet the assault began, the interval having been used for secret talks with Plator, whom Philip had put in command of the town's defences. The town has two citadels, or fortified heights, one right on the sea, the other in the centre, and from the latter a tunnel leads down to the shore, protected at its seaward end by a very remarkable five-storeyed tower. At that point a fierce struggle began, for the tower itself was equipped with all sorts of missiles, and catapults and siege-engines had been landed from the ships to attack it. Once attention had been concentrated on the fighting in this area, Plator seized his chance and let the Romans in through a gate of the other citadel, the one overlooking the sea, and in a moment the citadel itself was in their hands. The inhabitants attempted to reach the citadel in the town's centre, but found that men had been posted there to close the gates; unable to get in, they were surrounded and either killed or taken prisoner. The Macedonian garrison neither fled in disorder nor offered serious resistance, but stood massed under the wall of the citadel. Plator, with Sulpicius's permission, put them on shipboard and landed them at Demetrium in Phthiotis. He himself joined Attalus.

Elated by his easy success at Oreus, Sulpicius sailed with his victorious fleet to Chalcis, where things were to turn out very differently from what he expected. Broad to the north-west and south-east, the Euripus at Chalcis suddenly narrows and might well at first sight give the appearance of a double harbour with an entrance from either direction; but in fact it would be hard to find a more dangerous anchorage. Sudden and violent squalls come down from the high mountains on both sides of the strait, and the tidal stream does not change, as it is said to do, at regular periods seven times a day, but changes irregularly, like a shifting wind, and flows with the rapidity of a mountain torrent. So what with the fierce tides and the squalls a vessel cannot lie quiet either by day or by night. In addition to the dangerous nature of the anchorage, the town itself proved to be very strong – indeed, impregnable; defended by the sea on one side, on the other, landward, side it was admirably fortified, held by a powerful garrison and, what is more, secured by the loyalty of its military officers and leading men, unlike Oreus, where there had been no loyalty or steady pupose at all. The attempt on Chalcis had been undertaken without due consideration, so Sulpicius showed his good sense in refusing to waste his time, once he had informed himself of the difficulties which faced him; he promptly abandoned the enterprise and sailed across to Cynus in Locris, the market-town of the Opuntian Locrians, situated a mile inland.

7. Philip had been warned by signal-fires from Oreus, but they had been purposely raised too late by the treacherous Plator; moreover, his fleet being inferior in strength, approach to the island by sea was not easy. So after waiting a while he abandoned Oreus, and on receiving another signal hurried to the relief of Chalcis. This seemed to present less difficulty, for although Chalcis is, like Oreus, on the island of Euboea, it lies on so narrow a strait that it is joined to the mainland by a bridge and is thus easier to reach by land than by sea. Accordingly Philip marched from Demetrias to Scotussa and then on to Thermopylae, starting in the third watch; he dislodged the garrison, scattered the Aetolians who were guarding the pass, drove the enemy in confusion to Heraclea, and went on to Elataea in Phocis, covering over sixty miles in a single day. Just about that time the town of Opus was being sacked by Attalus – Sulpicius had granted him permission to do so because his troops had had no share in the loot at Oreus, which had been sacked by Roman soldiers a few days previously. When the Roman fleet had returned to Oreus, Attalus, knowing nothing of Philip's approach, was busy getting money out of the leading citizens of Opus, and might well have been surprised and overpowered by an unexpected attack, had not some Cretan soldiers on a foraging expedition some distance from the town caught sight of Philip's column while it was still a long way off. Attalus's men, who were unarmed, made a wild rush back to their ships, and while they were struggling to get them afloat Philip arrived on the scene and caused still further confusion amongst

the crews. He then returned to Opus bitterly cursing his luck in having had so great a prize snatched away from under his very eyes; nor did the men of Opus escape his wrath for having thrown in their hands at the first sight of the enemy when they might well have continued to hold out until his arrival.

Philip's next move was to Thronium. Attalus withdrew to Oreus, then, on receiving a report that Prusias, King of Bithynia, had invaded his territory, crossed over to Asia without further thought for the Aetolian war or the Roman interest. Sulpicius sailed back to Aegina where he had spent the previous winter. Philip captured Thronium as easily as Attalus had captured Opus. Thronium was inhabited by refugees from Thebes in Phthiotis; their town had been taken by Philip and they had sought the protection of the Aetolians, who allowed them to settle in Thronium – it had been desolated in a previous war with Philip and was consequently uninhabited. After the recovery of Thronium Philip took the small and unimportant Dorian towns of Tithronium and Drumiae; then he moved to Elataea, where the envoys from Ptolemy and the Rhodians had had orders to await him.[1] While discussions were going on about how to end the Aetolian war (the envoys had recently attended the council of the Romans and Aetolians at Heraclea) news came that Machanidas intended to attack the Eleans while they were preparing to celebrate the Olympic Games. To prevent this, Philip dismissed the envoys with a friendly answer – he had not, he said, been the aggressor in the war, and he would put no obstacle in the way of peace on fair and honourable terms. He then set out with his troops, marching light, through Boeotia to Megara, on to Corinth, and thence, after taking supplies, to Phlius and Pheneus. At Heraea he was informed that Machanidas had hurried back to Lacedaemon in alarm at his approach, so he withdrew to Aegium to attend the Achaean Council, at the same time believing that he would find there the Carthaginian squadron which he had sent for to give him striking power by sea as well as by land. A few days earlier, the Carthaginians had sailed over to the Oxeae islands and had then made for the Acarnanian ports on hearing that Attalus and the

1. cf. p. 469.

Romans had left Oreus, for they were afraid of being attacked and overwhelmed inside Rhion – the narrows at the entrance to the Gulf of Corinth.

8. Philip was exceedingly annoyed by his failure ever to have been on the spot in time, despite the promptness with which he had answered every call. Ill luck, it seemed, had continued to make a fool of him by snatching the chance of success from under his eyes. None the less he concealed his chagrin at the Council and made a grand speech in which he called heaven and earth to witness that at no time or place had he failed to hasten with the utmost speed to wherever the clash of enemy arms was heard. 'It is a nice point,' he declared, 'whether in this war I have been the more eager for a fight or the enemy more determined to avoid one. Attalus eluded my grasp at Opus, Sulpicius at Chalcis, and now Machanidas has done the same; flight from the field does not, however, always achieve its object; a war in which mere contact with the enemy is enough to give you victory can hardly be said to strain your resources; the great thing is that I have the enemy's admission that they are no match for me. Before long I shall win no uncertain victory: they will fight me, and the issue will be no better for them than (no doubt) they expected.'

Philip's allies listened to his speech with pleasure. He restored Heraea and Triphylia to the Achaeans, and Aliphera to Megalopolis because the Megalopolitans produced satisfactory evidence that it had once belonged to their territory. He then sailed to Anticyra with three quadriremes and three biremes furnished by the Achaeans, and from there, with seven quinqueremes and more than twenty light boats, previously sent to the Gulf of Corinth to join the Carthaginian squadron, he proceeded to Erythrae, near Eupalium in Aetolia, where he made a landing. As a surprise attack it was not successful: all the men on the farms or in the neighbouring fortresses at Potidania and Apollonia fled to the mountains and woods; but all cattle which, in the hurry to escape, could not be taken away by their owners, were seized and put on shipboard. The Achaean commander Nicias was sent with the cattle and other plunder to Aegium, and Philip, on reaching Corinth, ordered his army to march from there overland through Boeotia, while he himself embarked at Cenchreae and sailed along the Attic coast, past Sunium and right through the enemy fleets, to Chalcis. He congratulated the men of the town on their loyalty and courage, and on the steadfastness which would not yield to either hope or fear; and after urging them to remain as firmly his friends in the future, if they preferred their own lot to that of Oreus and Opus, he continued his voyage to Oreus, where he entrusted the defence of the town together with full authority to those of the leading men who, at its capture, had preferred to escape rather than surrender to the Romans. He then left Euboea and sailed back to Demetrias, the place he had started from in his various attempts to bring help to his allies. At Cassandria in Chalcidice he then laid the keels of 100 new ships of war and brought together a great number of shipwrights to complete the work, after which, as things were now quiet in Greece, thanks to Attalus's departure and his own promptitude in bringing help to his distressed allies, he returned to his own kingdom to deal with the Dardanian invasion.

9. At the end of the summer which saw these events in Greece, Quintus Fabius the younger was sent by Livius to advise the Senate that in his, the consul's, opinion, Lucius Porcius with the troops under his command would be quite sufficient for the protection of Gaul, and that he himself could therefore safely leave the area and withdraw his consular army. The Senate on receipt of the message sent instructions that not only Livius but also his colleague Nero were to return to Rome; the only difference in the two cases was that Livius's army was to be brought back with him, while Nero's legions were to remain on duty where they were, facing Hannibal. The two consuls communicated by letter and agreed that though they were coming from opposite ends of Italy they would approach the City together, just as they had fought together; whichever of them reached Praeneste first should there await his colleague. As it happened, they both arrived at Praeneste on the same day; and from there they sent their edict for a full meeting of the Senate three days later in the temple of Bellona. Crowds came out to meet them as they approached the City; mere words of welcome were not enough – every man in the dense throng wanted to touch each consul's conquering hand, as all together poured out their

congratulations and thanks for the service they had rendered in saving the country from disaster. In the Senate, following the precedent of all commanders back from a successful campaign, the two consuls gave an account of their actions and asked that in return for the brave and victorious conduct of the nation's affairs honour should first be paid to the gods and that they themselves should be permitted to enter the city in triumph. The Senate replied that it was indeed their will to grant these requests, acknowledging their debt first to the gods, then, after the gods, to the consuls themselves. In the name of both a public thanksgiving was decreed and both were granted a triumph. The two men, however, having fought side by side and with a common purpose, did not wish to be separated in this great ceremony; so they agreed together that, because the battle had been fought in Livius's province, and Livius had happened on that day to have had the 'auspices' and supreme command, and because Livius's army had returned with him to Rome while Nero's troops could not be withdrawn from duty, Livius should enter the city in a four-horse chariot followed by his soldiers, and Nero should ride in on horseback unaccompanied by troops.

The joint triumph shed its glory upon both, but did more to increase the fame of the man who had done the most and claimed the least reward. 'That man on horseback there,' the word went round, 'in six days marched from one end of Italy to the other; he fought hand to hand with Hasdrubal in Gaul when Hannibal still thought his troops were facing him in Apulia. It was he who did it all, in both parts of Italy, against two armies, two enemy generals, pitting his wits against one, his sword against the other! The mere name of Nero was enough to keep Hannibal within his camp; and as for Hasdrubal, what else but Nero's coming overwhelmed and destroyed him? Livius may ride high in his chariot, drawn by as many horses as he likes, but the true triumph is to ride on one horse's back through Rome – yes, and even if he had walked on his own feet, Nero will be for ever remembered both for the glory he won in the war and for the little account he has made of it today.' Talk of this kind amongst the spectators followed Nero all the way to the Capitol. Money deposited in the Treasury by the consuls amounted to

3,000,000 *sestertii* and 80,000 *asses*; Livius gave each of his men fifty-six *asses* and Nero undertook to give the same sum to his own men when he returned to Canusium. It has been noticed that on the day of the triumph the soldiers directed more of their affectionate ribaldries against Nero than against their own commander, and that the knights very warmly praised the two officers Lucius Veturius and Quintus Caecilius, urging the commons to elect them consuls for the following year; also that the consuls themselves added their authority to the knights' preliminary choice by holding an assembly next day and speaking of the brave and faithful support they had received in particular from their two seconds-in-command.

10. Election day was now approaching. The Senate decreed that a dictator should be appointed to preside, and the consul Nero named his colleague Livius for the office, and Livius, in his turn, named Quintus Caecilius his master of Horse. Quintus Caecilius Metellus (then master of Horse) and Lucius Veturius Philo were appointed to the consulship. The elections for praetors were then held, and the following appointed: Gaius Servilius, Marcus Caecilius Metellus, Tiberius Claudius Asellus, and Quintus Mamilius Turrinus, who was a plebeian aedile at the time. The elections over, the dictator laid down his office, disbanded his army, and set out for Etruria, where he had received instructions from the Senate to hold an inquiry and find out which of the Etruscan or Umbrian communities had planned to go over to Hasdrubal on his arrival in their territories and which had sent him aid in the form of men, supplies, or anything else. Such were the events of this year, at home and in the field.

The Roman Games were repeated three times in their entirety by the curule aediles Caepio and Lentulus; the Plebeian Games were similarly repeated once by the plebeian aediles Matho and Turrinus.

It was now the thirteenth year of the war and Philo and Metellus had entered upon their consulship. Both were assigned Bruttium as their sphere of operations, their task being to carry on hostilities against Hannibal. The praetors then drew for their assignments and the City praetorship fell to Marcus Metellus, the 'foreign' to Turrinus, Sicily to Servilius, Sardinia to Asellus. The distribution of the armed forces was as follows: one consul was to take the army commanded the previous year by Nero, the other the army commanded by the pro-praetor Quintus Claudius, both consisting of two legions; in Etruria the proconsul Livius, whose command had been prolonged for another year, was to take over from the pro-praetor Gaius Terentius the two legions of slave volunteers; Turrinus was to hand over his judicial responsibilities to his colleague the City praetor and to hold Gaul with the troops previously commanded by the praetor Lucius Porcius, with instructions to raid the territories of the Gauls who had gone over to Carthage on the arrival of Hasdrubal. The defence of Sicily with the two legions from Cannae was entrusted to Gaius Servilius, as before to Gaius Mamilius. The old army, which Aulus Hostilius had commanded, was withdrawn from Sardinia and the consuls enrolled a new legion to replace it under the command of Asellus. Quintus Claudius and Gaius Hostilius Tubulus both had their commands extended, the former to be responsible for Tarentum, the latter for Capua. The proconsul Valerius Laevinus, who had been in charge of the defence of the Sicilian coast, was ordered to hand over thirty ships to the praetor Servilius and return with the rest of his fleet to Rome.

11. It was inevitable that in critical times like these men should attribute everything that happened, whether favourable or adverse, to divine agency. Many prodigies were reported: the temple of Jupiter at Tarracina and of Mater Matuta at Satricum were struck by lightning; no less alarming at the latter town was the spectacle of two snakes gliding in through the door of the temple of Jupiter; from Antium came a report that the ears of grain seemed to have blood in them as they were being cut; a two-headed pig was born at Caere, and a lamb with both male and female organs; at Alba two suns were said to have been seen and there was a light in the night sky at Fregellae; in the country near Rome an ox talked and the altar of Neptune in the Circus Flaminius poured with sweat; the temples of Ceres, Salus, and Quirinus were all struck by lightning. The consuls received instructions by senatorial decree to make atonement for these prodigies by sacrifice of full-grown victims and to hold a day of prayer, and the instructions

were duly carried out. But more disconcerting than all the prodigies either reported from elsewhere or seen in the city was that the fire in the temple of Vesta went out. The Vestal who had had the duty of tending the fire that night was scourged by the order of Publius Licinius the *pontifex maximus*. Though this was in no sense a message from heaven, but merely an accident due to human negligence, it was decided none the less to atone for it by the sacrifice of full-grown victims and to observe a day of prayer at the temple of Vesta.

Before the consuls left Rome they were instructed by the Senate to do all they could to put the people back on their farms. The gods in their mercy had relieved Rome and Latium from the pressure of war; it was once more possible to live on the land without fear, and surely it could not be right to take more trouble over the cultivation of Sicily than of Italy. Nevertheless, despite these sentiments, resettlement was by no means easy for the people themselves. The free farmers had nearly all been wiped out in the war; slaves were scarce; cattle had been carried off and farmhouses destroyed or burned. A large part of the rural population was, however, forced by the consuls to return to the land. What had brought this matter up was a complaint lodged by representatives from Placentia and Cremona that their lands were being raided and ruined by the Gauls in the neighbourhood, and that a large part of the settlers in the two towns had dispersed, leaving them with an inadequate population and the countryside empty and neglected. Orders were accordingly given to the praetor Mamilius to protect these two settlements, and the consuls on the senate's authority issued an edict to the effect that all citizens of Cremona and Placentia were to return to their homes before a certain date.

At the beginning of spring the consuls left Rome for their duties in the field. Metellus took over Nero's army and Philo that of the pro-praetor Quintus Claudius, supplemented by recruits he had himself raised. They proceeded to Consentia in Bruttium, where they inflicted widespread depredation, and their column, loaded with captured material, was attacked in a narrow pass by a party of Bruttians and Numidian spearmen. In the confusion the column itself was in some danger, not to mention the plunder. However, there was little real fighting and the legions got safely out of the pass into open and cultivated country, having sent the plunder on ahead of them. They then turned north into Lucania, where the whole population, without any application of force, returned to its allegiance with Rome.

12. During this year there was no direct action against Hannibal. Because of the loss he had so recently sustained – a loss not only to his country but one which touched him personally as well – he did not himself offer battle; and the Romans were content to leave him alone so long as he remained inactive – such was the power they felt still to reside in this one man, even though everything around him was tumbling into ruin. Indeed I hardly know whether Hannibal was not more wonderful when fortune was against him than in his hours of success. Fighting for thirteen years in enemy territory, far from home, with varying fortunes and an army composed not of native troops but of a hotch-potch of the riff-raff of all nationalities, men who shared neither law nor custom nor language, who differed in manner, in dress, in equipment, who had in common neither the forms of religious observance nor even the gods they served, he yet was able, somehow or other, to weld this motley crowd so firmly together that they never quarrelled amongst themselves nor mutinied against their general, though money to pay them was often lacking and provisions to feed them were often short – deficiencies which in the first Carthaginian War had led to many acts of unspeakable atrocity by both officers and men. Surely it was an astonishing thing that there was no mutiny in the Carthaginian camp, at least when all hopes of victory had vanished with the death of Hasdrubal and the destruction of his army, and the abandonment of all Italy except for the one little corner of Bruttium. For in addition to everything else there was no prospect even of feeding the troops except with what could be got from the Bruttian countryside, and that was too small an area, even if it were all under cultivation, to supply so large a body of men. Moreover, most men of military age had been taken from the land to serve as soldiers, not to mention the vicious practice, inbred in the Bruttian people, of brigandage. Finally, Hannibal was receiving no supplies from home, as everyone there was concerned with

keeping a hold on Spain and seemed to fancy that in Italy all was well.

In Spain the general situation was in one respect much the same as in Italy, but in another very different. It resembled the situation in Italy in that the Carthaginians, defeated in battle with the loss of a commander, had been forced to withdraw to the Atlantic coast; and differed from it in that Spain by the nature of the country and the character of its people was better adapted than any other place in the world to making losses good for a renewal of hostilities. This is the reason why Spain, though it was the first mainland province to be entered by the Romans, was the last to be completely subdued, and held out till our own times, when it was finally conquered under the leadership and auspices of Augustus Caesar.

Hasdrubal son of Gisgo, the best and most distinguished general this war produced after the three sons of Hamilcar, had returned from Gades in the hope of offering further resistance, and with the help of Hamilcar's son Mago he set about raising fresh troops in Further Spain and succeeded in arming some 50,000 foot-soldiers and 4,500 horse. Most writers agree about the strength of his cavalry, but some state that the number of infantry brought to the town of Silpia[1] was 70,000. There in open country the two Carthaginian commanders established themselves, intending to resist any move that might be made against them.

13. On hearing that this immense force had been raised, Scipio did not think that with his Roman legions alone he would be a match for it, unless, if only for appearance's sake, he could also put into the field some foreign auxiliaries. At the same time he knew that he must not allow the auxiliaries to be sufficiently numerous to turn the scales in the event of their deserting to the enemy, the very thing which had brought disaster upon his father and uncle. Accordingly having sent Silanus to Culchas, a prince who ruled twenty-eight communities, to take over from him the troops, both horse and foot, which he had promised to raise during the winter, he himself set out from Tarraco and reached Castulo after collecting during his march a moderate force of auxiliaries from

1. More correctly, Ilipa.

the allied communities along the route. At Castulo he was joined by Silanus with the auxiliaries, 3,000 foot and 500 horse, and from there he proceeded to Baecula with the whole army, which, including Roman legionaries and allies, infantry and cavalry, amounted to 45,000 men. They were engaged in fortifying their camp when Mago and Masinissa attacked them with their cavalry in force,[1] and the Roman working-parties might have been roughly handled but for a timely and unexpected charge by a squadron of horse which Scipio had posted in concealment behind a convenient hill. Mago's leading cavalrymen were in loose order, and those of them who were quick enough to get close up to the rampart or actually amongst the working-parties were soon scattered by the Roman squadron; but with the rest who had been approaching in proper battle-order there was a more protracted struggle of which the issue was for a long time in doubt. However, Scipio called in the light cohorts on guard duty, withdrew his working-parties, and sent them into the line; more and more joined the fighting, fresh men coming to the aid of their weary comrades, until finally a powerful column of armed men was pouring from the camp to take part in the fray. This proved too much for the enemy; Carthaginians and Numidians alike admitted defeat and began to give way. At first their retreat was orderly enough and neither fear nor haste caused any confusion in their ranks; but later, when the Romans began to press harder at their rear and the weight of their attack proved irresistible, order was forgotten, the column broke to pieces, and it was a case of every man for himself in a wild rush to escape. The battle certainly gave a fillip to Roman morale, just as it discouraged the enemy; none the less for several days afterwards probing attacks by light or mounted troops continued without intermission.

14. Hasdrubal had used these minor clashes to test his strength, and as soon as he was satisfied he led out his main force into line of battle. The Romans followed suit. Each of the opposing armies stood ready in front of the rampart of its camp, neither of them making the first move to engage; the day drew towards evening; nothing happened, and first the Cartha-

1. Livy writes as if this attack was made near Baecula: but on p. 513, Mago and Masinissa are at Ilipa, over 100 miles to the west.

ginians, then the Romans, marched back into camp. For several days after the same process was repeated: each time it was the Carthaginian commander who first took the field and first gave his men, sick and weary as they were of doing nothing, the order to withdraw. Neither side made any forward movement, no missile was thrown, no sound was uttered. In Scipio's army the centre was held by Roman troops, facing native Carthaginians mixed with Africans; the wings in both armies were held by allied troops, in each case Spaniards; in front of the wings and in advance of the Carthaginian line were posted the elephants, looking, from a distance, like forts. Everyone in both armies naturally supposed that they would fight when the time came in the order in which, day after day, they had stood – that the two centres, Roman and Carthaginian, who were the real rivals, would meet in equal fight, sword against sword. Scipio, however, no sooner realized the universal conviction that this would happen than he deliberately changed everything for the day on which he intended to engage. On the previous evening he sent round an order that his men were to have their meal and the horses were to be groomed and fed before dawn; the cavalrymen, armed, were to keep their mounts bridled in readiness, with their saddle-cloths on.

It was hardly daylight when he ordered all his cavalry and light troops against the Carthaginian outposts; he then immediately advanced in person at the head of his heavy legionaries, and, contrary to what both his own men and the enemy confidently expected, posted Roman troops on the wings and allied troops in the centre. Hasdrubal hurried from his tent when he heard the cries of the Roman cavalrymen; seeing all in confusion outside the rampart of his camp, his own men running excitedly for their arms and in the distance the gleaming standards of the legions and the ground rapidly filling with enemy troops, he at once ordered out his whole cavalry strength against the Roman horsemen. At the same time he led his infantry out of camp, but made no change in the dispositions he had kept during the preceding days. For a time the cavalry struggle was indecisive, and could hardly have been otherwise because each of the opposing squadrons when overpowered, as happened more or less by turns, could safely withdraw to the protection of the infantry line. But a change was to come, for when the two lines were not more than five hundred paces apart, Scipio sounded the recall, opened his ranks, let through the cavalry and light troops and then, dividing them into two sections, posted them as reserves behind the wings. The moment for action had now come. Ordering the Spaniards, who formed the centre, to advance slowly, Scipio, from the right wing where he commanded in person, sent orders to Silanus and Marcius to watch his extension towards the right and to match it by a simultaneous extension of their own men towards the left, and to bring their light infantry and cavalry into action before the two centres had had time to engage. Thus with extended wings and three cohorts of infantry and three troops of cavalry on each, supported by light skirmishers, they advanced at a smart pace against the enemy, the rest following to complete the outflanking movement. The centre formed a concave line, where the Spanish auxiliaries were moving forward more slowly.

The wings came into action while the strong enemy centre, composed of veteran Carthaginian and African troops, was still not within range of missiles; these did not dare to go to the assistance of their comrades on the wings for fear of laying their centre open to the oncoming enemy; both wings were hard pressed and subjected to a double attack – on their flanks by the Roman cavalry, light troops, and skirmishers, and simultaneously on the front by the Roman infantry cohorts which were trying to cut them off from contact with the rest of the army. 15. In every part of the field the scales were heavily weighted in favour of Scipio, and especially because Spanish raw recruits and Balearic Islanders found themselves matched against Romans and Latins. Moreover, as the day wore on, Hasdrubal's men began to feel the effects of exhaustion, for they had been surprised by the unexpected alarm before dawn, and compelled to take the field in a hurry and on empty stomachs. Scipio had, indeed, deliberately contrived that the battle should be fought late in the day; it was round about noon when the infantry made their attack on the wings, and some time later when the fighting spread to the centre, so that even before they went into action Hasdrubal's men were beginning to flag from the heat of the midday sun and the strain of standing, hungry and thirsty, under arms, so much so indeed that they had to lean on their shields for support. In addition to everything else the elephants, scared by the rapid movements of the cavalry and light troops, had shifted from the wings into the centre. Tired and discouraged as a result of all this, the Carthaginians began their retreat; but it was still an orderly retreat with the appearance, at any rate, of a planned withdrawal by an unbroken line. But this was not to last, for when the victorious Romans saw their advantage they redoubled the weight of their attacks from every side. The Carthaginians could no longer hold them; Hasdrubal did all he could to keep them in hand and stop the rot, crying out again and again that if only they withdrew slowly and in order they could find safety amongst the hills in their rear. But panic proved stronger than discipline and, as their comrades in the van began to fall, the whole line suddenly faced about and took to flight. At the foot of the hills they paused, and the officers, when the Romans seemed to hesitate to advance up the slope, began to call the men back into their ranks; but soon they saw the Romans coming on again as fast as before, the scramble to escape was resumed, and they were driven in confusion into their camp. The pursuing Romans were close upon the rampart and in the speed of their advance would have captured it, but for a heavy rainstorm: the sun had been blazing through gaps in heavy clouds, when suddenly the downpour came, and with such extraordinary violence that the victorious soldiers could scarcely get back to their own camp, and there were even some amongst them who took the thing as an omen and shrank from making any further attempt that day. The Carthaginians, what with the stormy night, their own exhaustion, and the losses they had suffered, needed rest more than anything else; but their situation was a perilous one and the prospect of a fresh attack at dawn next morning gave them no time to relax their efforts. So they collected stones from the neighbouring valleys and increased the height of their rampart, hoping that fortification would provide the protection which their arms had failed to give. But their allies deserted, and then the only safety seemed to be in immediate flight.

The desertion began with Attenes, prince of the Turdetani, who went off with large numbers of his native troops; then two fortified towns with their garrisons were surrendered to Scipio by their commandants; and finally, to prevent the tendency to revolt, once started, from spreading further, Hasdrubal moved off in the silence of the following night.

16. At dawn the guards reported that the enemy had gone, and Scipio, sending his cavalry on ahead, gave the order to march. So rapid was their progress that they would undoubtedly have overtaken Hasdrubal if they had kept directly in his tracks; but they took the word of their guides that there was a short cut to the river Baetis, which would enable them to attack the Carthaginians as they were crossing it. Hasdrubal, finding his passage of the river closed, turned south-west towards the coast and, as his men hurried on more like fugitives than an army on the march, he soon put a good distance between himself and the Roman legions. None the less his attempt to escape was constantly held up by harassing attacks on flanks and rear by the Roman cavalry and light troops; soon they became so frequent that his column was forced to halt, and, while it was engaged either with the Roman cavalry or skirmishers and auxiliary foot, the legions arrived on the scene. With the coming of the legions what had been a field of battle was turned into a slaughterhouse, until the Carthaginian general was himself the first to confess defeat by making his escape to the nearest hills with some 6,000 half-armed men. The remainder were either killed or taken prisoner. The fugitive Carthaginians improvised some sort of defensive position on a high hill, and from it defended themselves without difficulty when the Roman attempt to scale the precipitous slope had failed. But surrounded as they were on a barren hill-top, with no source of supplies, their position in a few days became intolerable. Desertions began, and finally the general himself sent for ships – the sea was not far away – and abandoning his men made his escape by night to Gades.

When Scipio learned that Hasdrubal had fled he left a force of 10,000 foot and 1,000 horse with Silanus to maintain the siege of what was left of the Carthaginian army on the hill, and returned to Tarraco. The march thither took him seventy days, as he was constantly stopping on the way to inquire into the behaviour of the various communities and petty princes so as to be able to reward them on a proper estimate of their services. After he left, Masinissa entered into secret talks with Silanus, as a result of which he crossed with a few of his people to Africa, in order to ensure that his own nation would obediently follow him in his change of policy. The reason for his sudden change of sides was not, at the time, entirely clear; but that he had acted, even then, on reasonable grounds, was proved later by his unswerving loyalty to Rome down to his extreme old age.[1] Mago then made his way to Gades on the ships sent back by Hasdrubal; the remainder of the army, abandoned by its leaders, either deserted or dispersed amongst the neighbouring communities. No force of any significance, either in numbers or strength, was left.

Such was the series of events which led to the expulsion of the Carthaginians from Spain by Publius Scipio. It was the fourteenth year of the war and the fifth since Scipio took over command of operations in that country. Soon afterwards Silanus rejoined Scipio at Tarraco with the news that the Spanish war was over. 17. Lucius Scipio with many prisoners of noble rank was sent to Rome to report the liberation of the country from Carthaginian control.

Everyone was talking with boundless delight of the splendour of this achievement, except the one man who had brought it to to pass: he on the contrary, insatiable as he was in his hunger truly to deserve his country's praise, looked upon the conquest of Spain as a mere preliminary sketch of the great things which, in his noble ambition, he yet hoped to do. Already his thoughts were on Africa and Carthage and all the glory of that crowning campaign, gathered up as it were to shed a radiance on his name. He accordingly found it advisable to take certain preliminary steps, especially in the attempt to win the support of princes and their peoples. He began with Syphax, King of the Masaesulii, a tribe bordering the Mauri and on the coast more or less opposite New Carthage in Spain. Syphax had a treaty at the time with the Carthaginians, but Scipio, supposing it would have no more weight or sanctity with him than agreements ever do

1. He lived until 148 B.C. and reigned sixty years.

have with barbarians, who invariably support the winning side, sent Laelius, armed with valuable gifts, to put to him the Roman case. Syphax was delighted with the presents, and as things at the moment were everywhere going well for the Romans, while the Carthaginians were failing in Italy and had already utterly failed in Spain, he consented to accept the friendship of Rome. He would not, however, formally ratify any such agreement except in the presence of the Roman commander-in-chief. So Laelius returned to Scipio with a promise from Syphax that no danger would attend his visit, though nothing further was guaranteed.

For anyone planning an attempt upon Africa the attitude of Syphax was of great importance. He was the wealthiest of the African princes; he had already had experience of the Carthaginians in war, and geographically his dominions were situated conveniently with regard to Spain, being on the other side of a comparatively narrow strait. In view of this Scipio was convinced that a great risk was justifiable, since he could achieve his object in no other way; so he left Marcius and Silanus in charge of Spain – the former at Tarraco, the latter at New Carthage whither he had proceeded from Tarraco with all possible speed – and in company with Laelius set sail from New Carthage in two quinqueremes and made the passage to Africa, mostly under oars with a calm sea, occasionally helped by a light breeze. It so happened that precisely at the same time Hasdrubal, driven from Spain, entered the harbour with seven triremes. His anchors were down and he was bringing his ships in to the beach when the two quinqueremes were sighted; no one had any doubt that they were enemy vessels and might easily be overwhelmed by superior numbers before they could enter harbour, but beyond a lot of excitement and confusion amongst soldiers arming themselves and sailors trying to prepare the ships for action, nothing was done. Scipio's vessels, having found a better breeze, came into harbour before the Carthaginians had had time to raise their anchors, and after that no one ventured to cause any further disturbance in the king's harbour. Hasdrubal was the first to go ashore; soon Scipio and Laelius followed, and all three made their way to the king.
18. Syphax thought it a wonderful honour (as indeed it was)

that two generals of the two richest countries in the world should visit him together, on the same day, to ask from him peace and friendship. He invited both to be his guests, and since chance had willed that they should find themselves under one roof together, he tried to draw them into talks which might put an end to their quarrels. But Scipio declared, first that he felt no personal grudge against the Carthaginian such as might be ended by a conference, and secondly that he was unable to enter into any negotiations with an enemy of his country without instructions from the Senate. Thereupon the king, lest one of his guests should seem to be excluded from his table, urgently pressed Scipio to consent to share his dinner; Scipio did not refuse, and both men dined with the king. Indeed, to gratify him, they even shared the same couch. So perfect were Scipio's manners and so great his natural tact in dealing with all sorts of situations that he succeeded in charming by his conversation not only the barbaric Syphax, who knew nothing of Roman polite society, but even his bitterest enemy Hasdrubal. Hasdrubal indeed let it be seen that he found Scipio, when he met him face to face, an even more wonderful person than on the battlefield, and that his power of winning sympathy was so great that Syphax and his kingdom without any doubt would soon be in the power of the Romans. In his view therefore the Carthaginians ought not to consider how their Spanish provinces were lost so much as how Africa was to be retained; it was on no pleasure-trip, no idle excursion along delightful shores, that this great soldier had left his armies and the territories he had just acquired in order to cross to Africa with only two ships and risk his life in a hostile country, trusting himself to the unknown quantity of an African chieftain's word. On the contrary, it was because he cherished the hope of conquest. Moreover, this hope had long been in Scipio's mind; for a long time now he had been openly complaining that he was not, as Hannibal was, waging war on the enemy's soil.

A treaty was concluded between Syphax and Scipio, and Scipio left Africa. With variable winds and much stormy weather he reached New Carthage four days later.

19. The Spanish provinces were now relieved of the burden of the Carthaginian war, but it was clear none the less that

certain communities were abstaining from hostilities not so much out of loyalty to Rome as from fear engendered by a guilty conscience. Of these the most important, and the most guilty were Iliturgi and Castulo. The latter place had been allied to Rome while success attended her arms, but had gone over to Carthage after the death of the two Scipios and the destruction of their armies; Iliturgi had added crime to desertion by the betrayal and murder of the survivors of the defeat who had fled there for refuge. On Scipio's first arrival in Spain, when the fortunes of the country still hung in the balance, the punishment of these communities would have been just, though perhaps unwise; but now the situation was different: the war was over and the time for exacting the penalty seemed to have come, so Marcius was summoned from Tarraco and sent with a third of his forces to attack Castulo, while Scipio himself with the remaining two thirds marched to Iliturgi, making five stops on the way. The gates of the town were closed and everything prepared for resisting an attack. What need to wait for a declaration of war when the inhabitants already knew too well what they had deserved? It was this point which Scipio seized upon in opening the speech of encouragement he made to his men before the attack. 'By shutting their gates,' he said, 'the Spaniards have themselves shown how well justified are their fears. We must fight them with more hatred in our hearts than when we fought the Carthaginians; for against Carthage we felt but little anger, contending, as we were, for glory and empire; but these scoundrels here must be punished for the crimes of perfidy and murder. The time has come to avenge the brutal slaughter of our comrades and the treachery which would have awaited us too, if we had happened to seek refuge here; we must make an example of these traitors, and fix unalterably in men's minds the knowledge that no one may ever consider a Roman citizen and soldier, however desperate his plight, as fair game for insult and injury.'

All were fired by the general's speech, and immediately he ended, scaling-ladders were issued to selected men from different maniples; the army was divided, with Laelius in command of one section of it, and the assault began in two places simultaneously. What urged the townspeople to defend themselves –

and they did so with the utmost vigour – was not the command of a military officer or the exhortations of their leaders, but fear and the knowledge of their guilt. They told each other what each knew in his heart, that Scipio's object was not victory but punishment; that when every man must die, all that mattered was whether he died fighting in the line, where the common chances of war often raised the vanquished and crushed the victor, or whether later on amidst the smouldering ruins of the town, dishonoured by chains and tortured with the lash, he breathed his last before the eyes of wife and children, prisoners in the enemy's hands. Not only the men, young and old, rallied to the defence; women and boys helped too, doing work far beyond their strength, bringing up weapons for the fighters and carrying stones to the walls to help the working-parties strengthen them. Not only freedom was at stake – freedom, which whets the courage of brave men alone – but all had clear before their eyes the extreme penalty of a horrible death. The mere sight of one another, as each strove to do more, to risk more, than his neighbour, was a flame to kindle their determination. The battle began with so fierce an ardour that the famous army which had conquered the whole of Spain was again and again driven back from the walls by the fighting men of a single town and thrown into disorder in a manner by no means to its credit. Scipio, fearing that so many unsuccessful assaults might encourage the enemy and take the heart out of his own troops, determined to go into action himself and risk his own life with that of his men; so, with expressions of anger and contempt for their feeble performance, he ordered ladders to be brought and declared he would go up himself if the others hesitated to do so. He was already close under the walls and in no little danger, when on all sides a shout went up from his troops in their anxiety for their commander, and ladders were at once raised along a long section of the wall, while Laelius from the opposite side of the town exerted fresh pressure. It was the beginning of the end: resistance was broken, the defenders were dislodged, and the walls occupied.

During the confusion the citadel too was seized by attack on the side of it which was supposed to be impregnable. 20. This was the work of African deserters, then serving with the

Romans: while the inhabitants were engaged in the defence of those parts of the town which were obviously vulnerable, and Roman troops were making their way in wherever an opening presented itself, the Africans happened to notice a part of the town which was undefended either by fortifications or men. It stood very high, and the cliff which fell sheer away from it was evidently thought to be sufficient protection. They were light and active men, long trained to rapid movement, and, all of them carrying iron spikes, they began the climb, making use of such projections in the face of the cliff as they could find. Where the face was smooth and ascent impossible they drove in their spikes at short intervals to give a foothold, and, the leaders hauling up the men behind and each giving a hoist to the comrade above him, they succeeded in reaching the top. From there they rushed down with a yell into the part of the town which was already in Roman hands.

That it was rage and hatred which had inspired the assault was then all too apparent. No soldiers took prisoners or had a thought for plunder, though everything lay open to his hands; armed and unarmed citizens were butchered alike, women and men without distinction; they did not stop short in their beastly blood-lust even at the slaughter of infants. Then the buildings were set ablaze, and what would not burn was demolished. It was the victors' delight to blot out every trace of the hated town, to destroy the very memory of the place where their enemies had lived.

Scipio then marched to Castulo which was defended not only by Spanish refugees from other towns but by the remnants of the Carthaginian army which had collected there after its dispersal. Scipio's approach had been preceded by the news of the destruction of Iliturgi, which brought terror and desperation to the inhabitants. The interests of the Carthaginians and Spaniards were not the same, and as neither party had any regard for the fate of the other, provided that it could save itself, there was at first mutual, though unexpressed, suspicion, then an open quarrel and consequent split between them. The leader of the Spaniards, Cerdubelus, openly supported surrender; in command of the Carthaginian auxiliaries was Himilco, and he and his troops, together with the town, were betrayed into

Scipio's hands by the Spaniard, who had received a secret promise of mercy. This time there was much less bloodshed: the guilt had been less than in the case of Iliturgi, and voluntary surrender had done much to mitigate the anger of the Romans.

21. After this Marcius was commissioned to bring under the control of Rome any of the Spanish tribes which had not yet been completely subdued, and Scipio returned to New Carthage to pay his vows and exhibit the gladiatorial show which he intended to stage in honour of his dead father and uncle. The gladiators who took part in the spectacle were not of the usual sort provided by the trainers, bought slaves, that is, or free men willing to offer their blood for sale; every man fought voluntarily and without payment. Some had been sent by their tribal chiefs as examples of native valour; some offered to fight to gratify Scipio; others were led by the mere spirit of rivalry to offer, or accept, a challenge. There were also some who, unable or unwilling to end a difference by legal means, settled it by the sword on the understanding that the disputed property, or whatever it was, should go to the victor. Amongst the combatants were two cousins, Corbis and Orsua; far from being undistinguished, they belonged to a well-known and illustrious family, and were rivals for the chief office in a town called Ibes. They declared that they would fight for it. Corbis was the elder; Orsua's father had lately been chief, having inherited the position from an elder brother. Scipio wanted them to settle their difference by discussion and be friends, but both said that they had already refused their relatives the same request and would suffer no god or man but Mars himself to judge between them. The elder had the advantage in strength, his rival had the pride and confidence of youth; and each preferred death in combat to submission to the other's rule. Their ambition was madness, but nothing would make either give it up, and the spectacle they provided for the watching troops was a notable one, and a lesson too on the evil consequences of the passion for power. The older man by his experience and skill easily mastered the brute strength of his younger rival. The gladiatorial show was followed by funeral games, staged with such elaboration as local resources and the equipment of an army on service allowed.

22. Meanwhile Scipio's officers were no less active. Marcius crossed the river Baetis (known locally as the Certis) and received the surrender of two wealthy communities without bloodshed. Then came the action at Astapa; Astapa had always stood by the Carthaginians, but more annoying than its allegiance to Carthage was the personal hatred, beyond what was justified by the exigencies of war, which the inhabitants felt for the Romans. The town was neither well fortified nor situated in a strong position, such as might have inspired over-confidence in its people; their chief pleasure was in brigandage, and this had led them to raid the neighbouring territory of tribes allied to Rome and to pick up stray Roman soldiers or sutlers and merchants. On one occasion a large convoy – a small party would have run too obvious a risk – was waylaid in an awkward spot as it passed through their country, and was cut to pieces. When Marcius's army moved up to attack this town, the people, knowing that their walls and weapons would be inadequate to protect them, while surrender to so bitter an enemy would be certain death, were driven by their consciousness of guilt to a barbarous and horrible act of savagery against themselves. They collected all their most valuable possessions and made a pile of them in a prearranged spot in the forum; then, forcing the women and children to sit on the pile, they heaped logs and bundles of brushwood all round it. Fifty armed men were ordered to stand guard there over their treasures, and over those who were dearer even than their gold, so long as the issue of the battle remained in doubt; if they saw the fight was going against them and the town was on the point of falling, they were to understand that every man they saw going up into the line would certainly be killed; then a prayer was added in the name of all the gods above and below that they should remember their liberty, which that day was destined to end either in shameful slavery or honourable death, and leave nothing upon which the enemy might vent his rage. Fire and sword lay ready to their hands; rather than endure the triumphant mockery of a proud and cruel foe, would it not be better that friendly and faithful hands should destroy what in any case was doomed to perish? In such terms they urged the fifty to do their duty, and a terrible curse was invoked upon any one of

them who through vain hope or weakness might be turned from his purpose.

Then the gates were flung open and they rushed out with a great roar and trampling of feet. No Roman unit of any strength was in position to meet them, because a sally from the town was the last thing they expected. Two or three troops of cavalry and a contingent of light infantry hurriedly sent for the purpose encountered them. There was a battle of sorts, disorderly enough, but fought with dash and determination; the leading Roman cavalrymen were driven back and their repulse caused panic amongst the light infantry in their rear; fighting would have taken place right under the rampart of the town had not the Roman legionaries formed into line with unexampled rapidity. For a short time there was confusion in the front ranks even of the legions, so desperate was the courage with which the townspeople, blind with fury, hurled themselves upon the Roman swords; but soon those veteran soldiers, not to be shaken by such wild and undisciplined attacks, used their swords with effect and brought them to a standstill. A little later the legionaries took the offensive; but finding that no enemy soldier would yield an inch and that all were determined to die where they stood, they extended their line, as superior numbers enabled them easily to do, and then outflanked and finally surrounded their opponents. The circle gradually closed in, until every man of them was killed.

23. This bloody business was, at least, all in the normal process of war: the incensed Romans were fighting an armed enemy, capable of resistance. But far more horrible was the scene in the town itself, where hundreds of weak and defenceless woman and children were being slaughtered by their own friends. A fire had been kindled in the market-place, and the bodies, often still breathing, were flung into the flames, which were almost extinguished by the rivers of blood. Finally the appointed slaughterers, exhausted by their pitiful work, themselves leapt, sword in hand, into the fire. When the Romans appeared the butchery was complete. The sight brought them up short in astonishment and horror. For a moment they simply stood and stared; then, when amongst the heap of bodies and miscellaneous objects they saw the gleam of silver and gold,

natural greed overcame them and they tried to snatch the treasure from the flames. Those who stood nearest could not get back because of the surging and eager mass behind them: they were thrust forward, some right into the fire, while others were scorched by the fierce heat.

Such was the destruction of Astapa by fire and sword. The troops got nothing out of it whatever. Marcius frightened into surrender the other communities in the neighbourhood and then rejoined Scipio with his victorious army at New Carthage.

Just about this time deserters from Gades offered to betray the town together with the Carthaginian garrison and its commander and the fleet. Mago had stopped there after his escape from the battlefield, and having got together some ships on the Atlantic coast had collected with Hanno's help a number of reinforcements, some oversea from Africa and some from the neighbouring districts of Spain. Promises were exchanged with the deserters, and Marcius proceeded to Gades with a force of infantry, marching light, while Laelius was ordered to join him with seven triremes and a quinquereme for a combined operation by land and sea simultaneously.

24. At this juncture Scipio fell seriously ill, and the natural human passion for exaggerating rumours made out his complaint to be even worse than it actually was. The whole province at once became restless, especially in the more remote regions, and it was all too evident, since a mere rumour had stirred up such trouble, how serious the result would have been if the reported calamity had been true. Allied communities abandoned their allegiance, and the army refused duty. Mandonius and Indibilis, disappointed in their hope of a Spanish kingdom for themselves after the expulsion of the Carthaginians from the country, roused their countrymen (the Lacetani),[1] called out the Celtiberians and devastated by raids the territories of the Suessetani and Sedetani, both allied to Rome. Another outbreak, this time amongst Roman troops, took place in the camp near Sucro. There were 8,000 men in the camp, on duty as garrison for the tribes south of the Ebro; the trouble amongst

1. Probably Livy means the Laeetani of N.E. Spain in the region of Barcelona.

them had first started before they heard the rumours of Scipio's danger, and was the result in the first instance of the general deterioration of discipline which commonly follows a long period of inactivity. A contributory cause was the change from war-time plenty, when they had lived well on plunder, to the more restrictive conditions of peace. At first there were only whisperings and private complaints: if there was a war on, what were they doing here, where everything was quiet? If the war was finished and Spain finally subdued, why were they not allowed to return to Italy? Then came insolent demands for their pay, in terms not in keeping with the normal self-control of troops on active service; officers going the rounds were abused by the sentries, and men left camp at night to pick up what they could in the now peaceful countryside. Finally they began openly and by daylight to absent themselves without leave. The traditions and discipline of the service had broken down completely; nothing was done by the officers' orders, everywhere was do-as-you-please amongst the men. One thing, however, kept the outward form, at any rate, of a Roman camp, namely the men's hope that the military tribunes would be infected by the spirit of recklessness and take a share in the mutiny; and for this reason they allowed them to hear cases at headquarters, asked them for the password, and took their proper turns on outpost and sentry duty. So while in fact they had robbed their officers of real authority, they maintained an appearance of discipline, though the orders they obeyed were their own.

When it became apparent that the tribunes strongly disapproved of the men's action and were trying to oppose it, frankly refusing to take any part in such madness, the mutiny flared up in earnest. The tribunes were first refused the use of headquarters, then, a little later, they were turned out of the camp, and command was given by general consent to two private soldiers, Gaius Albius from Cales and an Umbrian called Gaius Atrius, who had led the mutiny. These men by no means rested content with the rank of military tribune but had the audacity to lay impious hands on the rods and axes, the insignia of supreme command, never pausing to imagine that those august emblems, which they had carried before them to overawe others, might soon be at work on their own backs and their own necks. Their belief in the report of Scipio's death blinded them, and they were convinced that once it was everywhere known that he was dead, all Spain would be ablaze; in the ensuing confusion money could be extorted from allies, neighbouring towns could be plundered, and what they themselves had done would, in the universal lawlessness and terror, be less conspicuous.

25. Every day now they were expecting news that Scipio was not only dead but buried. But none came; and when the rumour of his death, groundless from the first, began to lose hold, inquiries after the leaders of the mutiny began. The men one after another drew back, each hoping to give the impression that he had foolishly believed the story and had not been guilty of inventing it, so that the two leaders, left without support, began to dread their usurped insignia of office, knowing all too well that their shadow of power would soon be replaced by real and lawful authority, which would be used for their punishment. The mutiny petered out; trustworthy reports came that Scipio was not only alive but well, and seven military tribunes, sent by Scipio himself, arrived in the camp. At first they were received with resentment, but the troops soon calmed down when the tribunes began to speak with men they happended to know in conciliatory terms; they started by going round the men's quarters, then addressed groups which they saw talking together at headquarters or in the general's tent, not directly accusing them of misconduct but asking what were the grievances which had led to such unexpected and seditious behaviour. The usual reply was that they had not received their pay punctually, and that at the time of the murder of Roman troops at Iliturgi, after the loss of two Roman armies and the death of two commanders, it was by their valour that the Roman name had been defended and Spain had been held; yet, though the people of Iliturgi had been punished as they deserved, their own good service had been met with no thanks or sign of approval from anyone. The tribunes admitted that the complaints were justified and promised to report them to the commander-in-chief, adding that they were glad it was nothing more serious or less easy to put right. Scipio and the country

were, they said, by the grace of God in a position to show their gratitude.

Scipio, practised soldier though he was, had no experience in dealing with the sudden storms of a mutiny; his chief anxiety was to prevent the trouble from going too far and at the same time not to punish the offenders with unwise or excessive severity. He decided for the time being to continue his conciliatory measures and by sending collectors round the tributary states to increase the likelihood of being able to pay the men at an early date. He then issued an order for the troops to assemble at New Carthage to get their money, either in separate units or all together. The mutiny, already petering out of its own accord, was finally brought to an end by the sudden cessation of the Spanish rebellion; Mandonius and Indibilis, when they learned that Scipio was alive, had given up their attempt and returned to their own country; so there was now no one, Roman or foreigner, with whom the mutineers could share their desperate hopes. Considering all possibilities, they knew that they had only one way, and that not a very safe one, to escape the consequences of their folly – to surrender themselves to the just anger of their commander, or maybe, to the clemency they had not yet despaired of finding. How all too ready is the human mind to extenuate its own guilt! They told themselves how Scipio had pardoned even the enemies with whom he had fought; that their rebellion had caused no bloodshed, involved no violence, and could not therefore deserve a savage punishment. Their one doubt was whether it would be better to go for their pay in separate cohorts or all together. In the end the latter course was judged the safer and was consequently adopted.

26. Meanwhile a council was being held at New Carthage on the subject of the mutineers, the point at issue being whether to punish only the leaders – there were not more than thirty-five of them – or whether a larger number deserved to suffer punishment for what was, in effect, a shameful act of rebellion rather than a mere mutiny. The more lenient view prevailed that punishment should not go beyond the men who had been responsible for the outbreak; for the rest, a severe reprimand would suffice. When the council broke up, to conceal what had

in fact been the subject of discussion, orders were issued to the army at New Carthage to prepare several days' rations for an expedition against Mandonius and Indibilis; at the same time each of the seven tribunes who had previously gone to Sucro to quell the rising was given the names of five of the leaders and sent to meet the army, with further instructions to have the culprits invited by suitable persons, and with every outward appearance of friendliness, to dinner, where they were to be made sleepy with drink and then bound. The mutineers were not far from New Carthage, when the news, which they heard from people on the road, that the whole army was marching next day with Silanus against the Lacetani not only relieved them of the fears which were still lurking in their minds, but filled them with profound satisfaction, for they would have Scipio all by himself, and would not, they felt, be in his power. Just before sunset they entered the town, and saw the other army busy with its preparations to march. To maintain the deception, they were told by way of welcome that their arrival just before the departure of the other army[1] was most fortunate and opportune for the commander-in-chief. So they ate and rested without anxiety. The tribunes, without causing any disturbance, then had the leaders brought by suitable persons to visit them in their quarters, where they were seized and bound. In the latter part of the night the baggage-train of the army which was supposed to be marching on the morrow began to get away, and by dawn the standards were on the move; but at the gate the column was called to a halt and guards were posted to watch all the other gates and prevent anyone from leaving the town. The mutineers, who had been ordered to parade, truculently elbowed their way up to the general's platform, intending to intimidate him and shout him down when he started to speak; then, just as Scipio mounted the platform, the other army was brought back from the gates and drawn up in a semicircle behind the unarmed mutineers. Their confidence immediately collapsed and, as they afterwards admitted, nothing frightened them so much as the appearance and bearing of the commander: they had expected to see him a sick man, but he was as strong as ever, with the flush of health in his

1. i.e. the one about to march against Mandonius and Indibilis.

cheeks, and a look in his eyes which, they said, they did not remember to have seen even on the battlefield. He took his seat and for a moment said nothing, till word was brought him that the leaders of the mutiny had been led in and that everything was ready. 27. Then the herald called for silence and Scipio spoke as follows:

'I never thought that words in which to address my troops would fail me; not that I have ever been a man of words rather than of deeds, but because, having lived with the army almost from my boyhood, I know soldiers through and through. But now, in your presence, I do not know what to say or how to say it. I do not even know by what name I should address you. Citizens, when you have rebelled against your country? Or soldiers, when you have refused obedience to the high command and all that it implies, and violated the sanctity of your oath? Or enemies? I see in you the bodies, faces, clothes, appearance of Roman citizens, but your deeds, your words, your wishes, your hearts are those of enemies. Did you not share the hopes and desires of the Ilergetes and Lacetani? But they, at least, in their desperate attempt followed the leadership of princes – Mandonius and Indibilis; while you offered the supreme command to Atrius the Umbrian and Albius from Cales. Deny, my men, that it was all of you who did this thing, or approved it when it was done – I will accept your denial and willingly believe it was only the desperate madness of a few; for the crime was such that, were it shared by the whole army, it would call for a terrible sacrifice to wipe it out.

'Against my will I lay my finger on these sores; but unless they are touched and treated, they cannot be healed. When the Carthaginians were driven from Spain I did not think that there were any people, anywhere, in the whole country amongst whom my life was an object of hate, and surely the belief was justified by the way I had treated not friends only but enemies too. But how wrong I was! For here in my own camp the rumour that I was dead was not only believed, it was eagerly awaited. I do not accuse you all of this conduct; indeed, if I thought that every man in my army had desired my death I should die here at once before your eyes, for no life could give me pleasure if my fellow-citizens and soldiers found it a hateful thing. But a crowd is like the sea, of itself motionless, but stirred by winds, gentle or strong. You too have your calms and your storms; and the instigators of this act of madness were, as always, the sole cause of it and the fountainhead from which it flowed: you caught from them the contagion of insanity. And even now I hardly think you realize the magnitude of your folly, or the nature of the crime you have dared to commit against me, your country, your parents, and your children; against the gods who witnessed your oath of allegiance, and the auspices under which you serve; against traditional army discipline and all that is expected of a soldier, and in violation of the majesty of the supreme command.

'Of myself I say nothing. Let me grant you were fools rather than knaves when you believed me to be dead; let me admit that I am the sort of man whose command an army might reasonably enough grow sick of. But what of our country? What had she deserved of you, when you were trying to betray her in base alliance with Mandonius and Indibilis? What had the Roman people done to you that you should strip the popularly elected tribunes of their command and offer it to a couple of nobodies; nay more, not content with having them as officers, that you, a Roman army, should confer the *fasces* of your commander-in-chief upon rascals who have never even had the chance of commanding a household slave? Albius and Atrius took up their quarters in the general's tent; outside it the trumpet-calls were sounded; they were asked for the password and sat on Publius Scipio's tribunal. A lictor attended them and a way was cleared for them to pass; the rods and axes were carried in front of them. You think it against nature if it rains stones or a thunderbolt falls or animals produce the wrong sort of young; but *this* is a portent which neither sacrifice nor days of prayer can expiate, but only the blood of the men who perpetrated the crime.

28. 'No crime is based on reason, but I should like none the less to know, so far as can be known in any criminal act, what you had in mind, what your purpose really was. Some time ago a legion sent to garrison Rhegium murdered the leading men of that wealthy town and held it for ten years; in punishment for that act the entire legion – 4,000 men – were executed in the

forum at Rome. But those men, guilty though they were, did not follow the lead of Black Atrius of Umbria (what an ominous name!) but of the military tribune Decimus Vibellius; nor did they join the enemies of Rome, Pyrrhus or the Samnites or the Lucanians. You, on the contrary, shared your plans with Mandonius and Indibilis and meant to join them in arms as well. That legion intended to live in Rhegium permanently, like the Campanians in Capua when they had taken it from the Etruscans who used to live there, or the Mamertines in Messana in Sicily – they never proposed to make war upon Rome or her allies; but did *you* intend to make Sucro your home? Why, if I had left you there on my departure when the war was over, you would have had every right to raise heaven and earth to save you from the fate of not being allowed to return to your wives and children!

'No doubt you have forgotten that unhappy legion, just as you forgot your country – and me; none the less I want to trace the probable course of this plan of yours, a criminal plan, but not utterly insane. With me alive and the rest of my army intact – the army with which I took New Carthage in a single day, and utterly defeated and drove from Spain four Carthaginian generals and four Carthaginian armies – did you really propose, 8,000 of you, and all presumably of poorer stuff than Albius and Atrius to whose orders you submitted, to wrest Spain from the Roman people? Or leave me out of it altogether and suppose you have wronged me in nothing more serious than your readiness to believe me dead. Well, what then? If I had been dying, would the country have expired without me, or the power of Rome have fallen when I fell? God forbid that a city founded, with the blessing of all that is divine, to endure for ever should be supposed the equal of this frail and mortal body! Remember the many great commanders who have died in this war – Flaminius, Paullus, Gracchus, Postumius Albinus, Marcus Marcellus, Titus Quinctius Crispinus, Gnaeus Fulvius, the Scipios of my own family – yet the Roman people survive, and will continue to survive though a thousand others die by sickness or the sword. If I alone were buried, would Rome have been carried out to her grave? You yourselves here in Spain, after the death of the two army commanders, my father and my uncle, chose Marcius to lead you against the triumphant Carthaginians. But I speak as if the Spanish provinces, had I died, would have had no commander: far from it, for would Silanus, who was sent out here with the same authority as myself, or my two lieutenants, Laelius and my brother Lucius, have failed to vindicate the majesty of the high command? Could the two armies have been compared, or the leaders of them, or the leaders' rank, or the cause they would have fought for? Even if you had been the better in all these respects, would you have borne arms against your country and compatriots, or have wished Africa to rule Italy and Carthage to be the mistress of Rome? For what fault did your country deserve it? 29. Coriolanus, long ago, unjustly condemned to miserable exile, was driven by that undeserved punishment to march against his country; but the sacred bonds of family devotion stayed his treasonable hand. But you had no grievance, no reason for anger to drive you – unless you think a few days' delay in getting your money, during your general's sickness, a sufficient excuse for declaring war on your country, going over from Rome to the Ilergetes, leaving nothing, human or divine, free from the touch of your impious hands.

'Soldiers, you were out of your senses; your minds were no less sick than my body was. I shudder to recall what men believed, what they hoped for or desired. May it all vanish into oblivion, if that is possible, or at least be buried in silence. I would not deny that my words must have sounded harsh and bitter in your ears, but is what I have said any less cruel than what you have done? You think it right that I should endure your acts, but that I should even speak of them you find intolerable! But enough; vile though those acts have been, they will have no further reproaches from me. Would that you could forget them as easily as I! So far as most of you are concerned, I have punished you enough if you are sorry for your mistake; but Albius of Cales and Atrius the Umbrian and the other leaders of this wicked mutiny shall pay with their blood for what they have done. To the rest of you, if you are sane again, the spectacle of their punishment should bring not pain but joy, for to no one have they been bitterer or more cruel enemies than to yourselves.'

Scipio had scarcely finished speaking when terror, already prepared in all its shapes, audible and visible, revealed itself amongst them. The troops surrounding the mutinous army clashed their swords against their shields; the voice of the herald rang out calling the names of the condemned men; they were dragged, stripped, into the centre, and the instruments of punishment were brought out. Bound to the stake they were scourged and beheaded, while their watching comrades stood so numbed with fear that there was no cry of protest against the severity of the punishment, not even a groan. Then the bodies were dragged away, and when the ground had been cleansed the soldiers were called up individually by name and, in the the presence of the military tribunes, swore allegiance to Scipio. Each as he was called was given his pay.

30. About the same time as the mutiny at Sucro, which ended as I have described, Hanno, serving along the Baetis as a cavalry officer under Mago, was sent from Gades with a small party of Africans to raise troops, and by the offer of pay succeeded in arming some 4,000 Spaniards. He was shortly afterwards defeated by Marcius and his camp was taken; most of his men were lost during the confusion of the capture, and some were killed by the Roman cavalry as they were trying to make their escape. Hanno got away with a few survivors.

Meanwhile Laelius took his fleet through the Straits to Carteia, a town on the Atlantic coast where the sea begins to open out west of the narrow entrance. There had been a good chance, as I have already mentioned, of taking Gades without bloodshed, as representatives came to the Roman camp with a promise to betray it. But the plot came to light before it could be put into effect; Mago arrested the conspirators and handed them over to the magistrate Adherbal for deportation to Carthage. Adherbal shipped them in a quinquereme, which he sent on ahead as being the slower vessel, and himself followed not far behind with a squadron of eight triremes. The quinquereme was just entering the Straits when Laelius, also in a quinquereme and followed by seven triremes, came out of the harbour of Carteia and made for Adherbal and his triremes, confident that the quinquereme, once inside the Straits, would be unable to make its way back against the strong tide. The

Carthaginian, taken by surprise, was in two minds whether to follow his quinquereme or attack the enemy ships; but his mind was soon made up for him by the fact that the enemy was close aboard and well within range, so that to refuse battle was no longer possible. Besides, the ships once they were in the rush of tide were no longer under control. The battle which followed was by no means according to the book; no skill or strategy was possible, no planned manoeuvre of any kind. The tide took complete charge of everything, carrying vessels on to friends or enemies indiscriminately despite the efforts of the crews to keep them off. A vessel trying to escape pursuit would be swung right round and swept head-on against her victorious pursuers, and a vessel giving chase might at any moment find herself stern-on to the enemy, like a fugitive. In actual combat a ship trying to ram an enemy would turn broadside-on and be rammed herself; or another, with her broadside exposed, would suddenly swing and drive ahead to the attack. Chance ruled; but while the triremes were engaged in this indecisive manner, the Roman quinquereme – perhaps because her size steadied her, or because her more numerous banks of oars made her easier to control in the tide-rip – sank two triremes and sheered off the oars from one side of a third. She might have seriously damaged any others she closed with, but Adherbal, with the five ships he still had, made sail and got away to the African coast, leaving Laelius the victor.[1]

31. Returning to Carteia Laelius heard of what had happened at Gades – how the plot to betray the town had been exposed and the conspirators had been sent to Carthage with their object unaccomplished. He accordingly sent a message to Marcius saying that unless they wanted merely to waste time by hanging about at Gades they ought to rejoin the commander-in-chief at once. Marcius agreed, and a few days later both men returned to New Carthage. Mago, who had been threatened by both land and sea, was much relieved by their departure, and, what was even better, the news that the Ilergetes had risen against Rome gave him hopes of recovering control of Spain. With this in view he sent messengers to the senate in Carthage with

1. Livy as this passage shows, was sadly ignorant of nautical matters. (A. de S.)

instructions to exaggerate the mutiny in the Roman camp and the extent of the defection amongst the tribes allied to Rome in order to persuade them to send reinforcements by which the empire of Spain, inherited from their fathers, might be won back.

Mandonius and Indibilis returned home and remained for a time quietly awaiting news of the outcome of the mutiny, for they were reasonably confident that if the mutineers – Roman citizens – were pardoned for going astray, then their own misconduct, too, might well be forgiven. But once the extreme severity of the punishment became known, they could not but think that their own guilt deserved, in Roman eyes, a similar penalty; so once again they called their people to arms, collected such auxiliary forces as they had had before, and with 20,000 foot and 2,500 horse crossed into the territory of the Sedetani, where they had had a permanent camp at the beginning of the rebellion.

32. Scipio, by scrupulously paying his men, both the innocent and the guilty, and still more by the kindly looks and friendly words he bestowed on all alike, had quickly won back their respect and affection. Before leaving New Carthage he called an assembly and made a long speech inveighing against the treachery of the rebellious chieftains, and declaring that he was setting out to punish their crime with feelings very different from what they were when, a short time ago, he had administered medicine to cure an aberration on the part of his own troops. 'Then,' he said, 'when with groans and tears I atoned with the lives of thirty men for the folly or guilt of eight thousand, it was like a knife thrust into my own flesh; but now, on the march to slaughter the Ilergetes, I am filled with confidence and joy. The Ilergetes were not born in the same country as I; no ties bind us together – one did, the bond of honour and friendship but they have basely broken it. As to my own army, I am moved to see that all the men in it are Roman citizens or allies and Latins, and even more because there is hardly a soldier who has not been brought from Italy either by my uncle Gnaeus Scipio, the first Roman to enter Spain, or by my father the consul, or by myself. You are all familiar with the name and auspices of the Scipios, and it is my wish to take you home with

me to share my well-earned triumph, and my hope that you will support me when I stand for the consulship, as if it were an honour which belongs to us all.

'As for the expedition we have on hand at the moment, it is a mere nothing – anyone who calls it a war must have forgotten what we have already achieved. I am less concerned about the Ilergetes even than about Mago, who has escaped with a few ships to Gades on its Atlantic island beyond the limits of the world; for in that remote spot there is, at least, a Carthaginian general and a Carthaginian garrison, however small, while here there are only brigands and robber-captains, capable no doubt of raiding their neighbours' fields, burning their houses, and stealing their cattle, but quite powerless in a regular engagement with a hostile army. If they fight, they'll run, trusting their speed, not their swords. So it is not because I see danger in them, or think that their rebellion may lead to a more serious war, that I want them crushed before I leave my province; it is because, first, their criminal defection must not go unpunished, and, secondly, because it must not be said that any enemy has been left in a province we have so courageously and successfully reduced to subjection. So with God's good help follow me – not, indeed, to do battle with an enemy worthy of our steel, but to punish criminals as they deserve.'

33. After his speech Scipio dismissed his troops with orders to prepare to march on the following day. Reaching the Ebro in ten stages, he crossed the river and four days later pitched camp in sight of the enemy. In front of him was level ground enclosed on both sides by mountains; into the valley thus formed Scipio caused cattle to be driven – most of them stolen from the Spaniards themselves – to rouse the predatory instinct of the wild tribesmen; he then sent in a company of skirmishers, at the same time ordering Laelius to keep his cavalry concealed and in readiness; as soon as the skirmishers had the enemy engaged, Laelius was to charge. A convenient spur of the hills offered cover for the cavalry, and the fighting began at once: the Spaniards made a dash for the cattle as soon as they saw them, and while they were engaged in rounding them up Scipio's skirmishers attacked. Having tried the effect of missiles and found them more of an irritant than a weapon capable of

forcing a decision, they stopped using them and drew their swords; hand to hand fighting began and the two forces would have been evenly matched but for the arrival of the Roman cavalry. One section of it, in a frontal attack, rode the Spaniards down, while another making a detour round the bottom of the hill appeared in their rear, so that most of them found their escape barred and more were killed than is usually the case in minor scuffles of this kind.

For the Spaniards the result of their defeat was anger, not discouragement, and at dawn next morning, determined to show that their spirit was as high as ever, they formed once again for battle. The valley, as I have already said, was narrow – too narrow to allow the deployment of all their troops; about two thirds of their infantry, therefore, moved into line, together with the whole cavalry force; the remainder of the infantry were left straggling up the side of the hill. In Scipio's view the lack of room to manoeuvre was in his favour, both because fighting in a confined space was likely to suit Roman troops better than Spanish and because the enemy line had been driven to take up a position on ground which did not afford room for his whole force. Seeing therefore that his own cavalry could not, for lack of space, be used to protect his flanks, while the Spanish cavalry which had been brought down into the valley with the infantry would be quite useless, he made an unexpected tactical move, and ordered Laelius to take the Roman cavalry round the back of the hills by any route which would least expose them to view. The object of this move was to avoid mixing mounted and unmounted troops in the coming engagement and to keep the two arms, so far as possible, separate. Meanwhile Scipio ordered his whole infantry force to face the enemy, forming his front line of four cohorts, there being insufficient room to extend further. He then engaged at once, to distract attention from his mounted troops which were making their way round over the hills; nor, in fact, did the Spaniards realize they were outflanked until they heard the din of cavalry coming into action in their rear. The two arms, infantry and cavalry, were now separately engaged; down the narrow valley – too narrow to permit anything like a mixed action involving both together – two lines of foot and two squadrons of horse were in action against each other. On the Spanish side neither arm could support the other: the Spanish infantry, which had been rashly brought into its present position through reliance on cavalry support, was being cut to pieces, and the Spanish cavalry, outflanked and surrounded, could do nothing, now that their unmounted comrades had been wiped out, either against the Roman infantry in front of them or the Roman cavalry in their rear. They formed a circle and sat their horses, trying to defend themselves as long as they could, but in the end they were all killed. Of all who fought in that valley, not a single Spanish infantryman or cavalryman survived; only the remaining third of the Spanish force, which had stayed on the slope of the hill to watch the fight from a place of safety rather than take part in it, were enabled by their position to find an opportunity to escape. The two princes escaped with them, slipping away in the general confusion before the whole line could be surrounded.

34. On the same day the Spanish camp was captured, with about 3,000 men in addition to other booty. Roman and allied losses in the battle amounted to about 1,200 men killed and over 3,000 wounded; the victory would have been less costly if the fighting had been on more open ground where there would have been a better chance for the hard-pressed to make their escape.

Indibilis now abandoned all idea of armed rebellion and sent his brother Mandonius to Scipio in the belief that the safest course in his difficult position would be to trust to the Roman general's well-tried honour and clemency. Mandonius, flinging himself down at Scipio's knees, laid the blame for what had happened on the fatal madness of the times which, like some deadly contagion, had infected and driven crazy even the Roman army itself, not to mention the Ilergetes and Lacetani. To himself, he declared, and to his brother and the rest of his countrymen two courses only were now open: either, should Scipio so wish it, to surrender to him the breath of life they had already received at his hands, or, if they were twice spared, to devote for ever to his service the life they owed to him alone. Before they had known his clemency, they had had confidence in their cause; now, that confidence was gone and their only hope lay in the compassion of their conqueror.

It had long been the Roman practice in cases where no formal treaty on regular and equal terms was involved, not to exert the authority of a victor over a conquered enemy until everything human and divine had been surrendered, hostages received, weapons confiscated, and garrisons posted in his towns. Scipio acted differently. He did, indeed, use harsh language against Mandonius and his absent brother, declaring that they had fallen deservedly by their own criminal act and would now owe their lives to the merciful kindness of himself and the people of Rome. None the less he would not, he said, demand hostages or force them to surrender their arms; hostages, after all, were guarantees of men who feared a resumption of hostilities. 'No,' he continued; 'I am leaving you free; I am leaving you your arms to do with as you please. If you rebel, it will be yourselves I shall punish, not innocent hostages; I shall seek revenge not upon the helpless but upon an armed enemy. You have known me now both as enemy and friend: you may choose whether you prefer to have the Romans on your side, or ranged in anger against you.'

Mandonius was then dismissed with orders to furnish money only sufficient to cover the soldiers' pay. Marcius was sent on into Further Spain and Silanus was instructed to return to Tarraco, while Scipio himself, after a few days' delay to allow the Ilergetes to pay over the money which had been demanded, set off with troops marching light and overtook Marcius not far from the Atlantic coast.

35. Negotiations with Masinissa, already begun before this time, had been put off for one reason or another because he was determined at all costs to meet Scipio in person and clasp his hand upon any agreement they might make. It was also with a view to these negotiations that Scipio undertook his long and devious march. Masinissa while he was still in Gades had been informed by Marcius of Scipio's approach, and he succeeded in persuading Mago to allow him to cross to the mainland with the ostensible purpose of raiding Spanish territory in the neighbourhood. He argued, in order to obtain his request, that the horses were in bad condition from being shut up in the island: they were causing a general scarcity for everyone else

as well as suffering from it themselves, while at the same time prolonged inactivity was destroying the morale of the troopers. Once across on the mainland he sent on three Numidian chieftains to arrange a time and place for the interview. His instructions were that two of them should be retained by Scipio as hostages; the third was sent back to bring Masinissa to the agreed meeting-place, whither they came with a few attendants to hold the conference.

Masinissa already admired Scipio from what he had heard of his military successes, and had formed a picture of him in his mind as a man of powerful and impressive physique, but when he saw him face to face admiration deepened to awe. In addition to great natural dignity, Scipio's long hair lent him grace; his whole aspect and bearing, which owed nothing to studied elegance of dress or toilet, were truly virile and soldierly, and he was just of the age when his physical powers were at their height, seeming to be yet fuller and brighter by a sort of reflowering, after his illness, of his youthful bloom.

Masinissa was profoundly affected by the meeting. He thanked Scipio for sending back his nephew[1] and declared that ever since then he had sought the opportunity which he eagerly grasped when at last it was offered him by the favour of the gods. 'My desire,' he said, 'is so to labour for you and the people of Rome that no single foreigner shall ever have done better or more strenuous service to the Roman cause. This has long been my ambition, but I have been unable to do what I wished here in the strange and unknown land of Spain. However, to do it will be easy in the country where I was born and where I was brought up in the expectation of succeeding to my father's throne. If the Romans send Scipio to command their armies in Africa, I am confident that the hours of Carthage will be numbered.'

Scipio both saw and heard him with pleasure, knowing as he did that his mounted troops had been the very cream of the enemy's cavalry – not to mention the gallant aspect of the young chieftain himself. Pledges were given and received and Scipio started on his return journey to Tarraco. Masinissa carried out some raids in the neighbourhood, by permission of the

1. Massiva; cf. p. 455.

Romans, to disguise the real purpose of his crossing to the mainland, and then return to Gades.

36. Mago had been encouraged to hope for success in Spain first by the mutiny in the Roman army and then by the revolt of Indibilis. These hopes were now gone, and as he was preparing to cross to Africa orders reached him from the government in Carthage to take the fleet he had with him at Gades to Italy. He was then to recruit for pay as many Gallic and Ligurian fighting men as possible and join forces with Hannibal in order to prevent the Carthaginian war-effort, begun with great vigour and even greater success, from petering out. Money was brought him from Carthage for the purpose, and he himself wrung all he could from the people of Gades, not only emptying their treasury but robbing the temples and forcing every individual to contribute such gold and silver as he possessed.

Sailing along the Spanish coast, Mago landed troops not far from New Carthage for a raid on the countryside, and then put in with his fleet at the town itself. Keeping his men aboard during the day, he landed them after dark, and in the belief that the town was inadequately defended and that some of the inhabitants might well make trouble in the hope of throwing out the Romans, he moved up to the section of the wall at which the Romans had made their successful entry. But the enemy's arrival was already known in the town; men from the outlying farms had come in in great excitement with news of the raids and the flight of the farm-people; the fleet had been seen before darkness fell, and it was clear enough that its position in front of the town had not been chosen without reason. Accordingly troops were kept drawn up under arms inside the gate which faced the lagoon and the sea. The Carthaginians made their approach in no sort of order, soldiers and ships' crews all mixed together, and just as they were up to the walls, their bark being much worse than their bite, the Romans flung the gate open, raised their war-cry, and came out at the double. The Carthaginians were thrown into confusion; at the first charge and the first volley of missiles they turned tail and were chased back to the beach with much slaughter, and every man of them, fighting or trying to escape, would have been killed if the ships lying just off the beach had not been there to receive them. On the ships too there was much confusion. For fear that the Romans might get aboard together with their own people, they were shipping the gangways in a desperate hurry and cutting shore- and anchor-cables to avoid the delay involved in handling them properly. Many of their men swimming out to the ships and uncertain in the half-light what to look for and what to avoid perished miserably. Next day, when the fleet had gone safely back again to the open sea, some 800 bodies and 2,000 weapons were found between the wall and the shore.

37. Mago on his return to Gades found himself shut out of the town. Sailing in to Cimbii, which was not far distant, he sent representatives back to Gades to complain of the gates' being barred against a friend and ally; the people of the town tried to excuse themselves by saying it had been the work of a section of the populace which was enraged because the soldiers had stolen property of theirs when they went aboard ship; whereupon Mago enticed to a conference the *sufetes* of the town (the highest sort of Carthaginian magistrate) together with the treasurer, and, once they were in his power, had them scourged and crucified.

He then sailed for the island of Pityusa, which lies about 100 miles off the coast and was inhabited at that time by Carthaginians. His fleet was consequently welcomed with all friendliness; supplies were generously furnished and, in addition, weapons were given him and men to supplement the ships' crews. This addition to his strength encouraged him to sail for the Balearic Islands, fifty miles away.

There are two Balearic islands, one larger than the other and richer in men and arms. It has a harbour too, in which Mago judged (it now being the end of autumn) that he could conveniently lay up his ships for the winter. But his reception there was as rough as if the island's inhabitants had been Romans: the sling, still their chief weapon, was then their only one, and nobody in the world can use it with the surpassing skill possessed by every one of these islanders. The result was that as Mago's fleet drew in to the land, it was met by volleys of stones as thick as a violent hailstorm, so that they did not dare enter the harbour. Putting off to sea again they crossed to the smaller island, which, though the soil is rich, was not so populous or so well defended. They disembarked and established themselves in a strong position above the harbour; they took possession of the town and its adjacent lands without opposition, impressed and sent to Carthage 2,000 auxiliary troops, and hauled their ships ashore for the winter. The men of Gades, after Mago's departure from the Atlantic coast, surrendered to the Romans.

38. Such were the achievements in Spain under the leadership and auspices of Scipio. Scipio now handed over control to the pro-praetors Lucius Lentulus and Lucius Manlius Acidinus, and returned with ten ships to Rome. At a meeting of the Senate held for him outside the city in the temple of Bellona he gave an account of his Spanish campaigns, detailing the number of pitched battles fought, of enemy towns captured, and of Spanish peoples forced to acknowledge the dominion of Rome. He reminded the Senate that he had gone to Spain to face four enemy commanders and four victorious Carthaginian armies and had left not a single Carthaginian soldier in the country. For these services to his country he could not but hope for the honour of a triumph, though he would not persist in asking for it because everybody knew that up to the present time nobody who had commanded armies without holding a regular magistracy had ever celebrated a triumph. So the Senate was dismissed and Scipio entered the city preceded by his contribution to the treasury of 14,342 pounds weight of silver and a great quantity of silver coins. Lucius Veturius Philo then held the consular elections and all the centuries showed their enthusiastic and unanimous support in naming Publius Cornelius Scipio as consul. Publius Licinius Crassus, the *pontifex maximus*, was returned as his colleague. It is on record that the election drew a greater crowd of people than any other during the war; they had come not only to vote but to see Scipio, and great throngs followed him to his house and attended him to the Capitol to watch him sacrifice the hundred oxen which he had vowed to Jupiter while he was in Spain. They promised themselves that Scipio, like Lutatius before him in the first Punic war, should bring any fighting that was still to come to a successful conclusion, and that he should drive the Carthaginians from Italy as he had driven them from Spain. Indeed, they were

already in their thoughts giving him Africa as his field of operations, as if the war in Italy were over.

Elections for praetors were then held. Two men, Spurius Lucretius and Gnaeus Octavius, who were plebeian aediles at the time were elected, and two others, Gnaeus Servilius Caepio and Lucius Aemilius Papus, who held no office.

It was now the fourteenth year of the war. Scipio and Crassus having entered upon the consulship, their respective spheres of action were defined – Bruttium falling to Crassus and Sicily to Scipio. For the latter, lots were not drawn, Crassus making no objection because he, as *pontifex maximus*, was kept in Italy by his religious duties. The praetors' assignments were then drawn for; the City praetorship fell to Gnaeus Servilius; Ariminum (by which Gaul was meant) to Spurius Lucretius; Sicily to Lucius Aemilius, and Sardinia to Gnaeus Octavius.

The Senate met on the Capitol. On a motion of Scipio's a decree was passed enabling him to defray by the money he had himself brought into the treasury the expenses of the games which during the mutiny in Spain he had vowed to celebrate.
39. He then introduced the ambassadors from Saguntum, and the eldest of them addressed the Senate in the following terms: 'Although, gentlemen, to prove our unbounded loyalty to you we have faced the ultimate extreme of suffering, such have been the services rendered to us by you and your generals that we do not regret the miseries we have endured. It was on our account that you undertook this war; and now for fourteen years you have been fighting it with such determination that many a time you have both come yourselves, and brought the Carthaginian people, into a desperately critical situation. In spite of the fact that in Italy you had war to the death and Hannibal himself for your adversary, you sent an army under the command of a consul into Spain to salvage, as it were, the wreckage of our fortunes. The two elder Scipios, once they were in Spain, never ceased to act to our advantage and to the detriment of our enemies. First of all they gave us back our town; they sent all over Spain in search of our compatriots who had been sold into slavery, and restored them to liberty; then, when the desire of our hearts had all but returned to us after the miseries we had

suffered, your two great generals, Publius and Gnaeus Scipio both perished, bringing almost more grief to us than to you.

'Then it was that we felt we had been brought back from distant places to our old home only that we might die a second death and see our native town once again destroyed. There was no need for a Carthaginian army or general to effect our ruin – we could be blotted out easily enough by our old enemies the Turduli, who had been the cause of our former destruction. But at that moment, gentlemen, suddenly and beyond all expectation you sent us *this* Scipio, our hope, our strength, our salvation. We are the most fortunate of all our fellow-countrymen to see him declared consul, and to be able to tell our friends, on our return, of that most happy sight. This man, who captured countless towns belonging to your enemies in Spain, on every occasion separated citizens of Saguntum from the other prisoners and sent them home; and he finally inflicted on the Turdetani, a people who hated us so bitterly that while they remained strong Saguntum could never stand firm, a defeat so crushing that never again could they be an object of fear to us, nor yet (not to tempt providence by so rash a word!) to our descendants either. We see in ruins the city of a people for whose sake Hannibal had destroyed Saguntum; we receive as tribute the produce of their land, tribute pleasant enough as added wealth, but yet sweeter as revenge. For these benefits, greater than any we could hope or pray for, the senate and people of Saguntum have sent us, their ten legates, to thank you in their name, and at the same time to congratulate you on having fought during these years in Spain and Italy with such success that Spain is now subject to your armies not only as far south as the Ebro but to the remotest parts on the Atlantic coast, while in Italy you have left nothing in Carthaginian hands but the little circle within the rampart of their camp. We are bidden not only to render thanks for all these things to Jupiter Greatest and Best, Defender of the Capitol, but also to carry thither, if you permit it, this golden crown as a gift in recognition of your victory. We beg you to grant us this favour, and also, should it be your pleasure, to ratify in perpetuity the benefits which your generals have conferred upon us.'

In reply the Senate assured the Saguntine ambassadors that the destruction and restoration of Saguntum would be an example to the world of loyalty between allies honourably maintained by both; that the Roman generals had acted with absolute propriety and according to the Senate's will in restoring Saguntum and liberating its citizens from servitude, and that the Senate approved any further services the generals might have rendered. Finally, they gave permission for the gift to be deposited on the Capitol. Instructions were then issued for lodgings and all necessary comforts to be provided for the envoys, and for a sum of not less than 10,000 *asses* to be given as a personal present to each of them. After this the other delegations were admitted to the Senate and given a hearing; and as the envoys from Saguntum asked permission to see as much of Italy as they safely could, guides were provided and letters sent to the various towns with instructions that the Spaniards should be courteously received. The Senate then turned to the consideration of policy, the enrolment of troops, and the distribution of duties.

40. It was now common talk that Scipio was to dispense with the usual process of drawing lots with his colleague and was to take over Africa as his sphere of action – a province never before assigned to a Roman commander. He himself, no longer satisfied with such minor distinction as he had already won, was saying he had been named consul with the object not merely of conducting the war but of bringing it to an end; and this could be achieved only if he personally took an army across to Africa, which, he openly declared, he would do by the people's authority if the Senate opposed him. This plan of campaign was by no means approved by the leaders of the Senate, and while the rest expressed no definite opinion, either because they were afraid to do so or in the hope of ingratiating themselves with their betters, the question was put to Quintus Fabius Maximus, who replied in the following terms. 'I am aware, gentlemen, that many of you feel that we are debating today an issue which has already been decided and that to express an opinion upon fighting in Africa as if it were still an open question would be merely to waste words. But I for one fail to see how the assignment of Africa to our brave and energetic

consul can be taken as settled, when there has been no resolution in the Senate and no order from the people that it should be a theatre of operations for the coming year at all. If it is so, then, in my opinion, the consul is at fault who insults the Senate by pretending to bring a motion on a matter which is already settled, not the senator who takes his turn to speak on the subject under consideration.

'I know very well that in opposing this excessive hurry to invade Africa I shall have to face hostile criticism on two counts: first I shall be blamed for my natural tendency to avoid precipitate action, which the young are at liberty to call fear or indolence, provided they are still willing to recognize that though other men's strategy has always at first sight worn a more alluring look, mine has proved better in practice; secondly I shall incur the charge of ill-will and envy of the daily increasing fame of a brave consul. From this latter suspicion surely I am defended by my past life and character and by the distinctions I have won in my dictatorship and my five consulships, and so much honour as both soldier and statesman that I might well feel that I have had too much of it, not too little; and if that is no defence, then my age surely is; for how can I compete with a man who is younger even than my own son? Remember the attack made upon me by my master of Horse when I was dictator; yet, though I was still at the height of my powers and in the full tide of great events, no one either in the Senate or out of it heard me utter a word of protest against making his power equal with mine, a thing which had never been heard of before. I wanted by deeds not by words to force a man, who in the opinion of some had been put on a level with myself, to admit before many days were past that I was the better soldier. Is it then likely that now, at the end of my career, I should enter into jealous rivalry with one in the very flower of his manhood for the prize of this African campaign – that the task of conducting it, if refused to him, should be assigned to me, an old man worn out not by work only but by the sheer burden of many years? My duty is to live and die with such glory as I have already won. I prevented Hannibal from defeating us, and thus enabled you who are young and strong to bring him finally to his knees.

41. 'In my own case, Scipio, my country has always been more precious than what men might say of me; so in all fairness I ask you to pardon me if I do not rate even your glory above the welfare of Rome. If there were no war in Italy, or if the enemy on Italian soil were such that no glory could be won by his defeat, then indeed anyone who tried to keep you at home, even though he did so for the public good, might well seem determined to rob you of the possible glory of an African campaign. But our enemy is Hannibal; with an army still intact he has been entrenched in Italy for nearly fourteen years: can it be then that you, Scipio, will not be satisfied with your fame if during your consulship you rid Italy of an enemy who has inflicted upon us so much loss of life, so many defeats, and enjoy, like Gaius Lutatius in our former struggle with Carthage, the distinction of bringing the present war to a successful conclusion? It cannot be – unless indeed Hamilcar is supposed to be a better general than Hannibal, that war a greater one than this, and our former victory more splendid than our next is likely to be – only granted that, under your leadership, we win it. Would you rather have forced Hamilcar from Drepana, or down from Mount Eryx, than have driven Hannibal and the Carthaginians from Italy? Not even you – not even if you took more pleasure in glory won than in glory hoped for – would have been prouder of ending the war in Spain than of ending the war in Italy.

'Hannibal is formidable still: to prefer to fight elsewhere may well look more like fear than contempt. Why then do you not gird yourself for the campaign which lies before you? Tell us no more that when you have crossed to Africa Hannibal will surely follow you; cut short those devious ways; march direct to where Hannibal at this moment is, and fight him there. You want the victor's palm for ending the war with Carthage? Remember none the less that it is only natural to defend your own before attacking what is another's. Let there be peace in Italy before there is war in Africa; let us feel safe ourselves before we proceed to threaten others. If under your auspices and command both ends can be achieved, beat Hannibal here first, then cross the sea and capture Carthage; if one or the other of these victories must be left to your successors in the consulship, the first one will prove the greater and more famous, just as it will be the cause of the second.

'Situated as we now are, even apart from the fact that public funds cannot support two separate armies, one in Italy, one in Africa, and no resources are left for maintaining fleets and furnishing supplies, the magnitude of the danger we run is surely patent to everyone. Licinius will be fighting in Italy, Scipio in Africa: now just suppose – which God forbid: I shudder to speak of such a thing, but what has happened once may happen again – just suppose, I say, that Hannibal is victorious and marches on Rome, are we then, and not before, to recall you from Africa, as we did Fulvius from Capua?[1] Remember too that even in Africa the fortunes of war may be fickle; take warning from your own house, from your father and uncle, killed within thirty days of each other and their armies destroyed, and *that* in a country where by years of great achievement on land and sea they had won for your family and for Rome an honourable name amongst foreign nations. Time would fail me if I tried to enumerate all the kings and commanders who rashly invaded foreign soil with utter disaster to their armies and themselves: the Athenians, for instance, for once forgot their native prudence and, on the suggestion of a young citizen as venturesome in character as he was noble in blood,[2] abandoned the war in Greece and sailed with a great fleet to Sicily, where in a single naval defeat they brought irreparable ruin upon their once prosperous community.

42. 'But all this is far away and long ago. Let us take warning from this same Africa of yours and from Marcus Atilius Regulus, so notable an example of the fickleness of fortune. Believe me, Scipio, when you sight Africa from the sea, all your adventures in Spain will seem to have been no more than child's play. What comparison is there between the two? With no threat from hostile fleets you sailed along the coasts of Italy and Gaul, putting in at the friendly town of Emporiae; you landed your men and led them to friends and allies at Tarraco through country which held no hint of danger. From

1. See p. 365.
2. Alcibiades.

Tarraco your route lay past a chain of Roman strongposts; on the Ebro were the armies of your father and uncle, rendered all the more eager for battle by the very disaster of their generals' death; there too in command was that fine soldier Lucius Marcius, appointed, indeed, not in the regular course but by the mens' votes to meet the emergency, yet equal in all the arts of war to famous generals had he but possessed the distinction of noble blood and the normal course of promotion. You captured New Carthage at your leisure, for not one of the three Carthaginian armies attempted to defend their allies; as for your other achievements – and I do not belittle them – they are in no way to be compared with a campaign in Africa, where there is no harbour open to our fleet, no conquered territory, no allied settlement nor friendly king, nowhere to stand, nowhere to go, but wherever you turn your eyes nothing but hostility and danger.

'Perhaps you trust Syphax and the Numidians? You have done so once – beware of trusting them again. A bold move cannot always succeed; often treachery wins confidence in little things so that when the moment is ripe it may betray and reap a large reward. The enemy did not defeat your father and uncle on the field until their Celtiberian friends had first betrayed them; nor were you yourself in as much danger from the enemy's generals, Mago and Hasdrubal, as from Indibilis and Mandonius whom you had received under your protection. Can you trust the Numidians when your own troops have mutinied? Both Syphax and Masinissa would like to be supreme in Africa, while the Carthaginians themselves are naturally jealous of all rivalry; as things now are, while there is still no threat of foreign invasion, there is mutual suspicion and jealousy between them and every reason for conflict; but show them Roman arms and foreign troops and they will very soon unite to extinguish the fire which threatens to destroy them all. They will be the same Carthaginians who fought in defence of Spain, but very different will be the defence of their own city-walls, the temples of their gods, their altars and hearts, when trembling wives lead them from their homes on the way to the battlefield and little children fall tumbling in their way.

'And what again if the Carthaginians, deriving confidence

from the unanimity of Africa, the loyal support of allied princes, and the strength of their own walls, and seeing Italy denuded of the protection of your army, and yourself no longer there, should take the offensive again and send a fresh invading force against us, or order Mago, who is known to have left the Balearics and to be already sailing along the coast of the Alpine Ligurians, to join forces with Hannibal? We should be in the same sort of danger as we were not long ago when Hasdrubal made his descent into Italy – Hasdrubal, whom you, though you now propose to blockade not only Carthage but all Africa, allowed to slip through your fingers. You will say you had defeated him; then so much the less – for your own sake as well as the country's – should I have been willing to see a beaten man given a passage into Italy. Allow us to put down to your military skill everything which has turned out well for you and for Rome, and dismiss the failures as due to the chances of war and the instability of fortune: then the better and braver soldier you are, the more eager is your native city and all Italy to keep for themselves so potent a defender. Not even you can shut your eyes to the truth that the very head and seat of the war is where Hannibal is – indeed you claim that your object in going to Africa is to draw Hannibal after you. So whether you fight here or there, it is with Hannibal you will have to deal.

'Say then, will you be stronger alone in Africa or here in Italy, supported by your colleague's army? Is not the recent example of the consuls Nero and Livius sufficient proof of the difference? And as for Hannibal, in which circumstances is he likely to be the stronger, when he is boxed up in a corner of Bruttium, still vainly asking for reinforcements from home, or when he is close to Carthage with all Africa at his back? It is surely an odd sort of strategy to prefer to fight when your own numbers are cut by half and those of the enemy greatly increased, rather than when two armies of your own have the chance of dealing with a single enemy force already exhausted by the innumerable struggles of a long and exacting campaign.

'Remember and compare what you are proposing to do with what your father did. Your father started for Spain, but returned to Italy from his province in order to meet Hannibal as he came down from the Alps;[1] you, on the contrary, with Hannibal in Italy, are preparing to leave it, not because you think that such a move would help the country but rather that it would redound to your own glory and credit – just as without legal authorization or any decree of the Senate you, a general of the Roman people, left your province and army and entrusted to a couple of ships the fortunes of the State and the majesty of our empire, the safety of which was at the moment intimately bound up with your own.

'In my view, gentlemen of the Senate, Publius Cornelius Scipio has been made consul, not for his own personal benefit but to serve the country and us, and the armed forces have been raised for the protection of Rome and Italy, not for arrogant consuls who fancy themselves kings to whisk away to any part of the world they please.'

43. Apart from the aptness to the circumstances of Fabius's speech, his personal authority and his established reputation for soundness of judgement had a powerful effect upon a large part of the Senate, especially upon the senior members, who were more inclined to accept the advice of the old statesman and warrior than to praise the high and adventurous spirit of his young rival.

Scipio is said to have delivered the following address.

'Fabius himself, gentleman, at the beginning of his speech mentioned that he might be suspected of deliberate disparagement of myself; and though I should never venture to accuse so great a man of such a thing, none the less the suspicion of it has not been fully cleared away. Maybe his facts are wrong, maybe only his expression of them. To obviate the charge of envy he made a great deal of his own achievements and the high positions he has held, as if it were only from mere nobodies that I need fear rivalry, and not from a man who, because of his pre-eminence (a pre-eminence which I admit that I, too, am striving to attain) is unwilling that I should be thought his equal. Again, he has represented himself as an old man whose achievements are in the past, and me as even younger than his son, as if the desire for fame were coextensive only with the span of human life, and the greatest part of it were not what

1. See p. 56.

lives on in the memory of posterity. I myself am convinced that the noblest minds compare themselves not only with their contemporaries but with great men in every age; nor do I pretend, Fabius, that I do not wish to rival your fame – indeed, if you will pardon my saying so, my ambition is to surpass it if I can. I hope your attitude towards me, and mine towards younger men, may never be such that we are unwilling for anyone else to come in time to be as we are; for jealousy like that would be harmful not only to its immediate objects, but to the country as a whole – indeed to the world.

'Fabius remarked, gentlemen, on the danger I should encounter if I crossed into Africa, so that he seemed to be anxious about me personally as well as about my army and the welfare of our country. Whence this sudden solicitude for me? When my father and uncle were killed and their two armies almost annihilated; when the Spanish provinces were lost and four Carthaginian generals, each in command of an army, forcibly held the whole country in the grip of fear; when an officer was needed to take command and I was the only man to offer himself for the task, nobody else having dared to submit his name; when, finally, the Roman people conferred the supreme command upon me, at the age of four-and-twenty years, why was it that no one said one word about my youth, or the enemy's strength, or the difficulties that the campaign would involve, or the recent defeat of my father and uncle? Are we the victims today of some calamity in Africa even greater than what we had then suffered in Spain? Are there more powerful armies in Africa now, or more and better generals, than there were in Spain? Was I then an older and more experienced commander than I am now? Or does it seem more natural to fight the Carthaginians in Spain than in Africa? No doubt it is easy to belittle my achievements: the utter defeat of four Carthaginian armies, innumerable towns taken by storm or terrified into submission, the conquest of the entire country up to the Atlantic coast involving the surrender of countless fierce tribes and their petty kings, the complete recovery of Spain so that no trace of opposition is left in the country. And God knows it would be just as easy, should I return victorious from Africa, to belittle those very things of which the danger is now being so grossly exaggerated, in order to keep me at home.

'According to Fabius there is no means of approach to Africa and no open harbours. He reminds us of the capture of Regulus, as if Regulus had come to grief the moment he landed; but he does not seem to remember that even that most unlucky general found African harbours easily accessible and in the first year of his campaign was highly successful, remaining, so far as Carthaginian generals are concerned, unconquered to the end. So the supposed lack of harbours can be counted out as a deterrent! If that disaster had occurred in this war instead of the last, lately instead of forty years ago,[1] what could have stopped me from crossing to Africa after the capture of Regulus any more than from going to Spain after the death of the Scipios? I should not admit that the birth of the Spartan Xanthippus[2] was a luckier event for Carthage than mine was for Rome, and my confidence would grow by the very fact that the valour of a single man could put such weight into the scales. We also, apparently, have to be told how the Athenians neglected the danger on their doorstep and rashly undertook an expedition to Sicily. Well, as you have time to tell us tales from Greek history, why did you not rather choose the story of Agathocles, King of Syracuse, who, when Sicily had for a long time been suffering the devastations of a war with Carthage, crossed to this same Africa and successfully diverted hostilities to the country of the invaders?

44. 'But why bother to use old stories from foreign lands to show the value of taking the offensive, and, by removing the threat from oneself, of bringing the other man into peril? Can there be any better or more impressive illustration of this truth than Hannibal himself? There is a big difference between devastating your enemy's country and seeing your own ravaged with fire and sword; it is in the bosom of the aggressor, not the defender, that the heart beats highest. Moreover, the unknown always brings its especial dread – but once in the enemy's country, you can have a near view of his circumstances, good

1. Really, fifty years.

2. The Spartan commander who led the Carthaginian army in 255 B.C. See Polybius I. 32 ff.

and bad alike. Hannibal never hoped that so many of the Italian communities would join him, but they did so after our defeat at Cannae. In Africa the Carthaginians, treacherous friends, oppressive and tyrannical masters as they are, are far less likely even than we were to find the country stable and strong in their support. We, even when deserted by our allies, stood firm by our own strength, our native Roman soldiery; but Carthage has no native citizen troops; her soldiers are mercenaries, Africans or Numidians, all fickle as the wind, ready to change sides at a breath. Only let there be no delay at this end, and you will hear at the same moment that I have crossed the sea, that Africa is ablaze, and that Carthage is already beset – yes, and the very sound of Hannibal's fleet making its preparations to sail. You may expect more frequent and more encouraging dispatches from Africa than you used to receive from Spain. There is much to raise these hopes in my heart – the fortune of the Roman people, the gods who witnessed the violation of the treaty by our enemies, and the two princes Syphax and Masinissa upon whose word I shall rely, though not without due precautions to protect myself from treachery.

'Action on the spot will reveal many things which distance now renders obscure; it is the duty of a commander worth his salt to seize his good fortune when it offers and turn to good use any unexpected stroke of luck. Yes, Fabius, I shall have the antagonist you give me, Hannibal himself; but he won't keep me here, I shall draw him after me. I shall force him to fight on his native ground, and the prize of victory will be Carthage, not a handful of dilapidated Bruttian forts. Nor will the State suffer harm here in Italy while I am crossing the sea, landing my troops in Africa, and moving up towards Carthage; for would it not be an insult to suggest that the service which you, Fabius, were able to render to our country when the victorious Hannibal was here, there, and everywhere in Italy as the whim took him, could not now be rendered, when Hannibal is shaken and near to breaking, by our brave consul Publius Licinius, who has refused to draw lots for service abroad in order not to be absent from his religious duties in Rome as *pontifex maximus*?

'Even if the war were not more quickly ended by the strategy I propose, it would still be worth while; for the dignity and reputation of the Roman people would surely be heightened in the eyes of foreign princes and peoples once it was seen that we had the spirit to invade Africa as well as the courage to defend Italy. We must not let the belief spread that no Roman general dares to do what Hannibal did, or that while in the first Punic war, when we were fighting for Sicily, Africa was again and again attacked by Roman fleets and armies, now, in the second, when the prize is Italy, Africa is left without molestation.

'Italy has suffered long; let her for a while have rest. It is Africa's turn to be devastated by fire and sword. It is time a Roman army threatened the gates of Carthage, rather than that we should again see from our walls the rampart of an enemy camp. Let Africa be the theatre of war henceforward; for fourteen years all the horrors of war have fallen thick upon *us*, terror and defeat, the devastation of our farms, the desertion of our friends; it is *her* turn now to suffer the same.

'It is enough to have spoken of high policy, of the now imminent campaign and the division of duties under discussion. It would be a long speech and of little concern to you, gentlemen, if I, following Fabius's lead when he belittled what I did in Spain, tried to bring his military reputation into disrepute while bolstering up my own. I shall do neither, gentlemen; in moderation and restraint of speech, if in nothing else, you will see the young man surpass the old. Such has been the quality of my life and work that I am quite capable of saying no more, and of resting content with the opinion which you have formed without any help from me.'

45. Scipio's speech was received less favourably than it might have been, because it was generally reported that he intended immediately to bring a bill before the people if he failed to prevail on the Senate to grant him Africa as his province. Accordingly Quintus Fulvius, who had been four times consul as well as censor, demanded that Scipio should openly declare in the Senate whether or not he would permit the House to pass a decree about the assignment of duties, and whether he intended to abide by that decree or to bring a bill before the people. Scipio replied that he would do what was for the interest of the State; whereupon Fulvius said; When I asked the

question I knew what you would do and what your answer would be, since you are making it clear enough that you are not really consulting the Senate at all, but merely sounding it, and that unless we promptly grant you the province you want, you have your bill ready to bring before the people. Therefore,' he continued, turning to the people's tribunes, 'I demand your protection if I refuse to express an opinion because, even if the vote goes in my favour, the consul will not consider it valid.'

An argument then began in which the consul declared that it was not legal for the tribunes to use their veto to excuse a senator from expressing his opinion when called upon in his proper turn. The tribunes then gave the following ruling: 'If the consul allows the Senate to assign the provinces, he must abide by the Senate's decision, and we shall not permit a bill on that question to be brought before the people; if the consul does not grant that permission, we shall give our protection to any member who refuses to express an opinion on the matter.'

Scipio asked for a day's grace in order to consult his colleague, and on the day after gave the Senate his permission. The provinces were assigned as follows: one consul was to have Sicily and the thirty warships[1] which Gaius Servilius had commanded the previous year, and permission was given him to cross to Africa if he judged it to be in the public interest; the other consul was to have charge of operations against Hannibal in Bruttium, with whichever of the two armies he preferred. Veturius and Caecilius were to draw lots, or decide by agreement, which of them should carry on in Bruttium with the two legions which the consul left there, and whichever should have that province assigned to him was to have his command extended for a further year. Others also who had been in command of armies and provinces had their period of command extended. When lots were drawn it fell to Caecilius to join the consul in Bruttium for operations against Hannibal.

After this Scipio's Games were held and were attended by large and enthusiastic crowds. Marcus Pomponius Matho and Quintus Catius were sent as representatives to Delphi to present

1. A small fleet: 100 ships were assigned to Sicily in 208. See p. 459.

to the temple a gift from the spoils taken from Hasdrubal; it took the form of a golden crown 200 pounds in weight together with representations in silver of the spoils of war, weighing in all 1,000 pounds.

Scipio had not pressed for permission (which indeed was never granted him) to raise fresh troops; he did, however, have the Senate's consent to take volunteers and, because he had insisted that the fleet would cost the country nothing, to receive any contributions offered by allied communities towards the construction of new vessels. The peoples of Etruria were the first to promise aid to the consul in proportion to their respective means; Caere offered grain for the crews and supplies of all sorts; Populonium promised iron; Tarquinii sail-cloth; Volaterrae grain and timber for keels and garboards; Arretium 3,000 shields, 3,000 helmets, and a total of 50,000 pikes, javelins, and spears, an equal number of each, together with enough axes, shovels, sickles, basins, and hand-mills to equip forty warships; also 120,000 measures of wheat and a contribution towards travelling allowances of petty officers and oarsmen. Perusia, Clusium, and Rusellae offered fir for building and a large quantity of grain; Scipio also used fir from state-owned woods. The Umbrian communities, and also Nursia, Reate, Amiternum, and all the Sabine territory promised soldiers. Many Marsians, Paelignians, and Marrucini volunteered for service with the fleet; Camerinum, as a free community allied to Rome, sent an armed cohort, 600 strong. The keels of thirty ships – twenty quinqueremes and ten quadriremes – were laid, and Scipio in person so relentlessly kept the workmen at their task that forty-five days after the timber had been felled the ships were launched, fully equipped and rigged.

46. With the thirty warships, carrying some 7,000 volunteers, Scipio sailed for Sicily, while Licinius joined the two consular armies in Bruttium, and took over the command of the one previously commanded by the consul Veturius. He allowed Metellus to keep the command of his old legions in the belief that he would work more easily with men accustomed to his authority. The praetors also left Rome for their various assignments. As funds were short, the quaestors were instructed to sell that part of Campanian territory which stretches from the

Greek Dyke to the sea;[1] information was also allowed to be given about any land which had belonged to a Campanian citizen, so that it might become the property of the State. Informers were to have a reward equal to one tenth of the value of the land. Gnaeus Servilius, the City praetor, was entrusted with the task of seeing that Campanian citizens were all living in the districts allotted to them by the Senate's decree, and of punishing those who were found living elsewhere.

During the course of this summer Mago, the son of Hamilcar, had raised recruits from the smaller of the Balearic Islands where he had wintered, put them on shipboard, and, with a fleet some thirty strong accompanied by a large number of transports carrying in all 12,000 infantry and about 2,000 mounted troops, sailed to Italy and, as the coast was unguarded, succeeded by his sudden arrival in capturing Genoa. Thence he proceeded to the coast of Alpine, or western, Liguria, in the hope of causing a rising against Rome. The Ingauni, a Ligurian tribe, were at war at the time with the Epanterii Montani, a mountain tribe to the north of them; Mago accordingly deposited his plunder in the Alpine settlement of Savo,[2] left ten warships to guard it, and sent the rest of his fleet to Carthage to patrol the coast, as there was already a report that Scipio intended to cross. He then entered into an arrangement with the Ingauni, whose friendship he preferred to that of their opponents, and started hostilities against the Montani. His strength grew daily, his name being sufficient to bring the Gauls flocking to his standard from every side. These events were reported to the Senate in a dispatch from Spurius Lucretius and gave rise to acute anxiety lest the rejoicings over the destruction of Hasdrubal and his army two years previously should prove all in vain, if another threat should arise from the same quarter, equally serious and with nothing changed but the commander. Orders were therefore given to the proconsul Marcus Livius to move his force of slave volunteers from Etruria to Ariminum, and the praetor Servilius was instructed to appoint at his discretion, if he thought it advisable, a commander for the two

1. Near here was Scipio's home in his retirement, described by Seneca (*Letters* 86. 1–12).

2. Savona, on the coast at the foot of the Maritime Alps.

City legions and to order them out on service. Marcus Valerius Laevinus took them to Arretium.

About this time a fleet of about eighty Carthaginian transports was captured off Sardinia by Gnaeus Octavius, the officer in command there. According to the historian Coelius the ships were carrying grain and supplies to Hannibal, but Valerius Antias writes that they were conveying to Carthage the material captured in Etruria, and prisoners of war of the Ligurians and Montani. Nothing of importance occurred that year in Bruttium.

An epidemic had attacked both the Romans and the Carthaginians with equally devastating effect, save that the latter suffered not only from the disease but also from inadequate food-supplies. Hannibal passed the summer near the temple of Juno Lacinia, where he constructed and dedicated an altar with a long inscription containing a record of his achievements. The inscription was in Punic and Greek.[1]

1. See p. 62 and p. 234.

# BOOK XXIX

1. Arrived in Sicily, Scipio organized his volunteers into their ranks and centuries. He picked from them 300 men, all young and of exceptional physical strength and vigour, and kept them with him unarmed and ignorant of the reason why they were neither posted to centuries nor furnished with equipment. He then selected from all over Sicily 300 young horsemen, all of them men of good family and fortune, who were supposedly intended to accompany him to Africa, and for that purpose he named a day on which they were to present themselves with their horses and full military equipment. Now such a campaign, far from home and sure to bring much distress and fearful dangers both by land and sea, seemed highly disagreeable, and the young men's parents and relatives were no less tormented by anxiety about it than they were themselves. None the less on the appointed day they duly exhibited to Scipio their horses and equipment. Scipio thereupon remarked that people were telling him that certain of the Sicilian cavalrymen, feeling that the coming campaign would be unpleasantly exacting, shrank from taking part in it. If, he added, any of them shared that feeling, he would prefer them to say so at once rather than complain later and thus prove laggards in battle and useless to the State. 'Tell me what is in your mind,' he said. 'I am perfectly willing to listen.'

When one of them plucked up courage to say that, if he were really free to choose, he would prefer not to continue his service, Scipio replied: 'Because, young fellow, you have not concealed your feelings, I shall find you a substitute; you must hand over to him your weapons, horse, and other military equipment, take him home with you at once, train him, and see that he is properly instructed in horsemanship and the use of arms.' The conditions were gladly accepted, and Scipio assigned to the young man one of the 300 volunteers whom he was keeping unarmed about his person. When the other Sicilians saw their fellow-cavalryman discharged in this manner with the full consent of the commander-in-chief, they all excused themselves and accepted substitutes. Thus 300 Sicilians were replaced by Roman cavalrymen without costing the State a penny. Their instruction and training were all taken care of by the Sicilians, Scipio's orders being that any Sicilian who refused to comply would have to serve in his own person. It is said that this particular troop of horse turned out admirably and did the State good service in many battles.

On inspecting his legions Scipio selected from them the veteran soldiers who had the longest record of active service, especially those who had fought under Marcellus; these men, he believed, would be the best trained and, in particular, the most skilful in siege and assault operations as a result of what they had learned in the long siege of Syracuse. This was important, as the plans he already had in mind embraced nothing less than the destruction of Carthage. He then billeted his troops in various towns, requisitioned grain from the Sicilian states, using strict economy with the grain imported from Italy, patched up the old ships and sent Laelius with them on a raid on the African coast, and hauled his newly built ships ashore at Panormus. They had been built hurriedly with green timber, and it was necessary that they should not be left afloat through the winter.

When all his preparations were complete, he moved to Syracuse. The city, after the violent upheavals of the war, was not yet in a really settled condition: native Greeks and certain Italians were still at loggerheads, the former trying to recover property which had been conceded to them by the Senate, and the Italians holding on to it with as much determination as they had shown when they seized it originally during hostilities. Scipio, thinking the first essential was to honour his government's word, restored their property to the Syracusans, partly by edict, partly by giving judgements against Italians who persisted in maintaining unlawful possession. His handling of the situation was satisfactory, not only to the Greeks who personally benefited, but to all the Sicilian communities, which were thereby encouraged to assist his war preparations with greater energy.

In the course of this summer a new and very serious situation arose in Spain: Indibilis, the prince of the Ilergetes, rebelled, his sole reason being his admiration for Scipio which made every other Roman officer seem by comparison contemptible. He remembered how Scipio was the one Roman commander left when the others had been killed by Hannibal, and how Rome, after the death of the elder Scipios, had no other than him to take command in Spain; then again, under the pressure of a more serious war in Italy, he had been recalled to face Hannibal. Moreover, in addition to the fact that the Roman generals then in Spain were hardly more than names, the veteran troops had been withdrawn, everything was at sixes and sevens and in the hands of a mob of raw recruits. Never, surely, would such an opportunity for liberating Spain recur. Till then, Spain had been the slave either of Carthage or of Rome, not necessarily alternately but sometimes even to both at once. The Carthaginians had been expelled by the Romans, and now the Romans could be expelled in their turn by the Spaniards, if only they could work in concert, so that Spain, freed for ever from all foreign domination, could once more live her life as she had lived it in the past. By these and similar arguments Indibilis roused to action not only his own people but the neighbouring tribe of the Ausetani and others, too, either on his own borders or on theirs. Thus within a few days a force of 30,000 foot and some 4,000 horse assembled, according to Indibilis's instructions, in the territory of the Sedetani.

2. The Roman generals, Lucius Lentulus and Lucius Manlius Acidinus, were not slow to take counter measures: fearing that the menace would increase if they allowed the Spaniards' first moves to pass unnoticed, they united their forces and proceeded through the territory of the Ausetani, which was now enemy country. However, they abstained from hostile acts during the march until, reaching the spot where the Spaniards had established themselves, they took up a position three miles from their camp. They tried first by sending envoys to Indibilis to induce him to disband his forces; but the attempt failed, and soon afterwards Spanish cavalry made a surprise attack on a Roman foraging party. Roman cavalry was ordered up from the outposts, and the two forces engaged, but without notable advantage on either side. At dawn next day the Romans

were confronted with the spectacle of the entire Spanish force drawn up under arms and in battle order about a mile away.

The Ausetani held the centre; on the right wing were the Ilergetes, on the left the less important Spanish tribesmen. Between the wings and the centre they had left on each side a sufficient gap to allow the cavalry to pass through when the moment should come. The Romans, though their dispositions were in other respects according to usual practice, in one point followed the Spanish example and left lanes for the cavalry between the legions. It was clear to Lentulus that the advantage would lie with the side which was the first to send its cavalry forward through the gaps in the opposing line; so he instructed his military tribune Cornelius to pass the order to the cavalry to charge at the gallop through the open lanes in front of them. The struggle between the Spanish and Roman infantry had not started well; the Twelfth legion on the left, facing the Ilergetes, was giving ground, and Lentulus was compelled to reinforce it by bringing up the Thirteenth from the reserves. This was successful, and as soon as the balance in that sector was restored, Lentulus hurried to his colleague Acidinus, who was in the forefront of the battle encouraging his men and ordering up reserves wherever they were needed. He told him that all was now safe on the left wing; Cornelius had his orders and would soon surround the enemy with a whirlwind cavalry movement.

The words were hardly out of his mouth when the Roman cavalry charged, flinging the Spanish infantry into confusion and at the same time closing the passage by which the Spaniards had intended to send their own cavalry into action. This being no longer possible, the Spanish horsemen all dismounted, while the two Roman commanders, seeing the enemy lines breaking up, his standards wavering, and panic and confusion everywhere, urged their men with the utmost insistence to press their advantage and give the disintegrating enemy army no opportunity to pull itself together again. The wild tribesmen could never have withstood the weight of the attack which followed, if their prince Indibilis had not himself gallantly risked his life in advance of the front line together with his dismounted cavalrymen. For some time a bloody struggle continued, until at last Indibilis was fatally wounded; he was pinned to the ground with a lance through his body, and the soldiers who had been fighting to protect him were over-overwhelmed with missiles and all killed. That was the signal for a general rout. The Spanish losses were increased by the fact that there was no room for their cavalrymen to mount their horses, and also by the vigour of the Roman pressure on the already shattered line, a pressure which was not remitted until the enemy camp was also cleared. The Spanish dead amounted to 13,000, prisoners of war to about 1,800; of the Romans and their allies rather more than 200 were killed, mostly on the left wing. The Spaniards who were driven from their camp or who escaped with their lives from the battle scattered over the countryside, finally making their way home to their respective communities.

3. Later the rebels were summoned by Mandonius to a conference, where they complained bitterly of their disastrous failure, poured out their wrath on the men responsible for the rising, and voted that envoys should be dispatched to arrange a capitulation and the surrender of their arms. The envoys laid the responsibility for the rising upon Indibilis and the other chieftains, most of whom had been killed in the fighting, and when they offered to surrender their arms and themselves they were told in reply that a capitulation would be accepted only if they handed over Mandonius alive, together with any others who had helped to fan the flame of rebellion; otherwise, the Romans would march immediately into the territory of the Ilergetes and Ausetani, and would afterwards invade the territory of other tribes as well. The envoys reported to the conference the answer they had received. Mandonius and the other chieftains were arrested on the spot and handed over for punishment. Peace was restored to the Spanish peoples; the tribute for that year was doubled, a six months' supply of grain was requisitioned, together with cloaks and togas for the troops, and hostages were accepted from about thirty tribes.

Thus the Spanish rebellion having been raised and suppressed all within a few days and without any serious trouble, the whole weight of national anxiety was transferred to Africa. Laelius had reached Hippo Regius[1] during the night, and at

1. Livy means Hippo Diarrhytus (Bizerta).

dawn the following day took his troops, supported by the ships' crews, on a raid of the surrounding country. As none of the people was expecting trouble any more than in peacetime, great damage was done; wild reports that the Roman fleet with Scipio in command had arrived (the news of his crossing to Sicily had already been received) caused universal panic in Carthage. Nobody had any clear idea of the number of ships the messengers had seen and the size of the raiding force, and sheer fright drove them to exaggerate everything they heard; the result was a wave of terror, quickly followed by depression at the thought of the grievous change in their fortunes. Only lately, in the flush of victory, they had had an army before the walls of Rome; after the destruction of countless Roman armies they had accepted or compelled the surrender of all the Italian peoples, yet now the tide of war had turned and they were doomed to witness the devastation of Africa and the siege of Carthage. Nor had they the strength or resources which enabled the Romans to endure these calamities: for the Romans had their own populace and that of Latium to supply a greater and more numerous body of young soldiers continually growing up to take the place of their losses, however great; whereas both the city and the rural population of Carthage were utterly unwarlike – they were forced to hire mercenaries from the Africans, a fickle and untrustworthy people, swayed by the least breath which seemed to promise them some advantage. Of the neighbouring princes, Syphax had been alienated after his interview with Scipio, and Masinissa had openly thrown off his allegiance and was now their bitterest enemy; Mago in Gaul was neither causing a rising against Rome nor attempting to join Hannibal, and Hannibal himself was no longer the man he was either in reputation or in strength.

4. Such was the general gloom into which the news of the landing had plunged Carthage; soon, however, the apparent urgency of the danger recalled people to the need of discussing methods by which present perils could be met. It was decided to hold a hurried levy both within the city and in the country outside, to send officers to hire African troops, to strengthen the city's defences, bring in supplies of grain, provide a stock of arms, and, finally, equip a fleet to be sent against the Roman

squadron at Hippo. These preparations were already under way when another message arrived, to say that the invader was not Scipio but Laelius, that the forces he had brought were only enough for raiding purposes, and that the enemy's real strength was still in Sicily. This gave a brief respite, and missions were dispatched to Syphax and other princes in the hope of strengthening alliances. A delegation was also sent to King Philip, promising him 200 talents of silver as an inducement to invade either Sicily or Italy. Further delegations were sent to the Carthaginian commanders in Italy, to urge them to hold Scipio back by every possible threat, while to Mago were sent not merely envoys but twenty-five warships, 6,000 infantrymen, 800 cavalrymen, and seven elephants, not to mention a large sum of money to enable him to hire mercenaries, on the strength of which additional resources he was to move nearer to Rome and join forces with Hannibal.

During these preparations and discussions at Carthage, Masinissa, on hearing of the arrival of a Roman fleet, came with a small cavalry escort to Laelius, who was in the act of carrying off the rich haul of valuable material which he had taken from the unarmed and undefended country round. Masinissa complained of the lack of drive in Scipio's conduct of the war, in that he had not already invaded Africa while the Carthaginians were in a shaken condition and Syphax had his hands full with local wars. He said he was certain that Syphax would never loyally assist Rome in anything whatever, if he were given time to settle his immediate difficulties to his own satisfaction. Accordingly he begged Laelius to urge Scipio with every means in his power not to procrastinate, adding that he himself, although driven from his kingdom, would support him with a by no means contemptible force of infantry and cavalry. Moreover, Laelius himself ought not, he suggested, to hold on in Africa, as he had reason to believe that a fleet had sailed from Carthage which it would not be safe for him to engage in Scipio's absence. 5. After the interview Laelius took leave of Masinissa and on the following day sailed from Hippo with his cargo of spoils, and returning to Sicily, delivered Masinissa's messages to Scipio.

It was just about this time that the ships sent to Mago from

Carthage approached the coast between Genoa and the Ligurian tribe of the Albingauni. Mago, as it happened, also had his fleet in that locality; he listened to the envoys from Carthage urging him to raise as powerful a force as he possibly could, and promptly called a conference of Gauls and Ligurians, of whom very large numbers were present in the vicinity. He declared that he had been sent to restore them to liberty, and pointed to the reinforcements which were reaching him from Carthage; but, he added, the size and strength of the army with which that war of liberation would be waged depended upon them. There were two Roman armies, one in Gaul, the other in Etruria, and he was convinced that Lucretius intended to join forces with Livius; many thousands of men must therefore be raised and equipped if they were to be a match for the joint strength of two Roman commanders and their armies. In reply, the Gauls assured Mago that they were very willing to do as he asked, but, since one Roman army was actually in their territory and the other almost within sight over the Etrurian border, they would be immediately attacked by both if it became known that the Carthaginian general had received reinforcements from them. Mago, they urged, ought to require from the Gauls only such assistance as could be supplied secretly; the Ligurians, on the other hand, because the Roman forces were nowhere near their towns or territory, were free to do as they pleased – it was only right that they should arm their men of military age and take a fair share in the fighting.

The Ligurians did not refuse, but merely asked for two months' grace to enable them to raise troops. Mago meanwhile set about hiring Gallic soldiers, sending officers secretly into Gallic territory for the purpose; supplies of all kinds were also secretly reaching him from the various Gallic tribes.

Livius brought his army of slave volunteers from Etruria into Gaul and joined Lucretius, ready to encounter Mago should he move from Liguria in the direction of Rome. If, on the other hand, the Carthaginian remained inactive far away under the Alps, then he too would stay where he was, in the neighbourhood of Ariminum, for the defence of Italy.

6. On Laelius's return from Africa, Scipio was impressed by the adjurations of Masinissa; and his troops were fired with

enthusiasm to invade at the first possible moment by the sight of booty from enemy territory being landed from every ship in Laelius's fleet. But the grand design was temporarily interrupted by an operation of less importance, namely the recovering of Locri, which had joined the revolt of the Italian towns and gone over to the Carthaginians. A trivial incident kindled high hopes of success in this enterprise: the war in Bruttium had been a matter more of casual forays than of regular fighting, a sort of brigandage started by the Numidians and taken up by the Bruttians as much because it suited their character as because they were allied with the Carthaginian forces. Finally even the Roman soldiers caught the infection of a delight in plunder, and began raiding enemy farms with as much licence as their officers would grant them. It was by a Roman raiding-party that some men from Locri were rounded up and carried off to Rhegium. Amongst the prisoners were some workmen who had been employed by the Carthaginians on the citadel in Locri, and they were recognized by certain leading Locrian citizens who had taken refuge in Rhegium after being expelled by the opposite faction, which had betrayed Locri to Hannibal. On being asked the sort of questions people usually ask when they have been away for a long time, the workmen described what was happening in Locri and then raised hopes in their questioners that if they were ransomed and sent back they would betray the citadel to them. It was in the citadel that they lived, and the Carthaginians, they said, trusted them in everything.

The Locrians, who in addition to all the anguish of homesickness had a passionate desire for revenge upon their enemies, immediately paid the ransom money and sent the workmen back, having previously arranged with them how the thing should be done and what signals they should watch for outside the town; they themselves then went off to Syracuse to find Scipio with whom were some of the Locrian exiles, told him what the prisoners had promised to do, and raised in him a hope which gave reasonable prospect of success. As a result, the military tribunes Marcus Sergius and Publius Matienus were ordered to accompany them and to take a force of 3,000 men from Rhegium to Locri. The pro-praetor Quintus Pleminius also received written instructions to take charge of the operation.

The expedition left Rhegium carrying ladders specially made for what they had been told was the height of the citadel, and about midnight, at the prearranged spot, the fire-signal was raised for their accomplices in the town. They, in their turn, all ready and on the watch, let down specially prepared ladders of their own; up went the Roman soldiers in several places simultaneously, and, before a warning cry could be raised, fell upon the Carthaginian sentries, who, suspecting no such danger, were of course asleep. For a moment the only sound was the groans of the dying; then sleepers began to awake and there was sudden terror and running to and fro, though none yet knew what had happened, till at last the truth dawned as every man roused his neighbour, and there was a confused and general call to arms. 'The enemy hold the citadel!' the cry went up. 'The guards are being butchered!' The Roman party, far inferior in numbers, would certainly have been overwhelmed if the shouting from those outside the citadel had not made it difficult to be sure whence the danger had come, while imagined perils were exaggerated by the noise, confusion, and darkness all combined. Accordingly the Carthaginians, supposing the citadel to be completely occupied by enemy troops, broke off resistance and took refuge in the other citadel – there are two of them, not far apart. Between the two citadels, or fortresses, lay the town itself, the prize of victory, now held by the Locrian populace. Of the hostile forces in the citadels, Pleminius commanded the Roman, Hamilcar the Carthaginian, and daily skirmishes took place between them. Both sides were getting reinforcements from the neighbourhood and increasing their numbers, and finally Hannibal himself was known to be on the way. In these circumstances the Romans could not have held out but for the fact that the inhabitants of the town took their side in embittered protest against the tyranny and greed of the Carthaginians.

7. When Scipio was informed that the situation at Locri had become more critical and that Hannibal was moving on the town, he was anxious not only for the town itself but for the safety of its Roman garrison, as it was an awkward place to evacuate. Accordingly he left his brother Lucius in charge at

Messana and himself set sail as soon as the south-going tide began to run in the Straits. At the same time Hannibal, from the river Bulotus near Locri, sent forward a messenger to the town with orders that his troops should engage the Romans and Locrians at dawn next morning with all possible vigour, so that while attention was concentrated on the fight he himself might take the opportunity of delivering a surprise attack in the rear. However, when, at dawn, he found the action already begun, he was unwilling to shut himself up in the citadel where his men would not have enough room to manoeuvre, nor had he brought ladders with him to scale the walls. He ordered his men to pile their baggage, paraded his army close to the walls to inspire terror in the enemy, and with his Numidian horsemen rode round the town to find the best spot for an attack, while ladders and other assault-gear were being got ready. On one occasion when he had moved close up to the wall, the man who happened to be standing next to him was hit by a missile from a catapult; the incident was so alarming that he ordered the retreat to be sounded, and fortified a fresh position out of the range of missiles. The Roman squadron from Messana reached Locri when there were still some hours of daylight left; the troops were disembarked and entered the town before sunset.

Next morning the Carthaginians began operations from the citadel, and Hannibal, his ladders and other assault-gear being all in readiness, was in the act of moving up to the walls of the town when a gate was suddenly flung open and the Romans came out against him at the double. It was the last thing Hannibal had expected; his troops were taken completely off their guard and the Romans killed some 200 of them. Hannibal, when he realized that Scipio was present, withdrew the rest into camp, after sending a message to their comrades in the citadel that they must see to their own safety as best they could. He then broke camp under cover of darkness and moved off. The Carthaginians in the citadel fired the houses they were occupying in order to give themselves more time in the resulting confusion, and moving fast, like beaten men on the run, overtook the retreating column of their friends before nightfall.

8. When Scipio saw that the citadel had been evacuated by the enemy and that his camp was deserted, he summoned the Locrians to appear before him and severely reprimanded them for their defection. He executed the men responsible for the revolt, and handed over their property to the leaders of the opposite party as a reward for their notable loyalty to the Romans. As for the town as a whole, Scipio declared that it was not his business either to grant privileges or impose penalties; they must send a delegation to Rome and accept whatever fortune the Senate saw fit to grant them. One thing, Scipio added, he was sure of – that although the Locrians had not served the Roman people well, they would none the less be better off under the rule of an angry Rome than of a friendly Carthage. He then left Pleminius as his second-in-command to guard the town, together with the troops which had taken the citadel, and withdrew with his own force to Messana.

The Locrians after their revolt from Rome had been treated by the Carthaginians with such vicious arrogance and brutality that they might have welcomed mere ordinary ill-treatment not only with equanimity but even with pleasure. Unhappily, however, Pleminius and his Roman garrison so far surpassed Hamilcar and his Carthaginians in their vile and criminal rapacity that one might have supposed them rivals in vice rather than rivals in war. Of all the things which make the power of a master hateful to the helpless not one was omitted; between the officer in command and his men there was nothing to choose; and the unfortunate townspeople, together with their wives and children, suffered unspeakably at the hands of one and all. Soon the Romans' greed did not stop short even of robbing temples – many temples, including even the treasury of Proserpine which had always been inviolate, save for the one occasion when it was said to have been robbed by Pyrrhus, who after paying a heavy price for his sacrilege restored his loot to where it belonged. And indeed the parallel holds good; for just as on that occasion Pyrrhus's ships were wrecked and nothing was salved from them undamaged except the Goddess's sacred treasure which they were trying to carry away, so now that same treasure brought disaster of another kind upon the guilty, driving to madness all who were stained with the sin of violating the temple and turning officer against officer and man against man in the very fury of hatred.

9. Pleminius was the highest-ranking officer present, and in command of the troops he had brought from Rhegium; but there were also other troops under the military tribunes. One of Pleminius's men had stolen a silver cup from a citizen's house and was running away with it pursued by its owners, when he happened to meet the tribunes Sergius and Matienus. The tribunes ordered it to be taken away from him, and this gave rise to loud and angry abuse on both sides, and finally to a pitched battle between Pleminius's soldiers and those of the tribunes, while the crowd in the street grew larger and more out of hand as more and more people hurried to join their friends on one side or the other. Pleminius's men got the worst of it, and when, howling with pain and indignation, they ran to show him their bleeding wounds, telling him at the same time of the horrible insults hurled against him by their antagonists, he rushed out of his house in a flaming rage, called for the rods, and ordered the tribunes to be brought before him and stripped. Pulling their clothes off took time, as both men resisted and begged their soldiers to protect them; and during the process more soldiers, flushed with victory, suddenly came running up from here, there and everywhere as if in answer to a call to arms against an enemy. The sight of the tribunes' backs already bleeding from the rods redoubled their fury; in mad and uncontrollable rage they manhandled the lictors in a shameful manner and then, without regard for the dignity of his rank – not to mention ordinary decency – attacked Pleminius, their commanding officer. Separating him from his men, they slashed him about the body and left him half dead with his nose and ears mutilated.

When an account of these proceedings reached Messana, Scipio sailed to Locri a few days later in a *hexeris*.[1] Having heard the case between Pleminius and the tribunes, he acquitted Pleminius, and left him still in charge; he judged the tribunes to be guilty, and they were put under arrest to be sent to the Senate in Rome. Scipio then returned to Messana and from there crossed to Syracuse.

1. A ship with six banks of oars, very rarely used.

Pleminius was furious at this decision: he felt that Scipio had made far too little of the injury done him – indeed that nobody could really be capable of adequately punishing the tribunes' offence except the man who in his own person had felt the full horror of it. So he had the tribunes dragged into his presence, lacerated by every torture a body can endure, and then killed. Not satisfied with that, he punished their dead bodies too by having them thrown out and left unburied. He used similar savagery against the leading Locrians who were reported to him as having gone to Scipio with complaints of ill-treatment. The revolting crimes which had previously been prompted by lust and greed against a friendly community were now multiplied by rage, and brought odium and infamy not only upon the wretch who perpetrated them but also upon his commander-in-chief.

10. The time for the elections was already approaching, when a dispatch reached Rome from the consul Licinius, reporting that he and his army were in the grip of a severe epidemic, and that they could not have held out had not the enemy been attacked by a disease equally serious, or worse. Accordingly, since he could not himself attend, he proposed, with the Senate's approval, to name Quintus Caecilius Metellus as dictator to preside at the elections. It would be, he added, in the public interest to disband Metellus's army, since at the moment his troops were of no use. Hannibal had withdrawn into winter quarters and so serious an epidemic had found its way into Metellus's own camp that, unless the men were quickly disbanded, not one of them, it seemed, would be left alive. Licinius received permission from the Senate to do what he thought consistent with his duty and the public interest.

About this time a sudden wave of superstition swept over Rome. The Sibylline Books had been consulted because it had rained stones that year more often than usual, and in the Books a prophecy was found that if ever a foreign enemy should invade Italy, he could be defeated and driven out if Cybele, the Idaean Mother of the Gods, were brought from Pessinus to Rome. The effect upon the Senate of the discovery of this prophecy by the decemvirs was all the greater because the envoys who had taken the offering to Delphi declared that all the omens had been favourable when they sacrificed to the Pythian Apollo, and also that they had been granted a response by the oracle to the effect that a much greater victory was awaiting the Roman people than the one from the spoils of which they were bringing their offering. In support of these hopes the Senate was also inclined to adduce the sanguine temper of Scipio who, in that he had demanded the right to operate in Africa, seemed to be confidently anticipating the end of the war. So they began seriously to consider the best means of transferring the image of the Goddess to Rome, in order to enjoy as soon as possible the victory which so many omens and oracles portended – from Delphi, from the Sibylline Books, and from the inexplicable confidence of Scipio.

11. Rome had not as yet any allies amongst the Asiatic states. But the Romans remembered that once upon a time the aid of Aesculapius the Healer had been called in to deal with an epidemic while there was still no treaty of alliance with Greece, and also that at the present juncture they were on friendly terms with King Attalus because of their common quarrel with Philip. In the belief, therefore, that Attalus would do what he could for them, they decided to send him a deputation. The envoys selected were Marcus Valerius Laevinus, who had been twice consul and had seen active service in Greece, the ex-praetor Marcus Caecilius Metellus, the ex-aedile Servius Sulpicius Galba, and two former quaestors, Gnaeus Tremelius Flaccus and Marcus Valerius Falto. Five quinqueremes were assigned to the deputation so that in a manner worthy of the dignity of Rome it might approach lands where it was desirable that the Roman name should win for itself the highest respect. The envoys on their way to Asia went up to Delphi, where they consulted the oracle, inquiring what hope it foresaw for them and the Roman people of bringing their mission to a successful conclusion. The answer, so it is said, was that they would get what they wanted by the help of King Attalus, and that when they had brought the Goddess to Rome it would be necessary for them to make sure that she was hospitably welcomed by the best man in the City.

The envoys then visited Attalus in Pergamum. He received them courteously, escorted them to Pessinus in Phrygia, gave them the sacred stone supposed by the natives to represent the Mother of the Gods, and told them to take it back to Rome. Falto was sent in advance by the other envoys to announce that the Goddess was on the way and to tell people that the best man in the State must be sought out to give her due welcome.

Quintus Caecilius Metellus was named dictator by the consul in Bruttium to preside at the elections, and his army was disbanded. Lucius Veturius Philo was appointed his master of Horse. The elections were duly held; Marcus Cornelius Cethegus and Publius Sempronius Tuditanus were returned as consuls, the latter in his absence, as he was serving in Greece. The new praetors were Tiberius Claudius Nero, Marcus Marcius Ralla, Lucius Scribonius Libo, and Marcus Pomponius Matho. After the elections the dictator resigned from office.

The Roman Games were repeated on three, the Plebeian Games on seven days. The curule aediles were Gnaeus and Lucius Cornelius Lentulus; the latter was serving at the time in Spain, so he was not present either at his election or during his tenure of that office. The plebeian aediles were Tiberius Claudius Asellus and Marcus Junius Pennus. Marcellus dedicated this year the temple of Valour at the Porta Capena; it was sixteen years since it had been vowed by his father, in his first consulship, at Clastidium in Gaul. This year also saw the death of Marcus Aemilius Regillus, the priest of Mars.

12. For the past two years little attention had been paid to the situation in Greece. Philip, in consequence, compelled the Aetolians, abandoned as they were by the Romans, who had been their sole defence, to ask for peace and accept a settlement on his own terms. Had he not used every effort to bring this about promptly, he would have been surprised while still at war by the proconsul Sempronius, who had been sent out to relieve Sulpicius with a force of 10,000 infantry, 1,000 cavalry, and thirty-five warships – aid to Rome's allies of no negligible weight. Hardly had peace been made when Philip received the news that the Romans were at Dyrrachium, that the Parthini and other neighbouring peoples were up in arms in hope of a revolution, and that Dimallum was under siege. The Roman force had been sent to help the Aetolians, but had been diverted to Dimallum out of resentment against them for having made

peace contrary to the treaty and without Roman consent. Philip, on receiving the news, was anxious to prevent a more serious rising amongst neighbouring tribes and peoples; so he hurried to Apollonia on the track of Sempronius, who had gone there after sending his lieutenant Laetorius into Aetolia with a part of his forces and fifteen ships, to study the situation and upset the peace if he could. Philip devastated the outlying farms at Apollonia, marched up to the town and offered the Roman commander battle; but finding that Sempronius made no move, but contented himself with the defence of the walls, Philip, since he lacked confidence in his ability to storm the town and wanted peace with the Romans if he could get it, as well as with the Aetolians, or, failing peace, at least an armistice, withdrew to his own kingdom without further embittering relations with Rome by a fresh conflict.

About this time the Epirotes, sick of the long and tedious war, first assured themselves of Roman sympathy and then sent envoys to Philip to propose negotiating a general peace and to express their confidence that it would be agreed upon if he entered into personal talks with the Roman commander Sempronius. Philip, being by no means averse to peace, was easily persuaded to go to Epirus; at the town of Phoenice he held preliminary talks with the Epirote officials Aëropus, Derdas, and Philippus, and afterwards met Sempronius. Present at the conversation between the two leaders were Amynander, King of the Athamanians, and other high officials of the Epirotes and Acarnanians. The first to speak was the Epirote magistrate Philippus, who made a joint request to the king and the Roman commander to do his people the favour of stopping hostilities. Sempronius then laid down as the conditions of peace the cession to Rome of the Parthini, Dimallum, Bargullum, and Eugenium, and the annexation of Atintania to Macedon, provided that Philip sent envoys to Rome and obtained the Senate's permission. These terms being agreed upon, Prusias King of Bithynia, the Achaeans, Boeotians, Thessalians, Acarnanians, and Epirotes were written into the treaty as on Philip's side, with the Ilii, King Attalus, Pleuratus, Nabis tyrant of Lacedaemon, the Eleans, Messenians, and Athenians on the Roman. The treaty was put in writing and signed, and a two months' armistice was agreed upon, to allow envoys to be sent to Rome in order to obtain the people's sanction for the peace terms. All the tribes gave their consent, as now that the war looked like shifting to Africa, they wanted to be relieved for the time being of all military commitments elsewhere. Sempronius, when the settlement had been made, left for Rome to enter upon his consulship.

13. It was now the fifteenth year of the Carthaginian war; new consuls, Cornelius Cethegus and Sempronius Tuditanus, by decree of the Senate were given command respectively of Etruria, with the old army, and of Bruttium, with orders to raise fresh troops. The City praetorship fell by lot to Marcius; the 'Foreign' together with responsibility for Gaul to Libo; Sicily to Matho, and Sardinia to Nero. Scipio's command, together with the sea and land forces already under his control, was prolonged for a further year; the same was done in the case of Publius Licinius, who was to hold Bruttium with two legions for as long as the consul judged it expedient that he should remain there with full military powers. Livius and Lucretius also had their commands extended, each with the two legions with which they had defended Gaul against Mago, and Octavius's was extended with orders to hand over Sardinia and his legion to Nero, the new praetor, and with a fleet of forty ships to protect the coast within limits to be defined by the Senate. To Matho, the new praetor in Sicily, were assigned the two legions of the army of Cannae. Titus Quinctius[1] and Gaius Hostilius Tubulus, as pro-praetors, were to hold respectively Tarentum and Capua, as in the previous year and in each case with the old garrison. As to the command in Spain, the people were formally consulted about which two men they wished to be sent there with proconsular powers, and the tribes were unanimous in naming for that duty the same two men as in the previous year, Cornelius Lentulus and Manius Acidinus. The consuls then began the task of raising fresh troops, both for the new legions which were to serve in Bruttium and also, according to the Senate's instructions, to reinforce the other armies.

1. Titus Quinctius Flamininus who afterwards defeated Philip at the battle of Cynoscephalae in 197 B.C.

14. The Senate had never yet openly decreed that Roman armies were to operate in Africa; they were keeping the project dark, I fancy, in order to prevent the Carthaginians from getting wind of their intentions. Nevertheless all Rome was confidently expecting that there would be fighting that year in Africa and that the end of the war was at hand. This sense of an impending crisis had produced a wave of superstition, and there was general readiness both to report and to believe stories of unnatural phenomena. A great many such stories were consequently in circulation: two suns, for instance, had been seen; daylight had appeared during the night; at Setia a meteor was seen to cross the sky from east to west; at Tarracina a gate had been struck by lightning, and at Anagnia both a gate and also the wall in a number of places; a strange noise, accompanied by a frightful crash, had been heard in the temple of Juno Sospita at Lanuvium. A day of prayer was ordered as an act of propitiation, and to deal with the rain of stones a further nine days' religious ceremony was held. In addition to all this there were deliberations about the reception in Rome of the Idaean Mother; Marcus Valerius, one of the envoys, had hurried home in advance of the others to report that at any moment she would be in Italy, and another, more recent, message had arrived stating that she had already reached Tarracina. It was no easy question which the Senate had to decide – who, namely, was the best man in the State; and anyone would certainly have valued a clear victory in that contest above any high command or civil magistracy which might be offered him by the votes of Senate or people. The man whom the senate judged to be the best of good men in the whole community was Publius Scipio, son of the Gnaeus Scipio who was killed in Spain (and therefore cousin of the Scipio who was soon to lead his army into Africa), and a young man not yet old enough to hold the office of quaestor. What particular virtues led them to this judgement I should gladly pass on to posterity if only contemporary chroniclers had told us what they were; but I do not propose to put forward any views of my own, which could only be guesswork in a matter so remote in time and consequently so obscure. This young Scipio, then, was ordered to meet the Goddess at Ostia, accompanied by the married women of

Rome; he was to receive her out of the ship, carry her ashore, and deliver her into the matrons' hands. When his ship, according to instructions, reached the mouth of the Tiber, he sailed on out to sea, received the Goddess from the priests, and took her ashore. The leading women of Rome, of whom one distinguished name is that of Claudia Quinta, then took her from him – Claudia, whose previously dubious reputation, the story goes, has made her virtue all the more famous in after times as a result of this solemn service in the cause of religion. The women then passed the Goddess from hand to hand, one to another in succession, while all the population came thronging to meet her; censers were placed before the doorways on her route with burning incense, and many prayers were offered that she might enter the city of Rome with kindly purpose and benignant thoughts. So the procession moved on, till they brought her to the temple of Victory on the Palatine. It was the day before the Ides of April, and that day was held sacred. People crowded to the Palatine with gifts to the Goddess, and there was a Strewing of Couches and Games, called the Megalesia.

15. During the debate on the recruitment of the legions in the various theatres of war, some of the senators submitted that the time had come to put right a serious wrong: what, they said, the country had somehow or other been forced to tolerate in critical days ought no longer to be endured now that the immediate threat to Rome had, by the grace of God, at last been removed. At this the Senate was all ears, whereupon they went on to say that the twelve Latin colonies which in the consulship of Fabius and Fulvius had refused to supply troops[1] had now for some five years been enjoying exemption from military service, as if it were a special honour and favour, while good and obedient allies in all loyalty and proper submission to the Roman people had worn themselves out by providing men for the forces every year without fail.

This reminder not only recalled to the Senate a state of affairs now almost forgotten but also aroused its anger. Every other question was put aside, and a decree was passed ordering the consuls to summon to Rome the magistrates and ten leading

1. See p. 438.

citizens of the colonies concerned – Nepete, Sutrium, Ardea, Cales, Alba, Carseoli, Sora, Suessa, Setia, Circeii, Narnia, and Interamna. They were then to demand from each colony double the maximum number of infantry soldiers it had ever supplied since the enemy had been on Italian soil, as well as 120 cavalrymen; if any colony were unable to find that number of cavalrymen, it should be allowed to furnish three foot-soldiers in place of one horseman; both horse and foot were to be selected from men of the largest means and would be liable for service outside Italy wherever reinforcements were needed. In case of refusal, the magistrates and envoys of the defaulting colony were to be detained, and if they asked for a hearing in the Senate it should not be granted until they had done what was asked of them. Furthermore a tax was to be imposed and annually collected, at the rate of one *as* in every thousand, and a census taken in each of the twelve colonies according to an official form furnished by the Roman censors – the same form, in fact, as had to be filled in by the Roman people. It was to be sworn to by the censors of the colonies and brought to Rome before they laid down their office.

In accordance with this decree the magistrates and leading citizens of the colonies concerned received their summons to Rome, and the consuls demanded the money and the men. There was a chorus of protest: it was impossible that so many troops could be furnished; even if the number as originally agreed upon were asked for, they would have a struggle to comply; they besought the consuls for permission to get a hearing in the Senate, where they might plead their case. What crime had they committed that they deserved to perish? Yet if perish they must, neither their guilt nor the anger of Rome could make them produce more soldiers than they actually had. To these pathetic protests the consuls turned a deaf ear, ordering the envoys to be detained in Rome while the magistrates went home to raise the necessary troops. Unless the full number asked for were brought to Rome, nobody, the consuls declared, would grant the envoys a hearing in the Senate. That settled it: once there was no hope left of appearing before the Senate and pleading their cause, the twelve colonies held their levy; and, as the number of young men had increased during the long period of exemption from service, it was completed in every case with the utmost ease.

16. Another matter which had been left in abeyance for almost as long was brought up by Marcus Valerius Laevinus. It was only right, he suggested, that the monies voluntarily contributed when he and Marcellus were consuls[1] should now at last be paid back. No one, he added, need be surprised that he felt so strongly about a matter in which public credit was involved; for apart from the fact that some responsibility attached to the consul of the year in which those sums were contributed, it was he himself who had proposed that particular method of contribution at a time when the treasury was empty and the commons were unable to meet the demand upon them. Laevinus's reminder was welcomed by the Senate, and a decree, on a motion of the consuls, was passed authorizing the repayment of the money in three instalments, the first instalment to be paid in cash by the consuls of the present year, the other two at two-yearly intervals.

Hitherto no one had heard of the horrible events at Locri, but when with the arrival of representatives from the town the news spread round, all other concerns faded into the background. What roused people's anger was not so much the criminal behaviour of Pleminius as the attitude of Scipio, whether it was due to popularity-seeking or sheer negligence. The ten Locrian envoys made their appearance before the consuls in the Comitium in true Greek suppliant fashion, dressed in filthy rags, fillets on their brows, and branches of olive in their hands. Holding out the branches, they prostrated themselves before the consuls' tribunal with pitiful cries and floods of tears. In answer to the consul's question, they said: 'We are Locrians, and we have suffered at the hands of your commanding officer Pleminius and of Roman soldiers things which the Roman people would not wish even the Carthaginians to suffer. We beg you for leave to go before the Senate and there to lament our sorrows.'

17. Permission for an audience was granted, and the senior delegate addressed the Senate as follows. 'I know, gentlemen, that the value you attach to our complaints must be influenced

1. See p. 402.

more than anything by your being fully aware both of how Locri was betrayed to Hannibal and of how it was restored to your authority after the expulsion of Hannibal's troops. For if it should appear that the guilt of defection cannot be laid to the policy of our government, and that the subsequent return to your authority took place not only with our consent but with our active and courageous assistance, then surely you would be all the more indignant that good and faithful allies should suffer at the hands of your officer and his men such undeserved, such atrocious, injuries and insults. But the hearing of the case of how we abandoned first Rome and then Carthage ought, I think, to be postponed to another occasion, and that for two reasons: first, that it may take place in the presence of Publius Scipio, who recaptured Locri and can give evidence of everything we did, good and bad alike; secondly, because whatever we may be, we ought not to have been forced to endure what we did endure.

'We cannot pretend, gentlemen, that when our citadel was in the hands of Carthaginian troops we did not suffer much vile and abominable treatment from the garrison commander, Hamilcar, and his Numidian and African soldiers. But what was that compared with the miseries we endure today? Of your goodness, gentlemen, I beg you to listen to what, against my will, I am forced to say. At this moment the human race is at a crisis in its destiny, waiting to see whether Rome or Carthage is to be mistress of the world. If the rule of each is to be judged by what we in Locri suffered under Carthaginian domination and what we are suffering at this instant under yours, there is no one who would not rather have them as his masters than you. Yet consider how the Locrians have felt and acted towards you: though the treatment we received from the Carthaginians was so much less vile, it was to the commander of your troops that we turned for protection; though we are suffering from your soldiers injuries worse than an enemy could inflict, we have never brought our protests anywhere but to yourselves. Either, gentlemen, you will look with pity on our desperate plight, or there is nothing left for us to pray for even from the gods.

'Pleminius was sent in command of a military force to take

Locri back from the Carthaginians, and he was left with that same force to garrison the town. In this officer of yours – misery, gentlemen, has the courage to speak freely – there is nothing of humanity but the outward shape of a man, nothing of the Roman but the Latin language and the way he wears his clothes. He is a plague-spot, an unnatural monster, like those that the old tales tell us lurked once on either side of the Strait which divides us from Sicily, to the destruction of mariners. Had he been content to be the only one to exercise at your allies' expense his criminal appetites and his greed, our long-suffering might perhaps have filled up the gaping maw of his lust, however capacious and deep; but as it is he has made a Pleminius of every centurion and every private soldier, determined as he was that all his creatures should be stained equally with the filth of licence and dishonour. Every man of them robs, despoils, beats, murders; all of them debauch our women, our girls, our boys – and not slave-boys either – whom they tear from their parents' arms. Every day our city is captured, every day it is sacked; day and night there are heard in every street the anguished cries of women and children torn from their homes and carried away. Knowing this, one might wonder how we have strength to endure, or how it is that our cruel oppressors have not yet wearied and sickened of their own crimes. I cannot tell you, nor is it worth your while to hear, every detail of our miseries; let me then include them all in a single sentence: I declare that there is no house in Locri, no single human being exempt from injury; no kind of crime, no form of lust or greed remaining which has not been practised upon every possible victim. It is hard to decide which is the more damnable fate for a community, to be captured in war by an enemy, or to be forcibly held down by a merciless and deadly tyrant. We have suffered, gentlemen of the Senate, every horror known to captured cities; yes, and are suffering them still; every brutality inflicted by the cruellest and most savage tyrants on their oppressed subjects, Pleminius has inflicted upon us and upon our wives and children.

18. 'There is one particular thing, however, which we are driven by our natural religious feelings to resent, and which

we want you, gentlemen, to hear of in order that you may free your country, should you so wish, from the stain of impiety – for we have seen with what reverence you not only worship your own gods but even welcome others from other lands. We have a temple of Proserpine, and I think that some word of the sanctity of that temple reached you in the war with Pyrrhus. When Pyrrhus was sailing past Locri on his return from Sicily, amongst other brutal acts committed against us in revenge for our loyalty to Rome he robbed the treasury of Proserpine, never yet touched before that day, and loaded his ships with the stolen money, himself marching away by land. And what was the consequence, gentlemen? His fleet next day was battered by a terrible tempest, and every ship with any of the sacred money in her hold was driven ashore on our coast. Taught by this fearful calamity that the gods indeed exist, the proudest of kings ordered that all the money should be carefully recovered and taken back to the treasury of Proserpine. Nevertheless Pyrrhus never afterwards prospered; driven from Italy he met an ignoble and inglorious death in a rash attempt to enter Argos by night. Well, gentlemen, your officer Pleminius and his military tribunes heard all this, and a thousand other things which were repeated to them not as mere tales to fill them with superstitious dread, but as facts again and again brought home to us and our ancestors by the active and present power of the Goddess. Yet in spite of that they had the audacity to lay sacrilegious hands on that most holy treasure, and with their impious loot to contaminate their houses and themselves – and your soldiers too. Gentlemen of the Senate, for your conscience's sake I beseech you not to undertake any enterprise in Italy or Africa with these men, until you have first made atonement for their guilt; should you do so, they may well pay for their sacrilege not only with their own blood but with their country's ruin.

'Even as things are, gentlemen, the wrath of the Goddess is at this moment active amongst your officers and your men. More than once already they have fought each other, Pleminius leading one party, the two tribunes the other. Sword against sword they have fought it out as fiercely as ever they fought the Carthaginians, and their mad rage would have enabled Hannibal to recover Locri if Scipio had not intervened in answer to our call. You will admit, perhaps, that the guilt of sacrilege has driven the rank and file out of their senses; but what of the officers? In punishing *them*, you say, the power of the Goddess has nowhere been manifest. On the contrary, it was there that her power was most evident. The tribunes were scourged by Pleminius; Pleminius was then waylaid and trapped by the tribunes, half torn to pieces, and left for dead with his nose and ears slashed. But he recovered, flung the tribunes into chains, had them first beaten and afterwards tortured to death with every mode of torture one applies to slaves, and finally refused their bodies burial.

'These are the penalties the Goddess is exacting from the despoilers of her temple, and she will not cease to harry them with all the avenging furies until the sacred money is restored to her treasury. Time was when our ancestors, during a bitter struggle with the men of Croton, wanted to move that money from the temple, as it was outside our walls, to a place of safety within the town; but in the darkness of night a voice was heard from the shrine – "Hands off! The Goddess will defend her own." By this they were taught that to move the treasure would be an impious thing, so they planned to build a wall around the temple. The wall had already risen to a fair height, when it suddenly collapsed and fell. Both then and now and on many other occasions the Goddess has protected the temple where she dwells, or has heavily punished those who have profaned it; but to avenge what *we* have suffered, gentlemen of the Senate, there is no one in the world but you, nor do we want another protector. Your suppliants, we are here to beg your aid. It is all one to us whether you let Locri remain in charge of that officer of yours and his infamous garrison, or surrender it for punishment to the wrath of Hannibal and the Carthaginians. We do not ask you to believe us off-hand when we accuse a man in his absence, his cause as yet untried; let him come and hear the charges against him, and himself dispose of them, if he can. Then, if you find he has omitted to practise upon us any single villainy which a man can practise upon his fellows, we shall not refuse – granted the strength to do so – to suffer the same things all over again, while he, for his part, is acquitted of every crime against God or men.'

19. Such was the speech of the Locrian envoys. Fabius then asked them whether they had laid their complaints before Scipio, and they told him in reply that representatives had indeed been sent but that Scipio was busy with preparations for his campaign and had either sailed for Africa or was about to do so in a few days' time. The representatives had learned moreover of the extent of the influence which must have been exerted by Pleminius over Scipio when, after hearing the case between him and the tribunes, Scipio ordered the arrest of the latter while leaving the former in his position of command, in spite of the fact that Pleminius was equally guilty, if not more so.

When the delegation had been asked to leave the Senate-house, Scipio, as well as Pleminius, was the object of savage attacks by leading senators. Leading the onslaught was Quintus Fabius, who accused him of having all the qualities which inevitably lead to the ruin of military discipline. In Spain, he declared, almost more men had been lost through mutiny than had been killed in battle,[1] while Scipio, like some foreign despot, alternately treated his soldiers with absurd indulgence and extreme brutality. He then went on to formulate a resolution no less severe, namely that Pleminius should be brought to Rome in chains and plead his cause in chains, and that if the Locrians' complaints turned out to be justified he should be put to death in prison and his property confiscated. Scipio should be recalled for leaving his province without orders from the Senate, and arrangements should be made with the people's tribunes to bring forward a bill to deprive him of his command. The Senate, furthermore, should tell the Locrians openly that neither they nor the Roman people countenanced the injuries they complained of having received: on the contrary, the Locrians should be called good men, and friends and allies; their children, wives, and everything else they had been robbed of should be restored; all the money removed from the treasury of Proserpine should be carefully recovered,

1. An exaggeration. See p. 528.

and double the amount deposited in the temple; further, that rites of expiation should be performed, after consultation with the College of Pontiffs, who, in view of the fact that the sacred treasury had been disturbed, opened, and violated, would advise on the form of expiation, on the nature of the sacrificial victims, and to what deities they should be offered. Finally, that all the troops at present holding Locri should be moved to Sicily and should be replaced by four cohorts of Latin allies.

So strong was party feeling for and against Scipio that there was not time that day for every senator to be given the chance to speak. Apart from attacks on Pleminius's criminal conduct and the miseries of Locri, much was said also against the commander-in-chief himself – his dress and bearing were un-Roman, and not even soldierly; he strolled about the gymnasium in a Greek mantle and sandals, and wasted his time over books and physical exercise; his staff and friends were enjoying the amenities of Syracuse no less luxuriously, while Carthage and Hannibal seemed completely forgotten. The discipline of the whole army had gone to the dogs, just as at Sucro in Spain and again at Locri, so that it was more of a menace to its friends than its enemies.

20. Some of these accusations were true, while the half-truth in others rendered them plausible enough; nevertheless when Quintus Metellus expressed his agreement with Fabius in all he had said except in his charges against Scipio, his motion carried the day. Here, he pointed out, was a man whom, young though he was, the country had recently chosen as the one general capable of recovering Spain; whom, when that task was accomplished, his fellow-citizens had made consul to end the Punic war, confident that he would draw Hannibal from Italy and conquer Africa. That being so, it was not reasonable that such a man should be suddenly recalled from his province as if he were no better than Pleminius, and be already condemned, or nearly so, before his case was tried, in spite of the fact that the Locrians admitted that Scipio was not even there when the crimes they complained of were committed against them, and that so far as his sparing of Pleminius was concerned the only charge that could be brought against him was a

reluctance to take measures which might seem over-hasty or unnecessarily severe. Metellus proposed, accordingly, that Marcus Pomponius, the praetor who had been assigned to Sicily, should go there within the next three days, and that the consuls should select at discretion ten *legati*[1] from the Senate to accompany him, together with two people's tribunes and an aedile. With these as his advisers the praetor was to hold an inquiry, and Scipio should be ordered to leave his province if it were determined that what the Locrians complained of had been done by his orders or with his consent; if Scipio had already sailed for Africa, then the people's tribunes and the aedile should follow him there with two of the *legati* whom the praetor considered most suitable; the duty of the aedile and tribunes would be to bring Scipio back to Rome, and that of the *legati* to take temporary command of the army until the arrival of a new commander-in-chief. If on the other hand Pomponius and the ten *legati* found that the atrocities at Locri had taken place without Scipio's orders or consent, Scipio was to remain in command and carry on with the campaign in accordance with his plans. When this decree had been passed, the people's tribunes were asked to decide either by mutual agreement or by drawing lots which two of them should accompany the praetor and the *legati*. The College of Pontiffs was then consulted on the procedure for expiating the sacrilege in connexion with the violation and removal of the treasure in the temple of Proserpine at Locri.

The two tribunes who went with the praetor and the ten *legati* were Marcus Claudius Marcellus and Marcus Cincius Alimentus; they were accompanied also by a plebeian aedile, whose duty it would be to arrest Scipio on the tribunes' orders if he were still in Sicily and refused to obey the praetor, or if he had already crossed to Africa; the tribunes, by virtue of the sacrosanctity of their office, would then bring him back to Rome. Their plan was to visit Locri before going on to Messana.

21. There are two different accounts of what happened to

1. *Legatus* is here used in the sense both of a 'representative' (of the Senate) and of a military officer 'representing' his commander-in-chief on some special assignment (like Pleminius at Locri). (A. de S.)

Pleminius. According to one, on hearing of the proceedings in Rome he decided to go into exile at Naples, but on the way there he fell in with Quintus Metellus, one of the *legati*, who arrested him and took him back to Rhegium; the other story is that Scipio himself sent an officer with thirty cavalrymen of high rank to throw Pleminius into chains, and with him the other leaders in the disgraceful affair at Locri. They were all handed over to the men of Rhegium for safe keeping, either by Scipio's orders or, later, by the order of the praetor.

At Locri the praetor and the *legati*, according to the instructions they had received, turned their attention first of all to the religious issue: they replaced in the treasury all the sacred money which their search had discovered either in the hands of Pleminius or of the soldiers, together with the money they had brought with them, and performed the propitiatory rite. Then the praetor ordered the troops to parade, marched them out of town, and indicated a position where they were to encamp, at the same time issuing strict orders against any soldier who stayed in the town or brought out with him anything which was not his own property. According to these orders any Locrian who recognized a piece of property belonging to himself was permitted to take it, and to demand the restitution of anything which had disappeared; above all it was the praetor's intention that free persons should be immediately restored, and any man failing to restore them would be very severely punished.

The praetor then held an assembly of the Locrians and informed them that the Roman people gave back to them their liberty and laws, adding that anyone who wished to bring a charge against Pleminius or anybody else must go with him to Rhegium; if they wished in the name of their state to lay a formal complaint against Scipio, on the ground that the crimes committed at Locri against God and man had been committed either by his orders or with his consent, they must send a delegation to Messana, where he, the praetor, with his board of advisers would hold an inquiry. The Locrians expressed their gratitude to the praetor and the *legati*, and to the Senate and people of Rome, and declared their intention of going to

Rhegium to charge Pleminius; as for Scipio, though he had shown himself insufficiently sympathetic to their sufferings, he was none the less, they said, a man whom they would rather have as a friend than an enemy, and they were quite sure that none of the innumerable atrocities had taken place either by his orders or with his consent. Perhaps he had trusted Pleminius too much and himself too little; or it may have been merely that there are men who, though by nature averse to wrongdoing, lack the vigour and determination to punish it.

The praetor and his assistants were thus relieved of the burdensome duty of holding a court of inquiry into the actions of Scipio. They condemned Pleminius and about thirty-two others and sent them in chains to Rome, after which they continued their journey with the further intention of seeing for themselves, and reporting to Rome, what truth there was in the gossip about Scipio's dress and idleness and the lax discipline of his troops.

22. While they were on their way to Syracuse, Scipio made ready to provide visible evidence of his integrity and competence as a commander-in-chief. He ordered the whole army to assemble there and the fleet to be prepared for action as if there were to be on that very day a combined sea and land operation against the Carthaginians. The praetor and his advisers were hospitably welcomed on their arrival, and next day Scipio for their benefit put both his land and naval forces through their paces, the former not merely coming on parade but executing manoeuvres, and the latter, too, holding a mock sea-fight in the harbour. The praetor and the *legati* were then taken on a tour of inspection of the arsenals, magazines, and war-equipment generally; and such was their admiration for every detail in the grand total of what they saw that they were convinced that, if Scipio and his army could not defeat Carthage, assuredly nobody else could. They bade him therefore sail with God's blessing, and fulfil for the people of Rome as soon as might be the hopes they had conceived on the day when all the centuries had named him first to be their consul. Such was their joy as they started on their return journey that they might have been bringing to Rome the news not merely of impressive preparations for war but of victory already won.

Pleminius and the others who were involved in the Locrian affair were imprisoned immediately on their arrival in Rome. When they were first brought before the people by the tribunes for the first of the four successive appearances the law required, the horrors at Locri were still too fresh in everybody's mind to leave room for pity; but later, at subsequent appearances, when feeling against the culprits was beginning to lose its edge, much less anger was evident and the mere fact of Pleminius's changed appearance and the memory of the absent Scipio helped to win favour with the crowd. Pleminius, however, died in prison before the people's judgement could be finally passed upon him. Clodius Licinus in the third Book of his *Roman History*[1] says that Pleminius, during the votive Games held in Rome by Scipio Africanus (as he by then was) in his second consulship, bribed accomplices to set fire to the city in a number of places simultaneously, in order to give him an opportunity to break prison and get away; but the plot was discovered and he was transferred by order of the Senate to the Tullianum.[2] In Scipio's case no action was taken except in the Senate; here both *legati* and tribunes joined in praise of him and of his fleet and army, and the Senate voted in consequence that the expedition to Africa should take place at the earliest moment possible and that Scipio should be permitted to select from the forces in Sicily what troops to take with him and what to leave behind to garrison Sicily.

23. Meanwhile the Carthaginians had passed an anxious winter. Every promontory along the coast had its look-out; they had been constantly seeking information, and each piece of news as it came seemed more alarming than the last. Now however – and this was of no small moment in the defence of Africa – they had succeeded in procuring a pact with King Syphax, reliance upon whose support had, they thought, more than anything else encouraged the Romans to undertake the invasion. Not only was Hasdrubal son of Gisgo bound to Syphax by the ties of hospitality, which have already been

1. An unusually exact reference. Clodius Licinus was a younger contemporary of Livy's.

2. An underground chamber under the prison, where criminals were executed. (A. de S.)

mentioned in connexion with his arrival from Spain at the same time, as it happened, as the arrival of Scipio, but preliminary mention had also been made of a family connexion through the king's marriage to a daughter of Hasdrubal.[1] The girl was already of marriageable age, so Hasdrubal visited Syphax to see the arrangements completed and a time fixed for the ceremony; then, seeing that the king was aflame with desire – the Numidians surpass all other barbarian peoples in the violence of their appetites – he sent to Carthage for the young woman and hurried on the wedding. Congratulations were general, and, by way of strengthening the family tie by a national compact, a treaty of alliance between the people of Carthage and the king was declared and sworn to, guarantees being mutually exchanged that each would have the same friends and the same enemies.

But Hasdrubal none the less could not but remember the pact which Syphax had made with Scipio, and the fickleness and unreliability inherent in half-civilized peoples. He was afraid the marriage would prove but a feeble bond once Scipio was actually in Africa; so while he still had some influence over Syphax, before his passion had had time to cool, he induced him, with the help of some gentle persuasion from his young wife as well, to send envoys to Sicily to convey a warning to Scipio not to cross into Africa in reliance upon his former promises. They were to point out that he, Syphax, was bound to the Carthaginian people both by his marriage to a Carthaginian, the daughter of the Hasdrubal whom Scipio had seen as a guest in his own house, and also by a national compact; his first desire therefore was that the Romans should continue, as before, to fight Carthage far away from African soil, in which case it would not be necessary for him to be involved in their struggles nor to take sides with either one combatant or the other. If, on the other hand, Scipio refused to keep out of Africa and advanced against Carthage, Syphax would inevitably be compelled to fight in defence of the land in which he, too, had been born and for the native city of his wife and for her father and household gods.

24. Armed with these instructions the king's envoys met

1. Sophonisba.

Scipio in Syracuse. For Scipio it meant the collapse of a high hope and the loss of what might have been a decisive influence in his African campaign; nevertheless before the news could have time to spread he hastened to dispatch messengers to Africa with a letter to the king urging him with the utmost insistence not to play traitor to the bond of friendship which bound them to his alliance with the people of Rome, to the dictates of religion, and the handclasps which had sealed an honourable pledge, and to the gods themselves who are arbiters and witnesses of the compacts of men. But the Numidian envoys had already been all over the city, as well as making visits to headquarters, and it was impossible to conceal their presence; moreover if the object of their coming were passed over in silence, it was all too likely that the facts, simply because of the attempt to hide them, might somehow or other leak out by themselves, and fear begin to spread amongst the troops of having to fight the combined forces of Syphax and the Carthaginians. Scipio accordingly distracted attention from the unpleasant truth by filling his men up with lies, ordering a parade and telling them that there must be no more delay, because their allies, the African kings, were insisting that they must make the crossing immediately. Masinissa, he said, had taken the lead by visiting Laelius and complaining of the delays and waste of time, and now Syphax was sending over a delegation, puzzled as he was to understand the reason for such endless procrastination, and demanding either an immediate crossing of the Roman army at long last, or, if their plans were changed, that he should be informed of the fact to enable him to take measures for the safety of himself and his kingdom. Since everything, he ended, was now in complete readiness and the situation did not admit of any further hesitation, it was his intention to move the fleet to Lilybaeum, concentrate at that port all mounted and unmounted troops, and with God's blessing to sail for Africa with the first fair wind. At the same time he wrote to Pomponius asking him, if he thought fit, to come to Lilybaeum and discuss which legions and how many troops it would be wise to take to Africa. He also sent orders all round the coast for merchant vessels to be seized and brought to Lilybaeum.

Once all the troops in Sicily and every vessel in the fleet had been concentrated at Lilybaeum, making the town too small to contain the men and the harbour too small to contain the ships, such was the ardour in every breast to set sail for Africa that it seemed as if the prize of certain victory rather than a hard campaign awaited them at the end of the voyage. Above all it was the survivors of Cannae whose hopes were high, for they were sure that under their present commander and no other, they would be able, by doing good work for their country, to put an end to the ignominious conditions under which they had been serving.[1] Nor did Scipio himself in any way despise those particular units, knowing as he did that the defeat at Cannae had not been due to their cowardice, and that there were no other equally experienced soldiers in the Roman army or men with comparable knowledge of the various sorts of fighting, including, especially, siege warfare. The Cannae legions were the Fifth and Sixth; when Scipio had declared his intention of taking them to Africa, he inspected the men individually and supplied the place of those he thought unfit for service with others whom he had brought with him from Italy. Each of the two legions was in this way made up to a total strength of 6,200 foot and 300 horse. Scipio also chose Latin infantry and cavalry from the army of Cannae to accompany him.

25. The actual size of the army which sailed to Africa varies considerably in the accounts of different authors. In one I find an estimate of 10,000 foot and 2,200 horse; in another 16,000 foot and 1,600 horse; yet another account gives the numbers at more than double – mentioning the embarkation of 35,000 foot and horse combined. Some writers have made no statement of numbers, and since the question cannot be clearly determined I should prefer to follow their example. Coelius avoids any precise statement, but suggests enormous numbers by absurd exaggerations: he says, for instance, that the shouting of the soldiers brought birds tumbling to the ground, and so many men embarked that not a single soul seemed to be left in Italy or Sicily.

1. They had been retained in Sicily, but took part in no action. See pp. 299ff.

Scipio himself saw to the orderly and disciplined embarkation of the troops; Laelius, who commanded the fleet, ordered the crews aboard in good time, and kept them there; the praetor Pomponius was given instructions to load the stores – food for forty-five days, to include cooked rations for fifteen days. Once all the men were aboard, Scipio sent boats round the whole fleet with orders for the master and pilot of every ship together with two soldiers to assemble at headquarters for instructions; as soon as they had all reported, he asked if they had laid in as many days' supply of water, for men and animals, as food. The reply was that they all had water aboard for forty-five days, whereupon Scipio ordered the soldiers not to incommode the sailors in the performance of their duty, but to keep out of the way, not to make a disturbance, and to do as they were told. He and his brother Lucius with twenty warships on the right, Laelius, the admiral, with Marcus Porcius Cato (who was then quaestor) and another twenty warships on the left would act as escort to the transports. Warships were to carry a single light, transports two lights; the flagship was to show a distinguishing mark of three lights during the hours of darkness. The pilots' orders were to steer for the Emporia, a strip of coast south of Thapsus: the land there is very fertile, so there is plenty of everything in the neighbourhood, and the natives, as is commonly the case in rich country, are unwarlike and could, it was thought, be overpowered before help arrived from Carthage. When these instructions had been issued, they were ordered to return to their ships, and on the following day to cast off at the given signal and, with the gods' good help, to put to sea.

26. Many Roman fleets had previously sailed from Sicily, and from that port; yet not only in the present war (understandably enough, since most of the expeditions had merely been raids) but not even in the first Punic war had there been so spectacular a departure. To judge simply by the size of the fleet, it is true that two consuls and two consular armies had previously made the crossing, and there had been almost as many warships in those fleets as there were transports in Scipio's – Scipio, apart from his forty warships, used nearly 400 transports to carry his troops and their gear. But this second

war was felt by the Romans to be a much deadlier struggle than the first, partly because it was being fought on Italian soil and partly because of the frequent terrible losses in men and the death in battle of so many army commanders; Scipio himself, moreover, had fired the imagination of men both by his actual achievements and by a certain personal fortune of his own, which was no small element in the growth of his reputation, while added to all this there was the purpose he had formed, unlike any previous general during the course of the war, of invading Africa. Indeed he had publicly announced that the object of the invasion was to draw Hannibal from Italy and transfer the war to Africa, where it would be fought to a finish. A great crowd had flocked to the harbour to see the sight – not the inhabitants of Lilybaeum only, but all the delegations in Sicily which had met to escort Scipio as a mark of their respect, or which had followed the praetor of the province, Marcus Pomponius; while to swell the crowd yet further, the legions which were being left behind in Sicily had all turned out to see their comrades off. The dense throng at the water's edge made as thrilling a spectacle for the troops on board as the fleet itself made for the watchers on shore.

27. At dawn Scipio on board the flagship called for silence by a herald and said the following prayer: 'O Gods and Goddesses of the seas and lands, I pray and beseech you that whatsoever things have been done under my authority, are being done, and will be done, may prosper for me and for the people and commons of Rome, for our allies and for the Latins who follow my lead, authority, and auspices and those of the Roman people by land, river, and sea; and that you will graciously assist all these our enterprises and bless them with a rich increase. And I pray that you bring the victors home again safe and sound, enriched with spoils and laden with plunder to share my triumph when the enemy has been defeated; that you grant us the power of vengeance upon those whom we hate and our country's enemies, and give to me and to the Roman people means to inflict upon the Carthaginian state the sufferings which the Carthaginians have laboured to inflict on ours.'

After this prayer a victim was offered in sacrifice and Scipio, as the custom is, flung the raw entrails into the sea and gave by trumpet the signal to sail. A good fair wind quickly carried them out of sight of land, but soon after midday they ran into fog, which made it difficult to avoid collisions. Once they were well out to sea, the wind fell off somewhat, and throughout the ensuing night the fog closed down again, dispersing at sunrise when the breeze freshened. Soon land was sighted, and not long afterwards the pilot told Scipio that the African coast was not more than five miles distant; he said he could make out the Promontory of Mercury,[1] and if he had orders to steer for it the whole fleet would soon be in harbour. But Scipio, now that land was in sight, uttered a prayer that his glimpse of Africa might prove a blessing to himself and his country, and ordered more sail to be set and a different landing-place to be made for lower down the coast. The breeze held, but at about the same time as on the previous day the fog came down again, obscuring the land, and with the fog the wind dropped. Darkness fell, making their position uncertain and navigation difficult; so they anchored to avoid the danger of collisions or of running aground. With the return of daylight the breeze got up again, dispersing the fog and revealing the whole line of the coast. Scipio asked the name of the nearest headland, and on being told it was called the Cape of the Beautiful One,[2] exclaimed that the omen was good and gave orders to steer for it. The fleet came to land, and all the troops were disembarked.

Many Greek and Latin writers have recorded that the passage was a good one, without dangerous or alarming incidents, and I have followed their authority. Coelius is the one exception; according to his account, the fleet met every terror of wind and wave short of actual shipwreck; it was finally swept by a gale away from the African coast to the island of Aegimurus, from which it had great difficulty in getting on its proper course again; then, when the ships were in danger of foundering, the men, without waiting for orders, took to the boats and struggled ashore like castaways, without their arms and in the utmost terror and confusion.

28. After the landing the Romans established themselves on some high ground close to the sea. The sight of the fleet at

1. Cap Bon, the eastern arm of the bay of Tunis.
2. i.e. Apollo.

sea followed by the noise and bustle of disembarkation had already caused panic in the neighbouring towns as well as in the farms along the coastal strip; in addition to the crowds of people and jostling columns of women and boys which had blocked all the tracks for miles around, herds of cattle were being driven off to safety by the farmers, so that the impression was of a sudden evacuation of the whole countryside. To the towns the fugitives brought panic even worse than their own, to Carthage especially, where the terror and confusion were almost like that of a captured city. The panic was rendered all the more acute by the fact that since the landing, nearly fifty years previously, of the consuls Regulus and Manlius, the city folk had never seen a Roman army nor anything worse than marauding Roman fleets out for raids on the coastal farms, when the raiders would take what they were lucky enough to find and hurry back to their ships before a call to arms could arouse the farmers; and indeed there was another reason, namely, that they had no military force of any strength in the city and no general to lead the resistance. Hasdrubal son of Gisgo was the most eminent man in Carthage, by birth, reputation, wealth, and, at that time, also by his connexion with King Syphax; but they could not forget that in more than one battle in Spain he had been utterly defeated by the very Scipio who was threatening them now, and that the two commanders could no more be compared with each other than their own hastily raised irregular troops could be compared with the trained Roman army. So just as if Scipio intended an immediate attack, they called to arms what forces they had, hurriedly closed the gates, posted armed men on the walls, and stationed sentries and pickets. Throughout the night no one slept, and on the following day 500 horsemen, sent down to the coast to reconnoitre and to interfere so far as they could with the disembarkation, fell in with Roman outposts; for Scipio, having sent the fleet on towards Utica, had already moved forward a short distance inland and occupied the neighbouring heights. He had posted cavalry pickets in suitable places and sent other groups out to raid the farms. 29. These engaged the Carthaginian cavalry, killed a few of them in the first shock and many more in the subsequent pursuit, including their leader

Hanno, a young man of noble birth. Scipio not only devastated the neighbouring farms but took the nearest African town, a place of considerable wealth; in addition to captured material which was immediately loaded on to his transports and sent over to Sicily, 8,000 people, some free, some slaves, fell into his hands.

But what was most welcome to the Romans at the beginning of their campaign was the arrival of Masinissa. Some say he had with him no more than 200 horsemen; according to others he came with a force of 2,000. Since Masinissa was by far the greatest of all the kings of his time and rendered much the most valuable service to Rome, I feel that it is worth while to digress a little in order to tell the story of the ups and downs he encountered in the loss and recovery of his father's kingdom.[1]

While he was fighting for the Carthaginians in Spain, his father, Gala, died, and the kingdom passed according to Numidian custom to the dead king's brother Oezalces, then a very old man. Not long afterwards Oezalces also died and was succeeded by Capussa, the elder of his two sons, the second being still a boy. But since Capussa held the throne merely as the lawful successor and not by virtue of any strength of his own or influence with his people, there came forward a certain Mazaetullus, a man connected by blood with the royal house though belonging to a family always hostile to it, and constantly engaged with varying fortunes in a struggle for power with those who then occupied the throne. He roused the people, over whom his influence was great, because of the unpopularity of the kings, openly took the field, and compelled Capussa to accept the challenge and fight for his crown. In the ensuing battle Capussa and many of his chief men were killed. The whole nation of the Maesulii passed under sway of Mazaetullus, who nevertheless refrained from assuming the royal title and contented himself with the modest style of guardian, naming as King the boy Lacumazes, a surviving member of the royal house. He then married a noble Carthaginian, daughter of Hannibal's sister, who had been previously married to the king Oezalces; by this he hoped to ally himself with

1. This digression may come from a lost book of Polybius, who had known Masinissa.

Carthage, and at the same time he sent envoys and renewed his long-standing connexion with Syphax, all in preparation for his coming struggle with Masinissa.

30. But Masinissa did not remain inactive: on hearing of his uncle's death, followed by that of his cousin, he left Spain for Mauretania. The king of the Moors at that time was Baga; and Masinissa, unable to gain his assistance in his coming struggle, begged him with the most abject entreaties to allow him at least an escort for his journey. The request was successful and he was given 4,000 Moorish troops. When, thus escorted, he reached the frontier of his kingdom, having already sent on a messenger to his father's friends and his own to warn them of his coming, he was joined by some 500 Numidians. He sent back his Moorish escort according to his agreement with Baga, and although far fewer had joined him than he had hoped, and certainly not enough to justify confidence in his great enterprise, he none the less believed that by pressing vigorously on he would collect a force big enough for ultimate success. Near Thapsus he encountered Lacumazes, who was on his way to Syphax; the young king's column took fright and sought refuge in the town, which Masinissa then assaulted and captured, accepting the surrender of some of the king's escort and killing others who attempted resistance; most of them, however, took advantage of the confusion to escape with Lacumazes and complete their intended journey to Syphax.

News of this modest success at the beginning of his campaign induced the Numidians to join Masinissa; from all the surrounding farms and villages old soldiers who had served under Gala flocked to his standard and spurred him on to the recovery of his father's kingdom.

Mazaetullus had the advantage in point of numbers. He still had the army with which he had defeated Capussa and also some of Capussa's troops which he had taken over when the latter was killed, while young Lacumazes had, in addition, brought very powerful reinforcements from Syphax. His total force thus amounted to 15,000 foot and 10,000 horse, and that was the army with which he engaged Masinissa, whose strength in neither arm was anything like so great. Nevertheless victory went to the valour of experienced soldiers and the military skill of a leader who had learned his trade in the conflict between Roman and Carthaginian arms. The boy prince made his escape into Carthaginian territory with his guardian and a small company of Masaesulians.

Masinissa had recovered his kingdom. It was nevertheless clear to him that a much more serious struggle was awaiting him with Syphax, and in view of this he thought it best to seek a reconciliation with his cousin Lacumazes. He accordingly sent representatives to encourage the boy to hope that if he put himself under his, Masinissa's, protection he would enjoy a position no less honourable than Oezalces had previously enjoyed at the court of Gala; they were further to promise impunity to Mazaetullus together with the honourable restoration of all his property. In this way, in spite of the most vigorous opposition from Carthage, he drew them to his side, as both preferred a modest fortune in their own country to exile.

31. Hasdrubal, as it happened, was with Syphax while all this was going on. When the latter chanced to remark that, so far as he could see, it did not much matter to him whether the throne of the Maesulians was occupied by Lacumazes or Masinissa, Hasdrubal replied that he was greatly mistaken if he thought that Masinissa would remain content with what had satisfied his father Gala or his uncle Oezalces; Masinissa was a man of far loftier spirit and far greater ability than had ever been seen in anyone of his nation. While he was in Spain he had often given evidence to friends and enemies alike of a valour rare amongst men, and unless Syphax and the Carthaginians smothered that flame before it had time to spread they would soon be consumed in a mighty blaze, which they would no longer have the power to put out. At the moment, however, while he was still nursing a kingdom whose wounds had hardly healed, his resources were weak and frail. By urgent representations of this sort Hasdrubal goaded Syphax into moving his army to the Maesulian border, where he took up a position as if there were no possible question between himself and Gala as to his rights on territory the ownership of which had often been disputed, and even fought over. If, said Hasdrubal, anyone tried to keep him out, he must fight, which was just what he most needed; if Masinissa shrank from using force and with-

drew, then he must advance deep into his territory. The Maesulians would either surrender without opposition, or, if they fought, would prove in no way a match for him.

All this encouraged Syphax to attack Masinissa. His success was immediate; in the first engagement he heavily defeated the Maesulians, though Masinissa himself escaped with a few horsemen to a mountain known to the natives as Mount Bellus. A number of families followed him there with their tents and cattle, their only wealth; but the mass of the Maesulians surrendered to Syphax.

The hills which the fugitives had occupied are well provided with water and pasture, and because it was good country for cattle it furnished abundant food for men as well, accustomed as they were to living on meat and milk. From their stronghold they soon took to raiding, furtively at first and by night only, but they passed, as time went on, to open brigandage, until the whole neighbourhood was at their mercy. It was Carthaginian territory that suffered worst, because it contained more that was worth taking than was to be found amongst the Numidians, and because the taking of it was less dangerous. Before long the robbers were playing their game with such reckless abandon that they were taking their spoil down to the coast and selling it to traders who used to put in for the purpose, and more Carthaginians were being killed or captured than often happened in regular warfare.

The Carthaginians complained of all this to Syphax, and as he was himself far from pleased at what was going on they did their best to urge him to strike the final blow. Syphax, however, felt that it was hardly fit work for a king to go chasing a bandit about the mountains, so he selected for the task one of his officers, a vigorous and active soldier named Bucar. 32.
A force of 4,000 foot and 2,000 horse was put under his command, and he was buoyed up with hopes of an enormous reward if he brought back Masinissa's head or gave his master the inestimable pleasure of having him alive and a prisoner of war. Finding the enemy in disorder and off their guard, Bucar delivered a surprise attack, and, separating the masses of cattle and men from their armed escort, compelled Masinissa himself to take refuge with a few followers high up on the crest of the

mountain. It seemed to Bucar that the fight was almost over; not content with sending his prisoners and the captured cattle to Syphax, he also sent back the bulk of his army, as being much too numerous for what remained to be done, and with not more than 500 foot and 200 horse pursued Masinissa, who had by then left his perch, and shut him up in a gully with both ends blocked. The Maesulians suffered frightful losses, but Masinissa with at most fifty horsemen made his escape by unknown tracks winding amongst the recesses of the hills. Bucar none the less kept on his trail and caught him on open ground near the town of Clupea; surrounding the little band, he killed every one of them but four, whom, together with Masinissa himself, wounded though he was, he allowed in the heat of the moment to slip through his fingers. Away went the five fugitives still in full sight of the enemy: in a moment a troop of cavalry was after them, scattering widely, some veering away at a tangent to cut them off. Ahead lay a great river; unhesitatingly, knowing that a greater terror was behind, the fugitives plunged in without drawing rein and were swept by the current obliquely past their pursuers' eyes. Two, sucked down in the swirling waters, were drowned in sight of the enemy; Masinissa himself was believed to have perished, but with the other two survivors he managed to struggle out amongst the brush on the farther bank of the river. That, for Bucar, was the end of the chase, for he neither relished the prospect of entering the river nor imagined he had anyone left to pursue. He went back to the king to report, falsely, that Masinissa was drowned, and messengers were sent off to tell the glad news in Carthage. The story that Masinissa was dead, spreading all over Africa, had powerful repercussions, of joy or distress as the case might be.

For some days, while he was curing his wound with herbs, Masinissa lay hidden in a cave, living on what his two companions were able to bring him. Then with incredible audacity, as soon as the wound was closed and he thought he could endure the movement of a horse, he set out to recover his kingdom. On the way he collected some forty horsemen, not more, and thus accompanied rode on into Maesulian territory, now openly announcing his identity. And such was the strength of feeling aroused both by his former popularity and by the unexpected joy of seeing safe and sound the king they had thought to be dead, that within a few days an army of 6,000 foot and 4,000 horse flocked to join him. He was now not merely in possession once more of his father's kingdom but able to make devastating raids upon the tribes allied to Carthage and on the dominions of Syphax – the territory of the Masaesulians. Having thus provoked Syphax to war, he established himself in a very favourable position on a chain of hills between Cirta and Hippo.[1]

33. Syphax now recognized that the threat was too serious to be entrusted to his subordinate officers; he accordingly sent a section of his force under his young son Vermina with orders to make a detour and attack the enemy in the rear while his attention was occupied with the king's army in front of him. Vermina, who was to make the surprise attack, marched under cover of darkness; Syphax broke camp in daylight, marching by a route in full sight of the enemy and making no attempt to conceal his intention of a direct encounter. When he thought enough time had elapsed to allow Vermina's column to reach their objective, he began to move into action: relying on his superiority in numbers and the surprise attack about to be delivered in Masinissa's rear, he advanced towards the enemy in battle order up a gentle slope of the hill facing him. Masinissa also prepared for action, basing his hopes chiefly on the strength of the much more favourable position from which he would be fighting. The battle was a savage one and the issue for a long time in doubt, Masinissa having the advantage in position and in the valour of his men, Syphax in his greatly superior numbers. That enormous army, divided as it was into two sections, one pressing on the enemy's front, the other having moved round to cover his rear, gave Syphax no uncertain victory. Masinissa's men, penned in both front and rear, had not even a chance to escape. Most of his force, both mounted and unmounted, were either killed or captured. But there were about 200 horsemen whom he succeeded in rallying close round him, and these he divided into three troops and ordered to make a breakthrough, naming a rendezvous where, after getting away

1. Syphax's capital: and Hippo Regius.

in any direction they could, they were subsequently to meet. Masinissa himself broke through the flying spears and escaped in the direction he had determined on; two of his troops of horse failed to get through, one of them surrendering, the other, which offered more stubborn resistance, being overwhelmed with missiles and wiped out. Vermina pressed hard on the fugitives' heels, but Masinissa gave him the slip by continually turning off into a different and unexpected track, until he finally drove him to abandon the pursuit in sheer weariness and despair of success. Masinissa himself with his sixty horsemen made his way to the Lesser Syrtis, where, in the proud consciousness of his many attempts to regain his father's kingdom, he remained, somewhere in the region between the Punic Emporia and the Garamantes, until the arrival in Africa of Laelius and the Roman fleet. It is these facts which incline one to believe that Masinissa subsequently also came to Scipio with a small,[1] rather than a large, escort of cavalry; for surely the large estimate of some writers suits a reigning monarch, while the modest number I prefer is in keeping with an exile's fortune.

34. The Carthaginians, having lost a squadron of cavalry and its commander, held a levy to raise reinforcements and put Hanno son of Hamilcar in command. They then sent for Hasdrubal and Syphax, first by letter and messenger, but finally even going to the lengths of sending a delegation. Their instructions to Hasdrubal were to come to the relief of his native city now almost beleaguered; Syphax they besought to bring help to Carthage, indeed to all Africa. By now Scipio was encamped about a mile from Utica, after having moved there from the coast, where for a few days he had remained in close touch with the fleet. Hasdrubal's prime object was to increase the number of his cavalry by pressing anyone he could into the service, as the force he had been given was totally inadequate even to the task of checking enemy raids on the farmlands, not to mention the possibility of taking the initiative. Though willing enough to accept men from other tribes, he for the most part enlisted Numidians, who make by far the best mounted troops in all Africa. He had already raised his numbers to about 4,000, when he took a town called Salaeca about fifteen miles

1. This agrees with Polybius.

from the Roman position. Scipio on hearing the news is said to have exclaimed: 'What? Cavalry under roofs in summer? Who cares how many they are if *that* is the sort of leader they have!' Determined, therefore, to increase the vigour of his measures in direct proportion to the dilatoriness of his antagonist, he ordered Masinissa forward with a detachment of cavalry to ride up to the town gates and draw the enemy out to an engagement, adding further instructions that when the whole lot of them had come pouring out of the town and began to exert too great a pressure for him to withstand with any comfort, he was to retire gradually, and Scipio himself at the right moment would intervene. Scipio waited for what he thought was long enough to give Masinissa time for drawing out the enemy, and then followed with the main Roman cavalry, advancing under cover of the hills, which rose conveniently on either side of the winding track.

Masinissa carried out his orders: again and again he rode aggressively up to the gates of the town, only to retire as if in alarm at his own audacity, until finally, when his simulated timidity gave the enemy sufficient courage, he almost succeeded in luring them to a rash and ill-considered pursuit. Their sortie, however, was a badly organized affair and their leader was having a troublesome time of it; before they were all out, he had to wake some from a drunken sleep and drive them to arm themselves and bridle their horses, and to check others who were making a dash for the gates without any sort of order or discipline, or even their standards. But they managed some sort of a charge, which Masinissa met and held; soon they came out through one of the gates in greater numbers and Masinissa had all he could do to hold them, and finally their entire cavalry force was engaged. The weight of their attack was then too great for Masinissa to withstand and he began his withdrawal – not indeed in disorder but by a planned and gradual retreat, during which he held their attacks when he could, until he had drawn them to the hills behind which the Roman cavalry were concealed. Out they came on the instant, men and horses both fresh, and surrounded Hanno and his Africans, who were already feeling the strain of their running fight, while at the same moment Masinissa's men wheeled about and galloped back into the fray. Nearly a thousand men who had led the column and could not easily get away were cut off and killed, together with Hanno their commander; the rest, terrified by their leader's death, fled in disorder; for thirty miles the victors chased them, finally capturing or killing some 2,000 more. Amongst these it was generally admitted that there were not less than 200 Carthaginian horsemen, some of them belonging to wealthy and noble families.

35. The very day on which these events occurred the ships which had carried the captured material to Sicily returned with a cargo of provisions. It almost looked like second-sight, as if they had come on purpose to pick up a fresh cargo of spoils! That two Carthaginian commanders of the same name were killed in two cavalry engagements is not recorded by all the annalists – for fear, I suppose, that they might be unintentionally telling the same story twice. Coelius and Valerius both state that Hanno was taken prisoner.

Scipio conferred special gifts for gallantry upon his cavalry men and their officers, each according to the service he had rendered, and above all upon Masinissa. Leaving a strong garrison in Salaeca, he then marched with the rest of his army to continue his aggressive tactics. He not only devastated all the cultivated land he came across, but stormed and captured a number of towns and villages, spreading the horrors of war over a large area of the country; then, seven days after he had started, he returned to camp with every sort of booty, including a great number of men and cattle, and once again sent off his ships heavily laden with enemy spoils. After this he abandoned his raids and other minor operations and turned all his available resources to the siege of Utica, meaning to use the town, if he succeeded in taking it, as a base for the remainder of his campaign. On the side where the fleet lay, where the town is washed by the sea, marines were brought up, and the land forces at the same time were moved into position where high ground almost overhangs the town walls. In addition to the artillery and siege-engines Scipio had brought with him, others had been sent from Sicily with the supplies, while new ones were also being made in an arsenal where many expert craftsmen had been forcibly retained for the purpose.

The people of Utica, closely beset as they now were by these powerful forces, pinned all their hopes on Carthage, while Carthage, in its turn, looked solely to Hasdrubal, provided he could prevail upon Syphax to move. But everything was going much too slowly to satisfy the anxious longing of men badly in need of assistance. Hasdrubal had been recruiting with every means at his disposal, but though he had raised his numbers to 30,000 foot and 3,000 horse he still did not venture to take a position nearer the enemy until Syphax should have joined him. When, however, Syphax arrived with 50,000 foot and 10,000 horse, then at last Hasdrubal without further delay moved from Carthage, and established himself not far from the Roman lines at Utica. The result of the coming of these hostile armies was that Scipio, after about forty days spent in vain, despite every effort, on the attempt to reduce Utica, gave it up as useless and withdrew. Winter was now approaching, so his next move was to fortify a winter camp. He chose for its site a promontory which runs out some way into the sea and contracts to a narrow ridge where it joins the mainland.[1] A single earthwork served to protect the naval camp as well, where the ships lay hauled ashore; the camp of the legions was in the middle of the ridge, of which the northern side was held by the beached ships and their crews, and the southern slope, running down to the other shore, by the cavalry. Such was the course of events in Africa till the end of autumn.

36. In addition to the grain from the many plundered farms in the vicinity and the supplies brought from Sicily and Italy, the pro-praetor Gnaeus Octavius also brought an immense quantity of grain which had been sent from Sardinia by the praetor in charge there, Tiberius Claudius. Not only were Scipio's existing granaries filled, but new ones were constructed. The army was short of clothing, and Octavius was instructed to negotiate with Claudius and see if anything could be raised in Sardinia and sent over. This business was also carried out with dispatch, and within a short time 1,200 togas and 12,000 tunics were sent.

During the summer when these events took place in Africa, the consul Sempronius, who was acting in Bruttium,

1. Castra Corneliana: described by Caesar, *Civil Wars* II, 24.

encountered Hannibal on the march in the neighbourhood of Croton and engaged in a sort of running fight with him, neither army deploying into battle stations. The Romans got the worst of it. It was in no sense a regular action, but in the confused fighting Sempronius's army lost some 1,200 men. He hurriedly returned to camp, but the enemy did not venture an assault. In the silence of the following night Sempronius again left camp and joined forces with the proconsul Licinius, to whom he had sent orders to bring up his legions. Thus two commanders and two armies together returned to face Hannibal, and, as Sempronius's strength was now doubled and Hannibal was emboldened by his recent success, there was nothing on either side to postpone an immediate engagement. Sempronius moved up his legionaries into the front line, with Licinius's men stationed in reserve. Just before the fighting began, he vowed a temple to Fortuna Primigenia if he should defeat the enemy – and his prayer was answered. The Carthaginians were utterly routed; over 4,000 of them were killed; just under 300 taken alive together with forty horses and eleven military standards. The defeat forced Hannibal to withdraw to Croton.

Meanwhile, farther north, the consul Cornelius was engaged in holding Etruria, almost the whole of which was beginning to look to Mago and, through him, to the hope of throwing off its dependence upon Rome. He was doing this not by force but by a series of judicial inquiries, which he had been ordered by the Senate to conduct without any respect to persons. Many noble Etruscans who had either gone themselves to Mago to tell him of the readiness of their communities to revolt from Rome, or had sent others to do so, had appeared in court and been condemned, and later others whom a guilty conscience had driven into exile were sentenced in absence, thus avoiding the death penalty and leaving for the satisfaction of the law only such property as was liable to confiscation.

37. While the consuls were thus engaged in their respective spheres, in Rome the censors Livius and Claudius gave the official reading of the list of senators. Quintus Fabius Maximus was again chosen as *princeps*. Seven members received the 'black mark', but no one who had occupied a curule chair. The

censors next saw to the repair of public buildings with great fidelity and dispatch, and placed contracts for making a road from the Cattle Market, round the spectators' stands, to the temple of Venus, and for the erection of a shrine to the Great Mother on the Palatine. They also imposed a new tax on the annual production and sale of salt. At the time, the price of salt both in Rome and throughout Italy was one sixth of an *as*; the change, though the price in Rome remained the same, consisted in placing contracts for its sale at a higher price in market-towns and local trade-centres, the price varying in different districts. It was generally believed that this source of revenue was the private idea of one of the censors only, and arose from his anger with the people because he had formerly been unjustly condemned in court, and that the tribes responsible for his condemnation were the ones to suffer most heavily from the rise in price. It was from this incident that Livius got the cognomen of Salinator.

The quinquennial ceremony of Purification was later than usual because the censors had sent missions to the various provinces to ascertain and report the number of Roman citizens in the several armies. Including these, the total number returned in the census was 214,000. Gaius Claudius Nero concluded the rite of purification. They then received the census lists of the twelve colonies, brought to Rome by their own local censors; this had never been done before, and the object of it was to have a permanent record in the public archives of the resources of the colonies in men and money. A census of the knights was next begun. Now it so happened that both censors owned a horse provided by the State. When they came to the Pollia tribe, in which Livius's name was included, the herald, feeling it was unseemly to call a censor, hesitated; but Claudius would have none of it: 'Call Marcus Livius,' he said; then, either because he still remembered their old quarrel or because he prided himself on a very uncalled-for exhibition of severity, he ordered Livius, on the ground of his condemnation by the people, to sell his horse. Livius soon retaliated; when they came to the Arniensis tribe and the name of his colleague, he ordered Claudius to sell *his* horse – and that for two reasons: first because he had given false evidence against him, secondly because his subsequent reconciliation had been insincere. At the end of their censorship, too, they indulged in equally undignified competition to blacken each other's reputation at the expense of their own. When Claudius had taken the oath and gone up into the Treasury, he included his colleague's name amongst those he was leaving as *aerarii* – mere tax-payers, that is, without the right to vote. Livius then entered the Treasury and declared the entire Roman people, thirty-four tribes of them, as *aerarii* because they had unjustly condemned him and then, despite the condemnation, had made him first consul and then censor, so that they were caught in a cleft stick and would have to admit a mistake, either once in their verdict, or twice at the polls. The only tribe he excepted was the Maecia, which had not condemned him and had not voted for him when he stood either for the consulship or for the censorship. He added that the degradation of the thirty-four tribes to the status of *aerarii* would of course include Claudius; he would have mentioned him particularly by name, thus degrading him twice over, individually and collectively, if there were any precedent for it. As a squabble between the censors in giving 'black marks' this was a most improper proceeding, but as a sharp criticism of popular frivolity it was in the true tradition of the censors' office and worthy of the high seriousness of those days. The censors being in bad odour, the people's tribune, Gnaeus Baebius, saw a chance of advancing himself at their expense and issued a summons for both of them to appear before the people. The matter was quashed by the unanimous decision of the Senate, as it might have led to the future subjection of the censorship to popular caprice.

38. During this summer, Clampetia in Bruttium was stormed and taken by the consul Sempronius, and Consentia, Pandosia, and other unimportant communities accepted Roman control. Shortly before the date of the next elections it was decided to recall the consul Cornelius to Rome, rather than his colleague, because there were no military operations at the moment in Etruria. Cornelius accordingly presided, and named Gnaeus Servilius Caepio and Gaius Servilius Geminus as the new consuls. The election of praetors was then held, and the successful candidates were Publius Cornelius Lentulus, Publius

Quinctilius Varus, Publius Aelius Paetus, and Publius Villius Tappulus; the last two were plebeian aediles at the time of their election. The elections over, Cornelius rejoined his army in Etruria.

Death brought certain changes in the priesthoods during the course of this year: Tiberius Veturius Philo was elected and inaugurated as *flamen* of Mars in place of Marcus Aemilius Regillus, who had died the previous year; in place of Marcus Pomponius Matho, the augur and decemvir, Marcus Aurelius Cotta was made decemvir and Tiberius Sempronius Gracchus augur. The latter was a very young man, a fact which made his election to a priesthood most unusual. A gilded four-horse chariot was installed that year on the Capitol by the curule aediles Gaius Livius and Marcus Servilius Geminus, and the Roman Games were repeated for two days. The Plebeian Games were also repeated for two days by the aediles Aelius and Villius. To honour the Games a banquet for Jupiter was celebrated.

# BOOK XXX

1. The sixteenth year of the war was now beginning. When the new consuls, Caepio and Geminus, had brought up in the Senate the question of the state of the nation, the conduct of the war, and the assignment of provinces, a resolution was passed instructing the consuls to draw lots or determine by mutual agreement which of them should face Hannibal in Bruttium and which should operate in Etruria and Liguria. Whichever got Bruttium was to take over Sempronius's army, and Sempronius, whose command as proconsul was extended for another year, was to succeed Licinius, who, in his turn, was to return to Rome. Publius Licinius Crassus had by now a high military reputation in addition to his other accomplishments, with which no contemporary Roman was considered to be more richly endowed. Nature and fortune had heaped upon him every good gift possible for a man: aristocratic and wealthy, he had exceptionally good looks and physical strength; he was eloquent, both as a pleader in the courts and as a speaker when opportunity offered, on one side or the other of a question, either in the Senate or before the people; in knowledge of pontifical law he was deeply versed, and over and above all this his consulship had brought him the fame of a great soldier.[1]

A similar decision was taken about Etruria and Liguria as about Bruttium: Marcus Cornelius was ordered to hand over his army to the new consul, while he himself had his command extended with the duty of holding Gaul with the same troops as Scribonius had commanded there the previous year. Lots were then drawn to determine the assignment of provinces, and Bruttium fell to Caepio, Etruria to Geminus. In the drawing for the praetors' provinces, the City jurisdiction fell to Aelius Paetus; Sardinia to Lentulus; Sicily to Villius; Ariminum, with the two legions previously under the command of Spurius

1. A pointless and irrelevant panegyric: perhaps it came in here by accident. Crassus was consul two years previously, but achieved no notable success. (A. de S.)

Lucretius, to Quinctilius Varus. Lucretius also had his command extended to enable him to rebuild the town of Genoa which had been destroyed by Mago.[1] As for Scipio, the period of his command was not limited by a definite date but was to continue until the successful conclusion of his African campaign; and a decree was passed ordering a day of prayer that his crossing to Africa might bring a blessing to the Roman people and to him and his army.

2. Three thousand fresh troops were enrolled for Sicily, because the best troops in the island had been transferred to Africa; and in consequence of a decision to have forty ships for the defence of the Sicilian coast against any possible attack from Africa, the praetor Villius took thirteen new vessels with him and had the old ones which were already there given a thorough overhaul. Pomponius, who had been praetor the previous year, had his powers extended and was put in command of this fleet, which he manned with recruits brought over from Italy. The same number of ships, with the same extension of command, was assigned by decree to Gnaeus Octavius, also praetor in the preceding year, for the defence of the Sardinian coast, and the new praetor Lentulus received instructions to provide 2,000 soldiers to man them. As for the Italian coast, nobody knew where the Carthaginians might send a fleet, though it seemed likely that they would attack at any unguarded spot; defence, therefore, was entrusted to last year's praetor Marcius – again with forty ships. The consuls by decree of the Senate enrolled 3,000 soldiers to serve with this fleet, also two City legions for emergency duty. The Spanish provinces were assigned by decree to their old commanders, Lucius Lentulus and Lucius Manlius Acidinus, with their armies and full military authority. Rome's total military establishment that year was twenty legions and 160 warships.

The praetors were ordered to leave for their provinces; and the consuls had instructions to celebrate before they left Rome the Great Games, which the dictator Titus Manlius Torquatus had vowed to hold in four years' time, if the State should still survive unchanged.

At this juncture strange superstitious fears were aroused

1. See p. 563.

by reports of unnatural events from various places. Crows were believed to have pecked to pieces certain gold ornamentation on the Capitol, and even to have eaten it; at Antium mice gnawed a gold circlet; all the country round Capua was filled with swarms of locusts – so many that it was impossible to tell where they had come from; a foal at Reate was born with five feet; at Anagnia scattered fires were seen in the sky, followed by the blaze of a huge meteor; at Frusino there was a finely-drawn halo round the sun, and a little later, another circle, seemingly of sunlight, appeared to be inscribed outside of and round it. An area of level ground at Arpinum subsided, leaving a deep depression; finally, when one of the consuls was sacrificing his first victim, it was found that the liver had no head.[1]

The prodigies were expiated by the sacrifice of full-grown victims, the College of Pontiffs announcing to which gods the sacrifices should be offered.

3. The consuls and praetors were now free to leave for their various spheres of duty. But whatever their tasks, their thoughts were solely on Africa, as if it were there that their own duty lay; they knew that in Africa the final and conclusive campaign would be fought, and they wished, moreover, to gratify Scipio to whom the country had by now unanimously turned. In consequence it was not only from Sardinia, as was mentioned above, but from Sicily and Spain as well that clothing and grain were being sent over, and weapons, too, from Sicily and supplies of all kinds. Nor had Scipio, for his part, at any moment during the winter allowed any relaxation in his efforts; the number of tasks and anxieties he had simultaneously on hand were many: he was besieging Utica; his camp was in sight of Hasdrubal; the Carthaginians had launched a fleet which they were holding in readiness, fully equipped, to intercept his supplies; while in addition to all this he had not ceased to hope for a reconciliation with Syphax, should it so be that in his relations with his wife excessive indulgence had ended at last in satiety. But what Scipio heard from Syphax rather suggested possible peace terms between Rome and Carthage – that the Romans should withdraw from Africa and the Carthaginians

1. A head-shaped protuberance to which great importance was attached by the diviners.

from Italy – than gave any hope of his abandoning his support of Carthage if the war went on. I am more inclined to believe, with the majority of writers, that contact between Scipio and Syphax was through messengers than, as Valerius Antias states, that Syphax came to the Roman camp for a personal conference. At first Scipio would hardly even listen to the suggested terms; but later, to give his officers a plausible excuse for visiting the enemy's camp, he greatly modified the rigidity of his attitude and held out hopes that an agreement might be reached by frequent discussion of every side of the problem.

The winter camp of the Carthaginians had been built of any material that happened to come to hand in the neighbouring farmlands and was almost entirely of wood. The Numidians, especially, were living in reed huts, mostly under thatch, scattered about quite irregularly, some of them having even chosen on their own initiative and without orders a spot outside the fosse and rampart. This was reported to Scipio and raised his hopes of finding an opportunity to set the camp on fire. 4. His practice accordingly, when he sent envoys to Syphax, was to include in the party some centurions of proved intelligence and ability. These men were humbly dressed and made to look like servants, and while the envoys were in consultation they would wander separately about the camp, one here, one there, gathering information about the entrances and exits, the shape and layout both of the camp as a whole and of the separate portions occupied by the Numidians and Carthaginians, the distance between the two – Syphax's and Hasdrubal's – and also the way in which outposts and sentry-duty were organized, and whether they offered a better chance for a surprise attack by day or by night. The fact moreover that the consultations were numerous enabled more and more spies to be sent, with the deliberate object of familiarizing as many as possible with all the details.

When the frequency of the discussions began to make Syphax, and through him the Carthaginians, daily more certain that peace would come, the Roman envoys said that they had been forbidden to return to Scipio without a definite answer: if, therefore, his own mind was made up he must declare his decisions; if Hasdrubal and the Carthaginians had to be consulted, let him consult them, for the time had come either to settle terms of peace or to resort to an all-out trial of strength. Discussions ensued, and while Syphax conferred with Hasdrubal and Hasdrubal with the Carthaginians, the Roman spies had time to see all they wanted to see and Scipio was able to make all necessary preparations. Moreover, talk of peace and hopes of its conclusion led – as they often do – both Syphax and the Carthaginians into neglect of proper precautions against possible hostile action in the meantime. At last the answer was brought back to Scipio; it contained, as the Roman commander seemed excessively anxious for peace, certain exorbitant demands, deliberately included, and it was precisely these which gave Scipio, eager as he was to break the truce, the excuse he needed.[1] He told Syphax's messenger that he would consult his council, and on the following day declared that his solitary efforts had been all to no purpose and nobody else on his war-council had been in favour of peace; so he must inform his master Syphax that his only hope of peace with the Romans lay in his abandoning his support of Carthage. So the truce was broken – deliberately, to allow Scipio to carry out his purpose with a clear conscience. He launched his ships (it was by now the beginning of spring), got aboard the artillery and catapults as if he meant to attack Utica by sea, and sent 2,000 men to occupy the hill above the town as before. His object in all this was to distract the enemy's attention from his real designs and at the same time to guard against a sortie from the town against his own camp, left, as it would be, with only a light garrison when he himself had moved against Syphax and Hasdrubal.

5. These preparations made, Scipio called a council, and the spies were told to report the results of their investigations, a similar request being made to Masinissa, who had intimate knowledge of all the enemy's arrangements. Scipio then explained his plan for the following night and gave orders to the military tribunes to march the infantry out of camp as soon as the council was dismissed and the trumpets sounded the signal. Just before sunset, according to orders the march began; about the first watch the column was deployed, and by midnight the

1. Here Livy, or his Roman source, is trying to justify Scipio's conduct. Polybius says nothing about these demands.

seven miles had been covered and, moving at moderate speed, the Romans had reached the enemy's camp. At this point Scipio put Laelius in charge of a part of his forces, including Masinissa and his Numidians, and gave him the order to break into Syphax's camp and set it on fire; he then took both Laelius and Masinissa aside, one at a time, and earnestly impressed upon them how essential it was that attention to detail and constant alertness should be made to compensate for the lack of previous planning which in a night action was unavoidable. He himself, he told them, would be leading the assault on Hasdrubal and the Carthaginian camp, but he would not move until he had seen that Syphax's camp was ablaze.

Scipio was not kept waiting long: for when fire had been applied and the first huts began to burn, the flames immediately spread, first to the immediate surroundings and then with increasing swiftness throughout the entire camp. The terror and confusion were no less than could be expected in the circumstances, when the fire, at night, spread so rapidly and so far; but the troops imagined none the less that it was due not to enemy action but to accident, and rushing out from their quarters to extinguish the flames, without stopping to arm themselves, they encountered their armed enemy – especially the Numidian troops which Masinissa, from his knowledge of the camp's layout, had carefully posted at the various exits. Many were burned to death half asleep in their beds; many more were trampled to death in the narrow gateways in their wild rush to escape.

6. The Carthaginian sentries were the first to see the glare of the conflagration; the rest of the camp was soon awakened by the noise and confusion, and all, at the sight of the fire, made the same mistake as Syphax's men and supposed it to have been started by some natural cause. A further cause of bewilderment and error were the cries of wounded and dying men – cries which might, for all they knew, have been merely the result of a sudden emergency in the night. Without any suspicion, therefore, of enemy action, many of them on their own initiative hurried out of the nearest gate, unarmed and taking with them only what would help to put out the fire, and ran straight into the Roman column. All of them were killed, for, apart from

the ordinary heat of battle, it was essential that none should escape to tell his comrades in camp of the true state of affairs. Scipio then, without delay, thrust his way through the camp gates, which in the circumstances were of course unguarded. The nearest buildings were set alight: at first scattered fires blazed out at several points, but soon the creeping flames united until suddenly they devoured the whole camp in a single conflagration. Men and beasts badly burned blocked the lanes leading to the gates, first as they desperately tried to get away, then by their corpses; all who escaped the fire were cut down by the enemy, so that two camps were wiped out in a single disaster. However, both commanders escaped, and of the thousands of troops in the two camps 2,000 infantry and 500 cavalry got away with half their equipment, and many of them either wounded or severely burned. The killed, by fire or sword, amounted to 40,000 men; more than 5,000 were taken prisoner, including many Carthaginians of noble blood and eleven senators; 174 military standards were captured and over 2,700 Numidian horses; six elephants were taken alive, eight were either killed or burned to death. A great quantity of weapons also fell into Scipio's hand, all of which he dedicated to Vulcan and burned.

7. Hasdrubal after his escape had made his way with a few men to the nearest African town, and all the other survivors had followed him there. But he was afraid the place might surrender to Scipio, so he left it. Soon afterwards, its gates were, in fact, opened to admit the Romans, who, as the town had submitted voluntarily, took no hostile action. Two other towns were later taken and sacked and the plunder turned over to the troops, together with what had been rescued from the flames in the two camps. Syphax took up a position in a fortified place some eight miles distant, while Hasdrubal hurried to Carthage in the hope of preventing a weakening in the attitude of the authorities as a result of the recent disaster. At first the news had caused such terror that everyone was convinced that Scipio intended to let Utica go and immediately begin the siege of Carthage; the *sufetes*, accordingly (their power was more or less equivalent to the Roman consuls') called a meeting of the senate, at which three proposals were debated: one was to send envoys to

Scipio to treat for peace; another, to recall Hannibal to save his country from almost certain destruction; and a third – worthy of Rome herself for its steadfastness in adversity – was to replace the losses to their army and urge Syphax not to abandon his efforts in the common struggle. It was this last proposal which was adopted, because Hasdrubal, who was present in person, and the whole Barcine faction were in favour of war. Recruiting consequently began in the city and surrounding country, and envoys were sent to Syphax, who, as it happened, was himself already doing his utmost to make good his losses for the continuance of the war. His efforts were largely due to his wife, who had prevailed upon him not, indeed, with the old blandishments so effective with a lover, but with a passionate appeal to his pity, begging him with tears not to betray her father and the city where she was born, nor allow Carthage to be consumed in the same flames as had burned his camp to ashes. Moreover, opportune news brought further hope of success: envoys arrived with the information that a force of Celtiberians, 4,000 strong, had met them near a town named Obba – the men had been hired for service by their recruiting officers in Spain, and were all fine specimens; and Hasdrubal, too, would soon be on the spot with an army by no means contemptible. Syphax not only gave the envoys a friendly answer but showed them the large numbers of Numidian peasants whom he had recently equipped with arms and horses, and declared his intention of calling up every man of military age in his kingdom. He knew, he added, that their recent reverse was due to fire, not battle, and that in any war the loser was he who was conquered by force of arms. Such was his answer to the envoys, and a few days later Hasdrubal and Syphax once again joined forces. Their combined strength amounted to about 30,000 men.

8. Scipio had supposed that, so far as Syphax and the Carthaginian army were concerned, the war was as good as over. He was therefore intent upon the siege of Utica and was already moving his artillery up to the walls, when the report of a renewed threat forced him to change his plans. Leaving a small force – enough only to create the illusion that the siege was still being maintained by land and sea – he at once set out with the

main body of his troops to seek the enemy.[1] He first established himself on some high ground about four miles distant from Syphax's camp; then on the next day he moved down with his cavalry into what were known as the Great Plains, and spent the day in light skirmishes, the result of probing movements against the enemy's outposts. For a further two days the same sort of thing continued, one side or the other making minor and irregular attacks, without accomplishing anything worth mention; then, on the fourth day, the two hostile armies both went down into battle formation.

Scipio stationed the *principes* behind the leading companies of the *hastati*, with the *triarii*[2] in reserve; his Italian cavalry was sent to the right wing, with Masinissa and his Numidian horse on the left. Syphax and Hasdrubal posted their Numidians to face Scipio's Italian cavalry, and their Carthaginians to face Masinissa, with the Celtiberian contingent in the centre opposite the Roman legionaries. In this formation the fight began. At the first charge both enemy wings, Numidian and Carthaginian, were driven in; for the Numidians, who were mostly peasants, were no match for the Roman cavalry, and the Carthaginians, who also were raw troops, failed to stand up to Masinissa, rendered, as he was, a yet more terrible foe by his recent victory. The Celtiberians, stripped though they were of defence on both wings, continued to stand firm, partly because in the unfamiliar country flight would not have saved them, partly because they could hope for no mercy from Scipio, against whom they had come to Africa to fight for pay, in spite of the services he had rendered them and their nation. They were completely surrounded, and falling in heaps one upon another obstinately met their death. The Roman concentration on the Celtiberians gave Syphax and Hasdrubal time to escape, and both took advantage of it.[3] Darkness overtook the victors, exhausted by sheer butchery, which had lasted longer than the actual fighting.

1. A five-day march, which would take him about seventy-five miles south-west of Utica.

2. *Hastati, principes, triarii;* the three regular divisions of the Roman infantry. This was the normal order in which they were drawn up for battle. (A. de S.)

3. Syphax fled to Cirta, Hasdrubal to Carthage.

9. Next day Scipio sent Laelius and Masinissa with all the Roman and Numidian cavalry and light-armed infantry in pursuit of Syphax and Hasdrubal, and himself proceeded with the main body of his army to take over, sometimes by offering better conditions, sometimes by threats and sometimes by force, the neighbouring communities, all of which were subject to Carthage. In Carthage itself there was sheer panic; everyone was convinced that Scipio, on the march here, there and everywhere, would attack at any moment, once he had subdued all their neighbours in his lightning campaign. Work was at once begun on the repair of the walls and the construction of defences, and individual families brought in from their farms such supplies as would help them to face a long siege. Peace was seldom mentioned: more often one heard talk of the necessity of recalling Hannibal, and most people urged the dispatch of the fleet, which had been put in commission to intercept enemy supplies, for a surprise attack on the Roman ships lying off Utica. It might also be possible, they thought, to overwhelm the naval camp, which was only weakly defended. This was the plan which seemed to have most support, but they none the less passed a resolution to send a delegation to Hannibal, on the ground that while the siege of Utica might be partially relieved by a naval victory, the only adequate commander now left for the defence of Carthage was Hannibal, and the only troops those under Hannibal's command. So the ships were launched next day, and at the same time the delegation left for Italy: under the pressure of circumstances everything was done in haste, and there was not a man who did not feel a traitor to the state if he in any way relaxed his efforts.

Scipio's movements were by now somewhat impeded by the mass of plunder accumulated from all the towns he had taken; so he sent it, together with his prisoners of war, to his old camp at Utica, and then, as Carthage was now his prime objective, occupied Tunis. This place, which had been abandoned by its garrison, is about fifteen miles from Carthage, and was well defended both by fortifications and by its position; it can be seen from Carthage, and itself affords a clear view towards the city and over the sea which surrounds it. 10. From this point the Romans, while they were engaged in constructing a rampart, spotted the enemy fleet from Carthage making for Utica; work was promptly stopped, marching orders were given, and the column got on the move with all possible haste to prevent a surprise attack on their ships, which, as they were lying bows-on to the shore to facilitate their siege operations, were in no condition for a naval action. Ships cluttered up with artillery and siege-engines, and either turned over to transport work or lying close enough to the town walls to be a sort of equivalent to the earthwork and bridge used in land-operations for scaling the walls – ships in that condition could hardly have been expected to stand up to a fleet properly equipped with sea-going gear and capable of rapid manoeuvre.

In these circumstances Scipio on his arrival reversed the ordinary procedure in a sea-fight, sent the warships which might have been used to protect the other vessels to a position in the rear close in shore, and drew up the transports in line four deep in front of the town wall, to receive the enemy's attack. To prevent their regular formation from going to pieces in the heat of battle, he had the masts and yards laid across from one ship to another and the whole lashed together with stout ropes to form, as it were, a single unit; planks were then laid on top to enable men to pass right along the line, and gaps left underneath between one vessel and the next through which small assault-craft could pass for a rapid attack, and return again in safety. All this was hurriedly completed, and as adequately as lack of time allowed, and 1,000 selected fighting men were ordered aboard the transports. An immense quantity of weapons, mostly missiles, were amassed, enough to suffice for the most protracted engagement, and thus equipped all kept a sharp look-out for the enemy's approach.

The Carthaginians, if they had made reasonable speed, might well have found Scipio's men all at sixes and sevens in their haste to complete their preparations, and have carried all before them at the first assault; but the shock of their disasters on land had not yet worn off, with the result that they lacked confidence at sea too, where they were in fact superior. So they hung back, deliberately taking the whole day over the journey, and at sundown came to anchor in the harbour known locally as Rusucmon. Next morning at sunrise they sailed off shore again and took stations as for an ordinary naval engagement, expecting, presumably, that the Roman fleet would come out against them. When after a long wait in this position they still saw no movement on the enemy's part, then at last they sailed in to attack Scipio's transports.

What followed had no resemblance to a sea fight; it looked, if anything, more like ships attacking walls. The Roman transports were higher out of the water than their opponents, and the Carthaginians on their warships, forced as they were to lean back in order to discharge their missiles at a mark above their heads, failed more often than not to score a hit, whereas the striking power of their enemies' missiles was, from the fact of their position, much greater and more effective. The Roman assault-boats and other small craft which slipped out between the transports and underneath the covering planks were at first frequently sunk by the sheer weight and size of the Carthaginian warships, and as time went on they became a nuisance to their own fighting-men, who were often compelled, when the boats were mixed up with the enemy ships, to hold their fire for fear of missing their mark and hurting their friends. Finally the Carthaginians tried new tactics, and started throwing poles with an iron hook at one end ('snatchers', as the soldiers call them) on to the Roman transports. The Romans were unable to cut either the poles themselves or the chains attached to them as they were thrown, so that whenever a Carthaginian warship was backed by her oars and began to drag a Roman transport with her by the hook, you could see the latter's crew desperately trying to cut the ropes by which she was attached to her neighbours, while sometimes a whole line of vessels was towed away together. In this way the connecting plank-bridges over the transports were broken up and the men aboard were hardly given time to jump across on to the second line of ships. Some sixty of the Roman transports were towed off, stern first, to Carthage. The rejoicing at this success was greater than its importance justified; but it was all the more welcome to the Carthaginians in that after a series of continuous defeats and miseries one ray of sunshine, however small, had at last unexpectedly shone upon them, besides which they could not doubt that the Roman fleet had come near to destruction and was saved only by the dilatoriness of their own ships' captains and the timely arrival of Scipio.

11. Meanwhile Laelius and Masinissa after a journey of about fifteen days had reached Numidia, where the Maesulians, the subjects of Masinissa's father, accepted Masinissa as the king they had long waited for, and joyfully submitted to his rule. Syphax, after the expulsion of his troops and their commanders, confined himself to his old kingdom, though with no intention of remaining inactive. Still deeply in love with his wife, he was given no rest either by her or her father, and so great were the numbers both of men and horses available to him that the mere sight of the resources of a kingdom which had prospered for many years was enough to stir the ambition even of a less barbarous and passionate heart. So he assembled all the men fit for service, and equipped them with arms, horses, and missile weapons. The mounted troops he organized in squadrons, the infantry in cohorts, as he had learned, years ago, from the Roman centurions. Then with a force no less in numbers than his previous one, though composed almost entirely of raw and untrained men, he set out to meet the enemy. A position was taken up near them, and action began with cautious reconnaissance by a small party of horsemen from the outposts, who were driven off by missiles and hurried back to safety. Soon both sides started minor offensive movements, and the worsted, smarting under defeat, were joined by more and more of their comrades, thus starting the usual process by which cavalry actions develop, when the numbers engaged are gradually built up by the victors' confidence on the one side and the rage of the defeated on the other. So it was on this occasion: fighting began with a few men only, but in the end the entire cavalry strength of both sides was hurled into action by their zeal for the fray. So long as the battle had been confined to the cavalry, the sheer numbers of Syphax's men, the immense columns he sent continually into action, were almost irresistible; but the sudden intervention of the Roman light infantry, forcing its way into the gaps made for it by the cavalry squadrons, stabilized the line and checked the wild charges of the enemy. The effect of this was first (as has been said) to slow down the pace of the barbarians' attacks, then to bring them to a standstill in something

like bewilderment at a sort of fighting they did not understand; finally they not only gave ground before the Roman infantry, but even refused to face the cavalry, which by now had drawn fresh courage from the infantry's support.

At this point in the action the Roman legionaries were seen approaching. Syphax's Masaesulians did not even wait for their first attack: the mere sight of their arms and standards was more than they could endure, so great was the power of present fear, or perhaps of the memory of previous defeats.

12. While Syphax was riding up to the Roman squadrons, in a vain attempt to check the flight of his own troops by exposing himself to danger and putting them to shame, his horse was severely wounded and, as it fell, threw him. He was at once overpowered, taken prisoner, and dragged off alive to Laelius. To no one was the sight of him to give more satisfaction than to Masinissa.

Casualties in this battle were lighter than the importance of the victory might seem to justify, the reason being that the fighting was in fact confined to the cavalry. Not more than 5,000 men were killed, and less than half that number were captured in an attack on the camp in which the mass of fugitives had taken refuge after the loss of their king.

The capital of Syphax's kingdom was Cirta, and to that town a great many fugitives had found their way. Masinissa said that for himself he could imagine nothing more delightful at the moment than to visit, as victor, his father's kingdom, recovered at last after so many years, but that in good as in evil fortune no time could be spared for the relaxation of effort. If Laelius would allow him to ride on ahead to Cirta with the cavalry, taking Syphax with him in chains, he would carry all before him in the terror and confusion his sudden appearance would cause; Laelius himself could then follow with the infantry at his own pace. Laelius agreed to this proposal, and Masinissa upon reaching Cirta had the leading men of the town called out to a conference; they knew nothing of what had happened to the king, and Masinissa produced no effect upon them either by relating what had occurred, or by threats or persuasion, until Syphax was actually brought before their eyes in his chains. Then, at the dreadful sight, lamentations broke forth; many in terror abandoned the defence of the walls, others eager, as always, to toady to the man in power, suddenly gave in and opened the gates; whereupon Masinissa put guards at all the gates and at selected points along the walls to prevent escapes and rode in at the gallop to take possession of the palace.

As he entered the outer court, he was met on the threshold by Sophonisba,[1] the wife of Syphax and daughter of Hasdrubal the Carthaginian. Seeing Masinissa surrounded by his horsemen and conspicuous amongst them by the splendour of his dress and arms, and rightly supposing him to be the king, she clasped his knees and said: 'God and your own valour and happy fortune have given you power to do with us as you will; but if a captive may have leave to plead before the master of her life and death, if she may touch his knees and his victorious hand, I humbly beg by the royal majesty which but yesterday was ours, by the name of the Numidian people which you and Syphax shared, by the gods of this house whom I pray to receive you with kindlier omens than those with which they bade Syphax farewell, that you grant grace to me your suppliant and captive, and yourself determine my fate as your heart may prompt you, and not subject me to the arrogant and brutal whim of any Roman. Had I been nothing but the wife of Syphax, I should have preferred to trust the honour of a Numidian, born, as I was, here in Africa, than that of an alien and a foreigner. What a woman of Carthage – what a daughter of Hasdrubal – has to fear from a Roman is all too clear. If no other way is possible, then I earnestly entreat you to save me from the Romans' will by death.'

Sophonisba was in the full flower of her youthful beauty; as she clung to Masinissa's knees or clasped his hand, begging him to promise never to give her up to a Roman, her words grew little by little more like the blandishments of a lover than the supplication of a captive, and at this the conqueror's heart not only melted into pity but – with the characteristic inflammability of the Numidian race – was itself vanquished and led captive by love. As a pledge to fulfil her request he gave her his hand, and withdrew into the palace. Then he began to turn over in his mind how his promise could be kept, and, finding

1. Her traditional name: Sophoniba is the correct form.

no solution to his problem, allowed his passion to suggest a plan which was both reckless and unworthy of his honour. He immediately gave orders to prepare for a wedding that very day so as to leave no opportunity either to Laelius or Scipio of deciding what was to be done with her, as she would no longer be a prisoner of war, but Masinissa's wife. After the wedding Laelius arrived and was far from concealing his displeasure at what had been done: indeed, he even attempted to drag her from the marriage bed and send her to Scipio with Syphax and the other prisoners. But in the end he yielded to Masinissa's entreaties that he should refer to Scipio the decision as to which of the two kings should be granted the prize of Sophonisba. Syphax and the rest of the prisoners of war were then sent off, and Laelius with Masinissa's help took over the remaining communities of Numidia which were still held by Syphax's troops.

13. When the news arrived that Syphax was being brought into camp, the men poured in crowds from their quarters as if they were to witness the grand spectacle of a triumph. Syphax, in chains, led the procession; behind him came an assorted company of noble Numidians. The Roman onlookers by exaggerating their victory were soon doing all they could to add to the stature of Syphax and to the fame of his people, telling each other that he was the king to whose majesty both Rome and Carthage, the two most powerful nations in the world, paid such respect that Scipio, commander-in-chief of the former, left his army and the work he was doing in Spain and sailed with two quinqueremes to Africa solely to seek his friendship; while Hasdrubal, a Carthaginian army-commander, not only visited him in person in his kingdom but gave him his daughter in marriage. Thus at the same moment he had had in his power two commanders-in-chief, one Roman, one Carthaginian: both had sought by sacrifice the favour of the gods, and both had sought his friendship. So great had been his power that when Masinissa was driven from his throne Syphax had brought him to such a pass that his life was saved only by the report of his death and by his hiding in the woods, where he lived like the beasts on what he could catch.

In some such terms as these the watching crowd of soldiers

lauded Syphax to the skies. When he was brought to headquarters, Scipio, too, was not unmoved – both by the contrast between his past and his present fortune, and by the memory of their former guest-friendship, when they had clasped hands to confirm their pact in the name of their countries and of themselves. The same memories gave Syphax courage in addressing his conqueror; for when Scipio asked what had possessed him, not only to refuse the friendship of Rome but to wage aggressive war against her, he confessed that he had acted like a criminal and madman, though not only when he took arms against the Roman people: that, he declared, had been not the beginning, but the final result, of his madness. His reason had left him, and he had put from his mind the ties which bound him to Scipio together with the pact between their respective countries, at the moment when he received a woman of Carthage into his house. It was those nuptial torches which had set his palace aflame; she was the poison in his blood, the avenging Fury, who with her soft words and caresses had alienated his wits and sent him astray, not content until with her own hands she had nefariously armed him against one who was his guest and friend. But, in his desperate and abandoned state, he yet had one thing, he said, to solace his misery – the knowledge that this same monster of iniquity had transferred her corrupting influence to the house and home of his bitterest enemy. Masinissa, he ended, was no wiser, no more dependable, than Syphax was, and his youth made him more reckless; of the two marriages it was undoubtedly Masinissa's which had shown the greater folly and the more contemptible yielding to the moment's lust.

14. These words, wrung from Syphax not only by hatred of his enemy but by the torment of jealousy at seeing a beloved woman in a rival's house, caused Scipio the gravest anxiety. The charges against both Sophonisba and Masinissa were confirmed in his mind by the over-hasty marriage, almost, as it were, on the battlefield, by Masinissa's failure to wait till he could consult Laelius, and by the headlong precipitancy with which he had the marriage ceremony celebrated before the household gods of his enemy on the very day when he first saw her as his prisoner. Moreover, the whole business was the more

unsavoury in Scipio's opinion from the fact that in Spain, despite his youth, he himself had never once fallen a victim to the beauty of a female captive. He was thinking about this when Laelius and Masinissa rejoined him, and after welcoming them both with the greatest kindliness and congratulating them before a full council on their distinguished services, he drew Masinissa aside. 'I believe,' he said, 'that it was because you saw some good in me that you came to me first in Spain to win my friendship, and afterwards here in Africa put yourself and all your hopes into my hands. But of the virtues which might have made you wish to seek my friendship, there is none on which I should have prided myself as much as on self-control and superiority to the lusts of the flesh. How I wish, Masinissa, you had added this to your other excellent qualities! Believe me, for young men like us there is no peril from an armed foe to be compared with the peril of being surrounded with opportunities for sensual enjoyment. The man who has tamed and bridled the wild horses of lust has won himself more honour and a greater victory than is ours by the defeat of Syphax. All that you have done in my absence like a brave and active soldier I have been happy to remember and to mention before the council; as for the rest, I would rather you thought it over quietly than be forced to blush at my speaking of it. Syphax has been beaten under the auspices of the Roman people and is now a prisoner; therefore he, his wife, and kingdom, his land, towns, and the people who live in them – all those things which once were his – belong to the Roman people by right of conquest; and it would be our duty to send the king and his wife to Rome even if she were not a citizen of Carthage, even if we did not know her father to be a commander of our enemy's armies, and the Senate and people of Rome would have the right to decide the fate of a woman who is said to have estranged from us a king who was once our friend and driven him headlong into arms against us. Be master of yourself: do not spoil many fine qualities by one defect, nor ruin our gratitude for all your services by a fault so infinitely graver than its cause.'

15. Masinissa not only blushed for shame but wept at Scipio's words; then, saying he would remain under Scipio's orders and begging him to allow, so far as was possible in the

circumstances, the fulfilment of his rash promise not to give Sophonisba up into any man's hands – a promise he now admitted he had made – he withdrew, in deep trouble, to his own tent. There, with no one to see him, he stayed a long time sighing and uttering groans which he knew could be easily heard by anyone outside, and at last with a groan louder than all the rest called a trusty slave, in whose care was the poison which all kings keep against the changes and chances of fortune. He told the slave to mix the poison in a cup and carry it to Sophonisba, and tell her that Masinissa would gladly have kept the first promise which a husband owed to his wife, but that since those who had the power robbed him of the freedom to do so, he was keeping his second promise, not to let her fall alive into the hands of the Romans. Let her remember the general, her father, her country, and the two kings to whom she had been married – and do what she knew to be best.

When the slave had come to Sophonisba with Masinissa's message and the poisoned cup, she said, 'I accept this bridal gift – a gift not unwelcome if my husband has been unable to offer a greater one to his wife. But tell him this: that I should have died a better death if I had not married on the day of my funeral.' They were proud words, and no less proudly she took the cup and calmly drained it with no sign of perturbation.

When Scipio was told of this, he was afraid that grief might drive Masinissa, young and hot-blooded as he was, to some desperate act; so he sent for him at once and alternately consoled and gently rebuked him for having atoned for one rash action by another, and for importing into the whole affair a quite unnecessary note of tragedy. Next day, to divert Masinissa's thoughts from his immediate distress, he mounted the tribunal at headquarters and in the presence of the troops did him the signal honour first of addressing him by the title of King and praising him in the highest possible terms, and then of presenting him with a gold wreath, a gold bowl, a curule chair, an ivory staff, an embroidered toga, and a tunic embroidered with palm branches. As a further compliment he said that in Rome there was nothing felt to confer a more magnificent distinction than a triumph, and that for generals celebrating a triumph there was no decoration more splendid than the one which the Roman people thought Masinissa alone of foreigners to have deserved.

Scipio next congratulated Laelius, and conferred on him too a gold wreath; and finally other officers and men were decorated according to the nature of their services. Masinissa was mollified by these awards and encouraged to hope that before long, now that Syphax was out of the way, he would get possession of the whole of Numidia.

16. Scipio sent Laelius to Rome with Syphax and the other prisoners – accompanied also by Masinissa's envoys – and himself returned with his army to Tunis, where he completed the fortifications he had previously begun. The Carthaginians had been greatly delighted after their more or less successful attack on the Roman fleet; but it was a transitory and almost empty joy, for now they were once more profoundly shaken by the news of the capture of Syphax, in whom they had placed almost greater hopes than in Hasdrubal and his army. They refused any longer to listen to anyone who urged a continuation of the war, and sent the thirty senior members of their government to make overtures for peace. These men formed the Carthaginian Privy Council and had the greatest influence in directing the policy of the senate. When they entered Scipio's headquarters in camp, they prostrated themselves like the courtiers of an Eastern monarch (having I suppose, derived that practice from the country of their origin) and their words were fully in keeping with such fawning, as they proceeded, not to excuse their own error, but to transfer the original blame to Hannibal and the party which supported his power. They asked pardon for their country, now twice brought low by the reckless policy of its people, and able to be saved a second time only by the good will of its enemies. The Roman people, they said, wanted power over a vanquished enemy, but not his utter ruin; Scipio must lay upon them what commands he pleased, for they were ready to serve him in all obedience.

In reply, Scipio said he had come to Africa in the hope of bringing home not a peace treaty but a victory, and his hopes had been increased by the success of his campaign; all the same, now that victory was nearly within his grasp, he was willing to consider terms, so that all the world might know that the Roman people both began and ended their wars in accordance with justice. The terms he proposed were these: Carthage was to hand over all prisoners of war, deserters, and runaways; withdraw her armies from Italy and Gaul;[1] keep her hands off Spain; evacuate all the islands between Italy and Africa; surrender all ships of war except twenty, and supply 500,000 measures of wheat and 300,000 of barley. Authorities differ about the amount of money Scipio demanded: in one source I find 5,000 talents, in another 5,000 pounds of silver, in another double the soldiers' pay. 'You shall have three days,' he said, 'to determine whether or not you accept peace on these terms. If you do, you must then make an armistice with me while you send your envoys to the Senate in Rome.'

Dismissed with these words, the Carthaginians decided that no terms ought to be rejected, for they wanted time to allow Hannibal to cross into Africa; so they sent one delegation to Scipio to conclude the armistice and another to Rome to ask for peace; the latter took with them for the sake of appearances a few prisoners and deserters and runaways, hoping thereby to make their task easier.

17. Many days previously Laelius had arrived in Rome with Syphax and the most important Numidian prisoners. In the Senate, amidst great rejoicing and high hopes for the future, he gave a full and careful account of the operations in Africa, and the House, having discussed the matter, resolved that the king should be held under guard at Alba and that Laelius should be detained in Rome until the delegation arrived from Carthage. A thanksgiving, to last four days, was decreed. The praetor Publius Aelius dismissed the Senate, called a mass meeting of the people, and mounted the rostra with Laelius. The crowds, on hearing that the Carthaginian armies had been routed, a mighty and famous king beaten and taken prisoner, and all Numidia overrun in a succession of great victories, could not restrain the expression of their joy, but burst into cheering and such other signs of uncontrollable delight as men in the mass are wont to indulge in. The praetor gave orders to the temple wardens to open all the shrines in the City, so that the people

1. i.e. Cisalpine Gaul.

might have the opportunity all day long of going round the sacred places and of paying their respects and rendering their thanks to the gods.

Next day Masinissa's envoys were brought into the Senate. They began by congratulating the senators on Scipio's successes in Africa, and went on to thank them for Scipio's generous treatment of Masinissa, whom, as they put it, he had not only addressed by the title of king but had made a king in actual fact by restoring him to his father's throne, from which, now that Syphax was out of the way, he would henceforward rule – granted the good will of the Senate – without fear of opposition. They then added their thanks for Scipio's praise of him before the troops, and the splendid gifts he had conferred upon him, gifts to be worthy of which he had done his best, as he would continue to do thereafter. He asked the Senate, they said, to confirm by decree his royal title and the other gifts and favours Scipio had conferred on him, and added the further request, which he hoped would not meet objections, that they should send back the Numidian prisoners of war interned in Rome. This last would, he thought, much increase his standing with his own people.

In reply the envoys were assured that the Senate was no less ready to offer congratulations on the victories in Africa, and that Scipio had, in their judgement, acted with perfect propriety in saluting Masinissa by the name of king, while at the same time they heartily approved everything else he had done to gratify Masinissa. They further decreed that the envoys should take back to him certain gifts: two purple cloaks fastened by golden brooches, broad-striped tunics, two horses with breast-ornaments, two sets of cavalry equipment including cuirasses, and tents with furniture such as was usually provided for a consul on active service. The praetor was instructed to have all this sent to him; gifts were decreed for the envoys too: for each, not less than 5,000 *asses* and two suits of clothes; and for each of their attendants and the Numidians released from internment and restored to the king, 1,000 *asses* and one suit of clothes. Finally the envoys were provided with free lodging, seats in the Circus, and the usual comforts.

18. In the course of the same summer the praetor Quinctilius Varus and the proconsul Marcus Cornelius fought a pitched battle with Mago in Insubrian Gaul. The praetor's legions were in the front line; Cornelius kept his men in reserve, himself riding up to the front. In front of each wing, praetor and proconsul were doing their utmost to urge the troops to a vigorous attack, but to no purpose. No headway was made. Then Quinctilius said to Cornelius: 'As you see, this is slow work. Unexpected resistance has hardened them; soon they'll be ready for anything, if we don't look out. If we want really to shift them and throw them off balance, the only thing is a sudden cavalry charge. Either, then, let me lead the cavalry while you keep things going in the front line, or, if you prefer, I will command here while you organize the assault by the cavalry of the four legions.' The proconsul was willing to undertake whichever duty the praetor wished, so Quinctilius with his son Marcus, a fine young soldier, went to where the cavalry were waiting, ordered the men to mount, and sent them immediately into action. The excitement and clatter of the cavalry charge was increased by a cheer from the infantry, and the enemy line would never have stood if Mago had not brought his elephants into action. They had been kept in readiness for the first sign of movement by the Roman cavalry, whose assistance was now rendered useless, as all the horses were as much terrified by the aspect of the brutes as they were by their trumpeting and unfamiliar smell. At close quarters the Roman cavalry, when they could use the lance or sword, would have had the advantage, but not so in the present circumstances when their horses were bolting with them – at long range they found themselves out-shot by the Numidian javelins. At the same time, the Twelfth legion of foot had been badly cut up; it was hanging on out of a sense of duty, well beyond its strength, and would have been forced to retire if the Thirteenth had not been brought up from reserve and taken over just as the situation was touch-and-go. Mago too brought up a contingent of Gauls from his reserves to face the Roman Thirteenth; these, however, were quickly dispersed, and the *hastati* of the Eleventh legion then massed and attacked the elephants, which by now

were causing some havoc amongst the Roman infantry. The animals were all in a bunch, so hardly a lance missed its mark and they were all driven back to their own lines, four of them collapsing on the way from wounds. This was the turning point of the engagement: the enemy line was at last about to break, and all the Roman cavalry, once they saw the elephants repulsed, galloped into action to increase the terror and confusion. None the less the Carthaginians maintained an orderly and regular withdrawal so long as Mago kept his position in front of the standards; only when his thigh was pierced, and they saw him fallen and carried half dead off the field, did their fighting retreat turn suddenly into a rout. About 5,000 of the enemy fell in that action and twenty-two military standards were taken; but the Roman victory was not a bloodless one, 2,300 men, almost all of them from the Twelfth legion, being lost out of the praetor's army, including two military tribunes, Marcus Cosconius and Marcus Maevius. The Thirteenth legion, which came into action towards the end, lost Gaius Helvius, a military tribune, while they were stiffening the resistance of the exhausted Twelfth, and about twenty-two knights of the upper class who were trampled to death by the elephants, together with a number of centurions. The struggle would have lasted longer if Mago's wound had not brought his men to concede the victory.

19. In the dead of night Mago broke camp, and, extending his marches as much as his wound allowed, reached the coast in the territory of the Ligurian Ingauni. Here he was met by envoys from Carthage, who had landed a few days previously in the Gulf of Genoa and brought him orders to return to Africa at the earliest possible moment. They informed him that his brother Hannibal, who had also been visited by a similar delegation, would be doing the same, for the situation in which the Carthaginians now found themselves did not allow them to continue to hold Gaul and Italy. Even apart from his government's orders and the peril which threatened his country, Mago was afraid of increased pressure from the victorious enemy if he delayed his departure; moreover, the Ligurians, when they saw Italy being abandoned, might well transfer their allegiance to those who would soon be their masters. These considerations,

added to the hope that the motion on board ship would be easier on his wound than the jolting on roads, while there would be better opportunities for treatment, determined Mago to get away at once. He embarked his troops and set sail, but the fleet had hardly passed Sardinia when he died of his wound.[1] A number of the Carthaginian ships, which were sailing in no sort of formation, were captured by the Roman fleet stationed off Sardinia. Such were the events on land and sea in the Alpine districts of northern Italy.

The consul Gaius Servilius achieved no noteworthy successes in Etruria – or in Gaul, whither he had also gone. He did, however, rescue from slavery his father and Gaius Lutatius Catulus, who fifteen years before had been taken prisoner by the Boii near the village of Tannetum.[2] He thereupon returned to Rome, entering the city between the two of them. Though of no great national importance, this was a personal triumph and brought him distinction accordingly. A bill was brought before the people to clear Servilius from the charge of acting illegally in having held – contrary to the law as it then stood – the offices of tribune and aedile of the people while his father, who had occupied a curule chair, was still alive – a fact of which he was ignorant. The bill was passed into law and Servilius returned to his province.

In Bruttium a large number of unimportant communities, including Consentia, Aufugum, Bergae, Baesidiae, Ocriculum, Lymphaeum, Argentanum, and Clampetia, seeing that the war was almost over, threw in their lot with the other consul, Servilius Geminus. Geminus also fought a battle with Hannibal near Croton, though reports of the engagement are obscure. Valerius Antias says that 5,000 of the enemy were killed; but that would be an important victory, and either, it seems, Valerius must have shamelessly invented it, or other chroniclers must have been very careless in omitting to mention it. At any rate it is certain that nothing further was done by Hannibal in Italy; for it so happened that the emissaries from Carthage came to recall him to Africa just about the same time as they came to Mago. 20. The story goes that he groaned and gnashed his

1. There are several conflicting versions of Mago's death.
2. In 218. See p. 48 ff.

teeth and could hardly refrain from tears when he heard what the emissaries had to say. When their message was delivered, he said, 'For years past they have been trying to force me back by refusing me reinforcements and money; but now they recall me no longer by indirect means, but in plain words. Hannibal has been conquered not by the Roman people whom he defeated so many times in battle and put to flight, but by the envy and continual disparagement of the Carthaginian senate. At this unlovely and shameful return of mine it will not be Scipio who will be wild with triumph and delight, but rather Hanno, whose only way of ruining me and my house has been by ruining Carthage.'[1]

Hannibal had already foreseen his recall and in consequence had his ships in readiness. All his troops which were unfit for service he distributed, ostensibly for garrison duty, amongst the few Bruttian towns which fear rather than loyalty kept on his side, and all who were still serviceable he transported to Africa. Before he went, he had many Italians who had refused to go with him and had taken refuge in the hitherto inviolate shrine of Juno Lacinia brutally butchered in the very precincts of the temple.[2]

Seldom, we are told, has any exile left his native land with so heavy a heart as Hannibal's when he left the country of his enemies; again and again he looked back at the shores of Italy, accusing gods and men and calling down curses on his own head for not having led his armies straight to Rome when they were still bloody from the victorious field of Cannae. Scipio, who in his consulship had never seen a Carthaginian enemy in Italy, had had the audacity to march on Carthage, while he – when a hundred thousand Roman soldiers had been killed at Trasimene and Cannae – had been content to grow old in idleness at Casilinum and Cumae and Nola! Such were his self-accusations and expressions of distress as he was forced to surrender his long occupation of Italy.

21. News of the departure of both Mago and Hannibal reached Rome more or less at the same time; but two things

1. See p. 25. Hanno had been leader of the anti-Barca party, but it is unlikely that he was still alive.

2. Probably a fictitious story.

combined to lessen rejoicing at this doubly happy event. First, if was felt that the army commanders had lacked either the power or the initiative to keep them in Italy, though the Senate had ordered them to do so; and, secondly, people were anxious about the final outcome now that the entire weight of the war had to be borne by a single army and its commander.

About this time a delegation came from Saguntum with some Carthaginian recruiting officers whom they had caught, with their money, in Spain, where they had gone to hire auxiliaries. They deposited the money – 250 pounds of gold and 800 pounds of silver – in the courtyard of the Senate-house. The prisoners were accepted and put into confinement, but the gold and silver were given back and the envoys were thanked; in addition they were given presents, and ships were put at their disposal for the return voyage to Spain.

It was now that certain older members of the Senate remarked that people in general are slower to feel blessings than misfortunes: they well remembered the panic and terror when Hannibal crossed the Alps into Italy – what terrible disasters, what heartbreak, had followed! The enemy's camp within sight of the city walls, the national supplications and the agony of private prayer, the bitter question heard again and again in council when men raised their hands to heaven and asked if ever the day would come when they would see Italy free of the enemy and once more happy and at peace! Well, the gods at long last, after fifteen years, had granted that prayer, but was there a single man to propose that thanks be rendered them for their goodness? Alas, men were too little grateful even for a present blessing; still less did they remember the blessing that was past.

The effect was immediate: cries came from every part of the House calling upon the praetor Aelius to propose the motion, and a decree was passed ordering five days of public thanksgiving 'on all the couches' and the sacrifice of 120 full-grown victims.

When Laelius and Masinissa's envoys had been given permission to leave, news came that the Carthaginian peace delegation, on its way to the Senate, had been seen at Puteoli and intended to proceed overland to Rome. It was therefore decided to recall Laelius, so that the negotiations might take place in his presence.[1] Quintus Fulvius Gillo, one of Scipio's officers, brought the Carthaginian emissaries to Rome, and as they were forbidden to enter the city, they were lodged in the Villa Publica and granted a hearing before the Senate, sitting for the purpose in the temple of Bellona. 22. They put their case much as they had put it to Scipio, exculpating their government and shifting the whole responsibility for the war on to Hannibal. Hannibal, they declared, had, without orders from their senate, crossed both the Alps and the Ebro, and on his own private initiative had made war not on the Romans only but, before that, on Saguntum. The government and people of Carthage, on any proper view of the matter, had kept their treaty with Rome hitherto inviolate, and for that reason their instructions were, quite simply, to ask permission to abide by the last treaty concluded with Gaius Lutatius.[2] The praetor, following the traditional procedure, then invited the House to put any questions which any member might like to ask, and some senior members who had been present when the old treaties were being negotiated availed themselves of the opportunity; various questions were asked, and when the Carthaginian delegates, all of them young men, said they were not old enough to know the answers, there was a loud protest from all parts of the House that by a piece of characteristically Carthaginian trickery men who could remember nothing about the former peace treaty had been chosen to ask for its renewal.

23. The envoys were then told to withdraw and members were asked to express their opinions. Marcus Livius proposed sending for the consul Servilius Geminus, as the nearer of the two at the moment, to be present at the deliberations; for as there could be no subject of greater importance, he could not feel that the absence of one or both consuls from the discussion was really consonant with the dignity of the Roman people. Quintus Metellus, who had been consul three years before, and had also been dictator, put forward the view that peace should be accepted or rejected according to the advice of Scipio, and of

1. This conflicts with the account on p. 639.
2. In 241 B.C.: the end of the first Punic war.

nobody else; for Scipio was the man who by beating the Carthaginian armies and devastating their countryside had reduced them to the necessity of suing humbly for peace, and there was nobody better qualified to judge the temper in which the request was being made than the man who was now fighting before the gates of Carthage. Marcus Valerius Laevinus, who had been twice consul, accused the delegates of being no better than spies, and expressed the opinion that they should be ordered out of Italy and taken to their ships under guard, and that Scipio should be sent written instructions not to slacken his offensive operations. Laelius and Fulvius added that Scipio too had based his hope of peace on the supposition that Hannibal and Mago were not to be recalled from Italy; the Carthaginians, they were convinced, while waiting for those two generals and their armies, would make every sort of pretence, and then, when they had got them, would forget every treaty however recent, and all the gods in their heaven, and continue the war. This point induced a still larger number to support Laevinus, and the envoys were dismissed. They had not got their peace: indeed, their request had hardly even been answered.[1]

24. About this time the consul Servilius Caepio took it into his head that the glory of bringing peace to Italy belonged to no one but himself; fancying himself in pursuit of Hannibal, whom he alone had put to flight, he crossed to Sicily, intending to go on to Africa. When his behaviour became known in Rome, the Senate first voted that the praetor should inform him by letter that they judged it proper that he should come back to Italy; but when the praetor said he was sure that the letter would be ignored, the difficulty was got over by the appointment of Publius Sulpicius as dictator. Sulpicius, on the strength of his superior command, then ordered the consul back to Italy. The rest of the year he spent with Marcus Servilius, his master of Horse, in going round the Italian towns which by reason of the war had renounced their allegiance to Rome, and in inquiring individually into their cases.

During the armistice 100 transports sent by the praetor Lentulus from Sardinia and escorted by twenty warships sailed to Africa with supplies. They had fine weather for the crossing

1. Polybius states that the peace terms were ratified in Rome.

and met with no opposition. Gnaeus Octavius, on the other hand, on a trip from Sicily with 200 transports and thirty warships, was not so lucky. When he had sailed without mishap almost to within sight of the African coast, the wind dropped and then, with a sudden shift to the south-west, blew hard and scattered the convoy over a wide area. Octavius himself with the warships made the Promontory of Apollo, though only after a hard struggle at the oars against a head sea; most of the transports were carried out of their course to the island of Aegimurus, which lies about thirty miles from Carthage and closes the bay on which the city is situated, while the rest were driven to Aquae Calidae, right opposite the city. In Carthage itself, from which all this could be seen, there was an excited scramble for the forum; the magistrates called a meeting of the senate; crowds outside the senate-house angrily protested that such a splendid haul – right under their eyes and almost within their grasp – should not be allowed to escape. A few thought otherwise and pleaded the sanctity of the armistice, not yet expired, or of the peace negotiations. It was finally agreed, when there was little distinction to be made between a popular demonstration and the formal meeting of the senate, that Hasdrubal should first sail with fifty ships to Aegimurus and then collect such Roman ships as were scattered along the coast or in the harbours. All the Roman transports had been abandoned by their crews; and first those at Aegimurus, then the rest at Aquae Calidae, were towed stern-first to Carthage.

25. Since the envoys had not returned from Rome, nothing was yet known in Carthage of the attitude of the Roman Senate towards the question of peace or war, nor had the armistice expired; for these reasons it seemed to Scipio all the more unpardonable in men who had asked for peace and an armistice to have wrecked all hope of the one and violated the reality of the other. He accordingly sent at once to Carthage three representatives, Lucius Baebius, Lucius Sergius, and Lucius Fabius. On their arrival they came near to being manhandled by the mob, and since they saw that they would be no safer on the way back, they asked the authorities who had saved them from molestation to send ships to escort them. Two triremes were provided which went as far as the Bagradas river, from

which the Roman camp could be seen, and then returned to Carthage. The Carthaginian fleet was lying somewhere off Utica, and three quadriremes belonging to it suddenly attacked the Roman quinquereme from the seaward side as she rounded the promontory. Perhaps a secret order had been sent from Carthage to this effect, or it may be that Hasdrubal, who commanded the fleet, acted on his own initiative without the complicity of the government. However, the attacking vessels failed to ram the Roman, which was too quick for them, and the higher freeboard of the latter prevented the Carthaginian marines from jumping aboard her, not to mention the fact that she was most gallantly defended so long as the supply of missiles held out. When these began to fail, nothing could have saved the ship but the nearness of the shore and the soldiers in camp who crowded down to the water's edge to offer protection. The crew with a tremendous effort at the oars ran her hard aground, so that though the ship was lost, all on board got ashore safely. There was no doubt now that the armistice, by one act of treachery after another, had been broken. When Laelius and Fulvius arrived from Rome with the Carthaginian envoys, Scipio informed the latter that, though the Carthaginians had violated not only the armistice but also the law of nations in their treatment of his emissaries, he would himself, with regard to them, take no action which was unworthy of the traditions of the Roman people or at variance with his own sense of what was right. He then dismissed them and began his preparations for war.

When Hannibal was not far from Africa, a sailor was ordered aloft to see what part of the coast lay ahead. The man said they were making directly for a ruined tomb, whereupon Hannibal with a prayer to avert ill luck told his helmsman to steer a course past the ominous object, and put in at Leptis, where he disembarked his troops.

26. Such were the events of this year in Africa; what follows continues into the next year, in which the consuls were Tiberius Claudius Nero and Marcus Servilius Geminus – the latter, till then, being master of Horse.

Towards the end of the year we have been considering, delegations came to Rome from allied communities in Greece to complain that their territories had been devastated by the forces of King Philip, who had further refused to admit to his presence their own envoys who had come to demand reparations; at the same time they brought the news that 4,000 men under the command of Sopater were said to have sailed for Africa in support of Carthage, taking with them a considerable amount of money. In view of this the Senate voted to send a delegation to Philip to inform him that, in their opinion, his proceedings had constituted a violation of the treaty. The envoys were Gaius Terentius Varro, Gaius Mamilius, and Marcus Aurelius; three quinqueremes were put at their disposal.

The year was memorable for a great fire which completely destroyed the Clivus Publicius, and also for serious floods. Grain, however, was cheap, partly because all Italy was now open, as fighting had ceased, and partly because large supplies had been imported from Spain. These the curule aediles Falto and Buteo distributed amongst the country villages and the various quarters of the city at four *asses* the measure.

This year also saw the death of Quintus Fabius Maximus. He had reached a very great age, if it is true, as some writers have stated, that he held the office of augur for sixty-two years. What is indisputable is that he was worthy of the name Maximus, and would have deserved to be the first of his line to bear it. He held more magistracies than his father, and the same number as his grandfather. His grandfather Rullus enjoyed the fame of more victories and greater battles, but to have had Hannibal as one's enemy is enough to equal or outweigh them all. Fabius has been stigmatized as a cautious soldier, never quick to act; but though one may question whether he was a 'delayer' by nature or because delaying tactics happened to suit the campaigns he was engaged in, this, as least, is certain, that, as the poet Ennius wrote,

One man by his delaying saved the State.

His son[1] Quintus Fabius Maximus succeeded him as augur, and as *pontifex* (for he had held two priesthoods) he was succeeded by Servius Sulpicius Galba.

1. In fact, his grandson.

The Roman Games were repeated for one day, and the Plebeian Games, in their entirety, three times under the management of the aediles Sabinus and Flaccus. Both men were made praetors and Gaius Livius Salinator and Gaius Aurelius Cotta were elected as their colleagues. Owing to conflicting accounts in various writers it is uncertain whether the elections that year were presided over by the consul Servilius Geminus or by Publius Sulpicius who had been named by him dictator, because the consul was himself detained in Etruria by the inquiries he was conducting, on the Senate's instructions, into conspiracy amongst the leading citizens.

27. At the beginning of the next year the consuls Marcus Servilius and Tiberius Claudius called a meeting of the Senate on the Capitol and brought up the question of the spheres of command. Both men hoped to get Africa and proposed to let the lot decide; but chiefly owing to the efforts of Quintus Metellus, the decision between Italy and Africa was for the moment left in abeyance and the consuls were ordered to arrange with the people's tribunes – should they approve the measure – to bring the question of the African command before the people. This was done, and the tribes voted unanimously for Scipio. In spite of this, however, the consuls, by decree of the Senate, did draw lots for a command in Africa, and the lot fell to Claudius, who was to take across a fleet of fifty ships, all quinqueremes, and hold the title of *imperator* on a par with Scipio. The other consul, Marcus Servilius, drew Etruria as his province, and Gaius Servilius also had his command extended there in case the Senate decided that the consul should remain near Rome. Of the praetors, Marcus Sextius was allotted Gaul, the province and two legions to be handed over to him by Quinctilius Varus, Gaius Livius received Bruttium with the two legions commanded in the previous year by the proconsul Sempronius; Sicily fell to Gnaeus Tremelius, who was to take over the province and two legions from the last year's praetor Tappulus; Villius, as pro-praetor, was to guard the Sicilian coast with twenty warships and 1,000 soldiers; Marcus Pomponius with the other twenty ships was ordered to bring 1,500 troops back to Rome. The City praetorship fell to Gaius Aurelius Cotta. The rest of the praetors were to have their

commands extended, their provinces and forces remaining unchanged. The defence of the Empire that year was maintained by no more than sixteen legions in all. Lastly, to win the blessing of the gods on all the enterprises of the coming year, the consuls were ordered, before they left Rome on their military duties, to celebrate the Games which, in the consulship of Marcellus and Quinctius, the dictator Titus Manlius had vowed, together with the sacrifice of full-grown victims, if for five years 'the national fortune remained in the same state as it then was'. The Games were held accordingly in the Circus over a period of four days, and the sacrifices were offered to the gods to whom they had been vowed.

28. Meanwhile there was a growing conflict in men's minds between anxiety and hope. Which should take precedence – joy that Hannibal after sixteen years was gone at last and had left the Roman people in undisputed possession of Italy, or fear because he had reached Africa with his army still intact? The danger remained – it was only the place which was changed. In the mighty struggle still to come, the late Quintus Fabius, with prophetic words, often and not without reason foretold that Hannibal would prove a more terrible enemy in his own country than he had been in Italy; nor would Scipio have to deal with Syphax, king of a mob of undisciplined savages, whose armies used to be led by Statorius, a sort of army-cook, or with Syphax's father-in-law Hasdrubal, a general who showed his speed chiefly in retreat, or with irregulars hurriedly gathered together from a half-armed mob of country bumpkins. No, he would have Hannibal as his antagonist, Hannibal, who, one might say, was born at the headquarters of his father the mighty Hamilcar, was nursed amongst arms through his childhood years, and became a soldier while yet a boy and a commander in earliest manhood, and now, grown old by victories,[1] had filled Italy from the Alps to the Straits of Messana and the provinces of Spain and Gaul with monuments of his tremendous campaigns. Hannibal, moreover, was in command of an army which had been with him through all his years of fighting, an army toughened by hardships almost beyond human endurance, drenched a thousand times with Roman blood, and

1. He was not more than forty-five.

carrying with it the spoils not of soldiers only, but of generals. Many a man who would encounter Scipio in battle had with his own hand killed a praetor, a general, a Roman consul: many would be heroes decorated with the Mural or Vallarian[1] Crown, men who had strolled at their ease through captured Roman camps and cities. The *fasces* of all Roman magistrates put together at that moment would not equal in number those which Hannibal had captured from dead Roman generals and could proudly bear before him.

These were grim thoughts, and by brooding over them people only increased their fears and anxieties. There was another reason too, for whereas for years past they had grown accustomed to war being waged before their eyes now here, now there throughout the length of Italy – a war which raised no immediate hopes of any swift conclusion – now everyone was on tiptoe with excitement at the thought of Scipio and Hannibal facing one another for what would surely be the final struggle. Even those whose supreme confidence in Scipio assured them of victory were racked with anxiety in proportion to their longing that the victory should not be delayed. At Carthage, too, there were mixed feelings, and conflicting hopes and fears. Now, when they thought of Hannibal and the magnitude of his achievements, they regretted having sued for peace; and again, when they looked back on their two defeats in the field, on the capture of Syphax and the expulsion of their armies from Spain and Italy and knew that all this was the result of the brave and brilliant generalship of Scipio, they dreaded him as a man of destiny born to destroy them.

29. Hannibal had now reached Hadrumetum. After a few days spent there to allow his troops to recover from the effects of their voyage, alarmist reports of the occupation of all the country round Carthage forced him to move, and he hurried with all possible speed to Zama, which lies five days' march south-west of Carthage.[2] Scouts who had been sent from Zama

1. An award for bravery to the first man over the rampart (*vallum*) of the enemy's camp – as the Mural for the first man over a city's wall. (A. de S.)

2. There was an interval of several months between Hannibal's landing and his march to Zama.

ahead of the army were caught and brought by their Roman guards to Scipio, who handed them over to an officer and, telling them to have a good look at everything without fear of consequences, gave orders that they should be taken round the camp and shown whatever they wished to see. He then asked them if their investigations had been both comfortable and adequate, furnished them with an escort, and sent them back to Hannibal.

Nothing in the men's report gave Hannibal any pleasure to hear: for amongst other things they told him that Masinissa had joined Scipio that very day with 6,000 foot and 4,000 horse, though what he found most alarming was the enemy's confidence, which could hardly be entirely without foundation. Accordingly he sent to Scipio, and asked to be allowed a personal conference – in spite of the fact that he was himself responsible for the war, and by his arrival in Africa had violated the armistice and wrecked the hope of a treaty of peace. However, it seemed to him likely that he would get better terms from Scipio if he approached him while his army was still intact than after a defeat. Whether Hannibal took this step on his own initiative or by the instructions of his government, I cannot say with confidence; Valerius Antias related that he was beaten by Scipio in the first battle, in which he lost 12,000 men killed and 1,700 taken prisoner, and after that visited Scipio in his camp as an envoy of his government in company with ten others.

Scipio acceded to Hannibal's request for a conference, and the two generals agreed to advance the position of their respective camps so as to facilitate their meeting. Scipio established himself near Naraggara in a favourable position within javelin-range of water; Hannibal occupied a hill four miles away, safe and convenient enough except for its distance from water. Between the two positions a spot in full view from every side was chosen for the meeting, to ensure against a treacherous attack.

30. Exactly half-way between the opposing ranks of armed men, each attended by an interpreter,[1] the generals met. They were not only the two greatest soldiers of their time, but the equals of any king or commander in the whole history of the

1. Though both spoke Greek and Hannibal probably knew Latin.

world. For a minute mutual admiration struck them dumb, and they looked at each other in silence. Hannibal was the first to speak. 'If fate,' he said, 'has decreed that I who was the aggressor in the war with Rome, and so many times have had victory almost within my grasp, should of my own will come to ask for peace, I rejoice at least that destiny has given me you, and no other, from whom to ask it. You have many titles to honour, and amongst them, for you too, it will not be the least to have received the submission of Hannibal, to whom the gods gave victory over so many Roman generals, and to have brought to an end this war which was made memorable by your defeats before ever it was marked by ours. May it not also be a pretty example of the irony of fate that I took up arms when your father was consul, fought against him my first battle with a Roman general, and now come, unarmed, to his son to sue for peace? Assuredly it would have been best if the gods had given our fathers contentment with what was their own – you with ruling Italy, us with ruling Africa. Not even you can find Sicily and Sardinia adequate compensation for the loss of so many fleets and armies and the deaths of so many fine officers: but what is done is done – it may be censured, but it cannot be altered.

'Though we sought to win what did not belong to us, we are now fighting to defend our own, and the war has not been, for us, fought only in Italy, any more than for you it has been only in Africa. You too have seen the arms and standards of the enemy almost at your gates, just as now we can hear from Carthage the mutter and stir of a Roman camp. So in discussing terms of peace, it is you who can negotiate from strength – which is precisely what *you* most want, and *we* find most unfortunate. You and I have the most to gain by peace, and our respective governments will ratify whatever terms we decide on; the one essential thing is that we preserve in our negotiations a calm and rational temper.

'As for myself, an old man returning to the homeland I left in boyhood, the years with their burden of success and failure have so taught me that I would rather now follow the dictates of reason than hope for what luck may bring. You are young; fortune has always favoured you; and youth – unbrokenly successful – I fear may be too intolerant for the needs of cool and rational negotiation. The man whom fortune has never deceived cannot easily weigh the changes and chances of coming years: what I was at Trasimene and Cannae, you are today; you accepted a command when you were barely old enough for service; you shrank at nothing – and your luck has never failed you. By avenging your father and uncle you turned a personal sorrow into an opportunity for winning a splendid reputation for valour and for devotion to your family of the highest kind; you recovered the lost provinces of Spain, driving from them four Carthaginian armies; elected consul, while others lacked courage to defend Italy, you crossed to Africa – and with what result? Two armies cut to pieces on African soil, two camps captured and burnt within an hour, the mighty Syphax taken prisoner, countless towns in his kingdom seized and as many in ours – and, to crown all, your triumph in loosening the grip which for sixteen years I maintained upon Italy and forcing me to follow you here. A man's heart may well long for victory rather than for peace; I better understand the aspiring spirit than the politic brain, and once on me, too, smiled such fortune as is yours. None the less, if in prosperity the gods also gave us wisdom, we should consider not only what has happened in the past but what might happen in the future. To ignore all else, I alone am sufficient warning of what fate may bring: I, whom but yesterday you saw encamped between the Anio and Rome advancing my standards and on the point of scaling your city's walls – and whom now you see here, bereft of my two brothers – those famous generals, those valiant hearts – before the walls of my native city, already almost under siege, begging that she may be spared the terrors I so nearly inflicted upon yours.

'The greater a man's success, the less it must be trusted to endure. This is your hour of triumph, while for us all is dark; to you peace, if you grant it, will be a splendid thing and fair to look upon, but for us who sue for it, it will carry no honour but only the burden of necessity. Certain peace is better and safer than the uncertain hope of victory: the one is in your hands, the other in the hands of God. Do not stake the success of so many years upon the decision of a single hour; remember not only your own strength but the might of Fortune and the chances of war which we both must share. On both sides will be the sword, on both the bodies of mortal men – and nowhere less than in battle do results answer our hopes. If you win, you will not add as much glory to what you can have now by granting peace, as you will lose if things go against you. The luck of an hour can tumble to the ground the honours we have won, the honours we have hoped to win. In making peace, Publius Cornelius, everything is yours; refuse to make it, and you must take what the gods may please to give you. Amongst the few instances of valour rewarded by success would have been Regulus, here in Africa years ago, if only, after his victory, he had granted peace when our fathers sued for it. But he set no limit to his success – his luck ran away with him and he could not draw the rein: so the higher he rose, the more shameful was his fall.

'To define terms is the privilege of him who grants a peace, not of him who sues for it; but perhaps we of Carthage are not unworthy to lay a penalty upon ourselves. We do not object to leaving you in possession of everything for which we went to war – Sicily, Sardinia, Spain, and all the islands between Africa and Italy; let us be confined within the shores of Africa, and see you, since such is God's will, extending your sway over foreign countries, both by land and by sea. I would not deny that there was some lack of sincerity in our recent request for peace and our failure to wait for it, or that therefore the honour of Carthage has become suspect to you. Confidence that a peace will be kept depends, Scipio, largely upon the persons through whom the request for it is made; and I am told that your Senate, too, refused the peace partly, at any rate, because the envoys we sent were of insufficient importance. But now it is I, Hannibal, who have come to sue – and I should not seek peace unless I thought it for our good, and for the same reason I shall keep it. I was the aggressor in this war; and just as I did what I could, till the gods envied my success, to ensure that none of my people should regret it, so shall I strive that none may regret the peace obtained through my endeavours.'

31. To Hannibal's speech the Roman general replied somewhat as follows. 'It did not escape me, Hannibal, that it was the knowledge that you would soon be with them that emboldened

the Carthaginians to violate the armistice and wreck the hope of peace. Nor do you attempt to conceal this, when from the terms previously offered[1] you leave out everything except what has long been in our possession. But just as you want your countrymen to realize how great is the burden from which you have relieved them, so I, for my part, must do my best not to reward their perfidy by omitting any of the conditions to which they formerly agreed. Though you do not deserve peace even on the same terms as before, you are actually asking to better them by your dishonesty. Our fathers were not the aggressors in the war for Sicily, nor we ourselves in the war for Spain; in the former it was the peril of our allies, the Mamertines, in the latter the destruction of Saguntum which induced us to don the armour of loyalty and justice. That you were the aggressors you yourself admit, and the gods are our witnesses in that they granted for that war, even as they are granting and will grant for this, an ending in accordance with divine and human law.

'As for myself, I am aware of human infirmity; I do not ignore the might of Fortune, and I know well that all we do is subject to a thousand chances. If before you came to Africa – if while you were voluntarily evacuating Italy and had already embarked your army – you had come to me and I had turned a deaf ear to your request for peace, then, I confess, I should have been acting with outrageous insolence; but as things are, when on the brink of battle I have forced you to come here in spite of your most bitter reluctance, I am bound by no obligation to consider your feelings. If, therefore, to the terms upon which peace seemed likely to be made you wish to add some compensation for our ships which, with their cargoes, you took by force during the armistice, or for the violence you offered to our envoys, there will be something for me to bring before my council; if, on the contrary, you feel even that to be too great a burden, prepare to fight – for, evidently, you have found peace intolerable.'

Negotiation had failed. The two generals after the conference returned to their armies with the news that words had been in vain and the issue must be decided by blows. Each must accept the fortune which the gods chose to give. 32. Arrived in camp,

1. cf. p. 639.

Scipio and Hannibal each urged their men to prepare both heart and hand for the supreme struggle which, if Fortune smiled, would leave them victorious, not for a day only but for ever. Before the next night they would know whether Rome or Carthage was destined to give laws to the nations, for the prize of victory would be not Italy or Africa but the whole world, while a peril as great as the prize would be theirs whom the fortune of war opposed. To the Romans, in an unknown and foreign land, no way of escape was open; Carthage, her last reserves spent, was threatened with instant destruction.

Next day, to decide this great issue, the two most famous generals and the two mightiest armies of the two wealthiest nations in the world advanced to battle, doomed either to crown or to destroy the many triumphs each had won in the past. In all hearts were mixed feelings, confidence alternating with fear. As men surveyed their own and the enemy's ranks, weighing the strength of each merely by what their eyes could tell them, thoughts of joy and of foreboding jostled for pre-eminence in their minds. Such grounds for confidence as did not readily occur to the rank and file were supplied by the two commanders in words of admonition and encouragement, Hannibal reminding his men of their exploits in Italy during sixteen years of campaigning, of all the Roman generals killed, all the armies wiped out, and, when he came to a man who had distinguished himself in some particular battle, of the heroic deeds of individual soldiers. Scipio, for his part, spoke of the Spanish campaigns, of the recent battles in Africa, and of the enemy's admission of weakness and guilt, in that fear had forced them to sue for a peace which their ineradicable perfidy forbade them to keep. Furthermore, he made good use of his conference with Hannibal, which, as it had taken place without witnesses, he was free to misrepresent in any way he pleased. It was a good guess, he said, that the gods had given the Carthaginians, as they went out into line, the same omens as when their fathers fought off the Aegates Islands. Soon the war and all its hardships would be over; the spoils of Carthage were within their grasp, and they would all before long be at home again with parents, children, wives, and household gods. Scipio, as he spoke, stood so erect and wore on his face an expression of such calm happiness that you might have thought the victory already won.

The Roman army was then marshalled for battle, the *hastati* in the van, the *principes* behind them, and the *triarii* bringing up the rear. 33. Scipio did not mass his cohorts in the usual way, each in front of its own standards, but formed his line by maniples, leaving gaps between them to allow the enemy's elephants to pass through without breaking up the formation. Laelius, who had previously served as Scipio's second-in-command, but that year had been appointed quaestor – not by lot but by decree of the Senate – was given command of the Italian cavalry on the left wing, with Masinissa and the Numidian cavalry on the right. Scipio filled the gaps between the front-line maniples with *velites* (as the light-armed troops were then called) whose orders were either to retire to the rear as soon as the elephants charged, or to split up and wheel rapidly right and left to positions immediately behind the front-line troops, either of which manoeuvres would let the elephants through and bring them, at the same time, between two fires.

Hannibal in the hope of shaking his enemy's morale put his elephants – eighty of them, more than he had had in any previous battle – right in the van of his army; behind them were the Ligurian and Gallic auxiliaries with a certain proportion of troops from Mauretania and the Balearics. In the second line he stationed his Carthaginian and African troops together with the one legion from Macedonia; then, a moderate distance to the rear of these, came a reserve line of Italians, Bruttians mostly, of whom the majority had followed Hannibal of necessity and under compulsion, and by no means of their own free will, when he left Italy. Hannibal, like Scipio, stationed the cavalry on the wings, the Carthaginian on the right, the Numidian on the left. In an army composed of men who shared neither language, customs, laws, weapons, dress, appearance, nor even a common reason for serving, the best means of arousing the fighting spirit was no simple matter; hopes and fears, to suit the case, had to be dangled before their eyes: the auxiliaries, for instance, were offered their pay not only in cash but increased by a share in the plunder; the fire to kindle the Gauls was their peculiar and ingrained detestation of the

Romans; to the Ligurians was displayed the bait of the rich plains of Italy, once they had been brought down from their rugged mountains; Moors and Numidians were scared into courage by the prospect of Masinissa's tyrannical rule, while the Carthaginians were urged to keep before their eyes all they held dear – the walls of their native city, their household gods, the tombs of their ancestors, their children, parents, and trembling wives – and to remember the dread alternative, death and slavery on the one hand, world empire on the other, with no middle way, either for fear or hope, between those two extremes.

Hannibal was still addressing his Carthaginian contingent, and the various national leaders their own countrymen – mainly through interpreters because of the admixture of foreign troops – when from the Roman side the horns and trumpets blared out, and so tremendous a cheer was raised that the elephants panicked and turned against their own men, especially against the Moors and Numidians on the left wing. The ensuing confusion was easily increased by Masinissa, who stripped that end of the line of its cavalry support. A few of the elephants, who had not panicked, did charge, and caused frightful execution amongst the Roman *velites*, though suffering severe damage themselves; for the light troops, springing back behind the maniples to let the beasts through without trampling them to death, hurled their spears from right and left simultaneously, thus catching them in a cross-fire; the javelins of the front-line troops continued meanwhile to do their work, until under a hail of missiles from every side the elephants were driven out of the Roman line and, like the others, turned against their own men and even put to flight the Carthaginian cavalry on the right wing.

34. The Carthaginian army had been stripped of cavalry support on both sides when the infantry closed, and was no longer equal to the Roman forces either in hope or in strength. There were, moreover, factors which seem trivial to recall, but proved of great importance at the time of action. The Roman war-cry was louder and more terrifying because it was in unison, whereas the cries from the Carthaginian side were discordant, coming as they did from a mixed assortment of peoples with a

variety of mother-tongues. The Roman attack gained solidity as the men pressed on into the enemy by their own weight of numbers and that of their arms; on the other side, there were repeated charges with more speed than power behind them. Consequently the Romans immediately broke the enemy's line at the first attack; then they pressed on with their shoulders and shield-bosses, steadily advancing as the foe fell back, and making considerable progress as no one offered resistance. Then, as soon as they saw that the line confronting them had given way, the Roman rear line also began to press hard from behind, and this gave increased impetus to the rout of the enemy. On the other side, the second line of Africans and Carthaginians gave no support at all to the auxiliaries as they gave way; on the contrary, they fell back themselves for fear that the Romans would cut their way through those of the front line who offered firm resistance, and reach themselves. As a result, the auxiliaries suddenly turned and fled to mingle with their own men, some finding refuge in the second line, others cutting down their fellows who refused to let them through, crying that they had been given no support before and now were refused a place in the ranks. By this time there were almost two battles in one, as the Carthaginians were forced to fight both their enemy and their own men: nevertheless they refused to admit the auxiliaries who, maddened by terror, were forcing their way into the line, but closed up their ranks and drove them out towards the wings and the open plain outside the battle. By this they hoped to keep the panic running through the routed and wounded men from spreading to the part of the army which was still intact and in formation.

But such heaps of dead men and their arms filled the place where the auxiliaries had been standing a short time before that the Romans began to find it almost more difficult to make their way through them than it had been through the dense ranks of the enemy. Consequently, the *hastati* of the front-line broke up their maniples and ranks to pursue the enemy where they could over the piles of bodies and arms and through pools of blood. Then the maniples of the *principes* also began to break up, as they saw the first line losing formation. As soon as Scipio saw this, he ordered the recall to be sounded for the *hastati*, had the wounded men withdrawn to the rear, and led the *principes* and *triarii* out to the wings to protect and steady the centre, composed of *hastati* alone. Thus an entirely new battle began, for now the Romans had come to grips with their real enemies, the Carthaginian veterans, their equals in arms and experience of warfare, the fame of their exploits, and the extent of their hopes and perils. But the Romans had the advantage in numbers and in fighting spirit; they had already routed the Carthaginian cavalry and the elephants, and had broken up the front line, so that they were now engaged with the second.

35. Laelius and Masinissa had pursued the routed cavalry for a considerable distance; now at the right moment they wheeled round and charged into the rear of the enemy's line. It was this cavalry attack which finally defeated the Carthaginians. Many were surrounded and cut down where they stood; many were scattered in flight over the open plain, only to fall everywhere beneath the cavalry, the undisputed masters of the field. More than 20,000 of the Carthaginians and their allies were killed on that day, and about the same number captured, together with 132 military standards and eleven elephants. The Romans lost about 1,500 men.

In the confusion Hannibal escaped with a few horsemen and fled to Hadrumetum. He had tried everything he could both before and during the engagement before he withdrew from the battle, and on the admission even of Scipio as well as of all the military experts, he achieved the distinction of having drawn up his line on that day with remarkable skill. He had placed his elephants in the very front, so that their haphazard charge and irresistible weight should prevent the Romans from following their standards and keeping their ranks, tactics to which they attached the greatest importance; next came the auxiliaries, placed in front of the line of Carthaginians, so that the latter could block the possible retreat of these men drawn from the scum of any and every nation and held together by no loyal feelings but simply by the cash paid them. At the same time, the auxiliaries were to meet the first violence of the enemy's attack and to exhaust it, or, if nothing else, to blunt the enemy's swords by their own wounds. Then came the soldiers who represented Hannibal's highest hopes, the

Carthaginians and Africans, a match for the Romans in every other respect, and now to have the advantage of fighting fresh against tired and wounded men. Last of all were the Italians, placed in the rear and also some distance back, since their doubtful loyalty might prove them either friend or foe. This was the last creation of Hannibal's military genius. From his refuge in Hadrumetum he was summoned to Carthage – it was thirty-five years since he had left it as a boy – and there before the senate he admitted that this defeat in the battle was also total defeat in the war. He saw no hope for the future unless Carthage asked for terms of peace and was granted them.

36. Immediately after the battle Scipio stormed and plundered the enemy's camp and returned with an immense amount of booty to the sea and his ships, after he had received a message that Lentulus had arrived at Utica with fifty warships and a hundred transports bringing supplies of all kinds. This made him decide to strike terror into Carthage from all sides while she was still reeling from the blow she had received; so he sent Laelius to Rome with a report of the victory, ordered Gnaeus Octavius to bring the legions to Carthage by land, and set sail himself from Utica towards the harbour of Carthage with his original fleet augmented by the new ships brought by Lentulus. He was nearly there when he was met by a Carthaginian ship, hung with the woollen fillets and olive branches of supplication, which was carrying ten envoys, leading citizens of Carthage, sent by Hannibal's order to sue for peace. As they drew alongside the stern of the flagship they held out the symbols of supplication, begging and praying for mercy and protection. The only answer they received was an order to come to Tunis, where Scipio intended to move his camp. He then sailed on to look at the site of Carthage from the harbour, not so much with the intention of an immediate reconnaissance as to humiliate the enemy, and returned to Utica, to which place Octavius had been recalled.

While the Romans were on their way to Tunis news reached them that Vermina, the son of Syphax, was coming to the help of the Carthaginians with a force of infantry and a greater one of cavalry. Part of the Roman infantry and all the cavalry were sent to attack the column on the first day of the feast of the

Saturnalia,[1] with the result that the Numidians were routed after a short engagement; and with every way of escape cut off by the cavalry surrounding them on all sides, lost 15,000 men killed and 1,200 captured alive, along with 1,500 Numidian horses and seventy-two military standards. Vermina himself escaped with a few men in the general confusion. Then a camp was set up at Tunis on the same site as before, and thirty envoys from Carthage came to Scipio. Their pleading was even more piteous than before, constrained as they were by their misfortune, but the less likely to win pity when the memory of their treachery was still fresh in the minds of their hearers. A council was held, in which righteous indignation impelled everyone to urge the destruction of Carthage; however, second thoughts on the cost in time and effort of besieging a town with such fortifications and resources, in addition to Scipio's forebodings that a successor to himself was on the way to reap the reward of victory and to appropriate the glory of a war which had really been ended by another's effort and danger, brought them all round to the idea of peace.

37. On the following day the envoys were recalled and sternly rebuked for their perfidy: they were told that now that they had learned their lesson from repeated disasters, they should at long last believe in the existence of the gods and the sanctity of oaths. Terms of peace were put to them: they were to live as free men under their own laws, and to continue to hold the cities and territories which they had held before the war; the Romans from that day on would cease their raiding attacks. All deserters, runaway slaves, and prisoners-of-war were to be delivered to the Romans, all warships to be surrendered, with the exception of ten triremes, and all the trained elephants in their possession were to be handed over and no more to be trained. They were not to make war on anyone inside or outside Africa without permission from Rome; they were to make restitution to Masinissa and draw up a treaty with him; they must supply grain and pay to the allied troops until their own envoys had returned from Rome. They were to pay 10,000 talents of silver spread by equal instalments over fifty years, and to hand over 100 hostages of Scipio's choosing between the

1. 17 December: an unusually precise date.

ages of fourteen and thirty years. An armistice would be granted, provided that the transport ships captured during the previous time of peace were returned, together with their crews and cargoes: otherwise there would be no armistice nor any hope of peace. These then were the terms the envoys were told to take home.

When they were put before the Carthaginian assembly, a senator named Gisgo came forward to oppose the peace. The crowd listened, uneasy about the peace terms but anxious not to lose them, until Hannibal could bear it no longer – that words like that should gain a hearing at a time of such crisis – and pulled Gisgo down from the platform with his own hands. This was something new in a free state, and the murmur of indignation it roused left Hannibal, the disciplined soldier, astounded at the licence of a city mob. 'I was nine years old,' he said, 'when I left you, and after thirty-six years I have returned. Destiny, both personal and public, since boyhood has taught me all a soldier should know, and I think I have learned my lesson well; but it is left to you to train me in the rights, laws, and usages of the city and the forum.' After this apology for his ignorance, he spoke at length about the peace, showing that it was far from unfair and must be accepted. The greatest difficulty of all the terms imposed was that of the ships captured during the truce, since nothing was forthcoming except the ships themselves, and investigation was made difficult by the fact that anyone accused would oppose the peace. It was decided that the ships must be restored and the crews traced at all costs, and that it should be left to Scipio to assess the value of what was missing so that the Carthaginians could make restitution in cash.

Some historians say that Hannibal went straight from the battlefield to the coast, where a ship was ready to take him at once to King Antiochus;[1] and that when Scipio demanded Hannibal's surrender as a first essential, he was told that Hannibal was not in Africa.

38. After the envoys had returned to Scipio, the quaestors were ordered to make an inventory from the public accounts showing what public property had been on the ships, and the

1. His flight to Antiochus took place seven years later, in 195 B.C.

owners were told to declare the private property; then, in payment of the total sum, 25,000 pounds of silver were exacted on the spot. A three months' armistice was then granted the Carthaginians, with the additional clause that throughout the period of armistice they were not to send envoys to any other place than to Rome, and if any envoys came to Carthage they must not be sent away until the Roman commander had been informed who they were and why they came. The Carthaginian envoys were accompanied to Rome by Lucius Veturius Philo, Marcus Marcius Ralla, and Lucius Scipio, the general's brother. During this time supplies of grain from Sicily and Sardinia caused such a drop in price that merchants left some of the corn to the sailors in place of freight-money.

In Rome the first news that the Carthaginians had renewed hostilities had caused general alarm. Tiberius Claudius had been ordered to take his fleet promptly over to Sicily and thence to Africa, and the other consul, Marcus Servilius, to wait outside the city until more should be known about the situation in Africa. Claudius had not attempted to hurry on the preparations for assembling and launching the fleet, because the Senate had voted that the authority for settling terms of peace should rest with Scipio rather than the consul. Reports of prodigies following on the rumours of fresh hostilities had added to the country's fears: at Cumae the sun was partially eclipsed and it rained stones, and in the district of Velitrae the ground subsided in huge caverns where trees were sucked down into the depths; at Aricia the market-place and surrounding shops, and at Frusino the town wall in several places and a gate were struck by lightning; and on the Palatine hill there was a shower of stones. This last was expiated by a nine-day rite, in accordance with ancestral custom, and the rest by sacrifice of full-grown victims. Meanwhile the rivers rose to unusual height, and this too was interpreted as a portent; for the Tiber overflowed so far that the Games of Apollo had to be transferred from the flooded Circus Maximus to a site outside the Colline Gate, near the temple of Venus of Eryx. On the very day of the Games, however, fine weather returned and a message was brought that the floods had subsided from the Circus; the procession had already set out for the Colline Gate, but it was recalled and sent back. The restoration of the Games to their appropriate place added to the delight of the people and the numbers who attended.

39. The consul Claudius had left Rome at last, only to run into a violent storm between the harbours of Cosa and Loreta. Filled with alarm he made for Populonium and lay at anchor there until the rest of the storm should abate, then moved on to the island of Elba and from Elba to Corsica and Sardinia. There, as he was rounding the headland of the 'Mad Mountains', a much more furious storm hit him in a far more dangerous situation and scattered his fleet. Many of the vessels lost their rigging and began to ship water; some were wrecked; and in this battered and broken state the fleet reached Carales. There the ships were beached for repairs and winter overtook them. At the end of the year, when Claudius's command was not renewed, he could only resign it and bring the fleet back to Rome. Servilius named Gaius Servilius Geminus dictator, to avoid being recalled to Rome himself to hold elections, and went out to his province. The dictator named Publius Aelius Paetus as his master of Horse. A date for the elections was repeatedly announced, but each time had to be postponed because of stormy weather: consequently when the old magistrates retired on 14 March, the new ones had not been elected in their place, and the State was left without curule magistrates. Titus Manlius Torquatus, the pontiff, died that year, and Gaius Sulpicius Galba was elected in his place. The Roman Games were repeated three times in full by the curule aediles Lucius Licinius Lucullus and Quintus Fulvius. Certain clerks and messengers assigned to the aediles were convicted through an informer of having secretly taken money from the treasury, and the aedile Lucullus did not escape disgrace. Publius Aelius Tubero and Lucius Laetorius were elected people's aediles and then had to resign owing to a technical defect in their election, though they had first conducted the Plebeian Games and in connexion with these a banquet for Jupiter, and had set upon the Capitol three statues paid for out of money collected from fines. Games in honour of Ceres were held by the dictator and the master of Horse acting in accordance with the decree of the Senate.

40. The envoys from Africa, Roman and Carthaginian, arrived at Rome, and the Senate met in the temple of Bellona. There Lucius Veturius Philo, to the great joy of his hearers, described the battle – the last one the Carthaginians would ever fight – and the end which had come at last to their sufferings in the war. He told too how Syphax's son Vermina had been defeated, a small addition to a successful campaign. Upon this he was told to address the people outside so that all could share in the general rejoicing. Then all the temples throughout the city were opened for offering thanks, and three days of public thanksgiving were decreed. The Carthaginian envoys and those from King Philip (who had also arrived at this moment) applied for an audience in the Senate, but the dictator replied by order of the Senate that this would be granted to them by the new consuls. The elections were then held at once; Gnaeus Cornelius Lentulus and Publius Aelius Paetus were elected consuls, and the praetorships fell to Marcus Junius Pennus as City praetor, Marcus Valerius Falto, who drew Bruttium, and Marcus Fabius Buteo and Publius Aelius Tubero, who were assigned Sardinia and Sicily. No decision was to be made about the consuls' provinces until the envoys of King Philip and the Carthaginians had been heard; the Senate foresaw that if one war had ended, another was just beginning.

The consul Lentulus was consumed with a single desire – to have Africa for his province. There he hoped to win an easy victory if the war should continue, or alternatively the honour of having this great war end during his consulship if it were already in the last stages, and to this end he refused to allow any business to proceed until Africa was assigned him by formal decree. His colleague Paetus raised no objections; a moderate and reasonable man, he realized that this honour rightly belonged to Scipio, and no one could compete for it on fair or equal terms. Thermus and Glabrio, the people's tribunes, declared that Lentulus was attempting what the consul Tiberius Claudius[1] had tried unsuccessfully in the previous year, when the Senate had authorized the tribunes to put before the people the question of who should have supreme command in Africa, and all thirty-five tribes had voted for Scipio. The

1. See p. 651.

question was debated with some heat both in the Senate and before the people, until finally the decision was left to the Senate. The senators therefore bound themselves by oath, as had been agreed, and voted that the consuls must decide their provinces either by mutual agreement or by lot: one of them should have Italy, the other the fleet of fifty ships with which to sail to Sicily and thence to Africa, if peace terms had not yet been settled with the Carthaginians; there he should conduct operations by sea and Scipio by land, Scipio retaining his previous high command. If peace terms were agreed on, the tribunes must put to the people the question whether they should be ratified by the consul or by Scipio, and if the victorious army was to be brought back from Africa, who was to bring it. If it was the people's wish that Scipio should be the one to grant peace and bring back the army, the consul was not to cross from Sicily to Africa. The consul who drew Italy should receive two legions from the praetor Marcus Sextius.

41. Scipio's command in Africa was continued with the armies which he already had. Of the praetors, Marcus Valerius Falto was assigned the two legions in Bruttium which Gaius Livius had commanded the previous year; Publius Aelius was to take over two legions in Sicily from Gnaeus Tremelius, and Marcus Fabius the single legion in Sardinia which Publius Lentulus had had as pro-praetor. Marcus Servilius, the consul of the year before, had his command in Etruria renewed, also with his own two legions. With regard to the Spanish provinces, Lucius Cornelius Lentulus and Lucius Manlius Acidinus had already been there several years, and it was decided that the consuls should ask the tribunes to put before the people, if they thought fit, the question of who should be ordered to take up command in Spain. The general appointed should then enrol from the existing two armies enough Roman soldiers to form a single legion, and Latin allies for fifteen cohorts, with which to hold the province: the veteran soldiers should be brought back to Italy by Lentulus and Acidinus. The consul was assigned a fleet of fifty ships drawn from the fleet of Gnaeus Octavius which was off the coast of Africa, and that of Publius Villius which was guarding the coast of Sicily, the ships to be chosen by the consul. Scipio was to have the forty warships

which he had before; if he wished Gnaeus Octavius to continue in command of them, Octavius should have military authority as pro-praetor for the coming year, but if Scipio preferred to give the command to Laelius, Octavius must return to Rome and bring with him any ships which the consul did not need. Ten warships were also assigned to Marcus Fabius for Sardinia. The consuls were finally instructed to enrol two City legions, so that Rome's military establishment for the year would consist of fourteen legions and a fleet of one hundred ships.

42. The Senate then turned its attention to the envoys from King Philip and from Carthage, and decided to hear the Macedonians first. Their speeches dealt with several matters: some tried to answer the complaints made by the envoys sent from Rome to the king that allied territory in Greece had been devastated, while others went on to open accusation of the allies of the Roman people, singling out Marcus Aurelius for a violent attack: he had been one of three envoys sent to them, but, they said, had levied troops, stayed behind to make war in violation of the treaty, and frequently engaged their commanders in pitched battles. They also demanded the return of the Macedonians and their commander Sopater, who had fought as mercenaries for Hannibal and were now kept as prisoners in chains. In reply, Marcus Furius, who had been sent from Macedonia by Aurelius for that very purpose, maintained that Aurelius had been left behind solely to prevent the allied communities from being worn down by raids and acts of violence until they were forced to go over to the king's side: Aurelius had never left allied territory, and had concentrated on ensuring that raiding parties should not come in over the boundaries unscathed. Furius also declared that Sopater was a high official at the Macedonian court and a relative of the king's, and had been sent recently to Africa with money and four thousand Macedonians to support Hannibal.

The envoys when questioned about these points were evasive in their replies, and consequently received a stern answer. The king, they were told, was looking for war, and if he kept on doing so, he would find it all too soon. He had twice violated the treaty, firstly by wronging the allies of

Rome and harassing them in open warfare, secondly by assisting Rome's enemies with money and reinforcements. Publius Scipio had acted and was acting rightly and in order, in the opinion of the Senate, in keeping chained as enemies those men who had been taken prisoner while carrying arms against the Roman people; Marcus Aurelius, too, was acting in the best interests of the State, and the Senate was glad to know that he was defending the allies of the Roman people by force of arms, since the obligations of a treaty gave them no protection.

With these severe words the Macedonians were dismissed, and the Carthaginian envoys summoned. They were indisputably the leading citizens of their country, and as the senators observed their age and high rank there was not a man who was not convinced that this time they were genuinely seeking peace. The most conspicuous figure was that of Hasdrubal (popularly nicknamed 'the Kid') who had consistently opposed the Barcine party and worked for peace, and consequently on this occasion spoke with all the more authority when he sought to transfer the responsibility for the war from the Carthaginian people as a whole to the greed of the few. His tone ranged through the varying keys of emotion as he excused some charges, admitted others for fear of finding it harder to win pardon if they shamelessly denied known facts, and even presumed to advise the assembled Senate to make restrained and moderate use of their present good fortune. If the Carthaginians had listened to him and Hanno, he said, and had been willing to act at the right moment, they would have been granted the terms of peace which they were now seeking. It rarely happened that men were blessed with good fortune and good judgement at the same moment; but the Roman people was invincible for the very reason that in its hour of success it could remember to take counsel and be wise. It would indeed be surprising if this were not so; men for whom good fortune was some strange new thing were carried away beyond all control in their rejoicing, but the Roman people had such long experience of the joys of victory that familiarity might almost breed contempt; and they had extended their empire not so much by conquest as by sparing the vanquished. The remaining speeches aimed at even greater emotional appeal, as the speakers recounted the former great wealth of Carthage and the depths to which she had fallen; a short time ago their people had held practically the whole world by their arms, and now had nothing left but the walls of Carthage; from behind these they could look out on nothing on land and sea which was still subject to their rule, and even their city and ancestral homes would remain theirs only if the Roman people were willing to withhold its fury, and spare them the worst fate of all. When it was clear that this appeal was having its effect on the senators, one of their number, outraged by the notorious perfidy of the Carthaginians, is said to have risen with a cry: 'Who are the gods whose names they can take to sanction a treaty? The gods of their earlier one they have forsworn.' 'The same gods,' said Hasdrubal: 'since their hostility to treaty-breakers is now proved.'

43. The entire Senate was now prepared to make peace, when the consul Gnaeus Lentulus, to whom the fleet had been assigned, interposed his veto. Upon this the tribunes Manius Acilius and Quintus Minucius put before the people the questions, first whether it was their will and command that the Senate should pass a decree for peace to be made with Carthage, and secondly, whom they would instruct to ratify the peace and whom to bring back the army from Africa. To the first question all the tribes voted their assent; and voted too that Publius Scipio should be the one to grant peace, and also to bring back the army. The Senate accordingly decreed that Scipio should make peace with the people of Carthage upon such terms as seemed suitable to him and were in agreement with the opinion of a council of ten members. The Carthaginian envoys then thanked the Senate and begged permission to enter the City and speak to their fellow citizens who had been captured and imprisoned; some of them, they said, were men of high rank, their own relatives and friends, while for others they had messages from their relatives. When this was granted, they made the further request that they should be given the opportunity of ransoming certain chosen prisoners; and on request furnished some two hundred names. The Senate passed a decree that the ten Roman envoys should take to Scipio two hundred prisoners, selected by the Carthaginians, with instructions to

restore them to their own people without ransom if an agreement was reached about terms of peace. The Fetial priests[1] were then given their orders to go to Africa to draw up the peace treaty, and at their own request the decree was passed in these words: each priest should take with him one flint knife and one bunch of sacred herbs, so that when the Roman commander ordered them to make the treaty, they could formally demand of him the sacred herbs – such as are by tradition gathered on the summit of the Capitoline hill to be given to the Fetial priests.

The Carthaginians were accordingly dismissed, left Rome, and returned to Africa, where they presented themselves to Scipio and made peace on the terms I have mentioned. They surrendered their warships, elephants, deserters, and runaway slaves, and 4,000 prisoners-of-war, amongst whom was the senator Quintus Terentius Culleo. Scipio ordered the ships to be taken out to sea and burnt: according to some historians there were 500 of them, representing every type of vessel propelled by oars, and the conflagration, seen without warning, was as melancholy a sight for the Carthaginians as it would have been if their own city were in flames. The deserters were more harshly treated than the runaway slaves: Latin citizens were beheaded and Romans crucified.

44. It was forty years since peace had last been made with Carthage, in the year when Quintus Lutatius and Aulus Manlius were consuls.[2] The war which broke out twenty-three years later,[3] in the consulship of Publius Cornelius and Tiberius Sempronius, was brought to an end in its seventeenth year, in the consulship of Gnaeus Cornelius and Publius Aelius.[4] Tradition has it that later Scipio often said that it was the desire for fame, first of Tiberius Claudius and then of Gnaeus Cornelius, which prevented him from ending the war with the destruction of Carthage.

The raising of the first instalment of their indemnity seemed difficult to the Carthaginians, exhausted as they were by the long war, and there was general weeping and lamentation in

1. The college of priests in charge of the observances used in making peace or declaring war.

2. 241 B.C. 3. 218 B.C. 4. 201 B.C.

the senate. On this occasion Hannibal – so the story goes – was seen to be laughing. Hasdrubal ('the Kid') rebuked him for laughing while his people wept, when he himself was the cause of their tears. 'If eyes could see the mind within,' replied Hannibal, 'as they do the expression of a face, it would soon be apparent to you that this laughter you condemn springs not from a happy heart, but from one which is almost beside itself with its misfortunes; and yet laughter is far less untimely than your own irrational and misplaced tears. The time to weep was when our arms were taken from us, our ships were burnt, and we were forbidden foreign wars; that was when we received our death blow. You have no reason to believe that the Romans had any interest in your domestic peace, for peace can never stay for long in a great country. It will find an enemy at home if it lacks one abroad, just as a powerful body appears immune from any external infection but is strained by its own strength. How true it is that we feel public misfortune only in so far as it affects our private interests! And it takes a money loss to make us feel the pinch. So when the spoils of war were being stripped from vanquished Carthage, and you saw her left naked and unarmed amidst all the many armed tribes of Africa, no one raised a moan; but today, when contributions have to be made from private property, you behave like mourners at your country's funeral. All too soon, I fear, you will realize that it is the least of your troubles which has called forth these tears today.' These were Hannibal's words to his people.

Scipio called an assembly, and there, in addition to his own kingdom, Masinissa was presented with the city of Cirta and the remaining towns and lands which had passed from the kingdom of Syphax into the power of the Roman people. Gnaeus Octavius received orders to take the fleet to Sicily and hand it over to Gnaeus Cornelius the consul, and Carthaginian envoys were told to go to Rome, so that all Scipio's acts performed on the advice of his council of ten could be confirmed by the authority of the Senate and the people's command.

45. So peace was secured on land and sea. Scipio then embarked his army and crossed over to Lilybaeum in Sicily. From there he sent a large part of his troops by sea while he himself made his way through Italy. Everywhere he found rejoicing

as much on account of the peace as for victory, when the towns poured out to do him honour and crowds of peasants too held up his progress along the roads. He reached Rome and rode into the City in triumph–triumph such as had never been seen before. To the treasury he brought 123,000 pounds' weight of silver; to his soldiers he distributed 400 *asses* apiece. The death of Syphax – only recently at Tibur, where he had been transferred from Alba – took nothing from the glory of Scipio's triumph, though it denied the spectators part of the show; even so, his death attracted attention by the state funeral given him. (On the other hand, Polybius, an authority by no means to be despised,[1] relates that Syphax was led in the triumph.) Behind Scipio in the triumphal procession came Quintus Terentius Culleo wearing a freed slave's liberty cap; and for the rest of his life he honoured Scipio, as it was proper that he should, for restoring him to freedom.

As for the surname Africanus, I have not been able to find out how it became current – through the army's devotion to their general, or from popular favour; or it may have started with the flattery of his close friends, in the way, in our fathers' time, Sulla was called 'Fortunate' and Pompey 'the Great'. What is certain is that Scipio was the first general to be celebrated by the name of the people he conquered, though subsequently there were men far less renowned for their victories who took him as a precedent, and acquired titles of honour for their family portraits and distinguished surnames for their descendants.

1. Livy's sole reference to the great Greek historian whose history was his chief source for the war with Carthage.

# SPAIN DURING THE WAR WITH HANNIBAL

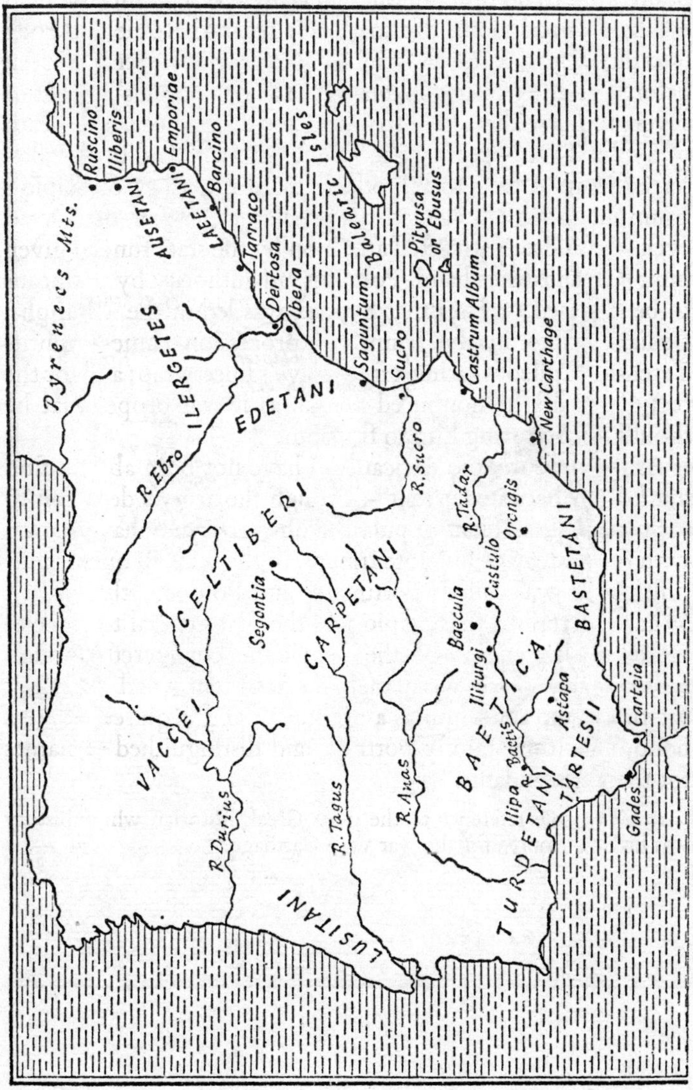

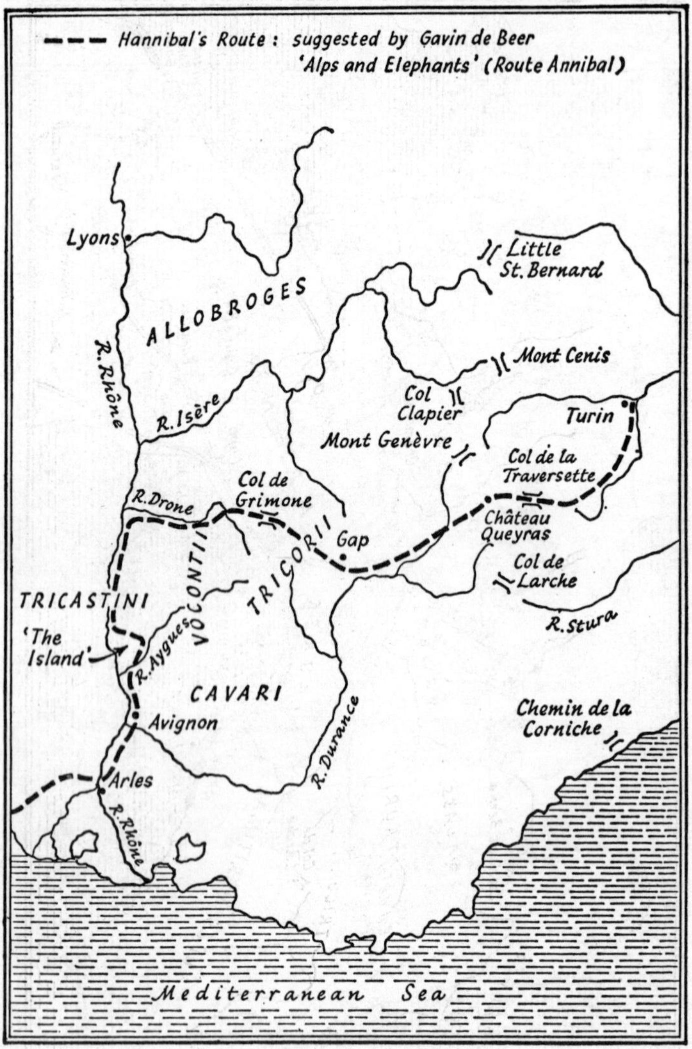
Hannibal's Route : suggested by Gavin de Beer
'Alps and Elephants' (Route Annibal)
Lyons
Little St. Bernard
ALLOBROGES
R. Rhône
Mont Cenis
Col Clapier
R. Isère
Turin
Mont Genèvre
Col de la Traversette
Col de Grimone
R. Drone
Château Queyras
Gap
Col de Larche
TRICASTINI
VOCONTII
TRICORII
R. Stura
'The Island'
R. Aygues
CAVARI
Chemin de la Corniche
Avignon
R. Durance
Arles
R. Rhône
Mediterranean Sea

# NORTH ITALY

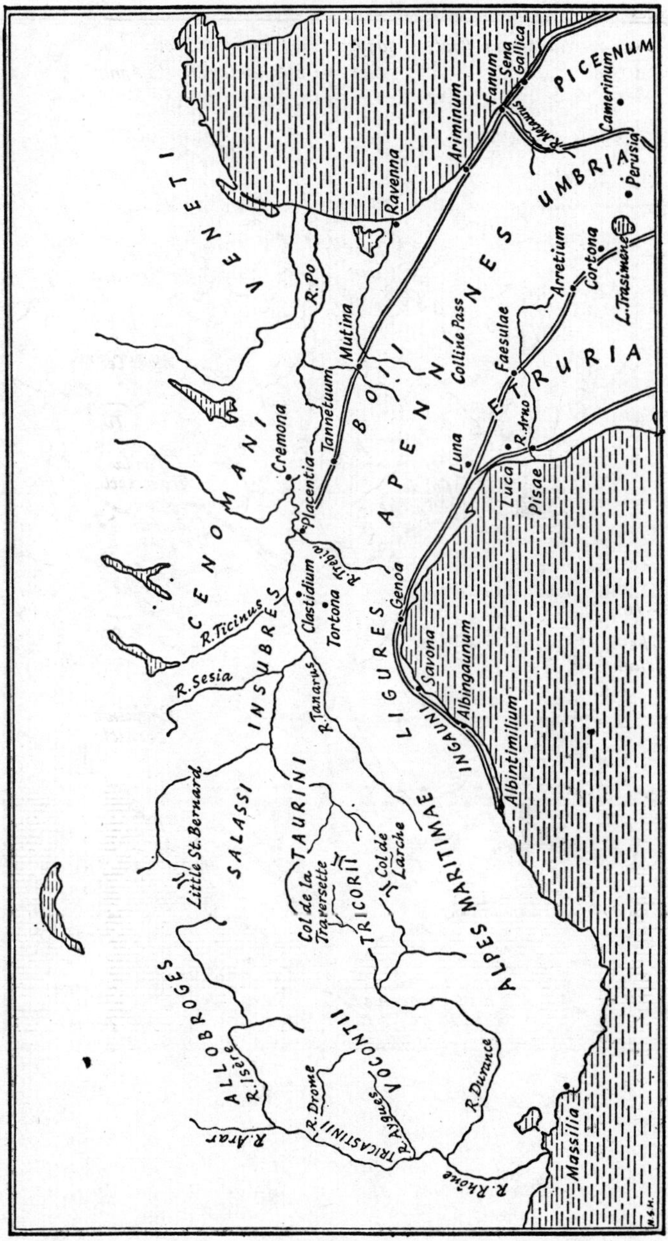
VENETI
CENOMANI
INSUBRES
SALASSI
TAURINI
TRICORII
ALLOBROGES
VOCONTII
TRICASTINII
ALPES MARITIMAE
LIGURES
INGAUNI
BOII
APENNINES
ETRURIA
UMBRIA
PICENUM
R. Po
R. Ticinus
R. Sesia
R. Tanarus
R. Trebia
R. Isère
R. Arar
R. Drome
R. Aygues
R. Durance
R. Rhône
R. Arno
R. Metaurus
Ravenna
Ariminum
Fanum
Sena Gallica
Camerinum
Perusia
Cortona
Arretium
L. Trasimene
Faesulae
Colline Pass
Mutina
Tannetuum
Placentia
Cremona
Clastidium
Tortona
Genoa
Savona
Albingaunum
Albintimilium
Luna
Luca
Pisae
Massilia
Little St. Bernard
Col de la Traversette
Col de Larche

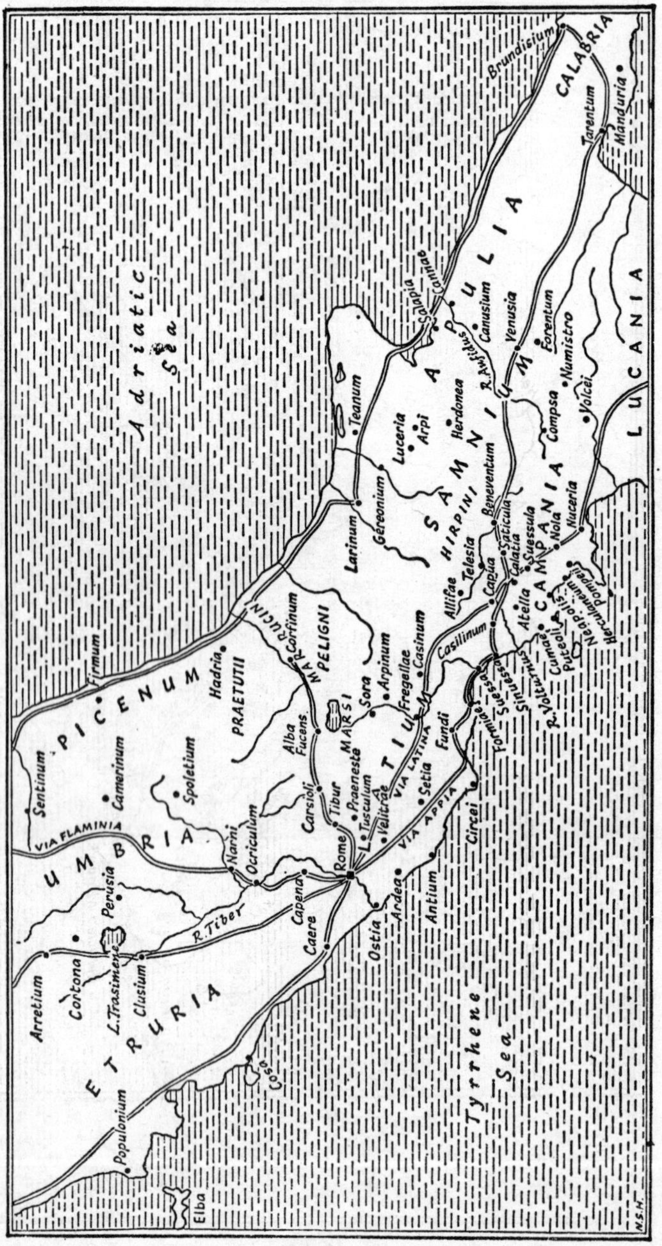
Adriatic Sea
Brundisium
CALABRIA
Tarentum
Manduria
APULIA
Salapia
Cannae
Canusium
Venusia
Forentum
Numistro
Volcei
LUCANIA
R. Aufidus
Herdonea
Arpi
Luceria
Teanum
SAMNIUM
Compsa
Beneventum
Gereonium
Larinum
HIRPINI
Telesia
Saticula
Calatia
Suessula
Nola
Nuceria
CAMPANIA
Capua
Allifae
Atella
Cumae
Puteoli
Neapolis
Herculaneum
Pompeii
Casilinum
Casinum
Sinuessa
Suessa
R. Volturnus
Formiae
Fundi
Fregellae
Arpinum
Sora
MARSI
PELIGNI
Corfinium
MARRUCINI
PRAETUTII
Hadria
Firmum
PICENUM
Sentinum
Camerinum
Spoletium
UMBRIA
VIA FLAMINIA
Narni
Ocriculum
Carsioli
Tibur
Praeneste
Tusculum
Velitrae
Alba Fucens
LATIUM
VIA LATINA
Setia
VIA APPIA
Circei
Antium
Ardea
Ostia
Rome
Capena
Caere
R. Tiber
Perusia
Cortona
L. Trasimene
Clusium
Arretium
ETRURIA
Cosa
Populonium
Elba
Tyrrhene Sea
N.S.H.

# SOUTH ITALY AND SICILY

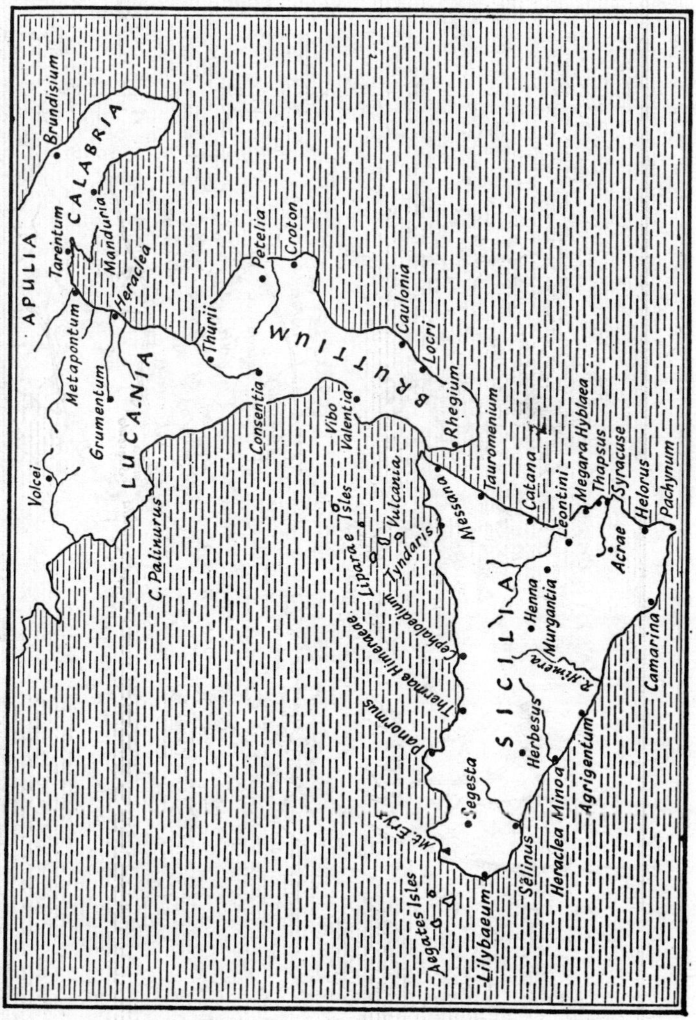

CENTRAL GREECE

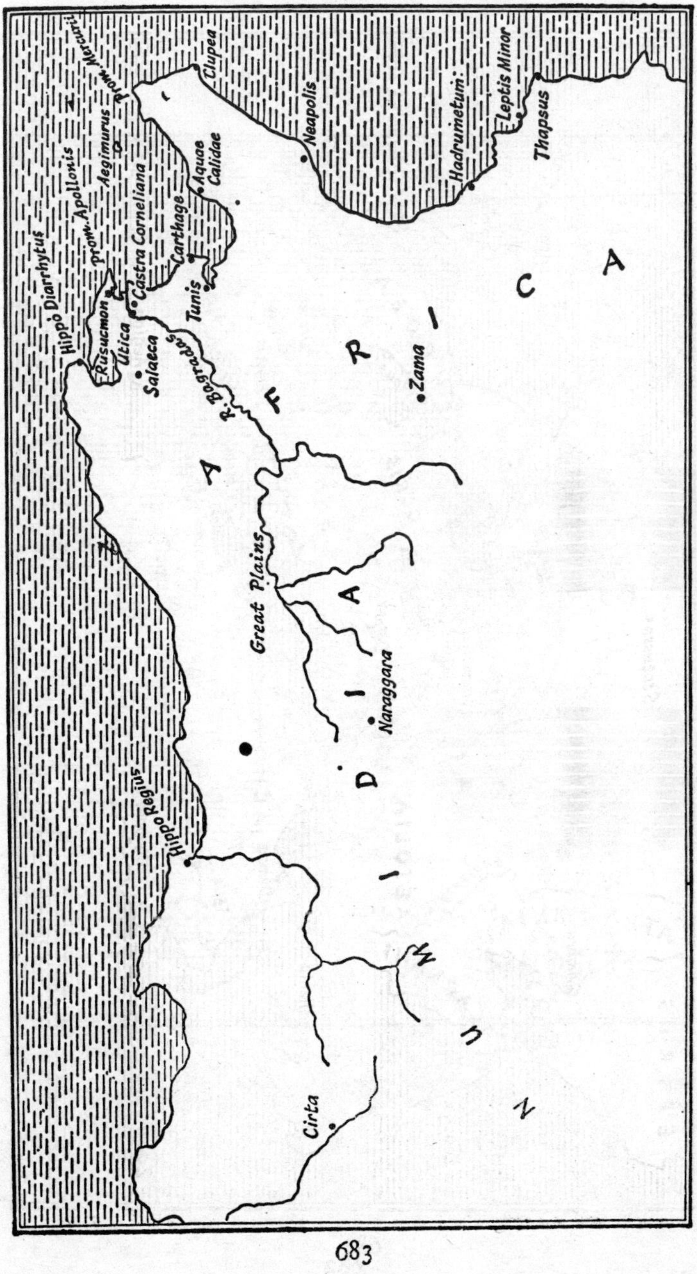
Hippo Diarrhytus
prom. Apollonis
Aegimurus
Prom. Mercurii
Clupea
Neapolis
Hadrumetum
Leptis Minor
Thapsus
Aquae Calidae
Carthage
Castra Corneliana
Tunis
Utica
Rusucmon
Salaeca
R. Bagradas
Zama
AFRICA
Great Plains
NUMIDIA
Naraggara
Hippo Regius
Cirta

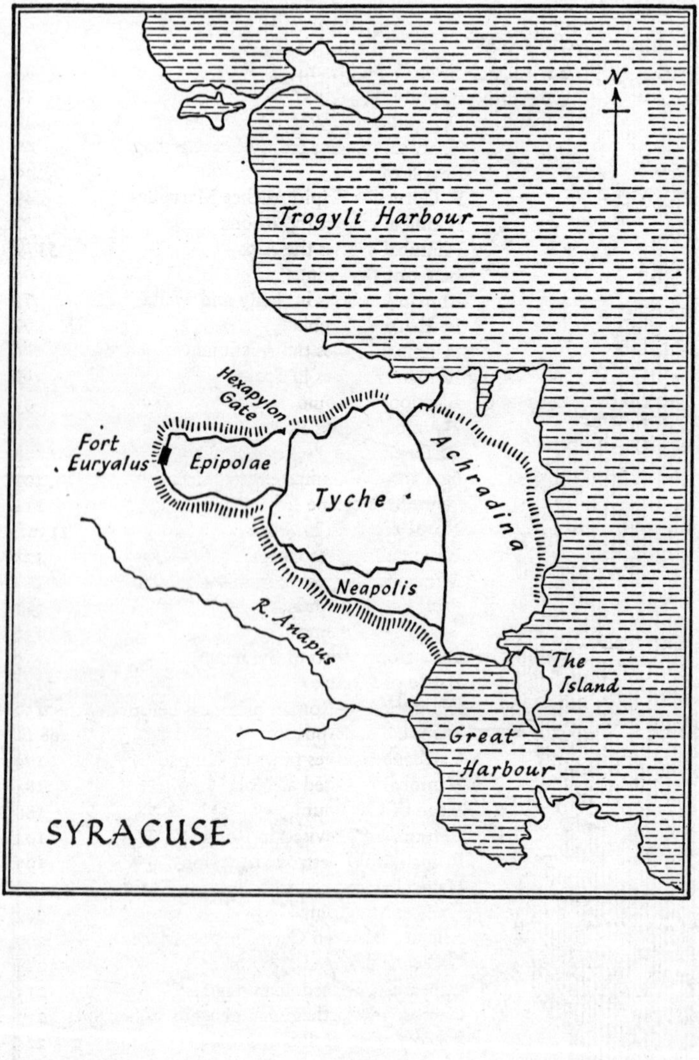
N
Trogyli Harbour
Hexapylon Gate
Fort Euryalus
Epipolae
Achradina
Tyche
Neapolis
R. Anapus
The Island
Great Harbour
SYRACUSE

# CHRONOLOGICAL INDEX

(Dates as given in Livy)


| | | | |
|---|---|---|---|
| BOOK XXI | 219 B.C. | Siege of Saguntum | 29 |
| | 218 B.C. | Capture of Saguntum | 38 |
| | | Declaration of War | 42 |
| | | Hannibal sets out from New Carthage | 46 |
| | | Revolt of Boii | 48 |
| | | P. Cornelius Scipio reaches Marseilles | 49 |
| | | Hannibal crosses the Rhône | 50 |
| | | Hannibal crosses the Alps | 53 ff. |
| | | Battle of R. Ticinus | 64 |
| | | Roman victories in Sicily and Malta | 75 |
| | | Battle of R. Trebia | 77 |
| | | Hannibal crosses the Apennines | 84 |
| | | Roman successes in Spain | 87 |
| BOOK XXII | 217 B.C. | Elections in Rome | 93 |
| | | Hannibal crosses R. Arno | 95 |
| | | Battle of Lake Trasimene | 98 |
| | | Q. Fabius Maximus elected dictator | 103 |
| | | Hannibal's escape from Campania | 112 |
| | | Naval victories in Spain | 115 ff. |
| | | Hannibal at Gereonium | 121 |
| | | Minucius's successes against Hannibal | 122 |
| | | Fabius saves Minucius | 127 |
| | 216 B.C. | Elections in Rome | 132 |
| | | Gifts from Hiero of Syracuse | 135 |
| | | Battle of Cannae | 144 |
| | | Delegation of Roman prisoners before Senate | 159 |
| BOOK XXIII | | Hannibal at Capua | 168 ff. |
| | | Carthage receives news of Cannae | 179 |
| | | Hannibal repulsed at Nola | 184 |
| | | Siege of Casilinum | 188 |
| | | Censors' lists revised in Rome | 194 |
| | | Roman army destroyed by Boii | 197 |
| | | Hasdrubal stopped from leaving Spain | 199 ff. |
| | 215 B.C. | Elections in Rome | 205 |
| | | Alliance between Carthage and Macedon | 209 |
| | | Gracchus besieged at Cumae | 214 |
| | | Capture of Macedonian envoys | 215 |
| | | Capture of Carthaginian generals in Sardinia | 217 |
| | | Success of Marcellus at Nola | 224 |
| | | More Roman successes in Spain | 228 |
| BOOK XXIV | | Fall of Croton | 232 |

| | | | |
|---|---|---|---|
| | | Events in Sicily after death of Hiero | 235 ff. |
| | 214 B.C. | Elections in Rome | 239 |
| | | Gracchus takes Beneventum | 247 |
| | | Fabius and Marcellus take Casilinum | 253 |
| | | Conspiracy in Syracuse | 256 ff. |
| | | Marcellus in Sicily | 264 |
| | | Roman attack on Syracuse | 271 |
| | | Massacre at Henna | 276 ff. |
| | | Romans land force at Apollonia (1st Macedonian War) | 279 |
| | | Roman recapture of Saguntum | 283 |
| | 213 B.C. | Elections in Rome | 283 |
| | | Recapture of Arpi | 287 |
| | | Roman overtures to king Syphax | 289 |
| BOOK XXV | 212 B.C. | Elections in Rome | 294 |
| | | War profiteering checked in Rome | 296 |
| | | Hannibal enters Tarentum | 305 |
| | | Carthaginians take Thurii | 315 |
| | | Tiberius Gracchus killed | 318 |
| | | Fulvius defeated in Apulia | 323 |
| | | Romans besiege Capua | 325 |
| | | Marcellus takes Syracuse | 326 ff. |
| | | Plague at Syracuse | 331 |
| | | Death of Archimedes | 338 |
| | | Defeat in Spain; death of the Scipios | 339 ff. |
| | | Lucius Marcius rallies Roman remnant in Spain | 344 |
| | | Marcellus victorious at Agrigentum | 351 |
| | 211 B.C. | Elections in Rome | 353 |
| BOOK XXVI | | Trial of Fulvius for his defeat | 356 |
| | | Hannibal marches to relieve Capua | 360 |
| | | Battle of R. Volturnus | 361 |
| | | Hannibal's march on Rome | 364 |
| | | Battle of R. Anio | 368 |
| | | Surrender of Capua to Romans | 373 |
| | | Hasdrubal's escape from Nero in Spain | 377 |
| | | Scipio volunteers to serve in Spain | 379 |
| | | Triumph of Marcellus | 382 |
| | 210 B.C. | Elections in Rome | 384 |
| | | Alliance between Rome, Aetolian League, and Pergamum | 386 |
| | | Fire in Rome | 390 |
| | | Sicilian and Capuan envoys before Senate | 394 ff. |
| | | Naval battle off Tarentum | 405 |
| | | Laevinus takes Agrigentum | 408 |
| | | End of War in Sicily | 409 |
| | | Scipio captures New Carthage | 412 ff. |

| | | | |
|---|---|---|---|
| | | Scipio and the girl captive | 420 |
| BOOK XXVII | | Hannibal destroys Herdonea | 426 |
| | | Envoys from Syphax in Rome | 429 |
| | | Raid on African coast | 430 |
| | 209 B.C. | Elections in Rome | 432 |
| | | Defection of twelve Latin colonies | 435 |
| | | Fabius recovers Tarentum | 447 |
| | | Scipio's victory at Baecula | 452 |
| | 208 B.C. | Elections in Rome | 457 |
| | | Death of Marcellus | 465 |
| | | Raid on African coast | 468 |
| | | Philip V intervenes in Greece | 468 ff. |
| | 207 B.C. | Elections in Rome | 473 |
| | | Hasdrubal crosses the Alps | 480 |
| | | Hasdrubal besieges Placentia | 481 |
| | | Hannibal routed at Grumentum | 483 |
| | | Hasdrubal's letter intercepted | 485 |
| | | Nero's march to join Livius | 486 ff. |
| | | Battle of R. Metaurus | 490 |
| | | Death of Hasdrubal | 493 |
| BOOK XXVIII | | Capture of Orongis in Spain | 499 |
| | | Successful raid on Utica | 501 |
| | | Romans capture Oreus in Greece | 503 |
| | | Philip at the Achaean Council | 505 |
| | | Triumph of Livius and Nero | 508 |
| | 206 B.C. | Elections in Rome | 509 |
| | | Livy's tribute to Hannibal | 512 |
| | | Scipio's victory at Ilipa | 515 |
| | | Masinissa joins the Romans | 519 |
| | | End of Carthaginian resistance in Spain | 519 |
| | | Scipio and Hasdrubal meet Syphax | 521 |
| | | Scipio reduces Iliturgi and Castulo | 522 |
| | | Slaughter at Astapa | 526 |
| | | Mutiny in army during Scipio's illness | 528 ff. |
| | | Revolt of Mandonius and Indibilis put down | 542 |
| | | Meeting between Scipio and Masinissa | 544 |
| | | Surrender of Gades | 545 |
| | | Scipio returns to Rome | 547 |
| | 205 B.C. | Elections in Rome | 547 |
| | | Fabius's attack on Scipio in Senate | 550 ff. |
| | | Scipio's reply | 556 |
| | | Contributions to expedition to Sicily | 562 |
| | | Mago raids Genoa | 563 |
| BOOK XXIX | | Scipio recruits men in Sicily | 565 |
| | | Rebellion in Spain put down | 567 |
| | | Laelius raids African coast | 569 |
| | | Scipio recovers Locri; Pleminius's atrocities | 573 ff. |

| | | | |
|---|---|---|---|
| | | Romans send delegation to Pergamum | 579 |
| | 204 B.C. | Elections in Rome | 580 |
| | | General peace in Greece | 581 |
| | | Statue of Cybele brought to Rome | 583 |
| | | Taxation of twelve seceding colonies | 584 |
| | | Locrian envoys before Senate | 586 |
| | | Settlement at Locri | 594 |
| | | Pact between Carthage and Syphax | 596 |
| | | Scipio crosses to Africa | 600 |
| | | Masinissa comes to join Scipio | 604 |
| | | Scipio fortifies Castra Corneliana | 613 |
| | | Hannibal defeated near Croton | 614 |
| | | Census taken in Rome | 615 |
| | 203 B.C. | Elections in Rome | 616 |
| BOOK XXX | | Burning of Carthaginian camp at Utica | 623 |
| | | Syphax defeated at Great Plains | 627 |
| | | Naval battle off Carthage | 629 |
| | | Final defeat and capture of Syphax | 632 |
| | | Masinissa enters Cirta and meets Sophonisba | 633 |
| | | Sophonisba's death | 637 |
| | | Carthaginian envoys ask for peace terms | 638 |
| | | Rome rejoices over African victories | 639 |
| | | Mago defeated in N. Italy | 641 |
| | | Mago and Hannibal recalled from Italy | 642 |
| | | Hannibal leaves Italy | 644 |
| | | Carthage breaks armistice | 649 |
| | | Hannibal lands at Leptis | 649 |
| | | Death of Q. Fabius Maximus | 650 |
| | 202 B.C. | Elections in Rome | 651 |
| | | Hannibal marches to Zama | 653 |
| | | Meeting between Scipio and Hannibal | 654 |
| | | Battle of Zama | 659 ff. |
| | | Scipio receives envoys from Carthage | 665 |
| | | Debate in Carthaginian assembly | 666 |
| | 201 B.C. | Elections in Rome | 668 |
| | | Macedonian and Carthaginian envoys before Senate | 671 |
| | | Triumph of Scipio | 679 |

# INDEX


Abelux, 118, 119, 120
Acarnania, Acarnanians, 386–9, 392, 501, 505, 581
Accaus, Vibius, 312, 313
Acerrae, 187–8, 191, 428
Achaea, Achaeans, 314, 468, 470–73, 502, 506, 581; Achaean Council, 469, 505–6
Acidinus, Lucius Manlius, 385, 429, 475, 494, 547, 567–8, 582, 620, 670
Acilius, *see* Glabrio
Acilius, Manius (envoy from Rome to Cleopatra), 429, 461
Acilius, Quintus, 48
Acrae, 275
Acrillae, 274
Acriminum, 548
Acuca, 255
Adherbal (magistrate at Gades), 537–8
Adranodorus (son-in-law to Hiero), 255–64
Adriatic, the, 77, 197, 215
Aecae, 255
Aegates islands, the, 33, 75, 155, 156, 182, 659
Aegimurus (island), 602, 648
Aegina, (island), 469, 473, 501, 505
Aegium, 469, 505, 506
Aelius, *see under* Paetus; Tubero
Aemilius, *see under* Lepidus; Numida; Papus; Paullus; Regillus
Aëropus (Epirote official), 581
Aeropus (in Macedonia), 472
Aesculapius the Healer, 579
Aesernia (Latin colony), 439
Aetolia, Aetolians, 327, 386–9, 392, 403, 447, 468–73, 501–2, 504–6, 580–81; alliance with Rome 210 B.C., 403, 501
Africa, Africans, 7, 12, 16, 18, 23, 24, 29, 40, 45, 66, 70, 129, 136, 155, 172, 184, 193, 205, 219, 241, 261, 275, 288–91, 293, 332–3, 407, 412, 413, 418, 429–30, 433, 435, 459, 468, 497, 501, 519–21, 528, 536, 538, 544–5, 548, 550–55, 557–61, 565–6, 569–72, 579, 582–3, 587, 589, 591–3, 596–9, 601, 614, 620–28, 634, 636, 638–40, 642–4, 647–52, 654–9, 669–71, 673–5; deserters to Romans, 523; troops (Carthaginian auxiliary), 45, 95, 98, 145, 147, 199, 203–4, 452, 454n., 455, 496, 515–16, 537, 559, 660, 662, 664–7
Agathocles, King of Syracuse, 558
Agathyrna, 409, 442
Agrianes, 502
Agrigentum, 274, 279, 326, 333, 351, 352, 407–8, 410, 430n.; falls to Rome 210 B.C., 408
Alba (Latin colony), 369, 438, 510, 585, 639, 676
Albingauni, the, 572
Albinus, Aulus Post(h)umius (consul 241 B.C.), 182
Albinus, Lucius Postumius (consul 234, 229 B.C.), 134, 197–8, 207, 357, 535
Albius, Gaius (soldier given command at Sucro mutiny), 529, 533–7
Alcibiades, 553n.
Alco (of Saguntum), 36
Alexander of Macedon (the Great), 380
Alexandria, 178, 263, 429
Alfius Marius (*medix tuticus*, chief Campanian magistrate), 213
Algidus, Mt., 89, 366
Alimentus, Lucius Cincius, 62, 63, 385, 392–3, 430, 434–5, 437, 463, 467, 468
Alimentus, Marcus Cincius, 593
Aliphera, 506
Allia, the, 149, 150, 159, 300
Allifae, 109, 114, 356
Allobroges, 55
Allucius (Celtiberian chieftain), 421, 422
Alorcus, 36
Alps, Alpine, 7, 14, 20, 47, 53, 54, 55, 56, 60, 62–4, 65, 66, 67, 69, 72, 79, 80, 105, 165, 202, 209, 224, 370, 410, 454n., 476, 477, 479, 480–81,

Alps, Alpine – *cont.* 497, 556, 572, 643, 645, 646, 652; tribes, 69, 481; Great St Bernard, 63n.; Little St Bernard, 63n.; Maritime, 563n.
Alsium settlement, 479
Altinius, Dasius, 285–6
Amiternum, 89, 285, 369, 562
Amtorgis, 339
Amusicus, chief of the Ausetani, 88
Amynander, King of the Athamanians, 469, 581
Anagnia, 366, 385, 429, 583, 621
Anapus, R., 275
Andronicus, Livius, 12, 478
Anicius, Marcus, 192
Aniensis tribe, 239, 241
Anio, R., 367–8, 372, 410, 656; bridge, 240
Annius, Titus, 48
Antias, Lucius Valerius, 211
Antias, Valerius (historian), 11, 350, 419, 564, 612, 622, 643, 654
Anticryra, 389, 506
Antiochus, King of Syria, 666
Antipater, Lucius Coelius (annalist), 11, 12, 63, 72–3, 130, 173, 419n., 465, 564, 599, 602, 612
Antistius, Lucius, 216
Antistius, Marcus, 91, 399
Antistius, Sextius, 476
Antium settlement, 94, 479, 510, 621
Anxur settlement, 479
Apennines, the, 79, 80, 85, 91, 93
Apollo, the Pythian, 179
Apollonia, Apollonians, 279–81, 387, 506, 581
Apollonides (Syracusan), 265
Appian (historian), 149n.
Apulia, Apulians, 15, 20, 103, 114, 139, 143, 152, 154, 165, 167, 179, 195, 198, 199, 209, 225, 227, 235, 243, 244, 256, 288, 295, 323, 353, 355, 356, 369, 383, 392, 428, 458, 463, 485, 490, 494, 508; partial defection to Carthage 216 B.C., 165
Apustius, Lucius, 216
Aquae Calidae, 648
Aquilius, Publius, 428
Aquinum, 365
Aratus (Achaean), 471
Arbocala, 27
Archimedes, artillery and military devices of, 272–3; killed at Syracuse, 338
Ardea (Latin colony), 29, 438, 585; forum at, 95
Ardiaei, 470
Aedoneae, 255
Argentanum (Bruttian community), 643
Argestaean plain, 472
Argive, 502
Argos, 469, 470–71, 589; Nemean Games at, 469, 470
Aricia, 135, 285, 667
Ariminum (Latin colony), 39, 77, 90, 91, 284, 434, 439, 563, 572, 619
Arines, 419
Aristo (Syracusan), 260
Aristomarchus, 233–5
army recruitment, 298–9
Arniensis tribe, 615
Arno, R., 95; swamps of, 103
Arpi, Arpini, 94, 103, 107, 225, 235, 245, 285–8, 314, 410; restored to Rome, 288, 410
Arpinum, 621
Arrenius, Gaius, 432
Arrenius, Lucius, 432, 464, 465
Arretum, 95, 96, 97, 457, 459, 460, 461, 562, 564
Arverni tribe, 481
Ascua, 200
Asellus, Claudius (cavalryman), 225–6, 240
Asellus, Tiberius Claudius, 483, 509–10
Asia, 387, 403, 468, 505, 579
Asina, Publius Cornelius (consul 221 B.C.), 48, 132, 364
Astapa, 526–8
Atanagrum, 88
Atella, Atellani tribe, 376, 399, 400, 428, 478; defect to Carthage, 165
Atellus, Gaius Mamilius (first plebeian chief *curio*), 435, 475, 477, 480, 510, 511, 650
Athamania, Athamanians, 469, 581
Athenians, 329, 335, 469, 553, 558, 581
Atilius, Lucius (garrison commander), 232
Atilius, Lucius (tribune), 399

Atilius, Lucius (quaestor), 149
Atilius, Marcus (envoy from Rome to Ptolemy), 429
Atilius, Marcus (legionary officer), 362
Atilius, *see also under* Regulus; Serranus
Atinius, Marcus, 314–15
Atintania, 470, 581
Atlantic, the, 68, 117, 291, 381, 454n., 456, 497, 499, 513, 528, 537, 540, 543, 549, 557
Atrinum, 288–9
Atrius, Gaius (soldier given command at Sucro mutiny), 529, 533–7
Attalus, King of Asia, 387, 403, 468–9, 473, 501–7, 579–80, 581
Attalus (Syracusan), 326
Attenes, prince of the Turdetani, 518
Attic coast, 507
Aufidus, R., 144–5
Aufugum (Bruttian community), 643
Augustus, 8
Aulius, Manius, 464–5
Aurelius, Gaius, 187
Aurelius, *see also under* Cotta
Aurinx, 282
Aurunculeius, Gaius, 432, 434–5, 459, 484
Ausetani tribe, 46, 88, 377, 567–9
Austicula, 217
Avernus, lake, 245, 255
Aygues, R., 55n.; *see also* Isaras, R.

Badius (Campanian), 319–20
Baebius, Lucius, 648
Baebius, *see also under* Herennius; Tamphilus
Baecula, 452, 455, 514
Baesidae (Bruttian community), 643
Baetica, 499
Baetis, R. (known locally as Certis), 339, 518, 526, 537
Baga, King of the Moors, 605
Bagradas, R., 648
Balearic Islands, 45, 117, 211, 218, 219, 456, 546, 555, 563; Balearic slingers (Carthaginian auxiliaries), 45, 81, 82, 98, 117, 136, 145, 427, 452, 516, 660
Bantia, 463
Bantius, Lucius, 185
Barca(e) family, 32, 218, 282
Barca party (in Carthaginian Senate), 25, 626
Barcelona, 528n.
Bargullum, 581
Bargusii, the, 42, 46
Bastetani people, 499
Belligenes, 383
Beneventum (Latin colony), 108, 245, 247–50, 251, 253, 254, 311, 312–13, 315–16, 318, 319, 321, 439; battle of, 248–9, 253, 357
Bergae (Bruttian community), 643
Bibaculus, Lucius Furius, 149
Bibulus, Gaius Publicius, 457
Bibulus, Lucius Publicius, 153
Bigerra, 282
Bithynia, 470, 505, 581
Blaesus, Gaius Sempronius, 129, 356, 358, 431
Blandae (Lucanian settlement), 255
Blattius (Salapian), 404
Blossius brothers (Capuans), 428
Blossus, Marius (Campanian magistrate), 174
Boeotia, 469, 472, 502, 505, 506, 581
Boii, the, 47–8, 53, 78, 131, 198, 458, 643
Bomilcar, 50, 219, 228, 275, 330, 332–3
Bostar, 119, 120, 210, 360, 370
Bottiaea, 388
Bovianum, 122, 311
Brancus, King of the Allobroges, 55
Brundisium (Latin colony), 74, 209, 227, 243–4, 246, 255, 279, 325, 439
Bruttium, Bruttians, 16, 179, 192–3, 204–5, 215, 219, 221, 225, 321–4, 242, 247–8, 254, 293, 311, 313–14, 360, 369–70, 409–10, 425, 434, 442, 446–9, 462–3, 467–8, 476–7, 480, 483, 485, 496, 509, 511–12, 548, 555, 559, 561–2, 564, 573, 580, 582, 613, 616, 619, 643–4, 651, 669–70; some remain loyal to Rome 216 B.C., 165; Carthaginian auxiliaries, 248–9, 660
Bubulcus, Gaius Junius (consul 291 B.C.), 432
Bucar (Numidian), 607–8
Bulotus, R., 575
Busa (woman of Apulia), 20, 152, 154

Buteo, Marcus Fabius (consul 245 B.C.), 195–6
Buteo, Marcus Fabius, 650, 669–71

Caecilius, *see under* Metellus
Caepio, Gnaeus Servilius (consul 203 B.C.), 294, 509, 548, 563, 616, 619, 647
Caere, 89, 94, 460, 510, 562
Caesar, Augustus, 513
Caesar (Gaius Julius), 613n.
Caesar, Sextus Julius, 457, 458, 459, 468
Calabria, 210, 244, 279, 293
Calatia, Calatini, 165, 184, 360, 376, 399, 400, 428; defected to Carthage 216 B.C., 165
Calavii (Capuan family), 390
Calavius, Pacuvius, 168, 169, 175–7
Calavius, Sthenius (brother of above), 175
Calenum, 123
Cales (Latin colony), 109, 111, 206, 214, 243, 247, 286, 365, 372, 374, 375, 376, 428, 529, 533, 585
Callicula, Mt, 111, 113
Callo, 237
Calor, R., 247, 318, 319
Calpurnius, Gaius, 164
Calpurnius, *see also under* Flamma; Piso
Calussa, Publius Cornelius, 298, 332
Camerinum, 562
Camillus, Marcus Furius, 97, 110, 297, 475
Campania, Campanians, 16, 108–9, 111, 123, 167, 169, 171–9, 184, 188, 191–2, 206, 210, 212–27, 231, 240, 245, 255, 285, 310–13, 315, 319, 325, 360, 369–71, 376, 398–400, 438, 460, 473, 535; sale of sequestered land by order of Roman Senate 205 B.C., 562–3
  troops: 216 B.C. with Roman forces in Sicily, 171, 173
    215 B.C. Roman auxiliaries, 207
    214 B.C. Carthaginian auxiliaries at Casilinum, 253–4
    211 B.C. Carthaginian auxiliaries at Capua, 359
Cannae, battle of (216 B.C.), 8–10, 13, 15–18, 20, 134, 158–60, 163, 165, 167, 171–2, 179, 181, 185, 188–9, 192n., 198–9, 205–6, 207n., 211, 220–22, 224, 227, 238, 241, 245, 251–2, 283–5, 299–302, 306, 309, 317, 324, 347, 352, 355, 357–8, 363–4, 370, 392, 410, 425–6, 434–5, 437, 441, 443, 459, 482, 493, 510, 559, 582, 599, 644, 656; casualties at, 149; Roman prisoners at, 149; village of, 104, 149, 156
Cantilius, Lucius, 157
Canusium, 20, 150, 151, 152, 154, 156, 157, 160, 161, 163, 171, 442, 485, 486–7, 490, 496, 509
Cape Leucata, 389
Cape of the Beautiful One (Africa), 602
Capena, 94, 368, 429–30
Capua, Capuans, 94, 108, 112, 168, 170–71, 173–4, 177–9, 183–4, 188, 190, 209, 211n., 213, 216, 222, 224–5, 240, 245, 254, 288, 310–11, 314–15, 319, 321, 323, 325–6, 353, 359, 360n., 378, 381, 386, 390–92, 395, 397–9, 400, 403, 410, 427–8, 431, 434, 440–42, 458, 461, 467, 476–8, 483, 486, 510, 535, 553, 582, 621; siege of 212 B.C., 322, 325, 355, 360–77; surrender to Roman forces of, 211 B.C., 373ff., 410
Capussa, son of Oezalces, 604–5
Carales (Cagliari), 217–19, 433, 668
Carpetani, 27, 28, 35, 47
Carseoli (Latin colony), 438, 585
Carteiea, 27, 537, 538
Carthage, naval affairs:
  217 B.C., 106, 110, 115, 116–17
  216 B.C., 123, 156, 199, 202
  215 B.C., 211, 218–19
  214 B.C., 264, 274–5
  212 B.C., 331–3, 335
  211 B.C., 381–3
  210 B.C., 431, 433
  209 B.C., 451
  208 B.C., 459, 468, 470
  207 B.C., 501, 505–6
  206 B.C., 520, 528, 537–8, 545–7
  205 B.C., 559, 563, 571–2
  204 B.C., 595
  203 B.C., 621, 628–31, 639, 643–4, 649
  210 B.C., destruction of fleet, 674

Carthage, political affairs:
the Senate, 18
222 B.C., 25
218 B.C., 32, 39, 40, 42
216 B.C., 180, 182, 201–2
206 B.C., 538
203 B.C., 625–6, 644, 648
210 B.C., 675
Privy Council
203 B.C., 638–9
negotiations for peace
202 B.C., envoys sue for peace, 664–5; Roman peace terms, 666; armistice granted by Rome, 667; 201 B.C., envoys to Rome, 669, 671–5; peace with Rome, 673–4
Carthalo (Carthaginian commander), 112, 149, 158, 159, 319, 449
Carvilius, Lucius, 296, 298
Carvilius, Spurius, 296, 298
Carvilius, *see also under* Maximus
Casca, Gaius Servilius, 296–7
Casilinum, 109, 111, 113, 123, 183, 184, 188–92, 194, 247, 253, 322, 325, 644; siege of, 253–4
Casinum, 108, 112, 365, 460
Cassandria, 507
Castra Corneliana, 613n.
Castulo, 282, 513–14, 522, 524; pass of, 117; forest of, 456
Catalia, 109
Catania, 437
Catius, Quintus, 433, 486, 561
Cato, Aulus Hostilius, 475, 477, 510
Cato, Gaius Hostilius, 475, 476, 477, 495
Cato, Marcius Porcius, 600
Catulus, Gaius Lutatius (consul 241 B.C.), 41, 42, 48, 110, 182, 547, 552, 643, 646, 674
Caudine Forks, the, 110, 300
Caudinus, Lucius Cornelius, 458
Caudinus, Publius Cornelius, 418–19
Caudium, 219, 254
Caulonia, 442, 447, 449
Celtiburia, Celtiburians, 68, 117, 118, 291, 411, 497, 528, 554; Carthaginian auxiliary troops, 497–9, 626, 627; deserted from Carthaginian force, 83; Roman allies 217 B.C., 118, 339–40, 497; Roman mercenaries, 291
Cenchreae, 507
Cenomani, Gallic troops (Roman auxiliaries), 81, 82
census:
of knights, 615
of Roman citizens in armies, 615
of twelve colonies, 615
Centennius, Gaius, 102
Centennius, Marcus (surnamed Paenula), 321–2, 324
Centho, Gaius Claudius (son of Appius Claudius Pulcher), 132, 294
Centumalus, Gnaeus Fulvius (consul 211 B.C.), 284, 288, 295, 353, 355, 356, 360–61, 363, 384, 392, 425, 426
Cercina, 129
Cerdubelus (at Castulo), 524–5
Certis, R., *see* Baetis, R.
Cethegus, Marcus Cornelius (consul 204 B.C.), 294, 295, 353, 383, 390, 392, 393, 441, 477, 580, 582, 586, 614, 616–17, 619, 641
Chalbus (Tartesian chieftain), 199–200
Chalcidice, 507
Chalcis, 469, 502, 503, 504, 506, 507
Chians, 469
Cicero (Marcus Tubius), 9, 10, 104n.
Cimbii, 546
Cincius, *see under* Alimentus
Circeii (Latin colony), 438, 585
Cirta, 609, 627n., 632, 675
Cissis, 87
'civic crown', 196
Clampetia (Bruttian community), 616, 643
Clastidium, 74, 462
Claudius, Emperor, 8
Claudius, Gaius, 386
Claudius, Publius (Prefect of the Allies), 483
Claudius, Quintus, 90, 457, 458, 468, 477, 480, 483, 485–6, 509, 510, 511
Claudius, *see also under* Asellus; Cento; Marcellus; Nero; Pulcher
Claustidium, 580
Clupea, 468, 608
Clusium, 562
Cluvia, Pacula, 398–9
Coelius, *see* Antipater
Cominium Ocritum, 313
Compsa, 167, 254, 285

Compulteria, 217, 254
Consentia (Bruttian community), 205, 293, 511, 616, 643; allegiance transferred from Carthage to Rome 212 B.C., 293
Cora, 365
Corbis (at New Carthage), 525
Corcyra, 387, 389, 447
Corinth, 470, 505, 506; gulf of, 389, 506
Coriolanus, Gnaeus Marcius, 536
Cornelius, Servius, 568
Cornelius, *see also under* Asina; Calussa; Caudinus; Cethegus; Dolabella; Lentulus; Mammula; Merenda; Scipio; Sulla
Cornus, 218–19
Corsica, 39, 129, 668
Cortona, 98
Cosa (Latin colony), 106, 439, 668
Cosconius, Marcus, 642
Cotta, Gaius Aurelius (consul 200 B.C.), 651
Cotta, Marcus Aurelius, 205, 325, 617, 650, 671–2
Crassus Dives, Publius Licinius (consul 205 B.C.), 298, 431, 433, 435, 457, 458, 474, 511, 547, 548, 559, 562, 578, 580, 582, 614, 619
Crassus, Titus Otacilius, 105, 130, 136, 156, 193, 194, 207, 219, 239, 240–44, 284, 338, 356, 384, 385, 386, 393, 433
Cremo, Mt, 63; *see also* Alpine (Little St Bernard)
Cremona (Latin colony), 48, 83, 439, 511
Crete, Cretans, 268–9; Roman auxiliaries, 268–9, 504
Crispinus, Titus Quinctius (consul 208 B.C.), 279, 319–21, 331, 432, 434, 457, 458, 460, 462–3, 464, 465–8, 473, 475, 535, 652
Crista, Quintus Naevius (Prefect of the Allies), 281
Crito (a Boeotian), 217
Croto, Marcus Metilius, 324
Croto, Titus Metilius, 206
Croton, Crotonians, 205, 209, 232–5, 405, 590, 614, 643; defected to Carthage 216 B.C., 165
Culchas (prince), 513
Culleo, Quintus Terentius, 674, 676
Cumae, 184, 192, 207, 212–14, 223, 227, 246, 302, 321, 357, 460, 644, 667; siege of, 214–15
Cursor, Lucius Papirius, 110
Cutiliae, 369
Cybele, Idaean Mother of the Gods, 578–9, 580, 583; *see also* Pessina
Cycliades, 471
Cyllene, 471
Cynoscepalae, battle of, 582n.
Cynus, 504
Cyrenae, 178

Damarata (daughter of Hiero, wife of Adranadorus), 258, 260, 262–3
Damippus (Lacedaemonian), 326–7
Dardania, Dardanians, 388, 472, 507
Dasius (Salapian), 404
Dassarettii, 472
Decimus, Numerius (Samnite), 122
Decimus, *see also under* Flavus
Decius, Publius (consul 295 B.C.), 242
Decius, Publius (tribune), 162
Delphi, the Oracle at, 157, 178, 561, 578–9
Demetrias, 472, 501, 502–4, 507
Demetrium, 503
Demetrius of Pharus, 131, 184n.
Democrates (Carthaginian commander), 405, 448–9
Derdas (Epirote official), 581
Digitius, Sextus, shares mural crown at New Carthage, 418–19
Dimallum, 580
Dinomenes, 239, 259, 268
Dionysius, 234, 236, 257n., 258
Dium, 389
Dives, *see under* Crassus, Publius Licinius
Dolabella, Gnaeus Cornelius, 477
Dorimachus (Aetolian), 386
Drepana, 552
Drome, R., 55n.; *see also* Druentia, R.
Druentia, R., 55, 56
Drumiae (Dorian town), 505
Ducarius, 100
Dymae, 471, 472
Dyrrachium, 580

Ebro, R., 24, 27, 28, 29, 39, 41, 42, 44, 46, 47, 53, 69, 70, 79, 87, 88, 115, 117, 118, 119, 123, 139, 199, 201, 202, 281, 345, 377, 381, 409, 411,

412, 528, 540, 549, 554, 646
Ebusus, island of, 117
Edesco, 450
Egypt, 262, 469
Elataea, 504, 505
Elba, 668
Elea, Eleans, 387, 471–2, 473, 505, 581
elephants, Carthaginian military, 14, 20, 27, 45, 51–2, 59, 60, 62, 73, 81, 82, 83, 85, 96, 182, 189, 204, 208, 219, 221, 225, 229, 274, 282–3, 353, 360, 361–3, 378, 382, 427, 445–6, 454, 484, 492–3, 515, 517, 571, 625, 641–2, 660, 661, 663, 665, 674
Elis, 471–2
Emporia (nr Thapsus), 600
Emporiae, 87, 88, 380, 553
Epanterii Montani, 563, 564
Epicydes (envoy from Hannibal to Syracuse), 237–8, 259–60, 264, 266–72, 274, 326–35, 351, 352, 394, 395, 407, 437
Epicydes (surnamed Sindon), 534
epidemics, 564, 578, 579
Epirus, Epirotes, 388, 581
Eretum, 369
Ergetium, 383
Erythrae, 506
Eryx (fortress), 33, 66
Eryx, Mt, 66, 552
Ethiopia, 7
Etna, Mt, 393
Etovissa, 46
Etruria, Etruscans, 16, 49, 84, 85, 91, 96, 101, 102, 172, 295, 314, 322, 325, 355, 380, 392, 428, 431, 434, 436, 457–8, 461, 464, 465, 475, 476–80, 509, 510, 535, 562, 563, 564, 572, 582, 614, 616–17, 619, 643, 651, 670
Euboea, 469, 472, 502–3, 504, 507
Eugenium, 581
Eupalium, 506
Euripus, 503
Europe, 468
Euryalus (Syracusan stronghold), 329–30

Fabius, Lucius, 648
Fabius, *see also under* Buteo; Maximus; Pictor; Rullus
Faesulae, 96
*falarica* (type of javelin), 31
Falerii, 94, 285
Falernum, Falernian territory, 109, 111, 123
Falto, Marcus Valerius, 579, 580, 650, 669, 670
Ferentinum, 366
Fetial priests, 674
Firmum (Latin colony), 439
Flaccus, Gaius Fulvius, 86
Flaccus, Gaius Fulvius (brother of Q. Fulvius), 360–61, 373, 398, 436
Flaccus, Gnaeus Fulvius (brother of Q. Fulvius), 295, 323, 355–9, 426, 434–5, 436, 535
Flaccus, Quintus Fulvius (consul 212, 209 B.C.), 106, 194, 197, 206, 209, 211, 219, 228, 242, 294, 297, 298, 311–13, 319, 321, 322, 325, 353, 355, 359, 360, 362, 364, 365–70, 372, 374–6, 390–91, 392–3, 395, 398, 399, 400, 401–2, 427, 428, 431, 432–4, 436, 438–9, 440–42, 446–7, 456–8, 460, 461, 476, 477, 483, 485, 553, 560–61, 584, 647, 649
Flaccus, Gaius Valerius, 435–6
Flaccus, Lucius Valerius (brother of Gaius), 435
Flaccus, Publius Valerius (consul 227 B.C.), 29, 34, 187, 210, 216, 227, 280, 365
Flaccus, Gnaeus Tremelius, 579, 651, 670
Flaccus, Valerius, 312
Flaminian Way, the, 106
Flamininus, Caeso Quinctius, 132
Flamininus, Lucius Quinctius, 294
Flamininus, Titus Quinctius, 582
Flaminius, Gaius (consul, 223, 220, 217 B.C.), 17, 39, 83, 90, 91, 93, 95, 96–9, 100, 101–4, 107, 115, 123, 135, 138, 142, 144, 183, 194, 196, 224, 244, 357, 473, 535
Flaminius, Gaius (consul 187 B.C.), (son of Gaius above), 417, 420
Flamma, Marcus Calpurnius, 162
Flavus, Gaius Decimus, 445–6
Flavus (leader of pro-Roman party in Lucania), 316–18
Floronia (Vestal Virgin), 157
Fonteius, Toberius, 341, 344, 377
Forest of Castulo (Spain), 381

Formiae, 112, 142
Fortuna Primigenia, (temple), 614
Foruli, 369
Forum Subertanum, 385
Fregellae (Latin colony), 365–6, 385, 439, 464–5, 510
Frentani, 486
Frusino, 366, 478, 621, 667
Fugifulae, 254
Fulvius, *see under* Centumalus; Flaccus; Gillo
Funditanius, *see under* Fundulus
Fundulus, Marcus Funditanius, 295
Furius, Marcus, 671
Furius, *see also under* Bibaculus; Camillus; Philus

Gaetulia, Gaetulians, 189
Gabii, 110, 243, 366
Gades (Cadiz), 45, 46, 291, 381, 413, 456, 497, 499, 501, 513, 518, 519, 528, 537–8, 540, 543, 545, 546–7
Gala (ruler of Maesulian part of Numidia), 290, 455, 604, 605, 606, 610, 631
Galaesus, R., 307
Galba, Gaius Sulpicius, 353, 355, 440, 668
Galba, Publius Sulpicius (son of Servius, consul 211, 200 B.C.), 353, 355, 356, 363, 384, 389, 392, 435, 440, 458, 459, 469, 470, 471, 473, 501–2, 505, 506, 580, 647, 651
Galba, Servius Sulpicius, 579, 650
Galeria century, 432
Gallic War, 242
Garamantes, 610
Gaul, Gauls, 197–8, 202, 240, 243–4, 256, 283, 295, 355, 380, 390, 410, 434, 440, 456, 459, 462, 475–7, 480, 487, 490, 507–8, 510–11, 548, 553, 563, 570, 572, 580, 582, 619, 641–2, 651–2
  Brixian, 49
  Cisalpine, 16, 40, 130n., 479, 494, 639
    defected to Carthage 216 B.C., 165
  Insubrian, 47, 63, 641
  Libuan, 63
  tribes (general), 481, 487, 545, 572
  military affairs:
    dress and weapons 216 B.C., 146
    spies for Carthage, 218 B.C., 80
    cavalry, Roman, 71, 73, 145, 159; Carthaginian, 73, 78, 79, 145–6, 305
    Carthaginian auxiliary forces, 492–3, 563, 660
Gelo (son of Hiero), 205, 236, 260, 261–2
Geminus, Gaius Servilius (land commissioner), 48, 643
Geminus, Gaius Servilius (consul 203 B.C., son of Gaius), 314, 433, 458, 473, 475, 477, 509–10, 561, 616, 619, 643, 646, 651, 668
Geminus, Gnaeus Servilius (consul 217 B.C.), 39, 83, 93, 95, 102, 103, 106, 129, 130, 139, 140, 143, 145, 149, 432, 433, 473
Geminus, Marcus Servilius (consul 202 B.C.), 386, 617, 647, 649, 651, 667, 668–9, 670
Genoa, 56, 63n., 563, 572, 620; gulf of, 642
Genucius, Lucius (ambassador to King Syphax), 429
Gereonium, 114, 121, 122, 131, 139, 144
Gillo, Quintus Fulvius, 646, 647, 649, 668
Gisgo (father of Hasdrubal), 76, 210, 339, 345, 381, 497, 513, 596, 603, 666
Glabrio, Manius Acilius, 669, 673
Gracchus, Tiberius Sempronius (consul 215, 213 B.C.), 190–91, 196–7, 198, 199, 205–6, 207, 208, 212–13, 214–15, 227, 235, 243, 244, 245, 247–51, 253–5, 283–5, 293, 295, 301, 315–16, 319, 321, 322, 357, 535; betrayal and death, 317–19
Gracchus, Tiberius Sempronius (probably son of above), 617
Great Plains, the, 627
Great Games, 104, 105, 473, 475, 620, 652
Greece, Greeks, 11, 12, 16, 210, 231, 232, 284, 296, 356, 380, 382, 387, 392, 395, 459, 468, 469, 475, 507, 553, 558, 566, 579, 580, 649–50, 671; Olympic festival, 475; Dyke, 563
Grove of Feronia (nr Rome), 368
Grumentum, 215, 473

# INDEX


Hadria (Latin colony), 103, 243, 439
Hadrumetum, 653, 663–4
Hamae, 212–14
Hamilcar Barca (father of Hannibal), 23–6, 32, 33, 66, 179, 281, 339, 342, 377, 381, 487, 493, 513, 552, 563, 652; killed in Spain, 281, 339
Hamilcar (son of Bomilcar), 228
Hamilcar (son of Gisgo), 76
Hamilcar (another, at Locri 215 B.C.)
Hamilcar (another, prefect), 433
Hamilcar (another, at Locri 205 B.C.), 574, 576, 587
Hamilcar (another), 610
Hampsicora, 208, 217–18, 219
Hannibal, 7–21, 198
- 222 B.C. Carthage, 23–5
- 219 B.C. Spain, 26–7
- 218 B.C. Saguntum, 28–31, 34–7
  - Carthage, 32–3, 40–41
  - Spain, 44–6
  - Gaul, 47
  - the Rhône, 49–52
  - the Alps, 53–6
  - North Italy, 62–3
  - Ticinus, 64–72
  - Placentia, 72–4
  - Trebia, 74, 77–82
- 217 B.C. wounded near Placentia, 83, 84
  - the Appenines, 85
  - Liguria, 86
  - the Arno, 95–6
  - loses sight of an eye, 96
  - Arretium, 96–8
  - Lake Trasimene, 98ff.
  - Central Italy, 102–3, 107–14, 121–2
  - Spain (tactics in), 118
- 216 B.C. Central Italy, 126–8, 129–30
  - Samnium, 140–41
  - Apulia, 142–3
  - Cannae, 144–52
  - Samnium, 167
  - Capua, 168, 173–8
  - relations with Carthage (Mago's report to senate), 179–82
  - Nola, 183–7
  - Acerrae, 187–8
  - Casilinum, 188–92
  - Petelia, 193
- 215 B.C. Campania, 210 (treaty with Philip of Macedon), 213, 215, 220–21
  - Nola, 222–5
  - instructions regarding Croton, 232–3
- 214 B.C. Campania, 245–6, 251
  - Nola, 251
  - Tarentum, 255–6
- 213 B.C. Arpi, 286–8
  - Tarentum, 293, 302–11, 314–15
  - funeral of Gracchus, 319
  - Capua, 321
- 212 B.C. Apulia, 323–4, 325
  - Capua, 325
- 211 B.C. crosses R. Volturnus, 365
  - within eight miles of Rome, 366
  - crosses R. Anio, 368
- 210 B.C. Salapia, 404–5
  - Lucania (Herdonea), 425–7
- 209 B.C. Apulia, 442–6
  - fails to save Tarentum, 449–50
- 208 B.C. Apulia, 462–3
  - Venusia, 463–6
  - Salapia, 466
  - Locri, 466–8
- 207 B.C. Bruttium, 467, 481–3, 496
  - Lucania, 483–4
  - Apulia, 485, 494
- 205 B.C. Liguria, 564
  - Locri, 573–5
  - Bruttium, 578
- 204 B.C. Croton, 614
- 203 B.C. Bruttium, 619
  - delegation sent from Carthage, 628
    - Croton, 643
  - returns to North Africa, 644
  - blamed by Carthaginian peace delegation to Rome, 646
  - arrives Leptis, 649
- 202 B.C. Zama, 653–61
  - Hadrumetum, 653, 663
  - summoned to Carthage, 664
  - flees to King Antiochus, 666 and n.

Hanno, (opponent of Barca faction in Carthage), 25, 32, 34, 180, 181, 182, 644, 672
Hanno (son of Bomilcar, nephew of Hannibal), 50, 51
Hanno (Carthaginian commander in Lucania), 215, 219, 221–2, 225,

Hanno – *contd*
231, 233–5, 247, 249, 254, 293, 296, 311–15
Hanno (cavalry officer under Mago), 528, 537
Hanno, in Spain 218 B.C., 46, 87; another at Agrigentum, 351–2, 407–8; another at Capua, 360, 370; another at Metapontum, 485; another in Spain 207 B.C., 497–8, 501; another, son of Hamilcar, killed at Salaeca 204 B.C., 610–12; another, killed in Africa, 603–4
Harmonia, daughter of Gelo, wife of Themistus, 261–2
Harpocrates, 326
Hasdrubal, son-in-law of Hamilcar Barca, 24–6, 41, 42
Hasdrubal Barca, son of Hamilcar Barca, brother of Hannibal, 45, 46, 56, 65, 87, 88, 113, 115–18, 134n., 146, 148, 199–204, 208, 218, 228, 281, 339, 342, 350, 377–8, 381, 410, 430–31, 434, 450–56, 476–7, 479, 480–81, 485, 486, 487, 489–97, 508, 509, 510, 512, 563; killed at the Metaurus, 563
Hasdrubal, son of Gisgo, 18, 281, 339, 342, 345–6, 381, 455–6, 497–9, 501, 513–20 *passim*, 554, 555, 562, 596–7, 603, 606, 610, 613, 621–8 *passim*, 633, 634, 636, 637, 638, 648, 649, 652
Hasdrubal Calvus (surnamed The Bald), 211, 218
Hasdrubal ('The Kid', opposed to Barcine party), 672–3, 675
Hegeas, 167
Helorus, 274
Helvius, Gaius, 642
Helvius, Marcus, 443
Henna, 17, 276–9
Heraclea (known as Minoa), 159, 256, 274, 299, 333, 352, 502, 504; council of Romans and Aetolians at, 502, 505
Heraclia, daughter of Hiero, 262–3
Heraclitus (surnamed Scotinus), 217
Heraea, 505, 506
Herbesus, 267–8, 274
Hercules, 66; pillars of, 68, 172
Herdonea, 323, 325, 425, 426
Herennius Gaius, 48
Herennius, Quintus Baebius, 132
Hermandica, 27
Herodotus, 16
Hiero, King of Syracuse, 75, 76, 136, 156, 194, 205, 216, 235–6, 238, 256, 258, 262, 265, 272, 284, 296, 329, 330, 334, 335, 337, 394, 395, 397, 437; death of, 235, 261
Hieronymus, grandson of Hiero, 235–8, 256, 258–9, 262–3, 265, 268, 334–5, 394; assassination, 239, 261–2, 239
Himera, R., 238, 351
Himilco, 35, 115, 180, 181, 200, 204, 274–5, 275, 278, 279, 326, 329, 331; death, 332
Himilco (Carthaginian commander at Castulo), 524
Hirpacra, 351
Hippo Regius (cited in error for Hippo Diarrhytus) (Bizerta), 14, 569, 571, 609
Hippocrates (envoy from Hannibal to Syracuse), 237, 238, 259–60, 264, 266–8, 269, 270–72, 274–5, 279, 329, 331, 334–5, 351, 394–5; death, 332
Hirpini, the, 108, 165, 167, 215, 219, 221, 446
defected to Carthage 216 B.C., 165
Horace, 8, 15
Hostilius, *see under* Cato; Mancinus; Tubulus
Hostus, son of Hampsicora, 217, 218
Hybla, 383

Iamphorynna, 388, 389
Ibera, 202–3
Ibes, 525
Ilergetes, 117, 420, 533, 536, 538–40, 542–3, 567–9; Carthaginian Spanish cavalry, 45–6, 88; surrendered at Atanagrum 218 B.C., 88
Iliberis, 47
Ilii people, 581
Ilipa, *see* Silpia
Iliturgi, 228–9, 282, 377, 522–5, 530
Illyria, Illyrians, 39, 256, 387
Illyricum, 388
Indibilis, Prince of the Ilergetes, 117, 341, 420, 450–52, 455, 528, 531, 532, 533–5, 539, 542, 554, 567–9; transfer of allegiance to Rome 209

B.C., 450–52; killed in Spain 205 B.C., 568–9
Ingauni (Ligurian tribe), 563, 642
Insubres, Insubrians, 70, 100, 131
Interamna (Latin colony), 365, 438, 585
Intibili, 229
Ionian Sea, 209
Isalcas, 189
Isaras, R., 55; *see* Aygues, R.
Istria, 39
Italy, Italians, 7, 12–16, 18, 24, 26, 33, 38–40, 43, 45–7, 53–6, 60, 62–4, 67, 69–70, 74, 77, 79, 86–7, 96–7, 100, 103, 109–10, 120, 129, 130–31, 133, 137–8, 144, 153–4, 167, 172–3, 177, 179, 181–2, 199, 201–6, 208–10, 215–16, 219, 222, 229, 233, 238–9, 241, 246, 248, 252, 275, 280, 283, 286, 288, 299, 301, 339, 355, 364, 371, 376, 378, 384, 386–7, 392–3, 401–3, 405, 408, 410–11, 425, 431, 434, 437–8, 442, 456–9, 461, 476, 479–80, 482, 485, 487, 491, 496, 497, 507–8, 511–12, 529, 536, 539, 545, 547–51, 553, 555–6, 559–60, 562–3, 566–7, 570–73, 578, 583–4, 589, 592, 599, 601, 613, 615, 620–21, 627–8, 639, 642–7, 650–53, 655–61, 664, 670, 675; cavalry (Roman auxiliary) at Beneventum 214 B.C., 248

Janiculum, the, 110
Julius, *see* Caesar
Junius, *see under* Bubulcus; Pennus; Pera; Silanus
Junius, Decimus, 324
Juno Lacinia, Temple of, 12, 62, 209, 210, 234, 564, 644
Juvenal, 7, 8, 9, 14, 22

Labici, 366
Lacedaemon, Lacedaemonians, 326–7, 387, 468, 502, 505, 581
Lacetani (probably Laeetani), 528, 532, 533, 542
Lacetania, 46
Lacinium, 12n., 462
Lacumazes, 604–6
Laeetani, the, 87, 88
Laelius, Gaius, 412, 417–19, 422, 433, 434, 451, 453–4, 520, 522–3, 528, 536–8, 540–41, 566, 569–70, 571–3, 598, 600, 610, 624, 628, 631, 632, 634–9, 645–6, 647, 649, 660, 663–4, 670
Laetorius, Lucius, 668
Laetorius, Gaius, 205, 324, 434, 581
Laevinus, Marcus Valerius (consul 210 B.C.), 197, 206, 209–10, 227, 240, 243–4, 255, 279–81, 284, 296, 356, 384, 385–7, 389–95, 397, 400–402, 407–9, 429–31, 434, 435, 442, 447, 459, 468, 474. 501, 510, 564, 579, 583, 586, 587, 647
Lamia, 469
Lanuvium, 207, 243; shrine of Juno Sospita, 89, 94, 243, 583
Larinum, 114, 121, 486
Larisa, 501, 502
Larisus, R., 471
Latins, the, 16, 188, 195, 297, 437, 516, 539, 592, 599, 601, 674; Latin confederacy, 194, 374, 376, 377, 399, 437; Latin colonies, 438, 670
Latin Way, the, 107, 365
Latium, 511, 570
Lavinium, 365
Lemnos, 501, 502
Lentulus, Gnaeus Cornelius, 319, 321, 580, 669, 673–5
Lentulus, Lucius Cornelius (*pontifex maximus*), 104, 294
Lentulus, Lucius Cornelius (praetor), 194, 353, 509, 547, 567, 568, 580, 582, 620, 670
Lentulus, Publius Cornelius, 243, 245, 284, 296, 299, 324, 356, 445, 616, 619, 620, 647 670
Lentulus, Servilius Cornelius, 509
Lentulus (tribune), 148–9
Leon, 279
Leontini, 238, 256, 258, 259, 266–72, 279, 394
Lepidus, Marcus Aemilius (consul 232, 220 B.C.), 75–7, 104, 132, 133, 205, 295; his sons, 205
Lepidus, Marcus Aemilius (son of above), 205, 283–4, 295, 296, 386
Leptis, 649
Lesser Syrtis, 610
Libo, Lucius Scribonius, 580, 582, 619
Libyphoenician horse (Carthaginian cavalry), 45
Licinius, Gaius, 40

Licinius, *see also under* Crassus; Lucullus; Pollio; Varus
Licinus, Clodius, 596
Licinus, Lucius Porcius, 433, 475, 477, 480, 489–92, 507, 510, 553
Liguria, Ligurians, 49, 85–6, 131, 572, 619; Alpine, 555, 563–4; troops (Carthaginian auxiliary), 45, 62–3, 86, 480, 492–4, 545, 660–61; *see also* Ingauni
Lilybaeum (Roman naval port), 75–7, 130, 156, 193, 219, 338, 430, 468, 501, 598–9, 601, 675
Liparae islands, 74
Liris, R., 365, 400
Litana, 197
Liternum, 112, 212
Livius, *see under* Macatus; Salinator
Livy (Titus Livius), 8, 9–21 *passim*, 54n., 63n., 73n., 136n., 149n., 180n., 190n., 211n., 233n., 240n., 420n., 437n., 514n., 528n., 596n., 623n.
Locri (Italy), Locrians, 17, 165, 205, 219, 231–3, 235, 260, 267, 462–3, 467, 573–8, 586–96; defected to Carthage 216 B.C., 165; treaty with Carthage 215 B.C., 232; besieged 208 B.C., 467; siege relieved by Hannibal, 467; envoys before Roman Senate 204 B.C., 586–91; Opuntine Locrians, 504; Treasury of Prosperine Temple at, 576, 589–90, 591–3
Locris (Greece), 389
Loeius, Seppius (last Campanian *medix tuticus*), 363, 371
Longuntica, 117
Longus, Tiberius Sempronius (consul 218 B.C.), 17, 28, 38–40, 74, 76–82, 83–6 *passim*, 90, 91, 107, 115, 144, 157, 215, 433, 674
Longus, Tiberius Sempronius (consul 194 B.C., son of above), 433
Longus, Tiberius Sempronius (son of Gaius), 433
Loreta, 668
Luca, 86
Lucania, Lucanians, 165, 179, 215, 242, 248, 254, 255, 285, 288, 293, 295–6, 316–19, 321–2, 369, 426, 434, 446–7, 462, 476, 483, 485–7, 496, 535; loyalties split 216 B.C., some defected to Carthage, 165, 179; return to allegiance to Rome 206 B.C., 512; Roman cavalry, 142; Carthaginian auxiliary troops, 248–9
Luceria (Latin colony), 103, 110, 209, 215, 227, 235, 243–5, 249, 255, 284, 295, 439
Lucretius, Marcus (tribune), 431
Lucretius, Marcus (another), 480
Lucretius, Lucius, 86
Lucretius, Spurius, 548, 563, 572, 582, 619–20
Lucullus, Lucius Licinius, 668
Lusitania, Lusitanians, 68, 117, 456; Carthaginian auxiliary troops, 83
Lutatius, Gaius (land commissioner), 48
Lutatius, *see also under* Catullus
Lychnidus, 472
Lymphaeum (Bruttian community), 643
Lyncus, 388

Macatus, Marcus Livius, 255, 405, 407, 462, 474
Macedonia, Macedonians, 210, 215, 216–17, 227, 246, 279, 280–81, 284, 384, 386, 388, 392, 434, 459, 469, 471–2, 502–3, 581, 671–2; fleet destroyed at Oricum 214 B.C., 281; Carthaginian auxiliary troops, 660
Machanidas (tyrant of Lacedaemon), 468, 502, 505, 506
Macilla, 383
Maecia tribe, 616
Maedi people, 388, 502
Maesesses (branch of Bastetani), 499
Maesuli, Maesulians, 604–9, 631–2
Maevius, Marcus, 642
Magalus, 53
Magius, Decius, 174, 175, 177, 178
Magius, Gnaeus (of Atella), 253
Mago, brother of Hannibal, 14, 16, 73, 80, 82, 95, 146. 167, 179, 180, 182, 208, 228, 281, 282, 339, 342, 350, 381, 455–6
Mago, member of Barca family, 218
Mago (representative from Hannibal to Philip of Macedon 215 B.C.), 210
Mago (Carthaginian commander) in Bruttium, 314, 316–19, 323; at Locri, 467

Mago (another), at New Carthage, 413–16, 419, 422
Maharbal, son of Himilco, 35, 70, 101, 109, 146, 151, 189
Malian gulf, 469, 502
Malta, 76
Mamertines, 535, 658
Mamilius, *see under* Atellus; Turrinus
Mammula, Aulus Cornelius, 193–4, 208, 211
Mancinus, Lucius Hostilius, 111, 112
Mandonius (Spaniard), 117, 420, 450–52, 528, 531, 532, 533–5, 539, 542, 543, 554, 569; transfers allegiance to Rome 209 B.C., 450–52
Manduria, 447
Manlius, Aulus, 464–5
Manlius, *see also under* Acidinus; Torquatus; Volso; Vulso Longus
Mantua, 243
Manus (a slave), 390–91
Marcelli, 335
Marcellus, Marcus Claudius, (consul 222, 214, 210, 208 B.C.), 12, 13, 17, 21, 134, 157, 183–7, 190, 196, 198, 199, 205–8, 214, 217, 219, 220, 221–5, 227, 242, 246–8, 251, 253, 254–6, 264, 266–7, 269, 272–5, 277, 279, 283, 284, 296, 299–302, 326–37, 351–3, 355, 382, 384, 389, 393–8, 404, 425–8, 431, 434, 440, 442–6, 449, 456–7, 458, 460, 462–3, 464–5, 466–8, 474, 477, 535, 566, 580, 586, 652; death in Venusia, 208 B.C., 465–6
Marcellus, Marcus Claudius, son of Marcus (consul 196, B.C.), 464–5, 467, 580, 593
Marcius, Marcus, 433, 477
Marcius (seer), 309
Marcius *see also under* Ralla
Marmoreae, 425
Marrucini, the, 103, 243, 369, 486, 562
Mars, 104, 525; Temple of, at Praeneste, 243
Marsi, the, 103, 369, 562
Martial, 9
Masinissa, King of Maesulia (son of Gala), 17, 18, 290–91, 340, 430, 455, 456, 514, 519, 543–5, 554, 559, 570, 571–2, 598, 604–12, 623–4, 627–8, 631, 632–8, 640, 645, 654, 660, 661, 663, 665, 675
Massicus, Mt, 109
Massilia (Marseilles), 44, 47, 49, 115, 380, 476
Massiva (grandson of Gala, nephew of Masinissa), 455, 544n.,
Maso, Gaius Papirius, 48
Maso, Gaius Papirius (son of Gaius), 294
Maso, Gaius Papirius (son of Lucius), 294
Matho, Marcus Pomponius (Master of Horse 216 B.C.), 101, 132, 134, 155, 243, 251, 380, 509, 617
Matho, Manlius Pomponius (praetor 204 B.C.), 561, 580, 583, 593, 598, 600, 601, 620, 651
Matienus, Publius, 573, 577–8
Mauretania, Mauretanians, 605; Carthaginians, 660
Mauri, 519
Maximus, Spurius Carvilius (consul 292, 272 B.C.), 242
Maximus, Spurius Carvilius (consul 234, 228 B.C.), 194–5, 386
Maximus, Quintus Fabius (consul 215, 214, 209 B.C.), 13, 18, 40, 41, 42, 103, 105–15 *passim*, 120–44 *passim*, 149, 155, 156, 194, 195, 205, 207, 208, 214, 225–7, 239, 242, 244, 245, 247–8, 253, 254–5, 283–4, 285–6, 295, 322, 364–5, 385, 432, 434–6, 438–42, 447, 448–9, 450, 456, 458, 461, 462, 474, 475, 482, 556–60, 584, 591, 592, 614, 650, 652; speech to Senate re Scipio Africanus, 550–56; death, 650
Maximus, Quintus Fabius (consul 213 B.C., son of above), 121, 153, 242, 244, 245, 283, 285, 286–8, 436, 468, 507
Maximus, Quintus Fabius (son of above), 650
Mazetullus, 604–6
Mediterranean, 412, 497
Megalopolis, Magalopolitans, 506
Megara, 268, 269, 274, 505
Megellus, Lucius Postumius (consul 291 B.C.), 432
Meles, 425
Menippus, 472, 502
Menix, island of, 129
Mens, 104, 105, 207, 209

Mentissa, 377
Mercury's Hill (New Carthage), 414
Merenda, Publius Cornelius, 133
Messalla, Marcus Valerius (Roman fleet commander), 430, 431, 433–7
Messana, 75, 76, 219, 232, 535, 575, 576–7, 593, 594, 652; Straits of, 652
Messene, Messenians, 470, 473, 581
Metapontum, Metapontines, 256, 308, 314, 406, 426, 450, 485, 496; defected to Carthage 216 B.C., 165, 314; population transferred to Bruttian territory, 496
Metaurus, R., 19, 134, 491
Metellus, Lucius Caecilius, 153, 252
Metellus, Marcus Caecilius, 283, 441,
Metellus, Quintus Caecilius (consul 206 B.C.), 194, 458, 477, 495, 509–11, 561–2, 578, 580, 592–4, 646, 651
477, 509–10, 579
Metilius, *see under* Croto
Metilius, Marcus, 123, 324
Metius, Statius, 253
Mincius, R., 243
Minurnae (Roman coast settlement), 477, 478, 479
Minucius, Marcus, 194
Minucius, Quintus, 398
Minucius, *see also under* Rufus; Thermus
Misenum, Cape, 9, 246
Moenicaptus (Gallic chieftain), 283
Moericus (in charge of Achradina, Syracuse 212 B.C.), 336–8, 383, 394–6
Mopsii (Samnite family), 167
Morocco, Moors, 7, 45, 110, 136, 172, 200, 204, 248, 256, 605, 661
Mount Bellus (Numidia), 607
Mount Victory, 281
Mucius, *see under* Scaevola
Munda, 282
mural crown, 189, 418–19, 653
Murgantia, 264, 276, 277, 279, 383
Mutina, 48, 458
Muttines of Hippacra, 351, 352, 383, 407, 408, 430, 437
Mylas, R., 267, 270

Nabis (of Lacedaemon), 581
Naevius, *see under* Crista
Naples, Neapolitans, 131, 135, 167, 168, 183, 184, 214, 225, 246, 251, 594; cavalry (Roman allies), 167
Naraggara, 654
Narnia (Latin colony), 438, 486, 494, 585
Nassus (Acarnania), 387, 388
Naupactus, 389, 468, 469, 470, 471
Navius, Quintus, 360, 361
Nepete (Latin colony), 400, 438, 585
Neptune, 415
Nero, Tiberius Claudius (consul 202 B.C.), 580, 582, 613, 649, 651, 667, 668, 669, 674
Nero, Gaius Claudius (consul 207 B.C.), 257, 295, 325, 326, 377–8, 380, 381, 445, 474–6, 477, 479–92, 495, 496, 507–11, 555, 614–16
New Carthage, 27, 38, 44, 46, 62, 115, 116, 412–23, 433–4, 451, 453, 459, 501, 519, 520, 521, 525, 528, 531–5, 538–9, 545, 554; besieged by Scipio Africanus 210 B.C., 412ff.; falls to him, 416
Nicaea, 503
Nicias (Achaean commander), 506
Nico (a Tarentine), 303, 305
Nico (at siege of Tarentum), 449
Nico (surnamed Percon), 406
Nile, R., 7
Ninni Celeres (Capuan family), 175
Nola, 183–7, 190–91, 208, 217, 220–25, 227, 246–7, 251, 253–5, 352; battle of, 223–5; reserves (Roman auxiliaries), 224, 644
Norba (Latin colony), 439
Nova Classis, 117
Nuceria, 16, 184, 185, 222, 428
Numida, Manlius Aemilius, 386
Numidia, Numidians, 16, 18, 45, 52–3, 110, 122, 150, 152, 172, 221, 256, 289, 318, 363, 370–71, 544, 554, 604–10, 624–5, 631, 633–4, 638, 660; send envoys to the Scipios 213 B.C., 290; send envoys to Scipio Africanus 204 B.C., 597–8; Maurusians, 291
(cavalry Carthaginian troops), 69–73, 78, 80–83, 95, 111–12, 142, 144–5, 147, 149, 167–8, 182, 200, 203–4, 245, 248, 304, 340–43, 351–2, 366, 383, 404–5, 407–8, 426, 430, 452, 464, 467,

485, 511, 514, 559, 573, 575, 587, 622, 635–7, 639–40, 660–61, 665; desert to Roman forces at Nola 215 B.C., 225, at Aventine (Rome) 211 B.C., 367, at Sicily 209 B.C., 437
cavalry (Roman troops), 480, 627–8, 641, 660; *see also under* Gala; Syphax; Masinissa
Numistro, 426–7
Nursia, 562

Obba, 626
Ocriculum (Bruttian community), 106, 643
Octavius, Gnaeus, 548, 564, 582, 613, 620, 648, 664, 670–71, 675
Oeniadae (Acarnania), 387, 388
Oezalces, brother of Gala, 604, 606
Olbia, 433
Ogulnius, Marcus, 428
Olcades, the, 27
Old Plains (Lucania): death of T. S. Gracchus, 318
Olympia, 387
Onusa, 116
Opimia (Vestal Virgin), 157
Oppia, Vestia (of Atella), 398–9
Opus, 504–7
Orbitanium, 254
Orestis, 472
Oretani, the, 35
Oreus, 503, 504–7
Oricum 279–81, 387
Orongis, 499–501
Orsua (combatant at New Carthage), 525
Ostia (Roman coast settlement), 106, 135, 157, 216, 322, 380, 449, 459, 460, 479, 583
Otacilius, *see under* Crassus
'ovation', ceremony of, 382
Ovid, 15
Oxeae islands, 505

Paccius (Bruttain noble), 447
Pachynum, Cape, 264, 274, 332–3
Paelignia, Paelignians, 369, 562
Paenula, *see under* Centennius
Paestum (Latin colony), 135, 405, 439
Paetus, Publius Aelius (consul 201 B.C.), 477, 617, 619, 639, 645, 668, 669, 674
Paetus, Quintus Aelius, 133, 194
Pandosia, 616
Panormus, 275, 566
Papirius, *see under* Cursor; Nasso
Papus, Lucius Aemilius (consul 225 B.C.), 194, 196, 244
Papus, Lucius Aemilius (praetor), 548
Papus, Marcus Aemilius, 433, 435
Parthini people, 580
Patavium (Padua), 8, 14; birthplace of Livy, 59 B.C., 8
Patrae (locally called Rhion), 468
Paullus, Lucius Aemilius (consul 216 B.C.), 17, 20, 40, 134, 137–45, 150, 152, 156, 194, 224, 357, 535; wounded at Cannae, 148; killed at Cannae, 149
Pedanius, Titus (third legion), 313
Pelagonia, 388
Peligni, the, 103, 114; Pelignian cohort, 312
Pella, 387–8, 389
Pennus, Marcus Junius, 580, 669
Penninus, 63
Pentri, the, 165 (Samnites loyal to Rome)
Peparethus, 502–3
Pera, Marcus Junius, 157, 159, 194, 196–7, 198–9, 207
Pergamum, 579
Perseus, 388
Persius, Gaius, 407
Perusia, 188, 192, 562
Pessinus, 578–9
Petelia, Petelini, 16, 192–3, 204–5, 463
Petrarch, 9, 10
Pettius, Herius, 222
Phalara, 469–70
Pheneus, 505
Phileas (a Tarentine), 302–3
Philemenus (a Tarentine), 303–5, 449
Philip V, King of Macedon, 13, 131, 209–11, 215–17, 227, 243, 246, 279–81, 326, 385–9, 392, 401, 403, 447, 468–73, 501–2, 504–7, 571, 579–81, 582n., 650, 669, 671; builds new fleet, 507; peace with Rome 204 B.C., 581
Philippus (Epirote official), 581
Philistio (Epicydes' nominee at Syracuse), 334
Philo, Lucius Veturius (censor 210 B.C.), 132, 433, 474

Philo, Lucius Veturius (consul 206 B.C.), 398, 432, 434, 440, 458, 495, 509, 510, 511, 547, 561–2, 580, 667, 669
Philo, Tiberius Veturius, 617
Phulodemus, an Argive, 329–30
Philopator, Ptolemy, 178
Phlus, Publius Furius (censor 214 B.C.), 134, 153, 155, 157, 193, 244, 283
Phlius, 505
Phocaea, 380
Phocis, 502, 504
Phoenice, 581
Phrygia, 579
Phthiotis, 503, 505
Picenum, 89, 103, 183, 209, 243–4, 284, 295, 486–7
Pictor, Quintus Fabius, 11, 101, 157, 178, 179
*pilum* (Roman legionary spear), 31
Pinarius, Lucius, 276–8
Pineus, Prince of the Illyrians, 131
Pisae, 63
Piso, Gaius Calpurnius, 353, 358, 367, 374–5, 382–3, 385, 392, 431, 434, 457, 458, 459
Pityusa, 546
Placentia (Latin colony), 48, 64, 72, 73, 82–5, 90, 439, 481, 485, 511
plague, at Syracuse, 331–2
Plator, 503–4
Pleiades, the, 60
Pleminius, Quintus, 17, 573–4, 576–8, 586–96
Pleuratus, King of Thrace, 387, 470, 502, 581
Pliny, 9
Plutarch, 9, 10, 429n.
Po, R., 14, 48–9, 56, 64, 68, 72–3, 77–8, 83; valley of the, 60
Poetilius, Publius (ambassador from Rome to Syphax), 429
Pollia tribe, 615
Pollio, Asinius, 8
Pollio, Lucius Licinius, 468
Polyaenus (Syracusan), 257, 258
Polybius, 11, 12, 14, 38n., 62n., 93n., 136n., 149n., 190n., 234n., 412n., 417n., 419n., 493n., 558n., 604n., 610n., 523n., 647n., 676
Polyclitus (Epicydes' nominee at Syracuse), 334
Polycratia (wife of Aratus), 471
Polyphantas, 472, 502
Pomponius, Sextus, 77
Pomponius, *see also under* Matho; Veientanus
Pontiae (Latin colony), 439
Popilius, Publius (ambassador from Rome to Syphax), 429
Popilius, Titus, 362
Populonium, 562, 668
Porcius, *see under* Cato; Licinus
Porsenna, 410
Postumius, Marcus, 296–8
Postumius, *see also under* Albinus; Megellus
Potidiana, 506
Praeneste, Praenestines, 94, 107, 188, 243, 507
Praetutia, 103, 486
Prefects of the Allies, 374, 461
Privernum, 440
Promontory of Apollo (African coast), 648
Promontory of Mercury (African coast), 602
Propertius, 15
Prusias, King in Bithynia, 470, 505, 581
Ptolemy, King of Egypt, 262, 469, 505; statue of, 178
Publicius, *see under* Bibulus
Pulcher, Appius Claudius (consul 212 B.C.), 153, 154, 168, 197, 206, 216, 219, 232, 238–9, 264–6, 267, 271, 275, 279, 294–5, 313, 321–2, 324–5, 352, 355, 360–61, 362, 372, 374, 375, 460; death 211 B.C., 375
Pulcher, Publius Claudius (consul 249 B.C.), 142
Punic Emporia, 610
Punic War: First, 23, 76, 121, 155n., 410, 512, 547, 552, 558, 560, 600, 646; Second, 120, 242, 558, 592, 600
Pupinia, 366
Pupius, Gaius, 132
Purpurio (at Numistro), 427
Pureoli, 239, 245–6, 322, 377, 380, 645
Pylus, 470
Pyrenees, the, 7, 46, 47, 49, 54, 87, 224, 380, 413, 454, 455

Pyrgi, 296
Pyrgus, 472
Pyrrhias (leader of Aetolians), 468–9
Pyrrhus (victor at Heraclea 280 B.C.), 159, 160, 174, 220, 233, 285, 299, 535, 576, 589

Quadrigarius, Claudius, 11
Quinctius, Decimus, 405–6
Quinctius, *see also under* Flamininus; Crispinus
Quinctilius, *see under* Varus
Quinta, Claudia, 584
Quintilian (historian), 8, 149n.
Quirinus, 240

Raecius, Marcus, 476
Ralla, Marcus Marcius, 580, 582, 620, 667
Reate, 302, 369, 385, 562, 621
Regillus, Marcus Aemilius, 239, 240
Regillus, Marcus Aemilius (priest of Mars), 580, 617
Regulus, Marcus Atilius (consul 267, 256, B.C.), 553, 558, 603, 657
Regulus, Marcus Atilius (consul 227, 217 B.C.), 139, 140, 194, 244, 283
Regulus, Marcus Atilius (praetor), 283, 362, 398
Rhegium, 16, 205, 231–2, 369–70, 405, 409, 442, 534–5, 573, 574, 577, 594–5
Rhion, 506; *see also* Patrae
Rhodians, 469, 505
Rhone, R., 49, 52, 54, 55, 56, 63, 64, 66, 68, 87, 480; valley of the, 54
Rome: civil administration
217 B.C. elections, 93
dictator elected, 103
216 B.C. elections, 132
Senate receive gifts from Hiero, 135
Senate condemn Cannae captives, 159ff.
Senate revise censors' lists
215 B.C. elections, 205
214 B.C. elections, 239
213 B.C. elections, 283
212 B.C. elections, 294
Senate control profiteering, 296
211 B.C. elections, 353
Senate try Fulvius for Apulia defeat, 356ff.
triumph for Marcellus, 382
210 B.C. elections, 384
alliances against Carthage, 386ff.
fire, 390–91
210 B.C. Senate receives envoys from Sicily, 394ff.; and from King Syphax, 429
209 B.C. elections, 432
Senate considers defection of colonies, 438
208 B.C. elections, 457
207 B.C. elections, 473
206 B.C. elections, 509
205 B.C. Rome receives and honours Scipio Africanus, 547
Scipio attacked in Senate, 550ff.
Senate send delegation to Pergamum, 579
204 B.C. elections, 580
Rome receives statue of Cybele, 583
Senate receive Locrian envoys, 586
census taken, 615
203 B.C. elections, 616
rejoicing over African victories, 639
mourning for Q. F. Maximus, 650
202 B.C. elections, 651
201 B.C. elections, 668
Senate receives envoys from Carthage and Macedonia, 669, 671
Senate decrees peace with Carthage, 673ff.
triumph for Scipio Africanus, 676
Rome, military formations: definition of, 361n.
Rome, naval affairs:
217 B.C., 115–18
216 B.C., 129
215 B.C., 210, 215, 227
214 B.C., 243–5, 255, 260, 264, 272, 275, 279–81
212 B.C., 330, 338
211 B.C., 380
210 B.C., 386–7, 392–3, 401–2, 405–6, 409, 412–14, 417, 422–3, 430–31
209 B.C., 435, 437, 447–8, 451

Rome, naval affairs – *contd*
208 B.C., 459, 463, 468–9, 471
207 B.C., 501, 503–4, 507
206 B.C., 510, 520, 528, 537–8
205 B.C., 547, 553–4, 560–62, 566, 570–72
204 B.C., 580–82, 596, 598–603, 610, 612
203 B.C., 620, 623, 628–31, 634, 638, 643, 647–8
202 B.C., 651, 658, 664–6
201 B.C., 668, 670–71, 673
Rome, political:
Commonwealth of the Quirites, the, 104
College of Pontiffs, the, 104, 400, 592, 593, 621
College of Praetors, the, 104
citizenship of, 195, 225, 383, 386, 399, 430
thirty-five tribes of, 181
Rome, religious affairs:
Board of Ten consults the Sacred Books, 89, 94, 104–5, 135, 157
'strewing of couches', ritual of (Lectisternium), 89, 94–5, 104, 105, 584, 645
Vestal Virgins, crime and punishment of, 157
Rufus, Marcus Minucius, 13, 103, 106, 108–9, 111–12, 114–15, 120, 121–9, 133, 140, 149, 551; killed at Cannae, 149
Rullus, Quintus Maximus (consul 295 B.C., grandfather of Q. F. Maximus), 242, 650
Ruscino, 47
Rusellae, 562
Rusucmon (harbour at Tunis), 629
Rutulians, 29

Sabatini, the, 399
Sabines, Sabine territory, 106, 135, 562
Sabinus, Marcus Sextius, 652, 670
Saguntum, Saguntines, 12, 25–43 *passim*, 54, 66, 69, 110, 118–19, 283, 381, 548–50, 645–6, 658; siege of, 12, 53; senate of, 37; forum of, 38; fall of, 39, 42, 44, 64, 189
Salaeca, 610, 612
Salapia, 256, 288, 404–5, 425, 466–7
Salassi, the, 63
Salinator, Gaius Livius (consul 188 B.C.), 386
Salinator, Marcus Livius (consul 219, 207 B.C.), 19, 40, 134, 168, 255, 474–6, 477, 479–82, 488–9, 490–92, 494–5, 507–10, 555, 563, 572, 582, 614–16, 646
Salinator, Gaius Livius (son of above), 617, 651, 670
Sallentia, Sallentini, 447, 477, 482–3; coast, 227, 256
Salyes mountains, 49
Samnium, Samnites, 15, 108–10, 112, 114, 122–3, 154, 162, 165, 167, 172, 179, 219–21, 242, 254, 300, 310–11, 369, 371, 410, 425–6, 535; Roman auxiliaries, 486; Samnites of Caudium, 219
Sapriportis, 405
Sardinia, Sardinians, 13, 23–4, 39, 65, 67–8, 70, 79, 94, 123, 129, 155, 193–4, 206, 208, 211, 217–19, 227, 243–4, 284, 296, 322, 325, 353, 356, 393, 410, 433–5, 459, 477, 509–10, 548, 565, 582, 613, 619–20, 643, 647, 655, 657, 667–70; Roman garrison in, 215 B.C., 211
Saticula, Battle of, 172; territory of (Latin colony), 184, 439
Satricum, 398, 510
Saturnalia, feast of, 664–5
Savo (Savona), 563
Scaevola, Publius Mucius, 11
Scaevola, Quintus Mucius, 197, 206, 211, 217, 243, 284, 296, 356, 435
Scantinius, Publius, 194
Scerdilaedus, king of Illyria, 387, 470, 473, 502
Scipio Calvus, Gnaeus Cornelius (consul 222 B.C., brother of Publius Cornelius), 56, 64, 86–9, 115, 117, 118, 199, 204, 227, 281–2, 289, 296, 339–49 *passim*, 356, 357, 378, 379, 403, 410, 411, 429, 482, 522, 525, 535–6, 539, 548–9, 553, 554, 557–8, 567, 656; killed in Spain 212 B.C., 344
Scipio Nasica, Publius Cornelius (consul 191 B.C., son of Gnaeus above, cousin of Scipio Africanus), 583–4

Scipio, Publius Cornelius (consul 218 B.C., father of Scipio Africanus), 28, 49, 53, 56, 63, 64–7, 69–74, 77–9, 83, 118–19, 199, 204, 227, 281–2, 289, 296, 339–42, 344, 345, 347, 355, 357, 378, 379, 403, 410–11, 429, 482, 522, 525, 535, 539, 548–9, 553, 554–8, 567, 655, 656, 674; killed in Spain 212 B.C., 341
Scipio Africanus, Publius Cornelius (consul 205, 194 B.C., uncle and adoptive father of Scipio Aemilianus), 9, 10, 13, 16–18, 21
218 B.C., saves father's life at Placentia, 72
216 B.C., takes joint command of Cannae survivors, 153–4
212 B.C., curule aedile, 295
211 B.C., given command in Spain, 379ff.
210 B.C., Spain, 409ff.
takes New Carthage, 412–23
Senate honours his successes in Spain, 434
209 B.C., Spain – victory at Baecula, 452
207 B.C., Spain, 497ff.
at Tarraco, 501
206 B.C., Spain, 513ff.
victory at Ilipa, 515
meets Hasdrubal and Syphax, 521
reduces Iliturgi and Castulo, 522
illness and army mutiny, 528ff.
meets Masinissa, 544
205 B.C., triumphal return to Rome, 547
elected consul, 547
attacked in Senate by Q. F. Maximus, 550ff.
reply to attack, 556ff.
raises troops in Sicily, 562, 565–6
recovers Locri, 573ff.
attacked in Senate over atrocities at Locri, 591–3
204 B.C., crosses to Africa, 599ff. Syracuse, 595, 597–8
joined by Masinissa, 604
fortifies Castra Corneliana, 613
203 B.C., peace discussions with Syphax fail, 621–3
burning of Carthagian camp at Utica, 624–5
defeats Syphax at Great Plains, 626–7
naval battle off Carthage, 629–31
visit from Syphax, 634ff.
Carthaginian envoys ask for peace terms, 638–9
violation of armistice by Carthage, 649
202 B.C., conference at Zama with Hannibal, 654–8
battle of Zama, 659ff.
receives envoys from Carthage, who later proceed to Rome, 665ff.
201 B.C., authorized by Senate to make peace with Carthage, 673
peace with Carthage concluded in Africa, 674
triumphal entry into Rome, 676
Scipio, Lucius Cornelius (consul 190 B.C., brother of Scipio Africanus), 499–500, 501, 519, 536, 574–5, 600, 667
Scipio Aemilianus, 14
Scopas (Aetolian chief magistrate), 386, 388, 389
Scotussa, 502, 504
Scribonius, Lucius, 164
Scribonius, *see also under* Libo
Sedetani, the, 528, 539, 567
Sempronius, *see under* Blaesus; Gracchus; Longus; Tuditanus
Sena – (Roman coast settlement), 479, 489
Seneca, 9, 10
Septimus, Lucius Marcius (commander of remnant of Roman army in Spain 212 B.C.), 344–8, 350, 356, 377, 381, 403, 516, 520, 522, 525–6, 528, 536, 537, 538, 543, 554
Septimius Lucius, 20
Sergius, Lucius, 648
Sergius Marcus, 573, 577–8
Serranus, Gaius Atilius, 49, 64, 89, 91, 130, 133, 194
Servilius, *see under* Caepio; Geminus
Setia (Latin colony), 365, 438, 583, 585
Sextilius, Marcus, 439
Sextius, *see under* Sabinus

Sibylline Books, the, 90, 104, 578–9; *see also* Rome, Board of Ten
Sicilinum, 215
Sicily, Sicilians, 13, 16, 18, 23, 39–40, 45, 65–8, 70, 74–7, 79, 83, 94, 123, 130, 136, 155–6, 171, 193, 199, 205–9, 216, 227, 234–5, 238–9, 243–5, 252, 256, 263, 266–7, 274–7, 279, 284, 294, 296, 299, 301, 308, 332–5, 350–51, 353, 355–7, 381–3, 385–6, 389–94, 396–8, 400, 401, 403, 405, 407–8, 410, 429–31, 434–7, 441–2, 458, 462–3, 467–8, 475, 477, 480, 482, 501, 509–12, 535, 548, 553, 558, 560–61, 565–6, 570–71, 582, 588–9, 592–3, 596–7, 599–601, 604, 612–13, 619–21, 647–8, 651, 655, 657–8, 667, 669–70, 675; seceded to Rome 210 B.C., 409; Carthaginian auxiliaries, 332–6; Roman auxiliary cavalry, 565–6
Sicyon, 470, 473
Sidicinum, Sidicini, 142, 172, 365
Signia (Latin colony), 439
Silanus, Marcus Junius, 184. 295, 322, 355, 380–81, 411, 419, 435, 459, 497, 499, 513–14, 516, 518, 519–20, 532, 536, 543
Silenus, 419
Silius Italicus, 9, 10
Silpia (more correctly Ilipa), 513, 514n.
Sintia, 388
Sinuessa (Roman coast settlement), 109, 207, 208, 212, 440, 478, 479
Sopater, 259, 261, 650, 671
Sophonisba (correctly Sophoniba), daughter of Hasdrubal son of Gisgo, wife of Syphax, 10, 17, 597n., 633–7
Sora (Latin colony), 438, 585
Sosis, 256–7, 259, 268, 329, 382–3, 394, 396
Sositheus of Magnesia, 217
Spain, Spaniards, 7–8, 12–14, 18, 20, 23–5, 28–9, 39, 42–7, 50, 53, 56, 64–5, 68–70, 79, 86–7, 106, 115, 117–20, 182, 199, 202, 204–5, 208, 227–9, 244n., 261, 281, 283, 289–90, 293, 296, 319, 336, 338–40, 350, 356, 361–3, 368, 377–81, 383, 403, 408–23, 425, 429–30, 434–5, 440, 450–51, 454n., 454–6, 459, 479, 482, 491, 497, 500, 513–25, 528ff.. 567, 580, 582, 591–2, 597, 603, 605–6, 620–21, 626, 639, 645, 650, 652–3, 656–9, 670
  death of Scipio brothers 212 B.C., 341–3
  dress and weapons of, 216 B.C., 146
  expulsion of Carthaginians from, 206 B.C., 519
  Further Spain, 456, 513, 543
  Hither Spain, 456, 501
  hostages (New Carthage 210 B.C.), 413, 417, 419–20
  troops: Carthaginian auxiliary, 44–5, 73, 95, 98, 114, 140, 143, 145–8, 203–4, 427, 445, 492–3, 515–16, 537
    Roman auxiliary, 119, 145, 200–201, 245, 291, 336, 339ff., 480, 515–19
    desertions to Roman forces:
    215 B.C., to Marcellus at Nola, 225
    213 B.C., to Q. F. Maximus at Arpi, 288
    212 B.C., Moericus at Syracuse, 336–8
Sparta, 558
Spoletium (Latin colony), 103, 243, 439
Statilius, Marius (the Lucanian), 142–3
Statorius, Quintus, 290, 652
Stella, plain of, 109
Sucro (mutiny at Roman camp), 528–30, 532, 535, 537, 592
Suessa (Latin colony), Suessetani, 341, 365, 438, 528, 585
Suessula, 184, 187, 206, 208, 225, 227, 247, 251, 284, 285–6, 288, 295, 302, 325, 361
Suetonius, 8
Sulla, Publius Cornelius, 295, 309, 314, 321, 324, 325, 353, 396, 460
Sulmo, 369
Sulpicius, *see under* Galba
Sunium, 507
Sura, Publius, 130
Sutrium (Latin colony), 400, 438, 585
Sybaris, *see* Thurii
Syracuse, Syracusans, 75, 135, 194n., 235–9, 256–74, 275, 279, 296, 301,

326–38 *passim*, 351, 353, 382–3, 386, 393–7 *passim*, 400, 410, 449, 558, 566, 573, 577, 592, 595, 598
215 B.C., breaks alliance with Rome, 237–8
alliance with Carthage, 238
214 B.C., falls to tyrants, 270–71
resists attack by Marcellus, 272–4
212 B.C., besieged and recaptured by Marcellus, 326ff., 350
death of Archemedes, 338
districts of:
the Island, 256–9, 261, 262, 329, 336, 337, 383
Tyche, 256, 330
Achradina, 257–9, 262, 271, 272, 328, 329, 331, 332, 336, 337
Hexapylon Gate, 256, 270–72, 279, 328
Epipolae, 328, 329
Citadel, 256–7
Neapolis, 330
Syphax, King of the Maesulii, 18, 289–91, 429, 519–21, 554, 559, 570–71, 596–8, 603, 605–10, 613, 621–8, 631–8, 639, 640, 652, 653, 656, 664, 669, 675; turns against Carthage, 289; infantry trained by Q. Statorius, 290; pact with Rome, 290; death, 676

Tacitus, 8, 16
Tagus, R., 27, 454
Tamphilus, Gnaeus Baebius (consul 182 B.C.), 616
Tamphilus, Quintus Baebius, 29, 40
Tannetum, 49, 643
Tappulus, Publius Villius, 517, 519, 620, 651, 670
Tarentum, Tarentines, 33, 159, 174, 209, 216, 242, 245–6, 251, 255, 293, 302–4, 305–10, 314, 325, 333, 360, 370, 381, 403, 405–8, 434–5, 437, 438, 440, 442, 447–9, 456, 458–62, 463, 468, 473, 475, 476–7, 480–83, 485, 510, 582; defected to Carthage 216 B.C., 165; entered by Hannibal, 304–5; recovered by Rome 209 B.C., 447ff.
Tarracina, 112, 285, 303, 429, 583; temple of Jupiter at, 510
Tarraco, 87–9, 115, 118, 377, 380–81, 409, 415, 423, 433, 451, 456, 501, 513, 518, 519, 520, 521, 543, 544, 553–4
Tarquinii, 359, 429, 562
Tartesii people, 199–200
Taurea, Vibellius (Campanian soldier), 175
Taurea, *see also under* Vibellius
Taurianum (Bruttian community), 293; allegiance transferred to Rome from Carthage 212 B.C., 293
Taurini, Ligurian, 63, 64
tax-farmers, dishonesty of, 293, 296–8
Teanum Sidicinum, 157, 197, 207, 374
Telesia, 108, 254
Terentius, *see under* Culleo; Varro
Thapsus, 600, 605
Thebes, 505
Themistus, son-in-law of Gelo, 260–62, 264
Theodotus, 237, 256–7, 259
Thermopylae, pass of, 502, 504
Thermus, Quintus Mincius, 669, 673
Thessaly, Thessalians, 388, 469, 472, 581
Thrace, 387, 388, 502
Thraso, 237
Thronium, 505
Thurii, 302, 314–15, 405n., 406, 426, 463; allegiance to Carthage, 314
Tiber, R., 54, 106, 209, 242, 380, 400, 584, 667
Tibur, 106, 676
Ticinus, battle of the, 8, 38, 64, 83; Ticinus, R., 70, 72
Tifata, 213–17, 221, 245, 360
Tisaeus, Mt, 502
Tithronium (Dorian town), 505
Torquatus, Aulus Manlius (consul 241 B.C.), 674
Torquatus, Titus Manlius (consul 347, 344, 340 B.C.), 240
Torquatus, Titus Manlius (consul 235, 224 B.C.), 161, 164, 195, 211, 217–19, 298, 384, 385, 397, 441, 473–5, 620, 652, 668
Tralles (Illyrians), 472
Trasimene, Lake (battle of), 8, 16, 17, 20, 101, 102, 106, 138, 145, 154, 158, 168, 189, 221, 224, 227, 241, 245,

Trasimene Lake, (battle of) – *contd* 268, 306, 370, 410, 432, 443, 482, 644, 656; lake, 98
Traversette, Col de la, 60
Trebellius, Quintus (shares mural crown at New Carthage), 418–19
Trebia, battle of, 8, 10, 17, 38, 39, 85, 146, 158, 189, 215n., 224, 410, 481; territory of, 184; River, 73, 74, 77, 78, 80, 83
Trebius, Statius (native of Compsa), 167
Trebula, 217
Tremelius, *see under* Flaccus
Tricastini, the, 55
Tricorii, the, 55
Triphylia, 506
Tubero, Publius Aelius, 668–70
Tubulus, Gaius Hostilius, 432, 434, 440, 458, 459, 460–61, 477, 482–3, 510, 582
Tuditanus, Publius Sempronius (consul 209, 204 B.C.), 20, 150, 161–3, 283–4, 288, 295, 355, 418–19, 441, 477, 580–81, 582, 586, 613–14, 616, 619, 651
Tunis, 628, 638, 664, 665
Turdetani tribe, 28, 36, 283, 518
Turduli people, 549
Turrinus, Quintus Mamilius, 509–10
Tusculum, 366, 429; temple of Jupiter at, 429
Tutia, R., 368

Umbria, Umbrian communities, 102, 103, 486, 494, 509, 529, 533, 562; Pass of Furli, 494n.
Utica, 338, 430, 501, 603, 610, 612, 613, 621, 623, 625, 626, 627n., 628–9, 649, 664
Uzentini, the, 165; (Samnites loyal to Rome 216 B.C.), 165

Vaccaei, the, 27
Vacuna, Temple of, 243
Valerius, Publius, 280
Valerius, *see also under* Falto; Flaccus; Laevinus; Messalla
Vallarian Crown, 653
Varro, Gaius Terentius (consul 216 B.C.), 91, 124, 132–3, 134, 137–45, 149–50, 154, 156–7, 161, 165, 171, 172, 173, 195, 198–9, 209, 216, 243, 244, 284, 295, 358, 460–61, 475, 477, 510, 650
Varus, Publius Licinius, 436, 457–60, 495
Varus, Publius Quinctilius, 616–17, 620, 641, 651; his son Marcus, 641
Veientanus, Titus Pomponius, Prefect of the Allies, 293, 296
Veii, 97, 110, 300, 400, 477
Velia, 405
Velitrae, 667
Venus Erycina, 104, 105, 205, 207
Venusia (Latin colony), 149, 154, 160, 161, 171, 300, 427, 439, 451, 458, 462–3, 467, 468, 483, 485
Veragri, the, 63
Vercellium, 215
Verginius, Lucius, 486
Vermina, son of Syphax, 609–10, 664–5, 669
Vesuvius, Mt, 9
Veturius, *see under* Philo
Vibellius, Cerrinus (surnamed Tuarea), 225–6, 240
Vibellius, Decimus, 535
Vibius (Bruttian noble), 447
Vibo, 77
Victumulae, 70, 84
Vicus Insteius, 243
Villius, *see under* Tappulus
Virgil, 8, 15, 17
Virrius, Vibius, 173, 371–3
Viscellium, 215
Vismarus (Gallic chieftain), 283
Vocontii, the, 55
Volaterrae, 562
Volcae people, 49–50
Volceii, 446
Volciani, the, 42
Volsinii, 460
Volso, Lucius Manlius, 40, 48, 49, 64, 131, 133, 164, 194
Volso, Publius Manlius, 385, 393, 433, 435
Volturnus, R., 109, 111, 184, 188, 191, 212, 214, 217, 247, 322, 325, 361, 364–5, 372, 400; Volturnum, 362 and n.
Volturnus (a wind, at Cannae), 146
Voturia tribe, 384
Vulcan Islands, 74, 77

Vulso Longus, Lucius Manlius (consul 256 B.C.), 603

White Fort, Spain (Hamilcar killed), 281

Xanthippus, 558

Xenophanes, 209–10

Zacynthus, island of, 29, 387

Zama, 653–64; battle of, 202 B.C., 8, 17, 18, 659–63

Zoippus, son-in-law to Hiero, 235, 237, 262–3